The Oxfam Handbook of Development and Relief

Deborah Eade

and

Suzanne Williams

Volume 2

Oxfam
UK and Ireland

ISBN for complete set of three volumes: 0 85598 273 X Hardback
0 85598 274 8 Paperbackk

ISBN for this volume: 0 85598 308 6

Available in Ireland from Oxfam in Ireland, 19 Clanwilliam Terrace, Dublin 2; tel. 01 661 8544.

Published by Oxfam (UK and Ireland), 274 Banbury Road, Oxford OX2 7DZ, UK.

Oxfam is registered as a charity No. 202918

Desiged and typeset in the Oxfam Design Department OX1032/PK/94

Contents of Volume 2

4 Production

1 General aspects of production 480
  1.1 Introduction 480

  1.2 Background 483
  1.3 NGO economic interventions 488
  1.4 Key questions 512

2 Agriculture 513
  2.1 Introduction 515
  2.2 Practical approaches to crop production 520
  2.3 Practical approaches to livestock production 537
  2.4 Support for rural organisations 555
  2.5 Key questions 560

3 Fishing 561
  3.1 Introduction: Fishing in developing countries 561
  3.2 Practical approaches 564
  3.3 Key questions 579

4 Trees and forestry 581
  4.1 Introduction 581
  4.2 Practical approaches 585
  4.3 Key questions 594

5 Small-scale industries 595
  5.1 Introduction 595
  5.2 Practical approaches 600
  5.3 Key questions 612

6 Resources 614

5 Health and development

1 **Introduction 625**
    1.1 The right to health 625
    1.2 Health and development 626
    1.3 The role of NGOs 627
    1.4 Chapter structure 629

2 **Background: approaches to health care 631**
    2.1 Primary health care 631
    2.2 Levels of health care 635
    2.3 NGO roles in secondary health care 637
    2.4 Infrastructure and equipment 638
    2.5 Vertical programmes 640
    2.6 Traditional, alternative, and informal health care 640
    2.7 Urban health 645

3 **Focusing on people: health needs of specific population groups 650**
    3.1 Introduction 650
    3.2 Women's health 651
    3.3 Child health 667
    3.4 Elderly people 672
    3.5 Disabled people 674

4 **Health care provision 677**
    4.1 Introduction
    4.2 Nutrition
    4.3 Environmental and public health: water and sanitation 688
    4.4 Immunisation 722
    4.5 Prevention and control of communicable diseases 727
    4.6 Birth planning 736
    4.7 HIV and AIDS 745
    4.8 The provision of essential drugs 756
    4.9 Mental and emotional well-being 759
    4.10 Emergencies and public health 763
    4.11 Health education and health promotion 767

5 **Financing, planning, and evaluating health programmes 773**
    5.1 Introduction 773
    5.2 Financing health care 773
    5.3 Planning and evaluating health programmes 781

6 **Resources 786**

6 Emergencies and development

1 Introduction 799
    1.1 Oxfam and emergencies 799
    1.2 Code of conduct for NGOs 801

2 Background: emergencies, conflict, and development 809
    2.1 Crises, disasters, and emergencies 809
    2.2 The changing nature of humanitarian response 815
    2.3 Information and advocacy 817
    2.4 The crisis of development practice and the need for new ideas 819
    2.5 The relationship between development and relief 824
    2.6 Reducing people's vulnerability to crisis 832

3 Emergencies deriving from war and armed conflict 840
    3.1 Introduction 840
    3.2 International legislation relating to armed conflict 842
    3.3 Armed conflict and NGOs 848
    3.4 Practical approaches 849
        impartiality, and independence 849
    3.5 Key questions 859

4 Assessment, co-ordination and consultation in emergencies 860
    4.1 Introduction 860
    4.2 Assessment of emergencies 862
    4.3 Inter-agency co-ordination 866
    4.4 Consulting and involving the affected population 878
    4.5 Assessing the situation of specific social groups 882
    4.6 Key questions 893

5 Health and nutrition in emergencies 894
    5.1 Introduction 894
    5.2 Background 895
    5.3 Assessment 896
    5.4 Practical approaches 900
    5.5 Health and nutrition surveillance 909
    5.6 Training programmes 912
    5.7 **Key questions 913**

6 Environmental health and physical infrastructure 914
    6.1 Introduction 914
    6.2 Settlements, housing, and shelter 915
    6.3 Water 919
    6.4 Sanitation 923
    6.5 Vector control 927
    6.6 Key questions 929

7 Food security, food aid, and food distribution in emergencies 930
7.1 Introduction 930
7.2 Security and vulnerability: entitlements and assets 931
7.3 Food aid in emergencies 936
7.4 Food supplies and distribution 942
7.5 Key questions 946

8 Oxfam procedures in emergency relief programmes 948
8.1 Introduction 948
8.2 Information and assessment 949
8.3 Relief supplies and logistics 961
8.4 Administration and staffing 970
8.5 Key questions 975

Appendix I Relief items for which local suppliers should be found 977
Appendix II Oxfam's emergencies stores 978
Appendix III Other relief items 979
Appendix IV Standard specifications for commonly required relief
    items 980
Appendix V Oxfam policy in emergencies 982
Appendix VI Oxfam water supply scheme for emergencies:
    the water packs 983
Appendix VII Oxfam emergency sanitation unit 985

9 Resources 986

Index to volume 1 and volume 2 989

Production

4

Contents

1 General aspects of production 480
  1.1 Introduction 480
    1.1.1 Poverty and economic interventions 480
    1.1.2 The role of NGOs 482
    1.1.3 Chapter summary 483
  1.2 Background 483
    1.2.1 Growth and modernisation 483
    1.2.2 Third World debt 485
    1.2.3 Structural adjustment policies (SAPs) 486
    1.2.4 The General Agreement on Tariffs and Trade (GATT) 487
  1.3 NGO economic interventions 488
    1.3.1 Basic principles of NGO economic interventions 489
    1.3.2 Sustainable livelihoods 490
    1.3.3 Gender and economic interventions 495
    1.3.4 Technology development 498
    1.3.5 Credit and savings support 502
    1.3.6 Marketing assistance 505
    1.3.7 Training and information exchange 508
    1.3.8 Participatory organisations 509
  1.4 Key questions 512

2 Agriculture 513
  2.1 Introduction 515
    2.1.1 Agricultural development and small-scale farmers 517
    2.1.2 Sustainable agriculture 518
  2.2 Practical approaches to crop production 520
    2.2.1 Access to and control of resources 520
    2.2.2 Increasing small-scale crop production 523
    2.2.3 Storage, processing, and preservation 527
    2.2.4 Small-scale cropping systems 530
    2.2.5 Low-external-input sustainable agriculture (LEISA) 532
    2.2.6 Vegetable production for landless people 535
  2.3 Practical approaches to livestock production 537
    2.3.1 Extensive livestock systems 538
    2.3.2 Small-scale livestock farming 541

4

2.3.3 Social and cultural considerations in livestock
    production 541
2.3.4 Division of labour and ownership rights 542
2.3.5 Women's role in livestock production 543
2.3.6 Increasing livestock production 544
2.3.7 General guidelines for pastoral development 547
2.3.8 Principal livestock species 549
2.3.9 Bees and beekeeping 554
2.4 Support for rural organisations 555
2.4.1 Pastoralist associations 556
2.4.2 Small-scale agricultural production groups and
    co-operatives 557
2.5 Key questions 560

3 Fishing 561
3.1 Introduction: Fishing in developing countries 561
3.1.1 The impact of fisheries development on fishworkers 562
3.2 Practical approaches 564
3.2.1 Small-scale fishing systems 565
3.2.2 Fishing communities 566
3.2.3 Women fishworkers 567
3.2.4 Technical support for small-scale fishing 569
3.2.5 Fish processing 576
3.2.6 Credit and marketing 577
3.2.7 Fishworker organisations 578
3.3 Key questions 579

4 Trees and forestry 581
4.1 Introduction 581
4.1.1 The historical context of forestry development 581
4.1.2 The 'deforestation' crisis 583
4.2 Practical approaches 585
4.2.1 The role of NGOs 585
4.2.2 Technical aspects of interventions 585
4.2.3 Tree planting 589
4.2.4 Ownership, control, and rights of use of trees and forests 591
4.2.5 Supporting forest users 592
4.3 Key questions 594

5 Small-scale industries 595
5.1 Introduction 595
5.1.1 The economic context of small-scale industries 596
5.1.2 NGO interventions and income-generation projects 598
5.1.3 Section summary 600
5.2 Practical approaches 600

5.2.1 Forms of NGO assistance 600
5.2.2 Social considerations in small-scale industry 602
5.2.3 Support for producer groups 604
5.2.4 Support for technology development 605
5.2.5 Marketing assistance 606
5.2.6 Credit 610
5.2.7 Training 611
  5.3 Key questions 612

6 Resources 614

Tables

4.1 Types of crops and their uses 525
4.2 Types of agriculture summarised 531
4.3 New directions for pastoral development in Africa 540
4.4 Women's economic enterprises 598
4.5 Types of small-scale industries 601

4

1 General aspects of production

1.1 Introduction 480
    1.1.1 Poverty and economic interventions 480
    1.1.2 The role of NGOs 482
    1.1.3 Chapter summary 483
1.2 Background 483
    1.2.1 Growth and modernisation 483
    1.2.2 Third World debt 485
    1.2.3 Structural adjustment policies (SAPs) 486
    1.2.4 The General Agreement on Tariffs and Trade (GATT) 487
1.3 NGO economic interventions 488
    1.3.1 Basic principles of NGO economic interventions 489
    1.3.2 Sustainable livelihoods 490
    1.3.3 Gender and economic interventions 495
    1.3.4 Technology development 498
    1.3.5 Credit and savings support 502
    1.3.6 Marketing assistance 505
    1.3.7 Training and information exchange 508
    1.3.8 Participatory organisations 509
1.4 Key questions 512

1.1 Introduction

1.1.1 Poverty and economic interventions

Poverty is a highly complex problem, with multiple causes and manifestations. It is conceived of in different terms in different societies, and poor people do not form an homogeneous group: 'the poor' is not a meaningful category. Poverty affects people in different ways, and its distribution is determined by many social, cultural and political factors. The links between material poverty, social discrimination and oppression, and socio-cultural expectations and assumptions about living standards, should always be analysed. Development workers should always question their own assumptions about poverty, when considering measures to alleviate it.

480

Among those who live in poverty, women are generally poorer than men, in terms of material deprivation and the social, cultural, and legal means to address that deprivation. The 'feminisation of poverty' refers to the fact that more and more women are forced into poverty, and increasing numbers of poor people are women, as women's poverty increases relative to men's. Poverty is also closely associated with racial, caste, ethnic, and class discrimination. Any analysis of poverty must take all these aspects of social and cultural differentiation into account. (See **2** Focusing on people.)

Definitions of poverty commonly focus on economic indicators such as levels of income, production and consumption. The World Bank, in its 1990 World Development Report on Poverty, defines poverty as 'the inability to attain a minimal standard of living'. The measurement of living standards is complicated and subjective: while quantitative data such as income and purchasing power can be measured and compared, people's expectations and levels of participation in social and economic life vary greatly in different parts of the world. In its report, the World Bank sets two variations of the 'poverty line' (the level of income below which people are said to be living in poverty) in order to take regional variations into account, and make quantitative comparisons between countries and regions. However, in order to plan interventions which aim to alleviate poverty, the analysis needs to be taken beyond quantitative indicators and to look at more complex social and political factors which affect the distribution of resources, and determine rights of access to them.

4

Oxfam believes that people's poverty is characterised not only by material deprivation but by the denial of basic human rights: to natural and social resources such as land and education, to participation in the decisions which affect their lives at the household, community, national and international levels, and to freedom from the discrimination and oppression which prevents people from making a living in peace. According to a recent report by the UN Committee on Economic, Social and Cultural Rights, the fact that one-fifth of the world's population is afflicted by poverty, hunger, disease, illiteracy, and insecurity 'is sufficient grounds for concluding that the economic, social and cultural rights of those persons are being denied on a massive scale'. Poverty and hunger are themselves gross violations of people's human rights. The alleviation of hunger has been on the UN agenda for the past 30 years, and yet hunger continues, in combination with poverty, to afflict increasing numbers of people. (See **1**.1 Principles of development and relief; and **1**.2. Human rights in development and relief work.)

Poverty is perceived very differently in different cultures, and is relative to perceived economic and social standards within any society. Poverty in Britain, for example, is measured against standards of wealth and control over resources and levels of education attainable by the majority of the British population, which could only be achieved by a tiny minority of people in many poor developing countries. However, while even poor people in Britain may have the possibility of access to food, health care and schooling that poor people in, for example, Malawi may lack, their rights of access to those social and economic benefits may be denied to them in similar ways in which they are denied to Malawians. Powerlessness is central to poverty, and may exist with very different levels of material welfare.

Oxfam's approach to economic interventions therefore seeks not only to improve the material conditions of people's lives, by supporting measures which increase food production or income-earning and employment opportunities, but also to tackle the structural causes of material deprivation. A production project to increase poor farmers' yields of maize, for example, will not be effective in alleviating poverty if farmers lack secure rights to cultivate the land, or if women among the farmers do not have equal rights with men to the land and its produce.

1.1.2 The role of NGOs

NGOs have an important role to play in supporting the efforts of poor people to tackle the causes and effects of poverty. However, their interventions are generally small-scale, and are only one, and usually a very minor one, of the processes of economic change affecting poor women and men. The major economic factors affecting poor people's access to resources are:

- the macro-economic policies of the powerful industrialised nations which create the conditions of world trade and global economic relations;
- the activities of large private industrial and landowning interests, and their influence on national policy;
- the economic development policies of national governments (with respect, for example, to credit and markets), and international financial institutions such as the World Bank or the International Monetary Fund (IMF).

These determine the economic and political climate within which NGO interventions take place and the scope for changes these interventions hope to promote. It is essential therefore that adequate analysis of these factors inform the planning stages of all NGO economic interventions, and are taken into account during monitoring and evaluation of them. Working only at the project level is unlikely to bring about the kind of changes required to alleviate poverty in the long term, and to address its causes.

However, successful economic interventions at the project level can help to strengthen the terms upon which people can negotiate for, and demand, the structural changes which are needed to address the causes of their poverty. NGOs also have a role in direct lobbying for changes in the economic policies — such as structural adjustment policies (SAPS) — of international institutions such as the World Bank and the IMF, and in international trading policies and agreements such as the General Agreement on Tariffs and Trade — GATT. Oxfam, with other donor agencies, campaigns and lobbies for policies which would alleviate the increasing poverty of millions of people in developing countries, and also supports lobbying and campaigning NGOs based in developing countries.

1.1.3 Chapter summary

This chapter is divided into five sections. Section 1 discusses the economic and policy context of NGO economic interventions, the basic principles underlying sustainable livelihood systems, and different forms of support for small-scale producers. It lays out general guidelines which should be taken into account when appraising proposals for economic interventions, and which should be referred to when reading sections 2 to 5 on particular types of production.

These sections discuss particular forms of NGO economic intervention, in the fields of agricultural production, fishing, forestry, and small-scale industries. They contain a certain amount of technical information, but it must be stressed that the technical information is of necessity highly selective, and cannot provide the level of detail required to assess particular proposals. They are intended to give the reader an indication of the kind of information which may be needed to appraise a project proposal, and where it may be found. Some key publications are listed in the Resources section at the end of this chapter, while organisations, institutes and resource centres, both international and regional, are listed in the Resources Directory. However, local sources of information and local practitioners, organisations, and publications, should always be consulted for appropriate advice.

A list of key questions will be found at the end of each section.

1.2 Background

1.2.1 Growth and modernisation

During the post-war period, and until the mid-1970s, many developing countries experienced some measure of increasing prosperity for much of the population. There were regional differences: East Asia and Latin America averaged much faster growth than either South Asia or sub-Saharan Africa. Nevertheless, during this period low- and middle-income economies achieved higher growth rates than the industrialised nations. In many countries, this growth was only achieved through high levels of borrowing from international banks and lending institutions, leading to the debt crisis of the 1980s. Some of these countries used the wealth generated to provide infrastructure for economic development. Some, including a number of low-income countries following socialist policies, such as Sri Lanka or Kerala State in India, also introduced a wide range of social welfare programmes leading to substantial improvements in health and education.

The effects of growth and modernisation policies have been very uneven both between and within countries. Some countries have undoubtedly benefited; and in some places popular pressure has led to improvements for poor people. In many countries, however, the preoccupation with growth and modernisation has increased the poverty of the poorest sections of the population. There has been a progressive concentration in ownership and control of productive resources. The increasing dependence of poor people on market activities, and particularly on wage labour, has increased their vulnerability to market fluctuations, both as producers and wage earners. This vulnerability has been further exacerbated in many countries by steep rises in the prices of basic commodities, and charges for services, following withdrawal of subsidies and state welfare provision under SAPs. Women have been particularly hard-hit as a consequence of the constraints on their control of resources, and their greater responsibility for non-market activities. State legislation and development policies have generally been premised upon a male household head, and have thereby increased rather than challenged gender inequalities within the household.

African countries, after decades of the ravages of debt and widespread armed conflict, have seen their hard-won gains in health and education reversed, their living standards decrease, and poverty deepen. In a recent report, Oxfam predicted that, based on current trends, the number of Africans living in poverty will total 300 million — half the continent's population — by the end of the 1990s. Africa has been in economic decline since the mid-1970s, and now contains 32 of the 47 countries ranked as the poorest by the UN.

In the early 1990s the increasing globalisation of production and markets and the growing power of transnational corporations, coupled with international debt burdens, is further eroding the scope for independent economic action by national governments. Low-income, developing countries continue to be disadvantaged in trade agreements,

484

loan conditions from international financial institutions, and international agreements on resource use. With the collapse of the Soviet Block at the beginning of the 1990s, neo-liberal growth policies have been extended to most countries formerly following socialist policies.

1.2.2 Third World debt

Before the early 1970s, the global oil market was not regulated and oil was cheap. After 1973, the oil-exporting countries began to regulate the supply of oil through the Organisation of Petroleum Exporting Countries (OPEC). This intergovernmental body dictated quotas of oil to be produced by each country, establishing control over world supply. The supply shrank and the price increased fourfold, bringing about world recession, and currency surpluses in OPEC countries. These 'petro-dollars' were recycled in many developing countries in the form of loans.

In the second half of the 1970s, a second rise in oil prices pushed the industrialised countries into recession, interest rates rose to almost three times the level of 1975, and imports from developing countries were cut back. By the end of the 1970s, with the recession continuing, creditors started to demand repayments; and debtor countries, crippled by interest rates, were unable to pay. In 1982 Mexico defaulted, and the World Bank and International Monetary Fund became involved, designing 'structural adjustment' plans for debtor countries to restore economic stability, increase the country's productive capacity, and enable it to service its debts.

During the 1980s, neo-liberalism, with its emphasis on unregulated market mechanisms, became the dominant influence in economic policy in many Western industrialised nations and the major international lending institutions. The global economy was still in recession. This posed serious difficulties for the governments of many developing countries, especially those with large debts. There were dramatic declines in world prices for primary commodities (minerals, raw materials, and agricultural goods such as sugar, cocoa, and coffee) upon which many developing countries depended. Many industrial countries, while advocating free markets in the developing world, introduced increasingly protectionist trading policies. Governments of poor countries were forced to borrow yet more money from international lending institutions, increasing the levels of their indebtedness.

The total amount of Third World debt doubled from the early 1980s to the early 1990s, when it reached approximately $1,500 billion. The human cost of the debt is measured in the lives of children — according to UNICEF's *State of the World's Children Report, 1992*, half a million

4

children die each year as a result of the debt crisis, as countries divert a high proportion of their national income from health and education to service their debts.

1.2.3 Structural adjustment policies (SAPs)

The policy package of SAPs varies somewhat from country to country, but generally involves privatisation of state enterprises, removal of subsidies on food, and cutting state expenditure on services, including health and education. Countries are also advised to increase export production, devalue their currencies, and 'open up the economy'. This includes encouraging investment by large multinational enterprises through the granting of preferential rights to exploit natural resources, and ensuring a cheap, unorganised labour force.

In sub-Saharan Africa, SAPs have achieved only modest results in their own terms, despite large exchange-rate devaluations, cuts in public spending, and credit squeezes. Critics of IMF policies claim that devaluation, for example, pushes up the local currency costs of debt servicing, making it more difficult for countries to achieve fiscal balance, while also failing to attract investment in production because of the collapse of infrastructure.

Combined with the abolition of food subsidies, and the deregulation of pricing policies, devaluation increases the price of imports, and prices for basic goods, such as fuel and food, have risen dramatically. The overall effect of SAPs generally has been to increase the poverty of poor people and exacerbate existing inequalities. They have failed to improve economic growth or to attract investment. In some countries they have led, not to economic stabilisation, but to increased inflation, affecting food prices and thus the health and nutrition of poor people. Since 1980, countries in sub-Saharan Africa have implemented over 240 SAPs — yet over the same period, their total debt has tripled, and in many countries there have been sharp rises in poverty-related diseases and both maternal and infant mortality rates. In Zimbabwe, for example, the withdrawal of food subsidies has raised the price of the staple, maize meal, by 200 per cent, while the minimum wage has fallen by 40 per cent. The result of this is that people have cut their food intake generally, and reduced their consumption of higher cost and nutritious foods, such as meat, dairy products, and fresh vegetables. (See 5.4.2 Nutrition.) Falling incomes also forced many of the workers surveyed by the Zimbabwe Confederation of Trades Unions (ZCTU) to withdraw their children from school. Unemployment is running at 50 per cent, and rising. The World Bank and the Zimbabwean government claim that the poorest people have been shielded from the worst effects of adjustment by a comprehensive social welfare safety-net encompassing health care, education, and food provision. However, the reduction of *per capita* spending on health by 30 per cent, and the introduction of charges for health services, has led to a deterioration in the standard of health provision, as well as making health care too expensive for poor people.

Oxfam accepts the overwhelming case for economic adjustment in countries facing chronic trade and budget deficits. However, SAPs have a profound influence on the livelihoods of poor people, on the position of women, and on the use of environmental resources. Urban people are particularly at risk, from job losses, the withdrawal of food subsidies, the erosion of social services, and the introduction of user fees in health and education. While rural people may in some cases benefit from increased income from export crops, the small-scale producers of subsistence food-crops suffer; poor farmers may be forced to leave the land as it is turned over to export crops, and they lose subsidies to credit and other inputs. Women, as the major staple food producers in many countries, are often the worst affected by the increased emphasis on export production. (See **2**.1 Gender.)

1.2.4 The General Agreement on Tariffs and Trade (GATT)

(To be read in conjunction with **1**.3.2.4 Trade, debt, and structural adjustment policies,.)

The General Agreement on Tariffs and Trade (GATT) is an international agreement which seeks to reduce trade barriers, such as tariffs and quotas, to allow the market to regulate the economic development of all countries involved. However, it is heavily weighted in favour of the rich industrialised nations and multinational companies based there, and the great majority of economic benefits from the agreement — including overall international income generated — will accrue to industrialised economies. Many developing countries will be net losers, and figures produced by the World Bank and OECD show that African countries may lose $2,600 million a year as a result of changes introduced by the final 'Uruguay' round of the GATT negotiations.

GATT failed to address central trade problems faced by developing countries, such as low commodity prices, and high foreign debt. Some of the trading agreements negotiated in favour of poor countries, such as preferential access to markets under the Lomé convention, will be jeopardised by the GATT liberalisation of markets in industrialised countries.

The world trade order after the Uruguay round will be dominated by a new organisation created by the GATT, the World Trade Organisation (WTO). This will be a more powerful body than the

GATT, empowered to force countries to comply with its rules, even when this means amending domestic legislation. It also allows countries to impose trade sanctions on goods if a trading partner does not comply with the deregulation of financial services and investment. Effectively, the WTO looks as though it will join the IMF and World Bank in becoming a powerful force for deregulation and liberalisation of the trade policies of developing countries, for the benefit of industrialised countries and multinational corporations, and to the detriment of the living standards of poor people everywhere.

1.3 NGO economic interventions

Throughout the 1980s, alongside global and national policies for economic growth, there has been an increasing emphasis on the potential role of NGOs in economic initiatives. On the one hand, multilateral aid agencies such as the World Bank have been interested in the role of NGOs in substituting for state provision within the process of 'rolling back the state'. There has also been increasing interest in the potential role of NGOs as intermediaries between poor people and government training and credit programmes. On the other hand, there has been a widespread increase in grassroots activism in developing countries in response to threats to their livelihoods and exploitative conditions of work. These grassroots movements have often been based on ideals of the empowerment of poor women and men, and the search for alternative forms of work organisation which more closely answer their needs. These movements, which may be NGOs such as co-operatives or trade unions, look to NGO donors for support.

Much of the emphasis of NGO and international donor agency funding in the economic and production sector is still on small-scale production and income-generation projects, implemented by a variety of national and local NGOs. Despite some successes, many of these project-based initiatives prove to be short-lived and fail to have a lasting impact on poverty. Some of the reasons for their lack of success may be:

- They have generally focused narrowly on technical interventions for particular types of production, without considering production and income-earning in the context of other roles and activities of poor women and men.
- They have been seen as an alternative, rather than a complementary, option to addressing the inequalities underlying poor women and men's lack of resources and income, and thus failed to challenge structural inequality.

- They have been limited by wider international and national economic and political processes and policies. These undermine poor people's rights to resources, and also determine the market context of small-scale production.
- They have failed to take into account the impact of national and international economic trends, such as high rates of inflation.

The problems are particularly acute in projects designed for women. These are often handicraft or small livestock projects, sometimes tacked on to bigger development projects under the leadership of men, or to women's health and family-planning projects. Many of these fail either to provide women with a significant level of income, or to address problems related to discrimination on the basis of gender. They also fail to take into account women's self-provisioning, which is the way women 'pay' themselves in goods which are the result of their own labour. This is often dismissed as unpaid work, or 'subsistence' labour, and undervalued, on the assumption that women would rather earn money (however little) by directing their labour into cash activities. But often women cannot control the cash they make. In such cases, they are likely to resist involvement in income-earning activities, preferring a reliable source of goods (replacing money they would otherwise have to spend) which they can produce for themselves through their own labour. (See 4.1.3.3, Gender and economic interventions, and 4.5.2.2 Social considerations in small-scale industry.)

Many development NGOs seek to address these problems through alternative economic strategies based on three interrelated principles of participation, equality, and sustainability. At the same time, NGOs are searching for ways of widening their impact, not only by increasing the impact of local-level initiatives, but by exploring the possibilities for changing prevailing conditions of inequality and injustice. Unless these wider issues are also addressed, experience has shown that small NGO economic interventions are unlikely to have any significant and lasting impact on poverty. They may indeed have a negative impact on the people they seek to help, by involving them in considerable effort and raising their expectations beyond the capacity of the project to deliver results.

1.3.1 Basic principles of NGO economic interventions
(To be read in conjunction with 1.1 Principles of development and relief work.)

Participation: participation is a vital element in the process of empowerment of poor women and men: participation and empowerment can be seen as different sides of the same coin.

489

Participation does not mean the mobilisation of people's efforts as a source of cheap labour in pre-planned development projects; on the contrary, it means the effective involvement of women and men in all stages of design and planning, implementation, and evaluation of development initiatives which are intended to benefit them.

Equity: inequalities in rights to and control of resources and power determine the nature and extent of participation, as well as the economic and political sustainability of any interventions. Strategies to counter the resulting inequities within households, families and communities must therefore be an integral part of any economic intervention. Careful analysis of rights of use and control should be conducted in every situation where economic projects are to be implemented.

Sustainability: Even successful short-term interventions are only useful if they contribute to longer-term impacts on poverty and well-being. Sustainability must be considered on at least four levels:

- **Social sustainability**: this refers to social relations within groups of people. If inequitable social relations are exacerbated or introduced by an intervention, the intervention will not be socially sustainable. Analysis into gender, race, and class relations should always be conducted to assess social sustainability.
- **Organisational sustainability**: experience has shown this is only possible where interventions to support capacity and institution-building are based on, and promote, participation and equity.
- **Environmental sustainability**: interventions can only be sustainable if they do not undermine the natural resources on which poor people depend and do not cause environmental damage which puts their health and other aspects of their livelihood at risk. This involves not only 'environment-friendly' technology but also equitable management of resources. (See 1.3.3.1 Sustainable livelihoods.)
- **Economic and political sustainability**: interventions must take into account the economic and market context, and whether participants are likely to have continued control of resources. Political conditions, such as respect for human rights, and the extent of people's participation in civil and political institutions, also determine the possibilities and impact of interventions.

1.3.2 Sustainable livelihoods

(To be read in conjunction with 1.3.1.1 Sustainable development, and 1.3.3.1 Sustainable livelihoods.)

Economic development has generally been concerned with increasing production and incomes, and increasing market integration of 'subsistence' producers. Western-influenced development thinking has assumed a progression from production for consumption to production for the market, and from diversified systems to specialised systems of production. Resistance to this has been attributed to backward traditions and lack of economic rationality. Such assumptions, which may also underlie NGO economic interventions, are based on a false understanding of the ways in which poor people live and survive. Although increased incomes and production are generally the prime aims of poor people, they also need to minimise risk. Subsistence producers may have relatively adequate and secure livelihoods, whereas those who are dependent upon the market are often very poor and face greater risks. Traditional diversified production systems are often technologically very complex, and well-adapted to prevailing conditions. It cannot therefore be assumed that 'modern' methods will necessarily increase production and incomes.

a. Assessing livelihood systems
The basis for assessing the appropriateness of any type of intervention is an understanding of livelihood systems and the strategies in which people are already engaged, the problems which they face, and the ways in which they are adapting to changing environmental and economic conditions. The notion of 'livelihood systems' takes into account the wide range of people's roles, activities, personal capacities, and resources, which make up the way they make a living; and how these elements are related to each other. There are three basic aspects to be considered in relation to livelihood systems and economic interventions: who owns what? Who does what? Who gets what?

4

Who owns what? Rights to resources, and the way they are differentiated, are critical in determining social and economic inequalities, and the potential for changing them. Typically there is a range of different rights to resources, governed by state legislation, customary and informal systems, and international agreements. These different systems may be in conflict with each other, and be undergoing changes. It is important to distinguish between:

- **Ownership rights** in the sense of being able to sell or give away resources, such as land, or animals. These generally belong to more powerful individuals or groups within societies, and to men within families. Individual ownership rights over land, for example, have often been re-enforced by state legislation and land reform.
- **Rights of access and use:** in customary systems people often have rights to cultivation of land or grazing rights even where they do not have ownership rights.

- **Rights of use of particular products**: in customary systems poor people are often entitled to certain products from land, forests areas and rivers on which they and their families depend for survival.

The rights of different groups of poor people may not be the same. The rights described above are usually differentiated by gender, age, race, class, and ethnic identity, and may be the basis of significant inequities.

Who does what? Livelihood systems involve a wide range of different tasks which together enable people to survive. Production itself may require many interdependent tasks, and is itself only part of a wider livelihood strategy, involving family and household provisioning, family and household maintenance, and family and community reproduction and care. It is therefore necessary to look at the range of different tasks and identify which are done by men, by women, by children, and old and young women and men, and how this varies according to race, class, and caste identity:

- **Market production**: this includes acquisition, manufacture and/or preparation of productive inputs, tasks involved in the production process itself, processing of products and by-products, marketing of products and by-products.
- **Family and household provisioning**: food gathering, fuel and water collection, production or purchase of household goods such as clothes, household utensils, and shelter.
- **Family and household maintenance:** cooking, washing, cleaning and mending of clothes and household goods, repair of house and care of immediate surroundings and domestic animals.
- **Family and community reproduction and care:** biological reproduction of children requiring considerable time and energy in pregnancy, breastfeeding, care of children, the sick and elderly; various types of community management such as working for collective resources and sharing responsibilities for community members who need support.

Who gets what? Men and women are involved in a range of social and economic relations within families, households and communities. Those who perform the labour do not necessarily enjoy the products. Benefit is largely determined by systems of ownership and allocation of goods, the division of labour and valuation of different tasks.

Rights to income are determined both by forms of remuneration for work, and by the way in which decisions are made about income distribution within families and households. Remuneration for work includes self-employment, wage labour, and systems of mutual labour exchange, including unpaid family labour:

- **Self-employment** covers a range of types of activity where workers own their means of production and exchange the produce on the market. 'Independent' self-employed women and men may have as little, and in some cases less, control over their conditions of work and levels of income than wage workers. Self-employment may be dependent on insecure markets and large-scale, powerful traders, and dependent on loans from traders and intermediaries, and may be more insecure and exploitative than wage labour. Self-employment is often dependent on the unpaid labour of other family members (particularly women and children), who may or may not have a say in decisions and a share of the income.
- In a system of **wage labour**, workers do not own their means of production but are paid an agreed amount in exchange for work. Wage labour is of many different types: paid in cash or kind, at daily rates or piece rates; permanent or casual. The relative benefits of different systems to workers depends on many factors; for example, in the case of cash versus kind, on the market price of basic foodstuffs and their seasonal fluctuation; in the case of daily versus piece rates, on the regularity of work; in the case of permanent versus casual labour, on the precise nature of permanent ties and the opportunities for other work.
- In informal systems of **labour exchange**, there is no direct remuneration, but performance of labour for others is central to maintaining support networks and rights to certain services and goods in reciprocal exchange. This includes various types of co-operative work groups and also unpaid family labour. Informal systems range from egalitarian systems of mutual benefit to extremely exploitative arrangements. Unpaid family labour, particularly that of women and children, is often 'invisible', and may be significantly increased by interventions aiming to increase production, while increased benefits may not be distributed to all the workers.

Within households there is often no direct relationship between work input or income earned, and control over income. Household budgeting arrangements vary both between and within societies, and even between different households within the same family. Although budgeting arrangements are often in practice quite fluid and subject to negotiation (and hence, potentially, to change by economic initiatives), there is a broad distinction between three forms of household budgeting:

- All family income is given to and controlled by the head of the household, who makes all decisions, with varying consultation with other members. Individuals, particularly older adult men, may retain

493

some money for personal expenditure. This appears to be the most common arrangement in most societies.

- Part or all of the income is given to women for household expenditure. Here women have more influence, but decisions are generally only taken within the boundaries set by other family members. This system is likely to be most common in very poor households where there is little surplus income once basic consumption needs have been met.
- Earners retain most of their income, paying some into a family pool and retaining responsibility for certain types of expenditure. This system is likely to be most common in households where most household members are earning.

Investigating livelihood systems and strategies can be very time-consuming and complicated, but is essential before any interventions are planned. (See **1.3.5 Livelihoods analysis.**) Interventions implemented at the level of 'the community' are often based upon assumptions that there will be a common benefit for all those contributing their labour to the project. This is particularly the case in environmental improvement schemes such as irrigation projects or social forestry. Analysis of the relations of production, and of power and control within the community, will show such assumptions to be false. Donor agencies must ensure that none of the initiatives they support exacerbate existing inequities, but seek instead to challenge them. It cannot be assumed that those putting most effort and time into economic activities will necessarily control or enjoy the benefits.

b. Changes in livelihood systems

The process of economic growth and modernisation has led to increasing concentration of power and ownership, and often to the degradation of resources. Resources which previously were regarded as common property (known as 'common property resources'), areas of land or forest, coastline or rivers on which poor women and men depend for survival in times of crisis, have often been taken over by private sector or state interests.

The increased emphasis on individual ownership has often led to disruption of traditional patterns of environmental management. Common ownership patterns were often based on effective resource conservation. In many cases it is after the disruption of such systems by state expropriation or large-scale private interests that degradation has occurred.

Within families, ownership of crucial resources such as land have generally been vested in older males through registration and land-titling measures, leading to erosion of use rights by other family members.

c. Interdependence of livelihood activities

For most poor people managing with very scarce resources, there is no fine line drawn between production and income earning and other activities.

Poor women and men are generally engaged in a wide range of activities, including market activities, household provisioning and maintenance, and family and community reproduction and care. All of these activities are interdependent and all are vital for survival. It is, for example, perfectly possible for interventions to increase people's cash incomes but to make them poorer because they are less able to withstand market fluctuations, particularly in the longer term.

The activities of particular individuals cannot be seen in isolation, but must be considered in the context of their relations with other people within families, households and communities. Concentrating solely on market activities or production alone for particular individuals may have adverse impacts on their ability to perform other tasks, and on other people.

1.3.3 Gender and economic interventions
(To be read in conjunction with 2.1 Gender.)

a. Gender inequality and livelihood systems

In most customary law and religious codes women are considered to be dependents of male family members, and under their authority. This means that women's interests are commonly seen, by women as well as men, as subordinate to those of the household and family. In most cultures this subordination is linked to and reinforced by attempts to control female sexuality. The definition of women as dependents and subordinates underlies many modern legal codes throughout the world. Gender subordination may be enforced within the household by domestic violence, and within the community by social ostracism or legal sanctions. It affects all aspects of women's economic activity in the following ways.

Unequal ownership and control of resources: Customary rules on ownership and use of resources are widely variable and often complex. A broad distinction is often made between patrilineal systems (where most productive resources pass from father to son) and matrilineal systems (where most productive resources pass from a woman's brother to her sons). In most systems women's rights of ownership and use of major productive resources are dependent on women's relationship to men. At the same time women may have separate rights to particular resources which pass between women. The amount of power and influence which individual women are able to exercise over the use of resources depends largely on how much control she has over her

495

marriage, the degree to which this enables her to have continuing interests in property in her natal village, the stability of marriage, and her ability to have continuing interest in property in her husband's village.

Gender division of labour: All societies allocate different tasks, roles and responsibilities to men and to women. These vary very much between and within societies and cultures, and change over time. They should always be carefully identified and analysed in any situation; no intervention should be based on assumptions about the gender division of labour which may themselves be based on experience in other societies. Because women bear children, it is universally considered a 'natural' consequence that women should take more responsibility than men for household maintenance and family care, including care of the sick and elderly. These are seen as an extension of their mothering role rather than 'work' as such. The association of women and motherhood influences all other aspects of their work, even for women and girls not currently of childbearing age or who cannot have children. Women's tasks are generally seen as less important than those of men. The burden of work in household maintenance and family care greatly increases women's hours of work.

Inequalities in income: Gender discrimination exists in nearly all forms of remuneration for work, because of restrictions on women's mobility and type of activities in the marketplace, exploitation of gender inequality by employers, and women's subordinate position in the family. This discrimination is reinforced by women's unequal access to resources, their heavy burden of work, and norms restricting female sexuality which often limit their opportunities for education and training. Systems of household budgeting generally give unequal rights to women. Both women's income and production are often controlled by men.

b. Gender-sensitive economic strategies

Gender inequality must not only be seen as a problem for women, but as *a matter of injustice which undermines all human relationships*, and increases levels of poverty for poor children and men as well as women.

Gender inequalities must be taken into account at *all* stages of project design, implementation, and evaluation. This requires the employment of at least some women staff, setting targets and standards for female participation, and ensuring women's representation in all stages of projects. In addition gender-aware strategies should include the following elements:

Strategies to increase women's control over resources: Women's unequal rights to resources must be borne in mind in all interventions. For example, membership regulations for participatory groups should not be based on ownership of resources such as land, which might exclude women. Ways of increasing women's control include measures to increase women's ownership of project resources (such as technologies), focusing on activities which strengthen women's control of resources, and linking with movements for change in property rights and legislation.

Strategies to decrease women's burden of unpaid work: All interventions should ensure that women's unpaid work is not increased, and, wherever possible, include measures to increase the efficiency of self-provisioning for consumption. Conventional approaches have included provision of creche and nursery facilities; introduction of labour-saving technology; and improvements in infrastructure such as water supply, housing, and sanitation. Other measures, which have been less frequently attempted but are equally important, are encouraging men to take greater responsibility for reproductive work through community pressure; organising women to pressure local authorities for adequate provision of childcare and other services; providing food-processing facilities or supplying certain processed food through co-operative marketing networks.

Strategies to increase income: For women the type of income and the ways in which it is earned may be as important as the actual levels of income. In some cases their labour and income may be appropriated by men; in others, increased income may lead to increased independence and status in the family. Women's control over the products of their work may vary depending on factors such as the productive resources which are being used and who controls these. Where the resources involved are controlled by men, they are likely to claim any income, and may attempt to increase women's unpaid labour. The income from other resources may be seen as legitimately belonging to women, but men may try to assert control if the productivity and income from these resources increase significantly.

The ways in which income is paid is also significant. There may be crucial differences in the degree of control which women can exercise over increased income depending on whether it is earned individually or by the household. In the latter case money is usually handed to the household head and women may have very little influence over how it is spent, even where they may perform most of the work. Where women's income is regular and of known amounts this is often paid into a 'family pool' over which men have the main control. Women may be more able secretly to put aside and control income which is paid irregularly and in varying amounts, although regular amounts of income give women more security and ability to save, where facilities exist.

Strategies to address gender subordination: These include support for organisations of self-employed women, who are trying to counter

497

gender discrimination in remuneration, and linking with wider movements for change in gender relations. They also include strategies to address inequalities in household budgeting arrangements through, for example, consciousness-raising of both women and men, and support for women who are trying to retain and save their income. All these strategies will also need to include measures to address women's lack of autonomy, including vulnerability to sexual violence and restrictions on their movements outside the home. (See **2.1** Gender.)

1.3.4 Technology development

Technology is a critical element in production. The introduction of new small- or large-scale technologies, or the development of existing technologies, profoundly affects all aspects of production. The transfer of technology from rich industrialised countries to developing, or poorer, countries, is constrained by many problems: the lack of will on the part of rich economies to share their most developed technology; the difficulties in adapting the technology to different conditions, and providing the skills transference which should accompany it; and the question of whether or not the technologies are appropriate to the new situations. The problems are similar for both small- and large-scale technology, but this section is concerned with the small-scale technology development supported by donor agencies and NGOs.

While the introduction of new technologies, or the improvement of existing ones, may bring great benefits to poor people, technology is also one of the areas in which most mistakes are made, and most damage done. This is mainly because technology is often seen as 'neutral': a value-free set of tools and techniques to solve certain kinds of technical problems. If these problems are defined in a mechanistic or one-dimensional way, without taking the social and cultural context into account, the solutions proposed may founder. Every donor agency has a long history of failed technological interventions, where expensive equipment (mechanised grain mills, tractors, pumps, trucks or sawmills) have literally ground to a halt because people could not maintain them or would not use them. At the root of many of these failures lie questions of the ownership and control of the technical inputs, which were not properly analysed at the planning stage.

NGO interventions in production often involve the introduction of new technologies, or development of existing technologies, such as new agricultural crops and production or processing techniques; new species of livestock, fish, and trees; and techniques of propagation and care; and new types of small-scale industry production. Technology development should not only be considered for production, but also for other aspects of people's livelihoods. For example, labour-saving technology for women's domestic tasks may have more impact on their ability to earn an income than technology for production.

Technology development cannot be divorced from considerations of ownership of and control over resources. It is never neutral in its effects, and its desirability can only be judged in relation to the aims, resources and constraints of those using it. What is efficient in one context, for some people, may fail to fulfil the needs of other people, in other contexts. Technological innovation which increases the productivity of labour may increase incomes or save time for some people, but lead to unemployment for others. It may also seriously increase the work burden of unpaid family workers in other tasks involved in the production process, without increasing their income. Technology introduced to increase the productivity of natural resources may lead to the erosion of informal use rights or appropriation of common resources, as those with power attempt to profit from the technology.

Many interventions using new technology focus on extension work with men, and on male tasks. Women are usually excluded from projects, leading to a 'gender technology gap', and increasing differences between women's and men's incomes. In other cases, where technology is introduced for tasks traditionally performed by women, it is often taken over by men, and women workers are displaced. Even where the technology increases women's production, they may not control the income. All technology interventions must therefore include strategies to protect women's interests, and be based on analysis of social and gender relations in the area where the intervention is to take place.

Technological interventions often take place without adequate consultation with women, and their needs are not taken into account. A classic example is that of a solar cooker which was introduced for women, with the idea of saving them time in fuelwood collection, and preserving fuelwood stocks. The women never used the cookers, because they cooked in the early morning before the sun came up, and in the evenings when returning from the fields. They had not been consulted. When they were, they said that what they really needed was a new variety of beans, which would cook more quickly, not a new type of cooker.

The introduction of new technologies may well need other types of support, including training in new skills, and access to credit, if it is to be successful. It is essential to research the market for products before introducing technology which may increase production. The local market may not be able to absorb the new or increased production, and producers may not be equipped for marketing elsewhere. A range of other issues may have to be addressed, such as storage of produce, transport, and new marketing outlets. All of these activities will have to

4

499

be taken on within a particular social context and according to the divisions of labour between women and men, young and old people, and different ethnic or race groups within the society. Class differences may be exacerbated by the increased production levels and higher income brought about by more efficient technologies, unless measures are taken to prevent that effect.

The advantages and disadvantages of different types of technology can be summarised as follows:

Existing, sometimes traditional, technologies: these are often technologically very complex and well-adapted to people's needs and environmental conditions, and their categorisation as 'simple' has often been based on the ignorance of outsiders. They should always be studied in detail before advocating any change. The questions to ask are who controls the technologies? Who uses them? What are the relations between people which are linked to these technologies?

Their advantages are that they are likely to have been tried and tested by users over a period of time, until they are appropriate to existing environmental, social, and economic needs, including the need to integrate different types of production to ensure steady income and labour demand. Tools may be made from locally-available materials, so are easy to repair and maintain.

Their problems are that they may perpetuate inequalities. Certain people may be excluded from using particular types of technology because of lack of skills and resources or social or cultural discrimination. The economic context may be undergoing rapid change; market competition due to changes in the local, national or international trading system may have seriously decreased the incomes of poor producers. Changing environmental conditions may require new production methods.

New 'intermediate' labour-intensive technologies: these are the type of technologies most commonly introduced by development NGOs. Many governments promote both technology design and extension work as part of poverty alleviation programmes. Formerly these technologies were mainly developed in Western countries or scientific laboratories in large urban areas, and were often inappropriate to the competitive markets in which producers had to operate. More successful programmes have focused on improving existing techniques and technologies, with the participation of the producers themselves. When new technologies are introduced, it is essential that *all* potential users and beneficiaries in the village or urban community are consulted. The questions to ask are Who needs what technology, for what purpose? How will the introduction of this technology affect social and economic relations in the area? Who will be in control of the technology? Who will maintain it? Who are the beneficiaries?

Appropriate technology tools and tchniques, in general:

- require only small amount of capital;
- emphasise the use of locally available materials, in order to lower costs and reduce supply problems;
- are relatively labour-intensive but more productive than many traditional technologies;
- are small enough in scale to be affordable to individual families or small groups of families;
- can be understood, controlled and maintained by villagers wherever possible, without a high level of specific training;
- can be produced in villages or small workshops;
- suppose that people can and will work together to bring improvements to communities;
- offer opportunities for local people to become involved in the modification and innovation process;
- are flexible, can be adapted to different places and changing circumstances;
- can be used in productive ways without doing harm to the environment.

The advantages are that intermediate — also called appropriate — technologies have been designed to require lower levels of investment than capital-intensive technologies, to give higher levels of production than existing technologies, and to be adaptable to local social and cultural conditions. Environmental impact has also generally been a consideration in their design.

Their problems are that they may require skills training and credit programmes, as the skills are likely to be different and the levels of investment higher than with existing technologies. They may still be unable to compete with large-scale capital-intensive technology. Where the technology leads to changes in product this may be unacceptable to existing markets.

High-input capital-intensive technologies: these have been the main focus of technology development by governments and international agencies until recently. Where the investment and skills are within the reach of poor people and extension facilities exist, these may increase incomes. It may therefore be desirable to assist poor women and men to acquire these facilities. However, the increased income may be short-lived unless poor people have sufficient resources to continue investment and production. These technologies often have adverse environmental impacts.

501

1.3.5 Credit and savings support

Many of the problems faced by poor producers are at least partly caused by lack of savings, and difficulties in obtaining credit. Without financial resources, people are unable to invest in improved technology, or benefit from economies of scale in production, marketing, raw material supply, or take advantage of low prices for bulk or seasonal purchases of basic necessities. Without savings, people are vulnerable to sudden and unforeseen expenses, such as the death of animals, sickness of family members, or destruction of crops by new diseases or pests. The provision of credit and savings facilities is thus a vital component of support for poor producers.

a. Forms of credit and savings
Various forms of indigenous or 'informal' savings and or credit institutions exist in most societies:
1 Informal and private provision
Savings may be in the form of hiding money; buying valuables or livestock; depositing money or valuables with a friend or broker; reciprocal arrangements with neighbours such as lending in the expectation of an equivalent return later.

Credit may be obtained from friends and neighbours possibly as part of a reciprocal arrangement, from moneylenders and traders, or landlords. It may involve highly exploitative relationships, leading in extreme forms to debt bondage, to systems of indebtedness to the 'company store' from which workers are unable to free themselves, and to the virtual enslavement of women to brothel-keepers.

Rotating savings and credit groups exist traditionally in many societies, the precise details of organisation depending on the size and purpose of the fund. The essential feature is that each member makes a payment into a central fund, the whole of which is then handed over to one of the members chosen either by drawing lots, auction or predetermined rotation. This fund then rotates until all members have received a lump sum.

2 Formal commercial or state savings and credit institutions These are the national Post Office network, and commercial or state banks.
3 Intermediary institutions
Revolving loan funds (RLFs) are often supported by donor agencies. A grant or loan is made to an organisation which lends money to its members and participants. The members repay their loans to the central revolving fund, so that further loans may be made. RLFs are vulnerable to the high rates of inflation common in many developing countries, and to currency devaluations. The real value of loans may fall rapidly, and RLFs require repeated 'topping-up' by donor agencies.

Saveway clubs are a particular model for savings groups. The basis of the Saveway system, first developed during the early 1970s in Zimbabwe, is the use of stamps to record deposits made by club members at weekly meetings. The cash is collected and placed in a post office or bank account in the name of the club. Variations of this system exist in other parts of the world.

Credit unions are a type of formal co-operative based on a nineteenth-century German model. The International Credit Union Movement has its headquarters in the USA, and this form of organisation has been promoted in a large number of developing countries through national credit union 'parent bodies'. A credit union helps members to save, and these savings are then made available to members as credit. It also channels other external credit funds to its members.

Alternative or intermediary banking systems have been funded by some large multilateral agencies to provide parallel banking systems or to act as intermediaries for groups excluded from the formal system. A well-known example of this is the Grameen Bank in Bangladesh. (See 4.5.2.6 Credit.)

b. Obstacles to obtaining credit

Poor people face a number of obstacles to obtaining credit, and when they do obtain it, it may be on relatively unfavourable terms. They are seen as less creditworthy because they lack resources for collateral for loans, and their activities are seen to be risky, so that high interest rates are demanded by moneylenders and traders.

Savings or credit needs may be too small to merit expensive trips to centres where formal institutions exist. Commercial and state banks are often unwilling to lend to small producers because the administration costs of small loans are high. This increases dependence on high-interest informal sources because these may disburse speedily and lend very small amounts. Even where preferential formal credit schemes for the poor exist these may be vulnerable to bribery and corruption of bank officials or those from whom references and guarantees are needed.

Women are particularly disadvantaged in access to credit on all these counts because of their lower earnings, lower levels of resources for security, restrictions on interactions with male moneylenders, and discrimination by moneylenders and banks in their assessment of women's capabilities. Women also lack information about credit. They do, however, often save and borrow small amounts, sometimes from richer women with whom they develop patronage relations, or from neighbours in reciprocal aid arrangements.

Women-only rotating savings and credit groups are also very common, particularly in West Africa and in India. These are generally smaller than those for men, and the social benefits of increasing friendship networks are often a major aim. Secure savings may enable women to increase their control over their income and property, and the process of obtaining credit in their own name may give them increased control over the productive activities concerned. However, unless women are fully involved in the process of obtaining credit, their name and signature may simply be used by men to get loans over which women may have very little control.

c. Assessing credit needs

The failure to understand the nature of poor people's credit needs, and a failure to link effectively with other informal and formal sources of savings and credit which might be made available has often led to the failure of credit schemes. A major problem with many credit schemes supported by NGOs or other agencies has been the tying of credit to particular purposes, such as a 'package' of inputs which enables people to adopt a particular technological innovation, for example, to buy improved seeds or to buy raw materials in bulk. Credit has only been given on production of receipts. These schemes may lead to manipulation of the loans by poor people so that they can use the money in accordance with their changing priorities; this may be characterised by the lending institutions as 'misuse'.

The conditions for repayment and the constraints poor people have in repaying loans must be carefully analysed. Poor people's lives are full of risk, and NGOs have to accept that their support often involves sharing those risks. For example, new technology is often risky; or the returns of the investment in production may not be enough to meet loan servicing and repayment requirements, due to crop failure, death of livestock or unfavourable market conditions.

For poor people, there may not always be a clear distinction between production and consumption, and the most helpful form of credit enables them to meet their most pressing need and, at the same time, results in an income large enough to enable them to repay their loan without hardship. They themselves are likely to be the best judges of what these needs and priorities are, and credit schemes should provide not only initial capital amounts, but working capital which can allow for sudden unexpected costs.

Poor people often need access to savings or credit urgently, sometimes for small amounts and with the minimum of formalities. These conditions may be best met by existing lenders, and NGOs should take care not to close off these avenues by introducing new credit facilities. They do not always charge exploitative rates, and often offer loans for 'unproductive' purposes, such as medical costs or marriage or funeral expenses.

There may be conflicts of interest within households over use of credit. Women may have very little control over the use of credit obtained in their name, unless they are fully involved in the process of obtaining it. Secure savings may enable women to increase their control over small amounts of income and property, such as dowry payments, which are theirs by law and custom but which in practice are controlled by men. Group credit schemes may offer some protection to women from males in the household.

Credit and savings available from small-scale projects are unlikely to be sufficient for all the production and consumption needs of poor people. Where possible they should also attempt to increase people's ability to use other formal and informal sources of credit to increase the range of options available to them.

d. The importance of participation
Some of the most successful credit and savings schemes have been small, participatory credit and loan groups. Repayment rates are always likely to be higher when the borrower has a sense of ownership and effective participation in the decisions of the institution.

Some notably successful schemes, in terms of rates of repayment, are the Self-Employed Women's Association (SEWA), and the Working Women's Forum and Annapurna Mandal in India, and the Bangladesh Rural Action Committee (BRAC) and the Grameen Bank in Bangladesh. However, the success of schemes such as the Grameen Bank depends largely on the fact that the main borrowers are women, who often prejudice their other activities in order to find the money to repay the loans. The Grameen Bank now prefers to lend to women, so that men who want loans may pressure their wives or other female relatives into getting the money for them; the women then have no control over the money borrowed, but are held responsible for paying it back. Other credit projects have involved NGOs acting as intermediaries with commercial or state banks. In some cases this has led to modifications and changes in bank attitudes and practices in favour of poor people.

1.3.6 Marketing assistance
(To be read in conjunction with 4.5.2.5 Marketing assistance.)

a. Assessing the market
The 'market' refers to any context in which the purchase, exchange or sale of goods and services takes place. There are different classifications of markets, and the nature of any particular market should be carefully researched. There are markets for inputs, for outputs, for credit, for technology, and so on. Issues in conventional market research include the

identification of consumers at a local, regional and international level; output prices; seasonal and regional price variations; sources of production inputs (raw materials, labour, technology); nature and prices of competitive products; and the physical accessibility of the market.

The market is far from being a passive entity; in fact it can rarely be used by resource-poor producers to capitalise on their so-called 'comparative advantages', such as climatic factors or advantageous location for the production of specific produce. Poor producers are likely to be at the mercy of local powerful elites, intermediaries, officials, landowners, and moneylenders. They are further constrained by ethnic, gender, class, racial, and other forms of discrimination; there is no such thing as the 'free' market for poor and disadvantaged people. Any producer who relies on the market knows only too well that technical skills and resources are only the starting point of production: much more is needed in terms of personal contacts and marketing experience in order to make an evaluation of realistic market opportunities.

Failure to take the market into account has been a major cause of failure of NGO production interventions: market behaviour, and the use that the poor producer makes of it, are two of the most powerful elements determining financial autonomy and ultimate sustainability. For example, new products may not be accepted by the targeted consumer; producers may not be equipped to cope with lower output prices; competition from large-scale production is too intense; or volatile markets lead to increased vulnerability of small-scale producers and the ultimate collapse of production projects of all types. It is therefore vital that a market feasibility assessment be included as part of the appraisal process of production interventions.

b. Forms of NGO marketing assistance

NGOs can offer assistance to producers and small traders in many different ways. Helping producers to improve their understanding of the market (degree of concentration, seasonal variation of prices, market chains) can be very valuable. There may also be scope for improving the supply of raw materials, and giving technical advice on methods of handling, storage, packing and transport methods, and transport and storage for finished goods for sale or consumption. The formation of small producer or trader organisations may be a way of increasing the power of individual producers, and giving them an advantage in relation to large traders.

Small associations may have a role in improving market places and trading institutions, to reduce monopoly power, through making markets more public, standardising and controlling weights and measures, introducing quality penalties, and in disseminating information through the radio or via handbills or newsletters.

NGOs can also have a wider role in support for changes in the economic and political context of small-scale production and marketing. This can be at the local level of lobbying and campaigning for changes in legislation regarding small-scale and informal sector trading to decrease bribery and extortion; or at the international level of lobbying and campaigning for changes in trading agreements, such as the GATT or WTO. NGOs such as Oxfam also support national and international alternative marketing organisations. (See 4.5.2.5 Marketing assistance.)

c. Problems faced by small producers

Problems faced by poor producers and traders include not only inadequate methods of and resources for marketing but also their economic and political vulnerability. They also face difficulties in the supply of raw materials and basic consumption goods. Marketing assistance should therefore include both these aspects. For women, these problems of poverty are compounded by gender inequalities.

It should not be assumed that poor producers and traders are operating inefficiently and that this can be solved by marketing training or feasibility studies. Often poor women and men are operating extremely efficiently within their constraints and needs. Training and small-scale credit support can therefore only be effective if based on detailed investigation of these.

The effectiveness of assistance to small-scale producers and traders may be seriously limited by the context within which they are forced to operate. Small-scale producers are often exploited by corrupt state marketing organisations and co-operatives, or face competition from large-scale traders and intermediaries. Large-scale traders may have a monopoly of the most lucrative types of trade, fixing prices of raw materials and basic commodities and controlling sale of produce through various exploitative means. They often wield considerable economic and political power, and their interests are often protected by the police, state bureaucracies, and legislation regulating small-scale and informal sector trading and hawking. Small-scale producers are often indebted to traders, intermediaries, and moneylenders, who provide credit at exorbitant rates of interest.

Finally, the scope for small-scale production (such as cash crops, textiles, and fishing) is often determined by international trade agreements which limit the amount which any country can export and favour larger-scale producers with the contacts and skills to negotiate with the authorities. Marketing assistance is therefore likely to need also to address the wider economic and political context. Lobbying and campaigning has often been a complement to the formation of participatory groups at the local level. (See 4.5.2.5.c Alternative trading organisations and Oxfam Bridge.)

4

1.3.7 Training and information exchange
(To be read in conjunction with **3**.1.2 Education and training.)

Training is a vital input to the development of production activities for poor women and men. A large proportion of Oxfam's development work all over the world includes some form of training and capacity-building. Types of training and approaches to it vary widely, from top-down, formally-structured programmes to participative, informal ways of transmitting skills and sharing knowledge and experience through networks of information exchange. The objectives of training in the production sector may be narrowly defined, to transmit very specific skills, such as those linked to particular technologies or needs; for example, the training of women and men in refugee camps to operate and maintain water pumps. Or they may concentrate on capacity-building, such as training in organisational and book-keeping skills to enhance the independence and efficiency of producer, credit or marketing organisations, and the participation and empowerment of the individuals who belong to them.

Training needs must always be vary carefully assessed, and based on consultation with those who require training, so that real needs are identified. The economic and social context must also be analysed: if, for example, the need for training in new skills to produce new products is not properly analysed, it may result in the oversaturation of markets with a narrow range of goods, and minimal incomes to those concerned. This may worsen the position of other, equally poor, workers already involved in small-scale industries.

Training programmes for women should be very carefully planned, as these are often based on wrong assumptions about women's training needs. There are many cases of women being taught skills seen by outsiders as 'appropriate to women' (such as tailoring, embroidery or basketmaking) which have not only failed to take into account the market context or to equip women to compete within it, but failed to respond to women's real training needs. These needs, like men's, may be in the areas of agricultural production, operating small machines, literacy, or book-keeping, rather than handcrafts.

a. Rural extension
'Extension' is the term applied to rural training programmes in which extension workers teach and train people in villages in a wide range of new ideas or techniques. They include programmes of agricultural technical assistance to improve crop yields or animal varieties, or health and nutrition. While many NGOs now recognise the value of participatory forms of learning, top-down extension is still promoted by governments in many countries. Successful forms of extension include

group learning, and exchanges between farmers, to enable them to compare experiences and transfer skills. (See **4.2.5.2** Small-scale agricultural production groups and co-operatives.)

A common problem in rural extension is that most training programmes assume that men are the farmers, while women are concerned only with childcare and at most, small-scale homestead gardens for domestic consumption. In fact most farmers are women. The failure of extension programmes to address the needs of women, and to target the training at those who would use it most, has negatively affected women's productivity and income, their control of land, and their social status in many developing countries. (See **2.**1 Gender.)

b. Information exchange
New agricultural and artisan skills often spread very rapidly by word of mouth, and informal demonstration to relatives and friends, without the need for training programmes; it is thus useful to link training with information exchange, where trainers learn from trainees and vice versa. Participatory teaching allows participants to learn as much or more from each other than from teachers. Networking has been supported by Oxfam in many parts of the world; the Arid Lands Information Network (ALIN), based in Senegal, is an example of an Oxfam-funded initiative which enables rural women and men to exchange ideas, experience and skills by means of a regular newsletter and regular visits between villages and regions. (See **3**.1.3.2 Networks and networking.)

There are a number of ways of exchanging information; these include participatory workshops and conferences where the emphasis is on participants forming networks to exchange information between themselves. Festivals and fairs can also be important venues for information exchange between producers. These networks can greatly increase the numbers of people gaining access to information and skills.

1.3.8 Participatory organisations
(To be read in conjunction with **3**.1 Social organisation and **3**.2 Institutional development. Only a very brief discussion of the issues is presented here.)

Economic interventions such as the introduction of new technology, provision of credit or training, and support for information exchanges, can be facilitated by the formation of some sort of participatory organisation. At the practical level there is a range of potential advantages to group formation, including economies of scale, benefits from pooling of resources and sharing expensive technology, and sharing information and knowledge. There are also important social benefits, such as increasing people's confidence and their ability to challenge social and economic inequalities.

Although there are numerous potential benefits to organising poor producers, experience has shown that this is far from easy. There are potential problems associated with levels of participation, and equity among the members. The problems of lack of skills and lack of time are also likely to be most acute for the poorest and most oppressed people within poor social groups.

A number of different types of participatory organisation are described below. They include traditional types of producer organisation based on kin and community ties, and membership organisations set up to pursue particular aims. Some are formal organisations, registered and governed by state legislation; others have resulted from grassroots co-operation, and resisted state regulation because of fears of state interference and manipulation. There are also popular movements for change. Oxfam supports a wide range of these kinds of organisations.

a. Types of production groups

People organise around a common interest in many different ways. Any analysis of socio-economic systems of production must include the way people are already organised, together with an assessment of their scope for social transformation. From the point of view of production activities, one or several of the following kinds of organisations may exist:

Informal production groups and associations: many societies have traditional forms of co-operative groups for production, savings and credit, marketing and resource management such as irrigation and forestry. Some of these are genuinely egalitarian and collective, for example, women sharing work on each other's plots; others may be more hierarchical and exploitative.

Many different types of informal production groups (marketing associations, credit and savings groups, information networks) have been introduced by development agencies. In some cases these have responded to the needs and priorities of those involved. In others structures have been imposed upon them.

Formal organisations: these include co-operatives, which are legally registered organisations with a formal structure, including membership, board of directors and official accounts. Most countries have legislation governing the establishment and running of co-operatives. This generally requires registration with a central Department of Co-operatives, compliance with a set of highly specific regulations governing such matters as the issuing of shares, the keeping of accounts, admission to membership, and the election of officers. Registration may also bring preferential credit and other benefits.

510

Trades unions are organisations to protect the rights of workers. In many countries these are part of a national trades union movement. Some trades unions have been set up by, and are dominated by, political parties or government. Others are formed as a result of grassroots activism, in defence of people's rights. In some countries there may be an extensive body of state legislation protecting workers' rights. In other countries the activities of trades unions may conflict with state legislation.

Multipurpose complex production organisations may themselves be termed NGOs. They have a number of professional staff and provide a range of services to poor producers. They may also have subsidiary local participatory organisations and projects affiliated to or supported by them.

Movements for change or popular organisations: these may campaign or lobby for changes in the conditions of production: changes in land rights and other legislation governing productive resources; the protection of environmental resources; and change in international trading agreements such as the GATT.

Other popular movements may campaign more broadly for social and political change on behalf of women, or oppressed race, caste or ethnic groups, in respect of their control over production resources.

b. Structure and activities of production organisations

Smaller and relatively homogeneous organisations often find it easier to operate and stay together. At the same time small size may limit the range of resources and skills available to the group and lead to dangers of marginalisation.

Producer organisations may have a number of different functions, such as: production; providing support for consumption, family provisioning and maintenance, care of community members to free producers for income earning; marketing and supplying goods; providing credit and savings facilities; lobbying and campaigning for change in the conditions of production. Many organisations may seek to cover more than one of these activities. However, in general the greater the range of activities then the greater the potential for conflicts of interest and the greater levels of resources, skills, and organisation needed.

The type of organisational structure best suited to the needs and priorities of poor people depends on their resources and skills and the size and intended activities of the organisation. In general, informal structures may be sufficient for very small local-level activities where levels of inequality between participants are low, but more formal structures may be needed as organisations grow. Much also depends on the types of state assistance which can be obtained through formal registration and the degree to which this may lead to state interference. These are widely variable between countries.

511

c. Gender considerations in organisations

All interventions will need to pay particular attention to gender inequalities which affect the degree to which women are able to participate or benefit. This involves gender awareness at all levels of project design, implementation, and evaluation. Women generally have fewer resources and less time than men, and less experience of formal types of organisation. Because of the pervasiveness of gender inequality, women's organisations may need assistance on many different levels, including confidence-building, dealing with domestic violence, or childcare.

Women are not a homogenous group; their needs vary and may conflict because of class, race and ethnic differences. Women's needs can only be assessed accurately after extensive consultation with them, and priorities may well change as women gain confidence and experience. They may start with immediate practical and achievable aims, but then find that gender inequalities in the family and wider society need to be tackled.

Women must have the flexibility to develop and organise themselves to respond to their changing needs and priorities. Women may find participation in women-only groups easier and more socially acceptable. However, unless these groups are assisted to gain significant skills and resources, their potential is limited, and they may in the end be demoralising to the participants. In community-based interventions, women's organisations are often regarded as marginal to the 'main' (i.e. men's) activities, and are included in project design as a token gesture to women's development. They often receive less funding and training. A strategy to counter the marginalisation of women in organisations can be to provide structures which include both women and men, but where women are able to organise to defend their particular interests.

1.4 Key questions

1 Has the national economic and political context been taken into account in the project proposal? What are the likely constraints and opportunities arising from both national and international economic policy, for the success of the intervention?

2 Has the project proposal been designed with the effective participation of the people who are to benefit from it? Have the interests of women and men, of different class or ethnic groups within the community been represented? Have existing conflicts of interest been identified, as well as common interests?

3 What is the relation of the participants in the particular intervention or project to other poor women and men in the community who

might be affected? Might there be a negative impact on the livelihoods of non-participants?

4 What natural and social resources are involved in the intervention? Who uses which resources, and who controls them? How will the products be distributed, and who controls the distribution?

5 What is the division of labour in the area? What work do women, men, and children do? Do people of different class or ethnic identities do different work, and what is it?

6 What is the additional work required by the project, and who will do it? Have ways of decreasing the unpaid workload of those involved or affected been considered?

7 Are technology inputs required? What existing technologies are used by women and men, and what social relationships are involved in their use? How will these relationships be affected by the new technologies? Will the technology inputs benefit both women and men? Have women's views and needs been expressed directly in relation to the proposal?

8 How will the new technology affect the sustainability of people's livelihoods? What will be the environmental impact? What is the likely effect on the workloads of those involved or affected? Is the proposed technology for production only? Has labour-saving technology in the areas of family provisioning (water and fuel collection, equipment for cooking and food processing) been considered?

9 Who will own and control the technology? Who will maintain it? Is training needed? What are the running costs? Can it be sustained financially?

10 What is the likely impact on the market of new produce, or increased production of existing goods? Has market research been carried out? What is the division of labour in marketing at present, and how will this be affected? If cash income is to increase, who will get it?

11 If training and credit is part of the proposal, many of the questions in relation to use and control, and social relationships also apply. Additional questions may be: Who needs the credit, and what is their full range of needs likely to be? Is there enough flexibility in the credit system? How do national economic factors (inflation, currency valuations) affect repayment? Who will control the credit system? Is the donor prepared to make a long-term commitment to credit provision if necessary?

12 Who needs what kind of training, and what for? What is the best way of ensuring that all those who need it will get it? Have different timetables and working hours, cultural and social factors such as mobility, been taken fully into account so that women have equal opportunities?

513

13 Is the organisation or group making the proposal formal or
   informal? What is the nature of its membership? Have members —
   both women and men — participated effectively in designing the
   proposal? How are decisions made, and who makes them? Does the
   organisation have the expertise to run the project, or is training
   needed in organisational skills, book-keeping, marketing or other
   areas?

2 Agriculture

2.1 Introduction 515
    2.1.1 Agricultural development and small-scale farmers 517
    2.1.2 Sustainable agriculture 518
2.2 Practical approaches to crop production 520
    2.2.1 Access to and control of resources 520
    2.2.2 Increasing small-scale crop production 523
    2.2.3 Storage, processing, and preservation 527
    2.2.4 Small-scale cropping systems 530
    2.2.5 Low-external-input sustainable agriculture (LEISA) 532
    2.2.6 Vegetable production for landless people 535
2.3 Practical approaches to livestock production 537
    2.3.1 Extensive livestock systems 538
    2.3.2 Small-scale livestock farming 541
    2.3.3 Social and cultural considerations in livestock production 541
    2.3.4 Division of labour and ownership rights 542
    2.3.5 Women's role in livestock production 543
    2.3.6 Increasing livestock production 544
    2.3.7 General guidelines for pastoral development 547
    2.3.8 Principal livestock species 549
    2.3.9 Bees and beekeeping 554
2.4 Support for rural organisations 555
    2.4.1 Pastoralist associations 556
    2.4.2 Small-scale agricultural production groups and co-operatives 557
2.5 Key questions

2.1 Introduction

According to the United Nations Development Programme (UNDP) two-thirds of the people in developing countries live in rural areas. Agricultural production is the main source of subsistence and income for the majority of these rural people, many of whom are small-scale farmers who own their own land, work the land of others as agricultural labourers, or graze their herds of animals on land which is 'common property'. At the heart of the viability of all these forms of rural livelihoods is the question of rights to resources, such as land, and rights over the produce or income which result from people's labour. The relationships of production at the 'micro' level of households and agricultural communities are organised according to customary and statutory rights, and understanding the different implications of these for women, men, and children, belonging to different race, class and ethnic groups, is essential for development workers attempting to intervene in agricultural production.

Risk is also a central feature of rural livelihoods. Rural people normally diversify their economic activities in order to spread their risks: they may combine crop or animal production with wage labour on farms or in local industries, or with income-earning activities on a self-employed basis. These risks may include loss of land, crop failure, death of animals, illness, and the impact of national and international economic policies. Large numbers of poor farmers have been adversely affected by capital-intensive agricultural development, which aims to 'modernise' production to increase yields, but seldom takes into account their skills, experience, and local knowledge, and the social organisation of production.

Oxfam supports the efforts of small-scale agricultural producers and agricultural wage-labourers to defend and improve their livelihoods, and to participate in the decisions which affect them. In the first place this means researching and identifying, in participatory ways, the skills and capacities, needs and priorities of women and men who make their living primarily from agriculture. The resulting practical interventions may be designed to increase agricultural production and improve marketing, fund training in production and marketing skills, or support the development of producer organisations, which may also lobby and campaign for land rights or fairer terms of trade. Whatever the particular form of intervention, donor agencies should always ensure that both women and men have participated in the planning stages, and that gender, and other social inequities, such as those linked to ethnic, race, class or caste identity, are addressed in the design and implementation of the work. (See **2.1** Gender, and **2.2** Ethnicity, race and caste.)

Although crop and animal production are closely linked in agricultural production systems — as they are with other ways of making a living in rural areas — this section focuses on crops and animals separately, in discussing production techniques and principles. Crop and livestock production are considered in a more integrated way in relation to other aspects of agricultural livelihoods, such as credit and training, and marketing of produce, and producer organisations.

2.1.1 Agricultural development and small-scale farmers

Agriculture is an important source of national income for most governments in developing countries. Capital-intensive agriculture promoted by governments and international agencies includes extensive development of cash crops for export, for example, sugar, cocoa, coffee, and tea. This is generally seen as a priority in developing countries because of their continuing dependence on primary exports and their need for foreign exchange to repay debts and finance other development programmes. Investment in cash crops has often meant the displacement of food crops from agricultural land, and consequent food shortages at the household level.

In the 1960s and 1970s, promotion of 'Green Revolution' technology based on a package of High Yielding Variety (HYV) seeds, high inputs of chemical fertilisers and pesticides for certain staple foods (particularly wheat, rice and maize) aimed to decrease dependence on food imports and the risk of famine. While in India the Green Revolution enabled the country to reach self-sufficiency in food grain production and build up stocks, the reliance on capital resources meant that while many rich farmers undoubtedly benefited, poor farmers were often left worse off than they had been. One of the main effects in India was to increase the gap between rich and poor. (See 1.3.5.1 Rural livelihoods.)

Capital-intensive agriculture has also promoted other 'improved' crop varieties, bred for particular properties such as resistance to disease or drought. More recently new varieties are being developed by traditional breeding, and through biotechnology and genetic engineering. Although these have considerable potential for assisting poor farmers, the research and promotion has so far been dominated by the interests of large agricultural concerns and agribusiness.

In some countries agricultural development strategies have led to an increase in both national food security and export earnings. However, they have failed to benefit many of the poorest people in rural areas, and have led to increasing poverty and landlessness.

National agricultural development strategies have often encouraged multinational companies and large-scale farming and plantation enterprises, which tend to appropriate the most fertile land, evicting small farmers and forcing them to occupy less productive or marginal areas. This in turn puts excessive pressure on fragile environments and leads to environmental degradation through over-exploitation — such as deforestation. In north-east Brazil, for example, pressure on land from the expansion of commercial agriculture has forced small farmers to turn to casual low-paid labour. While this trend cannot be reversed, a Brazilian NGO supported by Oxfam is trying to convince those remaining on the land that small-scale farming is not only viable but

4

may be a preferable alternative to wage labour or migration, by helping them to identify particular opportunities and demonstrating possible ways of improving their production system, using the best of traditional and new technologies.

Another effect of modernisation of agriculture is to mechanise many agricultural tasks, leading to widespread rural unemployment or underemployment. As a result, poor male farmers migrate to urban centres to seek work. This in turn leaves women solely responsible for the maintenance of the land and family subsistence. In many cases men send regular remittances back to help support the household, but often these remittances become fewer as time goes on, and as men set up new households in urban areas, or find themselves without work.

Agricultural development is often accompanied by land reform which distributes individual land ownership titles. In some cases these have increased the security of some small-scale, usually male, farmers, but have often been widely flouted and led to the eviction of tenant and sharecropping households. Land-titling programmes tend to ignore women's traditional use rights to land, and thus restrict or remove their access to land by registering it in the name of men. This increases the vulnerability of women farmers.

Where extension programmes of training and credit for small-scale farmers have been set up, they have often been unsuccessful. Training has been 'top-down', and inappropriate for local conditions, ignoring local farmers' own experience and skills. Conventional extension and training programmes typically assume that farmers are men, and women are excluded from them. Credit schemes, when implemented without the participation of farmer organisations, may be undermined by excessive bureaucracy and corruption.

2.1.2 Sustainable agriculture
(To be read in conjunction with 1.3.1.1 Sustainable development.)

Following the Brundtland Report presented by the World Commission on Environment and Development in 1986, there has been increasing emphasis in some development agencies on small farmer initiatives and the concept of 'sustainable development'. The report of the United Nations Conference on Environment and Development (UNCED) in June 1992 emphasised the importance of sustainable agriculture, and states:

Major adjustments are needed in agricultural, environmental and macroeconomic policy, at both national and international levels, in developed as well as developing countries, to create the conditions for sustainable agriculture and rural development(SARD). The major objective of SARD is to increase food production in a sustainable way and enhance food security. This will involve education initiatives, utilisation of economic incentives and the development of appropriate and new technologies, thus ensuring stable supplies of nutritionally adequate food, access to those supplies by vulnerable groups, and production for markets; employment and income generation to alleviate poverty; and natural resource management and environmental protection...The main tools of SARD are policy and agrarian reform, participation, income diversification, land conservation and improved management of inputs. The success of SARD will depend largely on the support and participation of rural people, national Governments, the private sector and international cooperation, including technical and scientific cooperation.

Alongside this official position, the NGO Sustainable Agriculture Treaty, also produced in June 1992, outlines the following central elements of sustainable agriculture:

- it is ecologically sound, economically viable, socially just, culturally appropriate and based on a holistic scientific approach;
- it is based on the preservation of biodiversity, producing diverse forms of high quality foods, fibres and medicines through methods which maintain soil fertility and water purity, conserve and improve soil quality, recycle natural resources and conserve energy;
- it uses locally available renewable resources and appropriate and affordable technologies, thus minimising the use of external and purchased inputs in support of local self-sufficiency and independence. It seeks to allow more people to stay on the land by ensuring stable sources of income;
- it respects the ecological principles of diversity and interdependence and farmers' traditional wisdom, seeking to use modern science to build on that wisdom rather than replace it.

One of the ways in which people's methods of making a living can be approached and analysed is through the concept of 'sustainable livelihoods'. (See **1.3.3.1** Sustainable livelihoods.) This concept includes the resources available to people; their capacities, which include capital, education, health, and social and economic networks; and the notion of equity in relation to their rights to and control of resources. Sustainability refers to people's ability to cope with sudden or gradual change, and adapt their livelihoods to new condition, without diminishing resources for future generations. The sustainable use of resources is central to the way this concept is applied to rural livelihoods.

2.2 Practical approaches to crop production

NGO economic interventions in crop production generally aim to support both landless labourers and marginal farmers adversely affected by agricultural growth policies and activities of large private farms and agribusinesses, and to assist resource-poor small-scale farmers in marginal areas to increase their production and incomes. In either case support is likely to be needed not only at the level of production, but also reproduction (the tasks concerned with bearing and rearing children and maintaining the household) and basic consumption, and increasing livelihood security. The question of rights over resources is central to all forms of production.

2.2.1 Access to and control of resources

Poverty in rural areas is not only a consequence of low levels of production, but depends crucially on systems of ownership and control which govern people's rights to resources and the distribution of produce. Crop production systems generally involve a wide range of customary and legal rights to land and other natural resources, as well as to labour and crops. These largely determine who is able to participate in particular initiatives, and who will benefit from them. They also determine the amounts of labour and investment which farmers are able or willing to put into improving particular types of production. For example, women who already work a 17-hour day in rural sub-Saharan Africa are not likely to wish to contribute their labour to process new crops over which they have no rights; and farmers without secure land rights are unlikely to be interested in investing a great deal of time and effort in improving soil quality in the long term.

a. Rights to land
Ownership rights: In some societies there are clear absolute individual rights where ownership, rights of sale and alienation, and rights of use are all vested in the same person. This is the concept of land ownership generally promoted in mainstream agricultural development and in land reform, and assumed to be vested in a male household head. Households headed or maintained by women are usually only taken into account if the women are officially recognised as heading the household (as widows, for example); women whose husbands have left them, or who maintain the household financially even though husbands live there, are usually not considered for land titles.
Usufruct rights: In many parts of pre-colonial Africa rights to land were based on usufruct: while villages of clans held the rights to the land,

members of individual households had usufruct rights, which meant they could farm the land and use the produce, but could not transfer land to others through sale or inheritance. During the colonial period these rights became gradually transformed by land reform measures into individual land-tenure systems. One of the results was that, as titles to land were generally granted to men, women lost their usufruct rights to it. In many societies today women may be the main cultivators and have usufruct rights under customary law, but their rights in such systems are dependent on their relationship to men and are thus insecure, particularly where divorce rates are increasing. In other parts of the world, for example in Latin America, while Amerindians have usufruct rights to their land, the State retains control and thus the right to exploit its mineral or other resources, or to sell concessions to do so to third parties.

Tenancy and sharecropping rights: In many parts of Asia and Latin America land is cultivated by tenant and share-cropper households with little security or freedom to improve production. Sharecropping and tenancy agreements are almost invariably held by male heads of households but usually assume the unpaid labour input of women and children.

b. Rights and access to other resources for production

Rights to capital for investment, agricultural inputs, and technology often reside in the owners rather than the cultivators of the land, and so to men rather than women. In addition women may lack the skills to use certain types of technology because of lack of training.

c. Rights to crops and income

Many different systems exist, such as:

- certain crops may belong to women, and others to men, even where both may be involved in their cultivation;
- gender differentiation may apply to different varieties of the same crop, where some types of rice or potato are preferred for household consumption, and grown by women, but other (often 'improved' varieties) are grown for sale by men;
- women are entitled to a share of the harvest for household provisioning while men are entitled to take any cash income;
- men and women may be entitled to both food and cash from crops which they cultivate.

Differential crop rights between women and men are often supported by ritual taboos and customs, and these should be researched and understood by development agencies when assessing the likely benefits of agricultural production interventions for women and men.

d. Rights to labour and assistance

Crop production involves a number of different inter-related stages, and is often integrated with other livelihood strategies, including livestock production, fishing, and small-scale industries. The timing of agricultural work is crucial for its success, and those with power within communities and households often have customary priority rights to the labour of others. These include rights of members within households to the labour of other household members. Men may control the labour of women and children. In other cases women may have considerable independence and also be able to call on the assistance of men, particularly younger men. In either case it cannot be assumed that women and men will benefit equally from their labour input.

Rights to labour are often included in tenancy and sharecropping agreements, and cover unpaid labour in production itself and other unpaid or underpaid labour for landlords. This affects the time which tenants and sharecropping households have for any small plots of land they may own, or use for their own production. Women and children are often called on to do unpaid work in the landlord's household, including domestic work.

Forms of co-operative labour exchange and mutual assistance between individuals and households are common for both women and men but vary widely in their form. They should always be carefully researched, and well-functioning co-operative work should be built upon, and not undermined by economic interventions or new institutions.

e. Rights to crop by-products

While certain people have the rights to the main crop, others may have customary rights to by-products such as straw from cereal crops, essential for feeding livestock or for fuel. Gleaning cereal fields is often a vital source of food for the poorest women and men. Increasing 'efficiency' on the part of landowners or changing to more profitable crops, such as short-strawed cereals, may deprive other people of their means of survival.

These different rights and inequalities must be assessed and taken into account at all stages of project design, implementation and evaluation. They are not static, but in a constant process of negotiation. Interventions should never increase inequalities, but build on existing formal and informal rights to lead to positive changes.

f. Rights and gender differentiation

Gender inequalities are common in all societies, and development workers should always analyse gender differences in rights to land, resources and crops. (See **2.1** Gender.) Attempts to increase production for land and crops owned and controlled by men may critically affect the time women have to work on their own fields and crops, and hence their income. In some cases women may be better-off in the short term assisting their husbands or male family members to increase production; but this is at the expense of their own longer-term security and independent sources of income. Helping women to improve crop yields on their own land, and strategies to save them labour time, may increase their income and independence.

It is equally important to examine work involved at all stages of crop production from land preparation through to cooking to ensure that attempts to increase particular types of production do not increase the unpaid work burden on women and children. Attempts to increase women's income should take into account whether or not they will require and can call on male assistance.

There are many forms of participatory appraisal, such as Participatory Rural Appraisal (PRA), Rapid Rural Appraisal (RRA), Participatory Learning Methods (PALM) which have been developed — and are constantly being adapted — to try to improve ways of gathering information from people about their activities, roles, aspirations and priorities. When effectively used, by informed and experienced practitioners, these information-gathering tools can enable those who are not usually able to make their views known — such as old or very young people, women, or people of low-status caste or ethnic groups — to participate in building up a picture of different views of a situation, and planning interventions. (See **1.4.3** Formal methods of information-gathering and appraisal and **1.3.4** Assessing the environment.)

4

2.2.2 *Increasing small-scale crop production*

a. Crop varieties

Much of the work of development agencies is concerned with assisting resource-poor farmers to increase production and incomes. In most cases there is a range of possible crops, crop varieties or combination of crops. There are numerous sub-species and varieties adapted to different circumstances. These fall into two main categories:

Locally-bred and traditional varieties: Women and men farmers often use a wide range of existing local varieties, bred and selected over generations for local needs and conditions; these are often neglected by development agencies and may not be known by all local people. It is possible to transfer locally-bred varieties between geographical areas of similar ecological conditions. These local varieties are often lower yielding but may have been selected for a wide variety of qualities, such as:

- higher resistance to drought;
- better flavour or cooking properties;

- greater pest resistance;
- out-of-main-season production, which spreads food availability, incomes and labour use throughout the year;
- lower labour or fertility requirements.

New exotic varieties: these are often bred in formal scientific research establishments. They include High Yielding Varieties (HYV), used in Green Revolution agriculture, bred for increased productivity per area of land; other hybrids, bred for increased pest-resistance, greater nutritional value or other purposes; and varieties bred by the use of new techniques such as biotechnology and genetic engineering.

Hybrid varieties may be valuable in some circumstances but increase the dependence of farmers on outside agencies because they cannot be used for seed production, and new seed has to be bought each year. Depending on the way in which they have been bred, hybrids may be more susceptible to local diseases and pests and less adapted to local climatic and ecological conditions. They may require inputs to correct these problems, such as fertilisers, pesticides, and irrigation, and succeed only on the most fertile land. The higher the inputs, the more these varieties may yield, but such a sustained level of investment is usually beyond the means of poor farmers.

There is also a wide range of different methods of cultivation and technology, from capital-intensive techniques with extensive use of machines and chemicals to labour-intensive methods using locally-available renewable natural resources. In many contexts a mix of capital- and labour-intensive techniques is possible. Certain crops or certain crop varieties may only perform to their full potential with particular techniques and inputs.

Given the variety of contexts in which NGOs work, and the varied needs and priorities of poor women and men, there can be no hard and fast rules about which type of crops or techniques will be most useful. It is vital to consult widely, with the cultivators in the programme area, local government sources, and experts in the field. Participatory appraisal techniques may be useful when consulting the cultivators about their needs and priorities.

Table 4.1. Types of crops and their uses

Food crops

Cereals	rice, maize/corn, bread wheat, durum wheat, sorghum, millets, barley, oats, rye, triticale (high-protein cross between wheat and rye).
Pulses and other edible legume seeds	peas, beans, lentils, soya beans, groundnuts, winged bean, tepany bean (for hot dry areas) and tarwi. Rich in protein and valuable for supplementing diets based on starchy crops such as cassavas, yams and sweet potatoes. Also obtain nitrogen from the air making it available in the soil for other crops, so they are useful for intercropping.
Roots and tubers	Cassava (manioc, tapioca), yam, taro, potato, sweet potato, winged bean (see legumes). Extremely important subsistence crops giving high starch and hence energy yields per acre. But excess cropping leads to loss of fertility unless steps are taken to replenish the soil.
Vegetables	Rich in vitamins and minerals. But high water and fertility and hence labour requirements. Good complement to night-yarding of cattle and small-scale fish-farming and good for schools projects.
Sweeteners Relishes	For example sugar cane. Waste materials from fields and factories are valuable cattle feeds and biomass for fuel production.

4

Fodder crops

Grasses	Grass planted on steep slopes between trees in reforestation programmes or along boundaries as part of soil preservation programmes can also provide fodder. Native pasture management is always the best option — controlling grazing, over-sowing with suitable legumes, applying small amounts of fertilisers — and possibly seeding into turf rather than replacing with new grass species.
Legumes	Provide fodder rich in protein and minerals, enrich the soil and increase animal consumption of natural pastures. As well as traditional varieties such as lucerne and clover some highly productive improved varieties are now available.
Other fodder and browse crops	Many so called weeds, including aquatic weeds such as water hyacinth, can also be used as fodder.

Crops with other uses

Fibre	Kenaf, jute, cotton, sisal, agave.
Oil crops	These include edible oils extracted from cropseeds such as rape, sunflower, olive, palm, linseed, cotton, coconut. Also non-edible oils for industrial use, for example the bean of the jojoba plant, which will grow in dry conditions. The residue after oil-extraction is usually useful either as an animal feed or as a soil conditioner.
Paper and board	Cereal straw makes very satisfactory paper and board. Water weeds (water hyacinth and salvina) have been successfully used for manufacturing high quality paper in India.
Fuel	There is some scope for small-scale biogas (methane) production from crops and crop by-products provided this does not conflict with other food and income needs.

b. Choice of crops

When a project proposal includes the introduction of new crops, or the increase in production of existing crops, social, economic and environmental factors which influence the choice of crops should be taken into account. Some of these may be:

Social factors: The structure of ownership and control of land, labour and resources by gender, ethnicity and class will affect the degree to which farmers are able or willing to invest time, and labour. Different crops and techniques have different labour requirements in production, processing and cooking. Crops which are labour-intensive at one or more of these stages may considerably increase the unpaid work burden of women and children without increasing their income.

Economic factors: The existence of a market for particular agricultural crops, the availability of credit, processing, storage, and transport facilities, the crop's suitability for storage and transport, and crop processing requirements.

Environmental factors: These include the type of soil, its structure and porosity, level of acidity, fertility, and factors that damage the soil structure. Some crops consume more nutrients than others, some do not thrive in conditions of excessive acidity or alkalinity, and some require water-retentive soils, while others develop root diseases or do not grow in water-logged soils. Climatic conditions, including rainfall pattern, temperature, day length, humidity, wind, altitude, and seasonal changes also influence the choice of crops. Finally, water sources and quality, drainage, irrigation systems, and salination will determine which crops are likely to thrive. (See 1.3.3.2 Sustaining natural resources.)

2.2.3 Storage, processing, and preservation

As well as improvements in crop production donor agencies have a role in supporting improvements in storage, processing and cooking. Storage facilities enable farmers to store produce for their own consumption, and for sale at times when the prices are higher than just after harvest. This leads to increased economic status and power; grain silos for women are also a critical indicator of status in the community in many parts of the world.

Cereal banks, run on a collective basis, not only provide some security against crop failures and hunger, but also enable villagers to store grain bought at lower prices during the harvest period, in order to sell it during times when grain is expensive. In Mali Oxfam supports an organisation which provided a five-year interest-free loan for setting up village-based cereal banks for storing and selling millet, sorghum and rice. Grain is sold to villagers and to others, and profits from sales invested in a village store. The village association buys basic necessities

527

wholesale and sells at prices lower than those in the local market. Secure storage is critical to such enterprises. However, interventions which enable some people to buy and sell advantageously *must* examine the context in which this is done, and the effect on other poor people who may not be involved in the scheme.

The sort of questions to ask are: Who are the producers from whom grain is bought at the lowest price? Who are the people who are having to pay the higher prices? Is the project simply reproducing a set of exploitative economic relationships?

Many foods require careful processing to make them more palatable and digestible, or to destroy bitter or toxic substances (such as exist in cassava). Processing and preservation of food is often very labour intensive and is a major part of women's work. It is therefore vital for development agencies to promote increased efficiency of cooking and food preservation methods, in terms of improved, labour-saving technology. Questions of the control of the technology, and whether it should be collective or household-based, are very important.

Storage: substantial crop losses are caused by poor storage. Adequate drying before storage is essential to avoid fungal diseases, and crops must be stored in dry hygienic conditions, and protected from damage by rodents and insects.

Traditional methods of storage include mud-brick or wicker-work stores above ground and sealed pits in the ground; they are cheap and effective provided they are properly maintained and strict hygiene is observed. Non-traditional building materials, such as concrete, metal or butyl rubber, are more expensive but may be more rodent resistant; and oil drums and old water tanks may be used for building stores. Bins or silos made from metal must not be exposed to the sun as this may lead to moisture condensation on the cool side of the container. Inflatable butyl balloon-type grain stores are now widely used for bulk or in-bag storage, and provide long-lasting storage. Their advantages are that they are fairly easy to transport and erect, they cost less per ton than concrete structures and they are hermetically sealed and thus difficult for insects or rodents to break into, or survive if they are already in the grain.

Expert advice should always be sought on construction and planning of storage buildings and permanent silos. A number of points need to be considered:

- Good ventilation is essential for storage of roots and tubers, and for all crops ventilation should be controllable.
- External paint should reflect light and heat; roots and tubers require shading from direct sunlight; interior paint should be of gloss type and not whitewash, which could react with insecticides.

- Walls should provide good thermal insulation, and roofs should overhang to protect walls from sun.
- The store must be rat-proof, with smooth walls and tight-fitting doors. Metal strips along the bottom prevent gnawing.
- The buildings should be easy to clean with no cracks or ledges to harbour insects.
- The site must be dry and well-drained and located away from fields of growing crops.
- Grain should be stacked so that inspection from all sides is possible, and bags should be stored on wooden pallets.
- Disease-free, undamaged produce should be selected for storage, and regular inspections should be carried out to identify and remove any damaged produce.

Processing and preservation: The processing and preservation of food crops (pounding or milling grain, hulling rice or maize, grating cassava, drying seeds, beans, fruit and vegetables and extracting oil from nuts and seeds) for sale or consumption is usually the work of women and children, as is cooking food. This entails the work, generally very time-consuming, of collecting water and fuel.

Development interventions which aim to increase crop production must look carefully at ways to support the processing of the increased volume of produce. This requires identification and analysis of all the tasks involved in growing, caring for, and harvesting the crops, and processing them for food or sale, and the identification of who does them, when they do them, and how they do them.

'Labour bottlenecks' can arise if technological improvements are applied to one part of the process only. For example, if mechanisation of the preparation of land, improved seed, and improved technologies for harvesting increase the area of land cultivated, and its crop yield, this will increase the time needed for other tasks such as weeding, which in many societies is the manual work of women. Women would face not only this extra work in the fields, but that of processing more crops for sale. To avoid this, careful studies of the time women and men spend on their tasks through the day are essential, and full consultation with both women and men about their production needs must be undertaken.

Without this information, the introduction of food-processing technologies can fail. In Brazil, for example, an NGO included increased production of the *babacu* palm nut in its wide-ranging programme of assistance to rural people. Traditionally, oil is extracted from the kernel of the small *babacu*, whose shell is as hard as coconut, by women and children, who break the nuts open and press the oil by hand. Attempts to introduce mechanised oil pressing have so far met with failure — not only does the technology itself require further work,

529

but the maintenance of the machines, and the cost of diesel fuel, have proved obstacles to its use.

Grain mills and dehullers are much favoured by donor agencies and NGOs seeking to alleviate rural women's work. The processing of coarse grains such as millet and sorghum is particularly time- and energy-consuming, and in West Africa, traditionally performed through pounding using wooden pestles and mortars. However, while there have been successes, particularly in urban areas where women are able to use the time they save to earn enough money to pay the costs of running the machines, in most rural areas poor women cannot earn enough money to use the technology regularly, and the machines are typically underused. Women continue to pound by hand.

If these interventions are to be successful, care must be taken to ensure that consumer demand can be translated into regular use; in other words, that potential users have the cash or surplus produce to pay for the use of the technology; that there are enough potential users in the area; and that prior consultation with everyone involved in the project has established an appropriate and acceptable way of setting up the service.

The management of the service should be set up through a participatory process, and appropriate training given. Care should be taken that the technology is not taken over by men. The technology itself should be reliable, with easily available spare parts, and low running costs. The responsibility for its maintenance must be clearly assigned, and appropriate training given.

2.2.4 Small-scale cropping systems

Since the mid-1970s a wealth of research on agricultural systems in resource-poor environments has shown that poor women and men cultivators have developed complex cropping systems and techniques adapted to their own needs and local ecological conditions. These systems generally combine diverse crops or crop varieties adapted to specific micro-climates and uses. Different varieties of staple crops are grown for different uses — some may be easier to cook, while others survive transport to markets better. A wide variety of crops are often grown to spread risks of crop failure, and spread the need for labour through the year. These forms of agriculture, adapted to difficult environments, and opportunistic in their responses to unpredictable changes, are sometimes known as 'complex, diverse and risk-prone' or CDR agriculture, one of the three types of agriculture identified by the Brundland Commission. Three forms are summarised in Table 4.2, opposite.

Table 4.2. Types of agriculture summarised (from *Farmer First*, Chambers, Pacey and Thrupp, 1989)

	Industrial	**Green Revolution**	**Third/CDR**
Main locations	Industrialised countries and specialised enclaves in Third World	Irrigated and stable rainfall, high potential areas in the Third World	Rainfed areas, hinterlands, most of sub-Saharan Africa, etc.
Main climatic zone	Temperate	Tropical	Tropical
Major type of farmer	Highly capitalised family farms and plantations	Large and small farmers	Small and poor farm households
Use of purchased inputs	Very high	High	Low
Farming system, relatively	Simple	Simple	Complex
Environmental diversity, relatively	Uniform	Uniform	Diverse
Production stability	Moderate risk	Moderate risk	High risk
Current production as percentage of sustainable production	Far too high	Near the limit	Low
Priority for production	Reduce production	Maintain production	Raise production

4

531

Many of the poorest of the world's farmers live and work in marginal environments. The farming models and recommendations coming out of conventional agricultural research stations and often based on stable environments have not in the past been helpful for agriculture in such environments. Useful interventions can only be identified by detailed research, which begins with the farmers' experience and analysis of problems commonly encountered in any particular area. Agricultural interventions should be based on forms of participatory research and appraisal which enable all farmers — women and men — to identify and communicate their own priorities, needs, and difficulties. Interventions which begin from this point and support farmers' own efforts are far more likely to be sustainable that those which attempt to impose techniques and strategies which have been developed in other situations.

2.2.5 Low-external-input sustainable agriculture (LEISA)

LEISA is not a single system of agriculture, but a cluster of ideas common to small-scale agriculture. Investigating LEI-systems requires the use of participatory techniques to investigate existing cropping systems and farmers' priorities, and to work with farmers in experimentation for improvement. The precise details of crops and techniques varies in accordance with particular characteristics of the environment and the needs of the farmers. The general principles of cultivation are outlined below, and are those used by resource-poor farmers in marginal environments all over the world. It provides a useful checklist for development workers investigating local cultivation systems. (See 1.3.5.1 Rural livelihoods.)

a. Maintaining fertility
There are a number of ways in which soil fertility can be maintained or increased:
Minimum tilling: ploughing is used to kill weeds, aerate and improve drainage of soils (particularly heavy soils), provide a good 'tilth' (soil structure), and bring insect larvae and pests to the surface where they may be eaten by predators. Disadvantages of frequent ploughing are damage to the soil structure, loss of nutrients, and a greater risk of soil erosion, particularly from ploughing up and down slopes. The ground underneath the tilled layer may become impacted, affecting rain infiltration.

Excessive tilling is best avoided; hand clearing has advantages, such as retaining more organic matter as mulch. The amount of tilling needed depends upon the season, the type of soil and the availability of labour. A key question is: how is this work organised, and who does it?

Soil conservation: in some environments a near-continuous ground cover is necessary to avoid erosion, and mixed annual and perennial cropping may be the most suitable system. Planting trees, preferably ones which give useful products, around the contours of fields can allow terraces to build up gradually.

Cropping systems: monocropping or continuous growing of one crop on the same land, encouraged on large-scale farms using mechanisation, requires irrigation, chemical fertilisers, pesticides and herbicides, and has adverse environmental effects. It increases soil erosion, reduces the ability of the soil to retain moisture and nutrients, and encourages the build-up of weeds, pests and diseases. Small-scale farmers using few external inputs are likely to use varied cropping systems, which include:

- **crop rotation**: different crops with different nutrient and seasonal requirements are planted on each plot each year;
- **intercropping** or 'companion planting': different crops — usually only two — are planted on the same land at the same time. This may be done in alternate rows, by mixed seeding, or in blocks, depending on the type of crops.

This maximises land use by growing quick-maturing crops in between those which take a long time to mature, spreading both food and income over the year; encourages pest-predators; suppresses weeds with appropriate crops as protection for other more valuable intercropped plants; takes advantage of complementary nutrient requirements of different plants — some plants 'fix' nutrients which can be used by others — and makes the best use of available light by planting crops with leaves at different angles and heights.

- **relay cropping**: a second crop is sown just before harvesting the first, mainly growing after the first crop is removed. For example, in parts of Central and South America farmers plant beans as the maize crop ripens so the beans climb up the maize stalks. The beans also in turn fix nitrogen in the soil for the following maize crop.
- **fallowing**: plots of land are left uncultivated for one or more years to allow the soil fertility to reestablish itself and to starve out pests and diseases. This is the principle of shifting cultivation systems. In settled agriculture systems livestock are pastured on fallow land and their dung adds to the nutrients available.

Use of organic fertilisers: these include animal waste, compost, and green manures, where plant crops are sown on fallow land for their nutrient value for the soil, and ploughed back in or harvested and composted.

b. Crop production

Farmers improve their crops according to their own priorities through seed selection and propagation techniques.

Seed selection: farmers in marginal and resource-poor areas rely on selecting and conserving their own seed for planting in the next season. Storage is critical, and may be supported by NGOs.

Propagation: some plants are best propagated by cuttings or other vegetative means; some can only be propagated in this way. Rooting of cuttings is enhanced by the use of (expensive) hormonal rooting powder or a simpler honey solution which contains organic growth substances.

Planting: farmers plan sowing of crops carefully in order to make use of seasonal supplies of water, ensure the maximum possible time for the plants to reach maturity, and allow the crops to reach the required stage to make maximum use of optimum day-length. Sowing time is vital, as day length fluctuates seasonally, and determines flowering which in turn affects yields. However, in marginal and risk-prone environments, many of these factors are unreliable, and support may be needed for farmers when, for example, the rains fail.

Optimum spacing and depth of planting, and placing fertilisers close to the roots of plants, can increase yields. Certain crops are best transplanted from nursery beds. However, this increases labour time, and whose labour time this is, and the impact it may have on other work, should always be investigated.

c. Pest control

Crops are subject to a wide variety of pests, particularly birds and rodents which eat them; insects and insect larvae which damage and attack various parts of plants; and fungal diseases. Chemical sprays are expensive, polluting, and may kill off benign insects and birds, and in time many pests and diseases become resistant to them. There are organic or biological methods of pest control and pest avoidance which are likely to be of greater help to resource-poor farmers because they are cheaper and minimise environmental damage. A form of integrated pest management (IPM) has been developed, with considerable success, by a team of researchers at Leon University in Nicaragua, in partnership with UNAG, the Farmers' Union. The Leon team identified a virus and a wasp which between them attack a number of pests which destroy basic grains. Technicians from the farming communities were trained in the use of the techniques, and the co-operatives which tried out IPM found that they were able to cut their use of chemical pesticides by half. The project, supported by Oxfam, has demonstrated that the technique of IPM is easy to use, reduces production costs, is safer in relation to human health, and does not damage the environment.

Some elements of pest and disease control are outlined below:

- Crop diversity, crop rotation, and intercropping helps to prevent the build-up of diseases and pests in the soil.
- Traditional seed varieties are often more resistant to disease than 'improved' hybrid seeds.
- Pest predators can be encouraged by providing them with habitats, for example by allowing vegetation to remain at the edges of fields to act as hiding, breeding, and feeding places. Companion planting with plants which provide food for predators encourage birds and insects which eat aphids and insect pest larvae.
- Many insect pests follow a particular breeding and growth cycle. By planting or harvesting crops at different times it is possible to avoid times of the year when pests are most active.
- Organic pesticides can be produced by farmers themselves from plants growing in the area; the seeds and leaves of the Indian Neem tree, for example, make an effective insecticide. All pesticides must be used with caution, because they can be poisonous to other beneficial plant and animal life, as well as to humans.

d. Weed control

Crop yield is strongly determined by the extent of weed competition in the early stages of crop growth. It is, after rainfall, perhaps the most important factor in determining yields.

Hand weeding is commonly a major task for women in farming households. Weeds should be removed early before they have time to get established and early in the life of the crop. They should also be removed after harvest and before they set seed to minimise problems in the following year.

Intercropping and continuous cultivation with vigorous crops, particularly those with large leaves, suppresses weed growth through depriving them of light and nutrients. Weeding of one crop can often be combined with planting of another.

Animals or plants which eat or suppress weeds and weed seeds can be encouraged, for example, in some systems of rice cultivation, ducks and fish in the rice fields help to keep down weeds and insect pests. Mulching with organic materials deprives growing weeds of light, and adds nutrients to the soil.

2.2.6 Vegetable production for landless people

Many of the techniques described above can be used in small gardens, and research has been done into ways of adapting small-scale cropping systems for very small areas of land around the homesteads of landless or near landless women and men in rural and semi-urban areas.

a. Integrated kitchen gardens

Small plots around homes may provide an important supplementary, or indeed the only, source of food for the household, and can provide a source of income. Landless labourers and tenant farmers often have small plots on which they are able to cultivate their own crops. For the smallest areas of land, in rural or urban areas, intensive cultivation of vegetables may be the best form of food production for consumption and sale, using organic matter from household waste, and purchased inputs. More efficient use of the land will be made by growing crops of different types and heights together.

Cultivation of such plots has been widely encouraged for landless people, many of whom are women. However, labour requirements must be taken into account: the demands can be high, and relentless: gardens in the dry season need daily attention, and may require large quantities of water, which may have to be carried from a distant water source. The management of small, intensively-cultivated gardens can be complicated and time-consuming, and require training and some external inputs if it is to be done successfully. Who is to do the work and when, and whether the work clashes with work which brings in greater income, are questions which must always be investigated, as well as how training will be provided, and other inputs funded. The intensive cultivation of small household plots should not, for example, be considered to be a simple extension of women's 'domestic' tasks.

b. Hydroponics and nutrient film technique

Hydroponics is the growing of crops without soil in a solution of nutrients. It is a highly specialised technique requiring high levels of management and is generally practised under glass or polythene. The nutrient film technique (NFT) involves growing crops, usually vegetables, in a continuously flowing shallow stream or film of nutrient solution. The solution is recycled so that the only loss of water and nutrients from the system is in that which is taken up by the plants or by evaporation. This is a very efficient use of water, but requires a high degree of hygiene as disease in the system will immediately be carried to all plants, together with constant monitoring and topping up of the solution. While using space intensively, hydroponics is generally capital- and technology-intensive and not suitable for poor households, who would become highly dependent on external inputs. It is also not suitable for producing food, but requires a stable market for high-priced produce in order to cover its running costs.

However, a practical adaptation of the NFT technique has been developed by National Organic Chemicals Industries of Delhi for use by landless or virtually landless people; the nutrient solution is contained in plastic-lined channels made in flat ground and re-

536

plenished by siphon from a tank, and the plants grow on capillary matting.

Oxfam has supported a number of small-scale peri-urban gardening initiatives around the world. In a communal gardens project in a shanty town of Lima, vegetables were grown in semi-desert conditions, using techniques which required a minimum of water. In Andhra Pradesh, an Indian NGO working with Scheduled Caste people has encouraged the use of intensive gardening techniques to raise vegetables in conditions where water is scarce.

2.3 Practical approaches to livestock production

Livestock production is the principal source of income for large numbers of people in some of the world's most difficult and least fertile environments. It is also an important subsidiary source of income and subsistence for many small-scale cultivators and landless people in rural and semi-urban areas. Raising livestock often provides a socially acceptable source of independent income for women. At least 60 per cent of the world's rangelands are unsuited for cultivation and can be exploited only by ruminant livestock or game; in Africa, 20 million pastoralists make the major part of their living by raising their animals on these rangelands.

Integrated small-scale farming involves the raising of animals and the cultivation of crops, for a wide range of products for sale and consumption. Animals ultimately killed for food may have other important roles: as draught animals, producers of milk or eggs, and sources of raw materials such as leather and wool for small-scale industry. Animal wastes are also an important source of fuel, and are used as fertiliser for low-input integrated systems. Waste products, such as fibrous roughage and crop by-products not suitable for human consumption, can be made use of for animal feed.

NGO interventions in livestock production are either in the context of mixed agricultural systems, particularly for landless women and men, or support people whose principal means of making a living is through raising animals. In both cases this involves direct support to production, marketing, and credit, and to the formation and strengthening of producer organisations through capacity-building, and information exchange.

Men and women raise animals in a wide range of ecological and socio-economic contexts. In this section we look at the two main categories of livestock production in which Oxfam is involved: extensive systems, such as pastoralism, and small-scale livestock farming.

2.3.1 Extensive livestock systems

Extensive livestock production is practised in many arid and semi-arid parts of the world, particularly in northern and sub-Saharan Africa. The major types of animals are camels, cattle, sheep and goats and, in the Andean countries of South America, llama and alpaca. Extensive grazing is generally practised in these systems in an environment which is subject to unpredictable seasonal and annual fluctuations in rainfall, and is unsuitable for agriculture. Because the conditions are so harsh it is essential that pastoralists and their animals are able to move for at least part of the time to find sufficient water and food. However, the movements of pastoralists have become severely restricted, both by development strategies which aim to sedentarise them or encroach upon their land with large-scale ranching or mechanised farming; and by political events, such as the closure of national boundaries, for example, between Senegal and Mauritania; and by armed conflict in, for example, Sudan.

Pastoralists are generally classified according to their patterns of migration and production systems. **Nomadic pastoralists** graze their herds over wide areas of land, and have no permanent settlements or base. **Transhumant** pastoralists are seasonal migrants, returning to a fixed base at certain times of the year. **Agropastoralists** are people for whom extensive livestock production is an important source of subsistence and income, but accounts for less than half of total needs. Such people may formerly have been pastoralists or agriculturalists.

Among pastoralists, there is considerable variation in the degree of dependence on their livestock, either as sources of subsistence or as sources of cash income. Men and women may obtain a supplementary, or even a major, part of their income from other occupations such as agriculture, small-scale settled livestock production, artisan production using animal products such as wool or leather, ancillary activities such as blacksmithing, or trading of milk and traditional medicines. Others also gain some income from employment as agricultural labourers or in urban jobs. Pastoralists' levels of wealth also vary widely: some own such large herds that they are rich even when compared with members of the urban elite, and may live in urban centres, while poor relatives and paid herdsmen look after their herds.

Pastoralists and their way of life have been, and still are, widely misunderstood. Pastoralists have sometimes been considered backward and conservative by development agencies and national governments, and blamed for progressive ecological degradation because of overgrazing of rangelands. Development programmes of governments and international agencies have been aimed mainly at converting these extensive systems into settled agriculture. Assistance directed to livestock production itself focused on large-scale programmes for water provision and vaccination campaigns, and distribution of food aid and restocking in times of severe drought.

These approaches are now widely questioned, and it is recognised that pastoralist systems are the best, and often the only, way of exploiting the most arid and infertile areas. Environmental degradation has often been worse on private ranches than under traditional systems. Such systems, far from being backward, are well adapted to difficult and unstable environments. Research found that overgrazing and desertification are usually associated not with traditional systems of extensive grazing, but with their breakdown. The causes are:

- increasing migration of settled agriculturalists and their animals onto marginal land previously only under extensive livestock production;
- political upheaval leading to large influxes of refugees and their animals into areas which cannot support them;
- the expansion of commercial ranching and the appropriation of the best land by governments;
- attempts by governments and development agencies to manage the rangelands and pastoral production according to inappropriate models involving fencing, ranching, and rotation, which tend to lead to rapid degradation of the land.

Policies for agricultural settlement in arid and semi-arid areas have led not only to environmental degradation, but also to increasing impoverishment among pastoralists, who have become more dependent on local markets to raise money for taxes, cereal foods, and other goods. This has increased their vulnerability to market fluctuations, particularly in times of drought. The increasing impoverishment of pastoralists has led to many of them selling livestock and becoming hired herders for settled livestock owners. Traditional exchanges between farmers and herders have broken down as a result of agricultural development, as settled farmers intensify their own livestock production.

Vaccination campaigns and water provision on their own were contributing to breakdown of traditional systems, by increasing the livestock numbers, in the absence of adequate management systems. The worst ecological damage was being caused around open-access water points, not around community-managed ones; and around settlements of ex-nomads rather than in remoter territories of pastoral nomadism. Relief measures such as food aid and distribution of animals in times of crisis were increasing dependency and doing little to increase livelihood security in the longer term.

New directions in policy for pastoral development, compared with old ones, are summarised in Table 4.3

Table 4.3. New directions for pastoral development in Africa (from 'Living with uncertainty', Scoones and Graham, *Development in Practice*, October 1994)

	'Old' Thinking	'New' Thinking
Focus on:	Improving commodity production, e.g. increasing meat offtake.	People: enhancing self-sufficiency and livelihoods of pastoralists.
Technical solutions:	Range management, e.g. pasture development, fencing, rotations. Emphasis on production.	Creating, improving, rehabilitating 'key' resources. Emphasis on tracking through mobility/flexibility; de-restocking, supplementary feeding etc.
Planning approach:	Blueprint planning.	Flexible, adaptive planning. Local involvement/feedback built in. Recognises uncertainty.
Drought response:	Drought years seen as separate from 'normal' years. Response often late/inadequate.	Drought seen as part of 'normal'. Safety net provision built-in.
Land rights:	Fixed tenure desirable. Privatisation or exclusive communal use encouraged. Conflict of interest largely ignored.	Flexible rights of access and use. Recognition of overlapping and integrated systems. Focus on conflict negotiation, mediation, arbitration.
Institutions and administration:	Services delivered through centralised extension agencies. Extension agents deliver technical packages.	Encourages pastoral organisations; emphasis on local management. Retraining of extension workers as 'institutional organisers'.

2.3.2 Small-scale livestock farming

Livestock are central to many small-scale integrated agricultural production systems, providing an important source of income for landless people and resource-poor farmers. Muslim women in a number of societies raise small animals, such as goats or poultry, to provide them with a traditionally acceptable source of income over which they may exercise some control. Raising animals also provides an important source of subsistence and income for the increasing numbers of poor people in semi-urban areas. In less densely-populated areas people often keep small numbers of sheep, goats, pigs or poultry, and let them scavenge around the house. In the more densely-settled areas, such as shanty-towns around large cities, poultry, rabbits, and guinea pigs are sometimes kept and fed on food wastes and garden forage.

Although the main emphasis in government policy tends to be on large-scale livestock development, small-scale livestock production is an important component of many poverty alleviation programmes. Credit schemes, training, and co-operative development for poor people may include livestock raising as part of the programme. Support for keeping small livestock is common in women's income-generation programmes. When interventions include the attempts to increase the productivity of traditional livestock through the introduction of new breeds and animals, more expensive feeds and improved veterinary care, they tend to run into the same problems as those outlined above in relation to high-input crop production. New breeds may be more vulnerable to disease and climatic conditions than traditional breeds, and the labour and money required for their care and keep is rarely offset by the increased income for their keepers. Some of these issues are discussed further in **4.2.3.8 Principal livestock species.**

Technological interventions should always be planned according to the analysis of costs and benefits within the social and cultural context. Donor agencies should carefully address social and cultural issues when considering the funding of livestock development.

2.3.3 Social and cultural considerations in livestock production

Animals have much more than monetary or food value: they have important social roles and significance, which vary from one society to another, change over time, and cannot therefore be substituted for other types of goods. For example, in many societies, the number of larger livestock owned is an important indicator of social status. Gifts or exchanges of livestock are often used to seal agreements between individuals and groups, as payment for work or services, or as brideprice. Animals have ritual functions: they are used in sacrifices to deities, for example. There are often religious rules governing the treatment and slaughter of certain animals.

Animals can provide an important form of investment where few other alternatives exist, which is why, when food is scarce, it is more rational to keep many animals in poor condition than a few in better condition, so that animals can be sold without depleting the herd too much. Animals also provide an emergency source of cash for unexpected or unusually high expenses, such as medicines and medical treatment, marriages or funerals, or costs of schooling.

2.3.4 Division of labour and ownership rights

Different individuals in households and social groups are usually responsible for different tasks in livestock production, with different rights to use or ownership of animals and their by-products. These different rights are usually subject to negotiation, and they may change over time and in response to different influences and events. NGO interventions can affect the basis of these rights, and can, for example, strengthen the terms upon which the poorest and most disadvantaged people negotiate. The tasks, responsibilities, and rights of different people in relation to livestock must be investigated and understood when planning an intervention.

There is generally a marked gender division of labour, which varies from one society to another, in the tasks associated with the care of livestock, some of which may be carried out by children. When planning interventions in livestock production it is therefore essential to answer the following questions:

Who owns the animals? Everything done to or for an animal should have the approval of the owner, although identifying the owners is not always easy. Ownership may not mean absolute rights to possession, but may involve more complex use and inheritance rights. Within households, different animals may be owned by women and by men and in many societies, including pastoralists, women may inherit and pass on livestock even where these are herded by men.

Animals in traditional pastoral systems may have several 'owners', sometimes from different age and kin groups; or be shared or leased under tenancy and share agreements. These are common where the gap between rich and poor pastoralists is large — poor herders care for the animals of richer people. They are also very common between landless people or marginal farmers and richer cultivators in settled agriculture systems.

Who has rights to animal by-products? People may have rights to the products of particular tasks for which they are responsible; women, for example, have the right to the milk of animals they do not own. Tenancy and share agreements vary, but may involve richer families supplying the animals, with poorer families taking responsibility for their care in return for a share of the by-products (milk, eggs) for their own consumption, and a share of the sale price.

Who owns the land? Ownership, and use rights to land, are critical in pastoralist systems, and in small-scale animal raising, and determine grazing and fodder collection rights. Many pastoralist systems involve communal ownership of land combined with private ownership of animals. In settled agricultural systems, grazing and fodder may be available from common land, or on privately-owned land at particular times of the year. In both cases management systems and agreements are necessary to prevent overgrazing and crop damage, and to safeguard people's rights to the resources they depend upon for the survival of their animals and their own livelihoods.

2.3.5 Women's role in livestock production

Women's role in livestock production and the types of animals, tasks and by-products for which they are responsible, are extremely variable between and within cultures. It is therefore important that women's roles and rights, and how these are changing, are not based on assumptions, but assessed carefully in each case.

Both pastoralist women and men own cattle and smaller animals, such as goats and sheep. Grazing and herding is usually the task of boys and, in some seasons, men. Women's work often includes milking and the production of butter oil, an important part of the diet in the rainy season, and also an important source of women's income. Among the Beja in the Red Sea Province, however, a woman may not milk her own animals, but calls upon a male relative to do it for her. Women are often responsible for the care of sick animals. If they have a role in milking, they are usually the first to notice any illness. Women's income is often used for vaccinations and other veterinary care. While men are usually responsible for watering the animals, this is sometimes done by women.

In addition to their work with animals, pastoralist women have other productive and reproductive tasks. They are engaged, with men, in agricultural work, but usually have sole responsibility for gathering activities, including the gathering of firewood, wild rice, wild grains, locust, wild berries, and palm leaves to make mats. Selling of firewood, mats and gathered food items may be an important source of income for women. Muslim Beja women, whose roles are private, weave blankets and baskets, but are not permitted into the public sphere to market them. Marketing of women's handcraft goods is thus a male task. In all societies, women are responsible for household maintenance

543

and childcare, including the daily provision of food, and in many pastoralist societies, it is their work to build houses or erect tents.

With changes in the pastoralist economy, women's roles have also changed, in different ways. For example, in Chad, among agriculturalists who have increased dependence on livestock production, women traditionally had a certain level of economic independence. They had their own fields inherited from their mothers or donated by husbands. They also had their own individual grain stores. They provided the daily food required by their family, earning additional income through the collection of wild fruits, and the production and exchange of household items such as mats and rope. When their production system slowly involved more livestock keeping, the women were able to continue their income-generating activities, adding milk products to their economic output.

Among pastoralists who have become increasingly dependent on agriculture, however, women's dependence increased with the changing system. As the people became more sedentary the women did not acquire their own fields or stores. Although they learned how to make household items, the quality was not sufficient for sale or exchange. As herds were smaller, their traditional income from milk or milk products declined; but they were still expected to find ways of providing daily food items, as men were now very reluctant to sell animals to provide for family needs outside the rainy (milking) season, as they had done before.

2.3.6 Increasing livestock production

Many NGO interventions aim to increase production of animals for meat and related products. This may be through increasing the profitability of existing animals by improved breeding, food and fodder, housing, and health care; and introducing new breeds. However, a narrow focus on increasing animal productivity through technical interventions may overlook the social and cultural factors influencing production systems. It is vital to assess existing systems of ownership and control of animals and incomes, and to analyse the different needs and priorities of individuals and groups. African pastoralists, for example, do not see their herds only in the narrow sense of producing meat; and interventions which concentrate on increasing meat production may be inappropriate.

The technical information given below must be assessed in relation to the particular system of livestock production, in consultation with the livestock producers themselves — women and men. General guidelines for pastoralist development are outlined in 4.2.3.7. The sections below refer generally to all livestock producers, and different kinds of animals.

a. Choice of livestock species and breeds

Indigenous animal species and breeds have generally been bred over centuries to be well-adapted to the local climate, reasonably resistant to local diseases, and to use locally available fodder and resources. Such animals may not be highly productive in terms of quantity of food, but fulfil a wide range of other uses.

Farmers usually improve their herds by mating best to best. If this process is repeated continuously, slow breed improvement can be expected. However, breed improvement is very difficult in small herds where every animal is required and there is little opportunity for selection, and disposal of poor quality stock. Repeated in-breeding is difficult to avoid, but in-bred herds and flocks tend to become less fertile and productive. Males may be exchanged with other breeders so they do not mate with their mothers or sisters; the males not suitable or required for breeding may be castrated. New breeds can be introduced by making available pure or crossbred exotic males for mating with local females, or by introducing entirely new animals.

Exotic breeds have generally been bred for higher productivity, for example high-milk yielding cattle, and larger and quicker-growing breeds for higher meat yields. Many governments have livestock development programmes involving training, credit, and extension, particularly for new breeds. The introduction of new breeds and animals has also been a common feature of programmes supported by NGOs. However, a number of factors need to be borne in mind:

- The animals must be able to adapt to the local climate and environment. Camels, for instance, are well-adapted to arid areas, but are more prone to disease in wetter areas. Cattle, sheep, and goats on the other hand may be adapted to a range of environments, but new breeds may have more specific requirements.
- Exotic breeds may have a greater susceptibility to disease and require higher levels of skills, resources, and care to avoid loss.
- New breeds may not fulfil other social, ritual or economic needs met by indigenous animals.
- The 'improved' livestock may require expensive inputs such as food, vaccines, and specialist health care. They may also divert household resources and labour from less profitable but more reliable existing forms of livestock production, particularly if interventions are planned with and for men, when women are in charge of domestic livestock production.
- Care should be taken that changing practices do not deprive poor women and men of free by-products, such as dung for fuel, or fodder, because of increased demand by new animals.

The suitability of animals and breeds for any particular environment depends on a wide variety of factors and must be considered with great care. Some issues in the care and requirements of particular animals are given below, but more detailed technical information should always be obtained from local and government sources. Some of the resources listed at the end of this chapter indicate further sources of technical information.

b. Nutrition

Grazers should be able to eat as much as possible of the foods which they are normally fed. High food intakes can be encouraged by allowing them frequent access to fresh, clean water, and ensuring they have sufficient grazing time. They may be herded to places where there are different grasses and shrubs to allow them to select as high a quality food as possible. Grazers may also need supplements of nutrients usually deficient in low-quality pasture, such as nitrogen, digestible cellulose or minerals. For cattle, buffaloes, sheep, and goats the most widely used supplements are different legume plants and a nitrogen-containing supplement, such as urea, mixed with molasses or another carrier substance.

Non-grazers are totally dependent on their keeper for their food. This is not a problem when the keeper can afford concentrated foods. But where grasses and low-quality foods are used, care is needed to provide a balanced diet. This can be done by choosing a variety of foods which include some of as high quality as possible, and collecting more food than the animal can eat and thus providing it with some opportunity for selection. Ensuring the food is fresh by feeding little and often is also important. However, all of these measures require extra time and labour, and exactly how this is to be managed, and by whom, must always be addressed.

Where concentrated food must be bought, such as cereal grains or balanced commercial concentrates, it will need to be stored in a dry, vermin-proof food store. Special troughs may have to be built or bought, and the amounts and type of concentrate carefully calculated and monitored. This may require training in new forms of management, and also require labour time. Technical advice should always be sought.

c. Health

Drugs and vaccines are often unavailable or too expensive for small farmers with few animals. Support should be given primarily for measures to maintain health and avoid disease. NGOs may do this by supporting production of indigenous breeds, good feeding of balanced diets, measures to minimise stresses (overcrowding, overworking, or extremes of temperature), and measures to reduce the number of disease organisms in the animal's environment (keeping food and water troughs clean and avoiding unnecessary mixing with other animals). Newly purchased animals should be free of illness and disease.

There are many contagious diseases which will affect, often fatally, healthy unstressed animals. Animals vary in their disease tolerance and resistance. When animals are constantly exposed to a disease they develop some natural tolerance to it. Animals most at risk include imported animals from other areas, regions or continents, particularly those imported from temperate continents into the tropics. Animals which have been routinely treated for internal and external parasites are at risk if such routine treatment stops. Expert advice should be sought on the use of vaccines to control the major contagious diseases such as rinderpest and foot-and-mouth disease.

d. Housing

Animal housing may range from a tree or hedge to a specially designed hutch or larger building. The overall objective of housing is to contribute to providing an optimum environment for the animals. They should be protected from extremes of temperature and wet conditions. Tropical climates, although hot during the day for much of the year, are often cold at night and in the rainy season. This puts new-born animals at risk. Dry floors avoid foot and parasite problems and provide comfortable lying conditions. Secure housing protects animals from predators and thieves. The use of locally available materials can reduce the cost of animal housing and shelters.

4

2.3.7 General guidelines for pastoral development

Pastoralist economies have always been based on flexibility and the opportunistic use of unpredictable pasture and water supplies. The freedom to move with herds is critical to the exploitation of these resources in a sustainable way. Pastoralists are used to adapting to change. However, in the last few decades pastoralist societies have had to face unprecedented and large-scale environmental, social and economic changes, such as land degradation, increasing population densities, restrictions on their traditional mobility, new forms of market economy, frequent droughts, and the resulting pressures on social and kin relationships. One of the results has been increasing differentiation within pastoralist societies, and the displacement of poorer herders from them.

In addition to this have been the misdirected policies and development strategies of governments and international agencies. This section outlines some major issues for future pastoral development policy, including a summary of the conclusions of an Oxfam publication based on the analysis of an Oxfam-supported pastoralist project in Somalia. (See resources list at the end of the chapter.)

a. Reducing the vulnerability of pastoral communities

Programmes have failed to address the vulnerability of pastoralists, regarding drought and famine as 'disasters' with cannot be prevented, and are inevitable. The following areas need urgent attention if pastoralists' vulnerability is to be addressed:

- development of government infrastructure and communications responsive to famine;
- improvements to food production rather than cash cropping, with soil and water conservation techniques;
- strengthening of traditional livestock production systems;
- development of appropriate credit schemes;
- decentralised famine early-warning systems, and community-based food security measures, including improvements to food storage capabilities;
- development support for democracy and a free press;
- lobbying on macro-economic issues such as limitations on military aid, and debt relief.

Reducing vulnerability should be part of all pastoral development programmes; increasing production will only contribute to this if increases benefit the poorest people among pastoralists, and produce can be stored to support long-term food security.

b. Supporting basic rights of pastoral communities

Measures should include securing pastoralists' rights to good quality pastoral land, and to move with their herds across regional and national boundaries. Water sources should be protected and provided in key areas used by pastoralists, and not only in settlement schemes. Programmes to create employment and develop alternative livelihoods for displaced pastoralists should be supported, where restocking is not viable.

Education and health services are poor in remote pastoral areas. Education should be a priority in building the capacity of pastoralists to participate in decisions about their future, and lobby for changes in policy.

In addition to these general policy measures, pastoralists need support in the areas of animal health and veterinary care, credit, marketing, and capacity-building through the formation of organisations and associations.

2.3.8 Principal livestock species

This section does not give exhaustive information about animal breeds, but indicates the kind of information which may be useful for the preliminary appraisal of project proposals. *Further technical information should always be sought, from the farmers themselves,* from local sources of expertise, and from specialised technical manuals on animal breeding and care. (See list of publications at the end of this chapter, and the Resources Directory for international and national institutions specialising in specific aspects of agricultural production.)

Cattle

The majority of tropical cattle are general-purpose breeds, which are milked, used for work and where religion and custom allow, killed for meat. The 'improved' specialised breeds are more productive but are more susceptible to disease, need higher levels of feeding, more expenditure and labour. Cattle are affected by a wide range of diseases. Control may be achieved by good nutrition, the use of vaccines and other measures. Indigenous cattle are normally more resistant to local diseases. Diseases include:

- Trypanosomiasis: spread by tsetse fly, widespread in Africa. Prophylactic drugs are available but expensive. Programmes to breed and release sterile male flies have been used in Nigeria.
- Rinderpest: now being brought under control in most parts of Africa. A vaccine is available.
- Contagious bovine pleuropneumonia (CBPP): still common in Africa. A vaccine is available.
- Foot-and-mouth disease: still found everywhere in Africa and in some parts of Asia and South America. Vaccines are available.
- Internal parasites: prevalent everywhere. Control measures are available.
- Tick-borne conditions such as East Coast Fever (East Africa only), heartwater, anaplasmosis and piroplasmosis. Avoided by the control of ticks, usually by frequent dipping of cattle, but this takes time, can reduce animal production, and ticks have begun to be resistant to the acaricides used. Some vaccines are available for some of the conditions.
- Bovine tuberculosis and brucellosis. These are common in many parts of the world. Vaccines are available.

In Ethiopia, the Sudan and other countries Oxfam supports paravet training, and the supplying of vaccines for large-scale cattle vaccination programmes.

Water buffaloes

There are two types of water buffaloes: river buffaloes found in the Indian sub-continent and as far west as Italy (good milk producers), and swamp buffaloes found in South-east Asia and as far east as the Philippines and Guam. Both types are used for meat. They are normally docile and important as draught animals. They are used widely in paddy rice cultivation.

Buffaloes suffer from exposure to hot sun; if worked or driven for long hours in the sun, they can suffer exhaustion or sudden death (young animals are particularly susceptible). They benefit from access to water for swimming or wallowing at the hottest times of the day. Many owners regularly bathe their animals and during work may wet them to prevent heat stress and improve skin health.

Buffaloes are generally susceptible to the same diseases as cattle but are more susceptible to rinderpest and less affected by foot-and-mouth disease. Greatest losses are among calves.

Sheep and goats

Sheep and goats are kept primarily for their meat, important for consumption and sale and in the celebration of many religious festivals, when their price can increase dramatically. The introduction of exotic breeds of milking goats has been attempted without much success, due to the lower hardiness of milking goats and the extra labour they require for their care.

Sheep thrive best in drier climates and when grazed on short pastures, though a few breeds do well in wetter climates. Sheep are primarily grazers and goats are primarily browsers, although both species are highly adaptable. Goats can thrive on coarser forage than sheep, but they are less tolerant of water deprivation. Both sheep and goats can often be left to forage for themselves. However they may need close herding or tethering during the growing season to prevent crop damage. Well-controlled goat herds can suppress unwanted forage species and improve grazing. Mixed flocks with cattle can make very good use of the available vegetation. Goats can also be reared in pens and fed on cut forage, as in many parts of Indonesia.

The major health problems of sheep and goats are internal parasites and to a lesser extent pneumonia. Sheep are also susceptible to diseases such as bluetongue, Nairobi sheep disease (Africa only) and sheep pox. Dosing regularly with anthelmintics and dipping are standard practices, but are expensive and may need funding.

Camels

Camels are being replaced as transport animals, but have a role as meat and milk-producing animals in very arid areas, to which they are well-adapted, and where they may replace cattle. They are also kept intensively in some countries.

The two major types are riding camels and baggagers; both are exceptionally tolerant of heat and of water deprivation. They prefer browsing to grazing, and move about constantly, which avoids overgrazing if the overall density of animals is not too great. Salt is particularly important for camels.

The healthy camel's hump should be firm and full. In arid areas they are not particularly subject to serious disease or parasitic attack, but skin conditions such as camel pox and mange are common. They are very susceptible to trypanosomiasis.

Llamoids

Llamas and Alpacas are important domestic livestock in the Andean countries of South America. They are used for meat, milk, wool and transport. Llamas and alpacas can thrive on very fibrous forage and do better than sheep at high altitudes in the tropics. They suffer from most diseases common to other ruminants, but are less susceptible to foot-and-mouth disease.

4

Donkeys

Most donkeys in the tropics are used as pack animals. Increasing effort is being given to designing suitable lightweight carts and equipment such as weeders and seeders to expand their use in semi-arid areas with light soils. Donkeys should carry no more than half of their weight; they commonly carry much more than this, which may lead to saddle sores and exhaustion, and increased susceptibility to internal parasites. Good feeding is essential if donkeys are worked hard.

Pigs

Pigs are an important class of livestock in some tropical regions, in societies where they are acceptable. Pigs are reared in a number of ways. Small indigenous pigs are allowed to scavenge for their own food. They may be given small amounts of supplement such as by-products of local brewing. The carcasses are often very fatty and may be infested with parasites which can also infect humans. In Asia pigs are often kept in integrated systems with fish and ducks. The faeces of the pigs are used to fertilise the algae in the pond upon which the fish and ducks feed. Whilst such systems may be successful in Asia they are very complex and require a high level of management skill.

Pigs provide high quality protein and are an important source of manure. When kept intensively they require high levels of management and care, and capital inputs to construct housing. It is important to feed them a well-balanced diet and keep them healthy. They need good housing design that gives each pig enough trough space and keeps them cool.

The major diseases of pigs in South-East Asia are swine plague and hog cholera. The latter can be controlled by vaccination. Pigs are very susceptible to internal parasites; kidney worm is a major cause of lack of growth and vigour in scavenging pigs and can be controlled if the animals are kept in clean pens.

Rabbits

Rabbits and other small herbivores have many advantages for small-scale producers. They provide a good protein food, require only a low capital outlay, have high reproductive and growth rates, consume many kinds of readily available foods, and have a good conversion rate of food to meat. Religious or cultural constraints must be investigated as rabbits are unacceptable in some cultures and alternatives (such as guinea pigs) may be preferable. The owners and their children sometimes become too fond of the rabbits to kill them, and this can be a problem in rabbit-rearing interventions. It is best to consider indigenous breeds because they are adapted to local conditions.

Wild rabbits spend a large part of each day carefully selecting a variety of food. Rabbit rearing based only on grass feeding gives poor results, as this diet is not of as high quality as that eaten in the wild. Locally available foods should be provided, such as broad-leaved weeds, grasses, banana leaves, vegetable wastes, and agricultural by-products. Legumes or other high quality plants may be planted to provide other food.

A good house (hutch), is essential, in a shaded and sheltered location protected from direct sunlight and heavy rain. Rabbits are very suscep-tible to diseases such as coccidiosis, pasteurella (snuffles), and lung infections in overcrowded or insanitary conditions. Good feeding and hutch cleanliness are very important as disease-prevention measures.

Guinea pigs

Guinea pigs are relatively docile creatures requiring virtually no capital or labour inputs. They are usually hardier and easier to manage than rabbits but less efficient than rabbits at converting food into meat. They are raised in captivity in the Andean region of South America where they are an important source of protein in cold and arid areas. In certain areas of Nigeria, domestic guinea pigs are popular. Among the main varieties of guinea pig are the Peruvian (very long-haired) and Abyssinian (smooth-haired).

Poultry

Poultry provides one of the most palatable and easily digested meats. It is high in protein and low in fat compared with other meats. Chickens also have ritual functions and are commonly used for religious offerings. Eggs are a good source of minerals, vitamins, and protein.

Chickens: Most breeds are originally descended from the jungle fowl of South-East Asia. Free-ranging chickens are usually fed once a day and left to scavenge for themselves, eating insects, seeds, and whatever else is available. Inputs are minimal and usually limited to a few scraps of kitchen waste. Housing may be a tree or a bush, or a shed to protect them from predators during the night.

In improved scavenging systems chickens may simply be restricted within a pen for part of the day when food supplements are given and the eggs collected regularly to discourage hens from becoming broody and encourage them to lay more eggs. In semi-intensive systems the chickens are more restricted, being kept in runs which can be moved about to allow the birds to find some of their own food. Vaccination programmes against Newcastle disease, fowl typhoid, and other diseases as recommended by veterinary staff, are advisable.

Ducks: The majority of ducks in the tropics are kept as scavengers. They are hardy and not as susceptible to disease as hens. There are a number of different types, but the Muscovy duck, technically a goose, is the most common type in tropical areas, and thrives under the toughest conditions. It is mainly useful for its meat. Unlike other types of duck it does not need access to water. Khaki Campbells or Indian Runners are high egg layers, and even under adverse conditions such as high rainfall, high temperature, excessive humidity, and poor housing, can still exceed the best laying strains of chickens. They need easy access to water.

Ducks can be profitably kept in conjunction with inland fisheries projects. Their manure stimulates the production of plankton and phytoplankton within the fish pond. Similarly they can be combined with paddy growing.

Geese: Geese make good use of grass and weeds. Access to water is not essential except to facilitate mating. Geese tend to be kept in family sets of one male goose (gander) and four or five female geese. They are kept for

553

eggs and meat. Their diet can consist largely of fresh growing green stuff. They need plenty of space to wander and forage. They are easy and cheap to keep, and also have a reputation as good homestead guards.

Guinea fowl: Guinea fowl are a scavenger species, able to escape predators by flying. Although wild birds, they can be encouraged to lay eggs in nestboxes if suitably handled. They forage for most of their food. They like to perch fairly high, and are excellent homestead guards.

Wildlife

In the past, wildlife and domestic animals have commonly been kept apart for reasons of disease transmission and competition for grazing. Grazing wildlife such as antelope may have an important role as a means of sustainable protein production. Their major attraction is their high level of adaptation to all aspects of the environment, including efficient utilisation of the available vegetation and resistance to prevailing diseases.

2.3.9 Bees and beekeeping

Beekeeping is common in tropical Africa and parts of Asia. Traditional techniques of keeping local bees are well-adapted to the local environment, but productivity is low and methods of collection often unnecessarily destructive. The economic return from beekeeping can be good provided there are adequate supplies of nectar and pollen close by. It should be possible for a beekeeper to pay off the capital cost of a manufactured hive in one or two years. Recurrent costs are normally small and the labour input only a few hours per hive per year.

Types of bee

- Tropical Africa: The indigenous honey bee is the same species as the European honey bee but is adapted to the tropical climate. It is productive but is very likely to sting, so its management can be difficult.
- Tropical Asia: There is a smaller species which produces only about one third as much honey as the European bee, but is well-adapted to the local environment. Two Asian species cannot be kept in hives, but honey is collected from them wild, throughout much of Southeast Asia.
- Latin America: There are no indigenous honey bees. European honey bees were introduced 150 years ago, and tropical African bees in 1956. The latter cause much trouble because of their stinging, but they produce larger amounts of honey. Stingless bees also produce

honey in smaller quantities collected in the wild; colonies are kept in hives in some areas.

Hives

These are of many types, of which two are commonly used in development projects:

- **movable-comb hives**: cheaper hives, originally adapted from a Greek basket hive built like a trough with sloping sides. Has the advantage that combs can be inspected and returned and management manipulations can be carried out without damage to the brood or colony as a whole;
- **movable-frame hives**: these have been less successful because of their much greater cost and complexity. To be successful they need close supervision.

Oxfam supports beekeeping in a number of countries. In the Gambia a regional seminar was supported which brought together individuals and organisations involved in beekeeping from all over West Africa to discuss common problems with beekeeping, appropriate technology in beekeeping, and the role of women in beekeeping development. Beekeeping supported by the Kagando Rural Development Centre in Uganda grew from a small apiary kept by a mission hospital. Honey produced by the participants in the beekeeping project is now sold in Uganda to shops, hotels, and supermarkets, and brings income to households in six parishes. In Vietnam Oxfam supports a Women's Union which has introduced beekeeping as a form of income-generation to two women's groups, from an ethnic minority group. The project has a strong focus on integrated training in all aspects of beekeeping, and generates training materials, which are usable in other mountain communities, which relate not only to keeping bees, but teach skills, such as marketing, applicable to other activities.

2.4 Support for rural organisations

(To be read in conjunction with **3**.1 Social organisation and **3**.2 Institutional development.)

There are many different kinds of organisations of rural workers and agriculturalists, ranging from informal co-operative networks based on kinship or residence, to rural trade unions, formal co-operatives, producer associations, credit unions and so on. These organisations may focus on sharing resources and labour in agricultural activities; defending the rights of agricultural workers in wage and land rights issues; the provision of consumer credit; and the marketing of produce.

A common form of support to producer groups is the rotating fund, which enables participants to obtain animals, seeds, tools, and other agricultural resources. Members are loaned the animals or seeds, and then pay back the loan with offspring or produce, which enables further loans to be made to other members.

Informal agricultural groups share labour on fields, or marketing facilities, and can more easily afford inputs such as health care and housing for animals or improvements in water sources such as wells or small dams. Many groups, however, organise in relation to issues such as land rights, rights to other resources, labour conditions on farms, environmental degradation and pollution, and agricultural or economic policies which negatively affect farmers.

Rural unions and organisations in many parts of the world have campaigned and taken positive action to resist eviction from land, to occupy uncultivated land owned by absentee landlords, and to fight for compensation when large projects, such as hydro-electric dams, force them to move. These actions often meet with state violence or violent actions from landowners or commercial 'bosses'. In Brazil, where Oxfam has supported rural trade unions and other peasant organisations for many years, including the national 'Movement of the Landless', many rural leaders have been assassinated by hired gunmen. One of the most well-known cases in recent times was the killing of Chico Mendes, the Brazilian trade-union leader who campaigned and organised on behalf of poor rubber-tappers and Indians to retain their rights to rubber trees in the north-west Amazon region.

The support of international NGOs and donor agencies can be crucial in such cases, to help to publicise the issues, and to campaign on behalf of rural workers, as well as offering them practical support. Often the most useful form of support is 'capacity building': funding training in skills such as literacy, book-keeping, running an organisation, and marketing, and funding networking to enable organisations to build solidarity with each other and exchange information. Oxfam has supported such initiatives in rural areas in most of the countries in which it works.

2.4.1 Pastoralist associations

In the 1980s development for pastoralists and other extensive livestock producers came to focus on the importance of participatory groups or pastoral associations (PAs). These were seen to have two functions:

- to provide legal structures through which governments could implement, manage and monitor pastoral development programmes;

- to give pastoralists organisational structures to safeguard and stabilise their threatened livelihoods, express their aspirations, and participate financially in development efforts and decision-making.

NGOs have been closely involved in the formation of pastoralist associations in a number of areas in Africa. These build on traditional forms of organisation of pastoralist men and women. Although they focus initially on livestock production, they aim to respond to changing needs and priorities. Pastoralist projects in which Oxfam has been involved in Sudan, Kenya and Chad have included a range of activities:

- technical support including para-vet training, agricultural programmes, environmental programmes and restocking in times of crisis;
- credit and setting up of revolving loan funds;
- assistance in marketing of livestock and other produce.

Recently, in recognition of women's important role in pastoralist economies and the failure of men's PAs to reach them, a number of projects have set up separate women's PAs. Pastoralist women may face a number of specific problems because of gender inequalities within pastoralist societies, including insecurity of rights to land and animals, where divorce is frequent, and difficulties in marketing their products.

Oxfam's experience with the setting up of women's PAs, who identify and implement their own priorities, has been positive. In Chad, for example, a number of women's PAs, initiated by a woman co-ordinator, saw little scope for increasing incomes from agricultural and livestock production, and concentrated on marketing. The women chose to focus on improving the sale of their produce (butter, oil, and mats) and the commercial production of household necessities like onions, garlic, and pepper. Although women own and are dependent on livestock, livestock improvement was seen as men's responsibility.

2.4.2 Small-scale agricultural production groups and co-operatives

Oxfam has supported many programmes developing small-scale agricultural production for various groups. These have included support for community poultry projects, for example, at Children's Homes in Ecuador and Colombia; a poultry-feed co-operative in Brazil, which started in schools and was subsequently taken on by village groups as well; women's groups producing, processing, and marketing sheanuts in West Africa. These groups may enable poor producers to obtain credit, and help them to market their produce more effectively. (See 4.1.3.5 Credit and savings support; and 4.1.3.6 Marketing assistance.)

557

a. Credit

Credit support may be in the form of revolving credit funds for purchasing seed, or agricultural tools, or for the distribution of animals. Credit is also needed by groups or individuals for improvements in crop or animal production by the introduction of improved breeds or building of improved houses and sheds. Credit to pastoralist organisations helps men and women to overcome price fluctuations on the market for both livestock and livestock products, and helps crop producers to cope with seasonal price fluctuation, enabling them to buy when prices are low at harvest time. Credit should be offered on a long-term basis, to provide poor producers not only with initial capital, but with working capital; this can also help them to become credit-worthy in the longer term, in the eyes of official lending institutions.

b. Marketing

Marketing is very important to all producers who raise income from their crops or livestock. Market research is indispensable in the planning stages of interventions, and training in financial management for producer organisations is essential. The storage and transport of produce is key to marketing, and there must be clarity about the allocation of income from the sale of produce. The questions to ask are: Who markets the produce? Who plays what role in the stages of preparing produce for marketing? Who gets what share of the income? Who has been trained in the financial aspects of marketing? How widespread is illiteracy and innumeracy, and is the marketing project addressing this?

For many pastoralists marketing assistance may be the most immediate priority. Prices for livestock and livestock produce are often highly seasonal, and credit may be a vital factor in increasing their incomes. Prices in the local markets are often controlled by a few businessmen; pastoralists' incomes may thus be significantly increased by improving transport facilities and bulk marketing in more distant urban areas.

In small-scale livestock projects marketing is also often a priority. Failure to consider marketing in choice of animals has often been a major cause of failure. Improving transport, storage, and packaging of livestock produce may be significant areas for intervention and support.

In Colombia the best land is controlled by cattle farmers who are members of a few powerful families, while the peasants produce on poorer land. One of the factors perpetuating the poverty of the peasants is lack of independent mechanisms for marketing. The State Marketing Board is controlled by corrupt functionaries linked to the landlords, and merchants who buy the poor farmers' produce below its real value, and sell inputs at a high price. The farmers formed a co-operative for the direct marketing of products and inputs, to lower the costs of production and improve incomes from sales, and also for the sale of basic foodstuffs (salt, cooking oil, soap). The co-operative suffered from vertical control imposed by peasant leaders, which led to low levels of participation. The intervention supported by Oxfam aimed to strengthen the economic capacity of the co-operative so that it could serve the surrounding communities, and to encourage the practice of participative decision-making in the management of the co-operative.

c. Training and extension
(To be read in conjunction with 4.1.3.7 Training and information exchange.)
Agricultural extension is the most familiar form of training in the sector, and new forms of participative learning with farmers are increasingly proposed and supported by NGOs to replace top-down forms of training which have proved to be inappropriate. 'Campesino a Campesino' (peasant to peasant) is a programme in Nicaragua which aims to support farmers in improving their lands and crops through small-scale experiments, diversification, and regular visits to exchange experience and information. Supported by Oxfam, Campesino a Campesino promotes regional exchanges and meetings, drawing as many as 200 farmers from different countries in Central America and the Caribbean to look at local farms, discuss methods and experiments, and exchange ideas.

Most livestock schemes benefit from training in animal breeding and care. In some cases this may be given to all participants, in others efforts may be concentrated on training individual men and women as paravets. Oxfam supports paravet training in many parts of the world. Where women are the main carers for animals, training programmes should ensure that they receive the appropriate training. As women have higher illiteracy rates than men, training programmes should build in literacy training if necessary. Failure to train women has often meant that many paravet training programmes have had negligible effects on the health of livestock.

In many cases, training groups rather than individuals has proved effective. Activities of groups may include competitions, visits to other farmers, and discussions about common problems and farmer-generated ideas. Livestock owners may also be encouraged to carry out simple trials to compare different animals and foods. Group extension has proved particularly valuable for women and provided a forum for them to discuss other problems and possible solutions. For example, the Pastoral Women's Workshops in Africa bring together women from a number of different pastoralist societies to exchange information about animal care, and explore forms of organisation and collective action to improve women's position within pastoralist communities.

559

2.5 Key questions

(Please refer to the Key questions at the end of **4.1** General aspects of production. The following questions are supplementary, and deal specifically with agricultural production.)

1 What is the division of labour, by gender, class and ethnic identity, among the agriculturalists who are to participate in the intervention? What is the structure of ownership and control of resources such as land, water sources, animals, and crops?

2 Is the technical advice needed for the intervention available locally? What is the best way of enabling farmers to obtain this advice?

3 Has full market research been carried out in relation to the particular crops and animals produced for cash?

4 Are the cropping or animal rearing methods sustainable, financially and in relation to environmental factors? Are there provisions for years of crop failure, low rainfall, animal disease, and so on, when people's livelihoods are at risk?

5 Have all aspects of production been considered: land preparation, sowing and harvesting, processing, cooking, storing, transporting, and selling the produce? Who does what? Who needs what support?

6 What is the structure of ownership and use of land, for crops and grazing animals?

7 What are the levels and forms of participation of women, the poorest farmers, and people of low caste or ethnic minority groups in the farmer's organisations involved in the interventions?

3 Fishing

3.1 Introduction: fishing in developing countries 561
    3.1.1 The impact of fisheries development on fishworkers 562
3.2 Practical approaches 564
    3.2.1 Small-scale fishing systems 565
    3.2.2 Fishing communities 566
    3.2.3 Women fishworkers 567
    3.2.4 Technical support for small-scale fishing 569
    3.2.5 Fish processing 576
    3.2.6 Credit and marketing 577
    3.2.7 Fishworker organisations 578
3.3 Key questions 579

3.1 Introduction: fishing in developing countries

(This section should be read in conjunction with the first section of this chapter, which discusses general principles of the social aspects of production more fully, and provides a fuller account of the general issues related to technology, credit, marketing and training.)

Small-scale fishing in developing countries produces about half of the world's fish catch of 100 million tonnes. In these countries fish is the main source of animal protein in the diets of most poor people, while fishing and allied activities provide important sources of income and employment for women and men in coastal, riverine and rural areas. It is estimated that 100 million people in poor countries throughout the world are directly dependent upon fishing for all or part of their livelihoods. Some are involved in small-scale fishing, while others are employed as labour or crew on large fishing boats, or are involved in fish processing, production of equipment or small-scale marketing.

Oxfam works with fishworkers and their organisations in Africa, Latin America, and Asia in a wide range of initiatives. The fishworkers with whom NGOs work are suffering increasing poverty and insecurity, and struggling to maintain their livelihoods in the face of modern large-scale fishing, national and international fishing policy, and industrial pollution of seas and rivers. In many societies, fishworkers are among the poorest people, often belonging to the lowest social class or caste. Fishing villages commonly lack basic services such as education, water, and housing, and among fishworkers literacy is often much lower and child mortality higher than in society at large. Fishworkers rarely own land or property. Women fishworkers are even more vulnerable than men: their traditional roles in all aspects of fish production have been more rapidly eroded, as a result of the introduction of capital-intensive technologies and centralised marketing.

3.1.1 The impact of fisheries development on fishworkers

While fish production steadily increased between the 1960s and 1990s in order to meet increased world demand, the local availability of fish resources for poor people declined as a result of national and international fisheries policies, uncontrolled fishing, and industrial pollution. Most specialists agree that conventional fish resources are either fully or over-exploited, and that further increases in fish production need to come from non-conventional fish resources such as deep-sea squid, or from fish farming, or aquaculture.

The boundaries of the world fish trade were redrawn with the establishment of Exclusive Economic Zones, when most maritime countries extended their sea boundaries and acquired new rights and responsibilities for the management of their marine resources. This has given rise to conflicts of interest in coastal waters where the traditional artisanal fishing activities have to compete not only with more industrialised fishing operations but with fish-farming, especially shrimp farming, and with tourism.

While global demand for fish has increased, the consumption of fish *per capita* in rich industrialised countries is still 3.5 times that of people in poor countries. At least 70 per cent of the world trade in fish flows from poor to rich countries, and as demand increases, the price of fish rises beyond the capacity of poor people to buy it.

Fish farming may offer a solution to the problem of maintaining fish supplies to the world's population, but the 'Blue Revolution' in fish farming techniques suffers from many of the same problems as the Green Revolution in agriculture. (See 1.3.5.1 Rural livelihoods.) Modern intensive fish-farming techniques tend to be environmentally damaging, producing high levels of biological waste, and pollution. Prawn culture in coastal areas in the Philippines, for example, endangers coastal ecosystems such as mangrove swamps, which are a vital breeding site for many species of fish and crustaceans. These forms of fish farming are inappropriate for poor people, for whom the levels of investment and management are beyond their means.

a. Capture fishing

During the 1970s and 1980s, national and international fisheries policies increased the vulnerability of small-scale fishers and fishworkers engaged in capture fishing (hunting fish in open waters). The availability of fish to local fishermen and women has greatly decreased, because capital-intensive methods of fishing, such as trawling and purse-seining for high-value fish such as tuna, prawns, and shrimps, have decimated local fish stocks. Large numbers of other fish, valuable for local consumption, are caught in the same nets and then thrown back dead into the sea. Most of the high-value fish caught is destined for export. The sea fisheries agreements drawn up under the Lomé Convention and the 1982 United Nations Law of the Sea Convention (UNLOSC) are based on national interest, and thus do not recognise the customary rights of local fishers. Where local fishing regulations are drawn up to protect stocks, they are widely flouted by powerful companies, but limit the activities of small-scale fishers.

Fishworkers are vulnerable in other ways. For example, traditional sea-fishermen may be pressured (and in some cases kidnapped) into low-paid employment as fishworkers on deep-sea fishing boats. The work is hazardous, vessels often lack safety equipment, and there may be no insurance for compensation in the case of accidents.

The increasing poverty of fishing communities has led to the breakdown of many traditional systems of regulation, and the over-exploitation of local fish resources. In the Philippines, for example, it is estimated that only 25 per cent of the coastal coral reefs remain in a fit state for fish to feed and breed in because of destructive fishing methods by local fishers (dynamite, poisons, and breaking reefs with rocks).

b. Fish farming (aquaculture)

Subsistence and small-scale fishing in inland areas is often dependent on insecure and informal fishing rights. The introduction of intensive, high-profit fish farming has had considerable environmental and social costs.

Inland fishing areas, which traditionally formed the major source of livelihood for many small-scale fisherwomen and men, are now being appropriated by big business for intensive shrimp and fish farming. Large areas, such as mangrove swamps in Brazil and the Philippines and 'backwaters' lagoon areas in Kerala, South India, have been cleared for fish farming. Fish farming has also led to the inundation of productive arable land and the displacement of people who are dependent upon this land for food and employment. Richer farmers and landlords assert rights over ponds and other small water resources formerly used by poor women and men for part-time or subsistence fishing. Intensive fish-farming produces large quantities of biological waste, and the excessive use of pesticides causes high levels of pollution.

Small-scale fishing is also adversely affected by other economic growth policies. In Brazil many coastal areas are being cleared to make way for tourist sites, while in the Amazon basin gold-mining operations and industrial development have poisoned the rivers over a huge area. In the Philippines, the fishing economy of Laguna Lake, the largest inland water tract in Asia, supporting 11,000 households, has been devastated by a flood-control programme, pollution, and over-fishing. On the coasts of Peru, the waste produced by mining and agro-industrial complexes has caused extensive pollution, poisoning the aquatic environment. In many countries high technology agriculture, with its intensive use of fertilisers and pesticides, has wiped out seasonal fish stocks on rice fields and other temporarily flooded land.

Oxfam supports fishworker organisations who are attempting to tackle such assaults on their livelihoods by organising with other fishworkers, campaigning and lobbying against policies and practices which damage and degrade the aquatic environment, and participating in the planning of more appropriate fisheries development. In Chile, for example, Oxfam supports the National Confederation of Fishworkers who run a training programme for representatives of fishworkers to enable them to participate more effectively in local and national fishing councils; and to use these official bodies to promote alternative fisheries development proposals to combat over-exploitation of fish, pollution of inshore areas, and the poor working and living conditions of fishworkers' families.

3.2 Practical approaches

NGO support for the development of fishing is likely to involve interventions in two different contexts: in villages in coastal areas or on rivers and lakes, where many people are dependent on fishing, and the principal focus of support is to protect fishworker's livelihoods and increase incomes through building on existing fishing systems; and in rural areas, where fishing may or may not already be important in the local economy, to improve incomes or food supplies for landless people or marginal farmers.

In either context, appropriate NGO interventions could include:

- support for small-scale participatory technology development, which builds on existing production techniques and should increase incomes without depleting fish stocks;
- providing credit and improving marketing;
- supporting production groups for fish-farming, fish processing, and production of fishing equipment;

- developing and strengthening organisations of fishworkers to defend their interests and influence the development agenda in their favour.

In assessing the different types of interventions it is important to consider:

- what kinds of fish culture and fishing activities already exist;
- existing and potential markets for different types and qualities of fish; small-scale fish farming species are often the same or similar to species obtained through fish capture and the additional costs (management, capital and labour inputs) may not be not balanced by increased prices;
- ownership and control of water sources and lands;
- the existing division of labour in fishing, between men and women, old and young people;
- the extent of capture fishing by women and men, and the possible effects of fish culture development on this;
- the impact increased fish production will have on the labour of processing and marketing fish.

In all cases women's and men's distinct roles in fishing, and their different needs and priorities, must be clearly identified. These may be addressed either in separate initiatives for women and men, or by ensuring that within all programmes, gender inequalities are addressed, and women and men participate equally.

3.2.1 Small-scale fishing systems

Fishing, like other production systems, involves a complex division of labour and social relations which entail differential ownership of and rights to equipment and produce. Fishing systems include not only fish capture or fish farming but also production of fishing boats and equipment, fish processing, and marketing.

These different aspects of fishing systems are all inter-related, and any interventions to assist people in one aspect will affect those involved in others. Development agencies should ensure that they understand the different roles and responsibilities of all those involved in different aspects of fishing, and pay particular attention to the division of labour, control over resources, and distribution of income and food among women and men, young and old people, and people of different classes, ethnic groups or race.

Fishing systems may be divided into two broad categories: capture fishing, a hunting activity to exploit an extremely vulnerable natural resource; and fish farming or aquaculture, using husbandry techniques.

565

a. Capture fishing

This is based on marine and fresh water resources. There are two main classes of fish, pelagic or surface fish, and demersal or bottom-living fish.

Pelagic fish, marine examples of which are sardines, tuna and herring, mackerel, barracuda and jacks, generally occur in large, very mobile shoals, which are highly seasonal in their occurrence and are largest at the time of reproduction. They are also prone to wide annual fluctuations according to the weather and oceanographic patterns. They often travel long distances through the territories of many states, and are extremely vulnerable to modern catching techniques, which can fish down to the very last shoal.

Demersal fish include reef examples, such as snappers, perches, some sharks and rays, and other bottom living-fish, such as shrimps and prawns, croakers, and grunters. In tropical waters there are many different species but small numbers of each species. Commercial fishing is particularly wasteful because of the catch-all techniques used. Fish not required are thrown back dead into the sea. In the case of prawn-trawling, between 50 per cent and 90 per cent of the catch may be rejected. In temperate waters bottom-living stocks can occur in large numbers, but there are relatively few species.

b. Fish farming

Aquaculture is the production of fish and other aquatic organisms for subsistence and commercial purposes, using husbandry techniques, and generally involving alteration of the natural environment. The system of production may be extensive or intensive.

Extensive production requires small amounts of inputs to increase natural or constructed aquatic environments, such as ponds, tanks or lagoons. Stocking levels of fish are slightly above natural levels, and capital investment is low, as are water requirements, labour, equipment and other input costs.

Intensive production requires purpose-built tanks, ponds, raceways, and other structures, stocking levels of fish are high, and large quantities of water are needed. Levels of fish production depend on feed and fertiliser inputs, and capital investment and running costs are high.

In addition to these two main types of fish-farming, another form is being developed, which creates artificial environments in fresh or sea water, to attract fish. These are known as 'nurture fisheries'. (See 4.3.2.4 Technical support for small-scale fishing.)

3.2.2 Fishing communities

Coastal and rural fishing villages are not homogeneous communities; those with an interest in fishing and fishery development may have very different needs and priorities. Different scales of operation often co-exist in the same community, with considerable income differentials between and within households, and between women and men. This leads to many different types of interdependence, and also to conflict and exploitation. Economic and social relationships should be identified and analysed by NGOs when planning any form of support to fishworkers.

In fishing itself there is a wide range in scale of operation and degree of capital investment, from small-scale artisan activity to large-scale capital-intensive production. Fishing may be a full-time, part-time, income-earning or subsistence activity, and people may be involved in a different way at different times of the year.

Many small-scale fishers do not own the means of production. The boats and fishing equipment are often owned by wealthier people to whom the fishers are indebted, sometimes working as bonded labourers. In rural inland areas, fishers from marginal farmer or landless households rarely own ponds or other water sources. This may vary from one part of the world to another, and 'ownership' can be defined in different ways.

The nature of the market for fish creates further sources of exploitation and differentiation within fishing villages. Fish is a highly perishable commodity, which needs to be processed and marketed quickly after capture. Where more capital-intensive technology is used, the quantities of fish caught are generally too large for local markets. In times of glut, prices in local markets are depressed.

The need to reach wider markets, and the use of new processing methods, coupled with the indebtedness and lack of capital of fishworkers, strengthens the power of moneylenders and intermediaries. Complex marketing and credit relationships exist between small-scale fishers and intermediaries, money lenders, and fish merchants. The money lender or intermediary may buy the fish catch at a low fixed rate, preventing fishers from receiving a fair return for their labour, and also preventing other fishworkers, often women, from earning an income in processing and marketing. Sometimes there is a system of debt-bondage, which may involve whole families and successive generations, where the fishworkers provide their labour at fixed low rates as payment against interest on loans received.

3.2.3 Women fishworkers

Women's role in fishing, their control over income, and the degree of independence they enjoy, varies widely. Although women may play an important role in processing fish (for example, working in small-scale or large smokeries or canneries), they do not generally work on boats, and

567

for this reason have frequently been overlooked in fishery development. Women play a number of important production roles in local and subsistence fishing, in processing and marketing of fish, and manufacture of fishing equipment. In some countries, such as the Philippines, women perform 50 to 75 per cent of pre- and post-harvest work, such as mending nets, and processing, marketing, and distributing the catch. In some areas, 15 to 20 per cent of women participate in fish capture as well.

In fishing communities, as elsewhere, women bear the major responsibility for a wide range of reproductive tasks and family subsistence activities, and may be alone for long periods when men are away fishing. Fish caught by male family members is essential for their own processing and marketing activities, and the loss of male partners or family members deprives them of their main source of livelihood. In sea-fishing villages the proportion of female-headed households is often high because of deaths in accidents at sea.

Where women are involved in catching fish, their access to fishing sites is often more restricted than men's because of lack of time to reach far-off fishing grounds, and gender-based household maintenance tasks. The fishing equipment women use is often inferior because they lack financial resources.

In marketing — with some notable exceptions — women are often unable to compete with male traders. In processing, they are being displaced because traditional processing methods of drying and curing are being replaced by freezing. The catches are often transported away from the fishing communities in bulk to distant factories for processing. For example, the bulk catches of oil sardines in South India by motorised ring seiners are causing the displacement of women processers. Where women are employed by larger enterprises, for example as 'prawn peelers', they are often poorly paid, and work in very bad conditions.

Throughout the world, women perform a wide variety of tasks in fishing systems. In north-east Brazil women fish for shrimp and other shellfish in estuaries while men fish at sea. In the South American Amazon region men and women work together scooping up and trapping fish which have previously been stunned with a vegetable poison. In Japan, women are pearl divers, and in South-East Asia, the Pacific Islands, and among the Okovanga in Southern Africa, women net and trap fish.

In West Bengal, low-caste women play an important role in subsistence fishing before the rice harvest. The small fish collected by women from the paddy fields are essential food when other food is scarce. Sale of this fish also contributes to income at a time when other employment opportunities for women are limited.

568

Traditionally, fish-processing is almost universally done by women: as unpaid family workers processing the men's catch; as independent processors and marketers catching or buying in fish; or employed as wage or piece-rate labour by male and female fish marketers.

Women make nets and other fishing equipment, generally for household fishing activity, but also for sale.

Women are commonly involved in fish marketing, particularly small-scale local marketing, and this may provide an important source of income. Women may sell their own or their husband's fish. In some cases richer women may have substantial fish marketing businesses: in West Africa (Senegal and Ghana) the 'Fish Mammies' who market the bulk of the fish catch, hold a very high social status, and may come from relatively rich families. The fishermen's wives who often process and sell the catch to these women are of much lower status. In India (Kerala) much of the small-scale fish marketing is done by women.

3.2.4 Technical support for small-scale fishing

Most fishery development, including some NGO projects, has involved the introduction of relatively large-scale capital-intensive fishing and processing technology. Modern capital-intensive techniques are extremely wasteful, and the greater the technical 'efficiency' the greater the damage to fish stocks. They are also beyond the capital and skill resources of small-scale fishermen and women.

Where development agencies have introduced new small-scale technologies, or improved existing ones, in capture fishing or fish farming, this has suffered from many of the problems outlined in 4.1.3.4 Technology development. Improvements have often been made to technologies controlled by men, for example, improved boats or fishing equipment; but increased fish production can cause a labour bottleneck, and will only be feasible if accompanied by measures to save labour time in processing and marketing.

a. Capture fisheries
Traditional fishing techniques, although less profitable, are generally based on an understanding of the importance of preserving fish stocks, and thus, the livelihoods of people dependent upon them. Fishermen and women often have knowledge, developed over many generations, of a wide variety of different types of fish and their relative abundance in particular fishing grounds, at different seasons.

Fishing is controlled by a complex set of customary regulations and taboos which allow time for fish to breed and grow before harvesting, such as limiting fishing seasons, and use of fishing grounds, and regulating fishing equipment (hook size or types of net).

569

Traditional fishing tends to be passive, relying on the fish coming into contact with the hook and line or nets, and allowing some fish to escape. To a certain extent, fishing is selective with only fish of the desired species and size being caught.

Any intervention which is designed to change or improve boats and fishing equipment must consider the effects which increased efficiency may have on the sustainability of fish stocks.

Motorisation of boats: technological improvements have often been concerned with increasing the catch through improving boats, often by the use of outboard motors and inboard engines. Motors alleviate the back-breaking tasks of rowing and sailing, and make it possible to fish further out to sea and reach more distant and less exploited fishing grounds. It also enables fishermen to carry more fishing gear, and make the journeys more quickly. This increases fishing time and leisure time and gets the fish to market faster.

However, there are many potential problems if fishers become dependent on imported technology. Traditional skills such as sailing may be undermined; spare parts, repairs and maintenance services may be expensive or unavailable; the returns from the fishing operation are often insufficient to cover the increased running costs, to pay back the principal and interest on the increased investment, and to set aside money for future repairs and maintenance. The use of motors can lead to overfishing of inland waters, as deeper waters are less productive, and may lead to inequities, with the poorest fishers, whose boats are non-motorised, being displaced.

In India, where Oxfam supports many fishworkers and their organisations, there has been a rapid increase in the number of small mechanised fishing boats in the past two decades. However, it has been calculated that fishermen using outboard motors have to catch seven times more fish than those without motors, to cover the costs of investment, maintenance, and fuel.

When considering support for the mechanisation of existing boats, all the above advantages and disadvantages should be carefully assessed in relation to the particular conditions in the area. Information about fish stocks, fishing grounds, and the socio-economic relations among the fishers, should be analysed.

Improved boat design: other attempts have been made to improve boats through using new designs and materials. Traditional boats are often built from large trunks of timber lashed together, or nailed together in the form of planks, or they may be simpler, dug out canoes. As timber becomes scarcer, these traditional boat-building materials become more expensive.

The use of new materials, such as fibre glass and other plastics, or steel, can create problems. The boat-building is removed from the local community, and traditional artisans de-skilled. Fishers become dependent upon future supplies of new materials and expertise from outside; boats made from the new materials are generally too expensive for poor fishers. In many cases the boats have been either too heavy or too light, and not versatile enough. Some of the high technology plastics and resins are hazardous to health, putting boat builders at risk.

For all these reasons, support to traditional boat-building with local materials is likely to be more successful. For example, the introduction of plywood boat-building was supported by Oxfam in South India, where the project built closely on local knowledge, and skills. The effectiveness of technological innovations, whether in the design and or motorisation of boats, will depend upon the extent to which they have a positive impact on the other aspects of fish production, and the women and men engaged in them.

For example, an organisation in Angola supported by Oxfam introduced boats and equipment to encourage fishermen to stay at sea for longer periods, and supported them with supplies taken to them in a larger boat. This increased their incomes, and also reduced male alcoholism, which had been a serious problem. Complementary improvements were also made in processing and conservation of fish, which was under the control of women.

An example of an intervention with unforeseen effects was a project on the Indonesian island of Lombok, which introduced fishing boats with a wider range. This resulted in male fishworkers migrating to another area of the coast. They formed a settlement there, and with the income they earned they 'bought' new wives and set up new homes. Their income was lost to their original households on the other side of the island, and this resulted in a great deal of hardship for their original wives and children.

b. Nurture fisheries

Nurture fishing is a recent development, which aims to concentrate fish in a zone where fishing can be regulated by organisations of local fishermen and women. Examples of techniques and technology associated with nurture fisheries include artificial reefs and fish aggregating devices (FADs), where an artificial habitat or shelter is provided. Oxfam supports the construction of artificial reefs in the Philippines.

The main advantages of artificial reefs and FADs are:

- They can be used to demarcate an area of water or sea over which exclusive access and fishing rights can be negotiated.
- Artificial reefs, if large enough, may prevent the use of destructive fishing techniques, like trawls.

- They can bring the community together to discuss issues of fisheries management, and these discussions may provide the basis for establishing committees to regulate fishing effort, negotiate with government, and strengthen community organisation.

However, the disadvantage of FADs and artificial reefs is that they attract fish to an area where they are easily caught, and this can lead to overfishing.

c. Fish farming or aquaculture

Traditional fish-farming systems include a wide range of different techniques, such as:

Polyculture whereby different fish species live at different levels in the water, occupying different ecological niches and following different feeding habits. This creates little competition for space or food between species, and maximum use of the natural productivity of the pond.

Fish and paddy cultivation, where rice is grown as a staple crop, small fish are introduced or encouraged in flooded rice fields. Some systems in India use the cycle of monsoon flooding alternately for shrimp farming and rice growing.

Integrated fish farming is common in China, and Vietnam. Here, fish, ducks, and pigs are raised in an integrated system, using the waste from pigs and ducks to provide fish food.

Increasing the availability and quality of local fish resources may be an extremely valuable part of a production strategy for marginal farmers and landless women and men. The introduction of fish farming, however, is not easy. Considerable extra labour may be involved in pond management; this raises the question of who will do it, and how they will find the time. Payment for this work may need to be considered, and ways to save labour in other areas. If these issues are not addressed carefully, it is likely that the value of the ponds will be marginal.

When new ponds and new types of fish are introduced interventions must include adequate training and provision of technical information for those who will be managing the ponds and fish.

Production levels of fish ponds: the levels of production which can be attained from fish farming depend very much on environmental factors, availability of capital, and capacity of the people to manage the ponds. These must be very carefully assessed.

It is possible for village ponds to produce 500-1,000 kilograms of fish per hectare annually, or 20 kg/year for a pond 200 square metres in area as long as conditions are favourable. Such ponds require negligible throughflow of water, minimal feed and fertiliser inputs, and a certain amount of management.

In purpose-constructed facilities, production levels of 4,000-6,000 Kg/ha/year are achievable if there are no constraints on the water availability, and if stocking with fish and feeding is carefully monitored and regulated. High inputs of feed and fertiliser are required, and careful and informed management is essential.

Much higher rates of production are achievable with large capital investment for example, on commercial trout farms and in research stations. However, the capital costs required for the construction of these facilities, the training costs, and the running costs required should only be considered if the management and maintenance of the ponds can be guaranteed, the processing and marketing of the fish can be handled, and the benefits will outweigh the costs.

General guidelines for NGO interventions: Appropriate interventions for NGOs are likely to be those which are extensive rather than intensive. Such interventions may aim to improve or construct water sources, or to optimise their use, to introduce or increase fish stocks, to improve the quality and hence increase the value of fish through improved feeding and water fertilisation, to decrease fish losses due to disease and degradation, to improve nutrition and income.

Improvement of ponds and water sources: In order to live and grow, fish need to have favourable environmental conditions and water supply.

- **Water quantity:** stocking levels are very dependent upon throughput of water: the higher the stocking density the more water is required. Water may be fed into ponds from streams, rivers and lakes, by gravity or using simple manually operated pumps. A permanent supply of water is essential to top up and maintain pond levels which drop through evaporation. Under ideal conditions ponds also should be drainable so that they can be cleaned and renewed.

- **Chemical composition:** the natural productivity of the water and its chemical balance will effect the levels of other inputs required. There are a number of factors which need to be considered in assessing the chemical suitability of the water supply, including its pH; its turbidity or amounts of suspended mud or silt; its hardness (particularly calcium hardness) and pollution levels; and the levels of some minerals, particularly iron, which can be harmful to some fish.

- **Water source:** the quantity and quality of the water is affected by its source. For example, the longer water has been settled in a pond or other water body, the more likely it is to be suitable for fish culture, and the less pretreatment it will require. However, water from deep wells is low in oxygen and needs to be settled and allowed to 'aerate' before use. It may also have a high salt or mineral level, particularly iron. Water from shallow wells may contain high levels of some salts.

Rain water may be too acidic, and is likely to require some pre-treatment, such as liming or fertilising, before it can be used.

- **Water temperature**: the growth rate of all fish is dependent upon temperature. Generally, up to a maximum of 25-35°C, growth rate increases with temperature, but each fish species has an optimum temperature. Wide daily and seasonal fluctuations in temperature can limit the potential of fish culture. Ponds need to be constructed to a minimum depth of one metre, to prevent wide daily temperature fluctuations and to prevent excessive weed growth. Oxygen levels decline as water temperature rises, causing fish to die.
- **Soil conditions**: these are particularly important where water sources have to be created. The main factors are whether or not the soil will hold water and whether or not the quality of the soil will affect the quality of the water.

There are three main types of ponds or water sources which can be created or modified:

- **Diversion ponds** where the water is diverted around each pond to feed into the next pond. The ponds are arranged in parallel rows with each pond effectively receiving its own independent water supply. This provides a stable water environment and gives complete control over stocking and harvesting of fish.
- **Barrage ponds** and **contour ponds** are built by placing an obstruction across a natural water course to make a dam. Barrage ponds are made by building a wall along the side of a stream, each pond having its own inlet or outlet or overflow pipe. Contour ponds are made on sloping ground; water enters from a stream or dam at the highest point and is held in by walls at the lower end. These ponds form a series: the water supply of the lower ponds comes from the ponds above. These ponds give less control over stocking and feeding the fish, and also increase the danger of the introduction and spreading of disease.
- **Paddy ponds** are paddy fields which are also used for fish growing on flat land surrounded by walls (bunds) on four sides. The cultivation of fish with rice is common in many Asian countries. However, the use of agricultural pesticides can kill off fish or limit their growth, and some fish can damage the rice crop.

Choice of fish species: selection of appropriate fish species is critical to successful fish culture.

The introduction of new fast-growing species has been a common policy in fish farming. However, this may seriously damage a country's ecosystem and local environment. A range of fish have been introduced in fish culture development: tilapia, carps, catfish, milk fish, buffalo fish, yellowtails, mullet, eels, salmon, trout, prawns and oysters. There are, however, many case studies of disastrous effects on the ecosystem of introducing new breeds — particularly with Nile Perch, tilapia and carp. There are many potential problems including:

- Introduced species such as tilapia are often chosen because of their tolerance of a wide variety of conditions and food, their precocious breeding habits, and rapid growth. However, for many environments they may breed much too rapidly and displace local species.
- New fish diseases can be introduced, against which local fish species have no resistance.
- Sources of fish seed (small fish for stocking), and the local capacity to grow the fish, must be assured. Hatcheries may be introduced, but these are often complex and difficult to manage, requiring imported technology and inputs (such as hormones). Their capital costs are relatively high.
- There are usually local preferences for particular types of fish and it must be ensured that there is a market for the introduced species and that it is acceptable in terms of taste, price and other factors.

It is therefore advisable to investigate fully the viability of local species before introducing exotic breeds.

Improvements in fish feed and water fertiliser: each fish species has particular feeding habits and preferences. Most fish require a high protein diet to grow fast and growth rates can be increased by adding feed. However, fish meal (a high protein food) can be relatively expensive and unless there is a very good local source available, it is unlikely to be a suitable food for low-cost fish culture. Natural productivity can also be enhanced by inputs of fertiliser such as lime, inorganic fertiliser, urea, manure and compost. However, these are also expensive and may not be readily available locally. Possible alternatives include:

- introduction of fish which feed on planktonic organisms; these can make best use of the natural productivity of pond water, but may not be a desired species for local consumption;
- encouraging the growth of aquatic weeds in the pond for fish such as tilapia and some carps;
- integrating fish culture with livestock production (integrated systems using the manure or droppings of ducks, chickens and pig farming are common traditional practices in many countries);
- use of agricultural and fisheries waste and by-products such as rice or maize bran and husks, oil cake (from groundnuts, sunflowers, mustard), brewing waste, shrimp factory waste, fish offal.

Decreasing fish losses: disease and depredation: losses from fish ponds through disease can be very high. Common diseases include fungal diseases such as gill rot. These may be introduced inadvertently through water inlets if these are not well-protected. The incidence of gill rot may be minimised by reducing feed intake, particularly of organic matter in periods of very hot weather. Parasites and worms also cause fish disease and these may be controlled by clearing and liming the pond.

Regular drainage is always advisable. If this is difficult, or impossible the introduction of some saline water may be a useful prophylactic provided the fish species are reasonably saline tolerant.

Losses from predation can also be very high. Frogs, snakes and birds can quickly fish out a pond. Losses are also frequent from poaching and in some cases poisoning where jealousies and rivalries lead to ponds being sabotaged. Some form of protection and guarding system is usually necessary.

3.2.5 Fish processing

Improvements in fish processing is a vital part of any fishery development. As processing is usually done by women, any extra demands on their labour time made by increasing the volume of fish for processing, or introducing new techniques, must be considered. Women have generally received little attention in development policy, because fish processing is often associated with other domestic activities and requires similar 'female' skills to those for domestic food preparation. Improved technologies should decrease labour time, or other measures should be built into the programme to decrease women's workload in agricultural production or household work.

There are a number of low-cost technologies which are appropriate, depending on local practices and conditions, and consumer preferences:

Gutting, washing and icing of fresh fish: fish is very perishable and toxins may develop quickly. If fish are to be sold fresh, spoilage may be decreased by careful gutting and washing as soon as they are caught. They should be kept as cold as possible, using ice if available, or held in an airy, sack-covered container and doused with water to benefit from the cooling effect of evaporation. Investigation of local preferences is vital because in many societies the removal of the head and viscera is not acceptable, as quality is judged by the colour of the gills and eyes, and the shape and texture of the underbelly. The use of ice and freezing has a bad reputation in many countries because the fish are often spoiled before they are processed, and iced or frozen fish may be rejected.

Salting: this depends on the availability, and cost, of salt. Dry-salting is more suitable for non-oily fish than oily fish. Salting fish is a very widely used method of preservation.

Sun-drying: this may be done with or without preliminary heating and with or without pre-salting. A hot climate and low humidity are essential.

Hot or cold smoking: this depends on a supply of fuelwood. Oily fish are more suitable than non-oily fish for hot smoking.

Unmarketable fish and offal may be collected for fish-meal production, if such processing facilities already exist in the vicinity and if quantities are sufficient. Alternatively small quantities can be made into fish silage for pig-feeding.

3.2.6 Credit and marketing

(To be read in conjunction with **4.**1.3.5 Credit and savings support and 4.1.3.6 Marketing assistance.)

There have been many attempts to set up marketing organisations for poor fishworkers, some of which have also involved providing credit. Women play an important role in small-scale fish marketing, often in unequal competition with fish merchants, who not only market much of the catch, but also provide the only source of credit in the fishing community. The debt relations between fishworkers and fish merchants give the merchant the power to buy the catch and determine its value. Thus the benefits of high prices in times of short supply are generally not passed on to women traders, or to those who have actually caught the fish. Capital constraints also generally make it impossible for local fishers to benefit from the high prices given for certain fish in luxury markets in big cities or countries of the North or compete with merchants to buy such fish for the local market. These marketing problems, and the marginalisation of women traders, have increased with large-scale fisheries development. Marketing organisations may encounter considerable resistance from merchants and moneylenders, and also in some cases from government officials who may benefit from pay-offs in existing systems.

Many marketing initiatives fail because fishworker organisations lack the strength to compete effectively. Fishing interventions which seek to break monopoly trading practices, stimulate small-scale marketing, and give the fishworkers a fairer return, must take account of the range of social and subsistence credit needs which intermediaries and moneylenders fulfil.

A number of programmes in India have Oxfam support: in Tamil Nadu, a federation of 2,500 fishworkers has successfully implemented a low-interest credit scheme for its members, negotiated better prices for export species such as prawns and lobster, and extended storage facilities to improve the fishworkers' bargaining power in the local market. Another Indian federation set up special credit schemes for

4

women, who are traditional fish vendors in the region, to enable them to bypass local money lenders. A Southern Indian Fishworkers' Federation holds fish auctions on the beach to ensure that prics are fair and fishers are paid on the same day.

Markets for fish should always be thoroughly researched when fish farming interventions are planned. There may be no existing marketing structure in areas where fish farming is new, and capture fishing is not practised; in which case, setting up fish farming may serve to diversify diet, but will not increase people's incomes or provide a livelihood.

3.2.7 Fishworker organisations

Capture fishing is often a highly individualistic and competitive activity. Where fish resources are scarce there is little incentive for fishworkers to co-operate in the capture of fish or to share their knowledge of successful fishing grounds with others. Nevertheless, organisations of fishermen and women can be effective in improving livelihoods, for example, by influencing legislation. Fishworkers' organisations campaign for changes in legislation governing small-scale fisheries, and oppose developments which increase the poverty and vulnerability of fishworkers.

Obtaining credit, and the marketing of fish, may be more effectively achieved through the formation of small production enterprises and co-operatives. These may also be the best way of developing allied activities, such as boat building, net making, and manufacture or purchase of other fishing inputs. Organisational development is particularly important for women, to increase their strength both within fishing societies and households, and to represent their interests as fishers, marketers, and processors.

Oxfam supports a number of fishworker organisations, associations and trade unions in India, Brazil, and the Philippines. In Maharashtra, for example, Oxfam supports the Fisherwomen Development Programme, which provides non-formal education, health education, and institution-building for fisherwomen's organisations. In Kerala marketing organisations or 'sangams' form the basis for a wider organisation of fishworkers through District Federations and the South Indian Federation of Fishermen Societies (SIFFS). The activities of these organisations are varied, and may include support to fish marketing, both local and for the export trade. Marketing is often organised around small auctions on the beach, open to all; the fishworkers contract independent auctioneers to sell their fish. In Brazil the Church Council for Fisherpeople and Justice and Peace Commission have worked to build strong and representative organisations of fisherpeople in many states of Brazil. Their activities include information on the rights and problems of fisherpeople and lobbying on their behalf. Campaigns have included:

- lobbying for an area to use as a free community fish market to bypass intermediaries;
- action against pollution from sugar distilleries and eviction from beaches;
- action against salt companies which were illegally damming up mangrove swamps;
- registration of fisherpeople's land titles to protect them and their beaches against tourist development;
- lobbying for pension rights for the widows of fishers.

They also produce a monthly magazine and radio programme for information sharing and networking, and 'fish for flour' barter systems have been set up with local farmers and community shops

In the Philippines conflicts between fishworkers and private commercial interests have been particularly intense, and local staff members of some of the organisations have been murdered. Oxfam supports a number of organisations, whose activities include lobbying and advocacy, the promotion of community resource management in response to fish stock depletion, and a gender-awareness programme, which includes gender-needs assessment and support for separate organisations of fisherwomen. These groups are working for a comprehensive gender-sensitive policy for the industry, and a federated fisherwomen's organisation.

In June 1994, Oxfam sponsored the participation of representatives from a number of fishworkers' organisations from different parts of the world in the Triennial Conference of the International Collective in Support of Fishworkers (ICSF). This is a global network of community organisers, teachers, technicians, researchers, and scientists working in close association with fishworkers' organisations. Basing its actions on the specific demands of fishworkers' organisations, the ICSF has campaigned for the sustainable an equitable use of fish resources, and against processes and policies which adversely affect the livelihoods of fishworkers.

3.3 Key questions

1 What is the division of labour among the fishworkers whom the intervention is intended to benefit? What is the work done by men, women, children, and people of different ethnic, race, class or caste groups? Who is left out of the proposal?
2 What is known about local and national fish stocks, if the intervention

is in capture fishing? If fish capture is to increase, what is the effect likely to be on other fishers, and on fish stocks? What obstacles are small fishing boats likely to encounter if they increase their fishing range and catch?

3 If aquaculture is proposed, is adequate training for management of the ponds included? Who will provide the training? Who will be trained? Who will manage the ponds, and who will provide the labour in, for example, draining and cleaning ponds, feeding the fish, caring for fish seed, dealing with disease? Is there capacity among women or men for this extra labour?

4 Does the organisation or group making the proposal have the necessary technical expertise? How can they be helped to obtain this?

5 Is there a market for the fish? Is it culturally acceptable, if a new variety? Who will market it, and how?

6 Who processes the fish (or will process the fish, if this is a new activity)? What support is offered for processing? Have suitable processing techniques been thoroughly explored, and is appropriate training planned? How will the extra labour time be formed?

7 What other activities are the people involved in? How is fishing linked to these?

8 Does the fishworker organisation require organisational support and capacity-building? Support for networking and campaigning activities?

4 Trees and forestry

4.1 Introduction 581
    4.1.1 The historical context of forestry development 581
    4.1.2 The 'deforestation' crisis 583
4.2 Practical approaches 585
    4.2.1 The role of NGOs 585
    4.2.2 Technical aspects of interventions 585
    4.2.3 Tree planting 589
    4.2.4 Ownership, control, and rights of use of trees and forests 591
    4.2.5 Supporting forest users 592
4.3 Key questions 594

4.1 Introduction

4

Trees provide a wide variety of important products, both for subsistence and as a source of income. Such products include timber, fuelwood, charcoal, food (including spices and condiments), fodder, fibre, and medicines. Trees also provide many additional benefits, such as shade and ornamentation, wind breaks and hedges, and a habitat for wildlife, and help in soil conservation. In urban and peri-urban locations, trees can improve the environment by trapping pollutants such as noise, fumes, and dust. At a global level, forests are widely recognised to have an important role as carbon sinks, and to contribute to climatic stability. There is increasing scientific evidence to support recent anxiety about the loss of the tropical rainforests and the effect of this upon global warming.

4.1.1 The historical context of forestry development

Approaches to forestry development have changed markedly over the last 40 years. During the 1960s, the main contribution of forestry to development was seen as the supply of raw materials for industry, chiefly in the form of timber, fuel or pulp for paper manufacture. The importance of trees and forests to local people only began to be widely recognised among forestry and development professionals in the late 1970s, in part as a result of the focus given to the topic in the Eighth

581

World Forestry Congress held in Jakarta in 1978. Fuelwood, as the 'energy source of the poor', was given particular prominence, reflecting concern at the time over rising oil prices and a perceived energy crisis. Various development agencies including the FAO and the World Bank announced the adoption of more 'people-oriented' forest policies. A number of large multilateral and bilateral forestry projects with this focus were instigated in the early 1980s, as were many smaller NGO-supported tree planting programmes.

Early social forestry or community forestry initiatives met with mixed results, some being extremely unsuccessful. Much of this may be attributed to a failure to discuss forestry issues with local men and women at project initiation. As a result, interventions were based on a misperception of local people's needs and a misunderstanding of local situations. In an attempt to remedy this, an important component of many early people-oriented forestry projects was education. Extension materials were prepared and personnel trained to teach local people about the importance of trees and forests. The early slogan for the large Community Development Forestry Project in Nepal, for example, exhorted villagers to 'Plant Trees, Protect the Forest'. It was subsequently found that, particularly in areas where there had been a recent decline in the availability of tree products from nearby forests, local people regularly plant trees. Their knowledge of propagation techniques for different species may exceed that of forestry professionals. In some cases villagers have also devised, agreed, and implemented various forest management systems. Forestry interventions in Nepal now aim to assist these initiatives where appropriate, and focus on supporting local users to manage forests in a sustainable and equitable way.

Forestry development in Nepal is particularly advanced in terms of genuine support for people's participation, and the country is often cited as an example to follow. Most forestry extension specialists would not now assume a need to teach village people how to plant trees or appreciate the value of forests. This may be necessary for new settlers to an area, but as in any other development sector, needs must be determined through discussions with the people who are to participate in, and be affected by, the intervention.

This obvious point is illustrated by donor response to the perceived fuelwood crisis of the early 1980s. The heavy emphasis on tree planting for fuelwood, particularly in drier parts of Africa, proved in many cases to be inappropriate, because fast-growing exotic tree species were planted to provide rapid yields, but the people who used them found their burning properties inferior to that of local species. In addition, chopped and split logs were in many cases unsuitable for local stoves designed to burn smaller twigs and branches. Although the most acute fuel shortage was often in urban areas, woodlots were planted in rural areas, where local people did not have a major fuel problem, as they obtained adequate supplies from gathered twigs, agricultural residues, and other sources. There was often no investigation of the ownership of land planted up with fast-growing fuelwood trees, resulting in confusion over rights and responsibilities for maintenance and harvesting.

4.1.2 The 'deforestation crisis'

The theory that a widespread fuelwood crisis threatens the developing world is now generally discredited, although local shortages do exist and need to be addressed in consultation with those experiencing them. There is, however, considerable concern about a global loss in forest cover. This is often expressed in terms of a 'deforestation crisis', in which deforestation refers to forest clearance of any type, whether the area felled is left to regenerate, replanted (often as a single species plantation), or put to an alternative land use. Each scenario has a different environmental impact, as well as differing consequences for local people; it is important to distinguish between them.

Logging activities do not usually amount to clear-felling, although if logging is carried out indiscriminately the forest can be very badly damaged. The bio-diversity of such a forest will be severely affected, but if it is left to regenerate, a rich plant and animal population may develop, which may be different from the original in species composition. Such secondary forests may well be highly valued and utilised by local people. If natural forests are felled and replanted by monoculture industrial plantations, their bio-diversity is lost, but they retain some value as a carbon sink and a vegetative cover against soil erosion. Some local employment may be provided, although in practice the pay and conditions are often very poor. The consequence of converting natural forests in the humid tropics to alternative uses, the most notorious being mining and cattle ranching, is almost invariably environmentally and socially disastrous.

Whilst many parts of the world are experiencing a loss of tree cover, or have done in the recent past, this is not true everywhere. Thus the belief, for example, that the Himalayas have been subject in recent years to a massive reduction in forest cover, causing downstream flooding and erosion, is not supported by available evidence. A further aspect in assessing overall changes in tree cover is the occurrence of trees on farm land. Studies from a variety of countries, including Kenya, India, Nepal, Bangladesh and Thailand, have shown that where access to communally used forests is limited, the density of on-farm trees is often high. Where people are able to respond to a shortage of tree products, they do, by planting their own trees.

The permanent loss of forest cover of greatest significance at global level, notably that occurring in the humid tropics and particularly in the Amazon basin, is usually well beyond the control of local people. In many cases powerful multi-national companies are involved, their activities being sanctioned by governments anxious to gain foreign exchange. The need to finance debt repayment has in some places resulted in increased logging operations. Governments have allowed land-hungry settlers to clear forest for cultivation, sometimes in state-sponsored 'colonisation' schemes, such as in the Brazilian Amazon region, and often in order to avoid land-reform programmes in other parts of the country. Since land cleared often remains productive for only a few years before the soil becomes so leached and eroded that it supports no agricultural production, the cycle of forest clearance is self-perpetuating.

Some countries rich in forest resources have recently adopted forest policies designed both to conserve bio-diversity and to protect the interests of forest dwellers and local forest users. Further to this, they have made legal provision for the participation of local people in forest management. For example, in the new national Forest Policy of India (approved in 1988) it is stated explicitly that: 'The people will be actively involved in programmes of protection, conservation and management of the forests.' The World Bank, conscious of criticism that its lending practices have sometimes had a negative environmental impact, is also trying to influence the forest policies of certain countries. A condition of the Structural Adjustment Programme (SAP) agreed with the government of Cameroon in 1988, for example, was that the country should reform its forestry sector, rewriting its forest policy and legislation. Cameroon now has forest legislation which allows for considerable participation by local people in the management of certain categories of forest.

Pressure to conserve tropical forests is also being exerted by consumers in the West. Various NGOs such as the Worldwide Fund for Nature (WWF) and Friends of the Earth have been influential in this regard. As a result of consumer demand, many timber product retailers are now seeking to supply 'sustainable harvested' timber.

Forestry development initiatives within less developed countries are now increasingly focusing on the promotion of sustainable forms of natural forest management. 'Sustainable' in this context encompasses both biological and social aspects. Tree-planting programmes are still of importance in many countries, although lessons learned from mistakes made during the 1980s (particularly with regard to matters of ownership and control, and species choice) should always be borne in mind.

4.2 Practical approaches

4.2.1 *The role of NGOs*

In some respects, the practical role of NGOs in the forestry sector is more limited than in agriculture. This is because in most countries the majority of forest land, whether natural forest or plantations, legally belongs to the State. Particularly in Africa and Asia, the control and management of forests is usually vested in a Forest Department run by forestry professionals. These professionals are responsible both for proper silvicultural management practices, and for ensuring the implementation of forest law — including occasions when this allows for the handing over of full or part control of forests to local people. While NGOs do not have the legal authority to make decisions about forest control and management, they may play an important role in other ways. These include acting as an intermediary between forest dwellers and users and government officials, campaigning for changes in forest policy, and supporting forest users in demanding better working conditions or a fairer marketing system for the products they harvest. NGOs are often involved in tree-planting initiatives, particularly on farms but also on areas of common land.

In the Indian state of Orissa, for example, Oxfam has provided funds for training, and for a tree nursery and seed-bank, a library, and a visitors' centre, to a movement formed to 're-green' the hills of the Puri district, which had been stripped of forest cover between 1940 and 1960. The core group of this movement (Friends of the Trees and Living Beings) was formed by people from villages in the district, and by developing a popular campaign, with local village councils in the area, to plant trees, and keep goats off the hillsides, they have been able to achieve remarkable results in reafforestation of the hills. Ten years after it was founded, the movement had reached 1,800 villages in the area, and its work in supporting tree nurseries and planting up the hillsides continues.

4.2.2 *Technical aspects of interventions*

For the purpose of discussion here, tree growing systems will be divided into three major categories: natural forests, plantations, and trees on farms. Tree planting initiatives are then considered.

a. Natural forests
There are many technical challenges posed by natural forest management; for example, appropriate levels of harvesting the wide

variety of non-timber forest products (NTFPs), such as fruit, nuts, honey, and latex, valued by forest users, are often unknown. There is also disagreement among forestry professionals and confusion among consumers regarding the definition of 'sustainable harvested' timber. While this is unresolved it is difficult for forestry programmes endeavouring to operate sustainable management practices to market their timber, and consumers cannot purchase it with confidence. The Forest Stewardship Council (FSC), a non-profit making, independent NGO established in 1993, may serve as a global regulatory body promoting the management of forests in ways that are environmentally appropriate, socially beneficial, and economically viable. To this end, it will evaluate, accredit, and monitor certification organisations that inspect forest and trading operations.

Donor governments and NGOs are becoming increasingly involved in assisting poor people who are forest users to manage forests on a sustainable basis. Some are also involved in assisting in the marketing of harvested timber or NTFPs. In Ghana, the Overseas Development Administration (ODA) supports a Collaborative Forest Management Project based in Kumasi which, although it began with purely technical silvicultural objectives, is now actively involving local people in forest management decisions. In another example, various organisations have been involved in assisting the people of El Pan in Ecuador to conduct forest inventories and thus draw up management plans and a sustainable harvesting programme. While in both these projects the intention is to harvest timber for sale to an export market, in other situations forest management may focus on the provision of forest products for local needs. This is largely the case in Nepal, for example, where maximising the production of products such as fodder and fuelwood is often a more important management objective than timber production.

In the north-west Amazon region of Brazil, where indigenous Indians and peasant families tap wild rubber from the forests, ranchers, government and private resettlement or colonisation programmes, and other commercial interests, such as logging, threaten the forest environment. The Rubber Tappers' Unions lobbied and campaigned for years, with the support of international agencies, including Oxfam, for the right to continue extracting forest products such as latex and brazil nuts, and proposed the creation of 'extractive reserves', where their livelihoods, and those of Indians in the region, would be protected. The first reserve was created in 1988, but whether or not the rubber tappers' way of life will survive in the face of cheaper latex from Malaysian plantations is uncertain.

b. Plantations

Large-scale industrial plantations are not generally funded by NGOs. However, there has been considerable involvement in the past in supporting community woodlots. These often failed, more for socio-economic than technical reasons, though the heavy emphasis on a few species (*Eucalyptus spp*, *Acacia auriculiformis*, and *Acacia mearnsii*) has technical drawbacks. It is often claimed, particularly in India, that some species of eucalyptus (notably *E tereticornix* hybrid) lower the water table. This is the subject of some controversy, but where water is very limited, eucalyptus species are probably best avoided.

NGOs may also support tree planting for soil conservation purposes on land used as common property resources (CPRs). It is important that such initiatives are technically well conceived, as tree planting is only likely to have a significant effect in reducing soil erosion if used in conjunction with other measures. Responsibility for tree maintenance must also be determined from the start, as weeding during early establishment, and protection from grazing animals is essential.

When large-scale deforestation has been carried out in the course of war or armed conflict, reafforestation of large areas may be supported by NGOs. In El Salvador, for example, Oxfam supports parts of a large programme to enable returned Salvadorean refugees to re-establish themselves on lands which have been devastated by 'scorched earth' tactics during the conflict. One aspect of the work is the setting up of tree nurseries, each with 20,000 trees, to provide food crops and timber for construction and sale. This is accompanied by educational work on preserving the region's natural resources.

4

c. Trees on farms

In some farming systems, particularly where agriculture is highly mechanised, trees are completely absent from fields. However, in many parts of the world, trees are grown on farms for a wide variety of purposes. Farmers clearing land to cultivate, either permanently or on a short-term rotational basis under swidden (shifting) agriculture, usually leave certain species which they value. Well-established fields often contain some trees that farmers have allowed to come up naturally, or which they have planted for specific purposes. Indians in Amazonia, such as the Yanomami, visit gardens left fallow to harvest the fruit of palm and other trees. Traditionally, before the Yanomami suffered large-scale land invasion, gardens were left fallow for ten to fifteen years before they were cleared and cultivated again. This permitted young fruit-bearing trees to grow and be harvested over the period.

In much of semi-arid Africa, *Acacia albida* trees are allowed to self-seed and grow on farm land, whilst in the Himalayan foothills trees such as *Ficus nemoralis* and *Grewia opposinfolia* are planted by farmers to provide dry-season fodder. Home gardens in many parts of the tropics are known for the rich diversity of plant species that they contain, maximum use of limited space being ensured by cultivating trees, shrubs, herbs, and plants with edible roots in close proximity. Classic examples are the Kandyan home gardens of Sri Lanka and the home-gardens of Java, Indonesia. These methods of combining trees and crops are examples of indigenous agro-forestry systems. Many are known to have been practised for generations, although agro-forestry as a scientific concept has only been widely recognised and studied for the past 20 years or so. The International Council for Research on Agro-forestry (ICRAF), based in Nairobi, Kenya, was set up in the late 1970s, and has had considerable influence.

A new agro-forestry system, which has been widely promoted in the tropics, is alley farming or alley cropping (strictly speaking, the former includes livestock whilst the latter does not). The concept of alley farming was developed by scientists at the International Institute for Tropical Agriculture (IITA) in Ibadan, Nigeria, as an alternative to swidden agriculture. Rows of fast-growing, usually nitrogen-fixing, trees are grown between rows of crops. The trees are regularly pruned, and their nutrient-rich leaves are used as a mulch for the crop, building up the humus content of the soil and improving its fertility. This is also enhanced directly by the tree roots, both through nitrogen fixation and by the recycling of minerals at lower soil levels.

The foliage of the tree species used is often highly palatable to livestock, and can therefore be used as a fodder, the animals' dung being returned to the fields as fertiliser. The woody branches form a convenient form of fuel. Proponents of alley farming argue that it is a sustainable form of agriculture that can be practised permanently on one plot. On sloping lands, soil conservation can be an additional benefit if the alleys are planted along contours.

Although alley farming has been shown to be technically feasible in certain circumstances, there are major drawbacks. To date, only a limited number of tree species have been found suitable for alley farming, and it is generally unwise to rely heavily on only one or two species in a new technology. Of the species known to be suitable, a number have particular limitations. (See 4.4.2.3 Tree planting.) The identification of appropriate tree species for acid soils is at an early stage of research. The best results have been obtained by intercropping maize with *Leucaena leucocephala*. For farming systems with other main crops, for example, cassava, alley farming may give poor results. In many farming systems women are the main labourers. Already over-burdened with work, they are not likely to have the time to spare for the labour-intensive technology of alley farming, unless they are freed from other work. The timing of labour inputs is inflexible; if the fast-growing trees are not pruned regularly, they will grow up and shade the crop, causing low yields. To introduce alley farming would require very careful planning, and interventions which free labour time at the right time, and for the right people.

If livestock are to be part of an alley farming system, they have to be tethered and stall-fed. Apart from the labour implications in areas where livestock are normally allowed to graze freely, perhaps with a child herder, livestock may be subject to more disease if penned closely together. This is a particular problem in the humid tropics, notably in West Africa. Whether the advantages of stall feeding outweigh the disadvantages may depend on the accessibility of veterinary services, and whether resource-poor farmers are able to afford the additional inputs.

Given these problems, alley farming is likely to be most successful:

• in semi-arid areas where maize is a main crop, and water availability is not a major constraint;
• on sloping lands, if soil erosion is a major problem and alley farming is used together with other soil conservation practices;
• in areas where labour supply is not a constraint.

4.2.3 Tree planting

The choice of species to be grown should always be made primarily by farmers, in discussion with forestry professionals. Trying out many new, exotic species is not necessarily desirable. It is often better to focus on species with which farmers are familiar and which are known to perform well in the locality. In the cases of new species, care should be taken to investigate whether they have ever been introduced nearby, and what the results were. A field visit by interested farmers before trying them themselves may be appropriate.

a. Multi-purpose trees
In recent years there has been much international forestry research focused on multi-purpose trees (MPTs). Typically these are fast-growing trees which can be used for fodder and fuel, and which have soil enhancing properties — usually through nitrogen-fixation. In environments to which they are suited, MPTs may give excellent results. However, their use should be promoted with caution, particularly with respect to nitrogen-fixing capacity: it is often mistakenly assumed that all leguminous trees fix nitrogen. Some species do not, and of those which do, their capacity varies considerably according to local conditions. A few species which are not legumes are capable of fixing nitrogen, a notable example being members of the genus *Casuarina*.

589

Many MPTs combine fast growth with prolific seed production, and have the capacity to become weeds; some MPTs are subject to severe damage by pests or disease. Attacks can be devastating if the tree has been planted in a virtual monoculture, allowing rapid spread of the problem. This has happened in some places with *Leucaena leucocephala* which is susceptible to a psyllid or leaf hopper.

Apart from the *Leucaena leucocephala*, some of the most commonly planted MPT's include *Gliricidia sepium. Calliandra calothyrsus, Cassia siamen, Aradirachra indica (neem)*, and *Prosopis spp*. Further details about these and other MPTs, are provided in some of the sources listed at the end of the chapter.

b. Seeds and seedlings

Whether exotic or indigenous tree species are to be planted, it is important to ensure a sustainable source of good quality seed. In the past, many tree-planting initiatives have been conducted by distributing seedlings from one or several centralised nurseries. There is a growing trend towards the decentralisation of plant production in the case of people-oriented forestry programmes. Small-scale nurseries have a number of advantages:

- more efficient and easier transportation of seedlings to numerous planting sites and to remote areas;
- better provision of the range of species and numbers of seedlings required by different farmers;
- wider distribution of the economic benefits to be gained from raising seedlings;
- promotion of sustainable forestry development by transferring the means of production to the people planting the trees.

Considerable investment in training is generally needed for small-scale nurseries to be effective. The ultimate form of decentralised plant production is the distribution of seed to farmers, who raise the trees they require themselves. The Kenya Agro-forestry Development Programme, for example, found the distribution of small amounts of MPT seeds in attractive packages to be very popular.

In order to encourage tree planting by local people, whether on private farms or communally accessible land, payment is sometimes offered. This may take the form of payment for seedlings produced in farmers' nurseries, wage labour for planting, a payment of a fixed sum per surviving seedling after an agreed period, or other mechanisms. Project planners following this strategy argue that they are providing local people with a source of income while contributing to environmental improvement. However, payment does not foster a sense of participation in programme planning, or tree ownership; and seedling survival is often low. Payment programmes are also inherently unsustainable.

Strategies which work with existing participation organisations are likely to be far more successful. For example, in Pakistan, Oxfam supports several NGOs working on agro-forestry projects with village organisations. Small-scale farm forestry, in which trees are planted for fuel, timber, and fruit, is based on collective action at village level, with technical assistance from the Agricultural and Forestry Workers' Association, and saplings provided by the government forestry department.

4.2.4 Ownership, control, and rights of use of trees and forests

The ownership, control, and rights of use of trees and forests can be highly complex, and must be fully investigated before any forestry intervention is initiated. All users should be consulted directly about their roles, needs, and priorities. A distinction may be made between tree ownership and ownership of the land on which the tree is growing. Tree planting may be symbolic of land ownership, with the result that tenants are not allowed to plant their own trees. Even if this is not the case, tenants will have little incentive to plant trees if they do not have long-term security of tenure. Sometimes the presence of trees on agricultural land may be taken to indicate that it was once forest. If all forest is state owned, this can be an incentive to remove all trees, clarifying ownership as agricultural land. The use, or control over the use, of trees may be determined by gender, economic status, and ethnic identity.

a. Gender
In many societies women have the responsibility for gathering forest products, particularly fuelwood and fodder. If new forms of community or collaborative forest management are being devised, it is essential that women are directly consulted and involved in project decisions, as they will be most affected by any changes.

Generally, tree planting is considered a male task — particularly in societies where tree planting gives an individual rights over land. The labour implications for women as well as men of increased tree production should be carefully investigated, as well as the rights to cash from sale of forest products. In some societies there are taboos against women planting trees, as is the case among the Luyia people of Kenya.

b. Economic status
Poor people are often far more dependent on the harvesting of forest products than richer people. Any changes in forest management

591

strategies will thus affect them deeply. For example, in Nepal proposed forest conservation and protection measures were sometimes supported by local elites, but opposed by poorer people whose livelihoods were threatened.

Tree planting on farm land tends to be practised by farmers who have a reasonable amount of land. Support for such activities is unlikely to benefit those who are landless, or own very little land.

In some countries, tree planting campaigns have curtailed poorer people's rights to gather fuel or herd their cattle on certain areas of land. Social forestry programmes in India, which reafforested vast areas of official wasteland, became notorious for this reason. In Pakistan, local elites deliberately used a tree-planting programme to gain control over land that was previously a common property resource.

c. Ethnic identity

In societies of mixed ethnicity, the collection of certain forest products may be ethnically determined. In India, for example, tribal peoples are generally far more dependent on the gathering of forest products for their livelihood than are high-caste villagers.

In the Amazonian region of south America, indigenous people have traditionally made their living exclusively from the forest and its products. While economic developments in the region are changing so rapidly, the survival of most Indian societies depends upon their continued ability to live in the forests.

4.2.5 Supporting forest users

In countries in which legislation permits the handing over of control of forests to local users, NGOs may have an important role in facilitating this process. Certain states in India, for example, now have legislation which allows for Joint Forest Management (JFM). Under JFM, the Forest Department and local users discuss and agree a forest management plan. Once this has been put in writing and signed on behalf of both parties, a forest management committee is responsible for its implementation. The committee is largely made up of local users, with a Forest Department representative. There is often considerable initial distrust between villagers and Forest Department officials, since in the past the latter have had a policing role. NGOs may play a valuable role in breaking down this initial mutual suspicion, and in ensuring that the users' priorities and needs are respected.

The forested area of Zambia's North Western Province supports some 1,500 households which rely on the forest for their livelihoods. Beekeeping is a long-established traditional means of earning a living in this area, and is supported by the Zambian government. Oxfam has supported the growth of beekeeper organisations, as the region is now threatened by local and foreign enterprises seeking to use the land for tourism, agricultural investment, logging, and mining. The widespread felling of trees for these enterprises would not only destroy the beekeepers' livelihoods but have a devastating long-term impact upon water supplies. Strengthening the beekeepers' organisations helps them to defend the forest more effectively, through establishing a stronger presence in the government-supported Rural Development Programme.

In countries where the rights of forest users are poorly acknowledged or ignored, NGOs may be able to offer support through political campaigning or through programmes of direct assistance. For nearly ten years, Oxfam has supported a literacy and numeracy training project for rubber tappers in Brazil, which formed the basis for the growth of a powerful movement of rubber tappers in the western Amazon region. In 1988, the Alliance of Forest Peoples was founded jointly by the National Council of Rubber Tappers and the National Union of Indians to strengthen their struggle to defend their forests and way of life. Oxfam, with other NGOs, has given support to the campaigning and lobbying activities of this organisation. The Indians proposed that the 'extractive reserves' proposed by the Rubber Tappers' Union form a protective green belt around the Indian areas. The growing co-operation between Indians and rubber tappers was formalised in the foundation of the Alliance of Forest People.

In the Urubamba valley in Peru, a Peruvian NGO, supported by Oxfam, has helped the Machiguenga Indians gain title to their lands. However, if these lands are judged by the government not to be used productively, they may be confiscated and given to settlers. Conflict between Indians and settlers over land led to the strategy of planting 'living boundaries' on the Indian land. The Indians planted coffee, cacao, and annatto trees, providing boundaries, proving the land was used productively, and providing standing cash crops.

Regeneration and reafforestation of degraded land on the basis of organisations of farmers and forest users is supported by Oxfam in Indonesia. The Indonesian NGO working on Sabu Island works with a large number of village organisations to strengthen their own capacity to run agro-forestry initiatives. Local fodder trees are grown in nurseries, and planted in conjunction with other species, and soil conservation measures, terracing, fencing, and well-digging are carried out. This is an example of support for community management of natural resources, and the successful use of local tree species, such as the fodder tree lantoro (*Leucaena*), coconut, banana, orange, mango, sour-sop, and cashew-nut trees. Village schools cultivate small tree-nurseries in addition to their school gardens, and pupils are encouraged to take seedlings home for planting in their own gardens.

593

4.3 Key questions

1 Who owns the land on which tree planting is proposed, and who uses it? Will any current uses of the land be curtailed by tree planting? If so, who will be affected, and how?

2 Who made the choice of species to be planted? Was it based on farmer priorities, or other factors such as seed availability? Were women and men consulted about their choices?

3 In new forest management initiatives, will any harvesting practices be restricted? Who will be affected most? Will the livelihoods of local people be affected differently according to their gender, economic status, or ethnic group?

4 If a project purports to sustainable forest management, how is this defined? Have environmental, social, and economic factors all been considered? Has a management plan been drawn up, and has it been professionally ratified? Is further technical advice available? If not, what steps may be taken to ensure that both farmer knowledge and other technical advice is taken into account?

5 Small-scale industries

5.1 Introduction 595
    5.1.1 The economic context of small-scale industries 596
    5.1.2 NGO interventions and income-generation projects (IGPs) 598
    5.1.3 Section summary 600
5.2 Practical approaches 600
    5.2.1 Forms of NGO assistance 600
    5.2.2 Social considerations in small-scale industry 602
    5.2.3 Support for producer groups 604
    5.2.4 Support for technology development 605
    5.2.5 Marketing assistance 606
    5.2.6 Credit 610
    5.2.7 Training 611
5.3 Key questions 612

4

5.1 Introduction

Small-scale industries provide a means of livelihood for millions of poor people in rural and urban areas around the world. These industries usually involve the production of goods and services for local markets, although they may also produce for export. They are low capital enterprises, labour intensive, and produce a relatively small volume of goods, or offer a small range of services. They are often constrained by lack of formal credit facilities, training opportunities, legal protection, and marketing outlets.

There is no clear way to define their scope — some small-scale industries producing high-value products with high capital investment can be extremely profitable. Usually, however, in the sector in which donor agencies assist small-scale production, these industries generate income which is barely worth the labour and effort people put in; but they may represent the only options open to women, men and children with few or no other productive resources. The aim of development agencies should be to support small-scale industries in order to make them more viable economically, while at the same time enabling the men and women making their living from them to build their capacity and skills. However, these small-scale industries have to survive within the national and international economic context, and it is essential to analyse the constraints and opportunities this places upon them.

5.1.1 The economic context of small-scale industries

Industrial development is generally seen as playing the leading role in national economic growth and, as such, has been a major focus of intervention by governments and aid agencies. In many countries this has been in the context of protected national markets, where certain products, and pay and working conditions in large-scale enterprises, were protected by legislation. In the 1980s, there was increasing emphasis on the export sector in developing countries, and a vast expansion in the activities of transnational corporations, attracted by a cheap and unorganised labour force, and fewer environmental controls on production methods, in these countries.

The liberalisation of developing economies has increased the vulnerability of workers as a result of the introduction of capital-intensive technology and the imposition of anti-union legislation, in an effort to compete in the world market and encourage transnational investment. Unemployment and underemployment have risen, and more and more poor people have had to make their livelihoods in the 'informal' economy, as self-employed workers producing goods and services, or working for small family or other enterprises outside the legal framework of the production sector.

The global production strategies of transnational corporations have also increased the availability of mass-produced cheap products. Many artisanal industries, such as pottery, carpentry, and tailoring, upon which millions of people depend for income, now face intense competition from cheaper mass-produced goods. The widespread introduction of new materials, such as plastics and synthetic fibres, has further decreased the demand for traditional products made from natural materials such as cotton, jute, and sisal.

Despite this competitive context, small-scale industries have an important role to play, particularly in alleviating some of the adverse effects of large-scale capital-intensive industrialisation. They provide employment, and may be the most efficient means of production where capital is scarce, or where the market cannot absorb mass-production. Small-scale industries may distribute wealth and enterprise skills more widely. The small-scale industry sector is therefore protected and encouraged in some countries, as part of poverty-alleviation programmes. Training, credit, technology development, and marketing support may be funded by national development programmes, and specific legislation and facilities for registered co-operatives is also provided.

However, small-scale industries are often legally exempt from whatever protective legislation for workers exists; much labour legislation relates only to firms employing more than a specific number of workers. Small-scale businesses often operate in ways which are unacceptable for organisations attempting to promote equitable development strategies. Workers may not be covered by protective legislation, minimum wages provisions or any other benefits, and are thus open to greater levels of exploitation than in large-scale industries. A large proportion of the workforce in the smallest, family-run, enterprises are unpaid family workers, particularly women and children. These workers are vulnerable to abuse, having no legal mechanisms for protection or redress. In very small industries profits may only be possible because of the avoidance of health and safety regulations for both workers and consumers, and the failure to pay taxes. Where these businesses operate in semi-clandestine conditions, it is extremely difficult for state authorities to monitor them and deal with infringements of the law.

Many small-scale industries are in fact not separate enterprises, but part of a long production chain controlled by large businesses and transnational corporations, who contract out the more risky and less lucrative parts of the production process, to home-workers and small firms, because it saves them the expense of providing working space, energy, and other facilities. This occurs particularly in the textile, leather, and electronics industries. The smaller sub-contracted businesses often operate illegally and clandestinely, and often employ children. Where work is done in the home, mostly by women at extremely low rates of pay, children contribute their labour to increase family income. If the manufacturers decide to reduce production when markets become unprofitable, they can simply withdraw orders from smaller firms or lay off outworkers. Women and children are employed as outworkers because of their lower rates of pay and lesser ability to organise to defend their interests.

The tendency to sub-contract has been increasing rapidly in recent years, often aided by national government policies. In the Philippines Oxfam supports an organisation working with homeworkers, mainly women, to bring their situation to the attention of policy-makers, government and the general public. This includes legal action and advocacy, as these women are usually not covered by any social security, and are largely unprotected by the law.

Small-scale industries attempting to run their businesses equitably and profitably are seriously constrained by competition from law-breaking, exploitative businesses. The market competition may be such that the scope for increasing incomes for poor producers through alternative production enterprises is very limited, even after assessing the range of possibilities discussed in this section.

597

5.1.2 NGO interventions and income-generation projects

Interventions on the part of NGOs or government agencies to support small-scale industries are often referred to as income-generation projects (IGPs), and are often associated with projects for women. Studies of IGPs for women have identified a number of common problems that development agencies should take into account when planning to intervene in this sector. A major problem is that IGPs not only seldom generate significant levels of income, but often result in loss. This may be due to inadequate research of the market, and the fact that the income generated is seldom offset against the real costs of women's labour time — which is typically undervalued.

Income generation for women may be seen, not as a serious economic activity, but a way for women to 'earn extra money in their spare time'. This is based on false assumptions that women have spare time, and that they are not already involved in productive activities. Often it is precisely because women are the beneficiaries of these small-scale economic projects that they are considered to be of marginal significance, and are called 'income-generation' rather than small-scale industrial production.

In fact, most women have no 'spare time'. They work, worldwide, longer hours than men, and on a wider range of tasks. (See 2.1 Gender.) In many cases, it would be far more helpful to women to support their existing productive work by providing technology, training, and productive inputs, and to address their lack of rights to land and other resources, rather than attempt to introduce new economic activities which may have limited profitability, increase their workload, and be unsustainable in the long term.

Table 4.4. Women's economic enterprises

- Many economic projects make no or only minimal profit. In many cases they simply increase workload and stress.
- The more successful economic projects are those that include elements of consciousness-raising. Building gender-awareness should be an integral part of any income-generation project.
- Many economic projects are still based on inaccurate conceptions of women's work and use of time. This severely limits their chances of success and long-term sustainability.
- NGOs need to have a programme approach and not fund projects in isolation.

- Economic enterprises should always be considered as part of the means of strengthening social organisation and empowering communities.
- NGOs should look one level up from the economic project; for example, consider the option of providing support services such as consumer/production co-operatives.
- NGOs need to appraise women's situation both at the micro and macro level. Substantive base-line data is needed. Gender-focused research techniques such as gender needs assessments are powerful tools in gaining accurate pictures of the women's needs.
- NGOs should look closely at what services women require in order to support their reproductive and community roles, to allow them to participate in economic enterprises more easily and effectively.
- Integrated (i.e. social, economic, etc) indicators for planning, appraisal and evaluation must be defined. These should reflect the women's perspectives.
- Training is essential. NGOs need to enhance their own institutional capacity in this field.
- Sound management should be recognised as crucial. Women in particular need support in learning leadership and organisation skills because of their limited experience in this are.
- Training in increased production techniques, marketing, etc are also vital.

(Based on an Oxfam workshop on Gender Considerations in Economic Enterprises, held in the Philippines in 1990.)

Many women's IGPs involve small income-generation schemes in traditional skills such as tailoring, embroidery, weaving, and food processing. Projects may be unable to survive the withdrawal of external funding because of fundamental weaknesses in planning. Projects which collapse can have a very damaging effect on the people involved. The reasons for failure may include poor assessment of the market for the products, a superficial understanding of social and cultural relations among the participants, the introduction of inappropriate technologies, lack of adequate skills training for the participants, and lack of organisational management of the enterprise.

Many of the problems which have been identified by studies of women's IGPs are faced by all small-scale industrial producers, while others are specific to women. The effectiveness of support to small-scale industries will depend upon the political and economic climate within which it takes place, and upon social and cultural relations among the people engaged in the work. Inequities based on race, ethnic identity, class, and gender limit poor people's rights to resources of all kinds, and determine the division of labour and distribution of benefits among them. Interventions which are planned on a 'micro' level must take all these factors into account at the design, implementation and evaluation stages, or they risk failing in their objectives to improve the living standards of poor people.

5.1.3 Section summary

This section looks at small-scale industries in relation to both rural and urban livelihoods, and at NGO interventions to support these forms of production. These activities include the production of manufactured goods for sale, sometimes using self-cultivated raw materials, or those purchased from other producers, and the provision of services such as hairdressing or gardening; and workers may be self-employed or employed, working as individuals or in productive organisations. The very wide range of economic activities loosely classified as part of the 'informal sector' are not dealt with in this section: for example, the work of adults and children employed as outworkers for large factories, or the work of street sellers, sex workers or people making their living through illegal economic activity, is not referred to, other than in the context of competition for small-scale industries. (See **1.3.5.2** Urban livelihoods.)

5.2 Practical approaches

5.2.1 Forms of NGO assistance

Oxfam supports a wide range of small-scale industries, in order to help people to escape from the cycle of low productivity and low income, through such measures as improving the supply of materials, access to credit and markets, technologies, forms of social and productive organisation, and the understanding of social and economic rights. Training in financial procedures and organisational management is critical to the success of small-scale industries, and when small-scale industries have failed, it is often due to lack of training and capacity-building of the participants in the enterprise.

Small-scale industries are very varied in their development potential and the ways in which outside intervention can be useful. Possible approaches for NGO interventions may be to assist workers and small-scale entrepreneurs to improve incomes, working conditions, and job security in existing small enterprises in the private sector, such as tile-making, small bakeries, or the manufacture of household utensils; to set up new enterprises for existing industries and products, where the market can absorb the additional production, such as new bakeries serving a different area or clientele; to set up new enterprises for new products in existing industries, building on existing skills and technology, such as for example, new kinds of processed and cooked foods, or different kinds of utensils or tools, using new materials; or to introduce completely new industries, products and skills.

The most appropriate option will depend on the industrial and market context and the needs, wishes, and skills of the producers. Working within existing structures, markets and ranges of skills should always be considered before introducing completely new industries and skills, as this is invariably problematic and risk-prone, and requires most resources. Where new products are introduced, market feasibility must first be assessed. The options listed above are not mutually exclusive, and producer groups may wish to change the type of activity in which they are involved, or to diversify their range of production, as they gain experience or as markets change. Information about the existing skills of different people in the society must be gathered, and the division of labour according to social and cultural factors must be understood, before any intervention is implemented.

4

Table 4.5 Types of small-scale industries

Food processing	bakery, bread, cakes, doughnuts, biscuits, sweets, snacks
	preserving, drying, canning and bottling fruit and vegetables fruit juices and drinks for local demand
	flour mill, for local or distant demand
	oil extraction e.g. from groundnuts, sunflower seeds, soya bean
	herbal medicines
Handcrafts	bamboowork and basketry
	pottery
	leatherwork
	embroidery
	textiles: batik, tie-and-dye, block printing, spinning, weaving, knitting
Small industries	tailoring
	housing and housing materials such as bricks, roofing tiles, etc
	production of energy-conserving cook-stoves

Small industries *continued*	household utensils e.g. water-pot filters farm equipment consumer goods eg candles, soap transport: rickshaws, bus company, trailers carpentry rope and twine products water pumps, solar heaters, windmills mechanics, plumbing, radio and bicycle repair
Petty trade	kiosks, stalls and retail shops restaurant/canteen/teashop e.g. for office workers, barracks, or for school lunches flower stalls
Entertainment	singing and dancing groups drama groups video and media groups
Recycling	waste collection production of household articles from waste materials collection of waste scraps of material from textile factories to make patchwork articles

5.2.2 Social considerations in small-scale industry

(To be read in conjunction with 4.1.3.2 Sustainable livelihoods, and 4.1.3.3 Gender and economic interventions.)

People have a wide range of different skills. In some societies particular skills are the traditional occupation of specific groups. An example of this is found in the Indian caste system, where some occupations are inherited within particular castes. In many societies, skills and traditional crafts are passed down from parent to child, which may be because certain crafts (such as pottery, tailoring, metalwork, and entertainment) require high levels of skill, which can only be learned over a period of years and thus involve long apprenticeships. Some crafts may have high symbolic and social status, and skills and markets may be jealously guarded by existing workers. Other kinds of work, such as waste collection and leatherwork, are considered particularly polluting or demeaning and so are confined to people with low social status.

In every society some roles and tasks are assigned to women and others to men. This gender division of labour is highly variable between societies, and between different class, caste and ethnic groups in the same society; and it also changes over time and according to changing economic and political circumstances. However, it is universally the case that most male tasks are assigned a higher social value than most female tasks; and that when female tasks are upgraded, for example through access to improved technology or credit facilities, they are often taken over by men. (See **2.1** Gender.)

For example, in most Indian Hindu and Muslim communities weaving is a male task, while women and children are involved in thread preparation such as spinning and bobbin-winding. In north-eastern India, as in northern Thailand and Vietnam, the preparation of cloth is a women's activity. Oxfam supports a linen-weaving co-operative in Vietnam where women process the flax, weave the cloth, and make clothes for the family; but men are the carpenters who make the looms. In many Asian and African societies commercial tailoring is a male preserve, and equipping women with sewing machines to make clothes may run into male opposition.

The division of labour leads to differences in ownership and control of productive resources, and income from production and social, and results in economic inequalities. Women workers are often confined to unskilled activities, and denied training, and promotion to better-paid activities. Even where they work alongside men, women are usually paid less and employed on less favourable terms. This is true in both industrialised and developing countries. Within family enterprises women often have little control over the income they earn. They may be excluded from marketing and major investment decisions.

The exclusion of women from training, higher skills, marketing and decision-making in the private sector, even where they form a major part of the workforce, makes entrepreneurship development for women particularly difficult. NGO interventions therefore need to pay particular attention to these problems in all aspects of their support. The distinction between women's practical and strategic gender needs is fully explained in **2.1** Gender. In relation to economic interventions this critical distinction is an essential planning tool. Because they lack information about different products, and find difficulty in improving their skills, women may need support in planning productive enterprises. They may also face marketing problems. These are practical needs and can be addressed with practical interventions. However, practical needs should always be addressed within the context of women's longer-term strategic needs, such as overcoming the barriers created by the sexual division of labour; and NGOs can contribute to this by supporting activities which do not reinforce gender stereotypes.

603

Planning support to women's IGPs, or to small-scale industries involving both women and men, must be based on careful appraisal of all the social and cultural factors governing different aspects of production, as well as the financial aspects. There is a wide range of methods of appraisal which may be drawn upon to facilitate this research, such as the analysis of use and control of productive resources set out in the Harvard Gender Framework Analysis described, among others, in **2.1.8.6 Resources and benefits: access and control**, and participatory forms of appraisal described in **1.4.3 Formal methods of information-gathering and appraisal**.

5.2.3 Support for producer groups
(To be read in conjunction with 4.1.3.8 Participatory organisations.)

Many potential economic, social, and political benefits to poor producers can result from joining or forming various types of group, co-operative or association. Producer groups can, for example, help individuals to cut the cost of raw materials by buying in bulk; can facilitate storage, transport, and marketing of goods; can give producers more muscle in negotiations with larger producer organisations and authorities; help to develop organisational skills and increased understanding of economic processes; and participate in wider movements for change through national and international networking and lobbying. However, these groups themselves need support and training.

In Mozambique, for example, Oxfam supports an organisation which offers help to small industries which were suffering from lack of training in organisational, management and bookkeeping skills, poor diversification of their products, and low product-quality. The Mozambican NGO provides marketing facilities for small co-operatives producing salt, garments, tin products, mats and wood carvings, while offering advice and support on technical and organisational aspects of their work. A critical issue for the mat producers, who are women, was transport of their goods to be marketed by the Centre. Previously mats were sold locally by men, who kept part of the proceeds; and women were unaware of the value of their own products.

There are a number of ways in which donor agencies can support the formation of small producer groups, and the effectiveness of organisations running small industries. Perhaps the most important is ensuring that the groups have appropriate training in the skills they will require to manage their enterprise. These may be managerial skills, bookkeeping, literacy, knowledge and understanding of financial management, and the organisational skills required to run a participative organisation whose leadership or management is accountable to its membership, and where trust and co-operation must be established. While traditional co-operative groups in many societies provide the most appropriate vehicle for small industry development, existing organisation may also be hierarchical and undemocratic, with unfair distribution of profits, and disaffection among members. This training is best provided by local NGOs with a training capacity, where these exist, or by other training organisations in the country. Donor agencies should seek out sources of appropriate training. Another useful intervention is to enable representatives from small producer groups to visit other similar groups and organisations, so that they can learn from each other's experience and form networks of support.

A workshop held in the Philippines on People's Cooperatives in 1990 set out a number of guiding principles for democratic groups relying on mutual cooperation, such as open and voluntary membership; autonomy and democracy; a commitment to education and training; and co-operation with other groups to build a national network. These principles arise from an approach which aims not only to enable poor people to have direct control over the means of production, but to strengthen their forms of social organisation and work towards an alternative economic system.

5.2.4 Support for technology development
(To be read in conjunction with 4.1.3.4 Technology development.)

Within each industry a range of technology is used; in small-scale industries, the type of technology is often crucial in claiming government facilities such as credit, training, and marketing provision. Before considering technology changes, the potential for government assistance should be investigated in detail.

In general, the more sophisticated the technology, the higher the potential levels of productivity, and hence income, to individual workers. However, new technology can also mean that the tasks of certain workers are supplanted — for example, buying in sophisticated weaving looms may put makers of traditional looms out of work. Higher levels of investment are required for complex technology, and its introduction may bring about changes in the organisation of production, and new business skills may be needed.

Training in these skills is indispensable if new technology is to lead to higher levels of production; and, of course, the introduction of new technology must be accompanied by appropriate training in its use and maintenance. The gender division of labour must be carefully considered, and measures introduced which will ensure that women are able to take advantage of training equally with men. Otherwise, men may take over new technologies, and women may lose control over production processes.

5.2.5 Marketing assistance
(To be read in conjunction with **4.1.3.6 Marketing assistance**.)

Producers in small-scale industries often experience considerable problems in marketing their goods. Many small-scale industry projects fail because they do not pay sufficient attention to market research and the planning of marketing strategies in the initial stages of project design.

a. Identifying the right market
The kind of market being aimed at must be clearly identified and defined. Markets for small-scale industrial products are of many different types and offer a wide variation in the price at which products can be sold. The price of the products in any particular market depends on the costs of production, the income which participants need to earn, their levels of skill, the time taken to produce particular products, the incomes of potential customers, and the price of other similar goods on the market.

The distance from producers is another important factor. Local markets may be more accessible and cut down on transport costs, but may be less profitable if local incomes are low. However, where local markets exist for a wide range of products, such as the Indian *melas* or craft bazaars, producers come together and exchange information, and may organise special markets on festival days. Access to distant domestic markets and export outlets depends upon the availability of transport, its cost, and rules governing trade between districts and countries.

Sometimes skills are 'upgraded' in expectation of higher incomes, but in fact there may be a very limited market for the improved product, and one which is completely unfamiliar to small-scale producers. There are, however, a number of ways in which incomes can be increased through changing products and markets. It is usually advisable to develop a variety of marketing alternatives, to maintain independence and accumulate experience, so that if one market fails another remains. There are also many 'intermediate' goods between cheap, mass-produced products and luxuries for the elite market. It is often advisable to start small, aiming at a local market, and gradually expand as market opportunities present themselves. Management and financial skills have to be gradually developed to cope with the complexity of the wider market.

b. Advantages and disadvantages of different markets
The markets for the types of products which small-scale industries produce may be divided into three broad categories: local market for cheap, mass-produced goods; local or urban market for expensive

luxury goods; and export market for expensive luxury goods. Each of these has potential advantages and disadvantages.

Outlets for the local market are direct sale from place of production; door-to-door sales and personal contacts; local shops; festivals and fairs; government shops; sales to public sector establishments.

The local mass market for cheap goods has the following advantages:

- Poor producers will themselves often be users of the products and so able to judge quality.
- Investment costs and skill requirements are likely to be low.
- It is easier for producers to monitor the market and to gauge changes in taste.
- Producers often have marketing contacts or are able to develop these.

The disadvantages of this market are:

- Items have to be produced quickly in bulk to yield sufficient income, and there may not be a large enough market.
- There may be intense competition from larger-scale mass production using very cheap labour or higher technology.

The local or urban elite market for luxury goods has the following advantages:

- Higher quality goods with added value from highly-skilled work may bring higher incomes from fewer products.
- In contrast with the export market, it is quicker and easier for producers to contact and understand; quicker to get products to and payments from; quality control is less severe; it is simpler to service than the export market — no documentation or special packaging is required, or foreign currency dealing.

The disadvantages of this market are:

- It may be less accessible to small-scale producers than that for cheap products, and restricted in size and price.
- Risks are high because tastes may change rapidly.
- Successful products may be taken up by larger-scale producers able to cut costs by the use of expensive technology and cheap labour.

The export market for expensive luxury goods can be reached through government and private export marketing agencies, alternative trading organisations (ATOs), or personal contacts. The advantage is:

- Prices may be higher for everyday handicraft items with 'ethnic' value.

607

The disadvantages of this market are:

* It is often fickle, as trends change quickly.
* Marketing is complicated by numerous regulations, and marketing costs are high; a high level of financial and management skills is needed.
* Currency exchange rates can fluctuate greatly.
* Quality control standards are stringent and there is intense competition.

c. Alternative trading organisations, including Oxfam Bridge
Although exporting is not easy, various sources of information exist to help potential exporters. For handcrafts and food products there are a number of alternative trading organisations (ATOs) to assist small producers. The largest in terms of sales turnover are:

* UK: Oxfam Trading, Traidcraft
* Germany: Gepa, Dritte-Welt-Laden
* USA: SERVV Self Help Handicrafts
* Netherlands: SOS Wereldhandel
* Australia: Community Aid Abroad Trading

There are also two main Fair Trade federations:
International Federation for Alternative Trade (IFAT), formed in 1989 with many ATOs and some producer groups in developing countries as members. Its principal activity is information exchange among its members and joint action to give voice to their concerns, and the organisation of a bi-annual conference on alternative trade.
European Fair Trade Organisation (EFTA), a smaller group of nine European ATOs who co-operate actively on orders, product development and producer services.

The ATO movement has grown steadily since the early 1970s and is now gaining momentum from the 'green' consumer movement. It uses a number of marketing outlets including fair trade shops, mail order catalogues, generally geared to the Christmas gift market, and informal markets such as fairs and church bazaars. Some are producer-oriented and give product and marketing advice to producers when they visit. Others emphasise the injustices of international economic relationships by providing information for consumers on the conditions of production or the goods they buy, and engaging in public education and campaigning work.

Oxfam Trading, Oxfam's commercial operation, is one of the largest of the UK ATOs. Under its Bridge scheme it imports crafts and foodstuffs from producer groups based in those countries where Oxfam works. A wide range of organisations are involved in the scheme, ranging from a marketing association in Bangladesh reaching out to several thousand women to a co-operative in Zaire with just six members. The criteria used in selecting suppliers for the Bridge scheme include:

- payment of reasonable wages and provision of reasonable working conditions;
- provision of social and economic benefits such as bonus payments, sick pay and savings schemes;
- participation of producers in decision-making;
- provision of social programmes such as literacy schemes and nutrition education;
- employment of people who are especially disadvantaged, for example, through disability or, in the case of women in seclusion, through women-only employment;
- whether the organisation or business is making products for which Oxfam has a market;
- the capacity of the organisation to supply products efficiently and reliably.

Eligible organisations are offered support in fulfilling orders and increasing their effectiveness in such areas as design, costing and marketing. Bridge staff are responsible for identifying products and give a range of services including advice on product development and export marketing. The Bridge Development Fund also makes small grants to producer groups needing assistance in such areas as design, training, technical assistance, equipment, networking and marketing. Any profits are covenanted to Oxfam and the proportion attributable to the Bridge programme is returned to Oxfam Trading for distribution to producer groups in the form of producer dividends (25 per cent of the profits) and grants from the Bridge Development Fund (75 per cent of the profits).

Initiatives by NGOs have often involved improving product design to respond to particular market demands and to be flexible to changing market situations. Such attempts must be market-led. A weaving programme in Thailand provides employment for women in the poverty-stricken north-east of the country, who may otherwise have migrated or been sold into the brothels of Bangkok. This has successfully revived the tradition of *matmee* weaving and now provides income to more than 300 weaving families and 54 tailors. This project has grown slowly, developed a reputation for reliability and quality, and has constantly adapted to the market. It now sells to a range of ATOs, including Oxfam Trading, but has also benefited from a growing tourist industry in the area.

5.2.6 Credit
(To be read in conjunction with **4.1.3.5 Credit and savings support**.)

Difficulty in production credit is often the major problem faced by small-scale producers. Many governments have credit schemes for small-scale producers who do not have other financial resources; and many development agencies fund a range of credit schemes. Some of these have been very successful, extending support to thousands of small-scale producers. Examples are the Self-employed Women's Association (SEWA) in India, which has a woman-run and fully independent bank, and Grameen Bank in Bangladesh. The Grameen Bank has helped nearly half a million people gain credit — 83 per cent of whom are women — and its loan recovery rates exceed 95 per cent. Its loans are used for a wide variety of purposes, including livestock raising and fisheries, crop cultivation and transport. The majority of trading and shopkeeping loans, over a third of the total, go to men, while women are the major borrowers in the area of processing and manufacturing. Lending to groups is an important aspect of these 'people's banks'.

Oxfam supports a number of smaller organisations to assist small-scale artisans through providing credit. Credit cannot be seen in isolation, however. Where activities involve self-employment, while repayment may be satisfactory, the actual increases in incomes are generally very small, and often non-existent. Initial loan amounts may be very small, but credit may be needed on a long-term basis, for a whole range of activities as enterprises grow, and some allowance must be made for this in the credit schemes. For example, a programme in Togo supported by Oxfam included advice on simple book-keeping systems, and on ways to reduce production costs, and technical and marketing advice on how to make goods competitive. Loan repayment was reasonable, but borrowers continued to be vulnerable to the problems of poverty, particularly to family illness, which required the use of loan funds, and to political and economic instability, which affected the profitability of their enterprises.

Women face particular difficulties in obtaining credit. Even when capital has been found to initiate an enterprise, working capital will be needed to enable it to operate, especially as many customers buy on credit, and working capital can go into consumption or emergency needs. Women often have little control over their income and it may be used by their husbands for their private requirements. When working capital is low, producers may be forced to sell at low prices, as they cannot hold out for better terms, and may not be able to buy the raw materials they need.

NGOs may help women — and other poor producers — by providing grants and loans, or setting up credit schemes, and by

610

supervising administration and repayment. Savings and loans schemes have proved very popular with women, and if these help to build up women's credit-worthiness, they may eventually be able to borrow from mainstream financing institutions. A complementary strategy is to support lobbying of banks and governments to make credit more available, and help women to gain information about financial institutions.

There remain serious limitations on the possibility of increasing incomes through self-employment; and attempts to expand operations, whether or not credit is involved, will face the problems of management and marketing described in **4.1.3.4** and **4.1.3.5**. Much of the success of organisations such as SEWA and the Grameen Bank has come as the result of accompanying organisational and campaigning activities, to change the wider context in which self-employed workers operate. As they have increased their impact in this way, they have also attracted funding from major donors, such as the World Bank, and been able to increase their effective support to more and more small-scale producers. Small producer organisations hoping to increase the scale of their operations will need a wide range of support, particularly in the areas of training and capacity-building, information exchange and networking, and the building of wider movements which try to change the economic and social context.

4

5.2.7 Training
(To be read in conjunction with **4.1.3.7** Training and information exchange; and **3.1.2** Education and Training.)

Training and educational assistance is a vital factor in the maintenance and sustainability of small-scale enterprises. Training should provide small-scale producers with the skills they need to run their organisations, the upgrading of existing skills, and the introduction of new ones. Before any training intervention is planned, the existing roles, activities and skills of women and men must be clearly understood, and the needs for skills training must be identified by producers themselves.

Much of the training supported by NGOs in relation to IGPs has been to upgrade handicraft skills, and success has been uneven. Training programmes for women have often concentrated on what are seen as 'traditional female skills', such as tailoring, embroidery and knitting. The perception that these are 'feminine' activities is often more a result of outsiders' assumptions than knowledge of the local situation. The introduction of sewing machines to women, for example, may be as alien as any other introduced skill; and tailoring programmes may run into serious difficulties because women are unable to sell products in societies where tailoring is a male-dominated industry. Even where these are traditional female skills, such training may only serve to equip women for very low-paid work, and worsen the situation for those already working in the industry by saturating the market.

Training should not only support traditional male or female tasks, and thus the existing gender division of labour, but be responsive to social and cultural changes, and offer training to men and women in non-traditional male or female tasks. The co-ordinator of a bakery project for miners' wives in Bolivia, supported by Oxfam, stressed the importance of both social and financial training for their enterprise. While the main objective of the project is to run the bakery at a profit without outside assistance, and women needed three years' training in various skills to accomplish this, social training is also a crucial component. An Oxfam report states:

She [the coordinator] sees gender awareness-building (examining violence, discrimination, injustice, fertility) as elementary and the most important part. Women have to know who they are and what they can do and need to educate children. Women must show society that they are not stupid. In addition it is not enough just to change women's role in the domestic sphere — there is a need to teach women to become involved in politics. She believes that both men and women need to change men.

Training is usually identified as a high priority in economic enterprises and should be seen as a long-term, ongoing process, with follow-up training and evaluation of its impact as part of the process.

5.3 Key questions

1 Is there an autonomous group or association that will manage the economic project? What is the nature of the participation of women and men in the group? If a mixed group, what does it need in terms of awareness training to ensure that women's development is promoted within the enterprise?

2 If this is a women's IGP, what are the skills and training needs of the women and how can these be met? Have all areas, such as management, financial administration, marketing, stock control, pricing, and so on, been addressed? Is there a need for literacy and numeracy training for members of the group so that all can participate on an equal basis, and the group's leaders be held accountable? Are men involved in any way in this project? Do they have control over any of the proceeds?

3 What practical and strategic needs (of women and men) does this enterprise address?

4 What extra labour is entailed by the enterprise, who will carry out the work, and what will be the impact on other activities?

5 Has the market for the products been thoroughly researched, both for new products and an increased volume or variety of existing products? Who does existing marketing — women or men, or both? How is cash distributed?

6 Is there a reliable supply of materials? Is transport needed, for materials and products? Who controls the means of transport?

7 How will the success, in financial and social terms, of the project be evaluated?

4

6 Resources

General

Boserup, E (1993) *The Conditions of Agricultural Growth*, Earthscan Publications, London.

Crow, B, Mackintosh, M and Martin, C (eds) (1990) *The Food Question: Profits versus People?*, Earthscan.

Campbell, B and Loxley, J (eds)(1989) *Structural Adjustment in Africa*, MacMillan Press.

Chambers, R, Pacey, A and Thrupp, L A (eds)(1989) *Farmer First: Farmer Innovation and Agricultural Research*, IT Publications, London.

Clark, A W (ed.)(1993) *Gender and Political Economy: Explorations of South Asian Systems*, OUP, Oxford.

Clark, J and Davies, M (1991) *A Simple Guide to Structural Adjustment*, Oxfam, Oxford.

Coote, B (1992) *The Trade Trap; Poverty and the Global Commodity Markets*, Oxfam, Oxford.

Drèze J, and Sen, A (eds)(1990) *The Political Economy of Hunger*, Vol I, II and III; United Nations University.

Duncan, Z and Howell, J (1992) *Structural Adjustment and the African Farmer*, Overseas Development Institute, London.

Evers, B (ed)(1994) *Women and Economic Policy*, Oxfam, Oxford.

Folbre, N (1994) *Who Pays for the Kids? Gender and the Structure of Constraint*, Routledge.

Haverkort, B, van der Kamp, J, and Waters-Bayer, A (eds) (1991) *Joining Farmers' Experiments: Experiences in Participatory Technology Development*, ILEIA Readings in Sustainable Agriculture Series.

Jeffery, P and Jeffery, R (1993) *Gender and Political Economy: Explorations of South Asian Systems*, Oxford University Press, Delhi; Oxford.

Karrow, K and Saxenian, M (1993) *Appropriate Technology Sourcebook: A Guide to Practical Books for Village and Small Community Technology*, Volunteers in Asia Publications, California, USA.

Korten, D C (1980) 'Community Organisation and Rural Developent: a learning process approach', *Public Administration Review* 20: 480-511.

Meadows, D H, Meadows, D L, Jorgen, R and Behrens III, W W (1972) *The Limits of Growth*, Pan Books.

Schumacher, E F (1973) *Small is Beautiful: A Study of Economics as if People Mattered*, Blond and Briggs, London.

The Open University Series (1992) *Poverty and Development in the 1990s, Industrialization and Development, Development Policy and Public Action, Rural Livelihoods: Crises and Responses.*

White, S C (1992) *Arguing with the Crocodile: Gender and Class in Rural Bangladesh*, Zed Books, London.

Whiteford, S and Ferguson, A E (1991) *Harvest of Want: Hunger and Food Security in Central America and Mexico*; Westview Press.

Wood, G and Palmer-Jones, R (1990) *The Water-Sellers: A Co-operative Venture by the Rural Poor*, Kumarian Press and IT Publications.

Woodward, D (1992) *Debt, Adjustment and Poverty in Developing Countries*, Vol I and II, Save the Children Fund UK.

World Bank and UNDP annual reports; in particular *World Development Report* 1986 and 1992.

Agriculture (crops and livestock)

Aaker, J (ed) (1994) *Livestock for a Small Earth: The role of Animals in a Just and Sustainable World*, Heifer Project International, Little Rock, Arkansas.

Altieri, M (1993) *Crop Protection Strategies for Subsistance Farmers*, IT Publications, London.

de Boef, W, Amanor, K, Wellard, K (1993) *Cultivating Knowledge: Genetic Diversity, Farmers' Experimentation and Crop Research*, IT Publications.

Carruthers, I, Rodriguez, M (eds) (1992) *Tools for Agriculture: A Buyer's Guide to Appropriate Equipment* (4th edition), IT Publications, London. (Also available in French.)

CGIAR (Consultative Group on International Agricultural Research and Development Centers) Publications; see addresses of member centres in the Resources Directory.

Lipton, M, Longhurst, R (1989) *New Seeds and Poor People*, Unwin Hyam, London.

Ministry of Agriculture and Fisheries (1985) *Agricultural Compendium for Rural Development in the Tropics and Subtropics*, Elsevier Science Publishers, The Hague, The Netherlands.

Prior, J (1994) *Pastoral Development Planning*, Development Guidelines Series 9, Oxfam, Oxford.

Reijntjes, C, Haverkort, B and Waters-Bayer, A (1992) *Farming for the Future: an Introduction to Low-External-Input and Sustainable Agriculture*, London/Leusden: MacMillan/ILEIA.

Scoones, I (1988) *Sustainable Pastoralism in Africa: An Annotated Bibliography*, IIED, London.

Sandford, S (1983) *Management of Pastoral Development in the Third World*, John Wiley and Sons, Chichester and ODI, London.

4

Fishing

Kurien, J (1988) *The Role of Fishermen's Organisations in Fisheries Management in Developing Countries*, FAO Fisheries Technical Paper No 300, FAO Rome.

Development and Change 20, October 1989, *Third World Fisheries: The Dynamics of Incorporation and Transformation*, SAGE Publications, The Hague, The Netherlands.

Panayotou, T (1982) *Management Concepts for Small-Scale Fisheries: Economic and Social Aspects*, FAO Fisheries Technical Paper No 228, FAO, Rome.

Tvedten, I and Hersoug, B (eds) (1992) *Fishing for Development: Small-scale Fisheries in Africa*, Nordiska Afriakinstitutet, Uppsala.

Forestry

Cernea, M M (1985) 'Alternative units of social organisations sustaining afforestation strategies' in Cernea M M (ed.) *Putting People First: Sociological Variables in Rural Development*, OUP for the World Bank.

Kerkhof P (1990) *Agroforestry in Africa: A Survey of Project Experience*, Panos.

Mendes, C (1989) *Fight for the Forest*, Latin America Bureau, London.

NAS (1983) *Firewood Crops: Shrubs and Tree Species for Energy Production* National Academy Press, Washington DC, USA.

Poore, D (1989) *No Timber without Trees: Sustainability in the Tropical Forests*, Earthscan.

Read, M (1994) *Truth or Trickery? Timber Labelling Past and Present*, WWF UK.

Shanks, E and Carter, J (1994) *The Organisation of Small-Scale Tree Nurseries*, Rural Development Forestry Study Guide 1, ODI, London.

Shepherd, G (1990) *Forestry, Social Forestry, Fuelwood and the Environment: A Tour of the Horizon*, Social Forestry Network Paper 11a, ODI, London.

Small-scale industries

Piza Lopez, E and March C (1991) *Gender Considerations in Economic Enterprises: Report of a Workshop held in the Philippines, November 1990*, Oxfam Discussion Paper 2, Oxfam, Oxford.

Buzzard, S and Edgcomb, E (eds)(1987) *Small-Business Project: A Step by Step Guide*, PACT, Madison, USA.

Devereux, S and Pares, H with Best, J (1990) *Credit and Savings for Development*, Development Guideline Series 1, Oxfam, Oxford.

Hewitt, T, Johnson, H and Wield, D (1992) *Industrialization and Development*, OUP and The Open University, Oxford, UK.

Hurley, D (1990) *Income Generation Schemes for the Urban Poor*, Development Guidelines Series 4, Oxfam, Oxford.

Levitsky, J (ed)(1989) *Microenterprises in Developing Countries: Papers and Proceedings of an International Conference*, IT Publications.

Millard, E (1988) *The Financial Management of a Small Handicraft Business*, Oxfam, Oxford.

Millard, E (1992) *Export Marketing for a Small Handicraft Business*, Oxfam, Oxford.

Smith, M (1993) *Why People Grow Drugs: Narcotics and Development in the Third World*, Panos.

4

CHAPTER 5

Health
and development

Contents

1 **Introduction 625**
   1.1 The right to health 625
   1.2 Health and development 626
   1.3 The role of NGOs 627
   1.4 Chapter structure 629

2 **Background: approaches to health care 631**
   2.1 Primary health care 631
       2.1.1 Principles and components of PHC 633
       2.1.2 The role of NGOs in PHC 633
   2.2 Levels of health care 635
   2.3 NGO roles in secondary health care 637
       2.3.1 District health teams 637
       2.3.2 Minimum activities package (MAP) 637
   2.4 Infrastructure and equipment 638
   2.5 Vertical programmes 640
   2.6 Traditional, alternative, and informal health care 640
       2.6.1 Introduction 640
       2.6.2 Forms of traditional health care 642
       2.6.3 NGO roles in traditional health care 642
       2.6.4 Key questions 644
   2.7 Urban health 645
       2.7.1 Health and urbanisation 645
       2.7.2 Facilities in urban areas 646
       2.7.3 Urban health problems 646
       2.7.4 The role of NGOs in urban health 648

3 **Focusing on people: health needs of specific population groups 650**
   3.1 Introduction 650
   3.2 Women's health 651
       3.2.1 Women in society 651
       3.2.2 The roles and health needs of women 652
       3.2.3 Maternal mortality and morbidity 653
       3.2.4 Women's reproductive health: MCH programmes 654
       3.2.5 Women's work-related health problems 659
       3.2.6 Women as carers and health workers 660

5

3.2.7 Sexuality and sex education 661
3.2.8 Sexually transmitted diseases (STDs) 661
3.2.9 Cultural aspects of women's health 662
3.2.10 Key questions 666
3.3 Child health 667
    3.3.1 Introduction 667
    3.3.2 Preconception care 668
    3.3.3 Antenatal care 669
    3.3.4 Perinatal care 669
    3.3.5 Under-fives 670
    3.3.6 'CHILD- to-child' 670
    3.3.7 Schools 671
    3.3.8 Key questions 671
3.4 Elderly people 672
    3.4.1 Introduction 672
    3.4.2 Age-related health issues 673
    3.4.3 Key questions 674
3.5 Disabled people 674
    3.5.1 Introduction 674
    3.5.2 Common causes of disability 675

4 Health care provision 677
4.1 Introduction 678
4.2 Nutrition 678
    4.2.1 Introduction 678
    4.2.2 Background 679
    4.2.3 Causes of malnutrition 679
    4.2.4 Types of malnutrition 682
    4.2.5 Nutrition interventions 686
    4.2.6 Key questions 688
4.3 Environmental and public health: water and sanitation 688
    4.3.1 Introduction 688
    4.3.2 Aims of environmental and public health programmes 689
    4.3.3 Urban environmental health 691
    4.3.4 A comprehensive approach to environmental health 693
    4.3.5 Water supply 695
    4.3.6 Sanitation 705
    4.3.7 Vector control 711
    4.3.8 Planning and evaluating environmental health
        programmes 714
4.4 Immunisation 722
    4.4.1 Background 722
    4.4.2 Immunisable diseases 722
    4.4.3 Immunisation schedule 724

4.4.4 The cold chain 724
4.4.5 Immunisation strategies 726
4.4.6 Key questions 726
4.5 Prevention and control of communicable diseases 727
4.5.1 Background 727
4.5.2 General prevention and control 727
4.5.3 Common communicable diseases 729
4.5.4 Epidemics 735
4.6 Birth planning 736
4.6.1 Introduction 736
4.6.2 Background 736
4.6.3 Oxfam's support for birth planning 738
4.6.4 Practical interventions 739
4.6.5 Birth-planning services 740
4.6.6 Birth-planning methods 741
4.6.7 Abortion 744
4.6.8 Key questions 745
4.7 HIV and AIDS 745
4.7.1 Introduction 745
4.7.2 Background 746
4.7.3 Practical interventions 750
4.7.4 Key questions 755
4.8 The provision of essential drugs 756
4.8.1 Introduction 756
4.8.2 Practical approaches 757
4.8.3 Advocacy, campaigning and networking 758
4.8.4 Key questions 758
4.9 Mental and emotional well-being 759
4.9.1 The role of NGOs 761
4.9.2 Key questions 763
4.10 Emergencies and public health 763
4.10.1 Health and nutrition surveillance 766
4.10.2 Key questions 767
4.11 Health education and health promotion 767
4.11.1 Introduction 767
4.11.2 Practical approaches 768
4.11.3 Key questions 772

5 **Financing, planning, and evaluating health programmes 773**
5.1 Introduction 773
5.2 Financing health care 773
5.2.1 Background 774
5.2.2 Principal methods of financing health care 776
5.2.3 Preventive versus curative services 778

5

5.2.4 Rational use of drugs 779
5.2.5 Revolving drug funds 779
5.2.6 Oxfam's approach to financing health care 780
5.2.7 Key questions 780
5.3 Planning and evaluating health programmes 781
5.3.1 Introduction781
5.3.2 Background 781
5.3.3 Baseline information 782
5.3.4 Evaluation 784
5.3.5 Key questions 785

6 Resources 786

Tables

5.1 Transmission patterns and preventive measures for diseases related to water and sanitation 690
5.2 Sanitation options 706

1 Introduction

1.1 The right to health
1.2 Health and development
1.3 The role of NGOs
1.4 Chapter structure

1.1 The right to health

Good health and a reasonable life span are among the most prized of human conditions. Health care is also a basic human right. While the care provided by formal and informal health services is indispensable for the achievement and maintenance of good health, there are many other conditions which are also necessary, including adequate daily food, safe and sufficient water supply, effective sanitation, education, reasonable shelter, employment or other means of gaining a livelihood; and guarantees of basic human rights and freedoms such as personal security, freedom from persecution, and gender equity.

The mere existence of health services, whether curative or preventive, is no guarantee that everyone in need will be able to use them or even benefit indirectly from them. Poor people all over the world are those who most need adequate health care, and they are the people whose requirements for health care remain most systematically unmet. In both urban and rural areas, the poorest people are likely to live furthest away from health centres, hospitals, and clinics, and be least visited by health workers. Where basic health care is not completely free of charge, poor people are likely to deny themselves treatment because of the cost. Furthermore, poor people are not a homogenous group, and among them, some are discriminated against because of class, caste, and race: this affects their health, and the health care they receive.

Social justice and equity are prerequisites for the achievement and maintenance of good health. Where people live and how they live, their opportunities and rights, are largely determined by political and economic forces, and are significant factors in their health. National health policies and priorities for investment in health affect the range of services provided, and where and how they are provided. Macro-

625

economic policies, such as the requirements of international lending institutions for adjustment of the economies of indebted countries, have a powerful impact on the health of poor people as public spending is cut. The cutting of health budgets by 50 per cent or more in some countries has led to severe decreases in health provision: in Tanzania, for example, the under-5 mortality rate (U5MR) increased from 193 per 1,000 in 1980 to 309 per 1,000 in 1987, while in Zambia child malnutrition has sharply increased, and child immunisation programmes have declined. It is always the poorest people, who have fewest resources, who suffer most.

1.2 Health and development

Average life expectancy in poor countries is commonly ten to twenty years shorter than in richer, industrialised countries. This is mainly the result of high infant and child mortality. Many of the health interventions and strategies promoted over the last two decades have therefore tried to ensure the survival of infants and young children. Outstanding examples are immunisation against six common childhood diseases, and programmes to control diarrhoeal diseases and respiratory infections, the most important killers of young children worldwide. However, according to the UNDP *1992 Human Development Report*, 14 million children die before they reach the age of five, infant mortality figures in the poorest nations are on average 115 per 1,000 live births (compared with 13 per 1,000 in industrialised countries), and 180 million young children are malnourished.

Although the provision of health services and safe water has improved over the last 20 years, 1.5 billion people (about one-third of the world's population) lack health services, 1.3 billion do not have safe water, and half the world's population have no sanitation. While gains have undoubtedly been made, the world is still a long way from the target of 'health for all by the year 2,000'.

Health is a critical factor in development: ill health affects productivity, and at the same time poverty causes ill health, setting up a vicious circle of increasing poverty and sickness. The ability of people to make a living depends on their capacities — their skills, knowledge, resources, and health. Unhealthy breadwinners affect the whole family: for example, among poor urban people in Bangladesh, sickness-induced loss of earnings has been found to be highest among the poorest people, and the families of sick breadwinners are the worst nourished. Whether the breadwinners are male or female also affects the health of household members. In sub-Saharan Africa, for example, there is evidence that in women-maintained households the nutritional status of children is better, because women are likely to prioritise feeding their dependants, while men commonly spend a greater proportion of household income on inessential personal items, such as alcohol or tobacco.

The health problems facing women and men differ according to their different biological roles; but also reflect their assigned social roles, and the unequal relations between them in social, economic, and political terms. For women, reproductive health is a major concern; the age at which a woman becomes sexually active, the number and frequency of her pregnancies, and the quality of her antenatal and postnatal care, are crucial factors in determining her general health status. Childbearing carries physical risks for the mother, as do many of the contraceptive measures that women adopt to control their fertility. Maternal mortality remains a leading cause of preventable death in many developing countries; and its incidence relates closely to the status of women in society.

For men, the situation is rather different. Physical violence has risen to become a major cause of premature death among men, often in the context of armed conflict, but death is often the outcome of violent personal conflicts, expecially in association with alcohol and substance abuse. Alcohol abuse is also closely associated with male violence against women and children; and with chronic ill health. Work-related and traffic accidents are also common causes of preventable deaths amongst men.

Unhealthy people may be unable to take advantage of the benefits of development, such as education or training; and their capacity to absorb new information may be hindered. Participation in collective activities such as meetings or social organisations may be affected by ill health, and people may thus lose opportunities to influence decisions which affect them. In all societies, it is women's time and energy which is generally devoted to caring for sick, elderly or disabled relatives, and this has an impact on their other activities, such as earning a living, participating in political and civil life, and food production and preparation, as well as on their own health.

1.3 The role of NGOs

The burdens of debt, economic recession, and structural adjustment policies have led to reduced health budgets, declining health services, and a deterioration of health in poor countries. In many parts of the world, war and internal armed conflict, often the result of economic or environmental pressures as well as political events, further erode health-care provision and the health status of the population. Health services are often destroyed or discontinued. Injuries and disabilities, emotional and mental trauma, and the loss of family members, as well as widespread hunger through loss or destruction of food sources, affect thousands of people throughout war-affected countries such as Afghanistan, Angola, Mozambique, Somalia, and former Yugoslavia.

This situation poses great challenges to NGOs such as Oxfam. The provision of health care is normally the responsibility of governments, and is supplemented by NGOs and the private sector. However, the quality of government provision varies greatly; and where it is declining, the non-governmental sector is often the main provider of health services. Donor agencies are now faced with new issues: as the State 'rolls back' from public services, should they step in and fund large-scale health programmes? (See **5.5.2** Financing Health Care.)

In all countries, traditional or informal systems of health care flourish alongside the formal government-funded health sector. In others, such as China and Vietnam, traditional health care (in the sense of indigenous, rather than modern, or imported from the West) such as acupuncture and herbal medicine, is provided by the state sector. In other parts of the world, traditional herbalism, spiritual healing, and other forms of indigenous medicine are frequently used as 'informal' treatments. Oxfam funds a wide range of informal or traditional health-care initiatives in many different countries (see **5.2.6** Traditional, alternative, and informal health care; also **2.2** Ethnicity, race, and culture.)

Donor agency support for health may include:

- funding capital expenditure for health facilities and equipment
- salaries for health workers
- drug supplies
- training traditional birth attendants (TBAs) and community health workers (CHWs)
- health education and awareness-raising
- lobbying and campaigning on health-related issues
- immunisation
- health-related activities such as encouragement for the growing of vegetables on small urban plots.

Health work may be undertaken within government programmes, in co-operation with UN agencies, mission hospitals, social organisations (such as trades unions), or with small local community or neighbourhood groups. There is a wide range of needs, ideas, and preoccupations in the field of health, and priorities vary in each national and local context. For Oxfam, however, the emphasis should always be on reaching the poorest and most marginalised people, who are most in need of assistance in obtaining health care. For this reason,

Oxfam places great emphasis on the specific health needs of women, both in their own right, and as the principal carers for children. Virtually all the women's organisations supported by Oxfam become involved in health issues to some extent, given the fact that health, including reproductive and emotional health, is such a major concern for women. It is less common for men to organise around health issues, or to choose to focus on their own or their children's health in development activities.

Oxfam seeks to be flexible in its response, supporting innovative ideas and pilot schemes which might lead to solutions to the many problems in health provision. While flexibility can be an asset, the disadvantage is that NGO work can be piecemeal, unstandardised, and uncontrolled: funding of health-care services should therefore seek to work within government guidelines. For example, standard national treatment protocols or immunisation schedules should be followed.

Supporting lobbying and campaigning at local, national, and international levels on specific health issues constitutes an important role for NGOs, which may take on advocacy themselves. For example, Oxfam was instrumental, through its own campaigning and the funding of other groups, in challenging the promotion of artificial baby milk in poor countries, in promoting breast-feeding, and working for policies on the rational use of drugs. Oxfam's campaigning on debt and structural adjustment policies (SAPs) is relevant to its health work, and the impact of debt and SAPs on already inadequate health services needs to be monitored.

1.4 Chapter structure

This chapter provides general guidelines on aspects of health and nutrition in development. It focuses on the principles of health care, and the problems development and relief workers may face when appraising projects or programmes in the field. It does not attempt to reproduce detailed technical information, which can be found in specialised publications (see Resources Section). The Background outlines different levels of formal health care in urban and rural areas, and traditional or informal systems of health. Section 3, Focus on people, stresses the importance of differentiating between the health needs of different sectors of the population. Section 4 presents guidelines on the provision of health care in a number of specific fields, and section 5 outlines issues in planning, monitoring and evaluation, and financing health care. There is a resources list for further reference on general and technical issues at the end of the chapter.

2 Background:
approaches to health care

2.1 Primary health care 631
  2.1.1 Principles and components of PHC 633
  2.1.2 The role of NGOs in PHC 633
2.2 Levels of health care 635
2.3 NGO roles in secondary health care 637
  2.3.1 District health teams 637
  2.3.2 Minimum activities package (MAP) 637
2.4 Infrastructure and equipment 638
2.5 Vertical programmes 640
2.6 Traditional, alternative, and informal health care 640
  2.6.1 Introduction 640
  2.6.2 Forms of traditional health care 642
  2.6.3 NGO roles in traditional health care 642
  2.6.4 Key questions 644
2.7 Urban health 645
  2.7.1 Health and urbanisation 645
  2.7.2 Facilities in urban areas 646
  2.7.3 Urban health problems 646
  2.7.4 The role of NGOs in urban health 648

5

This section outlines general approaches to health care. It discusses different levels of the health-care system (primary, secondary and tertiary), vertical programmes, traditional or informal health care, and approaches to health in rural and urban areas.

2.1 Primary health care

Primary Health Care (PHC) is a widely used concept, which is interpreted in many different ways. The 1978 international conference held in Alma Ata, former-USSR, defined it as follows:

PHC is essential health care based on practical, scientifically sound and socially acceptable methods and technology, made universally accessible to individuals and families in the community through their full participation and at a cost that

631

the community and country can afford to maintain at every stage of their development in the spirit of self-reliance and self-determination.

The conference recommended that national development plans should incorporate PHC in urban and rural health programmes, entailing a radical reorientation of health care away from large urban hospitals, advanced technologies, and medical professionals, towards community health centres and community health workers (CHWs). PHC stresses the extension of services to poor people and remote areas, the promotion of health and prevention of ill health rather than curative medicine, and the treatment of common conditions with inexpensive, simple interventions. It stresses the importance of people's participation, and of multi-sectoral collaboration for promoting and sustaining health.

PHC is conceived both as an integral part of a national health system, and its main focus. It is also integral to the overall social and economic development of the society. PHC is the first level of contact between people and the national health system, and aims to bring health care as close as possible to where they live and work. The role of secondary health services, such as district hospitals, is vital for referral of patients who cannot be treated at the primary level. However, health education, preventive health care, and efficient diagnosis and treatment, can minimise the number of referrals. Secondary level services can also provide supervision and support, facilitate distribution of drug supplies, and assist in training for health workers.

The form PHC takes in any particular country depends on the economic conditions, and social, cultural and political factors. It aims to address the main health problems in the country and match its promotional, preventive, curative, and rehabilitation services to them.

The PHC concept ushered in new thinking, and most governments have accepted its principles as outlined at Alma Ata and have enshrined them in their official health policies. However, practice has often lagged behind policy. Disproportionately large budgets are still allocated to urban hospitals and clinical training, in industrialised and developing countries alike. This may be due to vested interests within the medical profession, or to the wish of governments to satisfy middle- and upper-class demands for advanced facilities. With shrinking economies, even fewer resources are available for PHC.

2.1.1 Principles and components of PHC

Primary Health Care is based on the following principles:

- equitable distribution of resources;
- community participation: an active involvement of the constituency in decisions about its own health and health services;
- appropriate technology, acceptable and relevant to the conditions in which it will be used;
- inter-sectoral cooperation, because health is affected by policies in many other areas such as agriculture, education, and housing;
- promotion of health and prevention of disease should be emphasised while not excluding curative care.

The following were listed in the Alma Ata Declaration as the minimum components of PHC:

- health education;
- adequate food supply and promotion of good nutrition;
- safe water and basic sanitation;
- maternal and child health care, including birth planning;
- immunisation against the major infectious diseases;
- prevention and control of locally endemic diseases;
- appropriate treatment of common diseases and injuries;
- provision of essential drugs.

This is not an exhaustive list: several countries have added other components, such as mental health, rehabilitation and disability, and care of the elderly and chronically ill.

2.1.2 The role of NGOs in PHC

Since the adoption of PHC policies by many governments, much NGO work has concentrated on implementing them. However, problems have been encountered in extending the experience of small projects to national programmes. For example, CHWs often form the backbone of PHC work, and NGOs have frequently been involved in training, and supervising them. In small-scale local projects, volunteer motivation and supervision are relatively easy to maintain. However, in large national programmes, or over time, this is more difficult.

The formal health-service infrastructures in many developing countries have recently experienced serious problems due to a combination of local, regional, and international factors, ranging from the debt crisis and unfair trading practices, to weak infrastructures and lack of skills. Governments have had to rely on religious missions and other non-governmental organisations to fill gaps in the provision of

5

services, since these are often able to obtain foreign currency and trained personnel.

Oxfam and other donor agencies are increasingly faced with a dilemma in places where government infrastructure has failed to cope. They have to choose between supporting a collapsing, weak and often ineffective bureaucratic system, or working with other non-government structures and thus, at times, perpetuating the inherent inconsistencies and weaknesses of the system. Some argue that, while the government should maintain a controlling and normative function (for example, setting standard treatment protocols), it is acceptable to 'farm out' service delivery to NGOs. The choice is not easy, and depends on particular circumstances, and on the capacity of local people in urban and rural areas to be involved in decisions about how they want their health services to be run.

Oxfam aims to support local initiatives, but to avoid setting up parallel systems to those of the State. The PHC approach leads to a health-care system suitable and appropriate to local needs. International agencies can best participate by supporting people, in their efforts to improve their quality of life, and programmes and local initiatives which place PHC in the context of overall development.

In particular, national and international NGOs should:

- Ensure that programmes promote the participation of women as well as men at the household, village or urban community level, in design, planning, implementation, and evaluation. Participation means decision-making, not merely contributing resources. In Zimbabwe, Oxfam's support for health work included a special fund for community meetings for each district. These enabled people to voice their concerns to the health workers, and to identify problems and solutions. It is vital to ensure the genuine participation of women in identifying health-related problems and making decisions about solutions.
- Assist in the training of health workers, administrators, planners and other development workers. Training should be backed with support and follow-up and trainees must have conditions that allow them to practise what they have learned.
- Build on people's capacities, such as the skills and expertise of traditional healers and birth attendants; and on their institutions, such as neighbourhood committees, workers' or peasants' organisations, burial societies, women's organisations or savings clubs; and encourage appropriate links between these and the formal health services.
- Support sustainable and appropriate health technologies, innovations, and the use of local resources.

- Support methods of health education which enable people, individually and collectively, to take greater responsibility and control of their own health.
- Support the role of women in health care and health promotion within the overall context of development, ensuring their participation in training programmes and decision-making on priorities for health care.
- Build on health and development experience to develop and support advocacy and campaigning work on the damaging effect of macro-economic policies on poor people's health, and the promotion of policies which improve and strengthen existing health services.
- Promote the development and use of appropriate indicators for monitoring and evaluating health programmes, incorporating the lessons into future plans.
- Encourage operational research to solve specific problems.

PHC is increasingly under scrutiny. Some observers argue that the strategy has not worked and should be abandoned, whereas others suggest revising and improving the current approach. Oxfam believes that at the present time, PHC is the best way to make health care available to the poorest women, men, and children.

2.2 Levels of health care

In most countries health care is provided at three different levels: the **primary, secondary** and **tertiary**. Some countries also have an intermediate level between the secondary and tertiary levels.

5

a. Primary level
Health workers: CHWs, nurses, midwives, medical assistants, TBAs or healers, or other professionally trained health workers. There may be a single CHW, or a team. They work at the community level and in the primary level health facility.

Primary level health facilities: health posts, dispensaries, health centres or health clinics may be very rudimentary — one room, staffed by a CHW or a nurse — or quite large, with a team of professionally trained health workers. They serve a defined geographical area and are the basic units at the primary level. They are often the central places where community-based health workers come to report, meet with colleagues and supervisors, and replenish their supplies.

Services provided: health facilities often include a small pharmacy or medicines store, with basic drugs, vaccines (if there is a refrigerator), and equipment for simple laboratory tests. They may offer first-line diagnosis, minor medical procedures (stitching and dressing wounds, pulling teeth), antenatal care and contraceptive services, and health education materials; and keep patient records. Some health centres have beds for admitting a few patients and for normal births. They are supposed to be the first point of call for people within the catchment area. People with more serious health problems are referred to a secondary level facility.

b. Secondary level

It has been recognised in recent years that the primary and secondary levels are inextricably linked, and that PHC without secondary level back-up is not viable.

Health workers: district medical officers, doctors, nurses, pharmacists, midwives, laboratory technicians, health inspectors, and other health workers, who have more advanced diagnostic and therapeutic means at their disposal.

Secondary level health facilities: district — or equivalent — level hospitals which are the referral point for the primary level facility. Hospitals may have a large number of beds for in-patients, an operating theatre, and a laboratory.

Services provided: Casualty out-patient care, diagnosis with X-ray, complicated laboratory tests (such as for HIV, malaria, TB), surgery under anaesthesia, cold storage for vaccines. Apart from the care of in-patients, hospitals provide training, especially the continuing education of health workers, in administration, and in coordinating the district health programme.

Secondary level facilities deal with health conditions which cannot be handled at the primary level. However, they are often used as primary health centres by people living nearby, or on a direct transport route. These people often use the out-patient departments for conditions which should be taken to primary health centres. A well-functioning health system should be able to discourage this.

c. Tertiary level

Health workers: specialist doctors, surgeons, obstetricians, registrars, anaesthetists; nurses, midwives, teaching staff; administrators, orderlies.

Tertiary level health facilities: large hospitals with several wards (possibly up to 500 beds), operating theatres, laboratories, lecture theatre; nutrition centre, rehabilitation centre, and other special facilities.

Services provided: referral from district level; teaching hospitals; clinical equipment and staff to treat particular conditions; emergency and casualty departments, and out-patient clinics. Their emergency or casualty departments may also be used as a primary health centre by people living close by. Again, this should be discouraged.

2.3 NGO roles in secondary health care

Secondary or 'district' level care, which in most countries corresponds to a population of 100,000 to 250,000, is crucial to the support and implementation of PHC. The district health team is the link between the local and the national level, and is responsible for the management and support of the primary level. The lack of support at secondary level has often limited the successful implementation of PHC.

If PHC relies on district-level support, a strong district team is necessary and the national level has to decentralise many of its functions, including budgets, to the district level. Often, this fails to happen, or weak district health teams are created, with insufficient power or resources to make PHC effective.

2.3.1 District health teams

These are often made up of representatives from political parties relevant central government ministries, and the health professions, with local leaders, traditional healers, and others. The balance of power between different interests within the teams influences the way they make decisions and implement programmes.

The district health 'executive' team usually consists of the professionals in the district, such as the district medical officer, pharmacist, nursing officer, and administrator. It is responsible for the running of the service, and its tasks usually include:

- planning, monitoring and evaluating health programmes and promoting community involvement in health;
- day-to-day administration and management of all health programmes in the district, as well as resource allocation;
- training, supervision and support of all cadres of health workers;
- ensuring adequate provision of health services at primary and secondary level.

2.3.2 Minimum activities package (MAP)

This is a set of activities which the district teams should establish to facilitate planning on the basis of resources allocated by central government. Costs are minimised by adapting activities to the available technology. These activities should respond to local demands and needs.

The district provides:

- An organisational structure to facilitate communication between the

5

basic health services, their users, and CHWs including TBAs; and to promote inter-sectoral planning, local community involvement, and collaboration between government and non-government (private or informal) health services.

- Technical support for all the health workers' tasks and activities, such as patient care, environmental health, immunisation, and health education. This support should be co-ordinated at the district level.
- Personnel management including training, supervision, pay and working conditions for all health workers, including community health workers. While training and staff development is usually retained as a central Ministry of Health function, most in-service training should be a district function; external support for training may be needed in specific areas, for example in relation to HIV/AIDS or reproductive health.
- Administrative and logistic procedures, including monitoring and health information services, and ensuring supplies of drugs and equipment are regular and reliable.

2.4 Infrastructure and equipment

A health-care system which goes beyond locally prepared remedies needs an infrastructure of buildings, equipment, consumables, and transport. Much of the equipment and consumables used in health care are imported, especially in smaller developing countries. While NGOs cannot be responsible for major elements of infrastructure expenditure, a relatively modest contribution may mean that a whole health centre or hospital department serving thousands of people is able to function properly. Requests for such items should not be rejected by Oxfam because they are 'not primary health care'.

In considering the purchase or installation of infrastructural items, it is essential that maintenance and security are available and that the items can be used by existing staff; or that training in the use of equipment will be part of the programme.

a. Buildings
Oxfam would rarely consider funding the building of an entire hospital; but has often assisted at the health centre level, and in reconstruction, repair or additions to existing hospitals. The new or repaired facilities should extend health work in a priority area, for example, women's health or maternity services.

b. Diagnostic and investigative equipment

Clinics: even small health centres require simple diagnostic equipment, such as thermometers, adult and foetal stethoscopes, sphygmo-manometer for blood pressure measurement, and otoscopes for examining ears. Other essential low-cost items for diagnosis should be considered if these will improve the quality of diagnosis and treatment. Staff must be trained to use equipment correctly.

Laboratories: in many areas, no laboratory facilities are available at the primary level, yet simple tests are an important element in diagnosis and appropriate treatment. Correct diagnosis can reduce costs (to the patient and the system) of drugs and treatment. The tests required depend on local conditions and common infections, and only a small number of stool, urine, and blood tests are usually appropriate. Equipment would include microscopes, haemoglobinometers, centrifuges, dishes, and glassware. Laboratories at the district hospital level may require facilities for bacterial culture and matching blood. Specialist advice should be sought in funding of laboratory facilities.

X-rays and ultrasound scans: X-rays and ultrasound scans are important for general hospital use, and diagnosis of a wide range of conditions. Unfortunately, hospitals in developing countries are littered with machines which are broken or not in use because there is no-one to maintain them or because film is unavailable, or the electricity supply is unreliable. In assessing a request for X-ray or ultrasound equipment, it is important to ensure that there are staff who can use the equipment, and staff who can interpret X-rays and scans; and that maintenance and supplies of consumables will be available.

The use of X-ray machines for mass radiography in the diagnosis of TB is questionable, since microscopic examination of sputum is much cheaper and more reliable.

Sterilising and surgical equipment: asepsis and sterility is often a neglected area in clinical practice, and this has become more hazardous since the emergence of HIV/AIDS. Reliable equipment, ranging from stainless steel dishes to autoclaves, is essential for the process, and staff must be trained and motivated to use them. UNICEF produces a steam steriliser for syringes and needles that is useful at the primary level. Requests for more advanced equipment should be referred to a medical specialist.

Consumables: much medical equipment is useless without a regular supply of consumables. These may be impossible to supply on a tight health budget in a poor country lacking foreign exchange. Often there is no local substitute. Laboratories cannot function without stains, acids or alcohol; needs should be planned for when equipment is purchased. Patients sometimes have to scour the shops for their own wound suturing and dressing materials.

5

639

Transport: transport is needed for supplies, for health workers, for patients, and for supervision and support of health workers. Transport problems may have to do as much with terrain and road conditions as with vehicles. It is sometimes most efficient to choose local forms of transport — for example, donkeys or bicycles — which seldom break down, can be locally replaced, and are less costly to maintain. Provision of bus fares where public transport is available may be another solution.

Ambulances are seldom appropriate in NGO level health work, and a multi-purpose vehicle may be much more useful. (See **3**.2.7 Vehicles.)

2.5 Vertical programmes

Vertical programmes are initiatives which involve a specialised rather than a generalised health intervention. In the past, vertical programmes were much favoured. The best known was probably the malaria eradication programme under the overall supervision of WHO in the 1950s and 1960s. In each country, a specialised department with specialised teams worked down to the village level. A similar programme was the smallpox eradication programme, which came to a successful conclusion in 1979.

Vertical programmes by their nature lead to inefficiency and wastage, and are difficult to sustain without external funding. In most cases, the concept of eradication has been replaced by the more realistic goal of control. However, even this is difficult to achieve, as for example, in the case of malaria, which continues to resist the considerable efforts to control it.

More recent WHO programmes, such as the Expanded Programme for Immunisation (EPI), Control of Diarrhoeal Diseases (CDD), and Acute Respiratory Infections (ARI), also rely on specialist centres providing training material, research, and expertise, but attempt to integrate all these activities at the primary care level. However, because PHC so often consists mainly of international agency support for specific programmes, the false impression sometimes arises that PHC itself consists of a series of separate 'vertical' interventions.

2.6 Traditional, alternative, and informal health care

2.6.1 Introduction

WHO estimates that 80 per cent of the world's population rely entirely on traditional, alternative or 'informal' health care, either from choice or because there are no formal health facilities available to them. Formal, or 'modern' medicine may be the last of many treatments sought by sick people. For example, in Nepal, government and NGO health posts are under-used because people prefer indigenous *dhamis* and *jhankris*.

Oxfam uses the term 'traditional' mainly to describe the methods and remedies used by millions of people outside the formal health-care system, and as alternatives to modern drugs. However, the term does not cover all cases, because some alternative treatments may be new, or newly adopted in certain cases — for example, acupuncture is traditional Chinese medicine, but is a new alternative or complementary treatment in the West.

The term 'popular medicine' covers the vast array of remedies and treatments which are passed down from one generation to another, sometimes particular to a district, a village or a family. Its practices are not written down, as it is generally part of an oral tradition, both in urban and rural areas. Popular medicine also describes an approach to medicine which is closer to people and their traditions, which respects them, and their knowledge and skills. It is a form of treatment over which people have control; they can make the remedies themselves, often in the home, prescribe them, and treat themselves. Ideally, PHC and popular medicine would be integrated, and traditional and modern systems work co-operatively together.

A rational integration of modern and traditional systems has accompanied the official revival of traditional medicine in some countries. Chinese and Western medicine are now available together at different levels of health care in China and in Vietnam, for example. In Zimbabwe, TBAs are invited to bring their clients into government maternity clinics.

The Alma Ata Declaration expressed support for traditional medicines, and the WHO Traditional Medicine Programme helps to co-ordinate research and encourages governments to support traditional systems. For WHO and other agencies, an attraction of this was the vast labour reservoir of traditional healers who could become primary health workers with only a little informal training. Many MCH programmes have trained TBAs in hygienic birthing practices and the identification and referral of pregnant women who are at risk. In Zimbabwe, male traditional healers are being trained to refer people with HIV/AIDS and to distribute condoms. In Ghana, Uganda, and Malawi, there is cross-referral between traditional healers and hospitals in mental health work, and in care of people with HIV/AIDS.

The subject is vast and complex, and this section can only provide a general overview, focusing on the relationship of these systems to PHC, and outlining some of the factors to take into account when assessing proposals for this kind of health care.

5

641

2.6.2 Forms of traditional health care

There is an enormous variety of methods of health care and belief systems about illness. They can be divided into four broad categories:

- **Formal traditions**: such as Ayurved, Siddha, Unani, homeopathy, and acupuncture, which usually have written systems, and systematic training for professional practitioners.
- **Folk medicine and healing**: home cures or cures performed by traditional healers. People may become healers through inheritance, apprenticeship or religious experience. Some healers may specialise in, for example, midwifery, bone-setting, herbal medicine or healing through spirit possession.
- **Eclectic market medicine:** traders sell a range of substances from tetracycline capsules and bottles of tonics to amulets and herbs. These may be helpful, or harmless, or dangerous — particularly if the modern drugs sold are out of date, inappropriate, and sold in single but unmeasured doses, without guidance on their use.
- **Internationalised treatments and healing**: also known as complementary medicine, such as homeopathy, acupuncture, shiatsu, herbalism, and any form of therapy which becomes professionalised internationally.

2.6.3 NGO roles in traditional health care

NGOs have a certain freedom to explore methods of health care which do not neatly fit into the schemes of government services or the programmes of the multilateral agencies, which are increasingly pre-packaged and uniform. Oxfam, for example, has supported a wide range of different initiatives in Asia, Latin America and the Caribbean, and Africa, working on the development of herbal medicines, and with traditional practitioners. (See 2.2 Ethnicity, race, and culture.)

The following considerations are important for *any* health programme:

a. Collaboration
Many health programmes take little note of the cultural and social context in which they operate. Health workers, even at grass-roots level, are often better educated than the rest of the community, and not uncommonly they strive to establish their scientific credentials by criticising local traditions and beliefs relating to health and illness. Health workers should be familiar with and respect common local practices and remedies, and have a sympathetic understanding of beliefs surrounding health. Health workers should work with local

practitioners, and try to set up systems for mutual referral; this could be done informally, or through workshops and seminars, as has been the case with PHC programmes in Nepal, and Zimbabwe.

Health education should try to neutralise harmful practices, and build on and encourage beneficial ones. Practices to be discouraged would include the use of dubious alternative remedies for serious illnesses, such as TB, leprosy, and acute respiratory infection, for which proven treatment exists in orthodox medicine.

b. Assessing traditional and alternative practices

Many of the lesser-known traditional practices have not been studied or evaluated, and it is not always easy to assess their usefulness. Some forms of medicine, such as homeopathy or spirit healing, which are based on different belief systems from the positivist, scientific approach of Western medicine, cannot easily be evaluated against Western scientific criteria. They are often discounted for this reason, although people find them helpful and healing.

Problems arise when medicines are used outside the social and cultural context in which they were originally developed, resulting in their inappropriate use. This occurs in the case of both traditional and modern medicine: in poor countries it is common for local healers or pharmacists to offer injections of antibiotics, vitamin concoctions, and 'cocktails' of drugs for abortion, because people have come to believe that injections *per se* are the most powerful form of treatment.

The efficacy of traditional treatment has been questioned for the major, life-threatening diseases, although its supporters maintain that diseases such as cancer or cholera are responsive to such treatments, which sometimes succeed where modern scientific medicine fails. The medical profession argues that support for alternative medicine may divert energy and resources from what has been scientifically proven to be beneficial.

Diseases which kill large numbers of poor people, such as diarrhoea, pneumonia, measles, malaria, and tuberculosis, have proven Western preventive or curative measures, which are more easily delivered by government systems on a large scale, in combined strategies of public health improvements and the use of medicines. The efficacy of traditional therapy for these illnesses is not proven, and practitioners generally work on an individual level and are unable to deliver treatments for large numbers of people. Some traditional practices may be harmful, such as cutting and bleeding, or the avoidance of food linked to particular conditions, for example, for women after childbirth.

Oxfam has supported the dissemination of established home remedies for simple complaints, such as oral rehydration for diarrhoea or papaya fruit on wounds. Alternative therapies have been used with

5

some success in the treatment of drug addicts (acupuncture in Nepal and faith healers in Indonesia). Traditional healers are particularly useful for mental and emotional problems and often have greater success than Western mental-health workers, as they are better able to understand the culture and psychological make-up of their own people.

Traditional medicines, like modern drugs, should fulfil the agreed criteria for a medicine to qualify as essential: necessity, safety, and efficacy.

c. Practical support

Training: training should be promoted both for traditional practitioners and formal health workers, to increase mutual understanding, and broaden knowledge and skills. Health workers have been trained to incorporate aspects of traditional or alternative medicine into their work in a number of Oxfam-funded projects: for example, in Indonesia and the Philippines acupuncture and acupressure are part of health service training; TBAs have been trained in modern skills in Yemen, India, and Nicaragua; in Nepal, seminars for traditional practitioners encourage them to refer patients with TB symptoms to government health posts.

Research: pharmacological and biochemical research into traditional plant remedies is properly the domain of scientific establishments. However, action-oriented research into local health practices and beliefs may feed into health programmes and help with planning more appropriate interventions. Useful areas of research would be the links between the different systems and support mechanisms; and how and why individuals and families make decisions about using the different available forms of health care.

Co-operation: collaboration between traditional healers, TBAs, and others should be promoted. Funding of alternative health projects should be part of a broad-based health programme. Support for traditional health care should be based on the principles of PHC — including equity and participation.

2.6.4 Key questions

1 How will collaboration with the formal health sector be promoted?
2 How will accountability be ensured?
3 Is the project compatible with PHC principles?
4 What can the formal health sector learn from local traditional health customs?
5 What local practices are beneficial, harmless or harmful?

2.7 Urban health

(For fuller discussion of urbanisation, see **1.3.5.2** Urban livelihoods.)

2.7.1 Health and urbanisation

The last 40 years have seen the rapid expansion of the urban populations of poor countries, due both to natural increase of existing populations and to rural-urban migration. This has been particularly marked in Africa, where in cities like Lagos, Nairobi, and Khartoum, populations increased more than sixfold between 1950 and 1990. Latin America already has 11 cities with more than 3 million inhabitants; and Mexico City, the largest, has a population of over 20 million. In all but five countries in the region, more people now live in towns and cities than in the countryside. This expansion is projected to continue. Two-thirds of the population of developing countries currently live in rural areas; in another 40 years, this proportion is likely to be reversed, and two-thirds of the population of developing countries will live in urban areas.

Oxfam has tended to place greater emphasis on health provision in rural than in urban areas, on the grounds that the government health service is likely to have greater presence in towns and cities. However, as the cities of developing countries grow, it is increasingly obvious that, despite the existence of advanced health services in urban areas, poor people who live in the slums and peri-urban areas receive inadequate health care. While the provision for casualties and maternity emergencies may be adequate, neither private or state health systems seem willing or able to tackle the primary health problems of poor people.

Malnutrition is more prevalent in urban than in rural areas, and more severely malnourished children are to be found in cities and towns than in the countryside. Child mortality has been found to be higher in some urban areas, as is the incidence of certain diseases such as TB and parasitic infestation. Because the health differentials between rich and poor in cities tend to be greater than in rural areas, statistical averages can disguise the severity of the situation of the poorest people.

PHC has tended to be seen as a rurally-based strategy, but it is equally relevant to urban areas, and its central principles of equity, participation, appropriate health measures to the particular situation, and a preventive approach, should apply to urban health strategies.

Poverty may be experienced differently in rural and urban areas, and some of the particular problems may be peculiar to the city or to the countryside. However, many people would not classify themselves as either urban or rural, since they migrate between the two. Sometimes they are urban shanty-town dwellers, at other times they may be

5

landless labourers or share-cropping farmers: if they are poor and powerless, their health problems are those associated with lack of food, contaminated water, long hours of work and physical stress, the emotional and mental burden of struggling to make a living, and inadequate provision of health care.

2.7.2 Facilities in urban areas

There are various factors facilitating urban health provision, in comparison with rural areas. Doctors generally prefer to work in towns rather than in the countryside; and the vast majority of highly trained medical personnel in poor countries live and work in capital cities. This is partly because the capital is professionally a more rewarding place to work, with opportunities for promotion, further training, and contact with other health professionals and policy makers. Cities also offer a higher standard of living, more social facilities, and better opportunities for private practice. The lack of facilities and supplies is less acute in urban than in rural areas; there are usually more hospital beds, and drugs and vaccines are more widely available.

Communications and transport are less of a constraint in towns and cities than in rural areas. It is easier to establish a reliable and efficient cold chain in the urban environment, for example. If necessary, supplies of vaccine may be distributed daily from a central store to health posts, and the wastage rate of vaccines will be much lower than in the remoter rural areas

In spite of these advantages, the living conditions of millions of poor urban people threaten their health: overcrowding, inadequate housing, and lack of essential services such as drainage, sewage, and rubbish collection. Other problems include traffic congestion, air-pollution from traffic and factories, and water pollution through the unregulated discharge of waste from factories within residential areas, and the use of dangerous locations for housing such as areas prone to landslides or floods. There is greater exposure to crime, alcohol and drug abuse, stress and psycho-social illnesses.

2.7.3 Urban health problems

Crowding: In inner-city and shanty-town areas, over-crowding leads to an increase in the incidence of communicable diseases. Where it is combined with poor water supplies and inadequate sewage disposal, mosquito-borne diseases like malaria, dengue, elephantiasis, and certain haemorrhagic fevers may become more prevalent. The provision of clean water and the safe disposal of sewage should be a priority for NGOs, as well as low-cost housing schemes in certain circumstances.

646

Sewage disposal is usually beyond the scope of NGOs in urban areas, both for reasons of cost and because of the necessary involvement of a range of government ministries. However, following the hurricane which devastated the Atlantic Coast region of Nicaragua in 1987, Oxfam was involved in establishing a new municipal water system in Bluefields.

Working conditions: poor adults and children are more likely to be dependent on cash earnings in the city than in the countryside. In cities, they tend to work in conditions which are both inhumane and dangerous, whether in the formal or the informal sector. There are numerous health hazards arising from poor working conditions: chemical pollution, noise, and dangerous machinery.

Malnutrition: it is often claimed that food prices in Third World cities are maintained at an artificially low level by politicians fearful of discontent among urban populations, and thus that malnutrition is not a serious problem in urban areas. However, the more people depend on purchased foods, the more vulnerable they are to increases in food prices and shortages in supply. At times of stress, during periods of high inflation, or when harvests fail, poor urban people who depend exclusively on the cash economy are extremely vulnerable.

Homelessness and street life: extended family networks tend to break down in towns, especially among migrants, some of whom may have been displaced by war and armed conflict. The wider group of kin may lose contact with individual members, and group responsibility for weaker members is eroded. It is possible for individual households to suffer extreme hardship in a neighbourhood which is generally affluent. This, as well as other pressures, may lead to children or adults losing or leaving their homes to live on the streets.

Street dwellers and homeless people have special health needs. They are often isolated, and are usually poor, vulnerable, and marginalised, making a living from informal work, begging, sex work, scavenging, and theft. The situation of street dwellers makes it difficult to set up health programmes for them, because they are usually widely dispersed geographically and socially. They may also be very mobile — working and sleeping in different parts of the city from one week to the next. Conventional community-based health interventions are not likely to reach them. However, Oxfam has supported innovative work which aims to improve the health of such people, for example, a sex and health education programme for street girls in Recife, Brazil.

Alcohol and drug abuse: while alcoholism is prevalent in both rural and urban areas, alcohol and drug abuse, particularly by young people and children, may be more common in towns and cities, and associated with violence and injuries. Excessive alcohol consumption contributes to illnesses such as liver cirrhosis and is closely linked with road accidents, violence and rape, and in some cases with malnutrition and social

5

problems. Excessive alcohol intake during pregnancy may cause birth defects, including mental retardation.

Abuse of substances such as glue and intravenous drugs is also common in urban centres. The sharing of needles by intravenous drug users can spread diseases carried in the blood, including HIV. Substance abuse is a complex social and health issue, and the long-term impact of many interventions is uncertain. NGOs may support local organisations involved in campaigning on issues such as tobacco, alcohol or rehabilitation of drug users. Oxfam has funded programmes of rehabilitation for glue-sniffers in the slums of Chile, for intravenous drug users in Pakistan, and for education among young drug abusers in the Caribbean.

Accidents: with rapid urbanisation and fast-changing lifestyles, accidents are a growing problem in developing countries, and have led to a greater need for casualty facilities. The number of accidents is influenced by environmental, social, cultural, and other factors. Burns, falls, and poisoning with household items like kerosene and medicines are among the commonest. Road traffic accidents are assuming more prominence as the number of vehicles rises, and road networks increase.

The Assiut Burns programme in Egypt, supported by Oxfam, has an integrated approach to accident prevention and management. The programme provides care for burns to poor people (mostly children burnt by kerosene cooking stoves), and training for local health workers in the management and prevention of burns. Work is also done with families and communities in burns prevention, using street theatre, with semi-professional actors and musicians.

2.7.4 The role of NGOs in urban health

There is still a great deal to be understood about health provision in the urban environment, and a need to develop a coherent methodology for dealing with the health problems of poor urban households and communities. Health cannot be considered in isolation from the acute socio-economic problems facing people in towns and cities.

While in many rural areas the absence of services forced NGOs, volunteers, and community groups to create their own health infrastructure, there have been very few initiatives of this sort in urban areas, although NGO activity is increasing. Most city-dwellers go to the commercial pharmacist for advice and attention, visiting the hospital in an emergency. This inevitably means that an individualist, curative, rather than a collective, preventive, approach to health tends to prevail.

However, there are numerous examples of poor people organising and mobilising in connection with health issues. In many urban communities, NGOs work with poor people for the provision of clean water and safe sewage disposal, often by lobbying the local authorities. Oxfam supported a health project in a *favela* (shanty-town) in Brazil, providing basic health care and working with community organisations. After ten years the streets are paved, and water is available for each household. Sewage disposal remains a problem, and there is still a risk of landslides in some parts of the *favela*, but people are organised to press for better conditions.

Health often provides a good entry point to work in poor neighbourhoods, and mobilising community action. Some projects have grown from providing services to autonomous community-based movements, demanding from the local and central governments services such as water, lighting, sewage, and health care. Women, a high proportion of whom are heads-of-household in urban areas, often play an active role as members of neighbourhood committees in lobbying for better services, or working to improve health conditions themselves. For example, during the cholera outbreak in Peru, the community health workers were mostly women. They kept the epidemic under control, through their active involvement in health education, community mobilisation, and oral rehydration therapy, and there were few deaths. (See **1.3.5.2** Urban livelihoods.)

NGO roles in urban health could include:

- facilitating the development of local structures such as neighbourhood committees, women's groups, and workers' groups to form the basis of health programmes;
- documenting and raising awareness about specific health, social or environmental issues;
- strengthening the environmental health services, such as water supply, sanitation, waste management, and pollution control; and supporting groups lobbying for improvements;
- campaigning for investment in housing, sanitation, and clean water supply, to alleviate the problems of poor urban people.

5

3 Focusing on people: health needs of specific population groups

3.1 Introduction 650
3.2 Women's health 651
    3.2.1 Women in society 651
    3.2.2 The roles and health needs of women 652
    3.2.3 Maternal mortality and morbidity 653
    3.2.4 Women's reproductive health: MCH programmes 654
    3.2.5 Women's work-related health problems 659
    3.2.6 Women as carers and health workers 660
    3.2.7 Sexuality and sex education 661
    3.2.8 Sexually transmitted diseases (STDs) 661
    3.2.9 Cultural aspects of women's health 662
    3.2.10 Key questions 666
3.3 Child health 667
    3.3.1 Introduction 667
    3.3.2 Pre-conception care 668
    3.3.3 Antenatal care 669
    3.3.4 Perinatal care 669
    3.3.5 Under-fives 670
    3.3.6 'CHILD- to-child' 670
    3.3.7 Schools 671
    3.3.8 Key questions 671
3.4 Elderly people 672
    3.4.1 Introduction 672
    3.4.2 Age-related health issues 673
    3.4.3 Key questions 674
3.5 Disabled people 674
    3.5.1 Introduction 674
    3.5.2 Common causes of disability 675

3.1 Introduction

The health of all poor people suffers as a result of their lack of land and other resources, insecure employment and income, poor nutrition, the inadequate provision of water and sanitation, and bad housing conditions. However, their needs for health care are differentiated by gender, age, ethnicity, and other factors, such as disability. Health in relation to ethnicity and culture is addressed in **5**.2.6 Traditional, alternative, and informal health care. This section focuses on health care for women, children, the elderly and disabled people. It should be read in conjunction with **2** Focusing on people, which provides more detailed discussion of gender, childhood, ageing, and disability.

3.2 Women's health

This part of the section discusses women's health, and the needs which arise from their multiple roles in society, and different ways of addressing them. It concentrates on reproductive health, which is of special concern in countries where poverty, high parity (childbearing rate), and poor maternity and contraceptive services combine to make child bearing particularly hazardous. The low social and economic status of women adversely affects their health, through low levels of education, and overwork in arduous and poorly-paid jobs. There are also a number of harmful practices, both traditional and 'modern', which seriously affect women's health. The section looks briefly at the role of women as health workers, and the constraints they face in participating in health programmes. Birth planning, of major importance to women's health, but which also concerns, and must involve, men, is considered in **5**.4.6.

3.2.1 Women in society
(To be read in conjunction with **2**.1 Gender.)

Women's health is directly related to their position in society, their living conditions, and specific cultural beliefs and practices which vary widely around the world. According to the WHO, two of the most significant indicators of equity in any society are the disparities in health status between the sexes, and the actual health status of women. Levels of social justice and gender equality determine the health of women, from the moment they are born until they die. In some countries, they are in danger from the moment of conception: the life of the unborn girl child in India, for example, may be at risk simply because she is female, because of the high rate of abortion of female foetuses, following amniocentesis. The well-being of all children is affected by the health of their mother during pregnancy, and during their infancy and early life.

Gender-based discrimination against women the world over directly affects their health. In all countries, women have fewer opportunities than men for paid employment, and their incomes are lower; women work longer hours, yet have less food; women are the rearers and carers of children, yet receive less education; women are major food producers and processors, yet have less control over the use of land and natural resources.

The health care which women receive is restricted by a wide range of factors, from their lack of decision-making power over health resources, to their own lack of self-esteem, which leads them to undervalue their own health. A number of beliefs and cultural practices, or socially-sanctioned behaviour, in many parts of the world, are acutely damaging to women's health and well-being: examples are genital mutilation; food avoidance after childbirth; and the widespread occurrence of assaults on wives or partners, which are often condoned by society, although they may be officially illegal.

The internationally recognised rights to health and basic health care are often denied to women, simply on the grounds of their sex. Development and relief agencies working in the field of health should therefore always examine the social and cultural context of any programme, and address women's specific condition and needs within a context of promoting social justice, basic human rights, and fundamental freedoms.

3.2.2 The roles and health needs of women

Health programmes for women should take account of their multiple roles in production, in reproduction, as carers, as workers, and as social activists, as part of an overall strategy to improve women's health and status. Women are individuals, with a wide range of human skills and needs — they are not only mothers. A narrow focus on women's maternal role in the health sector has led not only to the neglect of other health and reproductive health problems, such as mental illness, work-related ill health, and sexually transmitted diseases, but also to a failure to build on women's existing experience, skills, and potential. Unless links are made between women's health, women's poverty, and women's powerlessness, health programmes will not address the roots of women's ill health. Working for women's empowerment is also a way of improving their health.

Most often, the only available services for women are Mother and Child Health (MCH) programmes, which may be very limited in scope. Since they are effective in reducing maternal morbidity and mortality, they will continue to be of great importance, and there is much that can be done to build on them. Women's health activists have been campaigning for many years for a more integrated view of women's health, and as a result the policies and programmes of some donor and international agencies now address reproductive health services and women's health, rather than focusing exclusively on MCH and 'family planning' services.

Oxfam has funded MCH care for many years, usually as part of a PHC programme, and at times as an outreach service from clinics or hospitals. Programmes should provide comprehensive reproductive health services, including birth planning, in a way that is sensitive to women's concerns. Oxfam also funds a range of women's organisations, many of which work on health outside the formal health system. They may provide health education, and services such as information on contraception, sex education, and counselling for victims of domestic violence. Their 'woman-centred approach' means that they respond to women's needs, and provide services that treat them with respect. Women's organisations may promote women's empowerment and collective action, through encouraging questioning by women of their own ill health, offering them the support of other women in action to improve their situations.

3.2.3 Maternal mortality and morbidity

For most women in poor countries, pregnancy, childbirth, and the period after delivery carry a high risk of death or illness. The maternal mortality ratio (the number of maternal deaths in relation to the number of live births) is extremely high in poor countries; it is the public health indicator which shows the greatest disparity between rich and poor countries.

According to a UN report, the 1980s saw big increases in maternal and infant mortality in some developing countries. Of the half a million women who die every year of causes related to pregnancy and childbirth, 99 per cent of them are in developing countries. Maternal mortality ratios are highest in Africa and South Asia, with an average of 640 and 566 maternal deaths per 100,000 live births respectively. In Latin America and the Caribbean the average is 270 per 100,000. This contrasts with an average of 10 per 100,000 in developed countries. For an individual woman, the risk of dying is affected by many factors, including her nutrition and health status, the number and spacing of her children, and the quality of health care available to her. The individual lifetime risk of maternal death is 1 in 20 in West Africa, but only 1 in 10,000 in northern Europe.

The most common causes of maternal deaths are obstetric haemorrhage, hypertensive disorders of pregnancy, infection, obstructed labour, and abortion. In many countries abortion is performed illegally in unhygienic conditions; in Latin America it is responsible for about half of all maternal deaths. For every woman who

5

dies as a result of an abortion, many more suffer permanent damage to their health and subsequent fertility. This underlines the well-documented, unmet need for contraception, and the inadequacy of contraceptive services, which are often inaccessible because of distance, cost, or lack of information, or are inappropriate. Contraceptive methods also fail. The provision of legal abortions carried out by skilled personnel in a hygienic clinic would save many women's lives. In countries where abortion is legal, such as Zambia and India, it is still not easily available or always safe.

Maternal death also has important implications for children; higher levels of infant and child mortality have been documented for motherless children. Illness also places an enormous strain on women caring for children, who are likely to suffer as a result of their mother's ill health. Many women suffer non-fatal complications of pregnancy, including severe anaemia, and obstetric infection. A significant proportion of women with infection develop serious illness, such as pelvic inflammatory disease, and are very likely to suffer infertility and ectopic pregnancy. Others develop fistulae, genital prolapse, and stress incontinence.

3.2.4 Women's reproductive health: MCH programmes

Women's reproductive health is most often addressed through MCH programmes, and these may provide the most appropriate 'entry point' for working for improvements in women's health.

However, reproductive health is not just health in pregnancy and childbirth, but also requires the ability to control fertility and to have sexual relationships free of fear of disease or unwanted pregnancy. Reproductive health programmes are usually wide ranging, and include the provision of sex education, information about the prevention and treatment of sexually transmitted diseases, and contraceptive services, as well as services for pregnancy, delivery, and postnatal care. (See **5.4** Health care provision.)

MCH, including 'family planning', is one of the components of PHC, addressing maternal as well as infant and child mortality and morbidity. The two are linked because the health of the newborn baby is affected by the health of the mother, and her care, during and after the birth, and women bear most of the responsibility for child care. Women in the reproductive age group (15–44 years) make up almost 20 per cent of the population, while in developing countries children under 15 comprise almost 50 per cent; in theory, programmes for women and children should reach almost 70 per cent of the population.

MCH programmes aim to reduce maternal, infant, and child mortality and emphasise prevention and education. They should provide care for both mother and child, but in practice, most MCH programmes concentrate on child survival. In an attempt to rectify this, and in response to the appalling rise in maternal mortality referred to earlier, in 1987 UNICEF and WHO launched the 'Safe Motherhood Initiative' or, 'putting the M back into MCH'. However, in spite of the growing concern over maternal health, many MCH programmes continue to focus only, or primarily, on antenatal care and clinics for children under five. In this section we discuss the aspects of MCH related to women's health: the aspects related to children are discussed in **5**.3.3 Child health.

The main maternal components of MCH programmes are antenatal care, delivery, postnatal care, birth planning, and training for TBAs.

a. Antenatal care (ANC)

The purpose of ANC is to monitor problems during the pregnancy, such as anaemia and high blood pressure, to provide tetanus immunisation and in some cases iron supplementation, and to identify high-risk pregnancies so that they can be referred to the appropriate facility. Ideally the person providing ANC also handles the delivery, but it is not uncommon for women to attend antenatal clinics and then to deliver at home. Alternatively, their first contact with maternity services may be at the birth. Since many women may attend an antenatal clinic only once, it is important to maximise the use of this contact.

The content of the ANC package may vary depending on the local prevalence of diseases, but among the most effective interventions are:

- tetanus immunisation, which helps to decrease neonatal tetanus significantly although it has no direct impact on maternal health;
- iron supplementation to prevent or treat anaemia, particularly in areas where malaria is common and where women are likely to be malnourished;
- screening for high blood pressure;
- treatment of sexually transmitted diseases and urinary tract infections.

ANC is often free, but some programmes have introduced charging schemes. For example, a pregnant woman may be expected to pay a lump sum entitling her to both ANC and maternity care. Sometimes a higher fee is demanded for delivery without ANC than for delivery after ANC, supposedly to encourage ANC attendance. Throughout the process of child bearing, from antenatal to postnatal stage, different cultural approaches and beliefs should be understood and respected — unless these are harmful to the health of the mother and baby. NGOs should be sensitive in their interventions, and should ensure that the programmes they support have been set up in consultation with women in the area.

5

655

b. Delivery

The most important features of delivery care are skilled and hygienic attendance at the birth, and facilities for the treatment or referral of emergencies. The main causes of death are haemorrhage, infection (sepsis), and toxaemia or 'pregnancy-induced hypertension' (women suffer from high-blood pressure, protein in the urine and convulsions, which can be detected early with adequate ANC). Genital mutilation increases the risks of complications (see 5.3.2.9.c Female genital mutilation.) Western modes of delivery should not be imposed on women who expect to give birth in traditional ways, for example, in semi-upright positions, or with the use of birthing stools.

Training of midwives, TBAs, and any others attending births in basic hygiene, while not solving all the problems, can reduce the incidence of infections in women and newborn babies. Simple birth kits for safe delivery, which can be prepared locally, contain soap, plastic sheeting or a clean woven mat, string or cotton tapes for tying the umbilical cord, clean razor blades, and two pieces of clean cloth (one for the baby and one for the mother).

Reliable transport is essential for emergencies. Many women die on their way to the health services and others die waiting for transport, either at home or at the roadside. Women who have experienced intimidation or poor services may be reluctant to use them again. When hospitals are only used for at-risk or emergency births, the rate of caesarian sections is higher. This may lead women to fear admission. Education, information, and a good relationship between health workers and women users of health services can alleviate this.

c. Postnatal care

This is care in the first six weeks after childbirth and is often neglected. Treatment and referral of complications is important. For example, post-partum haemorrhage needs to be detected early to avoid death. Women may also need advice and support about breastfeeding (see 5.4.2.5.b Encouragement of breast-feeding and good weaning practices), and childcare.

There are other long-term consequences of complications at delivery; the commonest are obstetric fistulae, pelvic inflammatory disease, and anaemia (see 5.4.2.4.b Specific mineral and vitamin deficiencies). Obstetric fistulae occur due to prolonged or obstructed labour, when an abnormal passage (fistula) erodes between bladder and vagina, sometimes even involving the rectum. They are very common where maternity services are poor or referral difficult, particularly among women who were malnourished in childhood, and in young girls who have not yet fully developed. Genital mutilation is usually associated with this complication. The resulting incontinence is a stigma, women may be rejected by their husbands and get little support from their families when they seek treatment. Gynaecological surgery is the only treatment and the funding of such surgical programmes can make an enormous difference to these women's lives.

d. Birth planning
Birth planning is a major component in women's health and development. Having too many children, too young, too often, or too old is the chief cause of women's illness and premature death. Enabling women to decide the number of children they want and when to have them, increases their own and their existing children's health. Birth-planning services should offer a wide choice of methods, provide information, encourage male responsibility and co-operation, treat women with respect, and, most importantly, raise women's status and promote their participation in programme design. (See 5.4.6 Birth planning.)

e. Training for TBAs and health workers
In many countries TBAs attend most deliveries, particularly in rural areas, and are likely to continue to do so. In other countries deliveries are normally attended by female relatives, and a different approach to supporting them may be needed.

In India, Oxfam funded a TBA training programme based on a thorough review and understanding of TBAs' practices and beliefs, and a clear identification of the health needs of women in the area. As with any community health workers, supervision, support, and referral centres will need to be provided for TBAs once they are trained. Careful selection of trainees is critical; and training itself may need to be adapted if TBAs are non-literate. In order to decrease maternal mortality, TBA training programmes must be backed by appropriate referral facilities and supervision by more skilled personnel. The training content should be culturally appropriate and based on what is locally feasible.

The roles and functions of TBAs vary greatly from one society to another. They may have a powerful role as community leaders, as well as providers of health care; or their standing may be low because their work is considered 'polluting'. TBAs may carry out genital mutilation, and one of their main functions may be to perform abortions, often by dangerous methods. These factors may affect their work even after they are trained, and need to be taken into account by planners and trainers. Sometimes young women may prefer to obtain maternity care from better educated women. Many programmes select inexperienced young women for training, who do not have the confidence of local women.

Nevertheless, wherever appropriate, PHC programmes should

consider TBAs when selecting community health workers, rather than train new cadres who may lack a TBA's experience and standing in the community.

f. Health education
In MCH programmes this usually includes information on nutrition, childbirth and childcare, and birth planning. In relation to child health it may include cooking demonstrations, information about the value of locally available foods, early detection of acute respiratory infection or malaria, and how to prepare oral rehydration solution. Often, however, health education messages are either inappropriate or accuse women of 'ignorance' or 'neglect', and undermine women's position, disempowering them and reducing their ability to learn. It is important to recognise the social and economic constraints that most women face and to support their efforts to deal with ill health. (See 5.4.11 Health education.)

In relation to maternal health, more training is needed to enable women themselves and the family or household members to recognise signs of ill health and dangerous conditions.

g. General issues related to MCH services
Practical issues that affect the use of services should be considered in programme design. It is especially difficult for pregnant women with small children to walk long distances. Services should be accessible by public transport, or as close to the village or community as possible. It is not uncommon in rural areas that services are not only distant, but that some centres provide different services at different times, so that a woman may walk 5–10km for her child's immunisation and then be told to come back another day for her antenatal visit. The result is that women may use the outpatient services when they need them, but not attend the preventive MCH services. Family difficulties or cultural factors, such as the staffing of health centres with only male health workers, may also affect women's uptake of services. Women's general lack of self-esteem, and low social status, mean that they do not give priority to their own health, and need for health care. They are unlikely to allocate scarce resources to pay for health care for themselves.

Women should always be encouraged to value their own health, and women's poverty should always be taken into account when fees are introduced for basic health care. It is also crucial that women should be consulted about their views of the practical aspects of the service: availability, quality of care, opening and closing times; and that these are considered when planning services.

Components of MCH programmes, such as immunisation, are sometimes introduced as vertical programmes, with their own resources and distribution systems. Efforts must be made to integrate MCH services into an overall PHC programme, so that the different aspects of it can be planned and implemented in a more efficient way.

3.2.5 Women's work-related health problems

Women play a crucial role in production at the household, community, and national level. In both rural and urban areas, their work contributes significantly to the survival of households as well as to national health. The number of women-maintained households, in which women are the main providers, is increasing. Whether they are engaged in formal employment or work in the informal sector, the health hazards related to women's and men's work have been inadequately explored and as a result are rarely addressed.

Women's domestic work is often extremely arduous, and includes feeding and caring for all household members, especially children, the sick, and the elderly; productive work in small plots, and care of small domestic animals (chickens, pigs, rabbits); preparing and cooking food; collecting water and firewood (in rural areas); cleaning and mending clothes; and cleaning and maintaining the dwelling. On average, women work longer hours than men even when they do not work to earn income, or work in the fields. Apart from the excessive working hours, carrying heavy loads like firewood or water frequently results in chronic back pain, particularly when women are suffering from malnutrition. Heavy physical work, combined with many and frequent pregnancies, can also increase malnutrition, which in turn leads to low-birth-weight babies. Low birth-weight is associated with stunting which, for women, is itself likely to lead to difficulties in labour and increased reproductive health problems.

Smoke-filled kitchens without adequate ventilation are a common cause of respiratory and eye problems. For women in factories, occupational hazards include chemical poisoning, exposure to fumes, and disablement from accidents. Protection for workers in newly industrialising countries is often totally inadequate in practice, even if protective laws exist. Women are usually the lowest paid, most unprotected workers, the first to be laid off and therefore the most vulnerable to abuse and exploitation. Agro-industry is often particularly unhealthy, exposing workers to agricultural chemicals and pesticides without adequate protective clothing and equipment, and forcing them to work long hours for minimal wages. (See Environmental dangers of agro-chemicals in **3.3.2** Sustaining natural resources; and **4.5.1.2** NGO intervention and income-generation projects.)

Domestic workers, the vast majority of whom are women, work very long hours, in isolation from each other and vulnerable to exploitation

5

or sexual abuse by their employer. They frequently suffer from exhaustion, stress, and chronic back problems.

Many women are forced to sell sexual services to support themselves, their children or extended families. Women in the sex trade are exposed to violence from their clients or the police as well as being at particular risk from infection by clients with sexually transmitted diseases, including HIV/AIDS. Oxfam supports work with prostitutes in Brazil, where the rate of self-abuse and attempted suicide among the women and girls is high. The programme supports prostitutes in organising themselves, and demanding, among other things, health care and pension rights.

3.2.6 Women as carers and health workers

Women are universally the main care givers, both in the family looking after children, the elderly and their husbands, and as workers in the health services. The cuts in social services which so often accompany structural adjustment policies increase the burden on women, who are expected to fill the resulting gaps in services with their unpaid labour.

In the primary health services the majority of health workers are nurses, most of them women. They are the backbone of PHC, and play an important role in support and supervision for community-based workers. Where they are hospital-based and oriented towards curative medicine, appropriate training can motivate them to provide invaluable support to PHC programmes. For example, Oxfam funded a three-month training programme for nurses in Zaire which introduced them to the principles and practice of PHC. This led the nurses to put more emphasis on preventive activities and increase their involvement with the community.

Many NGO programmes rely on women's voluntary work. However, it is unrealistic to expect already overworked women to undertake more unpaid work. When payment is introduced, men often take over the jobs; and programmes planning to pay women for their work in community health should be alert to this tendency. Women may not be selected as CHWs for many reasons, including their perceived lower status, their problems of mobility and family responsibilities, and opposition from husbands, fathers, and men in general. Women's literacy levels are likely to be lower than men's, due to discrimination against them in education, and this is often cited as a reason for non-selection.

Programmes which aim to increase women's involvement in health care should recognise the constraints women face. These include their excessive workload and consequent lack of time, their need for childcare provision, their lack of confidence and leadership skills, their lack of literacy and numeracy, or, as in the case of certain ethnic groups, their inability to speak the official language. Many of these problems can be avoided if women's real needs are carefully identified, and programmes planned to address them. Funding may be required for creches or other childcare arrangements, for literacy and numeracy training, for lightening women's workload, for learning languages, and for work with groups and organisations which increase women's confidence and self-esteem. These programmes are most likely to be successful if they are undertaken in a group context.

3.2.7 Sexuality and sex education

There is a close link between women's reproductive role, their sexuality, and their subordinate position in society. (See **2.1.6** Women's reproductive rights.) Their low status, low self-esteem, and the threats of violence from men, reduce their ability to act in their own defence, or preserve their own health. For example, although women may wish their partners to use condoms, for protection against HIV, they cannot always ensure this. Addressing women's reproductive health can open opportunities to work with women in other areas; and working with women's groups on other issues can usually provide good opportunities for addressing sexuality, reproductive health, and women's right to control their own bodies.

Oxfam supports women's groups in many places (India, Bangladesh, Brazil, Nicaragua, South Africa) which have run sexuality workshops as part of their health work. Enabling women to understand their bodies, and to be aware of their reproductive and other rights, gives them confidence in their relationships. These women's groups affirm women's knowledge, but also challenge myths and practices that maintain women's subordination, or damage their health. Dealing with sexuality and enabling women to control their fertility through birth planning contributes to their empowerment. (See **5.4.6** Birth planning.)

3.2.8 Sexually transmitted diseases (STDs)

STDs are a significant cause of illness and mortality for women, and can be the cause of infant deaths and disability. Studies of village women in India, Kenya, and Uganda have found rates of pelvic inflammatory disease (PID) as high as 20 per cent. STDs, particularly those that cause ulcers, facilitate the transmission of HIV. They are also related to cervical cancer, which is one of the leading causes of cancer deaths in women in many developing countries. The long-term complications of STDs include infertility, ectopic pregnancy, foetal death, low birth-weight or premature delivery. Infertility can have serious social and

661

economic consequences for women in many societies, where their status, and marriage is dependent upon the ability to bear children.

These infections can be prevented or treated and, with the exception of AIDS, can usually be cured. Better birth-planning programmes, early diagnosis, and prompt treatment, are essential. Screening of groups with high-risk behaviour, such as sex workers and especially their clients (who are more likely to infect the sex workers than the other way round), is in the short term a cost-effective intervention. Screening for syphilis is in some cases part of antenatal care, as is the use of silver nitrate in newborns to prevent gonorrhoeic ophthalmia of the newborn.

HIV/AIDS is a leading cause of death among young women in many countries and its importance as a women's health issue cannot be over-estimated. It is considered separately in 5.4.7 HIV/AIDS.

3.2.9 Cultural aspects of women's health

There are many traditional practices which are harmful to women, such as genital mutilation, as well as others which are helpful, such as giving birth in an upright position. Health programmes should build on good practices, and help women to question, or provide alternatives to, harmful ones. The misuse of modern drugs or medical practices is also harmful.

Groups are campaigning against some of these harmful practices in many countries. For example, the Inter-African Committee on Traditional Practices Affecting the Health of Women and Children has national committees in 20 countries in Africa. These committees encourage public mobilisation through information campaigns and training of health workers, and lobby governments to work towards the eradication of female genital mutilation, early marriage, nutritionally-dangerous taboos, and other harmful practices. In Asia, Oxfam supports women's groups actively campaigning against dowry, dowry murders, female foeticide, and the indiscriminate prescription and sale of drugs that are harmful to women's health.

In urban areas particularly, breast-feeding may be considered old-fashioned, unsophisticated or shameful. Women are discouraged from feeding their babies in public places. Where women are in employment, their maternity rights are likely to be non-existent or minimal, forcing them to abandon breast-feeding very early in the baby's life, or to forego it altogether.

a. Nutritional taboos and customs
There are many taboos relating to food during menstruation, pregnancy, and breast-feeding. These often restrict high protein foods at times when the intake of these is essential for the health of the woman

and her baby. In many cultures all over the world women are disadvantaged in their claims on the family food supply, as they are often the last to eat and are taught to serve themselves the least nutritious food portions, while the best are served to the men. Such customs have far-reaching effects on women's health and nutrition status. (See **5**.4.2. Nutrition.)

b. Early marriage and childbearing

In the Indian subcontinent, Middle East, and Africa, very early marriage is common. Childbearing as young as 12 years old is not uncommon, and leads to a high number of births. Such young bodies are not always sufficiently developed to bear children; for example, pelvic growth may not be complete, and the risks to health and life of very young mothers are considerable. The rate of birth complications and maternal mortality is high for young girls. It is well established that pregnancies which are 'too many, too early, and too soon' carry an increased risk of both maternal and infant mortality. Girls who are led into early marriage and childbearing are also less likely to be able to take advantage of educational, training, and income-earning opportunities, and other activities which may help to raise their status and self-esteem.

c. Female genital mutilation

The term female genital mutilation, previously referred to as 'female circumcision', is used to describe the practice of changing the appearance and structure of the female genitals by surgical intervention. There are three types practised in different cultures and parts of the world:

- sunna, in which the hood or foreskin of the clitoris is removed;
- clitoridectomy or excision, which involves the complete removal of the clitoris and most of the labia minora, and is the most common;
- infibulation or pharaonic circumcision, in which the labiamajora, labia minora, and clitoris are removed. What remains of the genitalia is stitched together. After the formation of scar tissue only a small opening for urine and menstrual flow remains.

More than 100 million women and girls living today have undergone genital mutilation. It is practised mainly in the south of the Arabian peninsula, some parts of Indonesia and Malaysia, and in parts of Africa, particularly the Horn of Africa.

Many people assume that the practice of female circumcision is directly associated with Islam. In fact, many of those who believe in the practice are not Muslim, and the majority of Muslims do not practise female genital mutilation. The reasons given for the custom vary

5

depending on the area, and are associated with religious, cultural, and moral values. It is often believed to discourage promiscuity, to maintain female virginity or improve fertility, as well as being hygienic. In areas where the custom is strong, it may be impossible for an uncircumcised girl to marry.

Surgery is usually performed on young girls between the ages of 7 and 12. It is often carried out in unhygienic conditions without anaesthesia, and is a considerable threat to the physical and emotional welfare of the child. Immediate risks include haemorrhage and infection, causing septicaemia or tetanus, which are life-threatening. The young girls suffer intense pain, trauma, and shock. Later in life, women may experience numerous problems as a result of the practice, including pain during intercourse, sterility, and frequent urinary infections. Childbirth may be prolonged and complicated by obstruction or haemorrhage due to scar tissue obstructing the birth passage. Apart from the danger to the mother, the child can suffer brain damage due to obstructions in the birth canal and lack of oxygen. The practice has profound consequences for women's sexuality and mental and emotional well-being, and affects the quality of her entire life.

Women who are victims of genital mutilation are increasingly speaking up about the impact of this experience on them. There are now a number of organisations and individuals in the countries affected who campaign against this and other traditional practices which are harmful to women and children. African and Arab women prepare and disseminate information and undertake education campaigns for both women and men. In 1990 the Organisation of African Unity approved a statement condemning all traditional practices harmful to children, and various heads of state in Africa have publicly supported efforts to eradicate female genital mutilation. These initiatives require the support of NGOs and governments alike.

Campaigns organised at an international level have sometimes ignored the social, economic, and cultural context of the problem. For example, as long as female genital mutilation is considered to be desirable for marriage, the very poor, who are unable to meet dowry payments, may be the last to abandon it, as it represents their only chance to enhance their daughters' marriage possibilities. In some countries, such as Sudan, it is the older women who are most anxious to continue the practice, because they see it as enhancing the status of their lineage. Women are trapped within sets of cultural beliefs and traditions which are dangerous and damaging to them, and this makes actions at the individual level extremely difficult.

Oxfam's approach is to promote better understanding of the custom and to support work in the countries where the practice takes place; for example, with some of the National Committees working on Traditional

Practices. The abolition of female genital mutilation must be part of broader social and cultural changes to improve women's status and address women's sexual and social subordination.

Where the practice is already being called into question or is on the wane, an appropriate intervention would be the provision of information. In Kenya for example, it is still widespread among pastoralists and farmers in remote areas, where control over girls is strong and bridewealth demands high. Efforts to encourage change could be made in urban areas, or at least in those rural areas not far from urban labour markets, where the introduction of cash crops and other innovations has brought about changes in social structures and cultural attitudes.

Support for adult education, or for programmes run by women's groups, is also appropriate, in the form of funding information packs or teaching materials which deal with the broader question of mother and child health or women's reproductive health, and more specifically with the dangers of genital mutilation. Oxfam has funded a theatrical production, and an accompanying training manual, outlining some of the risks of female genital mutilation. In many countries, women's groups have already prepared their own educational material, which may be available through the MCH or PHC structures. Support for education on genital mutilation can be combined with provision of birth planning, literacy, income-generation or any other programme which contributes to improving the status of women in society.

d. Violence against women
(See **2**.1.5 Violence against women and **1**.2 Human rights in development and relief work.)
Physical assaults on women by husbands, and rape, incest, and forced prostitution are common practices in many societies. When working with women, it is impossible not to be aware of the violence they suffer; women may often conceal it, for fear of retribution, but violence is a crucial issue in women's health and development, and should always be addressed. Apart from the physical damage they cause, the long-term effects on women's health, and the gross abuse of human rights they constitute, these 'crimes of gender' leave life-long emotional scars, cause unwanted pregnancies, and undermine women's self-confidence and sense of identity. This affects, in turn, women's ability to earn a living and to realise their own human potential through development opportunities.

Effective strategies to deal with the issue include, in the long term, improving the status of women, education, and increasing awareness of their human and legal rights. In the short term it is helpful to women to discuss the problem openly. Women's organisations in many countries

5

are active in this work, and provide an appropriate channel for donor agencies to tackle the problem of violence against women. Legal aid and education; refuges for the protection of women who are victims of domestic or social violence; counselling services; support or self-help groups; and lobbying for the prosecution of offenders, are other appropriate interventions for NGOs and donor agencies.

Oxfam supports a number of organisations that address the problem of violence, some through the provision of a safe and supportive environment where women can freely discuss the issue with other women, others through counselling, legal services, rape crisis centres, and refuges. In Uganda, for example, Oxfam supports a programme which provides counselling to women who have been raped, and other health services for them and their children. In Brazil, South Africa, Mexico, and India, Oxfam supports rape crisis centres, legal aid and education, mobile aid centres, and a range of information and advocacy work to address violence against women in all its manifestations.

3.2.10 Key questions

1 In any programme working with women, has health work been considered? Do women consider it a priority need? Why/why not?
2 What are the main health problems affecting women?
3 Are there cultural practices injurious to women's health? What are they? Has work on the issue been considered or carried out by any organisations?
4 Are women able to use existing local health facilities? Is special provision made for their needs (childcare, accessible opening times)?
5 Is MCH available and of good quality?
6 Are there other reproductive health services?
7 Are there referral facilities and means to refer?
8 Are there TBAs in the communities? What kind of practices do they have? Have they been trained? What is the content, duration, relevance of the training; is support and supervision provided? By whom and how?
9 What forms does violence against women take? What is the incidence of domestic violence? Is it being addressed? How? Are there women's organisations through which information could be obtained, and strategies worked out?

3.3 Child health

(This should be read in conjunction with **2**.3 Childhood.)

3.3.1 Introduction

About half the world's population is under 18 years of age. In developing countries, up to 20 per cent of the population may be under four years old. Generally, two out of three refugees and displaced persons are under the age of 15 years. The infant mortality rate (IMR) is the number of deaths of children under the age of one year per 1000 live births. The under-five mortality rate (U5MR) — the number of deaths of children under the age of five years per 1000 live births — is seen by UNICEF to be the principle indicator of human development. For example, in the UK the average IMR is 8 per 1000 live births, whereas in Tanzania it is 102 deaths per 1000. In France the U5MR is 9 per 1000, whereas in Malawi it is 28 times higher.

Every year, over 12 million children under the age of five die of poverty-related ailments: dehydration caused by diarrhoea, pneumonia, measles, and whooping cough. All of these deaths are preventable. Yet an average of one hundred times more is spent on the health care of a child in industrialised countries than on a child in a developing country.

Children are particularly vulnerable to a vicious cycle of infection and malnutrition. The six major childhood diseases — measles, whooping cough, polio, TB, diphtheria, and tetanus — can be prevented. International programmes to eradicate these are among the most significant interventions to improve child health and welfare. Until UNICEF's major immunisation programmes of the 1980s, measles was the main killer, also causing diarrhoea, pneumonia or blindness. UNICEF's Child Survival Programme was known as GOBI, because it focused on the four main areas of growth monitoring, oral rehydration therapy, breast-feeding, and immunisation. Later, two other vital components were added — female literacy and food.

Much of the work supported by Oxfam that focuses specifically on child health aims to reinforce the Child Survival approach. For example, Oxfam supports a Vaccination and Immunisation Centre for women and children in Afghanistan, an organisation in Malawi which works with Mozambican refugees suffering from polio, immunisation programmes in Mexico, Nepal, Sudan, Tanzania, and Yemen, as well as many MCH programmes around the world.

Children's health is influenced by a complex range of inter-related factors. These include material and emotional well-being and physical security, good nutrition, adequate health services (including reliable contraception for parents, and immunisation for children), and

5

667

recreational facilities. Other significant factors include the mother's educational background and health, level of household income, and a safe and hygienic environment, including safe water and sanitation. An improvement in any of these factors indirectly improves the well-being of children.

However, the reality is that many millions of children have few or none of these prerequisites for health. About one in three households are maintained solely by women, and these are among the poorest households, in every country in the world. Over 30 million children face the precariousness and distress of exile or displacement from their homes. In Brazil alone, over 8 million children endure a dangerous existence on the streets.

Gender is a crucial factor in child survival and good health. Discrimination may begin during pregnancy; in India son preference leads families who can afford it to pay for the selective abortion of female foetuses. In certain African countries, young girls face the physical and emotional trauma of genital mutilation. Many girl children in South-East Asia and elsewhere are forced into sex-work and prostitution, even before they are physically mature. Girls are more likely than boys to have stunted growth, since they are given less food. Girls are also less likely than boys to receive health care and immunisation, less likely to go to school, and less likely to complete their childhood without also being expected to work in the home. (See 2.1.3 Aspects of women's condition.)

3.3.2 Pre-conception care

The care of children is very much improved if parents are well-informed about sex and responsible parenthood and child care, and if children are conceived and born only if and when both mother and father want and are able to provide for them. The better the health of the parents, the more likely they are to have healthy babies.

Reality for most people is very different. Sexual behaviour is often ill-informed and frequently involves male coercion of women. Many adults of child-bearing age have inaccurate knowledge of the human reproductive system, and do not use reliable forms of contraception. While girls may have been involved with babies and children from an early age, beliefs about and customary practices of child-rearing are not always soundly based — for instance, the widespread abandonment of breast-feeding in favour of formula milk, in the belief that it is better for babies. Couples do not always negotiate fairly about having children, nor do most men take an active role in day-to-day childcare. The majority of women in the world do not have enough to eat, and are in poor health when they conceive.

In many countries, Oxfam funds programmes which address the issues of personal relationships, sexuality, and reproductive health, from the perspective of women. Examples include an organisation in Haiti which provides training in preventive health for women's groups, another in Nicaragua which offers sex education for adolescent girls, and a centre in South Africa researching women's health experiences and needs.

3.3.3 Antenatal care

The health of a pregnant woman affects her unborn child. Chronic malnutrition or anaemia, heavy work and exhaustion, increase the risk of producing a low-birth-weight baby, and leave fewer reserves for breast-feeding. Smoking in pregnancy also increases this risk. Low-birth-weight babies — under 2.5kg — are more likely to die. A balanced diet and rest contribute to good health, and routine antenatal checks should detect any major complications in pregnancy.

The importance of antenatal care is not always appreciated, nor is it always available to the women who need it most. Women employees are often not protected by labour law or membership of a union, and may not be allowed to take time off from work for medical appointments, or may be sacked if it is discovered that they are pregnant.

In the context of health education for women, and training for midwives and traditional birth attendants (TBAs), Oxfam supports a wide range of efforts in many countries to improve the provision of good antenatal care for poor women.

3.3.4 Perinatal care

The perinatal period (seven days before and seven days after birth) is a dangerous time for the baby as it moves from life in the mother's womb to an individual but dependent life outside.

Low-weight babies are especially vulnerable to infections, particularly respiratory and gastro-intestinal infections. Neonatal tetanus, known in some parts of the world as the 'seventh-day illness', caused by infection of the umbilical wound, is a common killer of new babies. Anti-tetanus vaccinations for pregnant women can reduce the risk of newborn tetanus, as can the provision of clean and sterile instruments to cut the cord. Breast-feeding from birth also builds up the baby's immunity to infection.

The vast majority of babies in developing countries are born outside the hospital system, with the assistance of a TBA or female relative. Oxfam's main area of support in perinatal care is therefore in training and back-up for midwives and TBAs: for instance, in Zaire, Oxfam funded refresher courses for nurses and TBAs attached to a maternity hospital. In Nicaragua, Oxfam funded a similar programme which gave TBAs a recognised role within the national health-care system. In Pakistan, Oxfam supports the educational work of a local NGO which assists non-literate TBAs. In Zaire and Burkina Faso, Oxfam has also funded the upgrading of maternity hospitals, largely through providing equipment and paying for rebuilding costs.

3.3.5 Under-fives

Clinics for infants and young children form part of most government health services, including mobile or outreach clinics, and many NGO health programmes. These cover:

* health education (see 5.4.11 Health Education)
* immunisations (see 5.4.4 Immunisation)
* growth monitoring (see 5.4.2 Nutrition)
* curative treatment (see 5.4.5 Prevention and control of communicable diseases).

Clinics which focus mainly on immunisation and growth monitoring tend to attract mothers and babies who are not at high risk. Single intervention programmes are also more wasteful of mothers' time, who may be disinclined to attend as a result. Clinics which offer a comprehensive range of services have more sustained contact with mothers and their children than those which deal with each intervention separately. In the former, a pregnant mother may receive routine antenatal care at the same time as her children are immunised, or checked for growth and general development.

3.3.6 'CHILD-to-child'

The worldwide 'CHILD-to-child' programme builds on the fact that school-age children — in particular girls — often have responsibility for their siblings. The programme teaches and encourages school-age children to concern themselves with the health of their younger brothers and sisters. They pass on what they learn to other children and to their families. The activities involve children, parents, teachers, and health workers. Subjects covered include: care of children with diarrhoea, accidents, better health habits, early signs of illness, improving the neighbourhood, and playing with young children. The programme produces simple activity sheets which may be adapted for use in schools and organisations such as church groups and local co-operatives.

CHILD-to-child can become a point of entry for other PHC and health education work, or reinforce existing programmes. One of its major strengths is that it teaches children to be observant and shows them from an early age that they are important, and can bring about valuable changes in their day-to-day lives. Oxfam has supported many local NGOs in various parts of the world which incorporate CHILD-to-child.

3.3.7 Schools

Schools are sometimes used as a focus of mass screening for particular diseases (such as TB or bilharzia), providing blanket coverage for immunisation programmes, or as distribution outlets for health education materials. Where school attendance of both girls and boys is high, this may be reasonably effective.

The HIV/AIDS epidemic has led to greater openness in addressing sex education in schools. The governments of Zimbabwe and Uganda have developed 'family life' modules for various age groups, which include discussions on sexuality and sexual behaviour, prevention of STDs, and related topics.

However, the children at highest risk of ill health are those least likely to attend school — children from low-income households, from oppressed ethnic groups or remote rural areas, street children, refugees and displaced persons, and girls. It is therefore vital to find imaginative ways to reach these children, other than through the formal education system.

For instance, Oxfam funds the Jamaican National Youth Council in its Caribbean-wide work on drug abuse with children and adolescents. Street children are difficult to reach, because they do not form a fixed group, and may avoid involvement with formal services. They are particularly vulnerable to health problems caused by drug or substance abuse, violence and sexual abuse, pregnancy and STDs, including HIV/AIDS. Oxfam supports an organisation in Haiti which works with street children, and one in Brazil which concentrates on health education for girls. Oxfam also supports numerous projects which offer health education and provision to ethnic minorities and oppressed groups, such as tribals and scheduled castes in India, and indigenous Indian communities in Latin American countries, such as Brazil, Colombia, Guatemala, Mexico, and Peru.

3.3.8 Key questions

1 What are the measurements for child health indicators for the area and for the country? For example: nutrition status, infant mortality, child mortality, maternal mortality, vaccination coverage.
2 What are the main health problems affecting girls and boys in the area?

3 Which children are at greatest risk? Are girls discriminated against?
4 What percentage of girls and boys are reached by the health services?
5 What are the principal causes of death of children? What are the underlying causes, and what efforts exist to address them?
6 Are integrated services provided to make the best use of resources? What has been the impact of the services?

3.4 Elderly people

(This should be read in conjunction with **2.4** Ageing.)

3.4.1 Introduction

Few development and relief programmes consider the special health needs of older women and men. Yet two-thirds of the world's people who are over 55 live in developing countries, and older people form an increasing percentage of all national populations. Among the elderly population, the majority are women.

As populations become older and increasingly urban, more elderly people live alone, without the care and support of their families. It is often assumed that older people's health needs are automatically met with those of young adults, and that the household or family network provides adequate social and economic support. These assumptions may be wrong. One weak and elderly person may be living alone, or caring for a partner, an adult child, or grand-children. Some health problems — for example, osteoporosis or cataracts — are not generally experienced by young adults. Elderly people may suffer a number of interacting complaints, such as poor eyesight, impaired hearing, and erratic physical co-ordination, which make day-to-day living more difficult. However, they may not seek treatment because they expect to cope with pain and discomfort, though their quality of life might be readily improved by simple aids, such as walking sticks or glasses. Alternatively, they may not attend clinics, not because they have no health problems, but because they cannot walk easily, because they prefer traditional healers, because they are confused or ignorant of their rights, or because they hold themselves in low esteem and do not seek care for their own health.

Health programmes which are designed to be accessible to all should both provide for the particular needs of elderly women and men and, where necessary, back up clinical services with visits to people's homes. In the case of refugee populations, which may include a higher than average proportion of older people, it is important to base health provision on a demographic survey which disaggregates information by age and sex. (See **6.4.5.4** Elderly people [in emergencies].)

3.4.2 Age-related health issues

a. Nutrition

Elderly people are susceptible to malnutrition, particularly to energy deficiency and to vitamin and mineral deficiencies. Malnutrition is more likely among people who are poor, unwell or immobile. Calcium deficiency leads to weak bones, vitamin C deficiency leads to delayed wound healing and scurvy, while low blood sugar (hypoglycaemia) and anaemia lead to malaise and fatigue. All of these can lead to accidents and falls.

Those especially prone to malnutrition are:

- people who are poor;
- people who are chronically sick, or who also have physical or mental disabilities;
- people living alone or caring for dependants;
- people with inadequate supplies of fuel and safe water;
- displaced persons, migrant workers, and refugees.

Elderly people may require a diet similar to that of small children — frequent meals, with high calorific value. They may need soft food if they do not have teeth, or if their gums are sore or inflamed.

b. Mobility

Joints and muscles change with age as the skeleton loses calcium, and joint cartilage shrinks. Where people customarily carry heavy loads on their heads, they often develop chronic back and joint pain, and difficulty in walking, as they grow older. Muscle wasting, thin skin which bruises easily, and reduced joint movement, are common complaints. Pain from rheumatic diseases can be worsened by depression, loneliness, or malnutrition. Pain and stiffness lead to reduced mobility, which in turn leads to muscle weakness, which further reduces mobility. After the menopause many women develop osteoporosis — thinning of the bones, which fracture easily. A high calcium diet (seldom available to poor women) will help to prevent this, while sunlight produces Vitamin D which keeps bones strong.

Older people can help to avoid falls and injuries by:

- taking regular gentle exercise;
- keeping the intake of alcohol or tobacco to a minimum;
- minimising hazards such as loose rugs, poor lighting, or uneven paths or steps;
- fitting handrails beside toilets, baths and steps;
- using walking aids if these are needed.

A person who cannot walk may become house-bound. To be socially and economically as well as physically dependent may itself be depressing

5

and humiliating. Rest, massage, and a good diet can help. Health workers can teach members of an elderly person's family how to provide massage, and help her or him to regain confidence and independence.

c. Eyesight

Failing eyesight is not inevitable in old age. Loss of vision can very often be prevented, cured or limited. Common eye problems in old age are long sight, cataracts, and glaucoma. Long sight can be corrected with glasses. Cataracts (clouding of the lens) can cause blindness, but can be reversed by a simple operation and a pair of glasses. Oxfam has funded programmes in Nepal and India to train health workers in such eye surgery, which has successfully restored vision to many elderly people. Glaucoma can be halted but not reversed. Early treatment is always needed to minimise the possibility of blindness.

d. HIV/AIDS

HIV/AIDS affects elderly people in two main ways. Firstly, they may have to care for their own dying adult children if these have AIDS, and then bring up their grand-children. Secondly, they are deprived of the care and support of their children. Programmes for AIDS carers need to include information, counselling and instruction in basic nursing care in a way that is appropriate for older, and less mobile, people.

3.4.3 Key questions

1 What percentage of the catchment population is aged 55 years or over, and how does this compare with the population at large? How many of these elderly women and men live on their own? How many are being cared for by other family members? How many are themselves caring for other dependants?
2 How have health workers assessed the needs of the elderly in the population for which they are responsible?
3 Are health workers trained to be aware of older people's needs?
4 Is specific provision made for elderly people, for example, cataract operations?

3.5 Disabled people

3.5.1 Introduction

Disabilities are thought to be more prevalent in urban than in rural areas. The WHO currently estimates that an average of 4 per cent of the populations of developing countries, and about 7 per cent of those in industrialised nations, have a disability of some kind. In any specific population group, the percentage may be considerably higher — as, for instance, among people who live in areas of Afghanistan, Angola, Cambodia, and Mozambique which are strewn with anti-personnel mines. As elderly people form a growing proportion of the world's population, so an increase in the number of people with age-related disabilities can also be expected.

Disabilities cover a broad range of physical, mental, sensory, and emotional or learning difficulties. These may be constant or intermittent; visible or hidden; present from birth or early infancy, or acquired during a person's life; caused by a chronic condition, or brought about by trauma or accident. Disabilities vary considerably in their seriousness and their impact on the lives of individuals, and their families.

In terms of health-focused interventions, Oxfam's priority is to contribute to the elimination of preventable and poverty-related disability, and to alleviate the impact of disabilities on the lives of poor women, men, and children. Since they are among the poorest and most vulnerable members of society, it is vital to analyse the specific needs of disabled women and girls; and to consider the role of women as (unremunerated) carers of disabled family members.

3.5.2 Common causes of disability

Some of the most common causes of preventable disabilities are:

* **Polio**: causes physical deformities which may be seriously and permanently disabling. In the early 1980s, some 500,000 children became crippled by polio each year. As a result of extensive immunisation programmes, the figure has since been halved. Polio is now less common though not entirely eradicated.
* **Iodine deficiency**: causes deafness and mental retardation, and can easily be prevented where water sources are iodine deficient.
* **Vitamin A deficiency**: causes blindness in 330,000 children each year, many of whom subsequently die. Balanced diets — which include carrots and green vegetables, dairy products, eggs, and fish — are rich in Vitamin A.
* **Vitamin D deficiency** : can cause rickets and is most common where children are wrapped or kept in the dark, so that they do not get enough sunlight.
* **Accidents**: deformities from burns and scalding are widespread where people cook on, or sleep near, open fires.
* **Amputations**: these are increasingly commonplace among civilian populations in areas where landmines have been disseminated. Oxfam has supported the work of UN/ICRC mine clearance operations.

5

Disability from TB, leprosy (Hanson's Disease), measles, malnutrition, and water-borne diseases are also common among people who live in extreme poverty, or in over-crowded and insanitary conditions such as refugee camps. Many AIDS sufferers become disabled as a result of their illness. Where disabilities are a symptom of social injustice and inequity, Oxfam believes that these root causes must be addressed. At the same time, Oxfam supports initiatives to minimise the devastating effect of these disabilities on people's lives, as for example in various leprosy rehabilitation programmes in India, or work with TB patients in Nepal.

The impact of a specific disability depends very much on the social, economic, and cultural context in which the disabled person must function. Impaired vision, for example, may be less critical for a fisher than for a worker in a micro-chip assembly plant; however, the loss of a leg might deprive the fisher of her livelihood, but not be so devastating for the factory worker. Oxfam supports humane efforts to ensure that disabilities are not more disabling than they must necessarily be. For instance, programmes in Cambodia and Uganda provide artificial limbs and physiotherapy for amputees, while in Bangladesh Oxfam supports the work of local NGOs which perform cataract operations on people who might otherwise lose their sight. Many community health programmes also include education about simple mobility aids, such as ramps or walking frames, for people whose mobility is restricted.

Local attitudes and beliefs affect how people see particular disabilities. For example, where people believe that epilepsy is the work of the devil, a child who has fits may be feared, teased, or concealed. Where leprosy is thought to be contagious, people with the disease may be ostracised and ridiculed. More dangerously, where people are frightened of being hurt or rejected in this way, they may disguise their problem or fail to seek help. Disabled women and girls are often at risk of physical or sexual abuse by men. Fear, ignorance, and lack of self-esteem are themselves also very disabling.

In the context of primary health care, and a concern that people take control over their own lives, Oxfam supports a considerable amount of disability-related work in the fields of education and awareness-raising. Much of this is through organisations of disabled people, who both lobby for their rights, and attack the prejudice and ignorance which surround them. Support for disability work of this kind is the major focus of Oxfam's programme in the Middle East, and is a significant component of its work in countries such as Zimbabwe and Sudan. In Uganda, the focus of education work is locally-based, in particular through community-based rehabilitation.

4 Health care provision

4.1 Introduction 678
4.2 Nutrition 678
    4.2.1 Introduction 678
    4.2.2 Background 679
    4.2.3 Causes of malnutrition 679
    4.2.4 Types of malnutrition 682
    4.2.5 Nutrition interventions 686
    4.2.6 Key questions 688
4.3 Environmental and public health: water and sanitation 688
    4.3.1 Introduction 688
    4.3.2 Aims of environmental and public health programmes 689
    4.3.3 Urban environmental health 691
    4.3.4 A comprehensive approach to environmental health 693
    4.3.5 Water supply 695
    4.3.6 Sanitation 705
    4.3.7 Vector control 711
    4.3.8 Planning and evaluating environmental health
        programmes 714
4.4 Immunisation 722
    4.4.1 Background 722
    4.4.2 Immunisable diseases 722
    4.4.3 Immunisation schedule 724
    4.4.4 The cold chain 724
    4.4.5 Immunisation strategies 726
    4.4.6 Key questions 726
4.5 Prevention and control of communicable diseases 729
    4.5.1 Background 727
    4.5.2 General prevention and control 727
    4.5.3 Common communicable diseases 729
    4.5.4 Epidemics 735
4.6 Birth planning 736
    4.6.1 Introduction 736
    4.6.2 Background 736
    4.6.3 Oxfam's support for birth planning 738
    4.6.4 Practical interventions 739
    4.6.5 Birth planning services 740

5

4.6.6 Birth planning methods 741
4.6.7 Abortion 744
4.6.8 Key questions 745
4.7 HIV and AIDS 745
4.7.1 Introduction 745
4.7.2 Background 746
4.7.3 Practical interventions 750
4.7.4 Key questions 755
4.8 The provision of essential drugs 756
4.8.1 Introduction 756
4.8.2 Practical approaches 757
4.8.3 Advocacy, campaigning, and networking 758
4.8.4 Key questions 758
4.9 Mental and emotional well-being 759
4.9.1 The role of NGOs 761
4.9.2 Key questions 763
4.10 Emergencies and public health 763
4.10.1 Health and nutrition surveillance 766
4.10.2 Key questions 767
4.11 Health education and health promotion 767
4.11.1 Introduction 767
4.11.2 Practical approaches 768
4.11.3 Key questions 772

4.1 Introduction

This section considers specific aspects of health care provision. These may form the focal point of a particular health intervention, or a programme may seek to integrate various components. While some areas of activity, such as health education, HIV and AIDS work, and advocacy, are often embarked on by groups that do not specialise in health care, others are likely to be relevant only in the context of health-specific programmes. This section provides an overview of the issues, and approaches. Detailed technical information of the level needed to implement health programmes should be sought from specialist sources.

4.2 Nutrition

4.2.1 Introduction

People become malnourished if they have too little to eat, their diets are wrongly balanced, or if they suffer prolonged illness and infection.

Malnutrition usually results from a combination of these factors, since malnutrition affects the incidence, severity, and duration of infections, while infections predispose a person to malnutrition. Malnourished mothers may produce low-birth-weight babies, who are in turn more vulnerable to illness.

This part of the section looks at the causes and types of malnutrition, including specific deficiency disorders, and certain possible interventions. Detailed information on assessing and measuring nutritional status can be found in 5.4.10.1 Health and nutrition surveillance.

4.2.2 Background

While lack of food in the right quantity and quality affects people of all ages, the capacity of an adult to withstand periods of inadequate food intake is far greater than that of young children, or very elderly people. In addition, young children are more susceptible to infections, especially at the weaning stage, when they are likely to be exposed to many common environmental pathogens for the first time. This is why the nutritional status of children under five is often used as a proxy indicator for the nutrition of the whole population group.

The principal consequence of malnutrition most frequently encountered by Oxfam is growth failure. This is due to low calorie intake, and may show up as stunting or wasting. Stunting means that children are short for their age, and indicates that their food intake has been inadequate for a long time. Wasting means that children weigh less than the standard for their height or length, and indicates that they are suffering from acute starvation or illness. Wasting is often seasonal, especially in subsistence economies; and while it is a sign of danger, it is readily reversed once the child has enough to eat. Conversely, stunting may not be reversible and children whose growth was stunted due to previous malnutrition may currently be completely healthy.

4.2.3 Causes of malnutrition

Malnutrition is almost always a consequence of poverty, and of ill health, though ignorance and poor education also play a role. Interventions should be based on an adequate understanding of the underlying socio-economic causes and cultural practices, as well as on particular factors at household level, such as the composition of the household, and differential control over resources of people within it. Ultimately, improving household food security is essential in order to decrease the vulnerability of families and communities to seasonal or recurrent malnutrition.

679

a. National and regional policies

Policies operating at regional and national level, such as food and fertiliser pricing and agricultural credit policies, are often weighted against the basic staples. In many cases, it is women farmers who are responsible for producing subsistence crops, while men are involved in the cash-crop economy. Women are also less likely than men to hold formal title to land, and are seldom offered government credit and extension services.

Policies for releasing or withholding stocked grain from the market can also influence the nutrition of a population. If food supplies are disrupted by production shortfalls during drought or flood, and it is not possible to import and distribute food to meet the deficit, widespread malnutrition may occur in the rural areas. In situations of armed conflict, food supplies and distribution systems might also be disrupted, and food is often deliberately withheld from civilian populations. In urban areas in particular, the discontinuation of subsidies for basic foods, often part of economic structural adjustment policies, has had a major impact on the nutrition of poor households.

b. Food availability

The supply of food to a household depends on whether the household has the necessary land, agricultural inputs, and labour to produce its own food; or has the means to acquire food, such as cash income or trading opportunities. It is also affected by market conditions, such as prices and availability of basic staples. These are all subject to seasonal variation, especially in subsistence economies. For example, the seasonality of food supply affects prices while the availability of work affects purchasing power — and both affect nutrition.

The distribution of food within societies and households is an important factor in determining the differentiated nutritional status of household members. In many societies in Asia and elsewhere, girls and women are the last ones to receive food, and when food is scarce are more likely than boys and men to go hungry, even though pregnant and breast-feeding women have additional energy requirements. Surveys in Bangladesh and India revealed higher malnutrition rates in girls than in boys, which emphasises the importance of disaggregating nutrition data by sex as well as age, and addressing factors that may discriminate against girls and women in the household distribution of food.

Women-headed households are often among the poorest and may have higher rates of malnutrition overall. However, women tend to prioritise feeding their children, whereas if men control the household income, they often use a disproportionate amount for their personal expenses.

c. Environmental factors

Environmental factors, such as water supply and sanitary provision, have a strong influence on the incidence of infections, especially diarrhoeal diseases; while poor housing and over-crowding may increase the incidence of respiratory infections and contagious diseases. Some infections are seasonally affected — for example, measles, malaria, diarrhoea, and respiratory infections. All of these in turn have an effect on people's nutritional well-being.

d. Health services and health care

The provision of appropriate, affordable health services is an important factor in the duration and severity of many infections, and their potential impact on nutritional well-being. Preventive services, such as measles immunisation, are of vital importance. Health information and education can influence practices such as weaning, food preparation, and personal hygiene, which can in turn help to prevent infections.

Whether people receive health care depends on the coverage and extent of the services available, and how well these are taken up in practice. Expensive health care services will not be of much real benefit to those who cannot afford them. The incidence of infections is often higher during the rainy season when health services may be inaccessible, and pre-harvest when people are least able to pay. Girls may be taken to health services less often or at a later stage than their brothers, and women are often less likely to spend time and money on their own health. For example, the immunisation coverage of female children in India is lower than that of males.

The type and availability of care in the home or at work may also affect children's nutrition and health status. Women may be obliged to leave children alone all day while they work outside the home, with slightly older children in charge of younger ones. This affects children's nourishment and increases the risk of infections and accidents. Oxfam has supported a great number of creches and childcare facilities around the world, to enable women to leave their children in safe hands during the day.

e. Social and cultural factors

In many societies, women and girls eat less than men and boys, especially of the more expensive and valued kinds of food, such as meat, eggs, and dairy products. There are also many taboos in relation to food during pregnancy. Maternal malnutrition is associated with low-birth-weight babies, and reduces the amount of milk a mother produces.

Women performing hard physical labour, or working away from home, may not start breast-feeding at all, be unable to breast-feed satisfactorily, or stop breast-feeding early. Given the value of breast-feeding, and its critical importance for child survival in poor countries, health information and education should promote it, and address those cultural, social or economic factors which limit women's opportunities to breast-feed their babies. Weaning practices also have a profound effect on the health and nutrition of young children.

4.2.4 Types of malnutrition

a. Protein-energy malnutrition

Protein-energy malnutrition (PEM) is a consequence of inadequate food intake. It presents itself in two different forms, or variations of the two.

Marasmus: (from Greek 'wither') this describes the state of a child who is severely undernourished and whose weight falls below 60 per cent of the expected weight for age, or 70 per cent or less of weight for height, without oedema (swelling). With progressive wasting as the child loses weight, the muscles become weak, the skin hangs loosely, due to loss of fatty tissue beneath the skin, and the child's face acquires an 'old man's' appearance.

Marasmus may follow the mother's death or illness, or her failure to breast-feed. Bottle feeding, often with diluted or contaminated milk, introduces the risk of infection, especially diarrhoea. Other contributory factors include repeated infections, a recent history of measles or whooping cough, and HIV/AIDS. Usually, household food supplies overall are inadequate, either because of poverty or other causes of hardship.

Kwashiorkor (a Ghanaian word meaning 'the child displaced from the breast'): the main and constant feature of kwashiorkor is oedema (swelling), especially of the child's legs and feet, and around the eyes, so that she or he looks puffy, with a distended stomach and 'stick-like' arms. Other features include failure to grow, muscle wasting but with retention of tissue fat, and apathy. The skin may be discoloured, or be affected by sores. The child's hair becomes thin, straight, brittle, discoloured and is easy to pluck. The child's weight usually falls to between 60-80 per cent of the expected weight for age.

Factors associated with kwashiorkor include abrupt weaning on to the household diet without any milk supplement — often precipitated by the arrival of a younger sibling — and a staple diet which is so bulky that the child cannot eat sufficient quantities to provide enough calories. A past history of an infection like measles, diarrhoea, or whooping cough is common.

The precise cause of kwashiorkor is still unclear. A possible cause may be toxic substances such as aflatoxin, a fungus which is found in humid climates and contaminates grain and groundnuts. Another theory is that toxic substances called 'free radicals' are released in the body, and subsequently damage the tissues.

Marasmic kwashiorkor: the child's weight falls below 60 per cent of the expected weight for age, and there is oedema. Children whose weight falls between 60–80 per cent of the expected weight for age *in the absence of oedema* are said to be 'under weight'. There is no explanation as yet for why some individuals develop kwashiorkor while others develop marasmus.

b. Specific mineral and vitamin deficiencies

The most common deficiencies are those of vitamin A, iron, and iodine. Among people completely dependent on delivered food supplies, for example in refugee camps or prisons, other deficiencies may appear, sometimes in epidemic proportions. These include vitamin C deficiency (scurvy), vitamin B1 deficiency (beri-beri), and niacin deficiency (pellagra). Rickets may be a problem in children deprived both of vitamin D and sunlight. (See 6.7.3 Food aid in emergencies.)

Vitamin A deficiency: this affects mainly young children whose liver stores of the vitamin are limited. The first warning sign is night blindness. Vitamin A deficiency is one of the world's leading causes of blindness. Vitamin A deficiency is also associated with the increased incidence, severity, and duration of infections, notably measles, diarrhoea and respiratory infections, and therefore contributes significantly to child illness, malnutrition, and death.

Vitamin A deficiency is prevented by a diet which includes sufficient green leafy or yellow vegetables. Where these are not readily available, supplementation is a feasible alternative. However, as with all supplementation programmes, distribution, reliability of supplies, and sustainability when external funding is discontinued, may be problematic. Vitamin supplements should not be given to pregnant women as they may cause congenital defects. However, it is recommended for children with measles in areas where vitamin A deficiency is prevalent. Immunisation programmes may also include vitamin A supplementation for children under five.

Iron deficiency anaemia: this is a common but often unnoticed condition among children and poor women of child-bearing age. An estimated 350 million women suffer from a degree of iron-deficiency anaemia. The commonest cause is a diet poor in iron, and anaemia is made worse by frequent pregnancies, which increase the body's iron requirements. Hookworm infestation is a common cause of iron-deficiency anaemia in children.

The severity of symptoms depends on the degree of anaemia, and include weakness, tiredness, dizziness, and shortness of breath. Anaemia can be identified clinically by the presence of pale mucous membranes

5

683

on the lower eyelids, but laboratory testing (measuring the level of haemoglobin) is required for a more precise diagnosis.

Causes for the particular susceptibility of women to nutritional anaemia are the increased iron requirements during pregnancy, breast-feeding, and menstruation; and the custom in some societies for women to eat last and less of the foods containing most iron, and protein foods such as dairy products, and meat. Anaemia is prevented through adequate dietary intake, particularly for vegetarians whose diets do not include dairy products or eggs. Supplementation during pregnancy with iron and folic acid tablets is widely practised where MCH services function, and may be distributed by TBAs or midwives.

Iodine deficiency: endemic goitre (growth of the thyroid) and cretinism are the visible consequences of iodine deficiency, and approximately 200 million people worldwide suffer from a recognisable iodine deficiency disorder (IDD). Many sufferers show less obvious mental impairment, for example decreased learning ability. Iodine deficiency in mothers contributes to the incidence of stillbirths and spontaneous abortions, and to perinatal mortality.

The main source of iodine is food, and most staples contain at least some iodine. The actual amount depends on the iodine content of the soil in which crops were grown. As iodine is concentrated in animal tissues, meat is a good dietary source. The richest natural source, however, is marine fish or other seafood.

Endemic iodine deficiency is common in mountain regions where iodine has been leached out of the soil, and is also found in lowlands where 'goitrogens' — dietary compounds which block the normal action of iodine in the body — are present. Cassava and cabbage may contain such goitrogens.

Health workers can be trained to recognise and grade goitre, but the method is subject to inconsistency, and goitre is difficult to recognise in infants and young children. Urine or blood samples are necessary for more precise surveys.

Iodine deficiency can be prevented by fortifying or supplementing food supplies. For example, iodisation of salt has been used for over 50 years to ensure an adequate supply in iodine-deficient areas. The problem is that such areas are often remote and isolated and thus difficult or expensive to reach. Where people subsist mostly on home-grown foods and salt comes from many small sources, supplementation is a possibility. Injections of iodised oil, which can be given in conjunction with immunisation programmes, last for four to five years. Oral oil has not been used as extensively, and may have to be given every two years. Oxfam has been involved in researching the use of oral oil in a goitrous area in Zaire.

Oxfam's Practical Health Guide 5, *Controlling Iodine Deficiency*

Disorders in Developing Countries contains more detailed information on the treatment of iodine deficiency. (See Resources section.)

d. Assessment of nutritional status

Individuals: in individuals, nutrition assessment can refer to the clinical assessment of sick or malnourished people. In emergencies, it may refer to screening. For example, children are commonly screened by measuring middle-upper-arm circumference (MUAC) or weight for height, to identify those in need of specific help.

Nutrition assessment can also refer to 'growth monitoring', that is the regular weighing of young children usually at MCH or under-5 clinics. This is intended to identify children at risk, and facilitate early intervention. Consistent growth monitoring requires comprehensive coverage from health services. Growth monitoring which involves the mothers themselves is the best way to ensure an awareness of the importance of nutritional well-being. Growth monitoring is one of the main elements of MCH programmes, and is most needed where levels of malnutrition and ill health are high. However, it is only of value if the information which is gathered is then used for planning interventions or monitoring their effectiveness.

Children are often identified as malnourished, but health workers are unable to address the underlying problems of lack of food. Oxfam has funded initiatives that try to address this through collective action, such as a scheme in Ghana where peanuts were grown communally and used for malnourished children whose families were too poor to provide protein-rich diets.

Populations: growth monitoring data are often collated and used to make statements about the nutritional status of the national population. However, the data may be unreliable, because of biases introduced through weighing children who attend MCH clinics, rather than all children in the community. Data may indicate the general trends in the levels of malnutrition in a particular area, but do not form the basis of accurate generalisations.

Nutritional assessment of populations is quite different from that of individuals. Since it is impossible to measure all children under five, except in very small populations, random surveys of a representative sample of individuals in the population are conducted.

Methods of survey and sampling must be selected and followed properly to ensure that the findings are statistically valid. Rather than one-off surveys, it is more valuable to carry out a series of repeat surveys using the same measurement which can look at trends over time, including seasonal changes. Surveys usually collect two types of data, that is nutrition measurements (anthropometry) and nutrition-related information, such as breast-feeding, and recent histories of infection.

5

They may also include aspects such as the availability of food, livestock or other assets in the household, as well as local market prices, and other indicators of the food-supply situation in the survey area.

Methods and criteria for the assessment of acute malnutrition are outlined **6**.5.5.4 Nutrition data. Anthropometric data should not be used in isolation; and technical input is usually needed for planning surveys and interpreting the results.

Uses of the nutritional assessment of populations: nutritional status may be used as a proxy for assessing other conditions, such as poverty levels. In areas where food supplies are chronically insecure, the nutritional status of the population can be used for early warning of life-threatening risks, and the planning of relief interventions. Data may be used in designing interventions to direct relief (including food aid programmes) to particular areas, and for evaluating the impact of a programme. Complicating factors, such as migration during the time between the initial and later evaluation survey, which might bias the results, should be noted.

4.2.5 Nutrition interventions

a. Indirect interventions

Improved housing, sanitation, and water; effective and accessible health services; and increased income, can all reduce ill health, and so improve nutritional status. Food-for-work or cash-for-work programmes may be implemented selectively for women-maintained households, since these are generally among the poorest and most vulnerable. In designing programmes intended to benefit women, as well as men, it is essential to consider indirect forms of assistance, such as childcare, to ensure that women are free to participate.

b. Encouragement of breast-feeding and good weaning practices

Women are bombarded with information implying that formula milk is better for their babies than their own breast-milk. Commercial advertising and peer pressure encourage bottle-feeding, as do employers who do not allow women to take adequate maternity leave, and fail to provide creche facilities to enable women to feed their babies during working hours. Although campaigning by UN and NGO bodies has resulted in a voluntary code for the promotion of baby milk, formula milk continues to be advertised aggressively, and the code is disregarded by many multinational companies.

Information about breast-feeding and nutrition should be made available through the health services, printed materials, television and radio, as well as through women's organisations. Breast-feeding should not be promoted in a way which blames mothers for their choice to bottle-feed. 'Breast is best' campaigns should help women to make better-informed choices about how to feed their babies. For example, women who work in factories or offices may opt for a combination of breast and bottle, while women subsistence farmers may decide to breast-feed for many months. If women believe that they do not produce enough milk, they should be reassured that by drinking fluid themselves, their milk supply will increase.

In designing health education programmes, it is crucial to establish why women interrupt breast-feeding, or withhold colostrum, and how these practices are linked to social, cultural and political influences. Often 'traditional' practices are in fact quite recent cultural innovations.

Infants and young children are often weaned straight on to the normal household diet, and the amount of a bulky staple food which they are able to eat does not usually provide them with enough energy. Health programmes may distribute or sell locally prepared dry mixtures of energy- and nutrient-dense weaning foods to the mothers of vulnerable or sick children. (See **6.7.3** Food aid in emergencies.)

c. Nutrition education

Growth monitoring is often part of a package which includes nutrition education: giving information about different food groups, and discussing with mothers the kinds of foods children need. Health education activities must be relevant to the local food situation, and sensitive to the problems poor women have in feeding their families, and controlling the way the household income is distributed. Women should not be blamed, nor should unrealistic suggestions be made, such as recommending foods they could not possibly obtain.

Oxfam supports a number of integrated health education and nutrition projects, often in the context of other activities. Nutrition education should be simple and relevant, and involve the participants directly, eliciting their own beliefs and practices concerning food. The underlying causes of malnutrition should be identified, and appropriate action to address them.

d. Nutritional rehabilitation units (NRUs)

NRU generally refers to a facility where mothers attend with their malnourished child for a period of several weeks in order to rehabilitate the child and educate the mother in how to prepare a more balanced diet with the foods available locally. NRUs may be useful for the management of severe malnutrition, especially for those at risk of developing complications, or with kwashiorkor which may require medical supervision in the first few days. However, they are not a long-term solution for the prevention or management of malnutrition.

5

687

In general, NRUs do little to help individuals or to decrease malnutrition within a community in the long term, because they do not tackle the social, political, economic, and cultural causes of malnutrition. The best response to malnutrition often requires a multi-disciplinary approach, with particular attention to means of improving household food security. The position of women, their own health and nutritional status, their workload and their control over resources, as well as cultural factors which influence food distribution among people according to age, gender and political position, are all fundamental in the maintenance of nutritional well-being, and the management of malnutrition.

4.2.6 Key questions

1 What are the local causes of malnutrition? Is it acute, seasonal or chronic? Have women been consulted about their views? What is their nutritional status? What are the breast-feeding practices?
2 How will malnutrition be measured? What methodology, sample, anthropometric indicator will be used?
3 What type of malnutrition is prevalent? Who is malnourished (by age, sex, race or ethnic group)?
4 Are there any specific nutrition problems, such as vitamin A or iodine deficiency? Is anaemia a common problem?
5 What are the constraints for household food security? How is food distributed within the household? What is the position of women with regard to control of resources and food distribution?
6 How will the nutrition programme be integrated with the local health services?
7 Are the interventions aimed at tackling the root causes of malnutrition? Are any long-term solutions being considered?

4.3 Environmental and public health: water and sanitation

4.3.1 Introduction

Environmental and public health is concerned with the management of aspects of the human environment which affect human health. These include domestic water supply, human waste disposal, solid waste and wastewater (sullage) disposal, drainage, and housing. It also includes the control of disease-carrying vectors, and issues relating to food hygiene, such as the domestic storage of water and cooked food. Larger-scale forms of contamination of the human environment, such as industrial and other forms of pollution of the air and sea, and dumping of nuclear waste, are also included in the term environmental health in its widest sense. This part of the section deals with domestic water supply and sanitation, and vector control.

Water supplies and sanitation are vital components of primary health care (PHC). Contaminated water and poor hygiene are the major causes of diarrhoeal diseases, the most common group of communicable diseases, highly prevalent among poor people living in crowded conditions with inadequate facilities. In consequence, these elements of environmental health are important factors in malnutrition, and are a major determinant of children's health and well-being. (See **5.2**.7 Urban Health; and **5**.3.3 Child Health.) The management of environmental health in emergencies, is considered in detail in **6**.6 Environmental health and physical infrastructure.

This section discusses the principles that lie behind an effective environmental health programme, and the practices and procedures which will help to bring about sustainable improvements in public health. The top-down approach to improving water supplies and sanitation has often led to the virtual exclusion of women from an area of work in which they are most centrally involved at the household level: the management of water. The section considers issues of social organisation, and in particular the involvement of women as the principal users and managers of domestic water supplies. It should be read in conjunction with **1**.1 Principles of relief and development; **2**.1 Gender; and **3**.2 Institutional development. Further technical materials are listed in the Resources Section.

4.3.2 Aims of environmental and public health programmes

Unsafe water and inadequate sanitation are main causes of human illness. Over 25 million people die every year from diseases related to inadequate water supplies and poor sanitation, and from diseases that are spread by vectors that have a close connection with water. Effective environmental health programmes could halve infant and child mortality, and greatly reduce the incidence of disease.

The primary aim of environmental health interventions is to reduce the spread of communicable diseases that are transmitted through water, faeces, and by insect and rodent vectors. This may be done through improving water supplies, improving sanitation facilities, preventing breeding of vectors, and by promoting appropriate changes in people's behaviour. The numerous, widespread and sometimes fatal diseases that are related to water and sanitation are listed in Table 1.

689

Table 5.1 Transmission patterns and preventive measures for diseases related to water and sanitation

Infection	Transmission pattern	Major preventive measures					
		Safe human excreta disposal	Personal hygiene (Needs adequate water)	Domestic hygiene	Food hygiene	Safe water consumption	Wastewater disposal and drainage
Various diarrhoeas, dysenteries, typhoid and paratyphoid	Human faeces to mouth, via faecally-contaminated water, fingers, food, soil and surfaces	●●●	●●●	●●●	●●●	●●	
Roundworm (ascariasis), whipworm (trichuriasis)	Worm eggs in human faeces to soil to mouth	●●●	●●●	●●●	●●●	●	
Hookworm	Human faeces to soil to skin (especially feet)	●●●	●	●	●●		
Schistosomiasis (bilharzia)	Eggs in faeces or urine to water to snails to water to skin	●●	●●	●●	●		
Guinea worm	Worm in human skin to water to mouth					●●●	●
Scabies, ringworm, yaws	Skin to skin, directly and through clothing, towels etc		●●●	●●			
Trachoma, conjunctivitis	Eyes to eyes, directly through discharges and through towels, clothing, washing water etc	●	●●●	●●			●
Louse-borne typhus and relapsing fever	Person to person via bites of typhus and body lice travelling directly and through clothes, bedclothes, etc		●●●	●●●			
Malaria, yellow fever, dengue	Person to person via bites of infected mosquitoes, which breed in standing water.			●			●●
Bancrofian filariasis	Person to person via bites of infected mosquitoes, which breed in dirty water.	●●			●		●●●

Environmental health activities try to improve people's health indirectly, through general improvements in their living conditions. A major part of women's lives is spent in collecting water for their families, often from distant and inadequate sources. By digging wells or protecting springs closer to where they live, or by building pipelines to bring water from distant sources, this potentially injurious heavy labour can be much reduced, and women's time and energy released. Improved water supplies may also lead to direct economic and nutritional benefits through, for example, small-scale horticulture.

The 1980s were proclaimed by the UN as the International Drinking Water Supply and Sanitation Decade. Much was achieved during the decade in providing new facilities and developing new, more appropriate, affordable technologies. A greater understanding emerged of the need for local-level involvement of women as well as men in designing and monitoring water and sanitation interventions, and for integrated strategies, in which health education was provided together with the construction of new facilities. There is now a much wider understanding of the need for appropriate community management systems to ensure the adequate running and maintenance of any new infrastructure.

However, the Decade did not achieve all that was hoped for. In the early 1990s, over 1.2 billion people still do not have a safe drinking water supply, and more than 1.7 billion people lack basic sanitation. The UN has set the goal of 'water, sanitation and health for all' by the year 2000, under the title of 'Safe Water 2000'. This ambitious goal could be achieved, by focusing efforts on the population groups most at risk, and by allocating resources on the principle of 'some for all, rather than more for some'.

National and international NGOs have played a vital role in this sector. Whilst Oxfam may be best known for its work in emergency water supplies — which account for 75 per cent of its spending in this area — water supply and sanitation improvements are incorporated in its development programmes around the world. This reflects the value that the people and organisations with whom Oxfam works, place upon improvements in water supplies.

4.3.3 Urban environmental health

The problems of environmental health in urban areas are more acute and difficult to manage than those in rural areas, because of the size and density of the population. Urban water supply and sanitation systems are generally inadequate, and deteriorating, as towns and cities rapidly expand. Water supplies are intermittent, and water quality poor, because of infiltration of contaminated ground or surface water through poorly joined and leaky pipes, particularly where sewerage pipes are situated within one metre of the water distribution pipes. Protection of groundwater or surface water sources is rarely adequate in the cities of developing countries. Supplies may have treatment or chlorination facilities, but they are not always operational.

Huge investment is required to provide sewerage systems to urban areas. (For instance, the Integrated Water and Sewerage System for Kathmandu will cost many million times more than Oxfam's entire income, for several years.) High premiums for land render on-site sanitation facilities expensive; poor households have no room for an outside latrine; and while people with larger houses may have enough space, the sewage system would not be able to deal with the flow from an increased number of facilities.

The water requirements of industry are generally low in developing countries, and their governments have placed few restrictions on increases in industrial water demand. On the contrary, industrial development has often been encouraged, and infrastructure in the form of water supply has frequently been provided by the government. In many cases, industries are allowed to develop their own supplies from the surface or groundwater, as an incentive for business. Demand for water for industrial and agricultural uses is likely to increase rapidly well into the next century, giving rise to conflicts over the allocation of water among agricultural, industrial, and domestic users. Rising demands in terms of both quality and quantity will oblige most governments to consider conservation and pollution-control measures in anticipation of future shortages.

The lack of controls on industry in developing countries means that industrial pollution has a serious effect on water supplies, and occurs in both modern and traditional industries. Processing of primary products, untreated wastes from agrochemical processes, and effluents from factories and workshops have destroyed fisheries, reduced available water supplies, and impaired agricultural productivity. Water sources in almost all major urban areas are polluted by untreated organic discharges from human and industrial activities.

The industries which cause widespread pollution of water are often those which process primary products for export, such as sugar, coffee and oilseed mills, and tanneries; or extract minerals. Levels of toxic pollutants associated with these industries have been found which exceed internationally recognised health standards. Where industrially polluted water sources are used for drinking water or for bathing, there can be serious health consequences. A high incidence of ulcers and skin disorders has been reported in communities living down-stream of coffee washing plants in Brazil and Kenya. Industrially polluted water should never be used for drinking purposes. Even with complicated and

692

expensive treatment techniques, such water is likely to be contaminated enough to pose health risks.

Water is not the only element of the environment contaminated by industry. Lack of controls over emissions into the atmosphere means that the air in cities in developing countries is often highly contaminated, resulting in a high incidence of respiratory tract infections and disorders. Air pollution contaminates the rain, which ultimately affects water supplies. In Mexico City, for example, a city of approximately 20 million people — a quarter of the national population — pollution levels are so high that private cars are forbidden to circulate for one day each week. Environmental lobby groups argue that much more drastic measures are required, to regulate the emissions of the many factories, and the large oil refinery, that are based within the city.

Uncontrolled run-off of rainfall can cause serious problems in urban areas. Drainage problems are accentuated by the construction of buildings, pavements, roads and other hard surfaces which restrict natural drainage and significantly increase the amount and rate of rainfall run-off. Nuisances may arise from standing water on roads and paths in public areas, with accompanying mud and deterioration of the surface. In many countries, standing water encourages the breeding of mosquitoes; and more direct health and environmental risks may arise from pollution of surface water run-off by excreta or industrial waste, or by spillage of toxic chemicals.

Small soakaways for individual properties, semi-porous paved areas, or large dedicated soakage areas may be effective, but often the surface water is best drained out of the area. This can be done using natural topography or by roadside drainage channels. Whatever system of drainage is used, natural drainage courses will need to be enlarged, straightened, lined or covered to deal with the increased flows, and with the loss of natural storage areas resulting from the encroachment of roads and buildings.

The technology for improving public health in growing conurbations is well understood, and, with appropriate local operation and maintenance, can lead to a striking improvement in living standards. However, the costs are high, and the social management of the problems are complicated by a lack of political will on the part of governments.

4.3.4 A comprehensive approach to environmental health

Little reduction in the prevalence of diarrhoea can be expected as a result of improvements in water supply alone, especially where faecal contamination of the environment is high: clean water collected from a well or spring may be contaminated later, as a result of poor domestic hygiene. Culturally sensitive sanitation measures, along with hygiene education, are also essential. The impact of water supply and sanitation activities is significantly less when it is not backed up with good health education.

Except in the prevention of guinea worm transmission — which is transmitted through water contaminated with the vector, a water-flea larva — improvements in the quality of drinking water are not as significant in improving community health as the safe disposal of excreta and the proper use of water for personal and domestic hygiene. Making more water available and accessible, so that people can keep themselves and their home environment clean, will have the greatest effect. The incidence of childhood diarrhoea is drastically reduced when adequate water supplies are brought close to home so that it is easier for people to wash their hands after defaecation and before eating.

However, people do not always use more water at home simply because the supply is closer and more accessible. Beyond a distance of about one kilometre, equivalent to a round-trip collection of 30 minutes, people do tend to increase the domestic use of water. At lesser distances, a plateau is reached, beyond which water consumption only increases when it is supplied directly to individual houses. This means that if the existing source of water is less than one kilometre away, the provision of a new source closer to the home may not lead to an increased use of that water, and thus may not affect the water-washed transmission of disease.

Human behaviour is a prime determinant of the success or failure of water and sanitation schemes. To use a new water supply or latrine, or to improve domestic hygiene, requires children as well as adults to change their behaviour to some extent. They may need little persuasion to do so, but they are most likely to make the change in a satisfactory way if there is good communication between them and the people who implement water and sanitation programmes. Including a communication process within a technical programme requires collaboration between several different people.

Communication is important both in achieving the full use of running water and sanitation facilities, and in their construction and maintenance. It is vital in sanitation schemes, where households are usually expected to build their own latrines. A latrine is part of a household's living space and relates to some of its most intimate habits. People will not use a latrine or be willing to build one or contribute to its cost unless they are convinced of its advantages. People who already have a latrine of their own are often best able to convince others.

It has been argued that the greatest benefits to health can be obtained by focusing on particular socio-economic groups, for example households with particular infant feeding practices or those below certain levels of education. However, the existing level of service seems to be a more significant factor. Where existing water and sanitation conditions are least hygienic, improvements in the level of service are likely to have the greatest impact. It is in keeping with Oxfam's concern for equity and social justice to give priority to the households and communities whose environmental conditions are worst; for example those whose water sources are furthest away or whose environment is most faecally polluted. These people are likely to be aware of the need to improve water and sanitation and therefore are most likely to contribute time and resources to make the improved facilities work, and also to change their own behaviour. However, they may not be the easiest people with whom to work, both because they are unlikely to be organised to press for improved services from government or NGOs; and because of the range of other pressing concerns they have, such as unemployment or inadequate income.

4.3.5 Water supply

The minimum daily water requirement for drinking and cooking is 3–5 litres per person. In addition, WHO recommends a domestic supply of at least 15–20 litres for all other uses, including hand-washing, bathing, clothes-washing and domestic hygiene. However, many poor households currently survive with a daily water supply of considerably less than 15 litres per head, due to the distance that water has to be transported, or because they have to pay for it to be delivered.

During the International Drinking Water Supply and Sanitation Decade in the 1980s, there was widespread debate about whether programmes should emphasise improvements in water quality or in the quantity available; or in the accessibility of water sources. There were also debates on whether all wells should be fitted with handpumps, or whether open wells, with protective walls and aprons built to avoid surface contamination, are more effective. Even the simplest handpumps are sometimes too difficult to maintain, and Oxfam favours the use of the simplest technology and improvements in water availability and accessibility, linked with the promotion of hygienic behaviour.

a. Water sources
The first step in designing or improving any water supply is the selection of a suitable source. Water that is available in rivers, streams, lakes, and marshes is called surface water. Water which has penetrated into the ground and, in some hilly and mountainous locations, emerges as springs, or can be lifted from wells or boreholes, is called ground-water. In general, surface water is very likely to be contaminated, and so

should always be considered to be unsafe without treatment. Groundwater, provided it is not contaminated by faeces, from nearby latrines or open defaecation, is usually safe. A third important potential source is rainwater. If rain falls in sufficient quantities, can be captured on clean surfaces and stored, it can provide a valuable source of safe water. The first step in considering potential water sources should be to discuss all possibilities with women and men from the user community. Women are most likely to know what water sources are available locally, at different seasons.

Springs: the point at which the water appears should be protected by construction of a masonry or concrete 'spring-box', which may include a storage tank, that will ensure that the full potential of a slow-flowing source can be exploited. Water can then either be taken directly from the protected spring or it can be piped, by gravity, nearer to the user community. Even though the cost of such a pipeline is often high, if it is correctly designed and well constructed, it should be available for several generations. Oxfam has assisted numerous community groups around the world to construct such schemes.

If springs are not available, groundwater can be brought to the surface. Groundwater may be found at relatively shallow depths, in which case it can be easily reached by hand excavation or by drilling a simple tube-well, unless a hard-rock layer obstructs the digging or drilling. Many village wells are no more than 20 metres deep, but, in some cases, such as in central Somalia, wells have been dug by hand to nearly 100 metres depth, and water lifted from these by bucket, for both humans and livestock.

Where water exists only at great depths, there will be a need for a heavy, mechanical drilling rig to drill a borehole. Such is the demand for water that most parts of the earth's surface have been the subject of some kind of hydrogeological survey. These should always be investigated before considering attempts to drill for deeper groundwater.

Hand-dug wells: in building or improving hand-dug wells, either by construction of a lining, a headwall and an apron, or by deepening, or by fitting a handpump, a few basic principles must be taken into account:

- The possibility of deepening an existing well, in order to increase its yield, or protecting it from contamination, should be considered before incurring the expense of building new wells.
- New wells should be built with a diameter sufficient to enable further work to deepen them if the water level drops.
- All wells should have a strong lining, at least close to the surface, and should be sealed so that surface contamination cannot enter the well.

- If a handpump is to be installed, access should always be left for a bucket to take water from the well, when the pump breaks down. All pumps break down; if there is no other means of taking water from the well, the users will be forced to return to previous, unsatisfactory sources of water.
- Appropriate village-level operation and maintenance handpumps (VLOM), and an appropriate management system involving a pump maintenance attendant, a local water committee, and sustainable supplies of spare parts, should be supported.
- Well construction must be carried out by competent, experienced workers. Excavating below the ground surface is a dangerous job since soil can easily collapse into the well and smother workers. Adequate knowledge of soil conditions, and methods to support the excavation, are essential.
- In order to ensure the most effective use of a well, it must be excavated below the lowest level of the ground water-table (the level at which water is found in the ground), which occurs at the end of the dry-season. Some means of lifting water out, whilst digging the well, is necessary, either by manual or mechanical pumping.

Oxfam's Manual on 'Safety in Wells', and a Safety Notice (in several languages), should be studied by all well-digging supervisors (see Resources Section). An adequate first-aid kit, and someone trained in basic first-aid and safety procedures, should always be available at well-digging and other construction sites.

Tubewells: relatively shallow groundwater can also be exploited by means of a small diameter tubewell. In suitable conditions, tubewells can be drilled to 200 metres. In the alluvial plains of the Ganges in Nepal, India, and Bangladesh, tubewells are regularly hand-jetted to depths of 40 metres. The chief disadvantage of the tubewell over the dug-well is that the former can only be exploited by means of a handpump. When the pump breaks down, the well cannot be used, until it has been repaired or replaced. In Bangladesh, where water exists at shallow depths below the surface, tubewells are the best way of exploiting groundwater for tens of thousands of villages.

Boreholes: if the only source of groundwater is at considerable depth, or if the ground is particularly hard, or contains boulders, it may be necessary to drill a borehole. This requires a relatively complex and expensive mechanical drilling rig, and may therefore be inappropriate. To make best use of a mechanically drilled borehole it is usually necessary to fit a mechanical pump, which entails recurrent running costs and maintenance. If the social and economic infrastructure does not exist to keep such a pump running, a borehole may not be a feasible water source.

Groundwater exploited by means of boreholes or tubewells often

5

contains high concentrations of iron. Although iron in water does not present a health hazard, it causes brown colouration of clothing washed in it, and iron imparts a taste to water and to food prepared with it. Iron can be partially removed by aeration of the water and subsequent sedimentation of the resulting deposits.

Surface water: if ground water is not available, or the cost of digging or drilling a well is too high, then surface water from rivers and lakes can be considered. Surface water is invariably contaminated and needs treatment; a first step in reducing contamination is to separate locations where drinking-water is taken from a surface-source, from places where livestock are watered and humans defaecate, and wash themselves and their clothing. In flowing sources, such as rivers or streams, drinking-water should always be drawn upstream of sources of contamination. Careful supervision and maintenance are needed if water is treated, in order to ensure the high quality necessary for drinking water. However, groundwater is likely to be accessible, at shallow depths, close to such surface water sources. Percolation through the ground, or through a permeable infiltration gallery, to a well located at least 10 metres away, should provide a level of treatment that renders the water safe for drinking. The microbiological quality of such water should be checked.

Rainwater: where rainfall patterns permit, rainwater harvesting should be considered, either as the primary water supply or as a supplementary supply during the dry season. Domestic use of rainwater requires a moderately large area of roof made of a uniform, impermeable material, such as galvanised steel, tiles or concrete; and a storage tank, which can be built underground or on the surface. Rainwater may be led from an area of ground covered with cement (which must be kept clean) to an underground tank. The first flush of rainwater during a shower will contain contamination and should be discarded for drinking purposes. Tanks, whether above or below the ground, must be covered to avoid mosquito-breeding. Rainwater used in this way may lack essential elements, such as iodine and calcium.

The capital cost of roof or ground-covering materials and a storage-tank may preclude domestic rainwater harvesting for poorer people. However, it may be possible to use communal buildings, such as schools and offices, for rainwater collection.

A form of rainwater harvesting that is widely used in parts of Africa involves the collection of rainfall in shallow depressions and behind small artificial dykes. If the soil is relatively impermeable, a small lake can be formed which provides a useful, readily accessible, source of water for both human consumption and for livestock, after the rainy season. As with other surface water sources, drinking water should be taken via some form of infiltration gallery, built under the bed of the lake to a well dug near the bank.

b. Water collection

Water can be contaminated when it is collected. Clean containers should be used to collect drinking water. In collecting water from wells, handpumps, where water is not subject to contamination, are preferable to buckets, which, if placed on the ground before being lowered into the well, can introduce contaminants into the well water. Windlasses can be used to lift water from the well using buckets which can not reach the ground, or rubber buckets which collapse, or round-bottomed buckets which fall over when placed on a hard surface. Water must then be poured directly into the water container for transportation. The bucket should be suspended above the ground when not in use

The simplest methods of transportation and distribution systems, to get water to people, are the easiest to maintain and the most likely to be successful. In Nepal, spring water in some areas was traditionally carried in split bamboo channels downhill up to 500 metres to households and small communities. The bamboo often leaked and the channels filled with leaves, requiring constant but easily managed repair by the householders. Piped gravity flow water increased supplies with less wastage, but at considerable cost. The expense of the pipelines and the time required to dig the trenches were minor problems compared to the disputes over water rights, and the difficulties of getting large numbers of people fully involved with the project management. In many cases, it may be more effective to upgrade traditional systems than to introduce new ones.

Taps on tapstands often leak, or are removed, and water flows out of the system continuously and may result in shortages. Where pipelines are not adequately buried, or soil is eroded and pipelines exposed, pipes easily become damaged and leak. When water slows or stops, people may be tempted to cut the pipe to obtain water where the leaks are obvious. Repairing broken taps and leaky pipes requires effort and motivation from all those using the water system, but particularly from the management committee and the maintenance workers. The success of piped systems is therefore highly dependent on social and community organisation.

A government survey in Nepal found that 92 per cent of piped water systems were in need of some rehabilitation. These projects had been all carried out with little community participation. A further survey of projects in which there had been significant local participation, where village maintenance workers were appointed, and users' committees set up, found that only 20 per cent were in a state of serious disrepair and not providing adequate service; 20 per cent were in need of some rehabilitation and were providing partial service; while the remaining 60 per cent were functioning satisfactorily. The good maintenance was related to people's perceptions that these systems improved their quality of life, rather than to affordability.

5

Where the water source cannot be piped by gravity, it must be lifted either by hand or with a pump. A system for maintaining the pump and providing fuel and suitable spare parts is necessary, together with some provision for people to be able to draw water when the pump is not working.

Collection vessels vary from traditional earthenware or brass pots to plastic jerry cans. Water is very heavy to carry, weighing 1kg per litre, and heavy pots increase the burden. The advantage of traditional pots is that they are often locally made, and have necks which are large enough to allow thorough cleaning of the inside of the vessel.

Storage of water within the household is highly variable. Some cultures do not permit water to be drunk after it has been stored for more than a few hours, while others encourage storage of water for several days before water is considered pure enough for drinking. Water from highly turbid sources may be considerably improved if it is left to settle. However, water which is high in organic material and contaminated with faecal bacteria can deteriorate if it is stored in warm environments. Water containers should be covered, to ensure that further contamination does not occur and that mosquitoes cannot use them as breeding sites. To prevent contamination of water during pouring, it is recommended that a clean vessel is used to scoop out the water, or that the water is poured directly from the storage vessel.

Where a new water source is brought into an area, attention must be paid to the provision of adequate drainage of the waste water from the water point and from the extra water discarded by the households. Inadequate drainage can provide conditions for mosquitoes to breed, and lead to the spread of filariasis, malaria, and dengue fever. Drainage can be improved by providing soakaway pits, or by using the waste water for irrigating kitchen gardens and other small-scale horticulture.

c. Water quality and testing

Water can be assessed in terms of microbiological, chemical, and physical quality. Strict standards for all three categories are set by water authorities in developed countries, where dangerous contamination is caused both by human and industrial waste. However, these standards are not universally feasible, particularly for rural water supplies in developing countries. The *WHO Guidelines for Drinking Water Quality* recommend that:

emphasis is placed first and foremost on the microbiological safety of drinking-water supplies; only a very limited number of physico-chemical parameters are considered to be of general significance for small-community supplies.

Microbiological quality: contamination by human excreta is likely to spread disease. Faecal contamination is indicated by the presence of the most common gastro-intestinal bacteria, the *Escherichia coli* (*E. coli*), and the presence of this indicator organism is universally used as the most important criterion in measuring water quality. Whilst the WHO Guideline for *E. coli* in all drinking water supplies remains at 0/100ml, huge numbers of people throughout developing countries are compelled to drink grossly contaminated water, with *E. coli* levels in the hundreds and thousands/100ml.

There are several portable water-testing kits which enable microbiological testing to be carried out in remote rural areas. The Delagua kit, for example, was developed by Oxfam and the Robens Institute at the University of Surrey. It provides a precise testing facility, that technicians can be trained to use quickly. It can be carried by hand, and needs to be connected to an external power supply to recharge the batteries weekly.

The visual inspection of water-sources, the human environment, and the hygienic practices of the population, should precede microbiological testing. A simple inspection will indicate whether the water-source is likely to be contaminated, and whether drinking water is likely to be contaminated while being carried to the home, or in storage.

Once the necessary improvements in water-sources, sanitation facilities, and hygienic practices have been achieved, a system of sanitary surveillance, by trained members of the local population (preferably assisted by CHWs), should be established. Sanitary inspection, and microbiological testing of water, should indicate where dangers are likely to arise, and where future improvements would be most effective.

Chemical quality: increasing use of agro-chemicals is a legitimate cause for concern, but the resulting health risk in developing countries is still insignificant in comparison to water-borne diseases spread by faecal contamination. However, four chemical constituents can affect people's health: iron, salinity, fluorides, and iodine.

Iron is commonly present in appreciable quantities in groundwater, giving an unpalatable taste, and discolouring food cooked in it, and clothes washed in it. Iron in water does not constitute a direct health risk. However, if such water is offered as an 'improved', safe, alternative supply to people, without considerable promotion of the health advantages, users may choose to return to their original, unsafe source. Iron content can be reduced by aeration of the water followed by settlement of the resulting sediment.

High levels of salinity, which may be due to incursion from sea-water or from salts naturally occurring in the ground, render water undrinkable. Salts can be removed by sophisticated processes, or by distillation with a simple solar still. It is usually better to find an alternative water source, sometimes at a different depth in the ground.

Long-term consumption of water with excessive levels of fluoride can

5

damage teeth and bones through fluorosis. Such water is mainly found underground in areas of flat, dry scrubland. Removal of fluoride requires processes that can only be achieved with reliable supplies of chemicals and adequate supervision. Alternative water sources should be sought.

The use of rainwater as a principal source of drinking and cooking water, which naturally has low iodine content, when combined with a diet low in iodine, may lead to iodine deficiency and to goitre. When considering schemes which make heavy use of rainwater, it is important to assess the need for supplementing the dietary intake of iodine. (See 5.4.2.4.b Specific mineral and vitamin deficiencies.)

Physical quality: the principal physical considerations in water quality are: turbidity (cloudiness), colour, taste, and odour. Whilst any of these may also be associated with poor microbiological or chemical quality, they all make water less pleasant to consume. Potential users may prefer alternative, less safe, sources.

d. Water treatment

Aeration, in which oxygen is mixed with water, is used to reduce the content of certain chemicals, such as iron or manganese. It can be carried out by spraying the water to be treated onto a bed of gravel and allowing it to trickle through.

Storage of water can bring about significant improvements in both physical and microbiological quality, especially when combined with exposure to the UV radiation of sunlight or with the addition of chemicals which increase the settlement of suspended matter to the bottom of the container. Such measures have been used for centuries in many societies, using local forms of the common additive, aluminium sulphate (alum). Larger-scale use of alum-dosing, to reduce turbidity and suspended solids, is common in water treatment works around the world.

Filtration is the most common form of water treatment, and takes several forms: slow sand filtration, rapid gravity filtration, and domestic filtration using 'candles'. Slow sand filtration provides a simple and effective method of treatment, combining physical removal of suspended material with biological treatment of faecal contamination. Slow sand filters yield clear and safe water, can be built from local materials, and do not require supplies of chemicals. However, they cannot cope with highly turbid water without pre-treatment, and require regular supervision to ensure reliability, as well as labour for periodic cleaning. Rapid filtration is used in more complex treatment plants, but such a process requires power for regular backwashing, and full-time technical supervision. Domestic 'candle' filters provide an effective, small-scale form of treatment, but cost precludes their widespread use.

Disinfection, in which microbiological organisms are destroyed by physical or chemical action, is commonly used as the final process in water treatment. A small amount of the active disinfectant should normally remain in the distributed water, to destroy subsequent contamination. Chlorine is the most common and most effective disinfectant. If chlorination is carried out, it is important to observe all safety procedures: chlorine products are dangerous, and careful control of dosing is essential. Boiling water for a few minutes is effective as a disinfection process, and water may be adequate for drinking after it has reached a rolling boil. However, it is not practical on a large scale.

e. Operation and maintenance of water supplies

The exclusion of women from the whole process of improving water supplies is perhaps the most significant factor in the disastrous failure rate in schemes to improve water supplies, and is a clear demonstration of how poorly-designed development programmes disempower women. If women are not included in the planning, implementation, and monitoring of the improved water supply, they may be disinclined to use and maintain it.

In many societies, men regard involvement with water and sanitation as demeaning for them. Their motivation to maintain the supply system in a state of good repair may also be limited, as Oxfam found among Miskito communities in Nicaragua, where the men who had been trained in maintenance and repairs later admitted that they found the suggestion that they assume responsibility for this area of work offensive.

Before and during construction, training should start for the teams or individuals who will be responsible for maintenance and supervision of the system. Since in most societies it is women who have the chief responsibility for domestic water supply and use, it is vital that women are well represented among the trainees.

The Community Water Supply and Sanitation (CWSS) programme, supported by the Government of Nepal and UNICEF, attempted to integrate sanitation and hygiene promotion along with water supply improvement, using technicians trained in water supply construction, health education, and community development. In each project, there was a motivation and promotion phase, emphasising hygiene improvement and environmental sanitation. Communities were expected to contribute to the project costs by carrying materials from the road-head, digging the pipe trenches, and so on. Voluntary Water Users' Committees were established for each project, each with at least two women members. Each Committee was responsible for planning and supervising the project, and ensuring that a village maintenance worker was appointed to keep the system in working order after

5

703

completion. CWSS water supplies were relatively well constructed and looked after by the communities, serving as a model for other NGO rural water supplies in Nepal. However, the sanitation elements were less successful. This was due to the lack of female technicians and extension workers to address and involve women at the village level.

In some districts, CWSS tried to involve women through appointing female extension workers to work directly with the women members of the Water Users' Committees. Since these were also members of a sanitation sub-committee, each representing the users of one water point, they were taught about the maintenance of the water system, and given a broad background introduction to personal, domestic, and environmental hygiene. They were also encouraged to share their knowledge with other water point users, and to suggest changes in poor hygiene behaviour.

The evaluation of this pilot project indicated that the better ratio of female extension workers had brought about a greater impact on hygiene-related behaviour. There was a reduction in the incidence of diarrhoea and intestinal worms. In addition, the women extension workers had raised the status and self-esteem of village women, enabling them to participate in decisions concerning water supply construction, and increasing their receptiveness to other development activities.

Training in the management of water and sanitation systems, and the promotion of hygiene education, cover matters which are often not publicly discussed. Children can be invaluable 'teaching aids', especially where informal methods are used. Teaching should be based on the following principles:

- encourage actions which are realistic and feasible within the constraints faced by the user-community;
- respect and build on existing ideas, concepts and practices, where these are beneficial to health and hygiene;
- exploit and adapt existing forms of communication such as songs, drama and story-telling;
- attract people's attention, and be entertaining;
- use straightforward and culturally appropriate language, emphasising the tangible benefits of actions that can be readily implemented;
- provide opportunities for dialogue and discussion to allow people to participate and give feedback;
- use demonstrations to show the benefits of adopting specific practices or behaviours, taking privacy and convenience into account;
- reinforce information, using a range of methods.

(See **5.4.11** Health education and health promotion, and **3.1.2** Education and training.)

4.3.6 Sanitation

Sanitation covers the control of public water supplies, excreta and wastewater disposal, refuse disposal, control of vectors of disease, housing conditions, food supplies and handling, atmospheric conditions, and the safety of the working environment. This section focuses on excreta and wastewater disposal. (See **6**.6 Environmental health and physical infrastructure on implementing sanitation and vector control in emergencies.)

Hygienic disposal of wastes should be the underlying objective of all sanitation programmes, and is vitally important in reducing the spread of diseases. Excreta must be contained and disposed of safely. WHO data show that 81 per cent of the world's rural populations, and 33 per cent of urban populations, lacked adequate sanitation in 1990. This situation poses an appalling threat to health, especially to poor and vulnerable people in developing countries.

a. Social and cultural issues

Bringing about effective and sustainable changes in sanitation practices involves much more than good engineering; it often requires changes in human behaviour. Defaecation practices are surrounded by cultural taboos and beliefs, which must be well understood before any sanitation programme can hope to be effective. Defaecation is a private matter, which adults are unwilling to discuss. Contact with faeces, for transport to a treatment or disposal site, or in cleaning of latrines, is often limited to the lowest class or caste in society. In most cultures, and most households, it is women rather than men who deal with their children's excreta. In public services, it is nurses — most of whom are women — who are expected to deal with the defaecation processes of patients under their care. Gender differences and constraints, such as the requirement in some societies for women to defaecate under cover of darkness, must be sensitively addressed. There are often taboos relating to women during menstruation, or in the post-partum period, when they may not share sanitary facilities with others.

Concepts of hygiene, cleanliness, and purity, and beliefs about sanitation and disease vary widely, but are often deeply ingrained through religious practice or culture. The word 'clean' may have quite distinct meanings to trained health promoters and members of the community with whom they are working. There are many different, traditional beliefs about the sources of disease, including spiritual concepts. Even when people associate excreta with the spread of disease, faeces of small children are often considered harmless, yet they are a frequent cause of dangerous contamination of the household, its water supply, and the food chain. In countries where water is used for washing after defaecation, the practice of using only dry toilet paper is

5

considered to be unclean and unhygienic. Provision of sanitation facilities cannot be based on assumptions that practices of industrialised societies are universally acceptable or appropriate.

A demand for improved sanitation can be translated into an effective technical intervention only through careful study, and by dialogue and the exchange of information between promoters and potential users. Individual users are the ultimate decision-makers in accepting or rejecting a new practice and a new technology. Women and men must first be convinced of the benefits of improved sanitation and of changes in their own behaviour. This essential process of two-way learning and promotion requires careful planning, proper resourcing, and adequate time. Latrine building programmes are often accepted by the community on the grounds of privacy or status before the community notices improvements in health.

b. Waste-disposal options

On-site disposal requires containment and/or treatment at the point of collection, in a latrine or septic tank. Off-site disposal requires either continuous transport (i.e. in water in a sewer system), or regular collection and transport (i.e. by emptying of night-soil buckets, or by pumping from a cess-pit) of waste to a treatment or disposal site. All off-site disposal systems suffer from serious disadvantages: night-soil systems create health hazards, smell bad, and attract flies, whilst pumped or sewered systems have high capital costs. Only on-site systems are considered in this section. Readers are referred to specialist books for further discussion of off-site systems. Table 5.2 presents the various on-site disposal options.

Table 5.2 Sanitation options

	Advantages	Disadavantages
Open defaecation	No cost. Often currently practised.	Serious health hazards, depending on weather conditions and population density.
Shallow pit	No cost. Benefit farmers as fertiliser.	Fly nuisance. Spread of hookworm larvae.
Simple pit latrine	Low cost. Can be built by householder. Needs no water for operation. Easily understood.	Smell. Fly nuisance, and mosquito nuisance if pit is wet (both can be controlled with a tight-fitting lid).
Borehole latrine	Can be excavated quickly if equipment available.	Sides liable to be fouled, hence fly nuisance. Short

	Suitable for short-term use, eg in emergencies.	life. Risk of groundwater pollution due to depth of hole.
Ventilated pit latrine	Can be built by householder. Needs no water for operation. Smells reduced. Control of flies.	Does not control mosquitoes. Extra cost of ventpipe. Extra maintenance of flyscreen. Need for dark interior. Complicated to build correctly.
Pour-flush latrine	Control of flies and mosquitoes. No smell. Pit contents not visible. Can be upgraded by connection to a sewer. Latrine can be in house with pit outside.	Reliable, unlimited water supply required. Unsuitable for use with solid anal-cleansing materials. Easily blocked and broken.
Composting latrine.	Valuable humus is provided. Convenience.Less expensive than a septic tank.	Careful operation essential. Urine should be collected separately in batch system. Ash or vegetable matter should be added.
Aqua-privy	Convenience. Less expensive than a septic tank.	Water must be available nearby. More expensive than any latrine. Sufficient water must be added to maintain seal. Regular desludging required. Permeable soil required.
Septic tank.	Convenience.	High cost. Reliable, ample water supply required. Only suitable for low-density housing. Regular desludging is required. Permeable soil is required.
Single vs double pit latrines.	**Single pit advantages** Will last for several years if large enough. Pits become more or less permanent.	**Double pit advantage** Easy removal of solids from shallow pits. Pit contents can be safely used as soil conditioner after 2 years.

5

The technical feasibility of a particular sanitation system depends on many factors, of which the following are the most important:

- cost and affordability
- communal or household facilities
- ground conditions
- population density
- upgrading potential
- reuse/recycling of waste
- anal cleansing materials
- timing
- maintenance.

Cost and affordability: in general, low-income groups do not spend more that 2-5 per cent of their income on excreta disposal. There is a greater perceived need for latrines in urban areas, arising in part from a need for privacy under dense housing conditions. Some communities have been known to spend large sums over short periods, especially if credit is available and the potential users fully understand and support the programme, and feel that they are involved and will benefit from it. For example, the VIP (Ventilated Improved Pit) latrine has been widely promoted since its development in Zimbabwe in the 1970s, as it has many advantages in reducing odour and fly nuisance, and is therefore acceptable to most users. However, the cost of a suitably dark superstructure and the essential vent-pipe and flyscreen often places this technology out of reach of poorer families. Small children may be frightened of the dark interior, and refuse to use it.

As with so many technological developments, sustainability may best be achieved by making small, affordable, incremental improvements. Providing the traditional pit latrine with a tight fitting cover to prevent access by flies and vermin is an efficient way of isolating excreta from the environment. A thin layer of cement plaster over the surface of the latrine floor makes it easy to clean and may increase the life of the slab. A small concrete slab, known as the *sanplat*, can be placed over the basic latrine to improve the squatting plate area. These simple and inexpensive improvements are feasible ways of improving latrine technology.

Experience with subsidised latrines is discouraging. As with any asset-improvement programme, wealthier people often benefit disproportionately, instead of the benefits reaching the poorest households, as had been intended. Subsidies for latrines run the risk of generating dependency, but there may be scope for the sensitive use of a revolving fund. Demand should be created through awareness raising rather than by monetary incentives.

Communal or household facilities: it is important that different population groups within a community are fully consulted about the type of sanitation facilities. What may seem appropriate to men may not be seen in the same way by women. Children, elderly or disabled people may have particular needs, which could be catered for if taken into account at the design stage.

Households often prefer to have their own individual latrines, which it invariably falls to women to clean and maintain. Some cultures demand that separate latrines be used by male and female members of a single family, and in these cases double latrines might be shared between a small number of families. Responsibility for looking after these latrines is not so clearly defined, and the households concerned may prefer to pay for someone to clean their latrines for them.

Communal facilities for more than a few households may not be maintained in a sanitary condition. The users lack any sense of ownership of the facility and no-one likes to use or clean a latrine after it has been fouled by someone else. In most societies, it is normal for separate communal facilities to be provided for men and women. Communal facilities are often the only solution in congested urban slum areas, where land is at a premium. Latrines run by an individual or a co-operative on a commercial basis are sometimes a clean, well-maintained, and viable option.

Ground conditions: the choice of latrine facilities often depends upon local soil conditions and the depth of groundwater. Unless water is extracted locally for domestic purposes, pollution of groundwater by latrines is preferable to the risks arising from defaecation in the open. However, where groundwater is abstracted from relatively shallow aquifers, *WHO recommends a minimum distance of 15 metres between a latrine or soakaway and a well or other source of drinking water*. Latrines should not be located uphill from a water source.

When considering the choice of latrine type the following points should be kept in mind:

- Sanitation problems are much greater in wet swampy areas than in dry conditions. In areas that are susceptible to flooding, above-ground latrines should be used.
- It is more difficult to provide adequate sanitation facilities on flat, undrained land than in hilly regions.
- Soils with good permeability are preferable to impermeable, either rocky or clay soils, since excess liquid will drain from the pit into surrounding soil. However, in ground that is excessively hard a suitable 'dry' sanitation technique may be used.
- Sandy or collapsing soils provide difficult and potentially dangerous conditions for construction, and necessitate the lining of pit latrines, raising the cost.

Population density: for individual households in relatively isolated sites, an 'on-site' disposal system, such as a family latrine, will be appropriate. However, in crowded urban situations, especially in slum areas of large towns or cities, or in refugee camps, the choice of sanitation system is likely to be different:

- There may not be sufficient space for on-site disposal.
- There may be an increased risk of groundwater contamination, and of pollution of local wells.
- More people can be served by a given length of sewer pipe so that sewered systems may prove to be cost-effective.
- There may not be enough space to build even a pit latrine in or near each house, in which case some type of communal latrine becomes unavoidable.

Upgrading: any sanitation programme should plan for people to upgrade and improve the facilities they have. It is unrealistic to assume that programmes for low-income groups will be able to upgrade their systems regularly, as most people will be unable to afford it. When there is sufficient training and local involvement, donor agencies can support projects for people to carry out modest improvements themselves.

Waste reuse: human waste in many societies is a valuable natural resource and is used in a number of ways:

- as an agricultural fertiliser, either straight or composted;
- for biogas production, usually by institutions;
- for aquaculture.

The way that waste is used varies according to local traditions and practices, and this will need to be taken into consideration when planning any new sanitation programme.

Anal cleansing methods: people use various materials for anal cleansing: corn cobs, rocks, paper, lumps of dry mud, and water. In some cultures this is a principle of religious code. There is little significant difference in the hygienic properties of any of these materials; hand washing after defaecation is the major hygiene factor. However, the kind of anal cleansing materials used determine the suitability of the waste disposal options. Water-seal latrines are only appropriate for the disposal of water and paper. Mud, stones and other large solid objects will block water-seal latrines; simple pits with lids, or VIP latrines, are more appropriate options for communities which use these.

The methods women use to deal with menstrual flow also need to be considered in relation to sanitation. In urban societies, there is a higher percentage of women who use disposable towels or tampons. Not all of these can safely be disposed of in water-seal latrines, in which case bins or other receptacles for disposal should be provided.

Timing: the duration and timing of specific interventions needs careful consideration. There are advantages in undertaking health education activities before the sanitation facilities are installed, so that people are motivated to become involved. However, to create extra demand which can not be satisfied before the facilities are available may cause resistance towards the extension workers, and the information they transmit. Promoting hygiene after facilities have been installed may mean the new facilities are used inappropriately, and habits may be harder to change at a later date. Commencing construction of facilities at the same time as motivating the intended users to become involved demands more resources initially, but people may be more receptive to health education messages and ready to change their own hygiene behaviours at the time that new facilities are actually being introduced. The most receptive people will participate first, and then others are likely to follow their example.

Maintenance: nobody willingly uses a latrine or toilet that has been fouled by someone else. Some daily cleaning is therefore essential. Individual household latrines are more readily kept clean by the users, though it is generally women household members who are expected to clean lavatories and bathrooms. Communal facilities are more complicated, and it is often better for them to be maintained by a caretaker, if a community is willing to pay for one.

Occasionally major repairs will be needed. Individual household latrines, particularly those built by the household, ought to be repaired by the owners. This may include the re-making of a well-fitting lid, or making sure that the fly screen is intact on the top of the vent pipe of a VIP latrine. Communal latrines regularly cleaned by a caretaker could be checked for other repairs as necessary. The caretaker or other repair worker should be adequately paid or reimbursed, and a schedule of checks made so that prompt repairs are undertaken.

Latrines, even ventilated pit latrines, can also provide breeding places for mosquitoes, particularly the *Culex* mosquitoes, which are the vectors for filariasis and encephalitis. One way to ensure that insect vectors cannot get to the pit contents is to fit covers over the squatting slab.

4.3.7 Vector control

a. Mosquitoes
Malaria is the single most important vector-borne disease world-wide in terms of the morbidity and mortality it causes. There are four types of malaria: *ovale, malariae, vivax,* and *falciparum.* Each is transmitted by the various species of *Anopheles* mosquito. Control programmes are highly specific to the species of mosquito involved in transmission. Residual spraying of insecticide on the inner walls of dwellings is the method of choice for malaria control where the vectors are known to rest indoors.

Anopheles mosquitoes all breed in still, stagnant but unpolluted water below 3000 metres altitude. Most of them feed on human beings at night, and fly up to 2km from their breeding site. It is possible to control these vectors in various ways.

The arboviral infections which cause major diseases include dengue and dengue haemorrhagic fever, yellow fever, and Japanese encephalitis. Arboviral diseases occur in non-human hosts, such as monkeys and pigs, and infect humans accidentally. Most are transmitted from their animal host by a range of mosquitoes or ticks. The mosquito *Aedes aegypti* is the most common urban vector of arboviral and filarial disease, and is found worldwide. It breeds in fabricated containers, such as water storage jars, pots, tin cans and tyres that contain water, and natural pools in leaf axils or tree holes. The eggs survive desiccation. It is nearly always associated with human habitats, and lives off human beings. It has a short flight range (30 metres), and most species bite and rest outdoors. Control of these mosquitoes entails covering water storage containers, and changing stored water on a weekly basis. Widespread popular mobilisation is needed if a control campaign is to be successful.

Methods of mosquito control are as follows:

- Remove mosquito breeding sites by unblocking gutters, emptying all water containers on a weekly basis and scrubbing them out before refilling, ensuring that all waste water drains into soakaways and that soakaways, grease traps, and latrine pits are tightly closed.
- Prevent the excessive production of waste water by regularly monitoring and repairing of faulty pipes to reduce the number of stagnant pools. Water saving taps can also reduce waste water.
- Use waste water by redirecting it into vegetable gardens. The amount of water required for washing is much greater than that required for drinking, and may result in stagnant pools being created or water being wasted in underground soak-away pits. Plants which are water-hungry, such as eucalyptus, papaya, and banana, can be planted in the area of run-off or by marshy ground in order to absorb the surface water.
- Screen or cover open water supply tanks to prevent mosquitoes getting in, with rust-resistant material like nylon, stainless steel or aluminium mesh.
- Drain or fill in puddles where fresh water collects.
- Fill breeding sites with fish, such as Gambusia, which eat larvae.
- Protect human beings from infection by using bed-nets or repellents.
- Apply insecticides to drinking water that are safe for humans and animals. Slow release briquets of these insecticides are available. Only three insecticides are approved by WHO for use in drinking water. These are Temephos (an organophosphate insecticide of very low

mammalian toxicity), Methoprene (a hormone which interferes with larval growth), and Bacillus thurinigensis (a bacterial insecticide). *No other insecticides should be used in drinking water.*

b. Flies

Fly-borne diseases are mainly diarrhoeal (shigella, salmonella, and cholera), and eye diseases (trachoma and conjunctivitis). Flies occur wherever there is breeding material and the environmental temperature and humidity suitable for development. Fly numbers increase in warm weather. Flies transmit diseases by treading and vomiting pathogens onto food, or into eye or wound excretions. Since flies are never the sole transmission route for any of the diseases that they transmit, it may be impossible to assess how important fly transmission is. However, since diarrhoeal diseases are often the major cause of death in small children, flies must be considered as a very serious health hazard.

Flies breed in organic matter: rubbish, animal and human faeces, corpses, and rotten plant material. Over 42,000 bluebottle larvae can be bred in 1kg of human faeces. One female adult housefly can lay 1200 eggs each day, and eight days later these hatch as flies. Wherever possible, control programmes should be based on providing suitable, effective sanitation, and rubbish disposal, and improved public and personal hygiene. Flies are able to develop resistance to insecticides extremely rapidly. Insecticides should be used only if absolutely necessary, and then only for a short period. Residual spraying is not recommended since it is likely to enhance the development of resistance.

Methods of fly control are as follows:

- Incinerate rubbish, hospital dressings, and dried manure. In some situations animal manure may be used as a fuel source. If the dung is spread thinly and dried then fly numbers should not be excessive.
- Destroy potential breeding sites for flies by burying rubbish and faeces to a minimum of 25 cm depth of compacted soil.
- Localise the organic matter in such a way that flies breeding in it are unable to escape, for instance by covering latrine squatting slabs with a tightly fitting cover.
- Treat with an insecticide, though only if absolutely necessary, and then only for a short time.
- Ensure effective participation by women and men in control schemes. It may be necessary to offer training in organisational skills, as well as health and hygiene promotion, in order for a fly-eradication campaign to be set up in a community.

5

4.3.8 Planning and evaluating environmental health programmes

Planning and evaluation are as vital to environmental health programmes as to any other development and relief interventions. However, there is a tendency to concentrate on the technical aspects of the activities, and to ignore the social, economic, and political dimensions. The general principles of planning, evaluation, and financial management are discussed in 3.2 Institutional development. Methods of information-gathering and initial assessment, including Participatory Rural Appraisal and Gender Framework Analysis are described in 1.4.3 Formal methods of information-gathering and appraisal. In what follows, only those issues of special relevance to environmental health programmes are highlighted.

a. Women, water and sanitation

(To be read in conjunction with 2.1 Gender.)

Managing the supply of water for domestic use, and household sanitation, are usually the responsibility of women. Men will often confirm this, laughing at the mere suggestion that they become involved in work relating to water or sanitation. However, most development planners and technical personnel, in government agencies and NGOs alike, are men. For the most part, agencies of every description have failed to realise how crucial it is for the success of local-level water and sanitation schemes to guarantee women a central role in decision-making and implementation.

In the mid-1970s, women were 'discovered' by development planners, and recognised as having a role in the water supply sector. However, in spite of the rhetoric about involving women, relatively little has been put into practice. Women's knowledge of and roles in water management must be respected, even where their social and economic status may not reflect the importance of their experience. Where societies are deeply polarised along gender lines, with women in a subordinate role to men, development and relief workers need to make determined efforts to ensure women's free and open participation in decisions affecting them, their children, and their households.

Women benefit directly from improved water supply and sanitation programmes, since in general they fetch and carry water for domestic use, process and cook food, take the major responsibility for the care of children and other household members, and are in charge of hygiene in the home. Many women in developing countries are in daily contact with polluted water and human faeces, and are therefore vulnerable to the associated diseases. Improving water supplies can significantly improve the health and well-being of women and children in particular.

Carrying water is one of the most arduous of tasks in the rural areas of developing countries, and is usually undertaken by women, and girls from as young as nine years of age. Carrying water on the head requires strength and considerable skill, as well as a great deal of energy. The average proportion of working time spent on water collection by women varies. For example, in East Africa it ranges from 12 per cent to 27 per cent in dry mountainous areas. The energy expended may consume up to a third of women's daily calorific intake. Women and children carrying water thus frequently suffer from malnutrition and anaemia, as well as water-related diseases.

A major problem arising from the carrying of water is the early ageing of the spine. Where children are concerned, this affects the growth of their bones. Often, very young children develop deformities in the spine or pelvis, particularly when water is carried on the hip or shoulder. Women carrying water on their backs with a head-strap often suffer from severe headaches and cranial depression. Other problems include fractures, slipped discs, and damage to the knees. Women who are pregnant are at greater risk of injury, because of the softening of the ligaments in the lumbar region. Women also suffer rheumatic problems in areas such as Central America where they customarily stand up to their waists in cold rivers in order to wash the household's clothes.

While animals, wheelbarrows or handcarts may be used to transport water, and so decrease the muscular strain suffered by women, they are expensive and may be difficult to obtain. The more equitable and sustainable option is to shorten the distance over which water must be carried by bringing a source of water nearer to households.

Women may regard firewood collection and grinding flour as more onerous tasks than collecting water. Indeed, it has sometimes been claimed that, since these activities are undertaken jointly with other women, they offer an opportunity to get away from the house and meet other people. There are, however, many other ways in which women could be involved in social and political life, which do not risk endangering their health and well-being.

It is frequently more difficult for women to find opportunities to wash or defaecate in private, than for men. In many societies, the bodily functions of women are regarded as 'shameful', and to be kept secret from other people. In others, women are not permitted to eat with the rest of the household while they are menstruating.

Women are often seen as the 'consumers' of water and sanitation schemes, who can contribute labour and implement innovations to achieve the goals of safer water and better health. However, women are often in fact marginalised and excluded from decision-making, and their customs and preferences are seldom taken into consideration in the technical design phase. Women may be co-managers of communal

5

water points, latrines, shower facilities, domestic waste collection, and recycling. However, this work is often taken for granted and denied its economic and social value. It is often helpful for female technicians or community workers to make links with local women, gather their opinions, and give them the confidence to become directly involved in policy decisions. If separate male and female committees are formed, this may perpetuate women's subordination to men. However, a great deal of back-up and support is usually needed to help women in mixed committees to challenge men's assumed role in leadership and public decision-making. Women's groups, which provide a forum for support and feedback for women committee members, may be of value.

The issue of voluntary involvement in community water and sanitation systems needs careful consideration. For example, the use of volunteer women caretakers instead of paid male mechanics may result in an increase in the number of handpumps in working order; in India, they rose from 50 per cent to 90 per cent. This was made possible by installing handpumps with lightweight components that were easy to assemble and dismantle. One evaluation survey found that, although the women were proud of their new role and improved status in the community, they regretted that the time spent as volunteers meant they had less time for paid employment and food production. They also pointed out that they were not rewarded on the same basis as men for the same work.

The emphasis on women's participation does not imply that activities should be carried out only by women, or by women as volunteers. It does, however, underline the need to analyse gender relations within the population group, and for men as well as women to address the issues arising from water and sanitation programmes. Techniques to assist with this process are summarised below:

Technical design:	• Community mapping
	• Women project staff
	• Women's groups
Design and implementation:	• Male and female representatives on management committees
	• Male and female involvement in planning meetings
Operation and maintenance:	• Users' committees
	• Fair remuneration
	• Equal pay for equal work

It is vital that women as well as men have proper technical and organisational training, since this will improve their chances of being accepted as community-based water and sanitation workers. If women fail as a result of lack of training, this may be interpreted as a general indication of their unsuitability for public office. (See **3**.1.2 Education and Training.)

b. Monitoring and evaluation
(To be read in conjunction with **3**.2.3 Evaluation and **5**.5.3 Planning and evaluating health programmes.)
Evaluation is an integral part of the implementation of a development or relief programme. The purpose of evaluation is to assess the effectiveness and impact of the intervention, and to identify issues and lessons of use in planning future interventions. Appropriate goals and standards must be established in advance, and monitoring systems designed that will ensure that an evaluation exercise is purposeful. It is vital to address the social, economic, and political dimensions of interventions with strong technical components.

Potential improvements from water and sanitation interventions include: better health, greater convenience, cleaner and tidier surroundings, more productive use of time and energy, more intensive use of land, improved earning capacity, and increased technical understanding; they may also provide a valuable experience in organisational management. However, interventions may have negative effects too: for example, they may change environmental conditions and encourage insect vectors of disease; or the health and economic benefits may be distributed unfairly, or to the disadvantage of poorer households. Some kind of ranking mechanism will be needed to weigh up the positive and negative impacts, and to disaggregate these by gender within households, and also by socio-economic status between households.

Water and sanitation projects are usually intended to improve health and well-being. The greatest health improvements arise where illness and death from water and sanitation-related diseases are high. Lasting impacts on health stem from changes in health-related behaviour made possible by water and sanitation facilities. Quantitative measures, such as noting the number of latrines built, are not good indicators of people's improved awareness of sanitation and hygiene issues. For instance, they do not reveal whether or not latrines are being correctly used or maintained; nor do they reflect any of the other preventive measures taken by individuals to stop the transmission of faecal-oral diseases. The same caution applies with data showing the availability of clean water.

Qualitative information on people's health may be obtainable from existing records. Alternatively, reports on the incidence and severity of diarrhoea amongst the user-community may be obtained from mothers, CHWs, traditional healers, TBAs, health clinic workers, extension workers, and teachers. Clear, unambiguous information provides

5

717

valuable feedback on the work being undertaken, and the basis for comparison of programmes and responses over time. (See **1.4** Exploring the context for development and relief work.)

c. Baseline information and monitoring indicators

Evaluations often reveal that not enough appropriate information was collected at the outset of a development or relief intervention. Ideally, especially in technically-oriented interventions, the implementing agency would start with an assessment of the existing situation (baseline data), together with an observation of the causal factors related to it. An intervention would then be planned and monitored. After a period of time, the situation would be re-assessed (outcome). The difference between the baseline and outcome could be attributed to the intervention variable, as substantiated by comparison with situations without the intervention (control).

In reality, it is rarely possible to establish ideal conditions for conducting Health Impact Evaluations (HIEs), and compromises are necessary. These issues are discussed in greater detail in **5.5.3** Planning and evaluating health programmes; and in **3.2.2** Planning and **3.2.3** Evaluation.

In the context of water and sanitation programmes, the following checklist can help to provide a sound baseline and to identify vital interventions:

Safe drinking water in adequate quantities
- quantity of water available for each purpose
- reliability and convenience of supply (including information on the major users)
- type of water source
- quality of water.

Healthy living environment
- provision and maintenance of sanitary defaecation site
- disposal of all faeces and anal cleansing materials
- re-use of animal and human faeces
- solid waste disposal
- waste water disposal and drainage.

Hygiene behaviours
- water collection, transport, storage and covering practices
- choice of defaecation sites (women, men, girls, boys)
- sanitary condition of defaecation sites
- methods of anal cleansing (women, men, girls, boys)
- washing of hands before eating, and after defaecating
- washing of face and body
- food handling, cooking, storage, reheating practices

- insect control (particularly flies)
- knowledge and usage of oral rehydration therapy (ORT).

Community awareness
- expressed needs of women and men in the user-community
- acceptance of proposed improvements (women, men)
- participation in implementing or managing improvements (women, men, girls, boys).

Contextual information
- historical (social, economic, political, cultural) background
- gender relations, and relations between socio-economic groups
- limitations of quantitative indicators
- beliefs or assumptions that affected implementation
- explanations for problems and/or achievements
- other relevant events or trends
- changes in availability of resources.

These data can be used as the basis for further adaptations or refinements of the programme. Effective monitoring is partly dependent on good record-keeping, and limiting the collection of information to relevant data. Collecting too little information may jeopardise the whole process, while collecting too much is both time-consuming and expensive, and may alienate project staff. In the case of semi-technical information, it is useful to present it graphically, so trends can be easily traced on a month-by-month basis.

d. Evaluation
For a final evaluation, or if a semi-formal exercise is planned, an external specialist may be helpful in drawing all the findings together. The evaluation should be done in as participative a way as possible, bearing in mind the crucial importance of behavioural changes in people's personal lives; and the extent to which long-term management responsibility must ultimately reside with the local community or neighbourhood committee. The need to allow adequate time for women and men from the user-community to be involved in the evaluation cannot be over-emphasised.

WHO has devised a Minimum Evaluation Procedure (MEP) for evaluation at three levels:

5

Are the facilities **functioning** properly?

 If **NO**, then ways of improving
this should be sought before a full evaluation.

If **YES**, then:
Are the facilities being **utilised** properly?

 If **NO**, then ways of improving utilisation
should be sought before a full evaluation.

If **YES**, then:
Are the optimum health, social and economic **impacts** being obtained?

 If **NO**, then what complementary inputs are
needed to improve impact?

If **YES**, then benefits can be analysed or assumed.

The checklist given above provides enough information to carry out the MEP process effectively.

When the MEP conditions have been met, health impact assessments should confirm what improvements have occurred.

e. Financial management and cost recovery

The role of subsidies in water and sanitation projects is a matter for debate. The high cost of installing infrastructure for water facilities cannot be recovered from low-income groups and communities. It is often assumed that by making a contribution of either money or labour, people will feel a sense of ownership for the scheme. This is not automatic, and depends on sensitive management.

In areas where people currently pay for water, it is relatively easy to continue to charge for water from an improved supply. Where the caretaker of the scheme is reimbursed by users for the use of the source at a predetermined fixed rate, the income can provide a modest stipend for the caretaker and provide enough money for spare parts and replacement tools. The caretaker relies on the users' payments, and they rely on the caretaker to maintain the facilities. Users' committees with clear management responsibilities are important to formalise the system and ensure that it runs smoothly. Even in areas where people do not normally pay for water, they may be willing to pay a contribution for running and maintenance to the caretaker or the management committee, provided that they are convinced of the benefits to them of the supply system.

Latrine provision is generally treated very differently from water supply systems. Latrine construction is often completely subsidised, because although the user-community has not expressed a need for latrines, the government or NGO regards them as vital. Coverage is often promoted by giving away construction materials, in the hope that households will build their own latrines. This may mean that latrines are built, but neither used nor maintained properly. Without supervision, construction materials find their way into markets for sale. Another potential anomaly is that the latrines may be better constructed and more expensive than the homes in which people live. However, communal latrines or public toilets are always difficult to maintain, so household latrines are preferred.

In Oxfam-supported programmes in Zimbabwe and Malawi, materials are given to householders in a systematic way. Only when the pit has been dug are households provided with a cement slab; when that has been installed properly, materials for the vent pipe and walls are given, until the structure is complete. This ensures adequate quality control during the construction of the latrine, and instils a degree of ownership because the household has provided all the labour. In Nepal, a system of flat-rate subsidies was developed in an area where cement linings were required in the pits to prevent collapse during the monsoon when water tables were high. A successful hygiene education campaign meant that people were keen to improve their latrines in this way, but they were not able to afford to line the pits. Subsidised pit linings were provided on demand, and households were enabled to build the latrine above the pits to a design to suit themselves, their status and their pockets. Where suitable materials are available locally, people can build adequate latrines without subsidies, and are thus in a position to repair and replace the latrines as the need arises.

Communal latrines and bathrooms can be modest sources of income for a few individuals in the community they serve. In Somalia and India, local entrepreneurs have constructed facilities for use by the local population. These are kept clean by paid attendants, and provide a profitable public convenience. In crowded urban areas or low-income communities, NGOs can be involved in constructing communal latrines and bathing facilities, as long as there are adequate organisational guarantees in place that profits will be re-invested in running and maintenance of the system. In Addis Ababa, a community bathroom supported by Oxfam provides funds which the local management committee uses for maintenance, and for general improvements in the living conditions of that urban neighbourhood.

5

4.4 Immunisation

4.4.1 Background

Immunisation is one of many effective strategies in the control of communicable diseases. Over the last ten years a large proportion of the world's children have been immunised against the six diseases selected by WHO/UNICEF's Expanded Programme for Immunisation (EPI), whose aim is to reach all children. Immunisation has been successful because it is a standardised technological intervention which can be applied without major social, environmental, and behavioural changes. By contrast, the control of diarrhoeal diseases, for example, requires fundamental changes in terms of clean water and sanitation provision, oral rehydration practice in homes, and improved health facilities.

Vaccines which are safe, confer lasting immunity, and are sufficiently cheap for mass application, exist for only a limited number of the many communicable diseases. Despite intensive research, there are as yet no useful vaccines against malaria and AIDS; and some vaccines, such as that for hepatitis B, are still too expensive to include in national programmes.

Before initiating an immunisation programme in any particular country, the department in charge of EPI at the Ministry of Health, together with the local WHO and UNICEF offices, should be consulted, in order to maximise efficiency and coverage, and avoid duplication. Sometimes immunisation programmes are considered in regions outside official government control, where UN organisations are unable to support programmes; Oxfam has in the past provided vaccines directly to Tigray and Eritrea, for example.

Usually, all vaccines have to be imported. International donor agencies should only attempt to import vaccines directly when all other possible channels have been exhausted, because it is difficult to avoid spoilage, the formalities tend to be complex, and the procedure is very expensive. It is better to use existing supply systems maintained by governments or UNICEF/WHO. Direct importation should be considered only for vaccines outside the standard EPI programmes, such as for meningitis epidemics.

4.4.2 Immunisable diseases

Six diseases — measles, polio, tetanus, diphtheria, whooping cough and tuberculosis — were selected by WHO as the most suitable for inclusion in standard immunisation programmes. This is because they are major causes of death and disability, and safe, effective, and relatively cheap vaccines protecting agains them are available. Programmes may include hepatitis B vaccine in areas with high prevalence.

a. Measles

Immunisation against measles should be given the highest priority in poor countries, because measeles is a serious illness in those who are not immunised, and mortality is high. It is particularly severe when associated with malnutrition, and blindness is a common sequel in children with vitamin A deficiency. A single dose can confer immunity, but when it is given before the age of nine months (recommended in areas where measles occurs in the very young), another dose is needed later, since maternal antibodies may interfere with the development of active immunity. High levels of coverage, between 80 and 90 per cent, are needed to prevent epidemics.

b. Polio

Polio is a major cause of disability and mortality in poor countries. The vaccine is cheap and is given by mouth. A minimum of three doses is needed to confer immunity. Subsequent boosters are recommended.

c. Tetanus

Tetanus is a major killer, especially of new born babies. As well as immunising young children with DPT (diphtheria, pertussis, tetanus) vaccine, it is important to immunise women of childbearing age, no later than seven months into their first pregnancy. At least two vaccinations are required, and should be included in antenatal care programmes.

d. Diphtheria

Diphtheria is not a major killer, but is still dangerous, particularly when associated with poverty and undernourishment. Children are immunised against it in combination with tetanus and whooping cough vaccines in the DPT vaccine.

e. Whooping cough

Whooping cough (pertussis) is the more dangerous the younger the child, and can result in death or permanent damage to the lungs. Immunisation is therefore scheduled as early as possible.

f. Tuberculosis

It is unclear how much immunity the vaccine BCG confers against pulmonary disease, but it appears to protect against the dangerous miliary form of TB and against tuberculous meningitis, both of which affect small children. It is given at, or as soon as possible after, birth.

4.4.3 Immunisation schedule

A basic course of immunisation should be given at the earliest possible age. The schedule should introduce effective vaccines, correctly spaced, and allow flexibility. Some governments have modified the standard schedule to suit local conditions. It must be simple enough to be understood by public and health workers.

Vaccines should be given before the child is in danger of getting the disease i.e. as soon as possible during the first year of life or after the child has lost the immunity conferred by the mother. If children have not been immunised, immunisation may be done after the recommended age. In some societies female children are immunised less often or at a later stage than boys. Health workers should try to ensure that parents bring *all* their children for immunisation.

Standard immunisation schedules for children and women of child-bearing age in developing countries are available in WHO/UNICEF training manuals, which are regularly updated, and may be locally modified to take account of particular conditions.

4.4.4 The cold chain

This is the process by which vaccines are kept at the correct temperature at all times, from the time of manufacture until they are used. This is essential because vaccines are very heat sensitive, and lose their potency if they are subjected to the wrong temperature. Vaccine that has lost its potency cannot protect against disease and must be discarded. Sunlight, spirit, soap, and detergents also damage vaccines. BCG, polio, and measles vaccines are the most vulnerable to heat and sunlight, while freezing will damage DPT, tetanus (TT) and diphtheria (DT).

The integrity of the cold chain depends crucially on adequately trained health workers, and on the equipment used to maintain the correct temperature.

a. Health workers

They need to know how to assess requirements of equipment, transport, and vaccines; how to store, distribute, and administer vaccines; and how to look after the vaccines and equipment. They also need to monitor the immunisation programme by recording the number of immunisations and vaccine stock levels, and checking vaccine temperature exposure and expiry dates. Immunisation records should note the sex of the child, to monitor for gender bias in the programme.

Estimating the amount of vaccine needed depends on the anticipated number of immunisations to be carried out; the time between delivery and collection of supplies; and the estimated vaccine wastage rates. Wastage depends on geographical factors, population density, number of health workers, type of vaccine, and whether vaccines are administered daily, among other factors.

b. Equipment

Appropriate equipment is essential for the safe storage and transport of vaccines. Different types of equipment are needed at different levels of the cold chain. Capacity must be correctly calculated for the amount of vaccine to be stored or transported. Equipment includes:

- refrigerator
- freezer — for making ice packs for transport equipment
- cold box — storage up to seven days
- vaccines carrier/flask — storage up to 24 hours.

Cold boxes and carriers must be well insulated: standard equipment has been designed and should be used wherever possible. The equipment must be compatible throughout the cold chain, for ice packs vary in shape and size and do not fit all boxes and carriers. Loose ice may be needed where flasks are used. Cold boxes are used to collect and transport large quantities of vaccine, while carriers and flasks are used for small quantities.

The correct temperature must be maintained at all times. It is important to choose the quickest route for distribution and to choose an immunisation site which is cool and shady. Thermometers which change colour if the temperature has at any time gone above a certain point are very useful and are available from UNICEF or WHO. DPT, TT, and DT must not be frozen. This can be achieved by placing insulating material like a newspaper between the ice and the vials. Measles, oral polio vaccine, and BCG will not be damaged by freezing.

It is impossible to eliminate vaccine wastage entirely: the main causes are cold chain failure, damage to the vials, expiry of the vaccines, and failure to use all the doses from an open vial. The latter is often unavoidable, and no child should be sent away unimmunised because a new vial has to be opened just for her or him.

Other equipment needed for immunisation is syringes, needles, and sterilising equipment. Syringes and needles must be thoroughly sterilised. UNICEF produces a useful steam steriliser which operates like a pressure cooker. It is particularly useful at the primary level. Disposable syringes and needles should not be reused as they deteriorate with boiling or steaming. They should be disposed of with care, preferably in an incinerator and in a special box for needles.

5

4.4.5 Immunisation strategies

a. Campaigns

If the level of immunisation in a population is low, and the health services are inadequate, a one-off mass immunisation campaign may be the most appropriate strategy. Support can be mobilised from voluntary groups, who motivate parents to bring their children for immunisation. Such campaigns may be useful in starting off a programme, but immunisation must then be incorporated into a continuing programme to maintain useful levels of immunity among the child population. Often this does not happen because there is no health infrastructure, and coverage rates fall off. Such campaigns can even be detrimental where they deflect health staff from their routine daily work, and the permanent health staff see outsiders come in for a few days, who may receive much higher pay.

b. Integrated programmes

Immunisation should be part of regular PHC activities. Vaccine storage is now practicable and standardised to provincial, and often district, level, so that vaccines can be transported in vaccine carriers even to quite remote health posts. This is best done on a set day each month, which becomes known in the community.

c. Emergencies

If there is a danger of an epidemic of an immunisable disease, or if an epidemic has already broken out, mass emergency immunisation against the disease may be necessary to contain and control it. Such epidemics constitute an emergency in themselves, but measles, especially, is often a threat among children in camps of refugee or displaced people, and emergency measles immunisation should always be instituted among such vulnerable children even if there are no current cases of measles. (See **6.5.4.7** Primary health interventions.)

4.4.6 Key questions

1 Is immunisation to be part of an integrated health programme?
2 Are vaccines available locally and regularly?
3 Can the project sustain the cold chain (from manufacturer to people to be immunised)? Are correct equipment and trained staff available for the whole immunisation process?
4 Has an effective and reliable method of recording immunisations been worked out (e.g. Road to Health charts and maternal health records)?
5 Does the programme follow the local immunisation schedule?

6 What efforts are made to motivate people for immunisation and to reach remote and poor households? Are girls being immunised?

7 How will the programme be monitored and evaluated?

8 Which other agencies are involved?

4.5 Prevention and control of communicable diseases

4.5.1 Background

Communicable diseases are those transmitted from person to person through direct contact (contagious) or indirect contact (infectious). Prevention and control strategies have to be specific to the particular disease concerned, and depend on the environment, the host, the vector, or the biology of the specific agent or pathogen. Correct diagnosis and complete early treatment, where this is available, is an integral part of the control strategy to reduce the disease reservoir.

4.5.2 General prevention and control

Prevention is the avoidance or elimination of any factor that might cause disease and inhibit the creation of a health-promoting environment. Many elements of daily life can contribute to prevention: a sufficient and varied diet; adequate housing; clean water and functioning sanitation. Overall improvements in diet and living standards contribute far more to the prevention of communicable diseases than specific prevention and control programmes or health services.

a. Immunisation

Immunisation is an important preventive strategy against diseases for which efficient, safe and affordable vaccines are available. It protects both the individual and, if sufficiently high coverage rates are achieved, entire social groups or settlements. (See **5**.4.4 Immunisation.)

b. Vector control

A vector is an animal carrier which transfers an infective agent from one host to another. Common vectors are: mosquitoes, for malaria, lymphatic filariasis, dengue, yellow fever etc; body lice for typhus and relapsing fever; tsetse fly for sleeping sickness; and fresh-water snails for bilharzia. (See **6**.6.5 Vector control.)

Before the 1950s, most control programmes were based on environmental management emphasising destruction of breeding sites by, for example, draining swamps and clearing bushes. In some cases, as in the bilharzia campaigns in post-revolutionary China, control measures concentrated on physical destruction of the vectors. But after the spectacular success of chemical control with DDT in the 1950s and 1960s, aimed at malaria mosquitoes, environmental control was all but forgotten. Although in some areas malaria was eradicated and has still not returned, elsewhere it reappeared in the 1970s, due to lack of continued funds, disruption of spraying schedules, and resistance of the vector to DDT and some anti-malarials. Other insecticides, like the pyrethroids, were more expensive, and most countries could not afford nationwide campaigns using them. At present there is a resurgence of malaria in many parts of the world.

A mixed approach to vector control is advisable:

- **environmental control**: appropriate design and maintenance of water projects for domestic use and for irrigation; denying breeding places to mosquitoes and snails; and selective use of insecticides and molluscicides;
- **information and advice to the public** on the connection between vector and disease, and how to minimise contact with mosquitoes; avoiding snail-infested water; and filtering water to avoid guinea worm;
- **appropriate technology** to avoid contact, such as bed nets impregnated with permethrin.

This integrated approach to vector control relies far more on local involvement than the chemical control programmes of the 1950s and 1960s, and is likely to make programmes far more acceptable and suitable to local conditions. However, integrated control can mean no control, and may allow national and international bodies to abdicate responsibility.

c. Case finding and treatment of infective cases
Early diagnosis and treatment is an important prevention and control measure, where treatment reduces the reservoir of infection, as for example in malaria and schistosomiasis. It requires trained staff, and availability of equipment and laboratory facilities.

d. Other control measures
Measures to limit the number of cases of a communicable disease include: notification, isolation and quarantine, identifying and protecting (or treating) contacts, eradicating carriage, investigating cases, and disinfection. With increasing knowledge and technology, such measures can be applied more selectively and rationally than was possible in the past. For example, tuberculosis and leprosy patients stop

728

being infective soon after they begin treatment, and the isolation that used to be imposed is no longer recommended.

4.5.3 Common communicable diseases

a. Diarrhoeal diseases

Worldwide, diarrhoea is a leading cause of mortality in children under five, and is responsible for an estimated four to five million deaths per year. Many different pathogens cause diarrhoea, and the most important route of transmission is faecal-oral. The underlying causes are inadequate water supplies, sanitation, and waste disposal; and poor food hygiene and personal hygiene. Diarrhoea is typically a disease of poor people living in crowded conditions with inadequate facilities. The three main categories of diarrhoea are acute, persistent, and bloody.

Acute diarrhoea is the most dangerous, as the resulting dehydration can kill young children within a very short time. It is caused by a range of different pathogens, including rotavirus and *Escherichia coli*, both very common in children, and *Vibrio cholerae*. For acute diarrhoea, including cholera, oral rehydration is an essential part of management.

Persistent diarrhoea, lasting more than fourteen days, is a major problem. In some areas it causes up to 50 per cent of the diarrhoea-associated deaths in children. It is a result of malabsorption precipitated by episodes of acute diarrhoea or other intestinal infections. Persistent diarrhoea can also be caused by *Giardia lamblia*, a parasite infection.

Bloody diarrhoea or dysentery is most commonly caused by various species of *shigella* (bacterial dysentery) or *Entamoeba histolytica* (amoebic dysentery). The latter is rare in young children. There are other pathogens, such as *Campylobacter*, which cause bloody diarrhoea. Apart from rehydration and maintenance of nutrition, treatment with antibiotics or antiamoebics is important in dysentery.

Nutrition and diarrhoea: Malnourished children have more episodes of diarrhoea, and diarrhoea tends to be more severe and last longer in such children. An episode of diarrhoea in its turn may increase pre-existing malnutrition; this is exacerbated if food is withheld from sick children because mothers believe that food prolongs and increases diarrhoea. Appropriate advice on nutrition is therefore an important part of management.

Bottle-feeding is a very common cause of diarrhoea and diarrhoea-associated deaths in infants. This is because of the lack of the antibodies which would be passed on from the mother in breast-milk; the contaminated water with which formula feeds are made up and the unsterile containers, bottles and teats used; and over-dilution of feeds to save milk powder, and consequent undernutrition. Encouraging breast-feeding is therefore a major component in the fight against diarrhoea,

5

729

and breast-feeding should always continue if a suckling child has diarrhoea.

Prevention and home treatment of dehydration: Although most episodes of diarrhoea are self-limiting, the actual cause of death in patients suffering from diarrhoea is dehydration. The discovery that oral rehydration therapy (ORT) with a simple solution of sugar and salt in water prevents death from diarrhoea was one of the major medical discoveries of the century. Health workers and parents are often reluctant to believe that something so simple can be so effective. It is commonly — and wrongly — believed that food and often also liquids should be stopped in patients with diarrhoea. Many people resort to drugs, which are mostly unnecessary, and sometimes dangerous. Pharmacists often prescribe these drugs over the counter.

Agencies, such as WHO and UNICEF, have concentrated their efforts on spreading the message of rehydration with the help of sachets, or home-made salt and sugar solutions.

Sachets are prepackaged envelopes containing exact measurements of various salts and glucose (simple sugar.) They are promoted by large national and international programmes. The advantages of sachets are that they standardise ingredients, while home-made sugar and salt solutions are sometimes made too salty and this could be dangerous in young children; sachets include elements such as potassium which contribute to the rehydration process and are not present in home-made ORS. Many families do not routinely have sugar or molasses with which to prepare ORS. Lastly, packaging confers prestige: health workers and parents are more likely to consider ORS as efficacious medicine when it comes in sachets.

There are also several arguments advanced against sachets. Instead of relying on sachets from the health centre, people should learn how to make the solution. If the health centre is closed, or not functioning properly, or the supply of sachets is unreliable, valuable time may be lost before rehydration or prevention of dehydration is started. Lastly, sachets, too, can be over or under-diluted and the solution can still be administered in the wrong concentration.

Home made sugar-salt solution is a remedy which does not depend on the existence of a functioning health service. The solution can be prepared at home from sugar or staple foods which most poor families can afford, and cereal-based ORS (from rice, oats, etc) is being increasingly recommended. ORT should not become dependent on the availability of a mass-produced product, but should be part of common knowledge. Home-made solutions are usually promoted by non governmental and other locally-based programmes which take a more comprehensive approach to PHC. Home made ORT promotion is integrated with other initiatives in health care and education which effectively strengthen the capacity of people to help themselves.

Drugs and diarrhoea: Even after two decades of promoting ORT as the main strategy in diarrhoea, and discouraging the inappropriate use of drugs, a 1990 WHO publication states that the 'appropriate treatment of diarrhoea often remains the exception rather than the rule.' WHO recommends the following as the rational use of drugs for treatment of acute diarrhoea in children:

- Antibiotics should be used only for dysentery and suspected cholera.
- Anti-parasitic drugs should be used only for amoebiasis and giardiasis.
- Anti-diarrhoeal drugs and anti-emetics should *not* be used.

Training of health workers: The training of health workers in the correct management of diarrhoea is crucial. It should be included in medical school curricula. It has proved difficult to convince health workers of the benefits of ORT and the limited usefulness of drugs in the management of diarrhoea.

NGO involvement: Diarrhoea still exacts an appalling toll among poor people. To help to reduce it, donor agencies can support:

- improvement of the general living conditions of poor people;
- improvements in water supply, sanitation, and waste disposal;
- health education programmes on household water handling, food hygiene, waste disposal, and personal hygiene;
- health services; inclusion of diarrhoea management in medical school training of health workers and in health education for parents;
- campaigning against bottle-feeding and breast-milk substitutes;
- campaigns on sale of anti-diarrhoeals, consumer information and education;
- epidemiological surveillance of for example, shigella or cholera, particularly in refugee camps or other emergency situations.

5

b. Respiratory infections

Acute Respiratory Infections (ARI), especially pneumonia, cause almost as many deaths among young children as diarrhoea. A quarter of the deaths could be prevented by immunisation against measles and whooping cough. The toll of the remaining cases in the children under five could be substantially reduced if early and correct treatment were available. The commonest pathogens are *Haemophilus influenzae* and *Streptococcus pneumoniae*, both of which are usually sensitive to relatively cheap antibiotics such as penicillin, cotrimoxazole, and chloramphenicol.

Programme considerations in relation to ARIs include training health workers in the diagnosis of ARIs and correct assessment of severity, and in the safe and efficient use of antibiotics. Careful observation of breathing movements gives a more reliable indication of the severity of respiratory infection in a child than using a stethoscope, and laboratory facilities are not essential at the primary level where most cases should be treated. Training protocols and manuals have been prepared by WHO for use and adaptation in national programmes, many of which address both respiratory infections and diarrhoeal diseases.

Information should be given to people caring for children on how to recognise the signs early, and take the child to the health centre for treatment. Supplies of appropriate antibiotics are still too expensive for many patients, and hardly ever regularly available at small government health centres.

c. Malaria

Malaria is caused by a parasite transmitted through the bite of a mosquito. Of the four species of the parasite, the most dangerous infection is caused by *Plasmodium falciparum*, which can cause cerebral malaria. Practically all deaths from malaria are due to falciparum infection. Malaria is particularly dangerous in pregnancy and is a significant cause of anaemia.

Laboratory diagnosis of malaria requires examination of blood under a microscope. However, in malarious areas where diagnostic facilities are not available, patients who have fever and shivering, and no other obvious infection, are often treated presumptively. This is justified, especially if the patient is treated with only chloroquine.

The treatment of malaria has become problematic with the increasing spread of forms of *Plasmodium falciparum* which are resistant to chloroquine, which is a cheap and safe drug. New drugs have been developed and more are under investigation. But resistance to newer drugs has already emerged in some areas, especially South-East Asia. There is some hope that a useful vaccine can be developed.

Specific problems for malaria control include the increased movements of people: for example, non-immune people moving to infested areas when clearing new lands or fleeing from conflict or natural disasters. In areas of conflict, spraying and other control measures are disrupted. Malaria became a major killer amongst the Yanomami Indians in Brazil when it was introduced by settlers and miners from other parts of the country, who invaded the Yanomami lands. As government posts were ill-equipped to deal with the problem, an NGO programme supported by Oxfam used helicopters and light planes, with mobile health personnel and materials to treat people in the remote forested areas.

Another problem is that control measures other than spraying require behaviour changes such as wearing protective clothes in the evening, and staying indoors during peak biting time. Bed nets may be expensive, inappropriate to people's sleeping customs, and unpopular.

The chemical vector control programmes of the 1950s and 1960s, consisting mainly of indoor spraying with DDT, were successful in eliminating or reducing the disease in large areas, making whole tracts, such as the Terai of Nepal, suitable for human habitation for the first time. However, the widespread use of these chemicals also created problems, such as residues of DDT in water and resistance to DDT developing in mosquitoes. With many of these programmes in abeyance, the situation has changed little or has actually worsened in the last 15 years, especially in sub-Saharan Africa.

d. Tuberculosis (TB)
With an estimated three million deaths each year from TB, the only other single-pathogen disease with a comparable death toll is measles. At any one time about 20 million people suffer from TB, most of them in the most productive age groups. The emergence of HIV has compounded the problem, as people who are HIV positive seem to be particularly susceptible to TB. Patients with symptoms of TB are often found to be HIV positive. (See **5.4.7**HIV and AIDS). TB control presents complex problems and the disease is likely to remain a major public health challenge for the foreseeable future.

TB is caused by a pathogen which is passed from person to person through droplet infection, and, to a lesser extent, is contracted from infected cattle. Only a small proportion of those infected develop the clinical disease. TB control is a particularly difficult problem because:

- Protection conferred by vaccination with BCG is variable and uncertain.
- TB occurs throughout the world and many infective people live undiagnosed in the community.
- Treatment takes a long time: six to eighteen months depending on the drug regime chosen.
- Patients feel better within a few weeks of starting therapy and frequently default on treatment.
- Only programmes with strong defaulter chasing achieve worthwhile cure rates. This is often not possible in ordinary government PHC services, especially in the under-serviced areas where many of the poorest patients live. Incomplete and incorrect treatment encourages resistance of the pathogen to drugs, making treatment of relapsed patients ever more difficult.

A reliable record system is essential for any TB programme, to make defaulter chasing possible. An additional complication is that drugs are often not available regularly, or are too expensive for patients. TB control is now increasingly integrated into the general health services. Although this is without doubt the only way by which TB control can be

5

brought to cover all the population, difficulties are inevitable: general PHC services often lack the technical skill, resources like microscopes and regular drug supplies, and organisation to maintain the work. Unless special efforts are made to strengthen PHC, and train health workers at the primary and secondary level in the diagnosis, treatment and follow up of tuberculosis, integration may threaten public health effort regarding tuberculosis. Oxfam has in the past often supported special TB programmes; given the right circumstances, such programmes can play a valuable role in assisting government services or other peripheral services to integrate TB control effectively. A good example is the work of the Britain-Nepal Medical Trust in Nepal.

e. Leprosy
Leprosy or Hansen's disease is caused by a pathogen similar to that of tuberculosis. The infected individual's antibody response determines whether there will be disease, and if so, what form the disease will take: there is a spectrum of disease from the 'tuberculoid', in which peripheral nerve involvement is the major feature, to the 'lepromatous' form which causes disfiguring lesions.

WHO estimates that there are approximately 10 to 12 million people with leprosy in the world, most of whom live in Asia and Africa. Four million patients are registered. The number has been declining especially since the introduction of Multi-Drug Therapy (MDT), which is encouraged and promoted by WHO. However, it is expensive and requires intensive supervision if worthwhile cure rates are to be achieved. Treatment has to continue for six months for tuberculoid leprosy and two years or more for lepromatous leprosy. Defaulting is therefore a problem, as with tuberculosis.

Early diagnosis is important to avoid or minimise deformity and disability, which includes blindness. While the patient with untreated clinical tuberculosis is likely to die soon, the patient with untreated leprosy may live for decades disabled, stigmatised, and ostracised in many societies. Public education is therefore important, as are rehabilitation programmes, which may include physiotherapy, and special appliances, for patients who have developed disabilities.

f. Other communicable diseases
In some areas of the world, other diseases than those listed above are more common and more life-threatening. They include some of the major vector-borne diseases, other than malaria, such as schistosomiasis (bilharzia), filariasis, which includes lymphatic filariasis (elephantiasis) and onchocerciasis (river blindness), South American trypanosomiasis (Chagas Disease), African trypanosomiasis (sleeping sickness) and mucocutaneous and visceral leishmaniasis (kala azar).

4.5.4 Epidemics

Many communicable diseases are endemic, that is they occur regularly and frequently especially among young children, but the population as a whole has acquired a degree of immunity to the disease concerned. For example, cholera is endemic in Bangladesh, and most cases of cholera are in children, usually indistinguishable from other types of acute diarrhoea.

An epidemic occurs if a new disease, or a new form of an old disease, spreads in a previously unaffected population, in which most individuals are not immune. In this situation, all age groups can be affected, and there may be very many cases of the disease at once. For example, malaria is endemic in many areas of the world, but if new settlers, gold diggers or refugees who were hitherto not exposed to it migrate to malarious areas, malaria among them may reach epidemic proportions; whereas the local population remain relatively unaffected. This sometimes makes it look as though the newcomers import the disease, and they may be blamed for it by the local people.

Over the past few years Oxfam has been involved in various activities related to epidemics. Oxfam supported preventive activities, and helped with preparedness against cholera in the refugee camps in East Sudan in the mid-1980s and in the 1990s in Peru, Nicaragua, and sub-Saharan Africa. In Vietnam some areas experienced a dramatic increase in malaria at the time when large numbers of soldiers returned home from Cambodia, and Oxfam helped to strengthen the capacity of the government's malaria control programme. It has also provided vaccine in meningitis epidemics in sub-Saharan Africa.

While epidemics are frightening, and tend to attract much attention, the fear and the attention is often disproportionate to the real danger involved. For example, according to WHO, it is estimated that during the first three weeks of the cholera outbreak in Peru in 1991, when 120 persons died of cholera, ten to twenty times more Peruvian children died during the same period from diarrhoea due to other causes. It is important during epidemics to keep a sense of proportion and not to disregard known epidemiology and established measures to treat existing illness.

Epidemics often stretch existing services, and dramatically show up inadequacies. Even so, it is usually far better to find out how existing services can be used, and strengthen them to bear the increased burden, than to import new structures.

5

4.6 Birth planning

4.6.1 Introduction

(To be read in conjunction with **2.1.6** Women's reproductive rights.)

Birth planning is an integral part of maternal and child health. However, it does not always receive adequate emphasis within MCH programmes. Birth-planning programmes are usually implemented independently, sometimes vertically, often related to national policies aiming to slow down population growth. This approach has often led to distortions, such as isolated and single-method programmes obsessed with achieving targets, and programmes using coercive measures.

Birth-planning programmes tend to focus on distributing contraceptives to women, while often disregarding their concerns and particular health and social needs. Women's health activists continue to highlight the abuses that take place. They argue that contraceptive services should be seen as part of a broader reproductive health framework with emphasis on women's reproductive rights: women's rights to regulate, control, and nurture the reproductive processes of their own bodies. When birth-planning interventions are considered, it is imperative that women are involved in programme planning and implementation, and that their right to make decisions about their own bodies and lives is defended and promoted. Because it is men, and male-dominated institutions, who seek to control women's fertility, it is also essential for the success of birth-planning interventions to involve men in educational programmes to help them to respect women's rights and to share responsibility for birth planning.

This section covers some general considerations for the provision of birth-planning services, the different methods of contraception available, and recommendations for gender-sensitive programmes. It also gives a brief overview of some of the controversies concerning population control.

4.6.2 Background

The World Fertility Survey and various health and demographic surveys have documented the 'unmet need' for contraception among women. Annually, 40-60 million abortions are carried out, approximately half of these outside authorised health services, and many of them could be avoided by the provision of improved facilities for birth planning.

a. Concepts and definitions

There can be few subjects where there is such a choice of terms, and where each term carries so much ideological baggage. This is because so many 'family planning' or 'birth control' programmes have amounted to population control programmes imposed by the industrialised, rich countries on poor developing nations. The most commonly used terms are 'family planning', 'child spacing', and 'birth control'. 'Fertility regulation' is used by some women's health groups. 'Family planning' is rejected by some because it does not address the needs of young sexually active people or of people who may not have or want a family. 'Birth control' is interpreted by many people, particularly in developing countries, as coercive and linked to population control. Oxfam has adopted the usage 'birth planning', because it seems the most comprehensive and least controversial, and it refers to the involvement of both women and men.

More significant is the shift in perception from the focus on 'family planning' and 'maternal health' to 'reproductive health' or 'sexual health'. This should include maternity, birth planning, reproductive morbidity, and sex education.

b. Population control and birth planning

Populations are described in terms of size, growth, distribution, and composition. But much of the debate has centred on population growth, and focused on 'overpopulation' in poor countries as a major world problem and the cause of poverty and underdevelopment. (See 1.3.2.1 The population issue.) Population growth is the outcome of reduced child mortality, longer life expectancy, and fertility; the control of women's fertility is therefore often promoted as an easy way to control population growth. For this reason, birth-planning policies and programmes may be viewed with suspicion and even rejected, particularly if promoted by international agencies. Some institutions, such as the Roman Catholic church, oppose artificial methods of birth-planning on religious grounds.

Programmes which have population control as their main aim tend to see women as producers of too many babies, and as targets or clients of contraceptive services. Such programmes have often failed or produced a backlash of widespread rejection among potential users.

To address population growth requires much more than regulating women's fertility through isolated interventions. Population growth is influenced by the socio-economic status of women, and their level of education, health service provision, infant mortality rates, and religious beliefs and cultural practices. These factors vary widely between and within countries. Women and men want to limit their family size when it makes economic sense for them to do so, but rational decisions are not

5

always possible when cultural traditions place a high value on large families, or on securing a male heir.

The availability of contraceptive and other reproductive health services is crucial for women's health, regardless of the demographic impact. Possessing the means to regulate their own fertility is central to women's empowerment, and essential to the securing of their rights over their own bodies. Birth-planning information and services should be available and accessible, and Oxfam should encourage all PHC programmes to provide good quality services.

4.6.3 Oxfam's support for birth planning

Birth-planning programmes must be sensitively designed as they touch upon some of the most personal aspects of women and men's lives. It is important to understand and differentiate between women's and men's attitudes towards motherhood, fatherhood, and fertility, patterns of decision-making in the community and household, and social and cultural beliefs and practices related to sex. The way people want to approach the issue may vary; women may want to discuss it with men, or prefer to discuss it in separate women-only groups; adolescents may prefer to discuss it without their elders present. Oxfam's approach is to analyse the particular needs and perceptions of individuals in relation to birth planning, and to support interventions which respect women's reproductive rights and promote women's reproductive health.

Oxfam recognises the importance of birth planning because:

- there is an expressed and unmet need for it, especially among women;
- it contributes to reduction of maternal deaths and to improving the health and well-being of women;
- it helps to improve the well-being of children;
- it allows women greater understanding and control of their bodies and their lives;
- it can increase opportunities for women's personal and social development.

Oxfam believes that it is a right of individuals, particularly of women, to be able to choose the number of children they want, when to have them, and when to stop having them. Birth planning services should:

- be available and accessible — physically, culturally and economically — to women and men, without any form of coercion or conditionality;
- consult and involve women in policy making and programme implementation;

- provide informed choice: a variety of methods should be made available, and enough information provided so that women and men can make informed choices according to their ages and personal circumstances;
- strongly recommend the use of condoms, given the increasing rates of HIV infection and AIDS;
- be backed up with adequate medical services to deal with side effects and/or contraceptive failure;
- recognise that needs differ, depending on the varying circumstances of, for example, single people and couples, childless people and parents, adolescents and older people;
- increase the awareness and participation of men, but without limiting women's ability to choose;
- support women when they challenge the structures and institutions in their societies which constrain their choices;
- strive to enhance women's education and self-awareness;
- be part of a broader programme of reproductive health care, including sex education for both women and men, particularly adolescent girls and boys;
- give greater priority to promoting women's reproductive rights and reproductive health.

4.6.4 Practical interventions

Oxfam has supported birth planning, usually as a component of a PHC programme, which includes raising awareness through health education, providing information about methods, and providing services. Some Catholic-run PHC programmes only provide information on natural methods, and should be encouraged to refer people wanting other methods to appropriate services. Oxfam supports women's groups in, for example, Bolivia, Nicaragua, and South Africa, many of which include among their activities awareness raising, information on methods of birth planning, sexuality workshops or sex education.

Oxfam has funded research and information work in connection with abuses of certain types of programmes such as those promoting incentives, sterilisation, and new methods (implants), as a contribution to the quality of programmes aiming to make safe, dignified, and suitable services available.

Oxfam supports a wide range of activities for the prevention of HIV infection and AIDS. Much of this work involves education and awareness raising, including the promotion of condoms which can have a dual role in contraception and in protecting against sexually transmitted diseases, including AIDS. (See 5.4.7 HIV andAIDS.)

5

The attitudes of staff in clinics or other health facilities may encourage or discourage women from using the services. A common reason given by women for discontinuation of contraceptive use is the lack of respect service providers show towards them. Health workers should be trained to listen to women's concerns and needs, and to treat them with respect.

Birth planning programmes need secure long-term funding, as people will need to use contraception for as long as they are fertile and do not want to have children. Most countries have to import contraceptives. Governments and international agencies often distribute contraceptives free of charge or at subsidised prices. The social marketing of condoms, particularly in areas where HIV/AIDS is prevalent, has been a successful form of intervention. Oxfam does not support social marketing of methods requiring back-up health services, such as the contraceptive pill.

4.6.5 Birth-planning services

Birth-planning services can be offered in several different ways. Birth planning is usually considered to be a medical intervention, offered in a medical setting — in clinics and hospitals — even though birth planning is for healthy people, and not all methods require health or medical workers to distribute them. Most contraceptive methods are required regularly; and social taboos mean that many people find discussing and acquiring contraceptives embarrassing. All users are different and require different types of services: adolescents, mothers, young couples, women with large families, single people, migrant workers. A range of services should be provided, with the back-up of well-trained health workers and medical care if necessary.

There are a number of different delivery systems for birth planning and the distribution of contraceptives, either through health facilities such as MCH or family-planning clinics or hospitals, or through individuals (Community Based Distributors), or via social marketing, whereby condoms are sold in public places with a small profit to the seller. All these systems have different advantages and disadvantages for different people, and should be carefully assessed when birth planning is supported.

The amount that people are prepared, or able, to pay for contraception depends upon their socio-economic and cultural status and on the importance they attach to averting pregnancy. Governments and international agencies often distribute contraceptives free of charge, or at subsidised prices. However, birth planning should never be encouraged by offering material incentives either to the user or the provider.

4.6.6 Birth-planning methods

The need for programmes to offer as wide a choice of methods as possible cannot be overemphasised. No one method of contraception can be universally recommended or is necessarily appropriate throughout an individual's entire fertile life. The most suitable and acceptable method for each person depends on age, number of children, state of health, civil status, social and cultural factors, and personal preference, where people, particularly women, are free to choose; in most societies they are not.

The social and cultural factors which determine the most appropriate or inappropriate methods to use, such as religious belief, sexual behaviour, nature of the relations between women and men, are not themselves static. Forms of birth planning which may be rejected (for example by religious authorities) may later become acceptable. In all cases, the socio-cultural constraints and opportunities for women in relation to birth planning should be carefully analysed and evaluated.

All methods have advantages and disadvantages and none is 100 per cent effective. In many countries there is a limited choice of methods, which leads to predominant use of one method even if it is not the most appropriate one. For example, sterilisation in Brazil accounts for 41 per cent of all contraception used, even in younger women. The only method provided by the state in Vietnam is intra-uterine devices (IUDs). Diaphragms are not available in Mexico.

In many programmes promoted by governments or international agencies, there is a marked preference for methods controlled by the provider, such as implants and injectable contraceptives, over user-controlled methods, such as condoms or the pill, which may require more information and counselling for their use. Barrier methods, particularly women-controlled methods such as the diaphragm or cap, have been similarly neglected. Yet, in industrialised countries, barrier methods make up 51.8 per cent of methods used, compared to 15.1 per cent in developing countries.

There is considerable controversy around the use of the injectable contraceptive, Depo-provera, and women's groups in many countries are strongly opposed to it. The evidence is that the risks of Depo-provera are not any higher than those of other hormonal contraceptives. Many poor women express a preference for it because it can be used without their husband's knowledge, and, unlike the pill, they do not need to remember to take it every day. However, all methods that are not user-controlled can be abused by the service providers, and Oxfam does not support programmes which use coercion in any way or in which people are not fully informed about the methods and their risks. Injectable contraceptives carry an added risk

741

because once injected, their effects are not reversible and may persist for months before the woman's body can begin to regulate its hormonal balance again. Poor women are often not effectively informed about the dangers, such as bleeding and other side-effects.

Condoms protect against HIV infection and other sexually transmitted diseases, and it is important to promote their use for protection against STDs as well as for contraception. Breast-feeding has an appreciable contraceptive effect during the first three to six months after delivery, particularly if it is the exclusive form of feeding; but its contraceptive effectiveness varies widely from one individual woman to another, and is not reliable. It plays an important role in child spacing, not least because in many cultures, sex is restricted while women are feeding a baby. Breast-feeding should be encouraged for this reason as well as for its beneficial effect on the child's health and nutrition, although it is no substitute for longer-term methods of contraception.

The main contraceptive methods with some of their characteristics are summarised below:

a. Traditional methods
These include breast-feeding, and traditional 'taboo periods'. For example, in some cultures, sex is forbidden until a child is two years old or until breast feeding is stopped. In others, intercourse is restricted to certain times. The reliability of abstention can be increased by various methods such as following the calendar (rhythm method), taking temperature measurements, and examining cervical mucus. Mucus examination is complicated by vaginal discharges which are caused by infections or illness; this makes the 'Billings' method difficult to use. Women do not always have the privacy to examine vaginal mucus at the appropriate times, and there may be cultural inhibitions against doing so. The advantages of 'natural' methods are that they carry no side-effects or risks, but even when care is taken, pregnancy rates remain high. These methods mean that only women take responsibility for contraception, but that they rely on male co-operation in observing periods of abstention. Withdrawal, where the male withdraws his penis before ejaculating, is very widely used, but is not a reliable method of contraception.

b. Barrier methods
These include the condom, sponge, diaphragm, cervical cap — most used together with spermicides. The role of condoms in the prevention of STDs is an advantage which does not apply to other barrier methods. The advantages of the other methods are that they carry no health risks apart from occasional irritation or allergy to spermicides, are readily reversible, and are controlled by the woman. Their effectiveness is

strongly influenced by the expertise of the user. Disadvantages for women may be resistance from men to using condoms. Condoms have the advantage of obliging men to share responsibility for contraception. The female condom has also been developed and has been used apparently with some success in Zimbabwe. It is not widely available or promoted more generally.

c. Hormonal methods

Oral contraceptives: combination pill and progesterone-only pill. Their advantages are high effectiveness when taken regularly, reversibility, and user-control. Their use is not related to intercourse. Disadvantages are that trained personnel are needed to check users, and there are health risks and side-effects. These include nausea, weight gain, increased risk of strokes and thrombosis with the combination pill, and menstrual irregularities and increased risk of ectopic pregnancy. All these affect women only, and do not require men to take responsibility for contraception.

Injectable: monthly or three-monthly injections. The advantages are that they are highly effective, not related to intercourse, and convenient. They are reversible, but conception is usually delayed, between 4 and 18 months. Disadvantages are that users do not control them, they can be abused, and health risks include heavy inter-menstrual bleeding. They may also cause amenorrhea. Like oral contraceptives, women take the health risks, and men take no responsibility for contraception.

Implants: silicone rods inserted under the skin of a woman's arm, that release hormones. The most common one is Norplant which lasts five years. They are the most recent hormonal method and hence not as much is known about potential long-term problems. They are highly effective, reversible and convenient, but not under user-control and their removal requires minor surgery. Side-effects and health risks to women are similar to those of other hormonals, but infection at the implant site is an added risk. Men are not required to take responsibility for contraception.

d. Intra-uterine devices (IUDs)

These are effective and reversible, not related to intercourse, but not controlled by the user. They are effectively abortion-provoking devices. Health risks include infection and perforation of uterus at insertion, increased menstrual bleeding often with pain, risk of pelvic inflammatory disease and local vaginal infection, such as thrush and chlamydia, and risk of ectopic pregnancy. They are not recommended for women who have never been pregnant or who are anaemic. Men are not required to take responsibility for contraception.

5

e. Sterilisation

Both male (vasectomy) and female (tubal ligation, tubectomy) sterilisations are highly effective, irreversible methods. They should only be considered when no more children are desired. Neither causes impairment of sexual function, and they do not carry health risks beyond the operative and post-operative period. Vasectomy is a minor operation, done under local anaesthetic, which carries little risk. Tubal ligation or tubectomy require opening the abdomen and are therefore far riskier, both during and after surgery. Sterilisation must be performed under sterile clinical conditions, with adequate surgical facilities, and by trained personnel.

4.6.7 Abortion

It is impossible to estimate, of the 40-60 million abortions worldwide women undergo each year — legal and illegal — how many cause women permanent damage, or kill them. Figures are usually under-estimated, because they are not available for illegal abortions. In South Africa, for example, 1,024 legal abortions were carried out in 1991; according to the Department of National Health and Population Development between 42,000 and 167,000 illegal abortions are carried out each year, and health workers treating women for complications from illegal abortions claim that the figure may be closer to 200,000.

Abortion is not a contraceptive method. However, it is an important back-up in the case of contraceptive failure. From a public health perspective, making abortion available, safe, and legal is a significant way of decreasing maternal mortality and improving women's health. Performed under adequate and hygienic conditions it is a safe and straightforward procedure, but where it is illegal it is often performed in unhygienic conditions and by unskilled people, and can lead to serious complications, including perforation, infection, and in many cases, death. In some countries where it is legal, such as India and Zambia, it is not easily available nor necessarily safe.

The most common methods used are surgical — dilatation and curettage (D and C) — and vacuum aspiration. Medical abortion has also been effected with a drug known as RU 486 (misepristone), an anti-progesterone which acts on the lining of the uterus to provoke rejection of an early pregnancy. It is taken orally in a single dose and followed 36-48 hours later by a further drug to cause dilation of the cervix. It is effective in 95 per cent of cases, but is only recommended for the first trimester. It is expensive, and requires longer-term care by trained health workers than surgical abortion. Its use in developing countries is under debate.

4.6.8 Key questions

1 Does the PHC programme offer birth planning services? If not, why not?
2 How are clients 'recruited'? Is it clear that no incentive, disincentive or other form of pressure is involved?
3 Is there a reasonable choice of methods?
4 Are follow-up and continuity of services and regular supplies assured? Are the facilities adequate?
5 Are health workers adequately trained for the methods they offer? Do they treat the women respectfully? Do they inform and counsel women and men who are users?
6 Are women well-informed about the possible side effects and complications of each method on offer?
7 Does health information and education work include sex education? Are efforts made to include men in this?
8 Does the programme promote women's choice and address their needs? Does it address women's reproductive rights? Have women been fully consulted about the services they require?

4.7 HIV and AIDS

4.7.1 Introduction

The Acquired Immune Deficiency Syndrome (AIDS) is a disease caused by the Human Immune Deficiency Virus (HIV). HIV and AIDS have far-reaching social and economic consequences for individuals and their families, for local communities, and for states. According to WHO, by the end of 1993 there were 15 million people infected with HIV. Of these, over one million were children; and, since almost half of newly infected adults are women, current estimates suggest that there will be 13 million women — and a correspondingly greater number of children — infected with HIV by the year 2000. The number of AIDS cases is expected by WHO to have quadrupled by the turn of the century.

The brunt of HIV/AIDS is felt in developing countries — particularly sub-Saharan Africa, but also in many parts of Latin America, the Caribbean, and Asia — where already overloaded health services are being stretched to breaking point. The majority of people with HIV infection and AIDS are in their most productive years: about 60 per cent of new infections are among 15-24 year olds. Thus the disease affects all aspects of the economy and development, from household to national level. While there is no known cure for AIDS, the prognosis and quality of life of sufferers in developing countries is far lower than in the industrialised nations.

745

In view of the scale of the HIV/AIDS epidemic, and the fact that HIV does not recognise gender, race, class or national borders, the impact of HIV/AIDS is inescapably a development issue. It compels individuals and societies to look critically and openly at their sexual behaviour and moral values, and to examine the kinds of relationships and social contexts within which sexual contact takes place. Only if they are based on a sensitive understanding of these issues can education and awareness-raising programmes be successful in promoting the changes in people's behaviour that will be necessary to contain the spread of HIV/AIDS.

4.7.2 Background

a. Appearance of the disease
AIDS was first recognised in 1981 in the USA as a disease affecting mainly male homosexuals. It was later recognised in other countries, particularly Central and Eastern Africa. In Uganda it was known as 'slim' disease. The virus was isolated in 1983 and a blood test to detect antibodies to the virus was developed in 1985. Recognition and knowledge of the disease has increased enormously since then. The WHO Global Programme on AIDS(GPA) helps governments to set up AIDS prevention and control programmes.

b. Magnitude of the problem
HIV and AIDS has spread to all continents, and is referred to as 'the AIDS pandemic'. There is a distinction between HIV-infected people, who are susceptible to AIDS, and AIDS cases. The number of AIDS cases reported to the WHO ignores those people who are infected, but asymptomatic. For every person with AIDS, there may be 50-100 HIV-positive people with AIDS antibodies, who can infect others.

Most HIV-positive people will develop AIDS. The eight-year incubation period of the disease means that seropositive people who are currently healthy can ignore, deny or be unaware of the problem until they are very sick.

WHO estimated at the end of 1993 that 15 million people were HIV-positive, 10 million of whom were in Africa. In one year alone, half a million Africans developed AIDS. In South and South-East Asia, over 1.5 million people were thought to be infected; and by the late 1990s more Asians than Africans will be infected each year. HIV has also spread to parts of North Africa and the Middle East, while in Latin America and the Caribbean 1.5 million adults are infected. (Figures taken from WHO EPI Update, November 1993.)

The true prevalence of HIV infection can be known only by carrying out antibody tests on random samples within each national population.

However, such testing raises ethical issues, as well being fraught with practical difficulties and financial constraints. Much of the available information uses blood surveys from particular social groups, such as women attending antenatal clinics, blood donors, or people whose behaviour is considered to be particularly at risk, such as those attending STD clinics, sex workers, and intravenous drug users. Results from such selective surveys cannot be extrapolated to apply to the whole population, since the prevalence of HIV may be exceptionally high among certain social groups.

c. What is HIV/AIDS?

HIV affects the immune system, which is the body's defence against diseases. AIDS exposes sufferers to a range of opportunistic illnesses, some of which do not cause serious problems when the immune system is working. AIDS itself is a fatal condition, with no known cure.

People with HIV infection may remain healthy for several years. Even after they develop symptoms of AIDS, it is possible to maintain their quality of life by appropriate treatment of the infections to which they become susceptible. However, people who already suffer chronic ill-health or malnutrition, or do not have good quality health care, have a much lower rate of survival.

AIDS affects mainly the sexually active sector of the population: those between 15 and 45 years of age. The number of women infected with HIV affects the number of children infected before or during birth. HIV is uncommon in older children or in elderly people. In developing countries the average peak prevalence is in women in the 20-24 years age group, and in men between 25 and 29 years. Children infected by their mothers usually die before the age of two (often much sooner), and may not be diagnosed as infected with HIV until the scheduled time for routine immunisations.

5

d. Testing for HIV

There are two types of HIV — HIV 1 and HIV 2 — each requiring different tests. The latter is found mainly in West Africa, but it is spreading to other areas. Both types are transmitted in the same way, and both cause AIDS.

The tests currently in use detect antibodies to HIV in the blood, rather than HIV itself. The most common is the Enzyme Linked Immuno-absorbent Assay (ELISA) test. It is highly specific, but may give some false positive results. For blood screening this is not important, but for individual diagnoses, supplementary tests are recommended. The Western Blot is expensive and difficult to carry out, and many health facilities repeat the ELISA test instead. Cheaper and easier tests on blood and saliva are being developed.

Antibodies to HIV take between 3 to 12 weeks to appear: the 'window period', during which a person could unwittingly be infected and transmitting HIV without being able to be detected.

HIV testing and blood surveys raise ethical questions. It may be argued that people have the right — and possibly the need — to know if they are HIV-positive; and that testing should lead to changes in their sexual behaviour. However, the evidence that people change their behaviour in response to such tests is not encouraging. Screening is difficult to justify when no treatment can be offered, and when the consequences of a positive result may be distressing and detrimental to the individuals concerned, and to their families.

Testing should not be performed without ensuring that those tested understand the potential consequences of a positive result, including the likelihood of being ostracised or discriminated against, for example, by losing their jobs, their homes, or any insurance or pension policies they might have. Sensitive pre- and post-test counselling and follow-up care are extremely important. As one HIV-positive man said:

Once you are told you are HIV-positive, there is no such thing as being asymptomatic. You may not have physical symptoms, but your life is forever changed. (Quoted in Berer, 1993.)

e. Transmission of HIV
Transmission mainly involves semen, vaginal fluids, and blood. HIV is sensitive to heat, to dryness, and to the sun. It does not spread easily from person to person, and is not transmitted through hand shaking, kissing, coughing or sneezing, sharing of eating utensils or of communal toilet facilities, or insect bites. HIV is transmitted in three main ways:

Sexual transmission: this is the most common form, and may be through vaginal or anal intercourse, whether heterosexual or homosexual. Heterosexual transmission is the most common form of transmission in sub-Saharan Africa and in other developing countries, and is increasing in industrialised nations such as USA and UK, where homosexual transmission had previously been more common. Sexually transmitted diseases (STDs), particularly those which are ulcerative, increase the risk of HIV transmission.

Infected blood, and infected needles, syringes, or tattooing instruments: blood transfusions can transmit HIV through infected whole blood and Factor 8, the blood clotting factor given to haemophiliacs. In developing countries, blood transfusions are more frequently required for women who are malnourished, anaemic, or haemorrhaging after miscarriages or childbirth. Reducing the rates of anaemia in pregnancy significantly reduces the need for transfusions, and thus, the chances of HIV transmission. Where HIV testing of blood donors is not possible, health workers must calculate the risks between death from loss of blood or HIV infection. Where only one unit of blood is required, oral or venal rehydration is preferable.

Intravenous drug users are frequently exposed to HIV infection, especially where needles are recycled or not sterile. Among groups of people who may be involved in drug abuse, such as street children or sex workers, the risk of HIV infection may be high.

Mother to child transmission: this occurs either in the womb through the placenta, or during birth through contact with the mother's infected blood. The risk of transmission is 25-30 per cent and is more likely if the mother has signs of AIDS. Diagnosis in babies is complicated by the fact that the HIV antibodies of the mother are present in the baby for up to 18 months. Children infected with HIV usually die within two years, from pneumonia and wasting. Many women discover that they themselves are HIV positive only when their child is diagnosed.

There may be some risk of transmission through breast-feeding, particularly if women have been recently infected, for example, by a blood transfusion at birth. WHO recommends that breast-feeding should nevertheless be encouraged. Women infected with HIV should continue to breast-feed their babies in countries where the risks of diarrhoea and malnutrition from bottle feeding outweigh the risk of HIV infection.

f. Signs and symptoms

AIDS is a series of opportunistic infections, so the signs and symptoms vary widely. TB and salmonellosis are common signs, but unspecific signs, such as chronic diarrhoea, weight loss or swollen lymph nodes, may also occur. Women often suffer gynaecological problems, including an increased risk of cervical cancer. The spread of AIDS has increased the prevalence of TB, sometimes in unusual forms.

g. Treatment

There is no cure for HIV/AIDS; and trauma, stress, and surgery can all precipitate HIV into AIDS. Appropriate treatment of the opportunistic infections associated with AIDS, combined with good nutrition, can help to prolong life. However, life expectancy is worse in poor countries, and among poor people in rich countries, partly because AIDS is likely to be diagnosed at a later stage. In addition, people who are socially or economically disadvantaged may already be suffering the illnesses of poverty, and be unable to obtain treatment and good food. For instance, in Africa the average time between diagnosis and death is 18 months, whereas in the USA it can be up to eight years.

There is no proof that Zidovudine or AZT prolongs life.

5

749

The Oxfam handbook of development and relief

4.7.3 Practical interventions

a. Prevention and control

Most countries have set up National AIDS Control Programmes with support from WHO and other donors. The emphasis is on information, education, and the promotion of behaviour change. All health programmes should incorporate HIV/AIDS prevention activities, focusing on education and awareness-raising, lobbying governments and religious authorities to take AIDS seriously, and urging the public and policy-makers to prevent a crisis from developing. In countries where the prevalence is extremely high, such as East and Central Africa, additional interventions may be necessary.

Many organisations funded by Oxfam are directly or indirectly involved in such work. For example, an association in Kenya runs a counselling service and drop-in centre for people infected with HIV, which includes group therapy sessions. A central aim is to challenge the stigma associated with the disease, and one of the results has been that more people have been prepared to admit their status in public and hence to change the climate of opinion surrounding HIV/AIDS. In Jamaica, Oxfam funds a research and education programme run by the University of the West Indies, in conjunction with the Ministries of Health and Education. The findings, which included that some children were sexually active from the age of 10 years, led to in-service training for teachers, to help them to offer sex education in a more enlightened way.

b. Education in AIDS awareness

(See 5.4.11 Health education and health provision; 2.1 Gender; and 3.1.2 Education and training.)

Practising safer sex or abstinence is the only way to reduce sexual transmission. However, as many women's organisations and activists have emphasised, safer sex can only be assured in the context of safer relationships. In practice, many women and girls do not have the right to exercise control over their own bodies, or to determine the sexual access that men should have to them. The imbalance in power between women and men — economically, socially, and physically — is responsible for much of the lack of safety in sexual relationships. Violence, and fear of violence or abuse, are frequently identified by women, both married and unmarried, as reasons why they do not insist on safer sex, even when they know there is a risk of HIV infection. For many women, sex work (or selling sexual services) is the only way to earn a living; and sex tourism involving young girls and boys is increasingly common in parts of South and South-East Asia. In such cases, the male clients often insist on 'unprotected sex', and refuse to use condoms.

HIV/AIDS is often a difficult subject to discuss, precisely because it forces people to admit to themselves — and to others — details about their sexual relationships that they may prefer to conceal. Men may be reluctant to admit to having had homosexual contact, or to being bisexual; they may also be unwilling to admit to buying sexual services from women, children or other men. Men and women alike may find it difficult to admit to sexual infidelities, or to having had a number of sexual partners in the past. Most people find it hard to accept that their most intimate lives may have exposed them to the risk of death: and fear and denial tend to reinforce each other.

The denial of personal risk makes it difficult to encourage changes in sexual behaviour. In tackling the issues surrounding HIV/AIDS, it is vital to help women and men to feel comfortable enough to discuss their personal relationships and sexual behaviour openly, in order to confront the problems they might face in protecting themselves from HIV infection. For many people, this is more acceptable in same-sex than in mixed groups. Women's organisations often include courses on reproductive health and sexuality within their overall empowerment approach. Men and adolescent boys may also find it easier to discuss aspects of their sexuality and emotional relationships with others who have shared similar experiences, and with whom they can identify. Men's anxieties about the use of condoms, for example, are often more readily shared in an all-male group. Whether it is undertaken in mixed or in same-sex groups, awareness-raising work should be aimed at enabling women and men to discuss the nature of their relationships *with each other*, in order to challenge the nature of oppressive gender and power relations. For instance, a women's legal education group in Uganda has supported women who refuse to have sex with their husbands, when they know that their husbands are sexually active with other women.

Public information and education campaigns, on which more focused education and awareness-raising work may draw, often include leaflets, radio slots, puppet shows, street theatre, videos, or television. Messages and approaches vary according to the needs of specific audiences, whether these are sexually active adolescents, school children, street children, mothers, sex-workers, trades unions, or church groups. Oxfam has supported activities ranging from the production of posters in Uganda, leaflets in Zaire, and a schools magazine in Ethiopia, to health education programmes using puppets in South Africa, theatre in Namibia, and video in Malawi. In many cases, these activities are also strengthened through the establishment of umbrella organisations, bringing together a number of NGOs and others concerned with HIV/AIDS education.

Messages that are intended to inform and to educate must be suitable for the intended audience, and based on what they know or believe

5

751

about HIV/AIDS. While mass media are invaluable in transmitting information or reinforcing messages, especially for non-literate populations, mass campaigns alone will not lead to changes in people's relationships and sexual behaviour. Small discussion groups, where people come together because they have something in common with each other, may be more appropriate. For example, Oxfam supports a voluntary agency in Brazil that runs a number of education programmes for specific population groups in rural and urban areas of the Bahia region. These include male and female prostitutes, homosexual and bisexual communities, adolescents in schools, and informal discussion circles organised through a federation of shanty-town associations. The work of the agency is supplemented through a telephone help-line, and publicised in a regular television programme.

Sex workers and their clients are population groups with whom it is important to work, given their exposure to STDs in general and to HIV in particular. Sex workers are much more likely to use protection with their clients than are the clients themselves in other sexual encounters, including with their own partners. Transmission generally is from client to sex worker, rather than the other way round. An important form of assistance is to help people who sell sexual services to have more control over their work conditions, in addition to offering information about safer sex. Where sex-workers are organised, as in the case of the Association of Prostitutes of Rio de Janeiro, they are in a better position to take collective action: for instance, by insisting that clients use condoms, and demanding legal and health services. In Haiti, one programme combined information about HIV/AIDS and condom distribution through beauty parlours that sex workers were known to frequent.

Education of health workers is an important facet of AIDS awareness-raising programmes. Health workers often have their own fears and prejudices about HIV/AIDS, and may discriminate against people who are infected. Training in both the traditional and the formal sectors should include information on transmission, sterilisation, disposal of needles and other material, hygiene, and care of people with AIDS. Health workers should practise the standard precautions for infection, whether a patient is HIV positive or not.

Caring for very sick or dying young people and babies is distressing, and NGOs may support interventions that offer the counselling and assistance that carers need.

c. Condoms

Apart from their use as contraceptives, condoms protect against STDs, including HIV. However, while they can be found in the capital cities of most developing countries, they may not always be readily obtainable, or affordable. A regular supply of condoms and a means to distribute them effectively should be provided by the State. NGO health programmes can lobby to ensure condoms are made available in the necessary quantities to those who need them, and people are taught how to use them.

The shelf-life of condoms depends upon storage conditions. Heat damages the rubber, and packaging varies in quality. Few developing countries can afford to test samples of imported condoms to check their quality; Zimbabwe is one of the few that has WHO-approved condom testing laboratories.

d. Promoting safe blood

Most countries have some form of blood screening for HIV, although this may not be done in all hospitals, particularly in rural areas. Shortages in supplies and trained staff may be a problem, particularly if large quantities of blood are needed suddenly. Oxfam has funded the provision of ELISA equipment for screening, but in most countries this is provided by national programmes. Where HIV is prevalent, much donated blood is likely to be in the 'window period' (see 5.4.7.2.d Testing for HIV/AIDS), and other ways of screening must be found. In Zimbabwe, for example, blood donors are first screened by interview: anyone considered a possible risk is not used.

It is generally advisable to keep transfusions to the minimum. In Zaire, the rate of transfusions was reduced by more than 50 per cent as a result of training health workers in appropriate treatment.

e. Mother to child transmission

At present, nothing prevents the transmission of HIV from mother to child, and mothers need special care and assistance in coming to terms with their situation. This should include consideration of their domestic circumstances, in particular if they are solely responsible for maintaining their household.

Many women may be diagnosed HIV-positive in antenatal or baby clinics, so counselling and support should be available. Where abortion is legal, it may be offered; but it is rarely an option and women often prefer to have the child, even knowing that the child will not survive for very long. Abortion could precipitate HIV into AIDS.

f. Care of people with HIV/AIDS

Where many people in the community suffer from AIDS, care becomes an integral part of prevention. Home-based care programmes can raise local awareness, and may encourage behaviour change at both individual and social level.

In the 1980s, many hospitals opened special AIDS wards. But as the

753

prevalence of HIV increased, it was realised that every patient might be HIV-positive — whether they had been admitted to TB, maternity or casualty wards — and these special wards were abandoned. Health workers should be trained to treat all patients as if they were HIV-positive, observing high standards of hygiene, and keeping blood transfusions and surgery to the necessary minimum.

Many hospitals in Africa, such as one funded by Oxfam in Uganda, run home-based care programmes. These involve counselling, medical treatment, nutritional or other support, and sometimes pastoral care, through home visits by teams of trained staff. Often, a network of volunteer supporters is also established to complement the work of the trained personnel. These programmes can be expensive, and incur high transport costs. They are nevertheless preferable in many respects to isolating AIDS sufferers in hospitals, far away from their homes, and with significant economic implications for them and their families. Economic assistance, or initiatives to generate some form of alternative income for carers and/or patients, may be needed to make home-based care viable.

Pre- and post-test counselling are important in helping people and their families to come to terms with a positive diagnosis, and then with death and bereavement. Voluntary organisations that provide these services have started in many countries. The AIDS Support Organisation (TASO) in Uganda is one of the best known, but there are many others such as GAPA (Grupo de Apoyo contra AIDS) in Brazil, TAPWAK in Kenya, and WAMATA in Tanzania.

The dependents of people with AIDS pose an increasing problem. In some areas of Africa, there is a significant number of AIDS orphans, whose care falls to grandparents who may be unable to feed them adequately, or to pay school fees. A family may remain together with the oldest child in charge, or the children may be absorbed by other family or community members.

However, the number of orphans may be so high that the community cannot absorb them, and many of the initiatives for orphans tend to be welfare oriented. Many orphans become street children or prostitutes and therefore at increased risk from HIV infection themselves. (See 2.3.3.4 Street children.) For widows too, especially where a man has several wives, the death of a husband can often mean destitution unless the legal and customary framework exists to ensure that she and her children are adequately catered for by other family members.

g. Human rights
HIV/AIDS has exposed many prejudices, and much ignorance and hypocrisy, about personal relationships, and sexual behaviour. There is

some potential for effective international and national advocacy work in protesting against the abuse of human rights of those suffering from HIV/AIDS. For example, joint NGO lobbying took place in response to the entry restrictions imposed by the US government on people with HIV who wished to attend an international AIDS conference in San Francisco. WHO no longer supports conferences where there are entry restrictions for people with HIV.

Initially, the specific concerns of women were not understood, and they tended to be treated as either transmitters or carers. There is now greater awareness of the need to look at the problem of HIV/AIDS in the context of gender and power relations, and full recognition of women's needs and rights. This in turn has led to more work with men, as well as with women, to change the attitudes and behaviour that place partners and children at risk.

Discrimination against people with HIV/AIDS is common worldwide. Any HIV/AIDS programmes supported by Oxfam must be based on respect for human rights, and a rejection of discriminatory practices.

4.7.4 Key questions

1 Are prevention and control of HIV and AIDS incorporated into health programmes? If not, why not? Are health workers trained to diagnose and treat STDs (including contact tracing)?
2 What are the government and existing health services doing for the prevention and control of HIV and AIDS? Do the proposed activities complement this?
3 If testing is offered, is pre- and post-test counselling part of the programme? What follow-up is offered to people who are HIV positive? Is care for the carers included?
4 Are the messages in education or information programmes appropriate to the intended audience? Do they address issues of gender and power relations in a sensitive way? Do the messages stress women's rights over their own bodies?
5 How are prevention and care integrated? Is the programme reaching only people with HIV/AIDS, or does it include people with other chronic or reproductive health diseases? Are essential drugs for common infections and symptoms available?
6 If changes in sexual attitudes and behaviour are proposed among specific sets of people, how are the different perspectives of women and men taken into account?
7 Are the various NGOs working on HIV/AIDS co-ordinating their work? Are there ways in which co-ordination among NGOs, and with international bodies, could be initiated or strengthened?

4.8 The provision of essential drugs

4.8.1 Introduction

The provision of safe and affordable drugs requires considerable organisation and collaboration on many fronts, at global, national and local level. National drug policies, the availability of appropriate and affordable drugs, good professional training, and accurate public information, all contribute to a situation where the supply and use of drugs supports people's health and well-being.

The solution to most avoidable ill health lies in removing the socio-economic and political factors that cause or contribute to it. However, correctly used, drugs alleviate suffering and save lives, and are an essential element in treating conditions with public health implications, such as TB, leprosy, and malaria. Treatment for the conditions related to HIV/AIDS would be impossible without them. Furthermore, the acceptance of PHC by people who use the services is strongly related to the provision of affordable drugs.

However, up to half the world's population are not given the drugs they need. Reasons for this include the real decline in international and national resources for health, political instability in many developing countries, and the increasing demand for certain drugs arising from the resurgence of some diseases in epidemic form.

As a consequence of international lobbying and campaigning over more than a decade, many governments have adopted partial national drugs policies, based on the concept of essential drugs in the public sector. However, severe resource constraints on public sector health services mean that drugs are often lacking at primary as well as secondary levels of care. Many governments do not have the resources to finance, regulate or manage pharmaceutical services on a continuing basis. The private sector is increasingly relied upon for all aspects of the drug supply chain, even though it is seldom integrated into comprehensive national drug policies. Some private companies continue to produce and promote inessential pharmaceuticals, with the result that quantities of undesirable and costly drugs continue to drain national budgets and erode the incomes of poor people. Poor prescribing and irrational use of drugs are widespread in both public and private sectors; and self-medication is commonplace where the sale of drugs is not restricted.

4.8.2 Practical approaches

a. WHO: the 'essential drugs' concept

WHO has provided the policy leadership and the practical framework for rationalisation of drug supply and use. The first model list of essential drugs (1977) sought to simplify drugs policy through drastically reducing numbers, selecting only those which matched priority health needs and which were acceptably safe, affordable, and of good quality. It established a core list of 250 drugs for national needs, and 30-40 for PHC. The list was intended to provide guidance for more specific adaptation to the requirements of individual countries. (See Resources Directory.)

The list, which has been revised several times, emphasises generic, rather than brand-name, drugs, and so has contributed to price reductions on the world market. Using generic names avoids the confusion that can arise when many different brands are sold. (For example, metronidazole, used for dysentery caused by amoebas and giardia, is sold under 25 different proprietary names.) The essential drugs list also discourages dangerous combinations of two or more drugs in one preparation — a marketing device often used to increase the price.

A selected list provides the basis for a comprehensive national drugs policy, simplifying all components of management, training, and rational use, in the interests of efficiency and safety. While many governments have followed WHO's lead and adapted the list to their specific disease patterns in the public sector, few have attempted to control the private sector.

b. Drug supply and availability

The economic crisis has made the provision of essential drugs on a sustainable basis increasingly difficult. It makes it more necessary for NGOs to adopt the essential drugs approach, rationalising drug use and saving costs by managing drug supply efficiently, whether or not a national policy exists.

To simplify drug supply and use, all health programmes supported by Oxfam should adopt a standard list of essential drugs using generic names, which conform with the Ministry of Health essential drugs list where one exists, or with WHO's model list. If drugs are imported directly, procurement agencies such as Equipment for Charity Hospitals Overseas (ECHO), and International Dispensary Association (IDA) (see Resources Directory), can help with selecting and purchasing good quality, low-cost, essential drugs. Procurement through agencies which can assure adequate quality as well as low cost is essential in view of the prevalence of sub-standard and counterfeit drugs. Manuals on managing drug supply are included in the Resources list.

757

c. Drug donations

The need for medicines often stimulates international organisations to send large quantities of drug samples to local hospitals. However, apart from undermining national drugs policies, this can cause considerable difficulties as the drugs come in many brands, labelled in different languages, and are in formulations and quantities which are not always appropriate. Frequently they are out of date and pose problems of disposal. Donations of drugs should conform with the guidelines established by the Christian Medical Commission of the World Council of Churches (see Resources Directory).

Inappropriate drug donations are also an unwelcome feature of emergency aid. The WHO *Emergency Health Kit* book lists recommended drugs and supplies, and provides additional information, as does the UNHCR *Technical Manual on Essential Drugs*. Ready-packed emergency health kits of drugs and supplies are held by ECHO and IDA.

d. Revolving drug funds

Oxfam has supported a number of health programmes incorporating revolving drug funds. These are discussed in greater detail in the 5.5.2.5 Revolving drug funds.

4.8.3 Advocacy, campaigning, and networking

Oxfam has been involved in advocacy and campaigning to draw attention to abuses in connection with the supply and use of drugs, and has actively promoted WHO's essential drugs concept as a framework for reform. The emphasis has been on influencing the responsible institutions and MNCs of industrialised countries, as well as fostering interest in developing countries through networking and information exchange.

In countries as varied as the Philippines, Bangladesh, India, Brazil, Bolivia, Nicaragua, Pakistan and Egypt, local groups of health professionals and NGOs have worked for many years to influence governments towards a rational drugs policy, and to support appropriate education for medical practitioners, and information for the public. Oxfam has supported these groups in various ways, and continues to see such networks as an important and cost-effective means to achieve and publicise results.

4.8.4 Key questions

1 Does the programme work with a drug list which conforms to national recommendations and/or WHO essential drug list?
2 Are there prescribing guidelines for health workers and are they followed?

3 Are health workers adequately trained and supervised in rational prescribing?
4 What does the programme do to educate people about the rational use of drugs?
5 Are there local groups working on drugs issues and do they need financial and other forms of support?

4.9 Mental and emotional well-being

Good health includes mental and emotional well-being. Mental ill health and emotional stress and disorder can be profoundly disabling, both for individuals and for the families and communities to which they belong. As such, mental health is a development issue which falls within the scope of primary health care.

There is a difference between promoting mental health and treating mental illness, or dealing with mental handicap. Oxfam's main concerns are to sensitise PHC workers to mental and emotional health issues, and to support initiatives which try to remove or alleviate the stress, social isolation, material deprivation, and forms of physical and mental abuse which can seriously affect people's emotional well-being. Oxfam is especially concerned with the long-term psycho-social effects of war and armed conflict increasingly borne by civilian populations.

The expression of mental distress and society's understanding of it is significantly affected by cultural and social values, and by people's economic and social status. For example, behaviour which is tolerated in young men — such as alcohol abuse and associated violence — may be regarded as evidence of mental derangement in elderly women. In other cases, people may be falsely diagnosed as mentally ill because they do not conform to social or religious mores. For example, in many countries, unmarried mothers, prostitutes, and 'illegitimate' or abandoned children, risk being consigned to mental hospitals or similar institutions. Finally, behaviour which is regarded as normal within a particular group of people — such as narcotics abuse by street children — may itself be a symptom of broader social problems.

Medical definitions of mental illness, and Western approaches to dealing with psychological suffering or disorder, will often not coincide with what people themselves believe to be the problem, or the best way to address it. For example, Western medicine has tended to see mental and physical health as separate domains, each subject to different clinical disciplines and expertise. Traditionally, Western forms of treatment have centred on individual therapy, and there is less experience in dealing with trauma on a mass scale, or using community-based approaches to promote awareness of mental health issues.

759

Focusing on the disorder rather than on the whole person can mean that wider social and economic factors affecting well-being are under-rated or ignored. For example, more than twice as many women as men in the UK are treated for depression with psychotropic drugs — a fact which may relate more to the specific social and economic situation of women, than to any innate propensity of women to depression. For instance in 1978, the Subpanel on Women to the US President's Commission on Mental Health stated:

Circumstances and conditions that society has come to accept as normal or ordinary led to profound unhappiness, anguish, and mental illness in women.

Understanding cultural concepts and assumptions about appropriate behaviour is not a simple matter. It is essential for NGO workers to have a comprehensive and sensitive insight into the broader social context before deciding whether and how to intervene in tackling perceived mental disorder.

Mental handicap is often confused with mental illness. The former is permanent, whether from birth or injury; and although much can be done for mentally handicapped people, they cannot be 'cured'. Mental illness includes certain physically attributable disorders (such as epilepsy) which may be contained through drug treatment, as well as those caused by specific circumstances — which may best be alleviated by drugs or therapy, or by removing the cause of distress. Depression may be acute and self-regulating, or chronic, requiring life-long treatment or care. Most people — men and women — suffer from depression or anxiety at some period of their lives, for many reasons. These may include inadequate housing, unemployment, deprivation, fatigue, insecurity, physical illness, or the breakdown or loss of an important relationship. At such times, people may come to rely on drugs (including forms of medication), alcohol, tobacco or other harmful substances. People — victims, soldiers, and aid workers alike — who have been involved in armed conflict, or other sorts of violence such as rape, child abuse or torture, may also suffer long-term psychological distress. Nightmares, insomnia, delusions, flashbacks, depression or paranoia are common symptoms of what is known as Post-Traumatic Stress Disorder (PTSD).

Mental health is often ignored in PHC programmes because priority is given to child-survival programmes and the prevention of common diseases. It may also be assumed that where people have access to traditional healers or religious leaders, those with mental illness will be properly helped. In reality, the treatment of mentally ill people may be harsh and inappropriate, and rely heavily on custodial containment. Often, those who suffer chronic mental illness are stigmatised or unable to find work, and so forced to beg, steal or live by prostitution. In times of social upheaval or catastrophe, or where health facilities are being cut back, people with mental illness are among the least likely to receive adequate support.

Where primary health workers are trained to promote mental well-being, and to recognise mental illness, they may be able to work together with traditional healers or religious leaders, who could ease some of the psychological and emotional problems which people are facing. Community health education programmes may look at specific issues such as domestic violence or substance abuse, which can have such disabling emotional and physical effects. For example, Oxfam has supported work on alcoholism in Mozambique, programmes for glue sniffers and drug abusers in Chile, and a detoxification and rehabilitation centre for heroin addicts in Pakistan.

People suffering psychotic disorders usually require specialist treatment. However, there may be few trained psychiatrists and psychologists outside hospitals in the capital city, while general health workers receive little or no training in mental and emotional health. In addition, mental hospitals are often overcrowded, ill-equipped and inadequately staffed, and frequently in extremely poor condition. Patients may be wrongly diagnosed, or inappropriately grouped together. It is not uncommon for elderly or disabled people, who are not suffering any mental illness, also to be kept in mental hospitals.

4.9.1 The role of NGOs

In both the promotion of mental health and in the caring for the sufferers of mental illness, there is a role for Oxfam to support humane and progressive initiatives. In Uganda, for example, Oxfam supplied materials and personnel for renewing an occupational therapy department in a mental hospital. In Rwanda, Oxfam funded training for psychiatric nurses. In South India, Oxfam funds a counselling service for the families of schizophrenics.

Almost half Oxfam's programme funding is related to armed conflict or to its consequences. The growing awareness of the psycho-social dimension of war and violence has revealed more about the human cost of such social upheaval. It is now recognised that people often suffer long-term psychological effects during and after being exposed to war and extreme violence. People who are particularly vulnerable are:

* women who have been widowed and/or lost a child or children;
* children, particularly those who have experienced violence either to themselves or to members of their families; or have lost or become separated from their families; and girls who have been sexually abused or raped;

- refugees or displaced persons who have lost their social network;
- people who have been tortured, raped or sexually abused.

Ex-combatants may also suffer serious emotional distress, and either find it difficult to reintegrate into civilian life, or come to rely on alcohol or other harmful substances.

The scale of such human suffering is immense and not fully understood. Individual NGO efforts can represent only a fraction of what is needed, particularly as people are often struggling to rebuild their lives in the midst of continuing hostilities, while the problems which gave rise to the violence remain unresolved. In civil conflicts, those responsible for raping, torturing or maiming people may be personally known to their victims — this was often so in former Yugoslavia, where Muslim women were gang-raped by Serbs who had previously been their neighbours. If a general amnesty is declared, as in El Salvador, the victims of human rights violations and their families have to cope with the knowledge that there will never be any legal redress for their suffering, and the perpetrators of terrible atrocities are exonerated.

Oxfam supports a wide range of initiatives to assist women, men, and children who are experiencing mental suffering as a result of violence, torture or rape. This kind of work is slow and long-term: there are no 'quick fix' answers, and it is irresponsible for NGOs to become involved in such programmes unless their commitment to them is also long-term. In Uganda, for example, Oxfam funds a counselling service for women who were raped during civil conflict in the early 1980s, and who still experience acute distress a decade later. The programme includes training for psychiatric nurses and other health workers in identifying and treating stress-related and other psychological disorders. In Mexico, Oxfam funded a programme for Guatemalan refugee women, who decided to train as mental health workers after experiencing the relief of assimilating their pain and trauma, rather than denying or suppressing it. Over several years, they saw how emotionally disabling this had been, and determined to help others to overcome their sense of fear and despair in the face of social injustice and political violence.

Mental health work often takes place in the context of human rights programmes, which may offer the means for victims to seek legal redress, or to meet other people in a similar situation. Oxfam funds a number of Chilean NGOs which bring together a range of human rights educational activities, including mutual support groups in the area of mental health. (See **6.3.4.2.b** Psycho-social aspects of armed conflict.)

4.9.2 Key questions

1 Does the programme promote integration of mental health and illness into the existing health system? Does it link with traditional healers or alternative health care?
2 How are issues of mental and emotional health and well-being defined, and what are the particular problems affecting the various social groups within the local population (alcoholism, domestic violence, marital rape, glue sniffing, drug addiction)?
3 How will the programme reduce any stigma attached to mental illness?
4 How will the programme ensure protection and humane treatment for the mentally ill?
5 How are the psycho-social dimensions of violence being taken into account in areas of armed conflict?

4.10 Emergencies and public health

This section provides only a brief summary of Oxfam's public health policy in the area of emergency relief. It should be read in conjunction with **6**.5 Health and nutrition in emergencies, and **6**.6 Environmental health and physical infrastructure, which present detailed guidance for assessing and implementing operational programmes.

People affected by major disasters are often already suffering the common health problems of poverty. An emergency may cause their conditions to deteriorate still further. For example, inadequate shelter and adverse weather conditions contribute to the incidence of acute respiratory infections. Pressure on water resources, and inadequate sanitation and waste disposal, provide the conditions for water-related diseases, such as diarrhoea, dysentery, typhoid, and scabies. Increased person-to-person contact in crowded refugee camps contributes to the spread of infectious diseases, such as measles or meningitis. Both the severity and incidence of common illnesses, such as diarrhoea, respiratory infections, and measles, are intensified by poor living conditions. Lack of food, as well as unfamiliar or inappropriate foods, may lead to malnutrition and lowered defences against disease.

War destroys health infrastructure, and disrupts the delivery of preventive and curative services. Distress migration increases people's exposure to infection, and reduces their chance of receiving health care. For displaced persons or people who are not settled in one place, there may be no health facilities available. The trauma associated with loss of home and livelihood, bereavement, torture, rape, terrorisation or political harassment, may result in problems which affect the emotional

5

well-being of victims for many years. (See 5.4.9 Mental and emotional well-being.)

Emergency health interventions must take a broad and long-term perspective, within the principles of primary health care (PHC). They should concentrate on the common conditions, not invest resources or plan for diseases which are rare or unlikely. The principal PHC interventions in acute emergencies are:

- measles immunisation
- management of diarrhoea and dehydration
- vitamin A supplementation
- management of acute respiratory infections (ARI)
- basic health information system.

Public and environmental health care in emergency relief programmes covers:

- water supplies
- sanitation
- waste disposal
- vector control
- hygiene and health education
- training and support for health workers
- shelter
- food supply and nutrition
- immunisation and preventive health
- basic curative services.

These are all inter-dependent. However, some areas may be overlooked or neglected, if several agencies are involved. Oxfam prefers to strengthen local capacity to implement emergency relief programmes, rather than taking operational responsibility for this work. However, when Oxfam undertakes the provision of water supplies, its policy guidelines recommend the deployment of an emergency health worker to review other aspects of public health. (See 6. Appendix V Oxfam policy in emergencies.)

Health and nutrition needs should be included in the overall assessment of an emergency. Basic demographic and health information may already be available, but additional details may be sought from government offices, UN organisations, NGOs familiar with the area, or local health practitioners. It is important also to identify any trained community health workers within the affected population. All such information should be disaggregated by sex and age.

The health assessment should cover:

- identification of risks to health

- identification of surviving health resources
- projected requirements, immediate and medium-term, including food and medical supplies, specifying types and quantities
- demographic information
- health care information
- nutrition and food security.

Major areas of public health intervention for Oxfam are providing adequate shelter; the control of communicable diseases (the majority of which are related to water and sanitation); and the provision of food.

Women, children, and elderly people may be particularly vulnerable in emergencies. Pregnant women and nursing mothers, and small children, have special nutritional requirements. Since women are primarily responsible for collecting and storing water, they are prone to water-borne diseases and to infection transmitted by insects which breed or feed near water, such as malaria, river blindness, dysentery, and infectious hepatitis. Reproductive health services for women are essential, to avert the complications in pregnancy and childbirth that are a major cause of maternal death.

Refugees or displaced persons may have suffered physical mutilation and so require special attention. Mental and physical trauma can affect the health and well-being of communities and individuals for many years. The extent and depth of adjustments which people are forced to make are also potential sources of distress or depression. (See **5.4.9 Mental and emotional well-being**; and **6.3.4.2.b Psycho-social consequences of war and armed conflict**.)

Health services should be appropriate and accessible. Adequate consultation with the women and men who will be using the health facilities must be built into the programme design stage. The failure to consult with women is one of the main reasons why their needs are not recognised or properly addressed. Monitoring the uptake of services enables health workers to detect gaps in coverage, and take steps to deal with them. For example, women may not wish to be treated by male health practitioners, and so may not make use of the facilities theoretically available to them. It may be necessary to recruit women health workers to ensure that women are offered effective health care. UNHCR recommends a ratio of not fewer than one health worker for every 200 households, and aims to ensure that at least 50 per cent of trainees are women.

Many emergency situations are prolonged for months or years. In training health workers, it is important to invest in people who will be able to apply their skills in the future. For example, it would be better to upgrade the abilities of traditional birth attendants (TBAs) — even if it seems slower at first to work with non-literate women — than to train

5

765

inexperienced male health workers in midwifery skills which they are unlikely to use.

4.10.1 Health and nutrition surveillance

Once an assessment has been completed, or a health intervention is being implemented, it is vital to monitor the situation in a systematic way, so that any changes can be acted upon swiftly. The most important areas of information are:

Population data: numbers and other relevant information concerning newcomers and departures, as well as births.

Mortality data: crude mortality rate (number of all deaths in the total population over a specified period) and under-5 mortality rates (U5MR) (number of deaths in the total under-5 population over a specified period). A daily crude mortality rate of 0.5 per 10,000 is considered normal in developing countries, and an emergency which is under control should not rise above 1 per 10,000 per day. A crude mortality rate of more than 5 per 10,000 per day indicates a major catastrophe.

Morbidity data: recording communicable diseases and nutrition-related conditions, including diarrhoea, ARIs, measles, malaria, meningitis, hepatitis, protein-energy malnutrition, vitamin A deficiency, and other specific deficiencies, such as scurvy and pellagra. Figures for children under five should be recorded separately.

Nutrition data: all newcomers between the ages of one and five years should be screened to ensure that their mid-upper arm circumference is not below a specified minimum (usually set as less than 13.5cm). Once supplementary feeding programmes are established, coverage and effectiveness should be monitored through routine information on numbers of admissions, discharges, referrals, re-admissions, and deaths.

Surveillance of nutritional status in the relief phase is usually through random sample nutrition surveys conducted every three months among the whole population. Professional advice is needed in designing surveys.

Health sector activities data: regular updates are needed on all health-related activities including:

- coverage
- immunisation
- out-patient attendances and in-patient bed occupancy
- water points established
- latrines built and functioning
- attendance at health-related training courses
- attendance at antenatal and reproductive-health services
- oral-rehydration centres and feeding centres.

This should be analysed alongside morbidity and mortality data.

General living conditions data: information on food supplies and distribution, and use of foods; availability of fuel for cooking and heating, and material for shelters. The construction and spacing of shelters should be monitored, with the aim of reducing over-crowded conditions. Information on water, sanitation, and refuse disposal is important in monitoring public health. Opportunities for vector control should be investigated and appropriate measures implemented and monitored.

4.10.2 Key questions

1 At what chronological stage is the emergency? In the case of displaced persons or refugees in fixed settlements, has registration been completed, with data disaggregated by sex and age? In the case of dispersed refugees or displaced persons, what is the approximate number of men, women, and children affected?

2 If an epidemiological assessment been conducted, by whom was this done (health authorities, trained health workers, camp officials) and what conclusions were drawn? What are currently the main causes of death and illness among the affected population? What is the nutritional status of the women, men, and children?

3 Are the existing or proposed interventions addressing the priority health and nutrition needs of women, men, and children, (measles, micronutrient deficiencies)? What are the specific needs of vulnerable people (elderly and disabled people, children, women of child-bearing age) and how are these being addressed?

4 How has health planning drawn on local capacity, including health workers from the affected population? How have gender-differentiated needs been addressed in the services to be provided and in the selection of health workers, both expatriate and local? What arrangements have been made for training of local health personnel?

5 What extra resources are required for health and nutrition programmes (technical expertise, equipment, food aid)? Have local sources for these been identified or do they need to be brought in from outside the affected area?

4.11 Health education and the promotion of healthy behaviour

4.11.1 Introduction

The aims of health education are to encourage and enable people to make informed decisions about their own health and behaviour; to take effective joint action for a healthier physical and social environment; to gain control of their own health; and to increase their influence over the content and quality of their health services.

In the past, health education was seen mainly as a means to change individual health-related behaviour. Education was thus largely confined to imparting information to passive recipients, and often fell into the trap of blaming people for problems caused by their environment, or by their behaviour. For example, mothers whose children had diarrhoea were blamed for not using boiled drinking water, and those with malnourished children were admonished for failing to feed them a balanced diet. Health education tended to disregard the underlying causes of ill health, such as discrimination against girls and women, inequitable distribution of resources, unemployment, poor housing, inadequate sanitation, and the broader social, economic, and cultural factors which create poverty and lead to ill health. It also failed to take into account the importance of building people's confidence and self-esteem.

This section looks at different approaches to health education, and discusses briefly the role of public education and campaigning in the context of health. It should be read in conjunction with 3.1.2 Education and training.

4.11.2 Practical approaches

To be effective in influencing people's health-related behaviour, health education must be based on an understanding of the complex factors affecting the health of individuals, communities, and societies. Health education is often aimed at adults, and it is essential that the approaches and techniques used are appropriate to their needs, interests, and motivation to learn.

a. Training for health education
Effective health education depends on the skills of the health workers and the methods they use, which in turn are strongly influenced by their own training. In local PHC programmes, health education is often the major task of CHWs, who themselves have perhaps received only minimum schooling. Relevant methods of adult education should be included in the training of CHWs. A frequently-encountered problem is that the people in charge of health programmes are health professionals, who may themselves not be familiar or comfortable with informal methods of adult education. Oxfam has funded work in Nicaragua and in India with medical students, on the use of participatory methods, which are more appropriate for non-specialist (sometimes non-literate) adult learners.

In many cases, health education is incorporated into activities which do not themselves focus on health. For instance, a literacy programme run by rural workers in Honduras included a range of teaching materials, of which one manual dealt with health and first-aid in the local community. The emphasis of the programme was primarily on stimulating interest in the literacy classes, rather than in conveying technical information about health. However, the teaching methods ensured that the manual generated considerable discussion about people's existing views and concerns relating to health; and was the first step in an effort to gather information about health conditions in the rural areas of the country.

b. Health education methods

Since health education aims to influence people's behaviour, it must take account of the audience's perceptions, beliefs, and practices about the topic under discussion. This should include an awareness of the ways in which women's experiences differ from, or are similar to, men's. Teaching methods and materials should be gender- and culturally-sensitive, and use the right language level for the particular group of learners.

Societies differ in their traditional beliefs and practices about particular illnesses. Sometimes these are helpful, such as cooling down a febrile child. Others may be harmful, such as not feeding a child who has measles. Health education should reinforce existing practices that are beneficial, and discourage those that are damaging.

To be relevant, health education must meet the needs, characteristics, and interests of the particular audience. For example, the tone and emphasis of education about HIV/AIDS will differ according to whether the information is aimed at established couples, adolescent girls, migrants, or sex workers; and whether the intended audience is elderly, or from a marginalised ethnic or cultural group; and whether people are literate, or non-literate.

Involving people in the production of their own materials can be an educational process in itself, as well as ensuring that materials are relevant and culturally appropriate. Materials should be piloted before they are used more widely. Visual materials in particular are effective only if the audience can identify with the people depicted in them. The use of images is not culture-free, and the same picture may be interpreted in very different ways by people from distinct backgrounds, or by women and men.

The three main approaches to health education are outlined below. These are not mutually exclusive, and health education is usually more effective if it draws on a range of approaches and methods:

Working directly with people: health workers' advice at clinics or

5

during home visits, public meetings and discussions, campaigning and pressure groups, practical demonstrations, health education work in schools and other institutions, and child-to-child activities.

It can be useful to involve influential local citizens or bodies, such as teachers, priests, healers, or TBAs, who may ensure that information is reinforced in a range of social structures. The existing health education activities of social organisations, local groups, and NGOs should be strengthened, where possible.

Working with teaching aids: printed materials, posters, films, slides, videos, murals, and flip-charts are among the most widely used teaching aids. Training courses may include methods of preparing these, in combination with other activities. Popular theatre, puppet shows and other forms of drama or role-play can also be highly persuasive ways to convey educational messages. For example, in India, Oxfam has funded the work of an arts centre which has staged plays on antenatal sex-determination at nine medical colleges, as part of its campaign to raise awareness among women and the medical profession about the rights of girl-children.

Working with mass media: radio, audio-cassettes, television, video, newspapers, and billboards. This is often attractive, partly because it is perceived to be modern. It can be particularly appropriate where there is widespread access to mass communication systems. For instance, in Pakistan, the health authorities have incorporated information about immunisation programmes in a popular television soap-opera, to positive effect. In Mexico City, organisations working on issues relating to HIV/AIDS have disseminated information through mass-circulation cartoon comics. Radio schools and programmes from Peru to Rwanda often include general health information and special health messages.

Mass media are better at reinforcing existing beliefs and behaviour than in helping people adopt new ways of doing things, for which personal contact and example are more effective.

Oxfam supports various forms of health education, often as part of a PHC programme, but also through organisations which do not specialise in health. While educational materials are useful for transmitting information — and are especially important as back-up for trainee community health workers — more inter-active methods are generally better for tackling specific issues, or for encouraging particular behavioural changes.

Oxfam has funded the translation or adaptation of existing material such as *Where There is no Doctor, Disabled Village Children, Where There is no Dentist,* and *Helping Health Workers Learn*. It is vital to ensure that technical material is correctly translated, or adapted. Good quality translations are expensive, and it is important to consider whether it is necessary to translate an entire text into another language. Wherever possible, and provided that the consistency and quality can be assured, existing material should be used if it can be appropriately adapted.

c. Impact of health education

Much so-called health education is limited to imparting knowledge, and it is questionable how far this is effective in changing behaviour. The mechanisms whereby people act on knowledge are complex and not clearly understood. This has become evident in the case of HIV/AIDS, where in spite of people knowing how HIV is transmitted, there is little evidence of significant changes in sexual behaviour. What is clear is that if people are ignorant about the possible impact of their actions, their options for deliberately changing their behaviour are reduced. Since a greater awareness of how to maintain good health and to avoid illness may lead to an increased demand on health services or supplies, appropriate follow-up should be guaranteed as part of a programme designed to change people's behaviour.

One of the most difficult aspects of health education is measuring changes in behaviour, and tracing trends over a period of time. For example, health educators can count how many condoms they distribute, but cannot count how many are used, when, or by whom. Before and after KAP (knowledge, attitude and practice) surveys are sometimes used to measure the impact of health education interventions. This points to the need to establish appropriate indicators of impact and change, in conjunction with the intended audience of a health education programme.

d. Public education and campaigning

Associations such as consumer groups and trades unions can play a vital role in health education, and encourage people to take action on the social, economic, political, and environmental factors affecting their health, such as cigarette advertising, hazards in the workplace, or pollution. A campaign might include collaborative action at various levels. For example, activities in support of breast-feeding may involve:

- encouraging breast-feeding through information (posters, leaflets, advice at MCH clinics and through maternity services);
- persuading clinics and maternity wards not to accept and distribute baby milk samples;
- campaigning nationally and internationally on the WHO voluntary code of practice, and monitoring breaches of the code;
- organising a boycott of companies breaching the WHO code of practice.

Oxfam has supported such activities, both through direct involvement and by funding other organisations, such as International

Baby Foods Action Network (IBFAN) and Baby Milk Action Coalition (BMAC) on breast-feeding. In the case of essential drugs, Oxfam was actively involved in initiating the Rational Health Campaign as well as in setting up Health Action International (HAI) in Europe, Latin America, and South-East Asia. (See 5.4.8 The provision of essential drugs.)

4.11.3 Key questions

1 Have the intended participants in a health education programme identified the issue being discussed as being important to them? Do the views of women and men coincide?
2 How are the messages relevant and appropriate to the lives of the participants? How has their sensitivity to cultural issues, and to gender differences been ensured?
3 If education material is being produced, how is it to be piloted?
4 What teaching methods have been selected and why?
5 Is health education raising expectations that cannot be fulfilled?
6 How and by whom will the impact of the health education be measured?

5 Financing, planning, and evaluating health programmes

5.1 Introduction 773
5.2 Financing health care 773
    5.2.1 Background 774
    5.2.2 Principal methods of financing health care 776
    5.2.3 Preventive versus curative services 778
    5.2.4 Rational use of drugs 779
    5.2.5 Revolving drug funds 779
    5.2.6 Oxfam's approach to financing health care 780
    5.2.7 Key questions 781
5.3 Planning and evaluating health programmes 781
    5.3.1 Introduction 781
    5.3.2 Background 781
    5.3.3 Baseline information 782
    5.3.4 Evaluation 784
    5.3.5 Key questions 785

5.1 Introduction

This section presents aspects of financing, planning, and evaluating health programmes, insofar as these are distinct from the general principles outlined in the main sections on these subjects. The various sub-sections should be read in conjunction with the more general tratement of the subject to be found elsewhere in the *Handbook*.

5.2 Financing health care

(This should be read in conjunction with **3**.2.4.Financial Planning and **3**.2.5 Financial Administration.)

The financing of health care relates to many aspects of health provision. While its prime concerns are how much money is used, how it is raised, how it is spent, and who controls it, the impact of these questions goes beyond mere matters of money. The means by which a health service is financed has significant implications for the way it is run and the care it provides. The issue of financing is thus a crucial issue in health care delivery. There is a difference in the care that people can expect if all costs of treatment are met by the State, through taxation and national insurance systems, as opposed to a situation in which individual patients have to meet the full costs of the tests, materials, drugs, and staff time required in their treatment. In the former, there may be little pressure on health practitioners to use resources efficiently. In the latter, however, the quality of health care will depend largely on the resources that patients and their families can mobilise.

5.2.1 Background

The issue of financing health care has become more urgent — and more contentious — in the context of widespread economic decline since the 1980s. In 1987, the World Bank published an influential policy document on financing health services, in which it advocated that users of government health facilities be charged fees (such that the government could recover a proportion of its recurrent expenditure on health), and that private health-care provision be encouraged. This fuelled an increasing interest in the idea of cost recovery in health care, particularly in situations where comprehensive state provision for health care was not a viable option.

However, for poverty-focused development agencies, for welfare-oriented governments, and for many health professionals in public service, the idea of financing health care at the expense of those most in need, and least able to pay, is objectionable on ethical as well as development grounds. Poverty and sickness are closely inter-related, as UNICEF's figures on infant mortality rates very clearly demonstrate. Prevention is always better, and usually cheaper, than cure; but people are often reluctant to spend money on routine medical and dental check-ups, preferring instead to wait until they have a problem. In the UK, for example, the introduction of charges for routine ophthalmic tests has discouraged people from having their sight tested. Apart from the cost in human terms, ill health is a major drain on a nation's economy, and undermines social justice and equity.

There is broad agreement across the political spectrum on the need to ensure that health care is provided efficiently and appropriately; and that services are as self-reliant as possible in their particular circumstances. It is also recognised that the State has a vital regulatory role in the health sector. For instance, patients must be assured of acceptable standards for the qualifications and conduct of registered health practitioners. Governments are responsible for health policy in areas such as screening and immunisation programmes, and national drug policies. They can also regulate standards of care, and be held accountable for the distribution of resources.

Good health care requires major investment, and incurs recurrent costs. While the costs of establishing and maintaining hospitals and clinics are more obvious, PHC should not be seen as a cheap alternative. Apart from capital investments, there are recurrents such as salaries, training, support and supervision, medical and drug supplies, and transport. As public health budgets are reduced, and donor agencies are increasingly concerned with the financial sustainability of the projects they fund, PHC has come under mounting pressure to prove itself economically viable.

PHC is based on the principle of 'health for all'. It thus focuses resources on simple preventive and curative health care for the majority, with the necessary referral and back-up facilities at hospital level. However, while the share of resources going to hospitals remains disproportionately large, the standard of hospital care has deteriorated in many countries, as there is no money to pay for maintaining facilities and equipment, or retaining and up-grading qualified staff. In several sub-Saharan countries, Oxfam has made grants for the purchase of basic obstetric and sterilising equipment, without which maternity hospitals can become a serious risk to the health of mothers and babies.

No health programme should be expected to change the basis on which it is financed without systematic consultation with the intended users, or without the opportunity to develop the necessary management and administrative structures. In terms of small-scale health projects, it is unrealistic to expect that poor individuals or even the broader catchment population can muster all the resources required to maintain a programme indefinitely. This does not mean that no effort should be made to find acceptable ways to share the costs of providing a service, with the people benefiting from it.

The choice of financing methods depends on what it is hoped to achieve with the health programme. If some form of 'cost sharing' system is to be introduced, different forms of financing health care should be measured against four criteria:

- viability and efficiency
- ability to raise revenue
- effects on service provision
- effects on equity.

For Oxfam, the issue of equity is paramount: no programme or intervention supported by Oxfam should deny the equal right to basic health care for all women, children, and men, irrespective of their social or economic status, or cultural background.

5.2.2 Principal methods of financing health care

a. NGO level

Any plans for financing health care should be realistic in an economic context which may be unstable. Even the most successful cost-recovery programmes raise only about 15 per cent of recurrents. Experience in most government facilities in Africa has been that only about 5 per cent of recurrents can be met through fees. Charging schemes may be progressive (so that the better-off pay more for a specific service); or regressive (so that payment for the same service takes a higher proportion of the income of a poorer person). Under the former, there is a transfer of resources from the better-off to the poorer, whereas the latter penalise people who are poor or chronically ill. Charging levels should ensure that no-one is denied access to basic health care because of inability to pay for it. Provision should be made for those who cannot afford to pay.

User fees: the term 'user fee' relates to a charge made to the patient or user of the health service, for a treatment or service received. Fees are most commonly charged for curative services, since people are generally more willing to pay for treatment than for preventive or information services. There are three common ways to design a fee structure:

- **Actual cost plus a percentage mark-up:** this may be preferred by the patient, because the calculation is clear and there are no hidden costs. On the other hand, the patient does not know in advance how much the treatment will cost. From an administrative viewpoint, the system is complicated because each patient's fee is different.
- **Fixed fee for treatment received:** either a standard fee for all diagnoses, or diagnoses banded into different groups, each with its own charge. The latter approach recognises that some conditions are far more costly to treat than others — for example, consultation for a common cold would cost less than treatment for pneumonia. Prices can be publicised in advance, and it is possible to set fees in such a way that the more expensive treatments are subsidised by the cheaper ones.
- **Fixed fee per episode of illness:** the user pays a fixed fee on the first visit, and nothing further provided that subsequent visits relate to the original diagnosis. The advantage over the other two systems is that this encourages people to complete the treatment, and to return if their condition does not improve.

Each of these systems could cater for price differentials or exemptions for certain categories of people, for example babies under one year of age, pregnant women, or people with a chronic condition.

Pre-payment (insurance): pre-payment schemes offer health care only to people who are members of them. On joining, members pay an initial pre-determined sum, followed by agreed instalments thereafter. In return, they receive health care for little or no extra charge when they need it. A major advantage is that the costs of providing health care are shared between sick and healthy people. Seasonal variations in ability to pay can also be incorporated into the payment schedules.

Schemes can be run at neighbourhood or village level, or at the workplace. However, it may be difficult to persuade people to join when they are in good health. In the event of a major unforeseen demand on services, the scheme would decapitalise.

Insurance schemes may be more or less comprehensive in what they cover. They are not easy to administer, it is difficult to set the right fees, and the degree to which they are equitable varies. Premiums often depend on the risk of ill health, so those at greater risk end up paying more. The perception that the service is free may also lead to an overuse of diagnostic tests and drugs.

Social insurance, which falls within the area of governments, operates according to the same principles.

Direct transfers and grants: these may be made by governments, or by international donors, and are either capital grants, or agreements to provide funding for recurrents such as salaries or drug supplies. The problems are that funding may be for a fixed period only, and that no flexibility is allowed in how the funds are applied.

Many NGOs are reluctant to enter into funding commitments of more than three years, since they do not want their own income to be tied on an open-ended basis to the same projects. This makes sense for the funder, but can be very disruptive for the organisers and beneficiaries of health programmes. Recipient organisations should resist the temptation to be funding-led, building up services which will make them more dependent than they need, or wish, to be on external donations. (See **3.2.4.6** Breaking the dependency cycle.)

Other methods of financing health care: in practice, 'cost sharing' is often achieved through the work that people do voluntarily, such as contributing labour for building a health post, or working as unsalaried health promoters or community health workers. 'Cost sharing' or 'cost recovery' schemes should reflect such non-financial inputs in drawing up their accounts. However, it is not realistic to assume that people will be able or willing to volunteer their time indefinitely without some form of compensation. The high turnover often associated with the use of voluntary labour can be costly in terms of training, since there will be a recurrent need to train newly-recruited volunteers.

b. Government level

In many developing countries, the revenue raised from income tax is negligible. Formal health insurance schemes, where these exist, usually

5

cover employees, whether in the public or private sector. People employed in the informal sector — such as many self-employed workers, domestic servants, and so on — are not covered. Nor, of course, are the large numbers of un- and under-employed people in urban and rural areas alike.

Recession, debt, and structural adjustment programmes have resulted in reduced health spending in many countries. Where a substantial part of health spending comes from multilateral and bilateral sources, these are influential in shaping health policies. For example, WHO-UNICEF sponsored the Bamako Initiative (so called, because it was first announced at a meeting of African Ministers of Health held in Bamako, Mali, in 1987), which proposed generating health revenue in sub-Saharan Africa through community-financing, by charging fees for essential drugs. Both drugs and revenue would be made continuously available by creating a revolving drugs fund, initially to be supported by the World Bank and the African Development Bank, in conjunction with UNICEF. It was hoped that the sale of drugs could subsidise the provision of other health services which had little or no income-earning potential. If a substantial mark-up on drug costs was allowed for when price-setting, a surplus would be generated which could be used to finance aspects of PHC. A particular emphasis was given to supporting MCH activities in this way.

Various NGOs, including Oxfam, highlighted the difficulties of this scheme. They argued that it was naive and simplistic, as well as 'top down'; it paid insufficient attention to the managerial and operational problems encountered in community drug sales; the ambitions for cost-recovery were unrealistically high; its assumptions were based selectively on the experience of a few small-scale projects, ignoring conflicting evidence from other similar projects; that successes from small-scale projects could not necessarily be replicated when implementation was expanded to national programmes; and that it shifts the major costs of PHC from the governments to the consumers. The other major concern was the flooding of African countries with unnecessary medicines by the pharmaceutical industry, in the face of foreign exchange shortages. The initiative has now been extensively modified and few countries have done more than adopt an *ad hoc* mixture of cost-recovery mechanisms.

5.2.3 Preventive versus curative services

People may be reluctant to invest in preventive health care, or health education, because there are no apparent benefits in doing so. Yet, as the case of HIV/AIDS education demonstrates, preventive health work may be of far greater impact in terms of saving lives, and improving the quality of life, than a curative approach for AIDS patients could possibly achieve. While money spent on prevention may mean that people will ultimately spend less on curative care, the pressure to maximise income can encourage health programmes to concentrate on curative services at the expense of preventive work.

Programmes should seek to subsidise preventive activities while encouraging people to benefit from them. For example, people may pay for a service such as immunisation, if it is seen to be effective and well administered. In Uganda, people were willing to contribute a small voluntary fee towards the petrol for an NGO mobile clinic which gave immunisation and antenatal care — though this was later stopped because it conflicted with the government's policy that such preventive services should be free of charge.

Willingness to pay is a complex issue. It depends partly on whether people actually have the disposable income — whether they are *able* to pay. It also depends on more subjective factors. For example, how patients view the quality, reliability, accessibility, and politeness of the care they receive, the availability of supplies, and the perceived value to individuals of using the health facilities as opposed to seeking some alternative form of care, such as a traditional healer or commercial drug-seller. There is a danger in concentrating on the financing of health care, without considering the programme as a whole.

5.2.4 Rational use of drugs

An emphasis on curative care and the income derived from it might encourage over-prescribing. This is already a major problem in those countries where control of medicines is poorly enforced. Direct charges for drugs, rather than charging patients per consultation, may also lead to over-prescribing, in order to increase revenue.

Prescribing practice and drug management are important features of many health programmes, and they become especially so if money is being raised through the sale of drugs. The International Network for Rational Use of Drugs (INRUD) has developed a series of indicators to monitor drug use.

5.2.5 Revolving drug funds

The idea of revolving drug funds is that donors provide the capital for a first batch of drugs, which are then sold at a slight profit to cover the costs of transport, storage and handling, and inflation. The money obtained is used to buy more drugs, and sometimes to pay for other services. Revolving drug funds should always be administered within the context of a broader health programme, not as isolated projects.

This is essentially a form of user charge, but the advantages of revolving funds are that they decrease the dependency on *ad hoc* donations, and guarantee regular supplies because the health programme is able to purchase in bulk. Where supplies are often a problem, the improved availability of generic drugs can lead to better use of health facilities and to better treatment.

The management of revolving funds is complex. There are often problems in calculating the profit margin needed to recover costs. Likely inflation or devaluation, foreign exchange transactions, taxes, import duties, storage, and transport, all need to be allowed for. There may occasionally be losses through damage or theft, which are an unanticipated expense and a disruption to the supply system. If the fund expands rapidly, it may become a victim of its own success, in that demand outstrips the capacity to supply. Excellent administration and financial book-keeping skills are needed to keep the records clear and up to date. In practice, 'top ups' are usually needed at regular intervals, to cover gradual decapitalisation.

Oxfam supports 'popular pharmacies' in Bolivia and El Salvador, and revolving drug funds in Guatemala, Zaire and Rwanda. In Mexico — a country where drugs are freely available over the counter — the revolving drug fund established by a national association of health programmes became a major supplier for non-governmental health programmes and mission hospitals throughout the country, and so implicitly promoted a rational drugs policy.

5.2.6 Oxfam's approach to financing health care

Oxfam believes that basic health care is the right of all women, men, and children, regardless of their social, economic or cultural background. A very wide range of health programmes are supported, from technical assistance for public sector health professionals, to training programmes for community health workers, capital expenditure for government health centres, and policy-oriented research. Many of these activities are self-defining, requiring only a limited amount of funds. As indicated above, Oxfam also supports a number of health programmes which manage revolving drug funds, most of which need regular top-ups over time.

Oxfam has also to respond to many requests for service-based programmes of an open-ended nature, where the scope for cost-recovery is very limited indeed. External funding may legitimately be needed beyond the conventional three- to five-year period of project funding, and this should be recognised before entering into such a commitment. In addition to seeking viable ways in which to share some of the costs, Oxfam can assist its counterparts to consider other ways in which they could generate funds, without distorting the services they offer. (See **3**.2.4 Financial Planning.) Oxfam can also help the agencies it supports to diversify their sources of funding. (See Resources Directory.) For example, components relating to national policy, such as immunisation or antenatal screening, might be covered by government contributions, leaving specialised NGOs to take on TB or leprosy control. This is in practice what happens in many situations, on an *ad hoc* basis. It is sometimes possible for agencies which usually send expatriate volunteers, such as VSO or CIIR, to meet the costs of a local health worker's salary.

5.2.7 Key questions

1 What are the capital and recurrent costs of a health programme, or health care service, and how are these to be financed? Examples of capital costs include: vehicles, equipment (refrigerators, sterilisers, scales, clinical implements, computers), and buildings (including storage facilities). Examples of recurrent costs include: personnel (salaried health workers, administrators, technicians, casual labour; insurance), supplies (drugs, vaccines, office stationery, teaching materials), travel, running and maintenance of buildings, equipment, and vehicles, communications (fax, telephone, postage).

2 If a cost-sharing approach is to be adopted, which method has been selected? Why, how, and by whom? How will people who are disadvantaged (either economically, or because of chronic illness) be protected?

5.3 Planning and evaluating health programmes

5.3.1 Introduction

Planning (including financial management) and evaluation are crucial elements in all development and relief interventions. The underlying principles and approaches are outlined in **3**.2.2 Planning and **3**.2.3 Evaluation, to which reference should be made. In this section, only those aspects of planning and evaluation that are of specific relevance to health care are presented. Issues in programmes involving water and sanitation are addressed in greater detail in **5**.4.3.8 Planning and evaluating environmental health programmes.

5.3.2 Background

Health programmes, just like any other development and relief activities, take place within a particular political, social, and cultural context. Beliefs and practices concerning health-related behaviour vary considerably from one situation and culture to another. For instance, in societies which place a strong taboo on sexual relations for women who are breast-feeding, mothers may prolong feeding beyond what is common in situations where no such cultural constraint exists, but where women do have access to reliable contraception. Where child-birth is strongly influenced by Western obstetric medicine, women may be expected to labour in the lithotomy position (lying on their backs, with their legs in stirrups), while in fact women usually labour more comfortably and efficiently if they are in a squatting or semi-upright position, as they have always done in most rural societies.

The assumed objectivity of the scientific and technical dimensions of medicine, does not mean that health programmes can be drawn up independently of the perceptions and circumstances of the women, men, and children intended to benefit from them. Health programmes should be based on a sensitive knowledge of existing practices and remedies, and a sympathetic understanding of local beliefs surrounding health. Health programmes should also have a clear and explicit relationship with government services, and with private health-care provision. It is better for NGO-sponsored health programmes to dovetail with formal and informal services, where it is appropriate to do so, than to be designed as if in a vacuum.

Eight out of ten people throughout the world rely at some point in their lives either on non-Western remedies and systems of health care, or on a combination of these and pharmacological medicines. In many cases, the patent tonics and treatments sold through pharmacies are of no value whatsoever. Furthermore, self-medication is rife, especially in those countries where pharmaceuticals are sold on the open market, rather than under medical prescription. For example, it is not uncommon for people to use antibiotics in an inappropriate and dangerous way — to 'cure' dysmenorrhoea, or to 'treat' intestinal worms. While health programmes should always challenge unsafe or unsound practices, they should also avoid undermining the good work and credibility of local health practitioners. Health workers should establish contact with non-formal practitioners, such as herbalists or traditional birth attendants, as well as with local nursing and medical personnel, and seek ways in which positive interventions for health might be reinforced. (See 5.2.6 Traditional, alternative, and informal health care.)

5.3.3 Baseline information

Without reliable baseline information, there is no way of ensuring that health programmes are designed to meet priority needs. Nor is there any way to measure impact, or to redirect efforts which are failing to reach the intended population, or which are not meeting their objectives. Routine monitoring ensures the work is on the right track, and that adjustments can be made as necessary; and provides the basis for sensitive and well-informed evaluation. Indicators should be determined with input from representatives of all the relevant parties, including the people intended to benefit from the programme. It is vital to incorporate the perceptions of those who use a health care service in monitoring and evaluating its impact on them.

General information is often available either through the formal health care system, or through the local offices of specialist agencies such as UNICEF or WHO. Additional surveys may be needed to gather specific details about a particular population group or geographical area, or in emergencies which involve large population flows. However, information is valuable only if it is used. Unless clear parameters and needs are defined from the outset, and kept under review, health workers may spend a disproportionate amount of time in record-keeping, and yet make little use of what has been recorded.

There must be a clear reason for gathering information, which is understood by those responsible for recording it. Health-related data should always be disaggregated by sex and age, to ensure that programmes are reaching the catchment population or to detect unintended biases. For planning and evaluation purposes, information is needed in the following areas:

General background: history; geographic and climatic conditions; economy; government and political structures; independent organisational capacity.

Demography: catchment population, by age and sex; births and deaths recorded; geographical distribution, migration patterns, and growth rate.

Morbidity and mortality: major causes of ill-health and death, and whether these differ from national statistics, or in terms of marked seasonal variations

Existing health systems: coverage and effectiveness of government and non-government facilities; availability of trained personnel, and the supervision and support provided for them; reliability of logistics and supplies; specific interventions such as immunisation programmes.

Health practices and beliefs: local or traditional health care practices and beliefs; perceptions of the role of health professionals and informal or community-based practitioners; expressed priorities or needs of specific population groups, such as elderly or disabled people, pregnant women, and children under five.

5

5.3.4 Evaluation

Everyone with a direct interest in a health care programme has a right to be satisfied that it is achieving its goals as effectively and efficiently as possible. This includes the catchment population first and foremost, other related health and welfare services (including health professionals in government service, and health practitioners outside the formal system), and funders. Evaluating performance helps to identify strengths and weaknesses, to determine if resources are being spent as intended, and to look at the costs and benefits of various options and interventions. Evaluation is only useful, however, if it is thorough and sensitive, and if it informs future plans. It must therefore be properly budgeted for as part of the planning process. The terms of reference (TOR) for evaluation should derive clearly from the programme's objectives. (See Table 3.2 Basic framework for TOR in 3.2.3.4 Organising an evaluation process.)

Methods of evaluation are described in detail in **3.2.3.3** Approaches to evaluation. As in all development work, it is vital not to rely solely on quantitative methods (such as surveys, questionnaires, or reviews of health records) which provide data for statistical analysis. It takes considerable skill and expertise to gather accurate information, particularly on issues such as sexual behaviour, about which people may not be truthful. Thus, assumptions based on statistical information can be seriously inaccurate if data are not gathered and interpreted sensitively. Qualitative information, gathered through informal interviews, group discussions or case studies, is always relevant for evaluating health programmes.

There are three principal ways of focusing evaluations of health programmes:

Impact evaluation is the most difficult to undertake, since it depends on reliable baseline data for comparative purposes, and to determine the exact changes that have taken place. Even with accurate data, it may be difficult to establish if the changes observed in the health of the intended beneficiaries of a community health programme were due to the specific intervention, or to a combination of factors.

Baseline studies include data on the overall health problems of the area, and of the health services available (state, voluntary sector, and non-formal practitioners). Basic statistical data on health enable a 'community diagnosis' to be formulated. Full studies are time-consuming and expensive, and may be more than is required for a small-scale health project. In most cases, existing data have to be used, together with whatever information can be readily obtained.

Process evaluation describes the implementation of a programme. It looks at what services are delivered, how are they are delivered, and who actually uses them. It examines whether the programme achieved its original objectives (or different objectives), and any changes required to achieve these.

It uses output measurements such as how many people were reached by a particular service: for example, how many of the women of child-bearing age had access to contraception, how many condoms were distributed and to whom, or the percentage of children who were immunised.

Outcome evaluation looks at the effects of an intervention, to determine if intended (or other) changes occurred as a result. It would reveal, for example, whether some sets of people had made more use of the services offered, and explore the reasons for this. For example, if an HIV/AIDS education programme is attended more by men than by women, this might be for practical reasons (such as the timing of clinic sessions), or because of a failure to convey to women the relevance of safer sex.

However, while the objectives of a health programme may include promoting behaviour change, it may be impossible to determine whether the intended impact has been felt within the timespan of implementation.

Evaluations may also attempt to monitor the quality of outputs — for instance, whether routine visits by mothers to an antenatal clinic were restricted to testing urine samples and blood pressure, or whether they were used as opportunities to make more general assessments about the women's well-being. An evaluation team may have to rely to a large extent on recollections and interpretations of what happened; and these may differ significantly among the people who use a service, and between these and the health workers themselves.

5.3.5 Key questions

1 How has the health programme improved the health of the intended population? Has its uptake and consequent impact been differentiated in terms of age and sex in ways that were intended, or in ways that are negative? Why?
2 Are the costs of the programme comparable to other types of intervention to reach similar objectives? Is the programme self-reliant in terms of organisational capacity, and financial security? If not, what are the implications?
3 How has the programme reinforced or challenged existing health provision? In what ways has it demonstrably expanded people's access to, and understanding of, good health care?
4 How are health workers selected, trained, compensated, supported, and supervised?

785

6 Resources

General

Allen T and Thomas A (1992) *Poverty and Development in the 1990s*, Oxford University Press, Oxford.

Amonoo Lartson R, et al (1984) *District Health Care*, Macmillan.

Chabot and Streeflald P H (1990) *Implementing Primary Health Care: Experiences in Alma Ata*, Royal Tropical Institute and Intermediate Technology, Amsterdam.

Dickson, M *Where there is no Dentist*, Macmillan.

Harpham T, Lusty T, Vaughan P (eds.) (1988) *In the Shadow of the City: Community Health and the Urban Poor*, Oxford University Press, Oxford.

Morley D, Lovel H (1986) *My Name is Today — An Illustrated Discussion of Child Health, Society and Poverty in Less Developed Countries*, Macmillan, London.

Morley D, Rohde J E , Williams G (1983) *Practising Health for All*, Oxford University Press, Oxford.

Open University (1985) *The Health of Nations*, Oxford University Press, Oxford.

Pryer J and Crook N (1988) *Cities of Hunger, Urban Malnutrition in Developing Countries*, Oxfam, Oxford.

Townsend, P (1993) *The International Analysis of Poverty*, Harvester/Wheatsheaf.

Walt G and Gilson L (eds.) (1990) *Community Health Workers in National Programmes: Just another pair of hands?*, Open University Press, Milton Keynes.

Werner D (1993, revised edition) *Where There is no Doctor: A Village Health Care Book*, Hesperian Foundation, Palo Alto, CA and Macmillan. (Available in many languages, including French, Spanish, Arabic, Bangla.)

Women's health

Hart R H, Belsey M A, Tarimo E (1990) *Integrating Maternal and Child Health with PHC: Practical Considerations*, WHO, Geneva.

Gender and Primary Health Care: Some Forward Looking Strategies, IDS Bulletin 23 (1), January 1992.

Phillips A and Rakusen J (1989) *The New Our Bodies Ourselves: A Health Book by and for Women*, Penguin Books.

Piaurki, H et al (1987) *Women as Providers of Health Care*, WHO, Geneva.

Royston E and Armstrong S (eds) (1989) *Preventing Maternal Deaths*, WHO, Geneva.

Smyke P (1991) *Women and Health*, Zed Books, London and New Jersey.

Turshen, M (ed) *Women and Health in Africa*, Africa World Press, New Jersey.

WHO (1992) *Women's Health: Across Age and Frontier*, WHO, Geneva.

WHO (1992) *Traditional Birth Attendants: A Joint WHO/UNFPA/UNICEF Statement*, WHO, Geneva.

Williams M (1986) (2nd Edition) *Training Local Midwives: Guidelines for Health Workers in Developing Countries*, CIIR, London.

Children, disabled and elderly people

See Resources for main Sections on Childhood, Disability, and Ageing in Chapter 3.

Nutrition

Berg (1987) *Malnutrition: What can be Done? Lessons from World Bank Experience*, Baltimore: Johns Hopkins University Press.

Biswas M R and Pinstrup-Andersen P (1985) *Nutrition and Development*, Oxford University Press, Oxford.

Cameron and Hofvander, 3rd edition (1983) *Manual on Feeding Infants and Young Children*, Oxford University Press, Oxford.

Jelliffe D B and Jelliffe E F P (1992) *Dietary management of Young Children with Acute Diarrhoea: A Practical Manual for District Programme Managers*, WHO, Geneva.

King, F S and Burgess, A (1993) *Nutrition for Developing Countries*, Oxford University Press, Oxford.

Lusty T and Diskett P (1984) *Selective Feeding Programmes*, Oxfam, Oxford.

Mamdani M and Ross D A (1988) *Vitamin A Supplementation and Child Survival: Magic Bullet or False Hope?*, EPC Publication No 19, Evaluation and Planning Centre, LSHTM, London.

Maxwell S (ed) (1990) *Food Security in Developing Countries*, IDS Bulletin; 21 (3), IDS, University of Sussex.

Phillips D I W (1989) *Controlling Iodine Deficiency Disorders in Developing Countries* Oxfam, Oxford.

Tomkins A and Watson F (1989) *Malnutrition and Infection*, Nutrition Policy Discussion Paper No 5, ACC/Subcommittee on Nutrition, UN Geneva.

Young H (1992) *Food Scarcity and Famine: Assessment and Response*, Oxfam, Oxford.

5

Environmental and public health: water and sanitation
Cairncross S and Feachem R G (1993) *Environmental Health Engineering in the Tropics: An Introductory Text*, John Wiley & Sons, Chichester.
RUHBC (Research Unit in Health and Behavioural Change, University of Edinburgh) (1989) *Changing the Public Health*, John Wiley, Chichester.
Thompson M C (forthcoming 1994) *Disease Vector Control in Refugee Camps*, Oxfam, Oxford.
WHO (1982) *Manual on Environmental Management for Mosquito Control (with special emphasis on malaria vectors)*, offset publication No 66.

Immunisation
Dick B (1985) *Issues in Immunisation in Developing Countries*, EPC Publications, London.
WHO (1989) *Immunisation in Practice: A Guide for Health Workers who Give Vaccines*, OUP, Oxford.

Endemic and communicable diseases
Benenson A S (1990) 15th Edition, *The Control of Communicable Diseases in Man: An official report of the American Public Health Association.*
Cheeseborough M (2nd edition, rev 1991) *Medical Laboratory Manual for Tropical Countries*, Tropical Health Technology/Butterworth-Heinemann, Oxford.
WHO (1993) *Guidelines for Cholera Control*, Geneva.
International Union against Tuberculosis and Lung Disease, (2nd edition, 1991) *Tuberculosis Guide for High Prevalence Countries*, Paris.
Jopling W H and McDougall A C (4th Ed 1988), *Handbook of Leprosy*, Heinemann, London.
McDougall A C (1988) *Implementing Multiple Drug Therapy for Leprosy*, Oxfam, Oxford.
Shan F (1988) *Respiratory Infections in Children: Management in Small Hospitals*, WHO, Geneva.
Shears P (1988) 2nd Edition, *Guidelines for Tuberculosis Control Programmes in Developing Countries*, Oxfam, Oxford.

AIDS
ActionAid, AMREF and World in Need, *Strategies for Hope Series*, available direct from contributing agencies. (English and French)
Berer M and Ray S (1993) *Women and HIV/AIDS: An International Resource Book*, Pandora, London.
Burns, J and Wright, C (1993) *A Trainer's Guide to Workshops on Young People and Sexuality in the Context of HIV/AIDS*, HMSO.
Evans, B, Sandberg, S and Watson, S (eds) (1993) *Healthy Alliances in HIV Prevention*, Health Education Authority.

Foster S and Lucas S (1991) *Socioeconomic Aspects of HIV and AIDS in Developing Countries: A Review and Annotated Bibliography*, LSHTM, London.

Gordon G and Klouda T (1988) *Talking AIDS: A Guide for Community Workers*, IPPF, Macmillan. (Available in French and Arabic.)

Latif A S, Marowa E and Choto R G (1990) *AIDS Counselling: A Manual for Primary Health Care Workers on AIDS*, Aids Control Programme, Ministry of Health, Harare, Zimbabwe.

Essential drugs

AHRTAG (1990), *Low Cost Medicine Packaging*.

Battersby A (1983) *How to Look After a Health Centre Store*, AHRTAG.

Christian Medical Commission (1991) *Guidelines for Donors and Recipients of Pharmaceuticals Donations*, World Council of Churches, Geneva.

Health Action International (1993) *Problem Drug Pack* (2nd Edition)

IDA Essential Drug Information Sheets; International Dispensary Association 1989; International Drug Price Indicator Guide 1991, Management Sciences for Health, 1992.

Melrose D (1982) *Bitter Pills: Medicines and the Third World Poor*, Oxfam, Oxford.

WHO (1988) *The World Drug Situation*.

WHO *The New Emergency Health Kit*, List of drugs and medical supplies for 10,000 people for 3 months, WHO DAP/90.1

WHO (1992) *The Use of Essential Drugs, Model List of Essential Drugs* (Seventh List), Technical Report Series 825.

Emergencies

(see also Resources Section of Chapter 6 Emergencies and Development)

Kelly N (1989) *Working with Refugee Women: A Practical Guide*, WHO, Geneva.

Lusty T and Diskett P (1984) *Selective Feeding Programmes*, Oxfam, Oxford.

Mears C and Chowdhury S (1994) *Health Care for Refugees and Displaced People*, Oxfam, Oxford.

Simmonds P and Vaughan P (1983) *Refugee Health Care*, Oxford University Press, Oxford.

UNHCR (1989) *Essential Drug Policy, Technical Manual*, Geneva.

UNHCR (1982) *Handbook for Emergencies*, Geneva. (Available in English, French and Spanish.)

Health education and promotion

Bunton, R and Macdonald, G (eds) (1992) *Health Promotion, Disciplines and Diversity*, Routledge.

789

Downie, R S, Fyfe, C and Tannahill, A (1990) *Health Promotion: Models and Values*, Oxford University Press, Oxford.

Werner D and Bower W (1982) *Helping Health Workers Learn*, Hesperian Foundation, Palo Alto, CA. (Available in Portuguese and Spanish; French in preparation.)

Mental health

Appleby, L and Araya, R (eds) (1991) *Mental Health Services for the Global Village*, Gaskell.

WHO (1990) *The Introduction of a Mental Health Component into Primary Health Care*, WHO, Geneva.

Financing, planning and evaluating health programmes

Feuerstein M-T (1986) *Partners in Evaluation*, MacMillan/TALC.

Green, A (1992) *An Introduction to Health Planning in Developing Countries*, Oxford University Press, Oxford.

Lankester, T (1992) *Setting up Community Health Programmes*, Macmillan.

McCuster J (1989) *How to Measure and Evaluate Community Health*, Macmillan/TALC.

Goodman H and Waddington C (1993) *Financing Health Care*, Oxfam, Oxford.

WHO (1988) *Managing Systems for Better Health*.

WHO (1991) *Community Involvement in Health Development: Challenging Health Services*, Technical Report Series 809, WHO, Geneva.

Periodicals, Newsletters, Journals, Series

AHRTAG publish a list of free international newsletters:

Dialogue on Diarrhoea (English, French, Portuguese, Spanish, Arabic).

ARI News (Acute Respiratory Infections) (English, French, Spanish).

AIDS Action (English, French, Portuguese, Spanish).

CBR News (Community-based Rehabilitation).

Other free newsletters include:

Child Survival - World Development Newsletter, Task Force for Child Survival and Development,Atlanta Georgia.

Community Eye Health, International Centre for Eye Health, 27-29 CaytonStreet, London, EC1V SEJ, UK.

Contact, Christian Medical Commission, 150 Route de Fernay, CH 1211 Geneva 20, Switzerland (English, French Portuguese, Spanish).

Drug Information Bulletin, (English, French) Pharmaceuticals Unit, WHO, Geneva.

Essential Drugs Monitor, WHO, Geneva.

Health Technology Directions, Programme for Appropriate Technology in Health , 4 Nickerson Street, Seattle, Washington 98109-1699, USA.

Ibfan Action News, International Baby Food Action Network, 3255 Hennepin Ave, Suite 230, Minneapolis, MN 55403 USA.

IPPF Medical Bulletin, IPPF.

Mothers and Children, Clearinghouse on Infant Feeding and Maternal Nutrition, American Public Health Association, 1015 Fifteenth Street, NW, Washington, DC 20005, USA.

Population Reports (Arabic, English, French, Portuguese, Spanish, Population Information programme, The Johns Hopkins University, 624 North Broadway Baltimore, MD 21205, USA.

Tobacco Alert, WHO, Geneva.

Women's Health Journal, (English and Spanish), Latin America and Caribbean Women's Health Network of Isis International.

Journals

Disasters: The Journal of Disaster Studies and Management [quarterly], Basil Blackwell, 108 Cowley Road, Oxford, OX4 1JF.

EPC publications, (covering topics such as District Health Planning and Management, Health and the Urban Poor, Issues in Immunisation, Traditional Medicine and Primary Health Care), Evaluation and Planning Unit, London School of Hygiene and Tropical Medicine, Keppel Street, London, UK

Health Alert, Health Action Information Network, Quezon City.

Health Policy and Planning [quarterly], Oxford University Press, Oxford.

Learning for Health, Intermediate Technology.

Pesticide News [quarterly], Pesticide Trust, 23 Beehive Place, London SW9 7QR.

Refugee Policy Group Series, Refugee Policy Group, Suite 401, 1424 16th Street NW, Washington DC 20036, USA.

Tropical Doctor, [quarterly], Royal Society of Medicine, 1 Wimpole Street, London, W1M 8AE, UK.

Waterlines, Intermediate Technology Publications, [quarterly].

World Health Forum, WHO, Geneva.

5

CHAPTER 6

Emergencies and development

6

Contents

1 Introduction 799
    1.1 Oxfam and emergencies 799
    1.2 Code of conduct for NGOs 801

2 Background: emergencies, conflict, and development 809
    2.1 Crises, disasters, and emergencies 809
        2.1.1 The changing nature of emergencies 812
        2.1.2 The causes of complex emergencies 813
        2.1.3 Emergencies and human rights 814
    2.2 The changing nature of humanitarian response 815
    2.3 Information and advocacy 817
        2.3.1 Information and vulnerability 817
        2.3.2 Information and public policy 818
    2.4 The crisis of development practice and the need for new ideas 819
        2.4.1 Planning for diversity and divergence 820
        2.4.2 Chaos and complexity: pictures of change 821
        2.4.3 The awareness of potential flash-points 823
    2.5 The relationship between development and relief 824
        2.5.1 The balance between short-term and long-term considerations 824
        2.5.2 Adapting development programmes to handle emergency relief 828
        2.5.3 Development as a response to crisis 829
        2.5.4 Supporting self-reliance 830
    2.6 Reducing people's vulnerability to crisis 832
        2.6.1 Capacities and Vulnerabilities Analysis 832
        2.6.2 Disaster mitigation 834
        2.6.3 Rehabilitation, reconstruction, and development 836

3 Emergencies deriving from war and armed conflict 840
    3.1 Introduction 840
    3.2 International legislation relating to armed conflict 842
        3.2.1 Refugees, asylum seekers, and displaced persons 843
        3.2.2 Rights of refugees 844
        3.2.3 Problems concerning the rights of refugees and displaced persons 846
        3.2.4 Civilians and the protection of victims of armed conflicts 847
        3.2.5 Non-international armed conflicts 848

6

3.3 Armed conflict and NGOs 848
3.4 Practical approaches 849
    3.4.1 Principles of humanitarian assistance: neutrality,
        impartiality, and independence 849
    3.4.2 Supporting civilians in situations of armed conflict 853
    3.4.3 Non-operational work 858
3.5 Key questions 859

4 Assessment, co-ordination and consultation in emergencies 860
4.1 Introduction 860
4.2 Assessment of emergencies 862
    4.2.1 Introduction and background 862
    4.2.2 Initial (general) assessment 863
    4.2.3 Detailed (technical) assessment 864
    4.2.4 Co-ordinating assessment with other agencies 864
    4.2.5 Preparedness and contingency plans 865
4.3 Inter-agency co-ordination 866
    4.3.1 Introduction and background 866
    4.3.2 International agencies involved in relief work 870
    4.3.3 Working with local authorities 874
    4.3.4 Working through local structures 875
    4.3.5 Working with dispersed populations 877
4.4 Consulting and involving the affected population 878
    4.4.1 Introduction and background 878
    4.4.2 Consulting women 880
4.5 Assessing the situation of specific social groups 882
    4.5.1 Introduction 882
    4.5.2 Women 883
    4.5.3 Children 886
    4.5.4 Elderly people 888
    4.5.5 Cultural considerations and minority groups 890
    4.5.6 People with disabilities 892
4.6 Key questions 893

5 Health and nutrition in emergencies 894
5.1 Introduction 894
5.2 Background 895
5.3 Assessment 896
    5.3.1 General assessment 896
    5.3.2 Assessment of sudden-onset emergencies 897
    5.3.3 Assessment of slow-onset emergencies 897
5.4 Practical approaches 900
    5.4.1 Response to sudden-onset emergencies 900
    5.4.2 Response to slow-onset and 'chronic' emergencies 902
    5.4.3 Food 903
    5.4.4 Gender considerations in food distribution 905

5.4.5 Water supply and excreta disposal 906
5.4.6 Health services 907
5.4.7 Primary health interventions 908
5.5 Health and nutrition surveillance 909
5.5.1 Population data 910
5.5.2 Mortality data 910
5.5.3 Morbidity data (cases of disease) 910
5.5.4 Nutrition data 910
5.5.5 Data on health sector activities 911
5.5.6 Data on general living conditions 911
5.6 Training programmes 912
5.7 Key questions 913

6 Environmental health and physical infrastructure 914
6.1 Introduction 914
6.2 Settlements, housing, and shelter 915
6.2.1 Settlements 915
6.2.2 Housing 916
6.2.3 Temporary shelter 916
6.2.4 Food storage facilities 917
6.2.5 Housing reconstruction 918
6.3 Water 919
6.3.1 Assessment of water needs 919
6.3.2 Priorities for the improvement of water supplies 920
6.3.3 Testing and disinfection of water 921
6.4 Sanitation 923
6.4.1 The dangers of faecal contamination 923
6.4.2 Social issues in sanitation 924
6.4.3 Immediate interventions 924
6.4.4 Latrines 925
6.4.5 Public health and personal hygiene 926
6.5 Vector control 927
6.6 Key questions 929

7 Food security, food aid, and food distribution in emergencies 930
7.1 Introduction 930
7.2 Security and vulnerability: entitlements and assets 931
7.2.1 Food production systems 933
7.2.2 Post-crisis recovery of food production systems 934
7.3 Food aid in emergencies 936
7.3.1 Types of food aid intervention 937
7.4 Food supplies and distribution 942
7.4.1 Food supplies 942
7.4.2 Distribution and monitoring 943
7.4.3 Monitoring the sale of food aid 945
7.5 Key questions 946

6

8 Oxfam procedures in emergency relief programmes 948
  8.1 Introduction 948
  8.2 Information and assessment 949
    8.2.1 Information needs 951
    8.2.2 Assessment 952
    8.2.3 Sources of funds for emergency programmes 953
    8.2.4 Recommending emergency grants 955
    8.2.5 Internal communications 955
    8.2.6 Reporting 959
    8.2.7 Liaison with other agencies 961
    8.2.8 Evaluation 961
  8.3 Relief supplies and logistics 961
    8.3.1 The importance of logistics 961
    8.3.2 Ordering supplies 962
    8.3.3 International transport 963
    8.3.4 Local transport, handling, and storage 966
    8.3.5 Distribution 969
  8.4 Administration and staffing 970
    8.4.1 Preparedness and contingency plans 970
    8.4.2 Financial procedures 971
    8.4.3 Staffing and recruitment 972
    8.4.4 Staff health and security 972
    8.4.5 Travel in hazardous situations 974
  8.5 Key questions 975
Appendix I Relief items for which local suppliers should be found 977
Appendix II Oxfam's emergencies stores 978
Appendix III Other relief items 979
Appendix IV Standard specifications for commonly required relief items 980
Appendix V Oxfam policy in emergencies 982
Appendix VI Oxfam water supply scheme for emergencies: the water packs 983
Appendix VII Oxfam emergency sanitation unit 985

9 Resources 986

Tables

6.1 The changing emphasis of support 827
6.2 Lessons from 41 case studies 833
6.3 Responsibilities, limitations, impacts and opportunities 867
6.4 Vectors which may pose significant health risks 928
6.5 Hierarchy of survival strategies 933
6.6 Framework for a situation report 959

1 Introduction

1.1 Oxfam and emergencies 799
1.2 Code of conduct for NGOs 801

1.1 Oxfam and emergencies

Since its inception, Oxfam has been involved in a wide variety of humanitarian relief programmes. Assistance has ranged from funding small-scale relief projects within the context of existing development work, to setting up and running large-scale operational emergency interventions. Oxfam views emergency relief as part of a range of humanitarian responses to poverty and suffering, which support people's capacity to take greater control over the forces that affect their lives. Advocacy and lobbying on issues of humanitarian aid policy and practice, and on sustainable peace-making initiatives, are an integral part of Oxfam's relief work, as of its development programmes. This is becoming an especially important aspect of Oxfam's work in view of the fact that many of the existing relief mechanisms of the international community are proving unable to cope with the changing demands made upon them.

The view of emergencies as temporary interruptions in the steady processes of development is changing, in response to a new understanding of the state of turbulence in many of the countries in which Oxfam works, where there is such fluidity and instability that the situation of poor people is one of virtually constant crisis. The role of aid agencies must, therefore, be to seek to lessen this underlying vulnerability, ensuring that their humanitarian relief efforts systematically address the root causes of crisis. (See 6.2.4 The crisis of development practice and the need for new ideas.)

Oxfam's expenditure on emergency relief has continued to rise in recent years, both in absolute terms and as a percentage of Oxfam's programme budget. Currently, at least half Oxfam's total allocation of funds goes towards emergency-related work. At any given time, Oxfam may be dealing with several major relief programmes around the world, usually involving work with refugees or displaced persons. Many such emergencies have arisen as a result of armed conflict. Recurrent

6

disasters, such as cyclones and floods, or sudden emergencies such as earthquakes or volcanic eruptions, also demand a humanitarian response. In addition, a large number of local emergency relief initiatives are managed within Oxfam's existing long-term programmes.

Emergency relief work is often subject to intense pressures, and it is easy to overlook the social and cultural aspects of people's lives in the rush to provide assistance. The urgency of human need compels swift action, and thorough assessment and planning may be impeded by constraints of many kinds. However, it is precisely because social structures and cultural traditions, and economic and political systems, are weakened by emergencies, that individuals are made more vulnerable to damage by ill-conceived interventions.

In Oxfam's experience, the conventional dichotomy between emergency relief and development work is a false and a dangerous one. The same basic principles and criteria govern any Oxfam intervention. Oxfam's approach is to strengthen the capacity of poor and disadvantaged people to bring about positive and sustainable changes in their lives; and to reduce their vulnerability to emergencies, or to any form of denial of their basic rights. This chapter should therefore be read in conjunction with Chapter 1 Oxfam's approach to development and relief, Chapter 2 Focusing on people, and Chapter 3 Capacity-building for development, which together represent a comprehensive guide to Oxfam's current policy and practice.

This chapter opens with a brief outline of current trends in the area of NGO humanitarian aid, as a background to the context in which Oxfam is working. The very nature of emergency work requires a continual adaptation to rapid and often unpredictable change. In addition, the formal roles of existing UN and other international humanitarian bodies are themselves subject to transformation in the face of the range and scale of demands upon them. Thus, while Oxfam believes in adhering to certain basic principles in all aspects of its work, it also aims to respond flexibly to different or changing needs. However, it is hoped that the holistic and integrated approach outlined in the opening sections will assist aid workers who are confronted with overwhelming emergencies or apparently impossible dilemmas, and enable development and relief workers better to understand the dynamics of crisis and turbulent change.

Issues relating to the assessment, planning, evaluation, and co-ordination of emergency relief programmes are then discussed. The remaining sections examine specific aspects of emergency relief work in which Oxfam has particular expertise, such as environmental public health, nutrition, and food security. These sections cover material that is presented in a more comprehensive and detailed way in Chapter 5 Health; and Chapter 4 Production, respectively; and should be read in conjunction with them. Finally, the chapter concludes with a summary of Oxfam's recommended procedures for emergency relief programmes, as a suggested guide to good practice. Key questions are included at the end of some sections, and further resources are grouped by section at the end of the chapter.

1.2 Code of conduct for NGOs

Many of the principles and ways of working which are described in this chapter have been set out as part of a code of conduct for NGOs recently drawn up by the Standing Committee for Humanitarian Response. Oxfam is one of the NGOs who are signatories to this code. It is reproduced here, because it illustrates the international nature of humanitarian response, and also because it provides a summary introduction for the reader to issues which will be dealt with in detail in the various sections of the chapter.

Code of Conduct for NGOs in Disaster Relief

Purpose
This Code of Conduct seeks to guard our standards of behaviour. It is not about operational details, such as how one should calculate food rations or set up a refugee camp. Rather, it seeks to maintain the high standards of independence, effectiveness and impact to which disaster response NGOs aspire. It is a voluntary code, enforced by the will of organisations accepting it to maintain the standards laid down in the Code.

In the event of armed conflict, the present Code of Conduct will be interpreted and applied in conformity with international humanitarian law.

The Code of Conduct is presented first. Attached to it are three annexes, describing the working environment that we would like to see created by host governments, donor governments and inter-governmental organisations in order to facilitate the effective delivery of humanitarian assistance.

Definitions
NGOs: NGOs (Non-Governmental Organisations) refers here to organisations, both national and international, which are constituted separately from the government of the country in which they are founded.
NGHAs: For the purposes of this text, the term Non Governmental Humanitarian Agencies (NGHAs) has been coined to encompass the

components of the International Red Cross and Red Crescent Movement — The International Committee of the Red Cross, The International Federation of Red Cross and Red Crescent Societies and its member National Societies — and the NGOs as defined above. This Code refers specifically to those NGHAs who are involved in disaster response.

IGO: IGOs (Inter-Governmental Organisations) refers to organisations constituted by two or more governments. It thus includes all United Nations agencies and regional organisations.

Disasters: A disaster is a calamitous event resulting in loss of life, great human suffering and distress, and large-scale material damage.

The Code of Conduct

1 The humanitarian imperative comes first.

The right to receive humanitarian assistance, and to offer it, is a fundamental humanitarian principle which should be enjoyed by all citizens of all countries. As members of the international community, we recognise our obligation to provide humanitarian assistance wherever it is needed. Hence the need for unimpeded access to affected populations, is of fundamental importance in exercising that responsibility.

The prime motivation of our response to disaster is to alleviate human suffering amongst those least able to withstand the stress caused by disaster. When we give humanitarian aid it is not a partisan or political act and should not be viewed as such.

2 Aid is given regardless of the race, creed or nationality of the recipients and without adverse distinction of any kind. Aid priorities are calculated on the basis of need alone.

Wherever possible, we will base the provision of relief aid upon thorough assessment of the needs of the disaster victims and the local capacities already in place to meet those needs.

Within the entirety of our programmes, we will reflect considerations of proportionality. Human suffering must be alleviated whenever it is found; life is as precious in one part of a country as another. Thus, our provision of aid will reflect the degree of suffering it seeks to alleviate.

In implementing this approach, we recognise the crucial role played by women in disaster prone communities and will ensure that this role is supported, not diminished, by our aid programmes.

The implementation of such a universal, impartial and independent policy, can only be effective if we and our partners have access to the necessary resources to provide for such equitable relief, and have equal access to all disaster victims.

3 Aid will not be used to further a particular political or religious stand-point.
Humanitarian aid will be given according to the need of individuals, families and communities. Notwithstanding the right of NGHAs to espouse particular political or religious opinions, we affirm that assistance will not be dependent on the adherence of the recipients to those opinions.

We will not tie the promise, delivery or distribution of assistance to the embracing or acceptance of a particular political or religious creed.

4 We shall endeavour not to act as instruments of government foreign policy.
NGHAs are agencies which act independently from governments. We therefore formulate our own policies and implementation strategies and do not seek to implement the policy of any government, except in so far as it coincides with our own independent policy.

We will never knowingly — or through negligence — allow ourselves, or our employees, to be used to gather information of a political, military or economically sensitive nature for governments or other bodies that may serve purposes other than those which are strictly humanitarian, nor will we act as instruments of foreign policy of donor governments.

We will use the assistance we receive to respond to needs and this assistance should not be driven by the need to dispose of donor commodity surpluses, nor by the political interest of any particular donor.

We value and promote the voluntary giving of labour and finances by concerned individuals to support our work and recognise the independence of action promoted by such voluntary motivation. In order to protect our independence we will seek to avoid dependence upon a single funding source.

5 We shall respect culture and custom.
We will endeavour to respect the culture, structures and customs of the communities and countries we are working in.

6 We shall attempt to build disaster response on local capacities.
All people and communities — even in disaster — possess capacities as well as vulnerabilities. Where possible, we will strengthen these capacities by employing local staff, purchasing local materials, and trading with local companies. Where possible, we will work through local NGHAs as partners in planning and implementation, and cooperate with local government structures where appropriate.

We will place a high priority on the proper coordination of our emergency responses. This is best done within the countries concerned by those most directly involved in the relief operations, and should include representatives of the relevant UN bodies.

803

7 Ways shall be found to involve programme beneficiaries in the management of relief aid.
Disaster response assistance should never be imposed upon the beneficiaries. Effective relief and lasting rehabilitation can best be achieved where the intended beneficiaries are involved in the design, management and implementation of the assistance programme. We will strive to achieve full community participation in our relief and rehabilitation programmes.

8 Relief aid must strive to reduce future vulnerabilities to disaster as well as meeting basic needs.
All relief actions affect the prospects for long-term development, either in a positive or a negative fashion. Recognising this, we will strive to implement relief programmes which actively reduce the beneficiaries' vulnerability to future disasters and help create sustainable lifestyles. We will pay particular attention to environmental concerns in the design and management of relief programmes. We will also endeavour to minimise the negative impact of humanitarian assistance, seeking to avoid long-term beneficiary dependence upon external aid.

9 We hold ourselves accountable to both those we seek to assist and those from whom we accept resources.
We often act as an institutional link in the partnership between those who wish to assist and those who need assistance during disasters. We therefore hold ourselves accountable to both constituencies.

All our dealings with donors and beneficiaries shall reflect an attitude of openness and transparency. We recognise the need to report on our activities, both from a financial perspective and the perspective of effectiveness.

We recognise the obligation to ensure appropriate monitoring of aid distributions and to carry out regular assessments of the impact of disaster assistance. We will also seek to report, in an open fashion, upon the impact of our work, and the factors limiting or enhancing that impact.

Our programmes will be based upon high standards of professionalism and expertise in order to minimise the wasting of valuable resources.

10 In our information, publicity and advertising activities, we shall recognise disaster victims as dignified humans, not hopeless objects.
Respect for the disaster victim as an equal partner in action should never be lost. In or public information we shall portray an objective image of the disaster situation where the capacities and aspirations of disaster victims are highlighted, and not just their vulnerabilities and fears.

While we will cooperate with the media in order to enhance public response, we will not allow external or internal demands for publicity to take precedence over the principle of maximising overall relief assistance.

We will avoid competing with other disaster response agencies for media coverage in situations where such coverage may be to the detriment of the service provided to the beneficiaries or to the security of our staff or the beneficiaries.

The working environment

Having agreed unilaterally to strive to abide by the Code laid out above, we present below some indicative guidelines which describe the working environment we would like to see created by donor governments, host governments and the inter-governmental organisations — principally the agencies of the United Nations — in order to facilitate the effective participation of NGHAs in disaster response. These guidelines are presented for guidance. They are not legally binding, nor do we expect governments and IGOs to indicate their acceptance of the guidelines through the signature of any document, although this may be a goal to work to in the future. They are presented in a spirit of openness and cooperation so that our partners will become aware of the ideal relationship we would seek with them.

Annex I Recommendations to the governments of disaster-affected countries

1 Governments should recognise and respect the independent humanitarian and impartial actions of NGHAs.

NGHAs are independent bodies. This independence and impartiality should be respected by host governments.

2 Host governments should facilitate rapid access to disaster victims for NGHAs.

If NGHAs are to act in full compliance with their humanitarian principles, they should be granted rapid and impartial access to disaster victims, for the purpose of delivering humanitarian assistance. It is the duty of the host government, as part of the exercising of sovereign responsibility, not to block such assistance, and to accept the impartial and apolitical action of NGHAs.

Host governments should facilitate the rapid entry of relief staff, particularly by waiving requirements for transit, entry and exit visas, or arranging that these are rapidly granted. Governments should grant over-flight permission and landing rights for aircraft transporting international relief supplies and personnel, for the duration of the emergency relief phase.

6

805

3 Governments should facilitate the timely flow of relief goods and information during disasters.
Relief supplies and equipment are brought into a country solely for the purpose of alleviating human suffering, not for commercial benefit or gain. Such supplies should normally be allowed free and unrestricted passage and should not be subject to requirements for consular certificates of origin or invoices, import and/or export licences or other restrictions, or to importation taxation, landing fees or port charges.

The temporary importation of necessary relief equipment, including vehicles, light aircraft and telecommunications equipment, should be facilitated by the receiving host government through the temporary waiving of licence or registration restrictions. Equally, governments should not restrict the re-exportation of relief equipment at the end of a relief operation.

To facilitate disaster communications, host governments are encouraged to designate certain radio frequencies, which relief organisations may use in-country and for international communications for the purpose of disaster communications, and to make such frequencies known to the disaster response community prior to the disaster. They should authorise relief personnel to utilise all means of communication required for their relief operations.

4 Governments should seek to provide a coordinated disaster information and planning service.
The overall planning and coordination of relief efforts is ultimately the responsibility of the host government. Planning and coordination can be greatly enhanced if NGHAs are provided with information on relief needs and government systems for planning and implementing relief efforts as well as information on potential security risks they may encounter. Governments are urged to provide such information to NGHAs.

To facilitate effective coordination and the efficient utilisation of relief efforts, host governments are urged to designate, prior to disaster, a single point-of-contact for incoming NGHAs to liaise with the national authorities.

5 Disaster relief in the event of armed conflict.
In the event of armed conflict, relief actions are governed by the relevant provisions of international humanitarian law.

Annex II Recommendations to donor governments

1 Donor governments should recognise and respect the independent, humanitarian and impartial actions of NGHAs.
NGHAs are independent bodies whose independence and impartiality

should be respected by donor governments. Donor governments should not use NGHAs to further any political or ideological aim.

2 Donor governments should provide funding with a guarantee of operational independence.
NGHAs accept funding and material assistance from donor governments in the same spirit as they render it to disaster victims; one of humanity and independence of action. The implementation of relief actions is ultimately the responsibility of the NGHA and will be carried out according to the policies of that NGHA.

3 Donor governments should use their good offices to assist NGHAs in obtaining access to disaster victims.
Donor governments should recognise the importance of accepting a level of responsibility for the security and freedom of access of NGHA staff to disaster sites. They should be prepared to exercise diplomacy with host governments on such issues if necessary.

Annex III   Recommendations   to   intergovernmental organisations

1 IGOs should recognise NGHAs, local and foreign, as valuable partners.
NGHAs are willing to work with UN and other inter-governmental agencies to effect better disaster response. They do so in a spirit of partnership which respects the integrity and independence of all partners. Inter-governmental agencies must respect the independence and impartiality of the NGHAs. NGHAs should be consulted by UN agencies in the preparation of relief plans.

2 IGOs should assist host governments in providing an overall coordinating framework for international and local disaster relief.
NGHAs do not usually have the mandate to provide the overall coordinating framework for disasters which require an international response. This responsibility falls to the host government and the relevant United Nations authorities. They are urged to provide this service in a timely and effective manner to serve the affected state and the national and international disaster response community. In any case, NGHAs should make all efforts to ensure the effective coordination of their own services.

In the event of armed conflict, relief actions are governed by the relevant provisions of international humanitarian law.

3 IGOs should extend security protection provided for UN organisations to NGHAs.
Where security services are provided for inter-governmental

6

organisations, this service should be extended to their operational NGHA partners where it is so requested.

4 IGOs should provide NGHAs with the same access to relevant information as it granted to UN organisations.

IGOs are urged to share all information, pertinent to the implementation of effective disaster response, with their operational NGHA partners.

2 Background: emergencies, conflict, and development

2.1 Crises, disasters, and emergencies 809
    2.1.1 The changing nature of emergencies 812
    2.1.2 The causes of complex emergencies 813
    2.1.3 Emergencies and human rights 814
2.2 The changing nature of humanitarian response 815
2.3 Information and advocacy 817
    2.3.1 Information and vulnerability 817
    2.3.2 Information and public policy 818
2.4 The crisis of development practice and the need for new ideas 819
    2.4.1 Planning for diversity and divergence 820
    2.4.2 Chaos and complexity; pictures of change 821
    2.4.3 The awareness of potential flash-points 823
2.5 The relationship between development and relief 824
    2.5.1 The balance between short-term and long-term
        considerations 824
    2.5.2 Adapting development programmes to handle emergency
        relief 828
    2.5.3 Development as a response to crisis 829
    2.5.4 Supporting self-reliance 830
2.6 Reducing people's vulnerability to crisis 832
    2.6.1 Capacities and Vulnerabilities Analysis 832
    2.6.2 Disaster mitigation 834
    2.6.3 Rehabilitation, reconstruction, and development 836

6

2.1 Crises, disasters, and emergencies

The focus of Oxfam's work is increasingly on defending and promoting the rights of poor people, and on supporting their own capacity to bring about sustainable improvements in every aspect of their lives. However, in the face of rapid and complex changes in the environments within which humanitarian agencies are working, it may be hard to keep sight of these basic aims, or to know how best to reach them. Prolonged crisis and unpredictable turbulence present aid agencies with major challenges, not only to their overall thinking and policy-making, but also to their capacity to plan ahead, or to determine what kind of actions are most appropriate in each situation. They are often tempted to see development and relief as different in kind, rather than as different facets of the same approach.

This section offers a brief survey of some of the critical shifts in the operating environment for agencies such as Oxfam, that have occurred at an accelerating pace since the end of the Cold War, and as a consequence of other major political changes of the late 1980s and early 1990s. This is necessarily selective, since it is beyond the scope of this *Handbook* to attempt an exhaustive account of the recent history of international humanitarian assistance. However, the Oxfam-supported 'Humanitarianism and War' project, run jointly by the Thomas J Watson Jr Institute for International Studies, Brown University, and the Refugee Policy Group in Washington DC, has produced a number of publications, including a series of detailed case-studies on emergencies in the Horn of Africa, the Persian Gulf, Central America, Cambodia, and Eastern and Central Europe: these are alluded to in this section, and are listed in the Resources Section of this chapter.

Oxfam's own thinking in the area of emergency-related work is also undergoing significant change. This is partly in response to challenges to the assumed relationship between development and relief raised by its long-term experience in areas that are emerging from prolonged conflict and political violence, such as Central America, Afghanistan, the Occupied Territories, or Southern Africa; as well as more recent involvement in Eastern and Central Europe. However, it also reflects the likelihood of major reforms in the policy environment, particularly in relation to the mandates of the UN agencies. These changes will, in turn, have an impact on the role of independent NGOs such as Oxfam. For these reasons, this section has concentrated on the general issues to be considered in framing an appropriate response to crisis, and has refrained from enumerating the recommendations for institutional reform within the inter-governmental organisations that Oxfam and other NGOs have been making in recent years.

A crisis may be defined as the point at which radical change becomes necessary — that is, when the *status quo* has become unsustainable. Not all crises give rise to emergencies; and change is by no means always negative. Indeed, the purpose of Oxfam's development work is both to assist poor people to bring about positive change, and to support their capacity to withstand adverse changes that affect their social and economic environments. However, for people or societies that are already vulnerable, even a small shift in their situation may give rise to a crisis that outstrips their capacity to cope — in other words, a disaster or emergency. Crisis does not refer therefore only to an unexpected catastrophe, but also to the culmination of a slow build-up of political, economic or environmental factors. The combination of these factors with a sudden event, such as an earthquake or a major accident, can prove overwhelming. It is therefore critical that relief interventions aim to address the underlying inequities that make people more vulnerable to extreme stress or crisis: these may range from broad and complex factors, such as the non-accountability of national political institutions or macro-economic systems, to highly practical considerations, such as poorly-constructed housing or inadequate flood-control measures.

Emergencies may be caused by natural phenomena, commonly referred to as 'disasters', such as earthquakes, floods, droughts, hurricanes, and volcanic eruptions; or by major accidents, as in the case of the Chernobyl nuclear plant. Inequity and poverty make people more vulnerable to the effects of natural and industrial hazards. Environmental degradation, which itself is often poverty-related, may exacerbate such hazards. They may also arise from broader patterns of social and economic injustice or discrimination against specific groups of people, which compound their vulnerability. In themselves, natural phenomena do not constitute disasters; it is their effect on human life that defines them as such.

Emergencies may also derive from a range of other causes, or more commonly, from a set of inter-related causes. These may be divided into:

- sudden-onset natural phenomena, such as cyclones, floods and earthquakes;
- slow-onset natural phenomena, such as droughts, or pest infestations;
- sudden-onset events, such as major accidents, war, or major civil unrest;
- slow-onset events, such as low-level conflicts or systematic discrimination against specific social groups.

However, these descriptive categories are of little help in predicting the impact of a crisis; or the longer-term political and social repercussions either of the disaster itself or of relief efforts. The physical disruption caused to people's lives, and the relief responses, may be similar, whatever the immediate or long-term causes of the disaster.

Any situation involving the severe disruption, distress, and suffering of large numbers of people constitutes an emergency that demands a humanitarian response. Oxfam's charitable purpose is *to relieve poverty, distress, and suffering in any part of the world...in particular to provide food, healing, clothing, shelter, training, and education.* Over the years, Oxfam's work has been focused on addressing inequities and alleviating poverty, to reduce people's vulnerability to future crises; and providing humanitarian relief for the victims of emergencies. For Oxfam, develop-

811

ment and relief are different facets of its overriding commitment to the eradication of poverty, and the suffering caused by social injustice.

2.1.1 The changing nature of emergencies

Oxfam is well known for its emergency relief work, which often commands a high international profile. Since the mid-1980s, most of the major emergencies in which Oxfam has been involved, and which have been the most difficult to address, have been associated with armed conflict. Oxfam's experience is not unique: a 1991 study on world hunger, sponsored by the US umbrella agency InterAction, concluded that while eradicating famine-associated mortality where civil strife does not exist is increasingly possible, 'the major obstacle to eliminating famine remains the destruction or interdiction of civilian food supplies in zones of armed conflict' (Minear, L, Weiss, T, Campbell (1991) *Humanitarianism and War: Learning the Lessons from Recent Conflicts, Occasional Paper* 8, Thomas J. Watson Jr. Institute for International Studies.) From the perspective of many humanitarian agencies, the major challenge facing the world community is how to respond to need, protect human rights, and promote lasting development in situations of conflict; and how to build sustainable peace in such contexts, and prevent armed conflict occurring or recurring.

To demonstrate the scale of the problem, in 1960 there were ten unresolved wars recognised by the UN; by 1993 there were 50 such wars, 30 of which were claiming more than 1000 lives each year. Almost 90 per cent of these wars were internal, and over half were defined by the UN as 'complex emergencies'. By this is meant major humanitarian crises of a multi-causal nature, that require a response across the entire UN system, including peace-keeping interventions. Unlike disasters caused by natural phenomena, complex emergencies are embedded in, and are expressions of, existing social, political, economic, and cultural structures. They are all-encompassing, and involve every dimension of a society, and the lives of the people who are part of it. For this reason, the design and delivery of humanitarian relief programmes cannot be insulated from the causes of the emergency to which they are a response. In the words of the paper prepared by the UN Department of Humanitarian Affairs (DHA) *Protection of Humanitarian Mandates in Conflict Situations*, '...given the inter-related causes and consequences of complex emergencies, humanitarian action cannot be fully effective unless it is related to a comprehensive strategy for peace and security, human rights and social and economic development.'

Issues of ethnicity and cultural intolerance were critical dimensions of almost all of these internal conflicts. Over the last three decades, long-running conflicts have been taking place in countries such as Angola,

Mozambique, Afghanistan, and Guatemala; and more recently in the former Soviet Union and Eastern and Central Europe. More wars started than ended each year, and they tended to last longer than in the past. The concept of the sovereign nation state is being contested in many areas of the world, and secessionist or resistance movements exist in over 60 countries; which could lead to internal conflicts breaking out in the future.

A tragic human consequence is that there are currently estimated to be about 20 million refugees, at least as many internally displaced persons, and approximately three times as many economic migrants, throughout the world. As the scale, frequency, and duration of armed conflict increases, so does the effect that such crises have on civilian populations. Most countries experiencing conflict will be in even greater need of assistance when peace is restored. It is thus predictable that Oxfam's expenditure on emergency-related work will continue to rise inexorably, both in absolute terms and as a percentage of Oxfam's programme budget.

2.1.2 The causes of complex emergencies

There are many inter-related factors behind the escalation in armed conflict. The end of the Cold War, combined with the collapse of the Soviet bloc, has profoundly changed the context for humanitarian assistance and for bilateral intervention in the affairs of sovereign states, and also the perceived role of the UN system. The collapse of nation states, and the resurgence of ethnicity and religious intolerance as elements of armed conflict, are also significant. Some analysts regard the predominance of the neo-liberal economic model as critical, while others emphasise environmental degradation, population growth, or the failure of some states to adhere to agreed covenants going unchallenged by the international community.

Whatever the immediate causes, it is increasingly clear that major crises and conflicts are not exceptional or static events, and are rooted in the past. They are a consequence of struggles over power, rights, and resources, and so represent only an intensification of broader processes of political, social, and economic change — processes which affect individuals and groups in very different ways. An aid agency cannot intervene in a strategic fashion without understanding the dynamics of change, to which there are many inter-related contributory factors, including:

- long-term processes producing patterns of vulnerability, such as environmental degradation, declining terms of trade, economic marginalisation, and the feminisation of poverty;
- contingent or proximate events producing reductions in resources or entitlements, such as the outbreak of war, or the onset of drought;

6

- specific local factors such as social structures, or control over resources, which give a particular character to vulnerability (for example, cultural or religious identities, or gender relations).

Conflicts do not occur in a vacuum, but within a context of inequities, and often in the absence of representative and responsive political structures at local, national, and international level. They are exacerbated by external factors, such as terms of trade or international debt, and by external interventions such as economic embargoes, or military blockades. Even relief efforts may be subverted, and actually have the effect of prolonging conflict. Humanitarian agencies are becoming increasingly aware that, since there are winners as well as losers in situations of conflict, it may be in the interests of some that repression, war or civil strife continue. In certain situations, violence and war may be a means for some groups to ensure their own economic and political survival, a point made by Michael Duffield in *Complex emergencies and the crisis of developmentalism*, IDS Bulletin 25: 3, 1994. For this reason, it is vital for aid agencies to be aware of the way in which humanitarian relief can be compromised by its relationship with violence, both structural and military.

2.1.3 Emergencies and human rights
(To be read in conjunction with **1**.2 Human rights in development and relief work; **6**.3 Emergencies deriving from war and armed conflict.)

Extreme deprivation (such as famine), conflict, the denial of political freedoms (including the right of access to information), and abuses of human rights, are inextricably linked. Agencies like Oxfam have a role to play in promoting the positive definitions of rights, which stress the obligations and responsibilities of national governments and of the international community. The current thinking which seeks to limit the role of the State may reinforce a negative definition of rights (i.e. 'freedom from..'), and may also encourage donor governments to condition aid allocations on rights-related agendas — such as 'good governance' or 'democratisation'; although donors may not necessarily change their own behaviour, or be prepared to meet their own domestic or international responsibilities in terms of respecting and promoting human rights. It is vital to take an integrated approach to human rights monitoring, bringing together civil and political rights as well as economic, cultural, and social rights. NGOs should seek to understand, and publicise, the rights dimensions of development and relief work, in the context of daily struggles for peace and material well-being, and the forces which shape such struggles.

2.2 The changing nature of humanitarian response

As the nature and scale of emergencies have changed, so too have the nature and scale of the response by humanitarian agencies. Since the Biafran war of 1968-70, when several medical volunteers spoke out against the behaviour of the Nigerian government, national and international NGOs have engaged in relief operations without the authorisation of host states. This occurred most notably in the Horn of Africa from the mid-1980s, where there were many cross-border operations; but also in other areas such as Afghanistan and Central America. While not always overtly supported by the UN and donor governments, these operations were marked by a degree of covert sub-contracting, by multilateral and bilateral bodies to NGOs, for the delivery of humanitarian assistance. This in turn led to negotiated access and 'corridors of tranquillity' — for example, in Sudan, Angola, and El Salvador — being developed by the UN, in consultation with governments and armed opposition movements. Again, it was often NGOs who were sub-contracted to deliver relief supplies.

The international intervention in Kurdistan following the end of the Gulf War in 1991 ushered in a period described by some as 'military humanitarianism'. This was characterised by the development of 'safe havens', the erosion of national sovereignty — ostensibly in order to protect human rights — the military enforcement of economic sanctions, and an uneasy tension between the humanitarian and military dimensions of peace-support operations. For instance, in 1992-93, economic pressure applied by the UN on the Federal Republic of Yugoslavia undercut the UN's own humanitarian work, by introducing significant delays in the delivery of relief shipments. During the same period, WHO and UNICEF protested that there were ten times as many civilians in Serbia and Montenegro affected by the collapse of the health-care system than the number of refugees for whom the UN programmes were intended. The picture is not uniformly negative: for example, in El Salvador, the UN peace-keeping forces (ONUSAL) played an important role in maintaining the momentum of the demobilisation process; and Oxfam actively encouraged the UN to allow the UN observers to remain for a further year after the first round of elections following the peace settlements. However, the fact remains that where the credibility of the UN's humanitarian and human rights interventions is undermined, the damaging impact is felt not only within the UN system, but within the aid community more generally.

The use of military personnel and supplies for humanitarian ends is not in itself new; past examples include the Berlin Airlift following the

815

1939-45 war. What is unprecedented is the inter-weaving of civilian humanitarian initiatives, through the UN, bilateral government agencies, and local and international NGOs, with military protection, as seen in Somalia, Bosnia, and Rwanda during the early 1990s.

Oxfam's experience suggests five criteria which are relevant in deciding whether military action is justified on humanitarian grounds. Underlying them all is the basic principle that the UN should authorise the use of force only where there is major loss of civilian life, or the real threat of it, and the level of this human suffering justifies the risks inherent in military action. Beyond this restriction, military action in humanitarian crises should not be authorised unless all of the following criteria can be met:

- All non-violent methods have failed, and the government or controlling authority has demonstrated its unwillingness or inability to end the civilian suffering. Peaceful means, including grassroots peace building, should always be attempted first, and given adequate time to work.
- It is limited to specific aims, and is impartially driven by humanitarian needs.
- There is evidence that the action would be welcomed by the people at risk.
- It is proportionate to humanitarian needs, and limited in scope to meeting those needs.
- It must be fully accountable to the UN.

Humanitarian agencies are sometimes the only viable channel for food and services in politically sensitive areas where governments and inter-governmental organisations are unable or unwilling to work. One unwelcome consequence has been that aid workers — from official and non-governmental agencies alike — are increasingly targeted by combatants; for example, the number of UN personnel killed in the course of duty rose fourfold between 1991 and 1993. Another potential problem is that NGOs may lose some of the flexibility that made them viable channels, either because they become over-dependent on official aid, or because the operational compromises they are forced to make undermine the trust between them and their local constituency. NGOs are often fearful of alienating governments, in both donor and recipient countries, and may be reluctant to speak out about the root causes of conflicts, because to do so might offend these governments.

NGOs can make a variety of responses to emergencies ranging from operational delivery of relief supplies, supporting the aid work of local organisations, to information, lobbying, and advocacy work. In any given situation, the response may consist of a combination of all of these. The specific emphasis depends largely on the nature and scale of the emergency, and also on how well the area and the people involved are already known to the agency, and whether there are other like-minded agencies with whom to work. Each crisis is different — although there may be important similarities between one situation and another — and is the product of inter-related macro-level and micro-level factors.

Sections 5, 6, 7 and 8 of this chapter describe some possible operational responses. But first, two crucial areas of non-operational response are considered: information and advocacy.

2.3 Information and advocacy

(To be read in conjunction with **1**.2 Human rights in development and relief work; and **3**.1.3 Communications in Development.)

Much of Oxfam's support for networks and coalitions revolves around the sharing of information — such as knowledge about hazardous agro-chemicals, or the effects of economic policies on low-income groups — on the basis of which people are better able to lobby for policy changes in the public interest. Similarly, Oxfam's extensive support for education and training activities is focused on equipping poor women and men with the knowledge and skills to defend their rights more effectively, and to press for greater accountability to them on the part of local, national, and international institutions.

The dissemination of accurate information is also of crucial importance in gaining support for Oxfam's work from the public in the UK and Ireland. Increasing public understanding of the causes of poverty is part of Oxfam's charitable purpose; all of Oxfam's work has an advocacy dimension. During emergencies, the provision of information to appropriate organisations within the affected country, as well as to other aid agencies and to the international media, should be seen as a major priority. (See **6**.8.2 Information and assessment.)

2.3.1 Information and vulnerability

The lack or denial of access to information concerning potential or actual crises is a major factor in determining the scope for effective and timely action to relieve suffering. The economist Amartya Sen has argued that censorship is so implicitly involved in the cause of famine that famine cannot occur in a country with a free press. The argument may be applied also to other disasters or crises which occur where people have neither the information nor the resources to deal with the problems, or to compel their government to do so.

The *1994 World Disasters Report,* published by the International Federation of Red Cross and Red Crescent Societies, states that the world

6

817

... appears to be awash with information but also with ever more people and communities vulnerable to disasters... One of the principles of a democracy, however defined, is that the people have a right to participate in decision-making and it follows from this that they must have access to information if they are to exercise this right responsibly.

The *Report* goes on to say that research following every major disaster over a decade, in industrialised and developing countries alike, has demonstrated that the risks were already known — and that in many cases, the remedies were also. Had there been a greater political commitment to placing this knowledge in the public domain, people would have been better placed to make informed choices, and to demand better protection from the risks to which they were exposed. In addition, if people are aware of their own rights as well as of the responsibilities of governments and international bodies in defending these, they are better able to use existing instruments, such as the press, or human rights legislation, to call the relevant institutions to account.

2.3.2 Information and public policy

By maintaining its independence and flexibility in complex situations that are often highly polarised, Oxfam may be able to play a role in galvanising others into action. Collecting, synthesising, and disseminating good quality, timely, and authoritative information is essential. This may involve sharing examples of good practice in small-scale activities with those capable of replicating them on a wider scale, for example, through the publication of research and evaluation findings. Alternatively, it may entail putting forward poverty-focused analyses of particular emergencies, and suggesting how other agencies might respond. For example, Oxfam's public policy position on the UN response to conflict-related humanitarian emergencies advocates changes to the UN's mandate, structure and funding, based on Oxfam's direct experience in Bosnia, Somalia, Sudan, Mozambique, Rwanda, Angola, Cambodia, Afghanistan, and Iraq. This policy outlines certain criteria to guide decisions about the use of UN-authorised force in humanitarian situations (see **6.2.2 The changing nature of humanitarian response**), and proposes changes in the UN's own management systems.

The international media are of crucial importance, not only in informing the public about emergency situations, but also in publicising the need for policy reforms within inter-governmental organisations and official bodies, and in generating pressure for rapid decisions and action. On many occasions, Oxfam co-operates closely with journalists, both in proactive advocacy work, and through providing briefings and poverty-focused information. Media coverage influences public opinion and attitudes in the UK and Ireland, and thus affects Oxfam's ability to raise funds for its work in major emergencies.

However, the media also present a double-edged sword to NGOs. For while they can help to galvanise recalcitrant governments and official bodies into action and provoke a degree of public pressure on agencies and governments to act, they may also sensationalise, trivialise, and oversimplify what are complex issues. The dynamics of media interest may not coincide either with the evolution of an emergency, or of the relief response: this is particularly so in the case of sudden-onset disasters. (See **6**.8.2 Information and assessment.) The very power of the media can mean that if a story is not told, in effect a disaster is deemed not to have occurred. Many journalists seek to promote awareness and provoke positive change, but there are others who present very one-sided accounts of events. Nevertheless, the media coverage of major crises, such as Rwanda in 1994, demonstrates the dedicated professionalism of journalists and war correspondents in continuing to report on the situation even when their lives are at risk. Oxfam would rarely contemplate major public advocacy work that did not incorporate a strong media component from the outset.

2.4 The crisis of development practice and the need for new ideas

Unpredictability and crisis are facts of life, in developing and industrialised countries alike. The changing nature of emergencies, and of the range of humanitarian responses to need and suffering, also represent a crisis for development thinking and practice. Aid agencies cannot continue to respond to unexpected change as they might have done in the past: either by ignoring it, or reacting after the event. Nor can they afford to overlook the fact that many years of development work have not succeeded in preventing conflicts and crises. Inappropriate forms of development may even have sown the seeds of conflict or exacerbated the inequalities that generate it.

Until quite recently, crises or disasters such as war and famine were seen by most aid agencies as temporary interruptions in the *status quo*, and the expectation was that — with appropriate assistance — 'normal' conditions would resume eventually. The conceptual framework for their interventions was that of a continuum of *relief — rehabilitation (or reconstruction) — development*, in which crises were viewed as setbacks to be weathered before continuing the journey along a defined path. It is now widely recognised that such linear assumptions about progress and development are unhelpful.

6

2.4.1 Planning for diversity and divergence
(To be read in conjunction with **1**.4 Exploring the context for development and relief work; **3**.2.2 Planning; and **3**.2.3 Evaluation.)

In recognising the diversity of situations in which it works, and the different impacts of its work on different groups of women, men, and children, Oxfam is increasingly aware of the need to avoid adopting definitions, policies, and procedures which close down future options, or reduce the scope for re-interpretation in the light of experience.

Uncertainty is inevitable, and actions taken to solve one problem will almost always create others. While some problems may be solved with enough data, analysis, and intelligence, many have no straightforward solutions. On the contrary, more information results in more, different, and often contradictory solutions. These are known as 'divergent' problems, and account for most of the insoluble dilemmas with which aid agencies and relief workers are grappling in emergency situations. Since knowledge about a situation is always incomplete, it is important that planning allows for flexibility in the face of a changing context, or a deepening understanding of that context. A rigidly designed response rules out the possibility of adaptation. However carefully plans are drawn up, it is not possible to eliminate all problems, or anticipate all opportunities that might arise. For aid agencies working in highly complex environments, the one certainty is that there will always be unpredictable problems, and mistakes will always occur. Plans should allow for this; and mechanisms should be built in for learning and adapting as necessary. In the words of a recent Word Bank report:

... the only way to learn is through action. The question to keep in mind is: does this process help generate information to solve problems identified, using methods that increase their capacity to solve problems in the future?...One of the most difficult challenges is giving up total control, or 'letting go' of the notion of the right way, the right order, the right answer.

Aid agencies should recognise that the best of intentions do not guarantee totally positive outcomes.

In all development or relief programmes, there is a danger of over-planning at the outset, and making inflexible commitments. As constructive dialogue and participatory planning become increasingly possible, activities and expenditure are likely to change. Consulting with local groups, and strengthening their capacity must be a priority — not at the expense of life-saving rescue operations but as a complement to them. Much of the kind of information ideally required in emergency situations cannot be collected and made available until certain activities actually start. It is unrealistic and self-defeating to expect maximum information at the beginning of a process of dialogue rather than after that process has begun. In the context of emergencies, just as in development activities, agencies should accept learning by doing as one key concept, and incremental learning as another.

Aid agencies should thus be open to change and ready to learn, and develop a culture that encourages challenges to their own thinking, from a range of different perspectives — especially those of the people they are trying to help. In most disasters, people survive through their own skills and capacities rather than through those of humanitarian agencies. In addition, local institutions have a crucial function in developing grassroots peace-building processes. In Somaliland, for example, the role of lineage leaders and traders in mobilising the withdrawal of support to local militia helped to create a fragile peace. In Central America, the actions of local NGOs and representative organisations of refugees and displaced persons, were critical to establishing the conditions for repatriation and subsequent peace settlements in El Salvador and Guatemala. In the context of local capacity-building, and the development of strong, accountable local institutions, Oxfam is committed to helping to create the conditions for such processes.

2.4.2 Chaos and complexity: pictures of change

Since development and relief are about engaging constructively with the processes of change, aid agencies need to learn from other areas and disciplines. There are new ways of thinking about, and managing, change — for example, in the areas of catastrophe, chaos, and complexity theories. For many years, natural and social sciences concentrated on those aspects of change that are smooth, linear, ordered, and predictable — in other words, those types of change that are easiest to analyse. But rapid, discontinuous, turbulent change, such as occurs when a *coup d'état* takes place, or a currency is suddenly devalued, has tended to be ignored, since it is more difficult to measure, predict, and handle. However, most emergencies involve just such types of discontinuous change. An analysis of this kind of change can illuminate how agencies can support people to cope with and promote positive change.

Interdependence and feedback: Major problems are not caused by one factor but by a combination of many interdependent ones. For instance, a famine can be caused by persistent drought, rising cereal prices, declining animal prices, poor roads, and lack of food aid, all at the same time.

Feedback concerns the effects of different factors and the links between them. This replaces the idea of unilinear cause and effect — for example, that A causes B — with the idea of interdependence, which

821

suggests that A and B may define each other through continuous interaction. There are two major types of feedback: negative feedback, where a change in one variable produces change in the opposite direction and therefore leads to stability; and positive feedback, which multiplies change. A well-known example of the use of feedback models was that of the Club of Rome's project on the *Limits to Growth*. This showed how world trends in population growth, pollution, and production could not be sustained if positive feedback systems did not have stabilising loops of negative feedback to counter their effects.

Understanding feedback loops can help to anticipate the potential impact of a given action, and to adapt to circumstances that vary rapidly and unpredictably. For aid agencies, this means that monitoring and a willingness to adapt are critical to coping with change.

Critical thresholds: Small inputs can lead to dramatically large consequences, as was exemplified in 1994 by the plane crash which killed the presidents of Rwanda and Burundi and which precipitated such tragic events. It is important to try to understand what happened at the outset of a period of turbulence, and what were the actual as opposed to the proximate causes. For example, in Niger in 1990, the fact that aid agencies did not provide food aid to nomads recently returned from Algeria led to demonstrations that eventually resulted in the rebellion in Mali. This small incident did not cause the rebellion, but was one of the sparks that provoked it. In essence, it triggered the processes of latent revolt in the area. There is often a critical threshold, beyond which catastrophic change takes place.

Patterns of change: The map-makers of the Middle Ages allowed great voyages to be undertaken because they boldly put forward their ideas without having seen the continents they drew. The shape was more important than the detail. If the exact details cannot be known, as is often the case in an emergency situation, what can be said about the overall shape? It is increasingly clear that an understanding of the broad dimensions of complex emergencies is required in order to provide the multiple and diverse actions that are needed in response. The inter-relatedness of causal factors and the mosaic or jigsaw nature of many emergencies needs to be understood in order to intervene in a strategic, and well-focused, manner. Aid agencies need to recognise that in many situations they will be acting in a state of 'optimal ignorance': when the information available is inadequate, but the best that can be obtained in the circumstances, and the urgency of the situation makes action imperative.

Stabilising points: These are points around which change occurs, or states to which a system eventually settles. For example, a tribe or a nation state may be stabilising points in terms of cultural evolution. There is no necessary progression between these; and many societies throughout history have achieved advanced levels of organisation, and then declined.

While emergency situations never repeat themselves exactly, there are similar stable points around which societies focus; and agencies should seek to build on these. For instance, in Somalia it is in many areas the elders that have proved to be the most stable element in the current crisis, and it is their ability to solve disputes at a local level which can deprive militia of support.

Thinking from the chaos and complexity debates challenges NGOs to analyse the nature and source of change of which they are a part, rather than viewing it as an external force with which they have to cope. As well as dealing with events in a reactive manner, they should also consider how they might shape and guide the forces which produce these events, in order positively to affect the nature of change itself.

2.4.3 The awareness of potential flash-points

Many of the countries in which aid agencies work are prone to the linked phenomena of variable climatic conditions, land degradation, conflict, and large-scale displacement. Such problems are compounded by geo-political considerations, and national and international power manoeuvres. It is important to be aware of:

- potential local problems that are likely to arise, and take great care to avoid activities that are likely to compound them;
- how conflict could be used by others within the country or sub-region (the state, rebel groups, or neighbouring governments) to further their own ends;
- who is providing support (moral, ideological, logistical or military) from within and outside the area.

While this awareness will not enable aid agencies to predict the future, it will enable them to identify potential flash-points which should be taken into account when programmes are being designed. Although international NGOs cannot possibly be aware of all the political complexities, cultural priorities, and social structures of the people affected, they should find out as much as they can before and during their involvement. Other local or international organisations familiar with the background and context should be actively approached in drawing up an analysis of the situation, and designing appropriate short-term interventions.

In view of the rapid and unpredictable changes in the situations in which Oxfam works, it is important to keep the focus of each programme under constant review, to ensure that appropriate adaptations can be made, and that the experience and new insights gained during the implementation phase can be used to modify programme priorities and project design. (See **6.8.4.1** Preparedness and contingency plans.)

2.5 The relationship between development and relief

Development and relief interventions are different ways in which aid agencies can help women and men to determine their own part in bringing about social justice and equity, whether at the household, local, national, or international level. Thus the fundamental criteria for long-term development work and for effective emergency relief efforts are the same. In Chapter 1 Oxfam's approach to development and relief, the basic principles are outlined that ensure that Oxfam's short- and long-term interventions strengthen people's existing capacities without undermining their potential to sustain themselves equitably in the future.

2.5.1 The balance between short-term and long-term considerations

In every emergency relief programme, there is a balance to be drawn between the timely delivery of assistance, and the longer-term implications of the way in which it is provided. The design, management, and evaluation of any aid intervention are just as important as the appropriateness of the goods and services being delivered. The impact of assistance varies according to social, economic, political, and cultural considerations. However, the greater emphasis on speed, and the tendency to see emergency programmes in terms of logistics, may mean that there is relatively little discussion in the initial stages with the people who are actually affected by relief assistance. Yet if development or relief programmes are implemented in ways which ignore local power relations, or which fail to take account of the distinct needs and perceptions of women as well as men, and of different social groups, Oxfam's experience is that the situation of women in particular is likely to be undermined. (See **6.4.4.2** Consulting women.)

Conflict and extreme deprivation are both caused by inequitable control over resources — whether these are political, social or material. If emergency or humanitarian assistance remains strictly defined in terms of material inputs, such as food aid and medical relief, it runs the risk of weakening and undermining people's existing capacities: local production systems, local organisations, and local self-esteem. This in turn may lead to a weaker civil society, and possibly reinforce the very factors which are the cause of the crisis. Emergency relief should not be narrowly defined as relief inputs, but also include more dynamic concepts such as 'relief production', 'relief employment', 'relief income generation', 'relief education and training', 'relief institutional development', or 'relief awareness-raising'. Another way of presenting these ideas is in the concept used in Central America during the 1980s: development for survival. This referred to the appeal by local NGOs and grassroots organisations to support activities of a long-term nature, such as agricultural production, immunisation campaigns, or literacy work, even though these were being conducted in highly unstable and insecure circumstances. To illustrate the point further, the elements of a welfare state, such as social security payments, low-cost public housing, or guaranteed employment schemes for vulnerable people, could in a sense be described as relief inputs, although many would see them as an essential facet of developed societies. For people who exist in conditions of extreme deprivation, the difference between normal life and what aid agencies define as an emergency may be marginal; poverty could be seen as a state of everyday, chronic emergency, which may intensify into crisis as a result of relatively small changes.

To be sustainable, development efforts must aim to strengthen the ability of people and local structures to cope with potential shocks and crises. Mid- and long-term plans should therefore accommodate short-term needs that either exist already, or that may be created by predictable and unpredictable shocks, such as climatic or civil disruption. It is equally important to assess whether long-term or development programmes will enable people to cope with crisis, as to ask whether short-term or relief activities will help in meeting long-term development objectives. If development work is not helping people to survive bad years or build sustainable peace, it is not long-term; because drought and conflict are structural problems that will recur unless the causes are eliminated. Similarly, unless relief activities strengthen people's capacity to overcome recurrent or structural crises in the longer term, then the overall impact may have intensified their vulnerability. In all areas of development and relief work, it is vital to respect and draw on the knowledge of the affected population, and to support their existing material and social capacities. The ability to identify and involve local NGOs and other social organisations from the earliest stage of a relief programme, may determine its short- and long-term success. (See 6.2.6.1 Capacities and Vulnerabilities Analysis.)

In Oxfam's experience, the conventional division of programmes into the categories of relief, rehabilitation or development is not only unhelpful but also — and more importantly — does not reflect the reality on the ground, where roles traditionally associated with development are possible in relief situations, and vice-versa. From

6

Bosnia to El Salvador or Somalia, Oxfam has supported many initiatives where local and international NGOs have undertaken innovative and creative reconstruction and development work even before peace has been achieved. As Drèze and Sen (1991) illustrate in their studies of famine-stricken countries, it is those governments which integrate relief, rehabilitation, and development, rather than dividing them into components of an imagined evolutionary process, that have been most successful in alleviating hunger. In the context of NGO work, the search is therefore for an appropriate mix of long- and short-term responses.

Such a mix requires a shift away from analysing situations in terms of exclusive 'either-or' options, towards more inclusive 'both-and' thinking. Instead of looking at problems as if there were only one solution, it is often more productive to assume that there may be more than one. While either-or propositions tend to lead to competition over the allocation of resources, both-and discussions tend to look for linkages, constructive collaboration, and comprehensive approaches. There are, of course, situations where difficult choices have to be made between mutually exclusive options; but routinely to adopt an exclusive rather than inclusive approach to problem-solving may hinder rather than stimulate creativity.

Table 6.1 illustrates that, although it is likely that the major focus of support may change over time, there are often important long-term or strategic activities that should be pursued in conjunction with meeting immediate needs, and vice-versa. Capacity building is as much a need in the face of severe crisis as in a more settled situation. Similarly, the strengthening of local coping mechanisms and political protection and lobbying are needed just as much by communities dealing with long-term trends as for those dealing with crisis. The dangers of concentrating on one area to the exclusion of the others can lead to undesirable results: for example, prolonging crises through ignoring opportunities to enable people to lobby for peace, or failing to relieve human suffering by ignoring short-term material needs.

Table 6.1 The changing emphasis of support

severe crisis	crisis pending	recovery	stable change

A represents support needs and roles related to: income-generation, enterprise development, savings and credit, sustainable health and education systems, environmental protection, capacity building, institutional development; encouraging strategic alliances, increasing ability to dialogue with the State and undertake national and international lobbying, preparing withdrawal; reinforcing women's entitlements and rights to gain access to credit, health, education, legal protection; promoting and strengthening women's ability as individuals and as groups, and developing networks and alliances with progressive agencies, legal services etc.

B represents support needs and roles related to: political stability, democracy at all levels, organising capacity, self-confidence, increased ability to deal with next crisis, securing and re-starting production, rehabilitating or establishing infrastructure; broad-based training, network building, strengthening people's ability to place demands on government, building economic foundations for group development; the readjustment and renegotiation of women's roles and gender relations; promoting and strengthening women's groups and women in mixed groups.

C represents support and roles related to: preparedness for possible crises, contingency planning, securing production, diversifying options, strengthening coping mechanisms; consolidating local control and management of resources by credit, training, support for organisational capacity; women as managers and consumers of shrinking resource base, directly involved and supported in all projects.

D represents support needs and roles related to: relief (eg food, shelter, medicine), preservation of local culture, strengthening of local coping mechanisms, political protection and lobbying, securing production; the provision of a liaison between community and external providers; thinking with community, 'being there', moral support, emphasis on life-enhancing principles, and avoiding dependency; women as guardians of family and culture, and as providers; protection, ensuring that although vulnerable, women are not seen as victims. (Source: ACORD 1991. See also *Development in Practice* 4:3.)

2.5.2 Adapting development programmes to handle emergency relief

Emergencies, particularly sudden-onset disasters, are likely to have a significant impact on existing programmes. Often the situation giving rise to a slow-onset emergency will have made it difficult to continue conventional long-term work in the region affected. In other cases, the impact of the emergency may be felt more widely than by those directly affected: for example, a large influx of refugees along a border area may have significant repercussions for the local population, especially if there are political or military implications. Where the emergency involves large-scale migration, there may be very high levels of women-maintained households. Such households are systematically among the poorest in most societies. (See **2.1.3.3** Women-maintained households.)

The prevailing emergency is thus likely to necessitate a change in priorities from longer-term work to meeting short-term needs. The extent of this shift will depend on the nature of the crisis, the existing social and material capacities of the people most severely affected, and the scale of the anticipated relief response.

NGOs often have difficulty in judging when or how to switch priorities, resource allocation, and programme focus. In other cases, a supervening catastrophe in the context of prevailing long-term crises may call for a 'double track' approach. For example, in Central America, the earthquakes in Mexico (1985) and El Salvador (1986), and Hurricane Joan in Nicaragua (1988) came on top of the complex emergency caused by armed conflicts, which had dominated Oxfam's programme priorities since the late 1970s. In each case, the challenge was to ensure that an appropriate response to the immediate crisis did not deflect attention unduly from the longer-term emergency priorities. It is inevitable that an emergency relief programme, especially in the context of a sudden-impact disaster, will require a re-allocation of resources; and that priorities may have to be redefined as a result. However, the existing programme commitments and style of work will affect the way in which a specific emergency is perceived and managed. For example, the 1985 earthquakes in Mexico City were severe, but localised in their impact, affecting only a very small area of the city. However, the extensive coverage in the international media gave an exaggerated impression of the situation, and this put a good deal of pressure on Oxfam's local staff to launch a high-profile relief programme. To do so would have been inconsistent both with existing priorities in the Central American region, and with Oxfam's role in Mexico. A substantial relief programme was implemented, but assistance was delivered largely through existing Oxfam contacts, and restricted to the emergency and immediate recovery stages. Even so, the medium-term consequences affected the regional programme for almost two years, because of the increased project load on staff.

When an emergency relief programme is likely to absorb significant resources in addition to existing commitments, it is advisable either to re-define those commitments, if this is feasible, or to seek additional or temporary staff, to handle the extra workload.

Oxfam's review of its own work in areas of conflict found that existing programmes go through a similar sequence of events as a crisis develops (Agerbak, 1991). This begins with shrinking of existing activities as the crisis looms, then moves through a phase of consolidation or enters a holding pattern, before arriving at an assessment of what can be done to deal with problems created by the crisis itself. In certain circumstances, where it is possible to do so, being there and remaining there, even if no tangible activities are feasible, is an important role for an aid agency. Its continuing presence can give moral support, provide a witness function, and be a symbol of normality; and allow the agency time to assess what role might be possible in future, and what new opportunities might emerge.

2.5.3 Development as a response to crisis

Experience suggests that the programmes which have adapted best in times of crisis have been those that have invested, over the years, in the development of people and organisations, who had the skills, capacities and, above all, self-confidence to propose and manage their own activities. When the margin between 'falling over the edge' and being able to survive without outside assistance is so small, programmes should concentrate on enabling people to avoid being caught in a downward spiral, by finding new economic niches. For instance, the market can play a role in precipitating or in preventing famine. Cash support to people who are vulnerable can enable them to make essential purchases, as well as stimulate demand. The knock-on effect for other vulnerable sectors can also be beneficial. For example, if those receiving support are thereby enabled to avoid 'distress livestock sales', this could benefit other livestock owners outside the relief system by preventing the collapse of livestock prices (Drèze, J and Sen, A, 1991).

In the face of crisis, the options for an existing programme may include the following:

- To either expand or increase the subsidy on existing activities (through reducing costs, such as in cereal bank programmes, or rescheduling credit; or through the provision of Food For Work; see **6.7.3.1** Types of food aid intervention).
- To exploit new, but temporary, opportunities that result from a crisis (such as the dried meat operations in Mali 1984–86; see **6.7.3.1** Types of food aid intervention); or supplying the aid economy, as in the case of an Oxfam-funded programme of support to the informal sector in Port Sudan in 1985–86 to supply pallets to aid agencies.
- To distribute key inputs (such as seeds and tools, animal feed) on a cost or subsidy basis, as a safety-net to avert distress sales, ensure production, or to compensate for a lost crop.
- To encourage diversified income opportunities through new activities (such as oasis gardening in the Sahel, or agriculture in siege towns) to respond to short-term needs: while these may not have any long-term business future, they provide skills and alternative strategies that can be drawn on in the long term, or reactivated in times of need

2.5.4 Supporting self-reliance

It is particularly important that pre-crisis support strengthens people's ability to cope with recurring and predictable events such as drought. So-called 'coping strategies' are a response to dwindling resources which are both anticipatory (insurance mechanisms) and reactive (disposal of assets). The effectiveness of coping strategies often depends on the range of entitlements on which people may call in a crisis. (Entitlements reflect the capacity of individuals and groups to guarantee their rights to a range of commodities. See **6.7.2** Security and vulnerability: entitlements and assets.) Strategic intervention in times of crisis demands an understanding of these processes.

Some of the coping strategies, and their sequencing, that people adopt during bad years include:

diversification of cropping patterns, livestock management, occupational choices;

exchange: acquiring cash or goods through the sale or barter of labour, animals, charcoal, craft work, assets, and superior foods;

dietary adjustments: eating less or worse food, gathering wild foods, are often responses to an early stage of a decline in food availability, before the sale of assets;

migration and employment: individual migration is often an early response to crisis, either to supplement household income or to decrease the demand on its resources; and the migration of entire households or families occurs as a last resort;

changes in intra-household resource distribution: in the early stages of a crisis, this usually results in children being protected and adults (particularly women and elderly dependants) eating less: cultural practices differ around the world, for instance in many Asian countries, boys are favoured over girls; in some situations, children may be discriminated against in favour of young men.

Agencies should be aware of these existing strategies, and ensure that activities undertaken during a crisis support them, rather than undermine them. However, survival strategies have a cost to those forced to resort to them. Even if they help to prevent famine in the short-term, they may damage long-term food security, be environmentally destructive, and in themselves involve a degree of suffering. The survivors have fewer assets, and may be in poorer health, and so will be more vulnerable when the next crisis threatens their livelihoods (Keen, 1993).

Appropriate contingencies should be built into long-term programmes. These should be based on a range of early-warning indicators that would signal the need to adapt. It is important not to focus on isolated variables (such as the decline in food production, changing prices, nutritional levels, wage levels), but to put these together to arrive at a coherent picture. Just as important as collecting information is to disseminate it, and to use it as a basis for pressurising others to act. 'There is no early warning without early will.' Such data collection systems, however imperfect, are in place in many countries, and agency staff should be aware of their results and incorporate these in their own analysis. Agencies should actively strengthen the long-term ability of local structures to organise, design, execute, and evaluate their own responses to short-term crises. (See 1.4 Exploring the context for development and relief work.)

It is important to present a realistic analysis of how far an agency can promote food security at the local level, resolve structural food deficits,

6

affect the market, and so on, given the external factors over which it has little control. This avoids raising false expectations. Oxfam's experience indicates it can and must adapt to each crisis in a flexible way, and that it does so best when it has reinforced the capacity of local structures to react. In the long term, it is hoped that such local structures will be able to influence wider change. But in many of the areas where Oxfam works this is not yet the case and will not be for some years. It is therefore vital in the short term that Oxfam has the flexibility, resources and commitment not only to move seamlessly from a long-term to short-term mode, but to apply pressure on those forces and institutions who make it necessary to do so. (See also **3**.1 Social Organisation.)

2.6 Reducing people's vulnerability to crisis

Linear thinking about the relief — rehabilitation (reconstruction) — development continuum tends to reinforce an approach to crisis that also divides activities into pre-emergency, emergency, and post-emergency stages. Reducing people's vulnerability to crisis requires a combination of short- and long-term responses that do not correspond neatly to mechanistic divisions between different stages in an emergency.

2.6.1 Capacities and Vulnerabilities Analysis

According to a major inter-agency project to establish a framework within which to combine development and relief more effectively (Anderson and Woodrow (1989); see **1**.4.3.2 Capacities and Vulnerabilities Analysis) aid agencies should analyse the long-term factors affecting people's ability to respond to events, which make them susceptible to crisis, in addition to needs, which refer to the immediate requirements for survival or recovery from a crisis. Vulnerabilities precede disasters, contribute to their severity, impede response, and continue after the immediate crisis. Examples of vulnerabilities are a lack of resources for subsistence, such as land; or forms of social and economic discrimination. Needs, by contrast, are generally shorter-term and immediate, such as a need for food or medicine; though they are themselves differentiated by the kinds of vulnerability to which different individuals, social groups, or communities are subject. For example, while an entire group of refugees may require food aid, the needs of very poor children who were already malnourished before the crisis may be more acute, and more urgent.

Analysing vulnerabilities may discourage any subsequent desire to return to normal, by revealing the extent to which the previous

832

situation involved long-term trends that held the seeds of future crises. In addition, it alerts aid agencies to the risk that their own interventions may unintentionally contribute to making people more vulnerable in the future. To avoid this, it is important also to look at people's existing capacities in order to know what strengths reside within a society, on which to build in future. In an emergency, a society's vulnerabilities are more noticeable than its capacities. However, taking a long-term and responsible approach to the ways in which agencies intervene in people's lives demands that agencies aim to understand both, in what is called a Capacities-Vulnerabilities Analysis (CVA). This relates both to material or physical factors, and also to the less tangible aspects of what makes a group of people stronger or weaker in the face of crisis; for example, whether they have some prior experience of social organisation; and whether they are motivated to act together. These factors vary according to gender, age, socio-economic status, and cultural or ethnic identity within the affected population. They also change over time, as people themselves adapt to changes in their situation. The aim of relief interventions should be to enable people to retain their existing capacities, and to develop new ones in the course of time. One of the strengths of this analysis is that it compels aid agencies to look both forwards and backwards, and not to focus exclusively on the present in designing and evaluating their work.

Carrying out an analysis in this way should enable aid agencies to make informed programme decisions, based on a number of basic principles. A summary of the lessons learnt from the project is given in Table 6.2.

Table 6.2 Lessons from 41 case studies
(Anderson and Woodrow (1989) *Rising from the Ashes: Development Strategies in Times of Disaster*)

6

Programming decisions
1 To do nothing is better than to do something badly. Agencies should not intervene in a crisis unless it is to support local capacities.
2 There is no such thing as relief projects that are neutral in terms of development. They either support it or undermine it.
3 Indigenous agencies are in a better position to respond developmentally than outside agencies. Outside agencies that are already present are better able to respond than those arriving to deal with the crisis.
4 Agencies that identify themselves as development agencies can provide creative relief in an emergency, especially in areas where they are already involved in long-term work.

5 Development agencies that work in areas prone to crisis should understand the need not only to anticipate the effects of disasters on their long-term work but also to address people's vulnerabilities through that work.

Principles

1 Relief work should be held to development standards. Thus every disaster response should be based on an appreciation of local capacities and should be designed to support and increase these.

2 Development work should be concerned with long-term sustainability. Thus every development programme and project should anticipate and be designed to prevent or mitigate disasters. Thus, they should identify and address the vulnerabilities of the people with whom they work and ensure that these are reduced over time.

3 Both relief and development should be more concerned with increasing local capacities and reducing vulnerabilities than with providing goods, services or technical assistance. In fact goods, services etc should be provided only insofar as they support sustainable development by increasing local capacities and reducing vulnerabilities.

4 The way that such resources are transferred must be held to the same test.

5 Programming must not be solely pre-occupied with meeting urgent needs but must integrate such needs into efforts that address the social/organisational and motivational/attitudinal elements as well.

2.6.2 Disaster mitigation

The combination of a short- and long-term view represented by CVA corresponds closely to Oxfam's analysis of poverty, and the approach to development and relief outlined in this *Handbook*. Vulnerability, poverty and marginalisation go together. For example, houses built in river gullies are prone to damage caused by floods or earthquakes. Settlements built on steep volcanic slopes may be subject to mud-slides or to eruptions. Subsistence farmers may cultivate land in fertile, but disaster-prone, areas such as flood plains; or in areas in which the environment is already severely degraded, such as deforested hillsides. Shanty-town dwellers may live in areas where the water is polluted by industrial or human waste, or where there is significant atmospheric contamination. Refugees may be compelled to stay in crowded and insanitary conditions for long periods of time; they may be forced to work in highly exploitative situations. Children may have to live on the streets, or become sex-workers, or become involved in military activities, in order to survive. People may or may not be aware that they are exposed to major hazards, to systematic violations of their basic rights, or to situations that will place them or their families at risk in the longer term. However, it is their powerlessness, and their lack of resources, which prevent them from either reducing the risks, or pressing the relevant institutions to do so; or from moving elsewhere.

In a narrow sense, *disaster mitigation* generally refers to practical measures to minimise the destructive or disruptive effects of natural hazards, and so lessen the magnitude of their impact. Reducing their vulnerability in this way enables individuals and communities better to survive and confront future disasters. Mitigation measures can be implemented at any time: before a disaster occurs, during an emergency, or as part of long-term rehabilitation and reconstruction. For example, a range of low-cost improvements in house design may be introduced to reduce potential earthquake or cyclone damage; or eroded hill slopes may be terraced, to prevent dangerous mudslides. People living in vulnerable environments can be helped to identify risks ('risk-mapping'), and to take action to reduce these. Oxfam has supported grassroots organisations and local NGOs in taking on specific aspects of disaster preparedness and mitigation. For example, the establishment of early-warning systems to enable economic and logistic measures to be put in place in anticipation of food shortfalls; or the construction of dykes or embankments to protect against flooding. Although disaster prevention and mitigation techniques may be introduced in the wake of a particular emergency, they are essentially of a long-term nature and should be accompanied by sensitive and socially-disaggregated analyses of the ways people currently survive, particularly if changes affecting their livelihoods are contemplated.

In a broader sense, the best form of disaster mitigation is through equitable social and economic development, that builds on people's strengths and tackles the causes of their vulnerability. (In this sense, most of Oxfam's work could be described as disaster mitigation.) The ways of doing this vary immensely in focus and in scope, though most are underpinned by social organisation and access to non-material as well as material resources. Strengthening the capacity of local organisations, in particular, is an essential element in helping poor people to be less vulnerable to future crises. International NGOs can assist by providing information on experiences elsewhere, and reinforcing learning skills for groups to decide their own rules, structures, and procedures. If local organisations are to respond to change, they have to retain their own capacity to change in the face of new situations. Many of the local institutions that Oxfam has supported as channels for emergency aid during situations of armed conflict have undergone this kind of self-questioning as they have had to function

6

within a new and less polarised environment. There is usually much more at stake than simply re-directing their programmes or areas of work: in some cases, such organisations have found that their erstwhile beneficiaries begin to question their legitimacy to continue as channels for international aid, now that the political arena has become more open. While it may be appropriate to support the establishment of formal institutions during periods of intense crisis, there is also a case for providing complementary support for informal alliances and networks whose role can perhaps adapt more easily to changes in the external environment.

2.6.3 Rehabilitation, reconstruction, and development

Any dividing line between relief, rehabilitation, and reconstruction phases is necessarily imprecise, especially when an emergency has been protracted over months, years or even decades. Rehabilitation and reconstruction are areas where relief and development become inseparable from each other. Since the underlying reasons for people's vulnerability are generally political or economic — for instance, they are living in wretched and dangerous conditions because of their lack of paid employment, land, education, food, or health care — rehabilitation means finding ways to address these inequities, and to help people to develop the organisational, material, and technical capacity they need in order to do so. The broader context within which rehabilitation is taking place is crucial. For instance, in a period of post-war reconstruction, the political and economic environment might continue to be unstable for some time. In the context of a sudden-onset natural catastrophe, the political situation might be relatively secure — and indeed the government may enjoy renewed popular support, if the crisis was seen to have been handled effectively.

Specific rehabilitation measures should also reduce the vulnerability of a population group to similar emergencies in the future. Anticipating the recurrence of a similar disaster may affect, for example, the types of crops grown in drought-prone areas, the way they are planted, where they are planted, and so on. In an area prone to earthquakes, specifications for new buildings might be modified to ensure that buildings are earthquake-proof.

Rehabilitation programmes should also focus on social or economic interventions as well as on improvements in material conditions. For example, after the tribal clashes in Assam in 1983, many households were left without looms, one of the major sources of income in the area. Looms were provided by Oxfam, thus helping to create conditions in which people could resume their previous economic activities. In the Horn of Africa, prolonged drought and famine had led to a loss of agricultural assets: seeds were eaten, livestock died or were sold at less than their usual market value to buy food, and so on. In order to recover, people needed to replenish such assets. Rehabilitation programmes supported by Oxfam involved the provision of seeds and tools to those whom famine and war had left completely impoverished; the purchase of livestock, or the provision of cash or loan funds to allow such purchases; and animal feeding and veterinary schemes. In Bangladesh, Oxfam was involved in rehabilitation work following the floods of 1987 and 1988. Relief and rehabilitation programmes included four elements: distribution of emergency cooked food, and of dry rations; agricultural rehabilitation (supply of seeds and fertilisers); employment-creation schemes, to compensate landless farm labourers for lost employment opportunity; and assistance with house reconstruction. These examples demonstrate the importance of defining rehabilitation in a broad and holistic way. (See **6**.7.2.2 Post-crisis rehabilitation of food production systems.)

The people in the area affected by an emergency are likely to know better than anyone else what action is required; but perhaps lack the resources to carry it out, may not be organised in any way to work together, or may need training in relevant techniques or organisational development. Agencies may be able either to provide, or to facilitate, appropriate training. For example, after the 1982 Yemen earthquake Oxfam co-funded a project for introducing people to new and safer building techniques, such as the use of ringbeams and L-shaped steel bars, following its experience in the Guatemalan earthquake of 1976. (See **3**.1.2 Education and Training.)

Rehabilitation and reconstruction following war and armed conflict entail an enormous range of social, political, and economic readjustments. One of the most significant is that people are unlikely to be returning, or even wishing to return, to exactly the same situation which prevailed before the outbreak of hostilities. It may indeed no longer exist in any recognisable form. The experience of the war, as well as its practical consequences, will also have altered certain aspects of people's lives profoundly, perhaps irrevocably. For example, there may be a significant number of amputees and people otherwise disabled as a direct result of the fighting. Ways in which people previously subsisted or earned a living may no longer be viable. Property rights may have changed significantly during, or as a result of, the war; and this will mean that survivors will need to develop new strategies to secure their livelihoods.

Social relations and expectations will also have undergone profound change. Refugees returning after years of exile in circumstances very unlike those which they left behind them, are not the same as they were when they fled. They may be returning with a wide range of new skills

6

and attitudes, which will not necessarily be shared by those who never left the country. Children who were born outside the country — for instance in refugee camps, or in urban squatter settlements — are probably not equipped to adopt the same way of life as their parents knew; and are likely to have different practical and organisational skills and social aspirations. Ex-combatants and former detainees may have difficulty in re-adjusting to civilian life, or in being accepted within their communities. People who left primarily for economic reasons will have perspectives which differ markedly from those who were political refugees, or who left because of direct persecution or repression. Rehabilitation is not so much a question of returning to normality, as a process of adapting to or creating a new set of norms.

Every case is different and requires sensitive analysis over a period of time to ensure that rehabilitation programmes are genuinely assisting people to cope with changed circumstances, rather than attempting to build on assumptions which are no longer accurate or relevant. Generalisations are of only limited value; however, it can be assumed that major changes will have taken place in the area of gender relations, since there is likely to be a higher proportion of women-maintained households after the fighting than before, and women may have been able to develop the skills and the confidence to take on a new range of civil and economic functions, in addition to those they traditionally carried. (See 2.1.4 Women in emergencies.)

In the case of agricultural rehabilitation programmes, changes in social and economic relations, and in the situation of women, may mean that issues such as access to land and credit, as well as specific inputs such as seeds and tools, need to be given prominent and active consideration. The new skills and confidence that people have acquired while in exile, for example, as teachers, health workers, or community organisers, will influence the way in which they cope on their return. They may not wish to revert to their former way of life, or submit to pressures on them to respect previous conventions or conservative traditions. For women and girl-children, a return to normality may mean disempowerment and subordination to men — pressures which they may wish to resist. Tensions arising from the roles and distribution of responsibilities between women and men, which may have been suppressed during a period of adversity, often become more pronounced once the situation has returned to normal.

Where former refugees or displaced people are reintegrating with others who never left the area where the fighting took place, there can be serious difficulties in establishing trust and mutual understanding. This is especially the case where the refugees enjoyed access to goods and services which the people who stayed behind did not. Refugees returning from Honduras to El Salvador took with them nine years of accumulated experience in dealing with international aid agencies, as well as the social and practical skills they had developed in exile. People who had never left the war zones, on the other hand, had suffered enormous physical hardship and had virtually no contact with the outside world over the same period of time. In this particular case, the considerable social cohesion between the two groups has been reinforced through their own efforts to transfer and complement each others' skills. Moreover, many of the same international agencies which worked in the refugee camps resumed their programmes, on an expanded scale, once the refugees returned. However, the exception proves the rule that good social relations cannot be automatically assumed in post-war reconstruction programmes.

3 Emergencies deriving from war and armed conflict

3.1 Introduction 840
3.2 International legislation relating to armed conflict 842
    3.2.1 Refugees, asylum seekers, and displaced persons 843
    3.2.2 Rights of refugees 844
    3.2.3 Problems concerning the rights of refugees and displaced
        persons 844
    3.2.4 Civilians and the protection of victims of armed conflicts 846
    3.2.5 Non-international armed conflicts 847
3.3 Armed conflict and NGOs 848
3.4 Practical approaches 849
    3.4.1 Principles of humanitarian assistance: Neutrality, impartiality
        and independence 849
    3.4.2 Supporting civilians in situations of armed conflict 853
    3.4.3 Non-operational work 858
3.5 Key questions 859

3.1 Introduction

As described in **6**.2 Background: Emergencies, conflict, and development, Oxfam is faced increasingly by situations of human need arising from, or complicated by, civil or international conflicts. Currently, more than half of Oxfam's emergency relief funding is related to armed conflict of some kind. Almost as much again is spent by Oxfam in activities dealing with the aftermath of fighting, and the social, economic, and infrastructural destruction brought about by war. While the precise combination of factors that causes war to break out is specific to each situation, inequity, poverty, and armed conflict are frequently interwoven, and mutually reinforcing.

There are obvious differences between armed conflict and sudden-onset disasters such as earthquakes, the impact of which is usually less socially destructive. Conflict is the playing out in violent form of political relations, which need to be understood by aid agencies if they are to avoid interventions which exacerbate the problems in the longer term.

840

Where extreme social inequalities exist, or where fundamental freedoms are systematically denied, armed conflict may ensue; and this generally causes still greater social and economic hardship for those who are already vulnerable, as well as for others. The war effort itself tends to divert human and financial resources from development programmes, both governmental and non-governmental. Infrastructure is destroyed and social welfare services, such as health and education, are subject to severe constraint — or are the target of deliberate attack, as in cases as different as Nicaragua, Mozambique, and former Yugoslavia. Economic infrastructure, such as production and distribution systems, may be destroyed, and the restriction of movement, and disruption of markets, further damage the economy. Since emergency supplies can easily been drawn into such dynamics, relief responses can have the unintended effect of fuelling and prolonging the conflict.

Fighting, and the denial of human rights associated with political violence and repression, cause immeasurable suffering. Individuals and societies remain profoundly damaged for many years after the cessation of hostilities. Where anti-personnel landmines have been extensively used, such as Afghanistan and Cambodia, the war continues to kill and maim people for decades after the fighting has stopped.

The economic consequences can also be devastating, and the investment in recovery may begin to approach the cost of the war itself. For example, during the decade of civil war in El Salvador, about one quarter of the population had to leave their homes and many thousands of civilians lost their lives. Material losses, *excluding* those of small farmers and workers in the informal sector, were conservatively estimated as the equivalent of two and a half times the annual operational budget of the Salvadoran government. The 16 years of fighting in Mozambique left at least one million people dead, and an economy which was already poor, shattered.

Women and children are usually the majority among civilian populations affected by emergencies, particularly those related to armed conflict. Women are already in a disadvantageous position in relation to men, are often not consulted about their needs and perspectives, and are rarely involved in planning or policy making for relief programmes. (See 2.1 Gender and 6.4.4.2 Consulting women.) In situations of crisis, social structures, including conventional gender roles, are severely affected and may break down altogether. While this social breakdown may cause distress and increase people's vulnerability in the short term, it can also open opportunities to work with them in innovative and creative ways. Effective emergency work can ensure not only that the basic needs of men, women, and children are addressed, but also, by recognising women's active and vital part in the process of recovery,

6

841

may equip them to take greater control over their lives in the longer term.

The scope for humanitarian assistance in the context of armed conflict is changing very rapidly, as outlined in the opening section of this chapter. In particular, the role of the UN system is likely to be redefined over the coming years, and the following paragraphs are therefore limited to describing some of the principal legal definitions that affect humanitarian aid, as a background for a brief presentation of the kinds of practical approaches that Oxfam can take in dealing with emergencies related to armed conflict. More detailed consideration of practical interventions and specific problems is given in the remaining sections of this chapter.

3.2 International legislation relating to armed conflict

While Article 10 of the Fourth Geneva Convention makes reference to the rights of an 'impartial humanitarian organisation', neither the definition of 'impartial' nor the exact nature of the rights conferred, are clear. Humanitarian bodies have traditionally assumed the right to offer relief and assistance to civilians in non-international conflicts; and this right is recognised in the international humanitarian law on armed conflict.

In practice, NGOs cite broad humanitarian principles to justify their work, rather than International Law. For example, Oxfam is committed to the relief of human suffering wherever it occurs; and to the policy of non-partisan support to people in need. Oxfam recognises that to fund organisations, or to work operationally, on either or both sides of a conflict, is to risk damaging relations with governments, and is likely to lead to other tensions. Nevertheless, Oxfam's paramount concern is to provide assistance to people in need, wherever it can reach them. Thus, political considerations should not in themselves determine the extent and nature of Oxfam's involvement in providing humanitarian relief.

While international law may offer only limited positive guidance to humanitarian aid agencies, there are nevertheless a number of detailed provisions concerning the rights of people with whom they work — refugees, asylum seekers, internally displaced persons, civilians and non-combatants in war and armed conflicts. These provisions influence the overall policy context and should inform NGO practice in the delivery of assistance, as well as in any lobbying or public policy work, at local or international level.

Details of essential documentation are included in the list of Resources at the end of this chapter. What follows is a selection of the most significant areas in which NGOs should ensure they are properly informed when implementing emergency relief programmes. These paragraphs should be read in conjunction with **1.2 Human rights in development and relief work.**

3.2.1 Refugees, asylum seekers, and displaced persons

Confusion and misunderstandings can readily arise where there are differing or incorrect interpretations of the status and rights of refugees, asylum seekers, and internally displaced persons. Various parties to the conflict may have an interest in either inflating, or under-estimating, the numbers involved. In addition, not all *de facto* refugees or displaced people are able or willing to register formally with the authorities. Accurate figures may be difficult to establish, further complicating the attempt to get a consistent picture of the situation.

The basic definitions contained within the 1950 Statute setting out the functions and responsibilities of UNHCR are as follows:

Refugees: are persons who

owing to a well-founded fear of being persecuted for reasons of race, religion, nationality, membership of a particular social group or political opinion [are] outside the country of [their] nationality and [are] unable or, owing to such a fear, unwilling to avail [themselves] of the protection of that country (1951 International Convention Relating to the Status of Refugees).

The UNHCR states that *'persons who meet this definition are refugees irrespective of whether or not they have been formally recognised as refugees by a national authority or by UNHCR'.*

The international protection afforded by UNHCR is intended to ensure that the treatment of refugees is in accordance with internationally accepted basic standards. In particular, UNHCR upholds the principle of non-refoulement. This means that *'refugees may not be forcibly returned to a country where they have reason to fear persecution.'*

Asylum seekers: are persons wishing to be admitted into a country as refugees. In some cases, they may be classed as refugees as a result of group, as opposed to individual, considerations. Where their status is unclear, the UNHCR will intervene on their behalf for temporary asylum, during which their status can be determined, and durable asylum secured.

Displaced persons: are people outside their place of habitual residence, who may not necessarily qualify as refugees, but who are nevertheless in refugee-like situations. UNHCR can act, at the specific request of a Secretary General of the UN, on behalf of *'persons displaced as a result of man-made* [sic] *disasters within the territorial limits of their country of origin'.* The involvement of UNHCR in such work is always determined on a

6

case-by-case basis, since its primary mandate is the protection of refugees explicit in the international recognition of the right to asylum. Internally displaced persons often refer to themselves as internal refugees.

3.2.2 Rights of refugees

The rights of refugees are extensive and derive from the Universal Declaration of Human Rights. (See Appendix 1.1.) Among these are the following basic standards, summarised by UNHCR in its *Handbook for Emergencies*:

- Refugees should not be penalised or exposed to any unfavourable treatment solely on the ground that their presence in the country is considered unlawful and they should not be subjected to restrictions on their movements other than those which are necessary in the interests of public health and order.
- Refugees should be treated as persons whose tragic plight requires special understanding and sympathy.
- There should be no discrimination on the grounds of race, religion, political opinion, nationality or country of origin.
- The location of asylum-seekers should be determined by their safety and well-being as well as by the security needs of the receiving State. Asylum seekers should, as far as possible, be located at a reasonable distance from the frontier of their country of origin. They should not become involved in subversive activities against their country of origin or any other State.
- Refugees should be provided with the basic necessities of life including food, shelter, and basic sanitary and health facilities.
- They should be granted all the necessary facilities to enable them to obtain a satisfactory durable solution.
- All steps should be taken to facilitate voluntary repatriation.

Many people who have fled their countries do not register for refugee status, and approximately 90 per cent of refugees and displaced persons return home spontaneously, *without any form of assistance*, either from the UN or from NGOs.

3.2.3 Problems concerning the rights of refugees and displaced persons

Upon request by the UN-Secretary-General, UNHCR can extend protection to displaced persons and repatriated refugees beyond its formal mandate, as defined in its Statute, in order to ensure that fundamental and internationally recognised humanitarian standards are observed. However, displaced persons are exceptionally vulnerable to human rights abuses, and may not receive proper assistance, since their status is unclear and they do not have any means of requesting formal protection from their government, or from an international authority. Along with illegal or undocumented refugees, or refugees who return without the papers they need to be able to move freely in their own country, displaced persons are also open to exploitation as workers. They may be forced to work in illegal, hazardous conditions, for little or no pay, in return for not being handed over to the authorities. In this way, many displaced women and girls end up as prostitutes or sex-workers in cities and border towns.

While women are often the victims of cruel or inhuman treatment for reasons related to their sex, persecution on the basis of sex is not explicitly recognised as part of the universal refugee definition. Thus, women fleeing threatened or actual rape, bride-burning, beatings and ill-treatment, or extra-judicial execution because they are deemed to have transgressed social or sexual mores, are not explicitly covered by the universal refugee definition.

The 1993 UN Human Rights Conference did, however, re-affirm that the rights of women and the girl-child are *'an inalienable, integral and indivisible part of universal human rights'*, and made specific reference to gender-based human rights violations, including *'genocide, "ethnic cleansing" and systematic rape of women in war situations, creating mass exodus of refugees and displaced persons'*.

Attempts to expand the interpretation of what constitutes persecution have included that of the European Parliament, which in 1984 called on States to consider women as 'a particular social group' within the meaning of the Convention. This was not successful, because some States considered that to do so would interfere with cultural or religious practices. The International NGO Working Group on Refugee Women recommends, nonetheless, that:

• States party to international and refugee conventions and protocols consider as refugees those who have been persecuted on the grounds of their sex; and,
• States recognise as forms of persecution leading to the granting of refugee status, social and institutional forms of repression which contravene international juridical standards and constitute a violation of human rights.

In fulfilling its protective function, UNHCR works closely with the ICRC, who may visit persons of concern to UNHCR, such as political detainees, but to whom the UN officials have no absolute right of access. It is, however, recognised under the Fourth Geneva Convention, that UNHCR officials should be able 'to go to all places where protected persons are, particularly to places of internment, detention and work'. The UNHCR is not competent to intervene on behalf of active combatants and persons bearing arms, responsibility for whom falls to the ICRC.

Family reunification is not a right conferred by the Refugee Convention. This means that States may use their discretion in deciding whether or not to provide for it. A particular problem for women who join their husbands in the country of asylum is that their own status as refugees often depends on his: if the family should break up, the wife may find herself threatened with deportation. In other cases, only male heads of household are registered as refugees. This means that if the men move on, as they often do, women and dependent children are left in a position where they not only have no refugee status in the country concerned, but also no access to ration cards and other essential services. It is essential that all the adult women in a household, including married and unmarried women, widows, additional wives, or mothers-in-law, are properly registered, *in their own right*, to ensure that they are not vulnerable to losing their entitlements as refugees. (See **2.1.4 Women in emergencies.**)

3.2.4 Civilians and the protection of victims of armed conflicts

Of the Geneva Conventions of 1949, it is the Fourth Convention concerning the Protection of Civilian Persons in Time of War, and the related Protocols of 1977, which are the most directly relevant to the work of humanitarian aid agencies and NGOs. Of particular relevance to much of the work in which Oxfam is involved, either during war or in its aftermath, are issues concerning the protection of civilian persons and property. Provisions include the following (taken from Articles 50, 51, 52 and 54 of the First Additional Protocol of 1977):

* *The presence within the civilian population of individuals who do not come within the definition of civilians does not deprive the population of its civilian character.*
* *The civilian population as such, as well as individual civilians, shall not be the object of attack. Acts or threats of violence the primary purpose of which is to spread terror among the civilian population are prohibited. (50)*
* *Indiscriminate attacks are prohibited. Indiscriminate attacks are:*
    those which are not directed at a specific military objective;
    those which employ a method or means of combat which cannot be directed at a specific military objective; or
    those which employ a method or means of combat the effects of which cannot be limited as required by this Protocol:

846

and consequently, in each such case, are of a nature to strike military objectives and civilians or civilian objects without distinction.

- Among others, the following types of attacks are to be considered as indiscriminate:

  an attack by bombardment by any methods or means which treats as a single military objective a number of clearly separated and distinct military objectives located in a city, town, village or other area containing a similar concentration of civilians or civilian objects; and

  an attack which may be expected to cause incidental loss of civilian life, injury to civilians, damage to civilian objects, or a combination thereof, which would be excessive in relation to the concrete and direct military advantage anticipated. (51)

- Civilian objects shall not be the object of attack or of reprisals...Attacks shall be limited strictly to military objectives...In case of doubt whether an object which is normally dedicated to civilian purposes, such as a place of worship, a house or other dwelling or school, is being used to make an effective contribution to military action, it shall be presumed not to be so used. (52)

- Starvation of civilians as a method of warfare is prohibited...It is prohibited to attack, destroy, remove or render useless objects indispensable to the survival of the civilian population, such as foodstuffs, crops, livestock, drinking water installations and supplies and irrigation works, for the specific purpose of denying them for their sustenance value to the civilian population or to the adverse Party, whatever the motive, whether in order to starve out civilians, to cause them to move away, or for any other motive. (54)

- Care shall be taken in warfare to protect the natural environment against widespread, long-term and severe damage. This protection includes a prohibition of the use of methods or means of warfare which are intended or may be expected to cause such damage to the natural environment and thereby to prejudice the health or survival of the population. (54)

3.2.5 Non-international armed conflicts

The Second Additional Protocol of 1977 concerns the protection of victims of non-international armed conflicts, and its provisions are virtually identical. The principal addition relates to the prohibition of forced movement of civilians (Article 17), which states:

6

The displacement of the civilian population shall not be ordered for reasons related to the conflict unless the security of the civilians involved or imperative military reasons so demand. Should such displacements have to be carried out, all possible measures shall be taken in order that the civilian population may be received under satisfactory conditions of shelter, hygiene, health, safety and nutrition...Civilians shall not be compelled to leave their own territory for reasons connected with the conflict.

847

Not all States are signatories both to the Conventions and the Protocols. Some which are have, nevertheless, prosecuted war in a way which flouted provisions, especially those concerning respect for life and livelihood of civilians: in contemporary armed conflicts, some 90 per cent of casualties are estimated to be civilian non-combatants. Much of the national and international lobbying work done by human rights organisations, as well as aid agencies, is concerned with such appalling discrepancies between the policies and practices of contracting States.

3.3 Armed conflict and NGOs

The chaotic social and political environment of war and armed conflict may create profound dilemmas for humanitarian aid agencies. For NGOs such as Oxfam that have a very wide mandate, there may be considerable internal debate about whether to concentrate on immediate relief, on low-profile interventions to address the underlying causes of the political violence, or on high-profile public lobbying for just and peaceful solutions. It is sometimes possible to pursue all three levels of response concurrently. Often, however, they may seem to be incompatible approaches, because of the different kinds of public profile required. Complex decisions have to be made about how to respond in the short term, at a time when it is hard to predict what implications these decisions will have upon future developments, or as the situation itself changes. The politics of international events will also have a major bearing on the way in which the conflict is presented and interpreted in the broader domain. The more complex the situation, the truer it is that a humanitarian response will only be as good as the analysis which informs it.

There are many issues to be considered before proceeding even with an apparently straightforward humanitarian relief response. These include questions such as the agency's actual and perceived autonomy in the specific circumstances or territory in question; and its capacity to function without compromising its basic standards of assessment, monitoring, and evaluation.

The physical security and well-being of local and expatriate staff must always be a paramount concern. Most aid agencies set clear limits on the risks they consider it acceptable for staff to take in the course of their work, though in practice these can be determined only on a case-by-case basis. It is sobering to note, however, that the number of UN personnel killed in the course of duty rose from one per month in 1992 to one per week in mid-1993.

Whatever the pressure to undertake site visits to unsafe areas, the highest priority must be given to the realistic assessment of risks and to detailed planning to avoid unnecessary exposure to danger. This may involve close liaison with the relevant UN, government or military authorities (or with similar authorities within the opposition forces), as well as other reliable sources of information. Precise guidelines will need to be drawn up for each situation. (See **6**.8.5 Staff health and security.)

In addition to physical risks, staff working in areas of armed conflict are also exposed to unusual levels of stress. They may witness atrocities and immense suffering; and may themselves be close to individuals who are killed, detained, tortured or bereaved. It can be very difficult for staff to rest or relax in the face of overwhelming moral and emotional pressure. Feelings of helplessness, guilt or anger are commonly experienced by aid workers in situations of extreme and prolonged stress. Appropriate support for relief staff should be built into programme plans and budgets. (See **6**.8.4.4 Staff health and security and **5**.4.9 Mental and emotional well-being.)

3.4 Practical approaches

The work that can be done in a country where there is war and armed conflict is not intrinsically different from relief or development work in peaceful situations. However, a situation of conflict accentuates certain moral questions, and operational problems; and obliges agencies to widen their horizons beyond the immediate responses, both in assessment and in implementation. There are particular challenges entailed in responding with a view to the longer term, especially where civilian populations are surviving in war zones, or where they are not concentrated in easily identifiable settlements. For example, the long-term impact of conflict-related trauma, both on individuals and at community level, is a subject about which relatively little is known.

3.4.1 Principles of humanitarian assistance: neutrality, impartiality, and independence

For a humanitarian relief agency, the main principle is to offer assistance to the civilian population without contributing to the war effort. The highly politicised context created by armed conflict makes it inevitable that one side or the other may seek to gain capital from the actual or presumed activities of independent NGOs. This is especially so in cases where the very notions of autonomy, impartiality or humanitarian assistance, are under threat.

Interpretations and motives may be erroneously ascribed to NGOs which insist on their right to provide humanitarian assistance to people in need, if those people are assumed to have affiliations in the conflict.

6

It is thus useful to be familiar with the international instruments on war and armed conflict, as well as with the definitions and rights of civilian populations including refugees, asylum seekers, and displaced persons, and with the formal mandates and roles of UNHCR and ICRC in particular.

Oxfam is not neutral, in that it is on the side of poor and disadvantaged people in their search for social justice and equitable development. Oxfam believes in people's right to determine their own values, aspirations, and priorities. Nor is Oxfam neutral in the sense of always seeking to have links with both sides in any given conflict.

Oxfam is, however, impartial and non-partisan. It intervenes to relieve human suffering, without regard to political, ethnic or national considerations. Equally unacceptable to Oxfam is oppression, on the basis of gender, race, age, disability, or any other human characteristic. Oxfam's independence of political institutions, both in the UK, and within the countries in which it is operating, is crucial in enabling Oxfam to function as an impartial humanitarian aid agency, in situations that may be highly polarised.

a. Dilemmas facing humanitarian agencies

There are many dilemmas to be faced in interpreting these principles in practice, examples of which include:

- whether it is morally tenable to withhold assistance if it appears that to do so might bring about a quicker end to the fighting; or, alternatively, whether there are situations in which to respect people's rights to food, medicine and shelter might prolong a conflict.
- whether humanitarian assistance should be extended or denied to the perpetrators of violence and repression, or their supporters; and whether there are circumstances in which it may appear to jeopardise the chances of reconciliation not to prosecute war criminals.
- whether humanitarian action is unacceptably compromised by being combined with peace enforcement and sanctions ('military humanitarianism'); or whether to seek to insulate it from military force is to ignore political realities.
- whether and how it is possible for NGOs to curb the potential of intervening powers to use humanitarian rationales for political and economic ends; and whether it is possible to ensure that humanitarian assistance is not used to fuel the conflict, either materially or morally.

While the resolution of these dilemmas is rarely the immediate or exclusive burden of NGOs, they must always be aware of the broader consequences of their decisions and the precedents that might be set. The international community must endeavour to enforce existing international covenants and mandates consistently and without prejudice. The NGO community has a role to play in applying pressure on governments to respect existing agreements, and to develop new international instruments to deal more effectively with the new challenges that are emerging.

For Oxfam, the fundamental principle for dealing with emergency situations is *the safeguarding of human life*. This involves protection and assistance, which are mutually reinforcing. They should be provided impartially and whenever they are needed, because *life is of equal value wherever it is threatened*: a principle which overrides narrow political or other interests.

b. Finding appropriate channels for humanitarian relief

Oxfam's assistance is not limited either to international or government-approved channels, or to non-governmental organisations. Oxfam will, if necessary, support work in areas of a country at war which are not controlled by the national government. In doing so, it will seek intermediary organisations that meet its usual criteria for channelling assistance:

• If the assistance requested is to be used in disputed territory, the organisation channelling it must have direct access to the affected population.
• The organisation serving as a channel for humanitarian assistance, whether operating in disputed territory or with refugees in a third country, should in Oxfam's judgement be offering assistance in an impartial manner, on the basis of need.
• Oxfam must be satisfied that the grants made will be used for the purposes agreed, as efficiently as possible.
• The organisation channelling the assistance must be able to demonstrate to Oxfam's satisfaction that it is accountable to the affected population, women as well as men.
• The organisation must be prepared to facilitate site visits by Oxfam personnel, security arrangements permitting.

In many cases, existing social organisations or local NGOs modify their normal activities to address the needs created by the emergency. While their technical experience in the field of humanitarian relief may be limited, they have the advantage of knowing, and enjoying the confidence of, the people affected by the fighting. They are often able to move relatively freely in the area as a result.

In assessing the suitability of an organisation to act as an impartial channel for humanitarian assistance, Oxfam must be clear about what activities are being funded, how these will relieve the suffering of the affected population, and why the organisation in question is the most appropriate means of providing assistance. Oxfam should also be aware of the danger of promoting dependency, if its support is critical in establishing or strengthening an organisation which could not sustain its activities without external financial assistance. It may not always be appropriate for emergency channels to formalise their structures and bureaucracies, and Oxfam should be sensitive to this. Often, the best channel for providing humanitarian assistance may be a local organisation with little prior experience in handling projects, or large amounts of money — for instance, the local branch of a farmers' association, or a diocesan or parish social-action committee. Oxfam's assistance should be provided with a view to the longer term, in a way that will enable the organisation to function as effectively as possible, and to develop practical and organisational skills that will be sustainable after the emergency has abated. This may include training, or practical assistance in planning or evaluation methods, or in drawing up project documentation; or it may include support for a basic organisational infrastructure, such as office equipment and stipends for community level workers who will be involved in distribution, or in monitoring and reporting on progress. (See **3**.1 Social organisation and **3**.2 Institutional development.)

c. Assessment and monitoring

Thorough assessment, appraisal and monitoring may be difficult, especially where there are serious security or logistical constraints. In the case of dispersed refugees or displaced persons, numbers are hard to ascertain, and statistics not necessarily reliable. For example, even formal refugee assistance programmes have no standard format for routinely registering the population by sex and age. Displaced persons and dispersed or unregistered refugees may not be settled in one place or area; or may wish to keep their whereabouts secret. Where there are logistical problems, costs may be much higher than would normally be acceptable. In Mozambique, for example, Oxfam staff had to travel almost entirely by air to monitor relief programmes, because road travel was too dangerous. Adequate resources must be secured in the operating budget to ensure reasonable monitoring.

A breakdown of normal markets may result in severe shortages of essential goods, leading to losses of relief goods from petty pilfering or organised looting. Such losses are significant for two reasons: not only does the relief fail to reach those for whom it was intended, but it potentially fuels the conflict by increasing the resources of the group diverting it. Extensive (and costly) monitoring, accounting, and security systems may be required to minimise the diversion of supplies.

852

While the intermediary or implementing agency should aim to provide Oxfam staff with reasonable access to the programme area, and to the affected population, there will be times when this is not feasible, for security or logistical reasons. In such cases, Oxfam must be satisfied that the monitoring and reporting provided by its counterpart organisation are of a reasonable standard in the circumstances. Unsatisfactory reporting may be a sufficient reason for Oxfam to suspend further funding.

3.4.2 Supporting civilians in situations of armed conflict

People often prefer to stay close to their places of origin or normal residence, even at considerable danger to themselves, whether as displaced persons, or as people having constantly to move from one place to another. In cases of civil or counter-insurgency wars, such civilians will commonly be categorised as 'subversive' or 'guerrilla sympathisers', or as government supporters, simply because of where they happen to live. Their very presence in war zones may be denied by government or military authorities who are fighting for control over territory, and over people. Aerial bombardments or 'search and destroy' missions against 'enemy territory' may ensue; and such disputed areas may in extreme cases become 'free fire zones'. Civilians living there are terrorised. If found, they may be tortured or killed; or compelled to live in displaced persons' camps, under strict surveillance. Children may be forced to witness acts of savagery, and even to participate in them, or to assist the military effort as soldiers or couriers. Atrocities may go unwitnessed, unreported, and denied by the guilty party, since independent journalists and aid workers are denied access.

The suffering of civilians subject to this kind of violence and repression is immense. Immediate needs range from acute medical attention, to food and shelter, as goods and services are not permitted to enter the area on any scale. Production and distribution systems, such as markets, are deliberately targeted by the opposing forces. Where people are having to flee from one place to another, under fire, their crops and livestock are neglected or destroyed. Surrounding vegetation may be bombed and burnt in order to destroy any possible hiding places for armed opposition forces. As time goes on, the general health and well-being of people deteriorates considerably. The extensive use of anti-personnel mines increases the physical dangers to which civilians are exposed, especially if they need to go beyond the immediate confines of their settlement or village. Children growing up in such an environment may be physically and emotionally scarred for life.

Situations like these pose serious problems for humanitarian agencies, given the severity of the need and the impossibility of insisting on

6

conventional methods or standards of project management, such as monitoring, reporting and evaluation. (See **6**.3.4.1.c Assessment and monitoring [in situations of armed conflict].) For instance, circumstances may dictate that people adopt high-cost and unsustainable practices in the short term, to ensure their survival, since they cannot operate on a long-term basis. Where their access to fields and crops is limited and irregular, farmers may not be able to contemplate adopting practices such as integrated pest management or the use of organic fertilisers, which require relative stability. In Central America, for instance, subsistence farmers living in war zones were fully aware that the way in which they were having to cultivate crops was neither desirable nor sustainable; but their immediate options were to compromise sustainability in the interests of physical survival, or to risk the uncertainty of fleeing the country to become dependent refugees.

Armed conflict will almost certainly interfere with traditional 'coping mechanisms', whether or not the population is able to remain relatively stable. (See 6.7.2 Security and vulnerability: entitlements and assets.) For example, in 1983–4 the fighting in Northern Ethiopia restricted the labour migration and trading that could have helped to reduce the effects of rain failure. In some cases, pressures on civilians are deliberately engineered, and may include starving a population in uncontrolled territory. A study commissioned by Oxfam in Africa concluded that the disruption of strategies on which local semi-subsistence economies depended was a major factor in the exacerbation of the effects of famine.

International law prohibits the use of famine as a method of warfare, but in practice this is rarely enforceable. (See **6**.3.2.4 Civilians and the protection of victims of armed conflicts.) The placing of restrictions on humanitarian aid may be indirect rather than overt, and so impossible to prove. Attempts by agencies to support people's survival strategies, or to provide material inputs such as food, may be deemed partisan. The inputs themselves may be diverted by one of the parties to the conflict, unless there are strong mechanisms in place to prevent this happening. These are all aspects of the complex and all-encompassing political climate of working in situations of armed conflict and political violence.

Other constraints to be taken into account include the practical impact of restrictions on people's freedom of movement or on introducing goods into the area where they are living. For example, it may be necessary to buy seeds, medicines or agro-chemicals in very small quantities, to be hand-carried if there is no transport available, or if civilians are not permitted to carry large amounts for fear of their being confiscated. Factors of this kind will inevitably affect project budgets, and may hinder plans and schedules of work, as well as the eventual outcomes. In supporting programmes of assistance in such difficult circumstances, it is all the more important to ensure that appraisal criteria and monitoring indicators are sensitive and realistic, and not imposed in a mechanistic way by the donor agency.

a. Women and armed conflict
(To be read in conjunction with **2**.1.4.3 Gender in armed conflict, and **6**.4.5 Assessing the situation of specific social groups.)
Women are not only victims of armed conflict, but are also widely involved in both combatant and non-fighting roles. However, in general, conflict is most likely to draw (or push) younger men and adolescent boys away from their home and thus increase existing burdens on women. An increased proportion of women-maintained households, and households with no males present, may result. The prevailing insecurity may restrict access to markets, fields, and water, making the burden of providing for everyday subsistence greater still. At the same time, it usually falls to women to hold household, community, and culture together during and in the aftermath of armed conflict.

Conditions of insecurity and the breakdown of normal social controls often leads to widespread or systematic looting, and assaults on civilian women, in addition to the atrocities inflicted on those considered to be accomplices with the opposing forces. Rape and sexual abuse of women and girls is frequently part of a deliberate strategy of terrorisation, humiliation, and social destruction, during and after war. The systematic use of rape as a weapon of war was specifically deplored at the 1993 UN Conference on Human Rights. (See **1**.2 Human rights in development and relief work.)

Information about refugee and displaced women is sparse, and existing data on refugee populations are not routinely disaggregated by sex. An understanding of the problems which they face in situations of armed conflict is neither systematic or comprehensive. Situations vary enormously from place to place, so that generalisations are difficult to make. However, the experiences of women, from their own perspective, are very often overlooked in both local and international aid responses. As a result, the specific needs of women, which they themselves may not be accustomed to articulating, are frequently ignored.

b. Psycho-social aspects of armed conflict
(See **5**.4.9 Mental and emotional well-being; and **1**.2 Human rights in development and relief work.)
Relatively little is known about the effects of collective trauma on people, or on the impact of prolonged trauma on communities in developing countries. For example, civil wars in countries such as Angola, Guatemala, and the Lebanon have lasted for well over a decade, leaving a legacy of social dislocation. While aid agencies may think of

people as victims, who have experienced terrible suffering, it is essential to recognise that they are also survivors: people who are resourceful and active before, during, and after their traumatic experiences.

Most research has focused on war victims from the industrialised world; and on the individual rather than on groups or on society as a whole. Formal methods for working with victims of Post-Traumatic Stress Disorder (PTSD) have been developed within a psycho-analytic model in which the sufferer is generally assumed to be verbally articulate. A study commissioned by Oxfam described the features of PTSD as:

... recurrent, painful and intrusive recollections of painful events, either in nightmares or in daytime 'flashbacks'. A disturbed sleep pattern...along with hypervigilance, often manifested as a tendency to startle easily, even in response to minor cues like small noises. Irritability, restlessness, explosive anger, and feelings of guilt, anxiety and depression may wax and wane.

There is an overlap with the features of chronic bereavement and in particular with certain kinds of depressive illness, and the onset of PTSD may be delayed for months or possibly years.

Clinical experience has developed mainly through treatment of ex-combatants and a handful of political asylum-seekers and refugees arriving in Europe, North America or Australia. Considerable experience has also been accumulated in working with and rehabilitating the individual victims of human rights abuses and their families, notably in Latin America. However, the deliberate traumatisation of large numbers of civilians, including children, is a relatively new feature of so-called low-intensity or counter-insurgency war. For many people suffering such agony, there is no prospect in sight of an end to the situation which is causing their suffering: approximately 90 per cent of refugees and displaced persons return to their homes without any guarantees of peace and safety, often with the underlying problems still unresolved.

While civilians — largely women and children — already form about 90 per cent of casualties of contemporary wars, the psycho-social dimensions of their experiences have scarcely begun to be acknowledged, much less understood. It is common even for 'progressive' or 'revolutionary' organisations to reproduce the oppressive attitudes to women that prevail in the very society that they hope to transform. People from ethnic minorities may also find that the organisations that are promoting the need for major social change are themselves insensitive to the specific needs and perspectives of communities who are not part of the dominant culture, and that their leadership is made up of the very sectors associated with their oppression. It can be devastating for people who have paid such a high price for their commitment to social change, to realise that the ideology they espouse leaves so many of their particular interests and needs out of account. This has been cited as a major cause of alienation and depression among women refugees and political exiles.

Humanitarian assistance may help to restore some of the essentials of daily life, such as clothes, shelter, food, and so on. It is not clear, however, how much this provision contributes to a process of emotional healing, or how aid could be made more sensitive to the effects of trauma. Programmes of individual counselling, family reunification, and care for orphans are valuable, but very limited, responses.

A great deal has yet to be learned about the way in which aid programmes can be made more effective and supportive in contributing to the process of healing on a wider scale. The inter-relationship between 'learned helplessness' and the kind of dependency-syndrome that can develop in camps of refugees or displaced persons, is not well understood. Similarly, it is not clear how other behavioural and social problems, such as depression, apathy, alcoholism, or aggression, are compounded by trauma. Oxfam's experience suggests that:

- it is helpful for appropriate people to listen to what the survivors of atrocities want to say;
- unconventional relief inputs (shrouds, funeral expenses; recreational or musical equipment; legal expenses) offer people the opportunity to acknowledge and channel their grief in a way they find appropriate;
- all cultures have a system of symbols and rituals, verbal and non-verbal, which are grounded in their social (often traditional or religious) values: people's ability to observe these is vital to their healing;
- human rights work and related activities can give a purposeful channel for anger, suffering, and distress, through documentation and lobbying.

For example, in Uganda, Oxfam funded the salaries of professionally qualified psychiatric workers experienced in counselling and therapy, whose role was to work with women who had been raped, and to train a cadre of local counsellors. In Central America, people relied heavily on existing networks of community health workers and on church structures for many of the listening and counselling functions. In Latin America more generally, where political 'disappearance' has been a systematic practice of political violence and repression, mutual support groups of 'families of the disappeared' have assumed a *de facto* listening function, as well as being involved in documentation and international lobbying. Oxfam has supported the work of many such committees and groups. The organisation of delegations to influential authorities can

6

857

also give some confidence that the suffering will not go unnoticed in the international arena. (See **1.2** Human rights in development and relief work.)

3.4.3 Non-operational work

As with any other crisis, the superficial causes of armed conflict may conceal issues of political and economic inequity, food insecurity, and international interventions, which may themselves be susceptible to resolution by a variety of means. Some humanitarian agencies may be in a position to initiate or become actively involved in a mediation process. Others may see their role more in terms of human rights issues than humanitarian relief. In extreme circumstances, some NGOs may prefer to close down their field operations in order to be able to denounce situations in which they feel powerless to be of effective help at an operational level.

In presenting a comprehensive analysis of the causes of conflict, Oxfam staff should identify major issues, such as human rights abuse, as well as noting any official or low-key mediation or reconciliation efforts that are under way. It may be decided that, if it is not already doing so, Oxfam should support the work of specialist human rights agencies as part of a comprehensive response to the situation, especially in circumstances where humanitarian work and aid workers become the targets of attack and repression.

Oxfam may also decide to become involved in lobbying for the international mobilisation of resources or for effective co-ordination of the relief effort by the UN or other relevant bodies. It may seek to identify practical steps which might be taken by parties to the conflict to minimise the adverse consequences to civilians of the fighting, such as to lobby for the right of access for the delivery of humanitarian assistance. For example, in May 1994, Oxfam placed an advertisement in the national press in the UK, which called on the Prime Minister to support action to open Tuzla airport, in Bosnia, to enable urgently-needed relief supplies to be flown in. (See **3.1.3.3** Advocacy.)

Oxfam's legitimacy and effectiveness in advocacy depends principally on the credibility it derives from its practical involvement. However, in highly polarised circumstances, that involvement may be jeopardised by a critical, public lobbying stance. For example, a government sensitive to criticism may close down a relief programme, expel the agencies concerned, or harass their personnel. A positive lobbying profile associated with one country may inhibit Oxfam's capacity to act in a neighbouring territory, in cases where the two governments are politically hostile to each other. Since there may be tensions between what it is appropriate to say about a situation and the security of staff *in situ,* communications plans must be informed by the insights of staff on the ground, and agreed with relevant staff in the Oxfam Head Office. Long- and short-term factors have to be carefully balanced, and the potential differences in perspectives and priorities reconciled. Oxfam's principal concern in reaching its decisions is always how best to support those who are suffering and in need of assistance.

3.5 Key questions

1 Does Oxfam have current or recent experience in the country or area affected by the emergency? If not, why does the situation warrant consideration of an emergency intervention by Oxfam? How reliable are the sources of information in this case, and which (if any) other humanitarian NGOs are likely to become involved?

2 What is the nature, severity, and extent of the emergency? Does Oxfam have any distinctive expertise in the kind of relief programme which will be required? Is other relief assistance available to the affected population, and by whom is this being provided? Might these be suitable channels or subjects of assistance from Oxfam?

3 What information exists about the differentiated impact of the emergency on women, men, and children? What is the additional information which would be required to disaggregate the data, and how will this be obtained?

4 Will it be possible for Oxfam staff to visit the affected area or to discuss the situation with people *in situ*? If not, how will Oxfam assess and monitor relief efforts conducted by local organisations?

5 If armed conflict is taking place, what are the security implications for Oxfam's personnel? What are the implications for other Oxfam programmes in the area or region which might be affected by involvement in the emergency?

6 What human and financial resources could be mobilised? Will additional resources be necessary for an emergency programme? If so, how will these be secured, immediately and subsequently?

7 Are there any communications or lobbying initiatives in which Oxfam might appropriately become involved?

6

4 Assessment, co-ordination, and consultation in emergencies

4.1 Introduction 860
4.2 Assessment of emergencies 862
    4.2.1 Introduction and background 862
    4.2.2 Initial (general) assessment 863
    4.2.3 Detailed (technical) assessment 864
    4.2.4 Coordinating assessment with other agencies 864
    4.2.5 Preparedness and contingency plans 865
4.3 Inter-agency co-ordination 866
    4.3.1 Introduction and background 866
    4.3.2 International agencies involved in relief work 870
    4.3.3 Working with local authorities 874
    4.3.4 Working through local structures 875
    4.3.5 Working with dispersed populations 877
4.4 Consulting and involving the affected population 878
    4.4.1 Introduction and background 878
    4.4.2 Consulting women 880
4.5 Assessing the situation of specific social groups 882
    4.5.1 Introduction 882
    4.5.2 Women 883
    4.5.3 Children 886
    4.5.4 Elderly people 888
    4.5.5 Cultural considerations and minority groups 890
    4.5.6 People with disabilities 892
4.6 Key questions 893

4.1 Introduction

Emergencies are characterised by large numbers of people in distress. The imperative to safeguard human life may require timely and appropriate assistance in areas such as the provision of food and support for agricultural production (seeds, tools, fertilisers); water supplies and primary health care; shelter (or housing materials); and immediate subsistence needs (clothing, cooking utensils, fuel, soap).

Relief programmes are not neutral in their long-term impact on people, or on social structures. Unless existing (and potential) local capacities are actively strengthened, the risk is that people and institutions may be left more vulnerable than they were before the emergency. The impulse to rush in and set up an operational relief programme must therefore be tempered by the need to draw on local and national structures which are, or should be, involved.

There are obviously constraints on the level of consultation which is possible in an emergency, and on the amount of information that can be gathered before a relief programme commences. The imminent risk of death to large numbers of people in a chaotic situation demands action to provide essential services on the basis of the best information available in a short time: for example, the establishment of feeding centres for severely malnourished children, or the siting and installation of water points for a population with no water. However, aid agencies should always aim to consult sufficiently to ensure that specific groups of people are not adversely affected by, or likely to be unintentionally excluded from, the services provided.

Consultation with the affected population may continue to be difficult after the immediate crisis, for various reasons. Normal social structures are often severely disrupted in emergencies, particularly where people have migrated or families have become separated. There may be language or cultural constraints that make it more difficult to elicit the views of specific sets of people, such as those from ethnic minority groups. National authorities may insist that the provision of relief be a 'top-down' operation, in which the people affected are seen to have no role other than as recipients. However, Oxfam believes in supporting people to recognise and develop their potential and to decide their own values and priorities. This means recognising the importance of listening to what women and men from the affected population say about their various needs and priorities, and helping them to organise themselves and to participate in decision-making and implementation of relief programmes.

The neighbouring or host communities in places of asylum may themselves be exceedingly poor. If all international relief efforts are focused on refugees from another country, this can cause tension and resentment. Humanitarian agencies have a responsibility to avoid exacerbating social or political tension. In establishing relief programmes, agencies should assess such potential dangers and seek all possible means to avert them.

This section deals with the broad issues concerning the assessment of emergencies, in order to ensure that a long-term vision is maintained even when the focus of the programme is short-term. Preparedness and

6

contingency plans are considered within this context. The section goes on to consider questions of co-ordination between NGOs and UN, and local government and non-governmental structures, and looks at ways in which to ensure effective consultation with the affected population. It ends by considering the particular problems and needs of marginalised groups in the affected community.

4.2 Assessment of emergencies

4.2.1 Introduction and background

It may be difficult to reconcile the careful and detailed assessment of emergencies, particularly sudden-onset crises such as cyclones, with the immediate but short-lived media coverage on which public appeals for funds are largely dependent. The international news media report disasters quickly, often with brief and high-profile visits to accessible areas. Coverage is usually dramatic, and likely to be inaccurate. In contrast, aid workers may face difficulties in travelling, and have to contact a range of local organisations and agencies dispersed over a wide area. It can take days or weeks to make the assessments on which to base detailed relief proposals. By that time, media interest is likely to have dropped. In slow-onset or chronic emergencies, aid agencies are in a position to prepare systematic assessments over a period of time. Even then, compromises have to be made between the speed and the comprehensiveness of reporting; it is important to provide relevant information to journalists, in the hope that media coverage will promote better international understanding of the nature of the emergency.

There are likely to be contradictory and competing expectations of an initial assessment, including pressure for it to be done quickly. Media coverage of sudden-onset or spectacular emergencies often sets up a public perception of 'obvious' priority needs. The pressure to respond immediately to these perceived needs may have to be resisted, to allow time for those *in situ* to make responsible recommendations for action. Oxfam staff may, however, be asked to give reports on their initial observations in advance of their considered assessment of the emergency, or before Oxfam's relief response has been fully defined. (See 6.8.2 Information and assessment.)

The response itself must be based on a detailed assessment of the situation, including information about what other agencies are doing. In fast-moving and complex situations, it will be necessary to re-assess a programme as needs change. Systematic monitoring should be built into any Oxfam programme, to allow for adaptations to be made as necessary.

Oxfam divides emergency assessment into two broad categories: initial (general) assessment, to decide whether an emergency warrants an Oxfam response; and detailed (technical) assessment, to determine exactly what that response should be. Both should be approached in the context of the issues discussed in Chapter 1 Oxfam's approach to development and relief; and in Chapter 2 Focusing on people; and 3.2.2 Planning, 3.2.3 Evaluation and 3.2.4 Financial planning. In making initial assessments, Oxfam depends in the first instance on its own locally-based staff, who are responsible for developing its in-country policy. In making technical assessments, Oxfam staff are sometimes assisted by in-house or external specialists.

4.2.2 Initial (general) assessment

The purpose of an initial (general) assessment is to gather sufficient information on which to decide *whether* Oxfam should respond to the emergency. This in turn depends on broader considerations such as existing geographical priorities, and existing local or national policy on emergencies. The assessment is usually made over a period of a few days by a mixed team of men and women, who combine experience in emergencies and a knowledge of local conditions. It may include a visit to the area affected and interviews with a range of local contacts.

An assessment team would consider the nature and scale of the emergency, the resources available locally to deal with it, and whether other local, national or international agencies are able to intervene. The team would seek basic information about the demographic composition of the affected population and preliminary consideration of the different needs of particular groups of people. It might also identify any culturally-determined priorities, where these differ from conventional Western assumptions about what might be needed. Finally, the assessment team would review Oxfam's situation, both local (existing experience, skills, contacts, and preparedness) and institutional (taking sectoral or technical expertise into consideration). (See 6.4.3 Inter-agency co-ordination; and 6.8.2.7 Liaison with other agencies.)

The team's recommendations would indicate whether Oxfam should proceed to implement an emergency programme, and include preliminary consideration of the staffing and financial resources that would be required in order to do so. An agency such as Oxfam, which has considerable experience in emergency relief, will be able to predict some of the needs which are certain to arise in emergency situations, even before a detailed assessment is completed. Advance arrangements to procure and transport vital relief goods, such as shelter materials and equipment for emergency water supplies, will make it possible to act quickly to save lives.

6

4.2.3 Detailed (technical) assessment

Whereas an initial assessment allows a policy decision to be made about *whether* Oxfam should become involved in an emergency programme, the detailed (technical) assessment always involves a site visit to determine *how* Oxfam should respond. Since a detailed assessment must be based on wide-ranging consultation, it may take two weeks or more to complete, following which a recommended course of action is agreed. In addition to people familiar with the local context, and with Oxfam's existing programme, an assessment team may include experts from a range of professional and technical fields. The team should be comprised of women and men, in order to facilitate effective consultation, and to ensure that the differing needs and priorities of women and men within the affected population can be adequately examined.

Since Oxfam is not restricted to working in a specific sector, technical assessments are as comprehensive as possible, covering both the main issues of immediate practical relevance — food, water, health, shelter, clothing, protection — and longer-term aspects of social organisation (such as the sexual division of labour, and existing decision-making structures or semi-formal bodies). (See **6**.2.6.1 Capacities and Vulnerabilities Analysis). The team would also explore the short- and medium-term concerns of the affected population, and the broader political context.

Detailed recommendations would outline a programme of responses, (including non-operational work), covering the major technical considerations, and proposing systems for co-ordination with other agencies. In particular, the assessment team would identify how the proposed course of action would build on existing local initiatives and institutions, and how it would strengthen the material, organisational, and motivational capacities of the affected population, and reduce their vulnerability to similar crises in the future. The recommendations would also cover staffing and other resource needs, and indicate a basic framework for monitoring and review.

4.2.4 Co-ordinating assessment with other agencies

Missions from different NGOs often arrive at the same time, during a period of disorganisation. Each wants to accompany and question the same local officials and relief staff, who are themselves preoccupied with their immediate work, as well as representatives of the affected population, who are also busy trying to get a measure of the situation themselves. Joint NGO assessments reduce duplication and unnecessary distraction of this kind, and can also enable agencies to develop a more comprehensive view than they would be able to do alone, and so detect and complement gaps in services.

In large-scale emergencies there is often an officially designated or generally recognised 'lead agency', usually one of the UN agencies, on whom the main burden of co-ordination falls. It is important for NGOs to share the findings of their own assessments, and to ensure that their proposed courses of action are broadly compatible with what other agencies are planning to do. For instance, it is useful for aid agencies to observe similar standards in the provision and delivery of basic services — such as food, health care, water supplies, or housing — to prevent problems that arise when one group of people receives goods and services from one agency which are evidently superior to those provided by another.

4.2.5 Preparedness and contingency plans

Assessment, co-ordination, and consultation are all improved if aid agencies already have a sound knowledge of locally available resources, and are aware of the disaster plans of government, UN, and local agencies; and an understanding of the social, political, and economic context of the people living in hazard-prone areas. For example, it is useful to have an existing idea of groups within the population who are likely to be especially vulnerable following an emergency (such as women-maintained households, unaccompanied children, or elderly people).

Within Oxfam, disaster preparedness involves the following elements:

- a preparedness plan for emergencies, assessing possible scenarios, and co-ordination with other agencies;
- assessment of emergency-related issues at a local or national level, such as the establishment of a national food reserve, local and national preparedness plans;
- a contingency plan for crises that may directly affect in-country staff, which should include detailed plans for security, communications, and evacuation;
- relevant training for all staff every two or threes years (or as staff turnover dictates).

Preparedness plans enable an aid agency to respond quickly, efficiently, and appropriately to a major emergency. Each aspect of the plan needs to be adapted to local conditions, and regularly updated. For example, if a conflict-related emergency is likely, then detailed security guidelines for staff should be part of the plan. A preparedness plan should be reviewed at least once a year, or more frequently if circumstances dictate. (See 6.8.4.1 Preparedness and contingency plans.)

6

4.3 Inter-agency co-ordination

4.3.1 Introduction and background

The rapidly changing international landscape of 'complex emergencies' and humanitarian relief means that there are no universally valid assumptions about the comparative advantage of one kind of aid agency over another, or about the appropriate division of roles and responsibilities between the UN, bilateral donors, NGOs (international, national or local), and national governments or civil authorities. Furthermore, the increasing use of non-governmental channels for official relief aid means that in the area of emergency work, some designated NGOs have more in common with major donors than with other voluntary agencies. In such a context, it may not be easy to agree what is meant by co-ordination.

A useful definition is that co-ordination is the systematic use of policy instruments to achieve cohesive and effective aid programmes. These instruments include information gathering and dissemination, planning and evaluation, mobilising resources and establishing systems of accountability, organising field activities, and negotiating a framework of action with the political authorities. The Oxfam-funded Humanitarianism and War research project (from which this definition is drawn) has developed comprehensive accounts and detailed case-studies of humanitarian relief in situations of conflict during the 1980s and 1990s. It concludes that since none of the relevant institutions is completely free of specific limitations, the central issue is to determine which 'by virtue of its mandate, its culture, or its accountability, is least limited and therefore most able to function in a given setting'. It proposes inter-agency co-ordination and collaboration based on the idea of principled pragmatism, whereby the aim is to maximise the range of channels rather than trying to centralise these into one all-purpose body.

The distinct characteristics of donor governments, UN peace-support operations, and NGOs are summarised in Table 6.3:

(Table 6.3 From a paper by Larry Minear, *Development within Conflict: The Challenge of Man-made Disasters*, given at a meeting between OECD donor governments and development NGOs, Paris, 1994. (See Resources Section for further details) Note: UN peace-support operations is an umbrella term for UN-associated peace-keeping, peace-making, and peace-building initiatives, which may involve enforcement (where troops or economic sanctions are imposed without the consent of the parties to the conflict); and multi-functional UN operations, including civil adminstration, human rights monitoring, and electoral responsibilities.)

Table 6.3 Responsibilities, limitations, impacts and opportunities (RLIO) grid

	Responsibilities	Limitations	Impacts	Opportunities
Donor governments	1 Fidelity to UN charters and covenants, Geneva Conventions and Additional Protocols, and other international instruments. 2 Historic ODA target of 0.7 per cent of GNP. 3 Management of bilateral and (indirectly) of multilateral aid operations. 4 Accountability to donor parliaments and publics.	1 Multiple agendas (e.g. foreign policy concerns or economic interests) may preempt, constrain, undercut or upstage development-related activities. 2 Political factors (sensitivities of sovereignty, relationships with one party or another in civil wars) may impede action. 3 Divergent interests of development, foreign affairs, and finance ministries within the same donor government may send mixed signals. 4 The aid apparatus of individual donors or the donor community may prove unwieldy. 5 Dependence upon support of parliaments and publics constrains freedom of action.	1 Donor governments often politicise the work of NGOs and UN agencies. 2 An excessive need for donor identification with on-the-ground activities may undercut the effectiveness of NGO and UN partners.	1 A more-focused application of an array of resources through a variety of channels. 2 Greater consistency of purpose in dealing with other actors. 3 Greater attention to conflict-prevention and prompt post-conflict action. 4 Greater solicitousness of the needs of NGO and UN partners for independence and space.

6

Table 6.3 Responsibilities, limitations, impacts and opportunities (RLIO) grid continued

	Responsibilities cont'd	Limitations cont'd	Impacts cont'd	Opportunities cont'd
UN peace–support operations	1 To implement Security Council decisions. 2 To interface with other UN activities: political, humanitarian, human rights, development. 3 To provide the presence of international personnel conveying the widest possible international concern.	1 As an organisation of governments, the UN has a structural bias against insurgents in civil wars. 2 The reluctance of governments to cede authority to multilateral institutions complicates their tasks. 3 An overextension of current peace-support activities in terms of resources, capacity, training, and expertise has undercut their effectiveness. 4 Traditional emphasis on the military side of peacekeeping activities works to the detriment of civilian tasks.	1 NGO activities may suffer from identification with UN troops and UN–blessed economic sanctions. 2 UN humanitarian activities may be undercut, as well as supported, by UN peacekeeping efforts. 3 Co-ordination and consistency has been a problem, even within UN peace–support operations.	1 Greater openness among governments to multilateral co–operation, despite specific problems such activities have encountered. 2 Greater UN sensitivity to the problems created for humanitarian and development actors by its peace–support activities. 3 Greater synergy of activities and effectiveness with other major actors.

	Responsibilities cont'd	Limitations cont'd	Impacts cont'd	Opportunities cont'd
Non-governmental organisations	1 A moral commitment to alleviate suffering and protect human rights, often as directly as possible.	1 The heterogeneity of the NGO universe, which includes a wide range of levels of competence and effectiveness, creates difficulties for concerted action.	1 NGO heterogeneity circumscribes effectiveness of NGO community and the broader international effort.	1 NGO capacity for creativity and risk-taking unconstrained by sensitivity to sovereignty and protocol..
	2 A connection with, and a perceived obligation to, NGO partner organisations engaged in common pursuits.	2 The perils of conflict situations create special vulnerability and uncertainty.	2 Competition for position among NGOs and between NGOs and other actors undercuts effectiveness of that effort.	2 Activities characterised by appropriateness and mutuality.
	3 A commitment to contributors to use resources cost-effectively.	3 Need for independence from parties to conflicts encounters difficulties in achieving the necessary humanitarian space.	3 NGO effectiveness may be diluted because of a lack of collegiality with the UN which would maximise NGO strengths.	3 Enlisting of citizen concerns and energies in development and conflict-resolution efforts.
		4 Traditional NGO preference for small- and medium-scale undertakings limits replication.		4 A commitment to improve their own functioning, with the help of donor governments an UN organisations.
		5 Lack of assured resources affects programming and risk-taking.		

6

869

While inter-agency coordination is something that Oxfam would generally seek to promote, it is important to be aware of the pitfalls that might compromise Oxfam's principles of impartiality and independence. (See **6.3.4.1** Principles of humanitarian assistance: neutrality, impartiality and independence.) Firstly, the relationship between NGOs and state structures (where these exist) in areas experiencing insecurity, is often double-edged. While a close working relationship may be obligatory for various practical reasons (such as travel permits and security considerations), the State may seek to capitalise on the appearance of 'normality' that a continued NGO presence might imply. NGOs may be aware of abuses against political opponents or supposed 'rebel sympathisers', but may feel powerless to do or say anything for fear of losing their right of access to the area or population concerned. Secondly, coordination with UN and official aid agencies has sometimes tended to inhibit NGOs' flexibility, as they find themselves cast in the role of implementing centrally-designed and unimaginative distribution plans.

At the same time, there are many benefits to be gained through appropriate co-ordination — not least because no single agency can possibly cover the range of activities required in dealing with situations of rapid and turbulent change. There are advantages in pooling information and resources, and in forming function-based alliances that allow each agency to contribute its distinctive competence in building up a more comprehensive response to crisis. Oxfam has participated in a wide variety of co-ordinating structures in the context of emergency programmes: these have included operational co-ordinating bodies in the Horn of Africa; establishing an NGO consortium in Cambodia; and to international NGO policy formulation for humanitarian work with refugees and displaced persons in Central America. Co-ordination does, however, require a commitment of time and effort. It may be appropriate to designate a lead agency, or establish an inter-agency secretariat, to ensure that the co-ordination works effectively and efficiently for all its members. (See also **3.1.3** Communications in development.) A Code of Conduct has been drawn up governing NGO assistance in emergencies, including co-ordination of response. (See **6.1.2** Code of conduct for NGOs in disaster relief.)

4.3.2 International agencies involved in relief work
(See Resources Directory for detailed descriptions, and addresses.)

As indicated in Table 6.3, the role of the UN agencies in relief work is multifaceted, and likely to change significantly in the coming years in the face of increasing calls for institutional and policy reform. For the purposes of this Handbook, however, the following descriptions of the

870

relevant UN agencies are limited to their existing formal functions rather than to speculations about possible changes in these. Similarly, the role of international NGOs in emergencies is also changing, as many of these increasingly serve as channels for multilateral and bilateral relief assistance. However, it is useful for aid workers to be aware of some of the principal international NGO networks that are involved in disaster relief.

a. UN agencies

Most developing countries have a United Nations Development Programme (UNDP) office, whose Resident Representative is the senior UN official in the country. The Representative usually has responsibility for co-ordinating all the UN agencies' relief operations at the time of a disaster. In the context of emergency-related programmes, the flexible operational mandate of the United Nations Children's Fund (UNICEF) also enables it to take on work that benefits the affected population generally. It is not restricted to direct assistance to children.

The UN Department for Humanitarian Affairs (DHA), headed by an Under-Secretary General, has responsibility for co-ordinating appeals and the UN response. It has a budget available for immediate humanitarian assistance. The UN Disaster Relief Office (UNDRO) is part of the DHA, and offers technical advice, through the local office of the UNDP. It may also channel funds through governments, other UN agencies, or occasionally through NGOs.

The Food and Agricultural Organisation (FAO) is concerned with evaluating the effect of disasters on food security, agriculture, and fisheries; and with offering assistance in agricultural reconstruction. The World Food Programme (WFP) evaluates food needs and supplies food staples on a large scale. Foodstuffs can be made available either direct to government or to NGOs, sometimes through food-for-work programmes. FAO's Global Information and Early Warning System arranges for detailed crop assessments and issues 'Alerts' to donors about threatening situations. It welcomes information from NGOs.

The World Health Organisation (WHO) takes action to combat epidemics and supports disease-eradication programmes, but more usually acts as consultant on health matters to other UN agencies.

The UN High Commissioner for Refugees (UNHCR) is primarily concerned with the international protection of refugees; with the search for permanent solutions for their problems; and, to the extent that funds are available, with their material welfare. It may also become involved with the resettlement phase of refugee repatriation programmes; and, at the specific request of the UN Secretary-General, in work with persons displaced within their own country. One of its principal roles is that of co-ordinating relief efforts for refugees.

6

However, it is important to bear in mind that many *de facto* refugees do not register with UNHCR; and 90 per cent of repatriations and returns are estimated to occur spontaneously, without assistance either from UN bodies or from NGOs.

UNHCR's work is facilitated when it operates in countries party to the international instruments governing the protection of refugees. However, even when an emergency occurs in a country not party to the international instruments, the provisions of Article 35 of the 1951 Convention Relating to the Status of Refugees define standards of treatment that are internationally recognised. (See **6.3.2** International legislation relating to armed conflict, and **1.2** Human rights in development and relief work.)

The UNHCR *Handbook for Emergencies* summarises policies and procedures for UNHCR field staff, together with the UNHCR *Policy on Refugee Women* and *Guidelines on the Protection of Refugee Women*. These free publications are available, in English, French and Spanish (see Resources Directory for details of how to obtain them). NGOs facing a refugee emergency, or likely to be co-operating with UNHCR or UNICEF in a relief operation, should consult these publications.

b. The International Red Cross and Red Crescent Movement

The Red Cross and Red Crescent Movement makes up an important sector of the NGOs involved in disaster relief. Different constituent parts of this organisation may be involved in relief operations, and it is important not to confuse their distinct roles.

The International Committee of the Red Cross (ICRC or CICR): This is a private Swiss organisation based in Geneva. As an impartial and neutral humanitarian institution, it undertakes the tasks incumbent under the 1947 Geneva Conventions, and 1977 Protocols, which frequently relate to war and armed conflicts: the treatment of prisoners of war; protection and assistance to civilian and military victims; tracing and reuniting divided families; and the provision of medical assistance to victims of conflicts.

The International Federation of Red Cross and Red Crescent Societies (IFRC or Federation: formerly called the League of Red Cross and Red Crescent Societies) The secretariat for the IFRC is based in Geneva. IFRC is the representative and co-ordinating arm of all national Red Cross and Red Crescent Societies. It is the organisation through which national Societies worldwide can channel aid and assistance to the national Society of the affected country.

National Red Cross and Red Crescent Societies: Each national society has independent status and participates in the Federation. National societies may have long-term programmes highly relevant to relief work, such as national blood banks, hospitals, and ambulance services.

Most have a network of volunteers, trained to various degrees in first aid and other aspects of basic health care.

c. NGOs and voluntary agencies

Some of the international NGOs experienced in disaster relief operations are organised into Federations, which are the central co-ordinating bodies of nationally based organisations.

The World Council of Churches (WCC): This is based in Geneva and brings together not only the mainstream Protestant churches but also the Orthodox (both Eastern and Western), the Anglican communion, and some independent churches, principally in Africa. It does not formally represent national Councils of Churches, although these may be affiliated, since these are not universally comprehensive or systematic groupings. For example, national Councils of Churches may include the Catholic church, while the WCC does not. The Lutheran churches are part of the WCC, though the Lutheran World Federation is a separate body (see below).

The WCC usually channels aid through the national Council of Churches service department in the affected country. The emergency desk of Programme Unit IV acts as a focal point for the co-ordination of relief through the WCC members (this department was formerly called the Commission on Inter-Church Aid Refugee and World Service). The WCC includes in its membership Department of World Service (DWS), Church World Service (CWS), the Division of Overseas Ministries of the American Council of Churches, and Christian Aid. Each of these organisations also runs and finances programmes independently of the WCC.

Caritas Internationalis: This is based in Rome, and is the main agency of the Roman Catholic Church. Its national counterpart societies may also be called Caritas, such as Deutsche Caritas in Germany, or Caritas Belgique in Belgium. In France it is Secours Catholique; in the United Kingdom, the Catholic Fund for Overseas Development (CAFOD); in Ireland, Tro'caire; in the United States, Catholic Relief Services (CRS), which operates a large food aid programme using US Government foodstuffs.

The Steering Committee for Humanitarian Response (formerly Licross-Volags Steering Committee for Disasters): This Committee is made up of the heads of the International Federation of Red Cross and Red Crescent Societies, World Council of Churches, Lutheran World Federation, Caritas Internationalis, International Alliance of SCFs, and Oxfam (UK/I). The Committee meets periodically to co-ordinate the disaster-relief activities of the member agencies.

The Lutheran World Federation (LWF): LWF is independent of the WCC, though the Lutheran churches themselves are bilaterally

6

affiliated to it. LWF is the formal grouping of the Lutheran churches. Its service agency is Lutheran World Service.

The International Council of Voluntary Agencies (ICVA): This is an umbrella organisation made up of over 80 NGOs, with a small Geneva-based secretariat. It provides the means for inter-agency consultation and co-operation, both through sharing information and, on occasion, facilitating specific interventions in connection with emergencies, such as international delegations, fact-finding missions, and lobbying initiatives.

Other agencies: There are many other non-governmental agencies and networks, some church-based, others secular; some generalist, others with technical expertise; some regionally-based, some international.

4.3.3 Working with local authorities

Where they exist, government and civil authorities usually have formal responsibilities both to undertake relief work and to co-ordinate operations. They are likely to be sensitive to popular perceptions of whether they are adequately fulfilling these roles. Although they may welcome international NGO assistance and contributions, they are likely to be suspicious of NGOs which are operating outside their co-ordination, or in ways which imply criticism of their own response. Sensitivities over responsibility for the causes of the emergency, and over the government response to it, may be heightened by media attention and international pressure. This is particularly so in the case of civil unrest or conflict, where the political stakes may be very high.

There are often complaints by governments about international NGOs ignoring or by-passing their authority, and operating unilaterally or without agreement. Equally, NGOs may be frustrated by regulations, delays, and restrictions on what they believe to be vital and urgent humanitarian work. International NGOs should, however, consult with the relevant authorities and establish protocols and working practice, in order to avoid duplication of effort or avoidable inconsistencies of approach. They must respect the fact that local government authorities have the responsibility, the authority, and often the technical competence to co-ordinate relief operations. For instance, following major earthquakes in Mexico and in India, the respective governments demanded that international agencies allow the civil authorities to handle the immediate search and rescue phase of the emergency, and to co-ordinate the subsequent relief efforts. International NGOs should aim to support competent and experienced local authorities, not to undermine or displace them.

In the immediate aftermath of an emergency, an early priority for Oxfam in-country staff is to contact the appropriate authorities for their assessment of the situation, and to advise them of Oxfam's assessment plans or proposals. Unlike UN agencies and the ICRC, NGOs have no special international status. Their staff are therefore subject to normal requirements for visas, travel permits, and so on. Similarly, the importation of vehicles, equipment, and relief supplies may not be duty free, or free of normal landing or port charges and import regulations, though sometimes these are eased for emergency relief items. It may be necessary to seek government or military permission to travel to and within the affected area. It is usually possible to co-operate with government co-ordinating structures through routine reporting of the progress of relief work, and attending or reporting to government or NGO co-ordination meetings.

In situations of armed conflict, there may be no recognised government authority, or it may be inappropriate for an independent humanitarian agency to co-operate with the government authorities. While it is important to be fully aware of the implications of working without government approval, or in areas where the government does not exercise control, Oxfam's response has to be determined by the needs of the people affected by an emergency, and how best to meet these. (See also **6**.3 Emergencies deriving from war and armed conflict.)

4.3.4 Working through local structures
(See also **3**.2 Institutional development.)

Oxfam prefers whenever possible to assist local organisations, supporting their work with funds or supplies, or seconding technical or professional personnel to work alongside local counterparts. The range of local organisations may be very wide: national, regional or local government departments; national, regional or local NGOs; local-level community or neighbourhood groups, popular organisations, trades unions, or religious structures.

In under-resourced government departments, there are often trained professionals who lack the means to mount effective relief operations. They may be overlooked as outside assistance arrives, on the assumption that there are no locally available personnel. Alternatively, such professionals may also be attracted out of local structures by international NGOs and other agencies that offer better terms and conditions of work, and career opportunities. Support through local channels should help to mobilise existing skills and resources in a sustainable way rather than displacing them with skills and services from abroad.

Working with local organisations ensures that they gain experience in relief work and extends their capacity to respond to future emergencies. This capacity can sometimes be developed in other ways.

6

For example, in 1992 Oxfam held a workshop in Uganda to train local engineers, including water authority engineers, in setting up emergency water supplies. The rationale was to lessen the need in future emergencies to fly in expatriate engineers unfamiliar with the country.

The involvement of local organisations brings the benefit of their experience and insights to the relief operation. Where these organisations are properly accountable to, and trusted by, the affected population, this helps to reduce the immediate risks of inappropriate action by international NGOs working in an area, or among a group of people, with which they are unfamiliar. To channel support through existing structures may also make outside NGOs more acceptable to local government authorities, and help to reduce the resentment that arises when local capacities are disregarded by outsiders confident that they know best how relief should be organised. The downwards accountability of international NGOs is also enhanced through such collaboration.

If the relief effort is to be effective in the short term, and to make a sustainable impact in the longer term, it is important to ensure that local organisations are given the additional support they need as they take on tasks that are outside their usual scope, or as they face sudden and unplanned expansion. Assistance in training, financial and other planning, project design, and organisational management may all be needed, to enable them to deal with these challenges.

There is a balance to be struck between the benefit of sharing expertise with less experienced departments and agencies, and the priority of meeting the immediate needs of people affected by the emergency. Although there can be frustrations in working with local structures, it is Oxfam's recommended policy, in relief as in development programmes, as the best way to strengthen their capacity to respond effectively in the longer term.

In major emergencies, existing local and national resources cannot always meet all the needs, and local agencies may be overwhelmed by the demands made on them. In such cases, it may be appropriate for Oxfam to assume operational responsibility for the relief programme.

Oxfam's operational relief work is normally undertaken on behalf of, and in close liaison with, a local government department, a national NGO or the UN system. For example, in Ethiopia Oxfam deployed engineers and emergency water supply equipment to meet the needs of Somali refugees, at the request of UNHCR. The programme was implemented in co-operation with the Ethiopian Water Works Construction Authority, the local government authorities, and the government bodies with responsibility for relief and refugee affairs. From the time when the programme was established, Oxfam worked towards handing it over to the local water authority. In Sudan's Red Sea

Province, Oxfam was a member of the Provincial Emergency Relief Committee set up in response to severe food shortage precipitated by drought. Through this arrangement, Oxfam worked with the government co-ordinating authority, and co-operated closely with other national NGOs involved in the targeting and monitoring of distributions of relief food undertaken by the WFP on behalf of the Committee. In Bangladesh, for example, Oxfam has mobilised teams of volunteers to prepare and deliver food to people made homeless by floods. In Zambia, Oxfam combined an operational response to the 1992-93 drought that included the distribution of food aid, with a long-term approach that involved mobilising local communities, municipal government officials, and civil servants, as well as the international media, to inform these about the impact of economic structural adjustment on food and livelihood security in the drought-stricken area. Local people were trained in simple information-gathering methods, while a network of community and aid workers transmitted this information to policy-makers at both government and aid agency level. The programme of activities included a massive letter-writing campaign, and so demonstrated to ordinary people that their vulnerability related to policies that they could, and should, challenge. (See **3.1.3.3** Advocacy.) An evaluation of the experience concluded that this has had a significant impact on people's confidence, and on the attitude of local government officials towards them. In every situation, the aim should be to develop local capacity to deal with similar crises in the future.

4.3.5 Working with dispersed populations

People affected by an emergency may not be concentrated in a large settlement. Often, refugees prefer to disperse among a sympathetic population on the other side of a national border, especially if there are economic, kinship, ethnic, or cultural links. It is estimated, for example, that from 1982 to 1991, there were up to ten times as many Guatemalan refugees *not* seeking recognition as such (and so ineligible for UNHCR assistance), as there were in the formal camps established many miles from the border. During the same period, tens of thousands of Salvadoran refugees lived for years in Mexico, though only a handful were legally registered or receiving assistance, and no camps were ever established.

As with displaced persons, there may be very compelling reasons for people not choosing to draw attention to themselves by registering with the authorities. In many cases, work with them is most appropriately done through mixed-population programmes which assist the most vulnerable, but not in such a way as to discriminate against what is often

6

877

a very poor host community. Local NGOs or religious structures are often in a position to help to identify needs, in a confidential manner.

In such situations, a relief response should always acknowledge the needs and priorities, and build sensitively on the strengths, of the women and men affected, and also of the host community. The main constraint for an international aid agency is that it may not be appropriate for their easily identifiable representatives to make personal visits to people whose survival depends on remaining inconspicuous. Distribution and monitoring of assistance is probably better undertaken by organisations representing the people themselves, or by a trusted local institution.

4.4 Consulting and involving the affected population
(To be read in conjunction with 1.4 Exploring the context for development and relief work.)

4.4.1 Introduction and background

Respect for local authorities and designated co-ordinating bodies, and the channelling of assistance through existing governmental and non-governmental structures, are important principles for international NGOs to follow. For Oxfam, it is a priority to enable people to participate more effectively in the decisions and processes that affect their lives, including any initiatives supported by Oxfam. In the context of an emergency, and under pressure to act fast, there is a greater risk of making assumptions about people's priorities, without adequate consultation with them. However, it is Oxfam's experience that relief programmes are significantly enhanced if the people affected are actively involved in all aspects of planning, implementation, and evaluation of relief programmes. While it may not be easy to institute effective consultation mechanisms in the initial stages, an attempt should be made to establish the *principle* of consultative planning, and then build on imperfect beginnings. It is more difficult to try to reorient programme priorities and methodologies that have already established their own top-down momentum.

Programmes should aim to reflect the diverse concerns of women as well as men, of older as well as younger people, and of people from the various social, ethnic or cultural backgrounds within the affected population. At the earliest possible stage, a routine of effective consultation should be established through co-ordination committees or existing structures, provided that these do not exclude or undermine the participation of any specific category of people. The majority of people may have little experience in social organisation, and considerable work and patience may be needed to enable different interest groups to articulate their demands effectively. Since most of the adults in refugee and displaced populations are women, there is no excuse for failing to make systematic efforts to elicit their views. Women have their own opinions about emergency and relief needs, even if they do not express these in the public arena. It can never be assumed that the priorities defined by men coincide with what women would identify, were they able, and encouraged, to articulate their views.

Occasionally, the affected population already has the cohesion and confidence to be able to assert itself effectively from an early stage. For example, on arriving in Honduras in 1981-2, Salvadoran refugees quickly established camp co-ordinating committees which took on the principal responsibility for ensuring that their concerns were represented before UNHCR and its NGO operational counterparts. In time, sub-committees were delegated to take on specific areas of programme design and management, including public health, construction, hygiene and sanitation, education and adult literacy, supplies and logistics. Refugees who had arrived as illiterate peasant farmers became increasingly effective in management, administration, and negotiation, along with acquiring vocational skills. In a situation of enforced captivity, these refugees used all the organisational tools at their disposal to develop sustainable and representative social structures on which they would build on their return to El Salvador.

International aid agencies are seldom compelled to be downwardly accountable to the people they aim to assist. Regular and systematic consultation and feedback with representatives of the affected population go some way to establishing an informal accountability. The pressure of work, whether practical and technical issues or meetings with government and other agencies, competes with the time needed for consultation. People's involvement in decision-making can also pose difficulties that agencies would rather evade. Relief workers may tend to avoid meeting people who they believe to be making unrealistic or inappropriate demands. On the other hand, the benefits of an active investment in training (in skills such as decision-making, budgeting, and evaluation) include the increased efficiency and sustainability of programmes.

6

Oxfam regards establishing *and respecting* consultative processes as a high priority. To enable this to happen, a member of Oxfam's staff, or a small mixed team, may take on responsibility for social organisation and motivation — sometimes called community liaison work — within an emergency programme. It is vital to ensure that the insights of these staff inform the development and management of the programme. (See **3**.2.3 Evaluation.)

4.4.2 Consulting women

(To be read in conjunction with 2.1 Gender; and 1.4.3 Formal methods of information-gathering and appraisal.)

Formal or traditional leadership positions are more likely to be held by men than by women, and camp officials or representatives tend to be male. The majority of local government as well as senior NGO workers and policy makers are men, as are most technical personnel. Frequently, therefore, dialogue takes place exclusively between men, even when they are discussing the specific needs of women, or areas of work for which women are primarily responsible.

The impact of such male bias, and of the gender-blindness that may result, is significant and damaging. Not only are women's needs, perspectives, and aspirations potentially omitted from programmes supposedly intended to benefit them, but their potential as human beings remains untapped and undeveloped. In the words of a 1993 report produced by Oxfam's office in Sudan:

Approaches to emergencies as they currently stand blatantly hand the power over women's traditional affairs to men ... running food distribution, water programmes, blanket, jerrycan and other distributions ... re-assigning the women's traditional responsibilities for food and shelter provision to men.

The practical impact of failing to incorporate the dimension of gender relations may even be dangerous, as the following example illustrates. In Jebal Kujur relief camp in southern Sudan, separate meetings were held with men and women of the Mundari, in which Oxfam staff consulted them about the use of pit latrines. Both agreed that while the latrines were necessary, latrines for men and women should be kept as far apart as possible, and divided according to tribal groupings. In the absence of such arrangements and with too few latrines, people continued to defaecate in open spaces, with serious health implications in an already over-crowded camp. In practice, severe shortage of space made the desired arrangements hard to achieve; but they would be taken into account in the planned re-siting of the camp.

Aid agencies may know little about women's lives before the emergency arose; and even less about how their lives and aspirations have changed as a result of it. Women themselves commonly underestimate the enormous range of burdens they bear; they may have negative self-images, and be unused to seeing themselves as strong and effective survivors, managing a very wide range of household and social responsibilities. (See 2.1 Gender and 3.1.2 Education and Training.) It is vital to ensure that:

• particular attention is paid to women's views in the assessment stage;

- women's actual responsibilities, both domestic (in terms of household subsistence, health, child care) as well as production and economic activity beyond the subsistence level, are taken into account in determining consultation processes;
- women representatives are included at all levels of planning, decision making, implementation, and evaluation;
- the particular constraints faced by women-maintained households are taken explicitly into account in designing and implementing relief programmes;
- the particular situation faced by unaccompanied women, lone parents, and widows is considered;
- issues of legal, sexual, physical and emotional protection are identified and properly addressed.

Methods of gathering this information need to be creative and sensitive. It should not be assumed that a direct question-and-answer approach will be appropriate. Many of the participatory approaches to information-gathering outlined in **1.4.3** are particularly valuable in situations of this kind. For instance, it may not be possible for women who have suffered rape, sexual torture, or physical abuse to talk freely about their experiences, for cultural, political, or emotional reasons. Indirect and unthreatening ways of allowing the problems to be expressed might include setting up a group on women's health needs; or a mutual support group for bereaved women. Interpreting information is also a crucial and sensitive matter. It may not be immediately apparent, for example, that households which have no adult males present may not qualify for employment and economic opportunities outside the camp settlement — and hence are significantly worse off than others which do.

For women to benefit equally with men from relief programmes, and to be able to contribute fully *on their own terms*, therefore requires a deliberate effort on the part of relief agencies. Where women are not accustomed to being consulted on their views, they may initially find it hard to articulate them. They frequently will not have the confidence to do so in mixed settings or in front of male or expatriate aid workers. Furthermore, their existing household responsibilities may mean that women have little free time available for lengthy consultation. With some imagination and sensitive planning, it is usually possible to facilitate their involvement — for example, by arranging for childcare during meetings, and making sure that these are held at a convenient hour. The initiative for this may initially depend on the efforts of aid workers.

Women are also likely to have fewer educational or language skills than men, and are more likely to be illiterate. Thus extra efforts may be

881

needed to adopt consultative and participatory approaches that do not depend, for example, on literacy and numeracy, or on knowledge of the national language. In the longer term, programme interventions might be designed to teach or upgrade existing skills and levels of confidence, so that women's capacities are strengthened as a result of their experience. (See **2.1.4** Women in emergencies; **3.1.2** Education and training.)

For relief workers to consult women, it may be necessary to hold separate meetings with them, or to ensure that female representatives in mixed forums are assisted by additional women-only discussion groups. Exchanges are usually more frank if the relief worker is female, and for discussions about menstruation, reproductive health, and gynaecological matters, this is *essential*. Oxfam recommends that women should always be included as members of survey and assessment teams, and if necessary recruited to work directly with women amongst the affected population. They may be able to assist in the formation of women's committees, or help to identify and mobilise those women's social structures that already exist. They may also encourage women to take on public roles, such as becoming refugee camp officials, community health workers or teachers. Women usually need help to get together and develop the confidence to express their views collectively, and in public. Methods might include establishing mutual support groups, for women who have been bereaved or who are alone; women's health discussion circles; female literacy classes; organisational training; vocational skills development. Less direct means include setting up support services such as creche and childcare facilities, or collective kitchens, without which women rarely have the chance to have time to themselves. Opportunities for women to express themselves might also need to be indirect, rather than the assumption being made that they can acquire the confidence overnight to speak their own minds, in public: theatre, socio-drama, role-play, painting, dance, music and song can all be effective vehicles for communication, none of which requires advanced levels of literacy.

4.5 Assessing the situation of specific social groups

4.5.1 Introduction

Situations of change and crisis affect people differently, according to their economic and social status, and their relationships with others within their society. Chapter 2, Focusing on People, examines in detail those aspects of people's identity — gender, ethnic and cultural background, age, and physical condition — that are *always* present, and which affect *every* dimension of their lives. These identities are dynamic, and may themselves change in the context of crisis. Such changes may have negative implications for some social groups — for instance, societies may respond to threat by reinforcing cultural traditions that oppress women and girls. On the other hand, crisis can often provide an opportunity for certain sets of people to take on new challenges, or learn new skills, and bring about lasting and positive changes in their lives.

Humanitarian aid agencies need to be aware of the various ways in which different people and social groups respond to, and are affected by, crisis and change. Interventions that ignore or are insensitive to existing social relations amongst the affected population run the danger of being ineffective, or even damaging the situation of those who are most vulnerable. However, in the context of an emergency, the pressure to act quickly increases the risk of making short-term interventions that fail to take these longer-term dynamics into account.

Emergency relief should always aim to be as sensitive as possible to the cultural and social expectations of the affected population, as well as to their longer-term human, social and economic development. Disaggregated data collection and needs assessment can provide an accurate representation of the refugee population, and so ensure that relief efforts are tailored to the different needs of specific social groups.

Many of the problems in consulting with women in order to find out their specific needs and perspectives, as described in the previous section (**6.4.4.2 Consulting women**), will also occur in relation to other groups within the affected population. Ethnic minority groups, for example, may not be able to communicate easily in the 'official' language; they may also be marginalised, and disempowered within their society, and be unaccustomed to being consulted about their situation. Children, elderly people, and people with disabilities may also need encouragement and specialised approaches on the part of aid workers if they are to be able to express their particular concerns, so that relief efforts can be designed to take these into account. This section looks specifically at the situations of social groups whose needs are commonly misunderstood or overlooked, and which therefore demand special attention in formulating a detailed and appropriate relief response. It should be read in conjunction with Chapter 2 Focusing on people.

4.5.2 *Women*

In every aspect of development and relief, if aid interventions are not good for women as well as for men, they have failed and are indefensible. The importance of talking directly to women cannot be stressed too strongly; men are usually unaware of exactly how women meet the wide range of responsibilities they carry within the household; and may know little about the other roles that women play, either in production or in terms of social or civic activities.

Women and children form the substantial majority (approximately four out of five persons) of most settled refugee populations, and a very high percentage of dispersed and displaced persons in situations of war and armed conflict. In relation to men and boys, women and girls are more likely to be malnourished, both when they arrive at their place of asylum and throughout their time away from their homes. Women are more likely than men to be illiterate, without formal education, and without experience in dealing with the outside world; and girls are less likely than boys to be enrolled in school classes even within the refugee camp or settlement. Many physical problems suffered by women relate to their reproductive health, and specifically to child-bearing. Large numbers of preventable deaths arise because of complications in pregnancy and childbirth.

In situations of social crisis, or major migration, an increased number of women assume sole responsibility for maintaining their household. This may mean caring not only for small children, but also for elderly relatives and others who are not able to work. Food production, particularly in Africa, is largely within the hands of women, as is almost all food preparation, cooking, and domestic distribution everywhere in the world. In emergencies, women may also have to tend the crops normally cultivated by men, often without the same support systems as men might have. For example, during the civil war in El Salvador, an association of abandoned or widowed women farmers were trying to take on additional responsibility for producing food staples such as beans, maize and rice. This was made more difficult for them by the fact that the fields were some distance away from their homes, and they had no-one to look after their children. While they might have been able to resolve childcare among themselves, what was far more incapacitating was the fact that, *because they were women*, they were not entitled to credit for agricultural inputs. Since fewer than 5 per cent of the membership were literate, they had difficulty even in setting up meetings to decide whether to approach Oxfam for support.

Refugees have frequently experienced not only physical hardship but also significant brutality and trauma during their flight to the place of asylum. They may already have lost close members of their family, as well as their homes and livelihoods. They may have witnessed, suffered, or been otherwise involved in atrocities. Their escape will have been a time of terror, with no certainty that a secure refuge would await them. For women and girls, in particular, the fear of rape and sexual abuse is a well-founded one before, during, and after their escape. Reports abound of even very tiny girls being raped by guards, members of the armed forces, or by the men who are taking them to supposed safety. Women are frequently pressed into becoming unpaid sex-workers, in return for being allowed safe conduct, or refuge for themselves and their children; or may turn to prostitution as the only way to gain a small income to maintain themselves and their children.

Women are seldom involved in decisions about the design and implementation of relief programmes, and this 'gender-blindness' on the part of aid workers can profoundly distort the way in which aid responses are formulated. Even where NGOs and relief workers do make a point of trying to consult women, this is frequently done in somewhat instrumentalist terms: women are seen as important principally as a means to ensure that specific interventions are not a complete failure — for example, to check that the proposed latrine arrangements will not be offensive to them — or as transmitters of information to and about children. They are rarely seen as people with their own rights, needs and perspectives; much less as agents either of social stability, or of change. If women's perspectives on the emergency are to be systematically incorporated into the processes by which programmes are designed, implemented, monitored, and evaluated, so that their needs are met and their capacities strengthened, aid workers must make conscious and sensitive efforts to enable women to communicate their ideas. (See **2**.1 Gender, and also **6**.4.4.2 Consulting women, and **2**.1.4.3 Gender in Armed Conflict.)

Oxfam's policy is to ensure that as a criterion of their recruitment all programme staff are aware of the gender-differentiated impact of work which is undertaken, or supported, by Oxfam; and committed to ensuring that Oxfam's work addresses those inequalities that place women at a disadvantage in relation to men. This means that all pro-gramme and decision-making staff involved in emergency programmes have a formal responsibility to analyse gender relations at all stages of relief interventions. Specifically, they have a responsibility to ensure that no intervention recommended to or supported by Oxfam overlooks the specific needs of women, or worsens their situation in relation to men. But Oxfam staff should aim well beyond this minimum standard of not exacerbating gender inequalities. Rather, they should identify and take forward those initiatives which actively encourage women to express themselves, which tackle gender inequalities, and which ensure that women's strengths and capacities are recognised and enhanced.

It is also Oxfam's recommended practice that teams involved in relief work (including short-term staff) should be made up of women and men, in order to ensure that proper consultation can take place with both sexes within the affected population.

6

4.5.3 Children

The needs of children in emergencies are distinct from, and often more extreme than, those faced by adults in the affected population. Children generally are more vulnerable to hardship and deprivation; and are physically as well as emotionally dependent on adults. The particular difficulties faced by girls are often exacerbated in emergency situations, and it is essential that relief interventions tackle discrimination against them, whether this is overt or implicit. Relief programmes should be designed in a way which is sensitive to children's specific needs, but without undermining those family and other social structures which already exist to give them care and protection.

It is preferable to avoid separating children from their families, community structures or kinship groups, in relief as well as in development programmes. This is especially so in view of the exceptional trauma and distress they may have suffered. It is relatively unusual for children to be completely unaccompanied, though the recruitment of child soldiers may account for the thousands of unaccompanied boys in some African countries. Where such separation has occurred, the process of reuniting them with their families is a complex matter that should be co-ordinated by the specialist agencies, such as ICRC or UNHCR. (See Resources Directory.) Similarly, the evacuation of children from danger zones usually requires the intervention of governmental or multilateral agencies; and is beyond the competence of non-specialist international NGOs such as Oxfam.

The global data on children who are refugees are generally inadequate and rarely differentiated by sex. The most commonly cited figure is that approximately 75-80 per cent of registered refugees are under the age of 15 years. Of the five million children receiving assistance from UNHCR, it is unknown how many are girls or boys, since there are no uniform standards for data collection. Good planning demands the differentiation of social and demographic data *by sex and age*; and NGOs should encourage this whenever possible.

Related to the issue of data collection is that of legal documentation. The lack of proper papers may limit the freedom of movement of child or adolescent refugees, or their rights to various services, either in the host country or in their country of origin. Children born in refugee camps may be entitled to the nationality of the host country, though it is perhaps not in their long-term interests to adopt it. While the matter of legal documentation is properly the concern of the competent authorities and specialist agencies, Oxfam staff should be aware of the problems which may arise from statelessness, especially when repatriation or other durable solutions are being proposed. It is important that parents or guardians understand their rights in this regard, and it may be appropriate to assist with legal information services.

Children are especially vulnerable to the effects of malnutrition and infectious diseases. Often, their illnesses predate the crisis. In other cases, they are the direct result of the emergency. In certain instances, problems have been exacerbated or even brought about by inadequate relief programmes. Issues relating to public health and specific nutrition interventions are discussed in **6**.5 Health and nutrition in emergencies; and **6**.7.3 Food aid in emergencies.

The problems arising from physical or sexual harassment of children may be more difficult to detect or address. Even very young girls may have been raped before they reach their place of asylum, or are subject to harassment by refugee camp officials; yet the long-term trauma, as well as the physical consequences, of their ordeal go unspoken and ignored. It may be easier for girls to disclose what they have experienced to women health workers, especially if these are drawn from among the affected population itself. Indeed, it may be impossible for rape victims to place their trust in male relief officials, whether these are local or expatriate.

Children may have been forced to witness or participate in atrocities which leave profound psychological scars on them. Boys in particular may have been forced to join the militia, act as informers, decoys or couriers, or be otherwise brutalised. Their process of social readjustment may be slow and difficult. Programme interventions to encourage expression and recreation may help, such as organised sport, musical events, theatre, and socio-drama or role-play. Being involved in other social activities will also assist children to reintegrate, though in some cases expert counselling might be needed.

The UN Convention Relating to the Status of Refugees provides that refugees should be accorded 'the same treatment as is accorded to nationals with respect to elementary education'. In practice, under 10 per cent of refugee children receiving UNHCR assistance are enrolled in schools. This figure masks an even worse situation for female children. For example, fewer than 0.01 per cent of Afghan refugee girls in Pakistan were enrolled in school. In the Horn of Africa, reports indicated that overall attendance rates were much lower than enrolment figures; and that virtually all of the pupils were boys.

Educational coverage in refugee camps can be made comprehensive; and female attendance rates enhanced. Where dispersed refugees and displaced persons are concerned, it may be appropriate to consider supporting self-run informal schools rather than assuming that refugee children will be able to register in the formal education system. In these areas, often regarded as non-essential to survival, NGOs may assist, for example, with provision of teachers' salaries, school books, and

6

educational materials. In the longer term, NGOs have funded training for adults from within the affected population to take on the role of teaching children. (See **3.1.2** Education and Training.)

The issue of cultural identity may become crucial to refugees, especially in situations where children are growing up outside their own country, or in the artificial situation of enclosed camps. There can be real tensions between the traditional expectations of their parents and the context in which the children are being brought up and socialised. For example, refugees who would have survived in their own country as subsistence farmers may be raising children whose skills are wide-ranging, but do not include agricultural techniques.

It is important to encourage efforts made by refugees to transmit their cultural identity to the children among them, even though such activities are unlikely to rank as essential to their immediate survival. In some cases, the traditions themselves may be 'rediscovered' in the context of the cultural threat to which the refugees feel exposed. While offering appropriate support, Oxfam staff should also be aware that, while boys are generally encouraged to be adaptive to new situations and challenges, considerable — and sometimes unwelcome — pressures are often placed on girls to preserve the cultural heritage of the group or community as a whole. (See **2.3** Childhood, and **2.2** Ethnicity, race, and culture.)

4.5.4 Elderly people

The importance of establishing reliable demographic data as a basis for sound programme design is very clear in the case of elderly women and men. People over 45 years — who may be classified as elderly in many contexts — form a significant percentage of the adult population in refugee camps. Their specific circumstances are thus relevant for overall management and monitoring both of the emergency, and of the relief effort. The situation of older people in normal times — a higher incidence of very elderly women than men, a higher percentage of female than male illiterates — may or may not be reflected in the refugee or displaced population.

In emergencies, it is likely that elderly people will have suffered bereavement, and will be without their partners and close family. In many cases, they make their way to refugee camps and settlements for displaced people precisely because they cannot fend for themselves; and because the normal household and family support mechanisms have broken down. This, in addition to the distress caused by being away from their familiar surroundings, can intensify the loneliness and depression that elderly people may experience.

Elderly people are especially vulnerable in situations where whole communities have to flee in search of asylum and assistance. If they are disabled or frail, they may remain in their homes rather than attempt to leave; although their chances of survival on their own may be very limited. If they try to join the exodus, they may die or be left behind on the journey. Nonetheless, the highest death rates among elderly people are recorded as occurring on arrival in refugee camps. This itself may reflect the low priority generally given in relief programmes to the specific needs of older women and men.

Older people are more vulnerable than young adults to the fatigue, malnutrition, and illness to which the affected population has been subject. The physically weak or disabled are also less able to compete for material resources or to make full use of the services available. Programmes which encourage self-reliance — such as supplying building materials for people to construct their own homes and shelters — may implicitly discriminate against unaccompanied elderly people who cannot construct their own housing without assistance. Food which is acceptable to younger adults will not necessarily be palatable to older people. The form in which food is distributed may also make it unavailable to people too frail, unwell or demoralised to collect it. Furthermore, the opportunities which young men have to supplement their income, and thus their diet, are less likely to be accessible to older people. While their physical dependence on the relief programme may be total, most elderly people would expect to lead active and productive lives for as long as they are able. In many societies, age is one of the factors which give women status, and elderly women often enjoy greater mobility and presence in the public arena. A disaster need not necessarily change that; but the attitude of relief workers often makes older people involuntarily dependent because of discrimination in favour of young, literate males, both for employment opportunities and for positions of responsibility and representation. For example, older women are rarely consulted — much less involved — in health programmes, in spite of the fact that they have considerable responsibility for health care and birth practices within their society.

The ways in which relief programmes are designed may, albeit unwittingly, cause offence and embarrassment to older people. For example, they may experience extreme humiliation in having inadequate clothing. Supervised feeding programmes which treat them as if they are small children, are not uncommon. The deference of aid officials to younger men may undermine the status and authority which elderly people might normally have enjoyed.

It is not uncommon for older people to be left out of economic or educational initiatives, and for these to be designed almost exclusively around the needs of able-bodied young men or children. Consequently, relief interventions largely fail to build on skills and knowledge which the elderly possess. They seldom enable them to develop new abilities or

889

adapt to changing situations. Older people may have experience of previous disasters. They may be able to provide a bridge for cultural continuity after the upheavals and disruptions of a crisis. Their active involvement in emergency relief programmes can, furthermore, contribute very greatly to the social cohesion which is so threatened in emergencies. It is not in the interests of the affected population at large for elderly people to be ignored. (See **2.4** Ageing.)

4.5.5 Cultural considerations and minority groups

Crises and emergencies tend to accentuate existing inequalities within a society. In cases of ethnic or religious tension, minority groups may be the only people directly affected, or affected disproportionately to their numbers. The emergency may consist in ethnic or religious persecution by more powerful members of the national society, by competing ethnic or cultural groups, or by state authorities. 'Ethnic cleansing' is a term currently used to describe the systematic persecution or massacre of people described as having a particular ethnic identity, in order to establish ethnically-homogenous territories. (See **2.2** Ethnicity, race, and caste.)

Political and military power do not always reside in numerical predominance of one population group over another, as the system of Apartheid demonstrated. In Guatemala, for example, the total number of Mayan Indians forms a majority within the national population; but the nature of political violence during the 1980s meant that it was Indians who were the principal targets of the massacres and destruction of villages and homes which took place throughout the mountainous Altiplano region.

Whether working in areas of past, current or potential conflict, ethnicity is inescapably a central issue for any humanitarian agency working in such countries as varied as Zaire, Rwanda, Somalia, Sudan, former Yugoslavia, the Philippines, Sri Lanka, the Occupied Territories, El Salvador, Guatemala, or Peru — to name but some of the countries which have been ravaged by internal conflict in the last decade. Ethnicity and war can reinforce each other, and positions harden where they were in the past more fluid. It is common to dehumanise the enemy, in order to strengthen the boundaries between distinct groups, and sanction the atrocities that are a feature of armed conflict.

While the conflict itself may be rooted in a struggle for political ascendency, nationhood, and control over resources or territory, it is the perceived 'difference' of particular groups — socially and culturally — that renders them vulnerable. They may be seen as marginal to the national economy, as for example with the pastoralist and nomadic societies in East Africa, which operate for the most part outside national structures. Such people may face constant pressure from the government authorities to settle in one place. In a drought or similar crisis, there may be an attempt to force people to settle as the price of relief.

Similar pressure may be applied on specific groups of people — usually ethnically defined — to be resettled in places and in ways that render them more easily controllable. Forcible resettlement is usually stated by governments as being 'for the people's own good' — perhaps for their protection from the effects of war or drought. An example of this was the attempt of the Ethiopian government during the 1980s to resettle people from the northern region — at that time contested with the rebel armies — to the south of the country, which was under government control. The main reason given was the insufficiency of natural resources in the north to sustain the population. While this in itself was not implausible, the strategic context was clear; and the resettlement programme was only able to proceed through coercion and terrorisation of the population concerned.

During the 'contra' war against the Nicaraguan government in the 1980s, the temporary evacuation of Miskito Indians from the Rio Coco on the Nicaraguan border was said to be for their own protection. It was, nevertheless, against the wishes of the Miskito community, for whom it was alien to their way of life to be housed in concentrated settlements far from the river. In fact, Oxfam-funded schemes to provide water tanks were undermined in part because of the lack of interest shown by Miskito men in maintaining them. As soon as they were able, the people returned to the river.

There is always a risk that relief interventions may play into broader strategic plans for involuntary resettlement — particularly in the case of ethnic or cultural minorities — in which the emergency is used as a pretext. Consultation with people familiar with the socio-political context, as well as with representatives of the people to be relocated, may help to avert these dangers. A knowledge of the growing body of international human rights legislation and instruments on involuntary resettlement, and of networks concerned with indigenous or ethnic rights, is also useful. (See **1.2** Human rights; and Resources Directory.)

Without an understanding of the overall issues, as well as of the customs, priorities, and way of life of the specific minority or marginalised groups in question, NGOs run a great risk of intervening in inappropriate ways. For instance, it may be incorrectly assumed that all members of an ethnically defined group share the same interests, or that those interests can be addressed in isolation, without reference to the broader political domain. As in any other area of development and relief work, it is important to analyse the various ways in which power

6

and access to resources are allocated within a distinct group, and not to assume that there are no internal conflicts or competing interests simply because members of a minority group or culture seem to form a self-defining 'community'. For instance, in the example of the Miskito Indians quoted above, Oxfam has since questioned whether the water tanks would have been operated more successfully had women, rather than men, been trained in their maintenance — given that women traditionally took responsibility for household water management, and men found it offensive to be associated with this aspect of community life. Since relief responses that are based on inaccurate views of the affected communities may do more harm than good, it is all the more important for aid workers to take all possible steps to understand the specific cultural context in which they are working, and to strengthen those cultural institutions and practices that will enable women and men to cope more effectively with the problems they face. (See **2.2** Ethnicity, race, and caste.)

An example of good practice, that is both culturally sensitive and gender-aware, is in Oxfam's work in the Turkana District of Kenya. This itself builds on earlier programme experience in Uganda and elsewhere in Kenya during the late 1980s and early 1990s, in which mechanisms had been developed to inform and involve food aid recipients, and specifically to take account of women's key role in food management within Turkana society. Food distribution systems are designed to recognise women's responsibility at the individual household level by registering women, and determining the number of rations according to the actual number of dependants for whom they are responsible. The food is distributed through the women, but in the presence of the elders' committees, in this way avoiding the danger of setting up parallel or competing systems of authority. Given the nomadic pastoralist culture, there is also a facility to move names from one register to another, and to establish a mutually-convenient distribution point for groups that are highly mobile, or that sub-divide as a means of surviving crisis.

4.5.6 People with disabilities

In emergencies, disabled people may become more dependent than usual on outside support unless their specific needs are given a high priority. Their disability may consequently become a double burden. This is especially true if they are immobile or have limited mobility, and where they are without family support. For women and girls, the disability may intensify other problems concerning protection. (See **2.5.3** Gender and disability.)

The number of disabled people within the affected population may be high; and the nature of the disability extensive. For example, many refugees may be amputees. In Cambodia, people returning to areas strewn with landmines are at risk of losing a limb, thus causing immeasurable disruption in their own lives, and also seriously affecting the post-war reconstruction efforts.

Only where the percentage of disabled people is exceptionally high, or the disabilities are particularly evident, is it common for aid programmes to incorporate specific attention to their needs, or to those who care for them. The access which disabled people have to the services provided — food, materials for shelter and clothing, as well as health care, education, and economic opportunities — may thus be unnecessarily curtailed. A conscious effort has to be made by aid workers both to find out what the specific disability-related needs are, and to design interventions in such a way as to facilitate access to services and provision of goods. (See **2**.5 Disability.)

4.6 Key questions

1 What structures and local organisations exist, within the affected population or within the area, through which Oxfam might be able to channel assistance; or on whose expertise Oxfam might draw?
2 What efforts have been made, and with what degree of success, to ensure that women and men from the affected population have been encouraged to articulate their own perceptions of the priority needs?
3 Are women's and men's perceptions identical and compatible? If not, what arrangements have been made to ensure that the situation of women is not undermined by any chosen intervention?
4 What is the involvement of women and men from the affected population in the design, implementation, monitoring, and evaluation of the relief effort; and how could this be enhanced?
5 What is known about gender relations, and about the specific situations of men and women, before the emergency? And what impact has the emergency had, directly or indirectly, on these? What are the implications in terms of differentiated needs in the imemdiate and medium term?
6 What are the impacts of the emergency on specific social groups (children, elderly people, ethnic minorities, people with disabilities)?
7 What other agencies are involved in relief interventions, and what co-ordinating mechanisms exist to ensure effective co-operation?
8 In the case of people returning to their country or place or origin, what is known about their experience while they were in a place of asylum? What impact has this had on them, and their capacity to reintegrate?

6

5 Health and nutrition in emergencies

5.1 Introduction 894
5.2 Background 895
5.3 Assessment 896
    5.3.1 General assessment 896
    5.3.2 Assessment of sudden-onset emergencies 897
    5.3.3 Assessment of slow-onset emergencies 897
5.4 Practical approaches 900
    5.4.1 Response to sudden-onset emergencies 900
    5.4.2 Response to slow-onset and 'chronic' emergencies 902
    5.4.3 Food 903
    5.4.4 Gender considerations in food distribution 905
    5.4.5 Water supply and excreta disposal 906
    5.4.6 Health services 907
    5.4.7 Primary health interventions 908
5.5 Health and nutrition surveillance 909
    5.5.1 Population data 910
    5.5.2 Mortality data 910
    5.5.3 Morbidity data (cases of disease) 910
    5.5.4 Nutrition data 910
    5.5.5 Data on health sector activities 911
    5.5.6 Data on general living conditions 911
5.6 Training programmes 912
5.7 Key questions 913

5.1 Introduction

People affected by major disasters are often already suffering the common health problems of poverty. An emergency may cause their health to deteriorate still further. For example, inadequate shelter and adverse weather conditions contribute to the incidence of acute respiratory infections. Pressure on water resources, and inadequate sanitation and waste disposal, provide the conditions for the spread of water-related diseases, such as diarrhoea, dysentery, typhoid, and scabies. Increased person-to-person contact in crowded refugee camps contributes to the spread of infectious diseases, such as measles or

894

meningitis. Both the severity and incidence of common illnesses such as diarrhoea, respiratory infections, and measles, are intensified by poor living conditions. Lack of food, as well as unfamiliar or inappropriate foods, may lead to malnutrition and lowered defences against disease.

War destroys health infrastructure, and disrupts the delivery of preventive and curative services. Distress migration increases people's exposure to infection, and limits their access to health care. Displaced persons or people who are not settled in one place, may not have any access to health facilities. The trauma associated with loss of home and livelihood, bereavement, torture, rape, terrorisation or political harassment, may result in problems which affect the emotional well-being of victims for many years. (See **6**.3.4.2.b Psycho-social aspects of armed conflict; and **5**.4.9 Mental and emotional well-being.)

Emergency health interventions must take a broad and long-term perspective, within the principles of primary health care (PHC). The role of women in managing the health care of themselves, their households, and their communities is crucial, but often overlooked in designing relief programmes. Similarly, emergency health care programmes often fail to take into account the health needs of women, especially their reproductive health needs.

Standard protocols have been established to handle health interventions in relief programmes. Although each emergency has its own particular features, which a thorough and sensitive assessment will identify, many of the protocols are universally applicable. Health care interventions should concentrate on the common conditions, not invest resources or plan for diseases which are rare or unlikely.

This section and section 6 on Environmental health and physical infrastructure cover the technical issues relating to assessment of an emergency, as well as the specific interventions necessary to ensure the maintenance of good public health in the longer term. The main focus is on the needs of people in concentrated settlements or camps, most of whom are generally women and children. Throughout, cross-reference should be made to Chapter 1 Oxfam's approach to development and relief, Chapter 2 Focusing on people, and Chapter 5 Health.

6

5.2 Background

In any emergency programme in which it is involved, Oxfam is committed to reviewing all aspects of public and environmental health, to ensure that these are adequately addressed in relief interventions. Health and nutrition needs should thus be included in both the general and the technical assessments of an emergency. (See **6**.4 Assessment, co-ordination and consultation in emergencies.) Basic demographic and health information may already be available, and should be disaggregated by sex and age. Additional details may be sought from government offices, UN organisations, NGOs familiar with the area, or local health practitioners. Trained or informal community health workers within the affected population are also vital sources of information and support.

The principal PHC interventions in acute emergencies are:

- measles immunisation
- management of diarrhoea and dehydration
- vitamin A supplementation
- management of acute respiratory infections (ARI)
- setting up a health information system.

Public and environmental health care in emergency relief programmes covers:

- water supplies
- sanitation
- waste disposal
- vector control
- hygiene and health education
- training and support for health workers
- shelter
- food supply and nutrition
- immunisation and preventive health
- basic curative services.

These are all interdependent. However, some areas may be overlooked or neglected, if several agencies are involved. Oxfam prefers to strengthen local capacity to implement emergency relief programmes, rather than take operational responsibility for this work. However, where Oxfam undertakes the provision of water supplies, its policy is to deploy an emergency health worker to review and recommend action on other aspects of public health. A summary of Oxfam's policy in emergencies is given as Appendix V.

5.3 Assessment
(To be read in conjunction with 1.4 Formal methods of information-gathering and appraisal.)

5.3.1 General assessment

It can be useful to distinguish between sudden-onset and slow-onset emergencies in assessing health needs. (See 6.2.1 Crises, disasters, and emergencies.) Oxfam's major contribution to health-related emergency work is in programmes associated with slow-onset emergencies and those of long duration. However, an emergency which begins as 'sudden-onset' may give rise to the same results as those of 'slow-onset', especially if the people affected are already vulnerable, or do not receive relief assistance in time.

A thorough review of health and nutrition needs is integral to deciding on an appropriate relief response, and must be part of the overall assessment of an emergency.

5.3.2 Assessment of sudden-onset emergencies

Sudden-onset emergencies may result in a high number of deaths. For example, earthquakes, bombardment, or cyclonic floods may cause many casualties, and there may be severely injured people requiring emergency surgery. Communicable diseases or food scarcity are not usually a concern in the short term. As time goes on, however, disrupted food supplies may become a problem, as may water and sanitation. In the case of floods, typhoons, or volcanic eruptions, current food stores as well as growing crops may be irretrievably lost.

The detailed assessment should include the following:

- identification of risks to health which would occur in normal circumstances; and explicit identification of the further risks to life or health which arise from the specific event, such as polluted water supplies, exposed power cables, or landmines;
- identification of surviving health resources (formal and informal) including personnel, buildings and equipment, drugs and materials, transport and communications systems, and related organisations; there may be a need for rehabilitation or reconstruction of infrastructure as part of the relief phase;
- projected requirements, immediate and medium-term, including food and medical supplies, with types and quantities specified; lead times should be considered when ordering supplies, and the fact that needs might change quite rapidly; 'time-marking', whereby the relief goods are requested along with an indication of the maximum and minimum delivery timetable, is a useful procedure.

5.3.3 Assessment of slow-onset emergencies

Basic background information is essential and should already be available within the Oxfam office covering the country, as well as from government departments, UN agencies, NGOs or local organisations in the area. The detailed assessment should include:

a. Demographic information

The total population, to be used as the denominator for estimating mortality, malnutrition, morbidity rates and total relief needs. This figure must be disaggregated by age and sex to allow for accurate identification of needs as well as specific programmes or provision of services, such as immunisation of children, supplementary feeding for pregnant and breastfeeding women, adequate sanitation facilities, and so on. It may also be appropriate to include information about ethnic identity of the population group, where discrimination along racial or cultural lines is a significant issue.

b. Health information

The health status, health service capacity, and emergency response programmes already under way. It is important to identify and describe the normal context compared with the current situation. The identification and quantification of the causes of death, and the prevalence of major causes of morbidity, will establish a baseline for comparison over time. It will also suggest indicators for monitoring progress, and evaluating health interventions.

Formal and informal structures and programmes in place before the emergency should be noted, particularly PHC activities such as immunisation, supply of essential drugs, and diarrhoea control. Information on the existence and coverage of such programmes will inform the health status assessment, and also indicate types of resources and skills available locally, as well as within the affected population.

The assessment should include relevant details of emergency health interventions already under way and the health agency responsible, for instance the Ministry of Health, UN agency, national NGO, national Red Cross or Red Crescent Society, or international NGO. The type of agency, its level of involvement, and details of co-ordination between agencies is essential to complete the picture, and ensure that gaps in provision are not overlooked.

c. Nutrition

Nutrition assessment is concerned not only with the nutritional status of the individual, household or community, but also with the processes leading to food shortage and malnutrition (including presence of infections and levels of health care), and the capacity of the affected population to recover from crises. Assessment must therefore include socio-economic, agricultural, anthropological, epidemiological, and political as well as anthropometric (human body measurements) variables. These help to identify causes and effects, and the responses of women, men and children within the affected population to adapt to pressures on food supplies.

Nutrition surveys establish the magnitude of the problem at the outset and provide a baseline for subsequent and comparative nutritional surveillance. The design of the survey is crucial to its validity and hence usefulness, so advice should be sought from a qualified statistician at the planning stage. Poor or inappropriate survey techniques produce inaccurate figures. The methodology chosen should reflect the opportunities for training, as well as the capacity to analyse results locally and make appropriate comparisons. A standard methodology must be used which is familiar to local health workers and relief institutions, or which can be readily taught. Unless numbers are very small, random sample surveys, using cluster sampling methods, are recommended.

An inadequate diet and/or infection may lead to weight loss. A child suffering weight loss becomes thin or wasted. This is known as acute malnutrition, and is reflected by the nutrition indices weight for height/length (WFH/L) and mid-upper arm circumference (MUAC).

Weight for height is the most common nutrition index used in emergency nutrition surveys. An individual's height and weight are compared with those of the reference population by calculating percentage weight for height/length (%WFH/L). This is the child's weight expressed as a percentage of the average weight of children of the same height or length.

An individual child's weight and height measurements may also be expressed as 'Z scores' or 'standard deviation' scores. These are statistically more accurate than percentages of the median, but are difficult to calculate in the field, and less easy to teach and to understand.

Mid-upper arm circumference (MUAC) is a quicker technique than WFH/L, and useful for rapid screening of children for nutritional rehabilitation programmes.

Whatever the index used, malnutrition is classified in three categories: adequately nourished, moderately malnourished, and severely malnourished. The different indices have cut-off points for defining malnutrition according to these categories:

Adequately nourished	>79.0%	WFH/L
	>-1.9	Z score
	>13.4cm	MUAC
Moderately malnourished	70% to 79%	WFH/L
	<-2 to >-2.9	Z score
	<13.4 to >12.4	MUAC
Severely malnourished	<70%	WFH/L
	<-3.0	Z score
	<12.5	MUAC

6

The results of MUAC and WFH/L surveys are not comparable, and MUAC tends to give larger estimates of the percentage malnourished than does WFH/L. Figures should not be used or quoted without reference to the *sampling method* and the *nutrition index* used. For more detail see *Food Scarcity and Famine: Assessment and Response, Oxfam Practical Health Guide No.7.* (See Resources Section.)

Malnutrition rates obtained from anthropometric surveys are useful indicators of general health and nutrition status. In camp settlements, they also help to identify at-risk groups who need to be included in supplementary feeding programmes. Figures should not be assessed in isolation, but used alongside other data such as mortality rates and incidence of infection. Comparisons with other situations are possible only if the same methods and measurements have been used. Information about the general context and other signs of nutritional stress — such as distress sales, relative market prices of meat and food staples — is essential to the accurate interpretation of anthropometric survey results.

5.4 Practical approaches

5.4.1 Response to sudden-onset emergencies

a. Search and rescue

After sudden-onset natural disasters, the search and rescue phase may last for several days. Most survivors are rescued by neighbours, family and friends; or by local first-aid teams, civil defence or military personnel. Foreign teams, sent out at great cost and often without knowledge of local conditions and language, save only a very small number of people in comparison.

Oxfam does not maintain or deploy international search and rescue teams, focusing instead on the relief and rehabilitation phases of such emergencies.

b. Management of immediate casualties

When there are mass casualties, the planning of effective triage is the most important element in achieving the best outcome for the most people. (Triage is defined by UNHCR as 'the selection and classification of the sick and wounded patients for attention in the face of overwhelming needs and insufficient resources'.) The aim is to provide priority assistance to those most likely to benefit.

Classification is usually by three categories 'those who cannot benefit from the treatment under emergency conditions and are therefore not treated; the seriously ill or injured, who should be attended to first; and those who, after initial first aid, can wait for medical attention until after the second category'. (UNHCR *Handbook for Emergencies.*)

Oxfam has little experience of this type of work, but has assisted other agencies in mounting programmes. In wars and armed conflicts, the ICRC is the most experienced agency. The national Red Cross and Red Crescent Societies, as well as Médecins sans Frontières, work in many types of emergency, though their experience in the specific type of emergency may be limited.

Most of the immediate medical and surgical care in sudden-onset emergencies will be provided by local services. By the time outside teams arrive on the scene, the search and rescue phase is usually over.

c. Shelter

Adequate shelter is essential to protect people's health, especially against acute respiratory infections which can quickly kill very young and elderly people. Emergency and temporary shelters are discussed elsewhere in this chapter. (See **6**.6.2.3 Temporary shelter.)

d. Communicable disease control

The most serious problems are related to water and sanitation, whether from damage to existing systems or lack of provision. Contamination may arise where bodies and carcasses have not been disposed of or safely buried. The priorities are provision of adequate safe water, and organisation of excreta disposal, together with related health-promotion activities. Health education may be especially important where unfamiliar systems are introduced, for instance, to people who have previously lived in isolated homesteads and have no experience of the collective water and sanitation arrangements which are necessary when large numbers live closely together.

Water and sanitation-related diseases are most likely to be the 'simple' diarrhoeas. There are few instances where epidemics of cholera and typhoid occur in association with an emergency. When they do occur, such epidemics are considered emergencies in themselves. Management of diarrhoeal diseases, including cholera, involves swift action to reduce transmission, particularly environmental health interventions, as well as organisational measures. Prompt treatment by oral rehydration therapy (ORT) is required, for which training may be necessary, along with community and individual hygiene education. The maintenance of adequate supplies for these interventions is also essential. (See **6**.8.3 Relief supplies and logistics.)

e. Food

This is likely to involve planning food supplies to maintain nutrition, rather than emergency programmes to treat malnutrition, a distinction

6

that is not always made. There may be a need for cooking pots and utensils, and water containers. In some situations, there is an immediate need for cooked food, which can be provided by local people, if given financial assistance. For instance, Oxfam assisted in distributing locally-cooked *chapatis* among people marooned by floods in Bangladesh. Local foods, when available, are always preferable. Biscuits (high-energy or high-protein) may be distributed, but their use should be reserved for malnourished children in supervised feeding programmes. (See **6.7.4** Food supplies and distribution.)

5.4.2 Response to slow-onset and 'chronic' emergencies

a. Non-displaced people

Famines in Africa during the mid-1980s elicited little response from the international community until large numbers of people were driven from their homes in search of food. Following this, NGOs have become increasingly involved in programmes attempting to prevent the 'distress migration' which frequently leads to camps of destitute, displaced persons depending entirely on relief. Such camps, crowded, often without adequate shelter or food supply, create their own severe health problems; and every effort must be made to avoid the need for them.

When information about an incipient food crisis is received, an assessment may result in recommending measures designed to help people survive the crisis without leaving home. These may include food aid, food-for-work or cash-for-work programmes. Oxfam may assist with distribution, monitoring or administration. In such circumstances, people are not entirely destitute. Food aid is not designed to supply a complete household 'food basket', but to supplement a shortfall, and prevent the need to sell assets such as animals, land, and valuables. One of the problems with such preventive food programmes is deciding when to stop, since there is no natural cut-off point such as that which may occur when a camp disperses and the refugees or displaced return home.

Many food aid programmes do not include an obvious health and nutrition component. However, there have been cases when they included, or even concentrated on, setting up nutritional surveillance to monitor people's access to food and the risks to health caused by the changing situation. Such information helps to identify people in need, and vulnerable areas. It can be used at government and international level to guide policy on resource allocation. It may also be used to identify appropriate interventions, for example, free food, supplementary food, food-for-work programmes, vitamin A distribution, provision of water and sanitation, and strengthening of health services. Interventions may be highly selective: for example there has been some success with vitamin A distribution, and supplementing basic cereal rations with dry porridge mixes for vulnerable groups.

The lack of an adequate basic health service to deal with health crises arising from food-related emergencies may be a major cause of excess mortality rates in some famine situations. Health interventions, such as extended programmes of immunisation, should be promoted within a context of efforts to strengthen existing PHC services.

b. Refugees and displaced persons

The essential elements of a relief programme for dependent, famine-affected people who have no alternative sources of support are: food, water supply and sanitation facilities, and basic health education and referral services.

5.4.3 Food

(See 6.7 Food security, food aid, and food distribution in emergencies.)

a. General rations

The minimum daily calorie requirement per person established by international agreement is 1,950 kilocalories. This figure is calculated as an overall average, and so does not reflect the extra needs arising from previous nutritional status, from cold weather or strenuous physical activity. Neither does it cover the needs of women who are pregnant or breast-feeding, for extra calories.

Over the longer term, the human body also needs basic amounts of protein, and micronutrients (vitamins and minerals). It has been calculated that the daily requirement of iron in women of child-bearing age may be as much as three times higher than that of men. Iron deficiency results in anaemia which, in turn, gives rise to fatigue and susceptibility to disease. Pregnant and breast-feeding women are at special risk of problems arising from deficiencies in iron, calcium, iodine, and vitamin C.

Rations are usually provided in the form of cereals. Other components of an adequate diet, such as oil and beans, are sometimes more difficult to obtain, and may only be included in the ration after intensive lobbying. Provision of the general ration is usually the responsibility of the government, in co-operation with multilateral or bilateral donors.

NGOs are often involved in food-distribution programmes. The method of distribution is usually a 'dry' ration, where the refugees take the ration home and prepare the food as they wish. This method requires that cooking pots, fuel, and utensils have been previously distributed; and that the food is in a form which can be cooked. Where individual household facilities are not available, cooking may be

6

collectively organised, and cooked food or 'wet' rations are then distributed. This is extremely time-consuming and often unpopular with recipients. In some cases, a combination of the two methods is used: for example, Salvadoran refugees in Honduras organised the preparation of major staples (maize *tortillas* and beans) collectively as a means of economising on fuel, and relieving women from some aspects of domestic drudgery. Other foods were prepared by individual women for their own household.

b. Supplementary foods

These usually consist of processed foods of high caloric and protein value, such as corn-soya milk (CCSM), 'Unimix', or locally prepared mixes such as *faffa* in Ethiopia or *Incaparina* in Central America. They are used:

* to rehabilitate malnourished people;
* where the general ration does not provide a balanced diet or consists of food which may be unsuitable for some groups e.g. unmilled or crudely milled cereal for children of weaning age. In such cases, supplementary rations are provided to selected groups, usually under-fives, pregnant and breast-feeding women, the elderly, and the sick.

Supplementary foods are given in addition to an adequate general ration. Otherwise, where large numbers of people are malnourished and resources inadequate, supplementary rations will not be sufficient to prevent widespread death. If such a situation arises, pressure for an adequate general ration must go hand in hand with supplementary feeding programmes. Where high levels of malnutrition are recorded, supplementary feeding is *essential,* as malnourished people will not recover on the general ration alone.

Supplementary feeding programmes need clearly defined objectives to avoid becoming institutionalised. For example, In Bangladesh in 1984, Oxfam funded a supplementary feeding programme for about twenty malnourished children within a fishing community. The programme was organised by women and ran for two months, which was sufficient to ensure that the children's condition did not deteriorate below the level from which they could be expected to recover.

c. Therapeutic feeding

This is for the severely malnourished (<70% WFH/L with or without kwashiorkor), and consists of frequent feeds, usually of high-energy milk. Many patients who need therapeutic feeding also have other health problems, including anaemia and vitamin deficiency diseases (xerophthalmia, scurvy, pellagra). Medical care must be integral to such feeding programmes.

Therapeutic feeding is expensive in staff time and may divert resources from other important interventions. Where only a small number of people are severely malnourished, it may be possible for such cases to be managed at the local referral health facility.

5.4.4 Gender considerations in food distribution

Major problems associated with the effective distribution of food relate to gender relations and inequalities. Although many male refugees are malnourished, the incidence of malnutrition is far higher among women. Decisions about food distribution are often made by host governments and international agencies, at best in consultation with male camp or community 'leaders' or assumed heads of household. Many households are maintained by women; and men generally hold little or no responsibility within the household for the processing and preparation of food, and may have only limited knowledge or understanding of what it entails. In many cultures, the best and largest portions of food are given to men and boys within the household, while women and girls have less to eat.

While women are responsible for preparing and cooking the food within the household, their own low status in the hierarchy of intra-household food distribution means that often they are not receiving the full adult ration, much less the additional food, minerals, and vitamins they need during pregnancy and breast-feeding. Children, especially girls, may also not be receiving their fair ration.

It is not uncommon for food distributed through male networks to be diverted onto the parallel market or to support armed fighters. Food, like any other resource, can also be used to blackmail or exert control over those who depend on it.

Pregnant and breast-feeding women have additional food needs. (See 5.4.2.5.b Encouragement of breast-feeding and good weaning practices.) Women who are themselves malnourished may fear that they cannot produce enough milk — in cases of severe stress, they may stop lactating — and turn to free milk powder as a substitute. Where women do not have access to sterile water for mixing the powder, or for cleaning containers, or do not fully understand the quantities required, this can result in an increase in infant diarrhoea and associated problems. It is usually preferable in such circumstances for the mother to drink the milk, and continue to breast-feed her child.

It is vital for women to be actively involved in decisions about food programmes and, preferably, in controlling the actual distribution of rations. The specific monitoring of the nutritional status of women and children should form part of health surveillance. Where possible, this should be done by women health workers, ideally from among the

6

affected population. Persistent problems in ensuring the fair distribution of adequate food can thus be detected more comprehensively, and steps taken to address them.

5.4.5 Water supply and excreta disposal

A water supply of sufficient quantity and quality is essential to good health. (See **6**.6.3 Water.) Health promotion and education relating to water is often a neglected area. Yet however good the quality of the water at source, it will become contaminated if no suitable containers are available, if the containers are not kept clean, or if personal hygiene is not observed.

Where people live in concentrated settlements or crowded conditions, safe disposal of excreta becomes crucial. However, defaecation areas are often assigned, pits dug, and superstructures built, but the latrines are left unused. They may become health hazards in themselves if they are not cleaned and regularly emptied, if education in their use is neglected, and responsibility for maintenance left unclear. These tasks are unpopular and unglamorous, but of great importance for public health, especially in a large settlement. (See **5**.4.3.6 Sanitation.)

Sanitation provision and refuse disposal must involve gender, social, and cultural considerations. Chores relating to water management (water collection and washing) are largely the responsibility of women and girls. However, decisions about supply systems are often made by male agency workers, in consultation with men in the affected population. The UNHCR recognises this as a major problem and recommends that women should be specifically consulted about water supply systems and pumps, before installation. Women should also be trained in maintenance and repair tasks, which are more likely to be seen as a priority by them.

Sanitation facilities must be based on the needs of the user population. In most cases, women form the large majority in the adult population in refugee camps. Their domestic and childcare responsibilities may make it inconvenient for them to have to walk long distances to latrines, showers or laundry areas. Women's needs in relation to menstruation are usually overlooked. They need to be sensitively discussed with women, and adequately taken into account in designing sanitation provision for them. This may entail ensuring the provision of appropriate privacy and washing facilities, as well as extra cloth, paper or towels.

5.4.6 Health services

In the acute, early phase of an emergency, it may be necessary to place emphasis on nutrition and specific public health interventions. However, the essential components of PHC programmes, especially preventive care and health education, should be incorporated as early as possible.

Women and children are particularly vulnerable in emergencies. The special nutritional needs of pregnant and breast-feeding women, as well as children, have been referred to above. Given their responsibility for collecting and storing water, women are also particularly prone to water-borne diseases and to infection transmitted by insects which breed or feed near water, such as malaria, river blindness, dysentery, and infectious hepatitis. Their closer involvement with dealing with their children's excreta also exposes women to diarrhoeal disease. Ante-natal, birth planning and gynaecological services, as well as information about sexually transmitted diseases, including HIV, are essential for women. These issues should not be overlooked, especially since avoidable complications in pregnancy and childbirth are a leading cause of death among women of childbearing age.

Where refugees or displaced persons have suffered physical mutilation, they may require special attention, such as orthopaedic treatment. People may suffer emotional as well as physical trauma as a result of an emergency: bereavement, torture, rape, and deliberate terrorisation are widespread, but also very personal, experiences which affect the health and well-being of communities and individuals. The extent and depth of adjustments which people are forced to make may be potential sources of distress or depression.

Mental health should be taken into consideration in the planning and implementation of health services for refugees and displaced persons. Professional counselling may be an important component of health services, with special attention to the needs of children as well as adults who have been involved in, or forced to witness, acts of extreme violence. (See 5.4.9 Mental and emotional well-being; and 6.3.4.2.b Psycho-social aspects of armed conflict.)

Inappropriate or inaccessible health services are obstacles to good health. Every step needs to be taken to ensure that adequate consultation with the women and men who will be using them takes place during the programme design stage. Monitoring of the use of services will enable health workers to detect gaps in coverage and take steps to deal with them. For example, women may be reluctant — or forbidden — to be treated by male health workers, and so not make use of the facilities theoretically available to them. It may be necessary to recruit additional female health-personnel to ensure that women are effectively provided with health care.

6

Often, there are trained community health workers within the affected population. Health services should identify and support these people, and draw on their existing skills. The UNHCR recommends that at least 50 per cent of new trainees should be women, even if this means overcoming initial obstacles, such as offering protection when going to and from work, or negotiating agreement with male relatives where women are in seclusion. Female health workers should be actively sought for clinical services aimed at women, especially antenatal and birth care. If necessary, additional training in literacy and organisational skills may be required to enable them to take on these roles.

In dealing with refugees, UNHCR's standard operational practice is to begin training community health workers from as soon as one month after commencing the programme.

In all UNHCR-funded health programmes...education and training of refugee health workers are standard requirements included in formal inter-agency agreements, with government and NGO implementing partners. (From the conclusion of the 39th Session of Executive Committee of UNHCR in 1989 on refugee women.)

The target is set at one health worker per 200 families. In a number of programmes, most of the health workers (including midwives) are women. This approach is seen as a major means of ensuring that health services are made genuinely accessible to women among the affected population; and that continuity is ensured beyond the acute emergency phase.

5.4.7 Primary health interventions

a. Measles immunisation
Measles can be a major killer, particularly in association with malnutrition. An epidemic in a crowded camp with many at-risk children can be devastating. Immunisation against measles should always be undertaken as an emergency measure, as it is one of the few genuinely life-saving interventions available. To prevent an epidemic, extremely high coverage rates (over 95 per cent) need to be achieved and maintained. Immunisation against the other five common infectious diseases (tuberculosis, polio, diphtheria, whooping cough, tetanus) are not emergency measures, but should be included as soon as the priority interventions have been implemented. (See 5.4.4 Immunisation.)

b. Management of diarrhoea and dehydration
The prevention and prompt management of dehydration by

administering oral rehydration solution saves lives. Although the treatment is cheap and simple, it can be difficult to convince health workers and carers of the efficacy and importance of the treatment. When health workers are not themselves convinced, they may offer treatment with inappropriate antibiotics or anti-diarrhoea mixtures.

c. Vitamin A supplementation
Vitamin A deficiency is associated with increased incidence, severity, and duration of measles, diarrhoea, and respiratory infections. In populations living in crowded, insanitary conditions, the distribution of vitamin A supplements to all children under five is a major priority.

d. Management of acute respiratory infections (ARIs)
A simple protocol should be worked out for health workers to enable them to diagnose and effectively treat respiratory infections — though it makes sense to institute such measures only if a regular supply of standard antibiotics is ensured. Training and instruction will be necessary to ensure that protocols are followed. Health education should include information on how to recognise signs of ARIs in young children.

e. A basic health-information system
This must be an integral part of the health care provided in any camp settlement and should be instituted as early as possible. Record-keeping and surveillance should be part of the daily tasks of the health workers. Maintaining adequate data should not take up much time as long as only the most important information is collected, and a consistent standardised system is used.

5.5 Health and nutrition surveillance

The initial emergency assessment provides the basis for decision-making, but it is equally important to set up a system for collecting simple data regularly, once the relief programme is under way. Every emergency is a rapidly changing situation. Hence reliable data are needed to ensure that the programme is managed appropriately, to alert workers to problems as they arise, and to procure adequate supplies. Only by providing such data is it possible to persuade donors of new or changing needs. Information on population, mortality, morbidity, nutrition, health sector activities, and general living conditions, should be collected systematically.

6

909

5.5.1 Population data

Data should include numbers of newcomers and those leaving, *counted and categorised by age and sex*, and if appropriate and feasible, by other variables such as clan, language, religion, and ethnic group. Births may need to be recorded separately, through the maternal and child health (MCH) services.

5.5.2 Mortality data

Data should include crude mortality rate (number of all deaths as a percentage of the total population over a given period of time) and under-five mortality rates (number of deaths in under-fives as a percentage of the total number of under-fives over given period of time). Deaths at health centres will not give a complete figure. Community representatives, religious leaders or community health workers may know about deaths which have taken place in homes and shelters. In some cases, grave-watchers have been employed as the only way to get complete information. They have to be given a 24-hour rota, and be closely supervised and trained to identify five main causes of death.

Accurate mortality data are important because they provide basic information about the health of the people in the camp. For example, a daily crude mortality rate of 0.5 per 10,000 is considered normal for developing countries. An emergency which is under control should have a crude mortality rate of less than 1 per 10,000 per day. Anything above this indicates a serious situation. A mortality rate of more than 5 per 10,000 per day would be a major catastrophe.

5.5.3 Morbidity data (cases of disease)

The most important diseases to record are communicable diseases and nutrition-related conditions. These include: diarrhoea, ARIs, measles, malaria, meningitis, hepatitis, protein-energy malnutrition, vitamin A deficiency, and other specific deficiencies, such as scurvy and pellagra. Initially, the figures need to be broken down only for under-fives and over-fives. Later, it may be useful to record attendance of specific groups, such as women, so that coverage and access can be improved if found to be inadequate.

5.5.4 Nutrition data

All newcomers between one and five years should be screened by MUAC, and referred to nutritional rehabilitation if their arm circumference is below a specified minimum. This is usually set as less than 13.5cm (in some extreme situations this has been set at 12.5cm). Ideally, children qualifying for feeding according to MUAC should subsequently be assessed by weight-for-height or length. This is not always possible. For example, children may be admitted according to MUAC only, because the proportion of severely malnourished is high, intervention is urgently required, and the operating period is not secure. Once feeding programmes have been established, coverage and effectiveness should be monitored through routine information on numbers of admissions, discharges, referrals, and deaths.

Surveillance of nutritional status in the relief phase, is usually through random sample nutrition surveys carried out every three months among the whole population. Professional help should be sought for survey design and sampling method.

5.5.5 Data on health sector activities

Data should include information at regular intervals on health-related activities including:

- coverage
- immunisation
- numbers of out-patient attendances and in-patient bed occupancy
- numbers of water points established
- latrines built and functioning
- numbers attending health-related training courses
- attendance at antenatal and reproductive health care services
- oral rehydration centres and feeding centres.

The data should be used to investigate gaps or inadequacies in health service provision, and be analysed alongside other information, especially morbidity and mortality data.

5.5.6 Data on general living conditions

Information on food available in the general ration, and the camp distribution system, should be gathered, as well as distribution at household level and use of available food products.

Information should be routinely collected on the availability of fuel for cooking and possibly heating, as well as that of material for shelters. The construction and spacing of shelters should be monitored. Crowding is often a problem in camps, but good planning can mitigate the serious risks of fire and increased transmission rates of communicable disease. Intense crowding will also increase the risk of domestic accidents, particularly burns in children. Male violence against

6

women and children, alcoholism, and psychological stress may be heightened when conditions are very cramped.

Information on water, sanitation, and refuse disposal is important in monitoring public health. In addition, opportunities for vector control should be investigated and appropriate measures implemented and monitored. Special campaigns may be required to deal with problems of lice infestation or rampant scabies. Knowledge of the local environment and ecology must inform such interventions, and their effectiveness must be continually monitored. Careful monitoring can also identify specific risks, such as areas where mosquitoes might breed, or the symptoms of trypanosomiasis.

5.6 Training programmes

Training at all levels is a crucial component of health and nutrition work in emergencies. Disaster-preparedness workshops are held periodically for Oxfam staff. These usually include the principles of health and nutrition interventions in emergencies, and information about the support resources available.

Most relief programmes suffer from a shortage of trained personnel. Technical staff recruited for operational programmes should seek or create formal and informal opportunities for sharing their skills and expertise with local counterpart organisations, and with women and men from the affected population. It is important that trainees will be able to use what they have learned. For example, it would clearly be inappropriate to train inexperienced or male health workers in midwifery skills which they are unlikely to put into practice.

It may be appropriate to consider offering training activities within government ministries. More commonly, however, the immediate priorities are to train health workers for community or clinic work, teach nutritional surveillance techniques, or give instruction in consistent and accurate mixing of supplementary food ingredients. Methods — participatory, directive, on-the-job — should be appropriate to the stated objectives and to the needs of the trainees. Where health workers are semi-literate or illiterate, or where their knowledge of the national language is limited, teaching materials and methodologies need to be adapted accordingly. (See 3.1.2 Education and Training; and 5.4.11 Health education and health promotion.)

Although the type and length of training will be dictated by the needs of the particular emergency situation, it should fit wherever possible with the national curricula for health workers, especially since many emergency situations turn out to be very long-term.

5.7 Key questions

1 At what chronological stage is the emergency? In the case of displaced persons or refugees in fixed settlements, has registration been completed, with data disaggregated by sex and age? What is the approximate number of men, women and children affected?

2 If an epidemiological assessment been conducted, by whom was this done (health authorities, trained health workers, camp officials) and what conclusions were drawn? What are currently the main causes of death and illness among the affected population?

3 What is the nutritional status of the women, men and children? Are the existing or proposed interventions addressing their priority needs? What are the specific needs of vulnerable groups — elderly and disabled people, children, women of child-bearing age — and how are these being addressed?

4 How has health planning drawn on local capacity, including health workers from the affected population? How have gender-differentiated needs been addressed in the services to be provided and in the selection of health workers (both expatriate and local)? What arrangements have been made for training of local health personnel?

5 What extra resources are required for health and nutrition programmes — technical expertise, equipment, food aid? Have sources for these been identified?

6

6 Environmental health and physical infrastructure

6.1 Introduction 914
6.2 Settlements, housing, and shelter 915
    6.2.1 Settlements 915
    6.2.2 Housing 915
    6.2.3 Temporary shelter 916
    6.2.4 Food storage facilities 917
    6.2.5 Housing reconstruction 918
6.3 Water 919
    6.3.1 Assessment of water needs 919
    6.3.2 Priorities for the improvement of water supplies 920
    6.3.3 Testing and disinfection of water 921
6.4 Sanitation 923
    6.4.1 The dangers of faecal contamination 923
    6.4.2 Social issues in sanitation 924
    6.4.3 Immediate interventions 924
    6.4.4 Latrines 925
    6.4.5 Public health and personal hygiene 926
6.5 Vector control 927
6.6 Key questions 929

6.1 Introduction

This section deals with the environmental health issues, and especially public infrastructure, associated with large human settlements following disasters, or in emergencies. When people are displaced from their own homes, they may not be permitted to choose the site where they are to stay, and may have little idea of when they will be able to return. Often, camps which were intended to provide only temporary refuge become people's homes for many years, or have to accommodate much larger populations than those for which they were planned. Settlements may be open, with people able to come and go as they please; or they may be under strict military surveillance, as concentration camps. As time goes

914

by, so the needs and expectations of the affected population change. Infrastructural arrangements for water supplies, sanitation, shelter, waste disposal, vector control, and hygiene, which were appropriate in the immediate term, may need to be substantially modified as the settlement becomes semi-permanent or as more people arrive.

In the case of emergencies which do not cause large-scale human displacement, but which bring about extensive damage to homes and public infrastructure, the problems are rather different. Nevertheless, the risks to environmental health are similar, and relief programmes must take these into account.

Oxfam's public health policy for emergencies represents a commitment to examining all aspects of public health when assessing overall needs and determining an appropriate response. The policy also states that a Public Health Adviser should be deployed with other technical staff, such as water or sanitation engineers, when assessing an emergency or implementing a water or sanitation component within a relief programme. (See **6** Appendix V Oxfam Policy in Emergencies.) This comprehensive approach aims to review all aspects of public health prior to determining Oxfam's specific input, and to ensure that there are no major gaps in provision.

This section should be read in conjunction with others in this chapter, in particular **6**.5 Health and nutrition in emergencies, and with reference to Chapter 1 Oxfam's approach to development and relief and Chapter 5 Health. While it includes a substantial amount of technical detail, practical interventions in these areas should be assessed by people with relevant technical and medical expertise, for which this general *Handbook* cannot substitute.

6.2 Settlements, housing, and shelter

6.2.1 Settlements

It is unusual for refugees or displaced people, or the NGOs assisting them, freely to choose settlement sites. There is invariably a range of constraints and conflicting priorities to be reconciled; and a compromise will have to be sought between the needs of the affected population, the sites available, and the concerns of the host government or relevant authorities.

Populations affected by emergencies, in particular refugees and internally displaced persons, have already faced considerable uncertainty and upheaval in their lives. They may have little idea how long their period of asylum will last; and are not always treated as welcome, either by the host government or by surrounding communities. The rapid establishment of suitable sites for settlement can help considerably in enhancing their own sense of security. However, unsatisfactory temporary arrangements can be very difficult to change once established.

Criteria for site selection include social, political, and physical factors. UNHCR recommends that:

...in addition to considerations specific to the refugees and their background, criteria should include water supply, topography and drainage, adequate surface area, security and protection, accessibility, environmental and soil conditions, vegetation and land rights. (UNHCR *Handbook for Emergencies*; see Resources Section.)

Consideration should be given to the cultural background and normal livelihoods of the affected population, and to their usual ways of life. The needs and expectations of, for example, pastoral people will differ from those of people from a large city, or from small fishing or farming communities.

6.2.2 Housing

Natural disasters such as earthquakes, floods or hurricanes often result in the widespread destruction of homes and public infrastructure. The people affected are usually reluctant to move away from their homes, and will start to salvage their household belongings as soon as they are able. Whenever possible, they will use materials from their destroyed houses to build makeshift shelters. Often, what is most urgently needed is roofing: galvanized sheets or plastic sheeting to provide shelter for people and their belongings. Weather conditions usually dictate what the most appropriate materials will be; and how urgently they are needed.

Oxfam frequently provides assistance in this type of crisis, usually channelling assistance through a local organisation or NGO. Often, materials can be purchased locally or regionally. Occasionally it is necessary to import them. In some cases, the best form of assistance may be to provide technical expertise to assist in the reconstruction phase, to introduce low-cost measures to improve the safety aspects of housing design. For example, following the earthquake in San Salvador in 1986, Oxfam sent in two Mexican experts with whom contact had been established following the 1985 earthquakes there.

6.2.3 Temporary shelter

While people rebuild their permanent housing, temporary shelters are needed. There is an increasing demand for these as a result of the growing numbers of refugees and displaced persons around the world.

Oxfam has developed a temporary shelter of which a stock is maintained at its UK-based Emergency Stores. The shelters, made of reinforced plastic sheeting, can house about ten people. They are approximately four times more economical than conventional tents of the same size. These multi-purpose shelters come in a kit and can be easily adapted for use as a cover or fly sheet; or can be adapted to water proof local shelters when people build to their own specifications, with locally available materials.

a. Tents
Tents are the main form of emergency shelter, stockpiled by donor countries and the governments of vulnerable regions (often with the national Red Cross or Red Crescent Society, or the military). Their usefulness is generally limited to the initial phase of a relief programme; and their evidently temporary nature reduces the risk of their becoming semi-permanent. However, they are costly, usually too small, and cannot be enlarged.

b. Plastic sheeting
Plastic sheeting can be used to provide shelters, stores, workshops, feeding centres, hospitals, and so on, as well as ground sheets and temporary cover for food stocks. Oxfam keeps a large quantity in its UK-based Emergency Stores; and Oxfam offices in vulnerable areas are encouraged to keep a stock, as part of their disaster preparedness. Details of an Oxfam booklet on the use of plastic sheeting are given in the Resources Section.

c. Commercial emergency housing
Many commercial companies produce 'emergency housing'. In most cases, the individual units are costly, difficult to transport to site, and generally not appropriate to local people's needs. Occasionally, such housing may be suitable for the use of relief teams.

6.2.4 Food storage facilities

When people are concentrated in camps or settlements, food storage facilities are always needed. The large 'Rubb-Hall' type of fabric-covered tubular frame shelters are strong, and can stand up to adverse conditions. They are quickly erected, but some technical supervision is needed. They are also suitable for use as temporary hospitals.

a. Grinding facilities
Food staples, such as maize, beans or other grains are frequently distributed in an unprocessed state. Refugees and displaced persons

6

917

may have no means of grinding these foodstuffs, and it is therefore essential to provide a large-scale grinding facility for collective use. The use and maintenance of such a facility requires proper supervision and relies on a degree of social organisation among the users.

6.2.5 Housing reconstruction

Disasters are most disruptive to the poor and vulnerable in society. At the same time, such people — whether subsistence farmers or shanty-town dwellers — usually expect and know how to build their own houses: relief agencies should not undermine their capacities by doing this for them.

Any housing reconstruction programme must take into account the particular needs of disadvantaged people. For example, a woman maintaining a household may not have the time available for reconstruction; widows, elderly, infirm or disabled people may also need additional help. In some cases, these needs might be addressed by providing a fund enabling such people to pay others to undertake the reconstruction work for them. Where the community or social group is reasonable cohesive, it may be possible to ensure that help is given on a voluntary basis.

Reconstruction programmes must involve women and men in the affected population and incorporate their own ideas and priorities as much as possible. This not only saves financial resources, but also supports people's own efforts to rebuild their lives. It also enables them to practise and test any new building techniques which may be introduced, as well as ensuring that any innovations suit their needs. Locally-available materials, whether natural or manufactured, are always preferable to imported materials. In the event of a future disaster, materials not destroyed will be re-used in subsequent reconstruction.

Training should be considered for people living in areas vulnerable to cyclones and earthquakes, since simple improvements in building methods can save lives and reduce the amount of physical destruction to housing. For example, courses on the use of ring beams, L-shaped steel bars, and other straightforward, relatively low-cost technical improvements to make houses more stable, can be incorporated in disaster mitigation programmes.

Any new building styles, techniques or materials used should be appropriate to the setting, and acceptable to the population. For example, galvanised or corrugated iron sheeting can be lethal in cyclone-prone areas: these sheets may be picked up by the wind, and scythe through anything in their path. Training must aim to be sustainable so that when it ceases, people will be both technically and financially able to continue. As far as possible, it should respect

918

traditional techniques and not conflict with existing methods and designs. (See **3**.1.2 Education and training.)

6.3 Water

(To be read in conjunction with **5**.4.3 Environmental and public health; and **6** Appendix VI Oxfam water supply scheme for emergencies.)

Water is an absolute need. A supply of sufficient clean, safe water is vital to people's health and well-being. When water and sanitation facilities break down, public health is immediately at serious risk. The availability of adequate water supplies is one of the essential criteria in determining sites for displaced persons or refugees.

The World Health Organisation (WHO) sets the following minimum standards for determining water needs:

- 3-5 litres per person per day for drinking and cooking;
- at least 15-20 litres per person per day for all needs, including drinking, cooking, personal hygiene and washing of clothes and cooking utensils.

Water and sanitation needs are inter-related: each has a significant bearing on the other, and together they are the most important single element in determining community and public health.

6.3.1 Assessment of water needs

There are a number of practical and social considerations to be addressed in assessing the water needs of a particular human settlement following an emergency. Where comprehensive registration of the population has not been undertaken, the assessment will initially have to be based on observation, approximation, and consultation.

Prior to committing any response, information will be required on:

- the number of people in the settlement or camp, and the quantity of water being used;
- the quality of the water being used; most importantly, evidence of contamination with human or animal faeces;
- accessibility of the water source.

The quality of the water can be visually assessed and biologically tested for contact with human and animal faeces. Any such contamination is potentially dangerous. In general, groundwater from below the surface, from wells and boreholes, is safe as long as no latrines are built within 30 metres of the water source. It is vital to check the water for salinity after flooding, and wells may have to be subsequently decontaminated or abandoned. Surface water is invariably contaminated in crowded camps. For biological testing, portable test kits are available, such as the Oxfam/Delagua kit. Alternatively, the services of a local laboratory might be used.

The nearer the water source is to the settlement or camp, the more water people are likely to use. Women generally collect and use water more than men do; and are also likely to be more restricted in their freedom of movement than men, either because of cultural constraints on them, or because of childcare and other domestic responsibilities. Thus accessibility of a safe water source is crucial. Clean water is often contaminated during collection, transportation, and storage, so that it is rendered unsafe for drinking. Carrying and storage containers may have to be provided, and the assessment should indicate this. Containers should be sensibly designed to allow people to hold them while simultaneously working the water pump.

Assessment of water supply requires not only a survey of the practical needs, but also discussion with representatives of the affected population about the provision of water. Women generally carry the principal responsibility for household water management and must, therefore, be thoroughly consulted and involved in planning. Women and men have different personal needs, as well as distinct responsibilities, with regard to water and sanitation. In addition, women are often subject to cultural constraints concerning personal hygiene requirements.

Social structures are threatened and often break down when people become displaced or refugees; and it may be some time before these are restored. In some cases, these structures are irretrievably lost or destroyed, especially where significant demographic distortions have occurred as a result of the emergency. Efforts should nevertheless be made at the earliest opportunity to encourage and enable women and men to give their advice, by whatever means are available, and be involved with the implementation of their water supplies and sanitation. Consultation with women about water and sanitation often needs to be undertaken separately from discussion with men, preferably by a woman relief worker.

6.3.2 Priorities for the improvement of water supplies

In emergencies, lives are at stake without a safe and reliable water supply. It is more important to provide more water, even of only moderate quality, than to limit the supply to a very small amount of high quality water. Immediate, relatively simple improvements are almost always necessary. It is better to start with a programme of incremental measures, than to design the optimum system and then lose time while it is being implemented.

The local water authority should be approached as a source of valuable information and resources. People in nearby settlements, particularly women, may also be able to identify water sources, such as springs and surface sources, in addition to wells and boreholes. Members of the affected population may also be technically skilled in water and sanitation: these people and new trainees should be actively involved as much as possible in the design, construction, operation and maintenance of the water system.

The main priorities are to identify an unpolluted water source, if possible; and to protect it from further contamination. Essentially, this means taking the water to the people rather than the people to the water. It is vital to keep people and animals as far as possible from sources to be used for drinking water; and protect wells from contamination from the surface. Every household should have a container for collecting water: plastic jerry cans should be provided if necessary. UNHCR provides 10 litre containers as standard provision in all its programmes.

If contaminated water must be used, the simplest form of minimum treatment is storage in tanks for at least six hours before distribution. If water has to be transported by tanker, it should not be distributed directly but should first be unloaded into a separate tank, and only then distributed. The most straightforward and rapidly deployed system may involve a flexible rubber 'pillow' tank, and a tapstand. Sedimentation using aluminium sulphate (alum), followed by chlorination with hypochlorite, can also be carried out in any tank, such as the Oxfam storage tanks. (See **6.6.3.3** Testing and disinfection of water.) If the water supply is to be chlorinated, this should be done in such a way as to achieve a chlorine residual in the domestic water container.

6.3.3 Testing and disinfection of water

Where people are crowded together, as in refugee camps, the risk of faecal contamination and hence the spread of infectious diseases, is much higher than in normal circumstances. Although groundwater is normally clean, all water should be regarded as potentially dangerous in such conditions. Regular quality-surveillance procedures must be established. The Oxfam/DelAgua Water Testing Kit provides an effective means of testing the most important quality parameter, faecal contamination. Drinking water must be treated if such contamination is found.

Water treatment can comprise any combination of sedimentation, filtration, and disinfection, depending on the chemical and biological quality of the raw water and the means available.

Sedimentation is used to settle suspended solid particles from cloudy or muddy water. Such solids often carry with them a large number of

921

micro-organisms, so that water that has been treated in this way is not only physically but also biologically cleaner. Turbidity or cloudiness makes disinfection more difficult, so that sedimentation is often a useful precursor to effective disinfection. Sedimentation is facilitated by the addition of aluminium sulphate (alum).

Slow-sand-filtration provides a very simple method of removal of both physical and biological impurities. However, it is not practical to consider filtration of water for very large numbers of people. Establishment of effective filtration requires at least two weeks, so that interim treatment measures may be needed. Oxfam's Treatment Pack can provide filtered water for 5,000-20,000 people.

Disinfection is used to purify water of any disease-transmitting micro-organisms. It can be either physical or chemical.

a. Physical disinfection

Boiling water for several minutes is effective in destroying most disease-transmitting micro-organisms. Whilst it is practicable at household level, boiling does not normally provide a workable method of disinfection on a large scale, because of the need for large amounts of fuel. It may be feasible to boil water in a feeding centre or hospital facility, where safe water is needed regularly.

Ultraviolet light: the sun's radiation provides some disinfection of clear water, but its effectiveness is significantly reduced when the water is turbid (cloudy) or contains particular chemical constituents. Storage of water for several hours in relatively shallow tanks that are open to the sun provides a useful first method of water treatment.

Neither of these methods can protect the water against further contamination, for example, by domestic containers.

b. Chemical disinfection

Chlorine is the most common chemical disinfectant. It is widely available at reasonable cost, acts rapidly and effectively, and can produce a residual to protect against further contamination. Chlorine is available in gaseous and liquid states as well as in the form of hypochlorite granules, powder, tablets, and liquid solution. All forms of chlorine require care in transport, handling, and storage; but the gas is particularly dangerous and is not suitable for emergency use.

The most convenient forms of chlorine compounds for emergency use are 'bleaching powder' (calcium hypochlorite); 'high test hypochlorite' in granules or tablets; slow release chlorine tablets (as used in swimming pools); and liquid laundry bleach (Javel). All require experimentation and testing to find the correct level of dosage, which should be chosen such as to leave a small residual level of chlorine in domestic water containers.

Iodine is also effective as a chemical disinfectant, but it requires high doses and is not effective with water that is turbid or highly coloured. Iodine is the active constituent in many 'personal' water sterilising tablets.

c. Mobile drinking-water units
Trailer-mounted drinking-water units, comprising motorised pumps, pressure filters, and chlorinators, are available in a range of sizes from 2,000 to 50,000 litres per hour. They produce good quality water. However, such units are expensive, need supplies of chemicals, and require expert personnel to operate them. Nevertheless, mobile units have proved valuable in sudden-impact disasters, especially in urban areas.

6.4 Sanitation

When water and sanitation facilities break down, public health is immediately at risk. The sanitary disposal of excreta may pose particular and urgent problems in two kinds of situation:

- when municipal sewerage systems or other arrangement are damaged or disrupted in urban areas; and
- when displaced persons or refugees are living in crowded conditions, whether in rural or urban areas.

Water and health facilities are seriously undermined by the insanitary disposal of excreta. If no sanitation facilities are provided, people will defaecate wherever they can around the camp or surrounding area. Often, time elapses before sanitation is addressed, either because expertise is not immediately available or because the provision of clean water and health facilities are wrongly seen as being of a higher priority. The affected population may have no previous experience of living in such large settlements, and be unfamiliar with the sanitation problems this raises. It is essential that temporary arrangements are made at the earliest opportunity to prevent the resulting public health hazards.

6.4.1 The dangers of faecal contamination

Dangerous infectious diseases are transmitted through human faeces which, if not isolated and treated, may contaminate water supplies. Uncovered excreta also provide a breeding ground for insects which act as disease transmitters, and attract rats and other vermin. Faecally-transmitted diseases include typhoid, cholera, bacillary and amoebic dysentery, infectious hepatitis, polio, bilharzia, roundworm, hookworm, miscellaneous diarrhoeas, and gastro-enteritis. Diarrhoea affects and debilitates adults and children alike. However, children are more likely to die of the resulting dehydration.

Human faeces are more dangerous than human urine or animal waste; and children's faeces are more dangerous than adults'. Sanitation systems must, therefore, be as appropriate for children as for adults.

6.4.2 Social issues in sanitation

The management of human excreta and waste always raises sensitivities relating to traditions, accepted behaviour or inhibitions, as well as cultural or religious beliefs and practices. There are invariably differences in the cultural constraints placed on women and men concerning personal hygiene and privacy. They also have distinct physical needs. For example, there are practical issues relating to menstruation which have to be considered in establishing appropriate sanitation facilities. Women and men may need private and segregated latrine and bathing facilities. It is often not culturally acceptable for women to wash either in public or in front of men. Women may require facilities which are adequately screened, so that they are not exposed to embarrassment or vulnerable to harassment or attack. Gender-differentiated needs are seldom understood by male relief or government officials, and may have to be raised by NGO aid workers.

Representatives of the affected population as well as local health or sanitation staff should assist in the planning of sanitation facilities. Initially, it may be difficult to identify any leadership within the population, and establish a coherent policy. Until the situation settles, local government officials, relief workers or camp organisers may play a more significant role in determining immediate needs.

As they arrive, people usually camp close to a water source. Consequently, this water often becomes the major source of infection because people often defaecate where they draw their water, bathe, wash their clothes, and water their animals. Alternatively, people may settle on quite scattered areas, in which case a zone-by-zone approach is needed to decide what sanitation and water facilities are suitable for each grouping.

6.4.3 Immediate interventions

a. Open-surface defaecation
The first priority is to designate an area for people to excrete — known as controlled surface defaecation. This requires careful management and supervision to keep pollution to a minimum. Men, women, and

particularly children must be encouraged to use these areas, and not defaecate near dwellings, or in or around water supplies.

The defaecation area must be situated down-wind from houses and shelters, and not in the path of any surface run-off during rain. It should be fenced, with cut-off ditches to protect it from flooding. In hot, dry climates, where sufficient space is available, open-surface defaecation may be adequate as a short-term measure, since the heat and sunlight eventually render the faeces harmless. However, if the ground is flooded or marshy, or there is a high water-table, the risks to public health are very high. Pending a proper latrine-contained system, simple raised platforms can be constructed so that people do not themselves become contaminated by excreta.

The area must be kept as clean as possible. Teams of people should be organised to remove all excreta on a regular basis, to avoid attracting rats and insects.

b. Trench defaecation

Open-surface defaecation can be much improved by digging shallow trenches into which people excrete directly. The advantages are that walkways can be kept free of excreta, and fresh faeces can be covered daily by a layer of clean soil. Proper management and supervision arrangements are needed as for open-surface defaecation.

6.4.4 Latrines

(To be read in conjunction with **5.4.3** Environmental and public health.)

In planning a longer-term sanitation programme, it is imperative to involve both men and women who can represent the affected population in discussing the most appropriate and culturally acceptable options.

Social factors to be considered include:

*   customary sanitation arrangements for men, women and children;
*   materials used for anal cleansing;
*   preferred defaecation position of men and women;
*   women's needs during menstruation;
*   need for privacy;
*   need to segregate the sexes;
*   cultural taboos or preferences;
*   social factors including likelihood of organised action to ensure proper use of proposed system;
*   constraints on siting of latrines, for example the freedom of movement of women and men around the settlement;
*   acceptability of collective or shared latrines.

6

925

The physical limitations imposed by the soil also have to be taken into consideration:

- pit latrines are difficult to excavate in rocky ground;
- sandy soil demands special measures to prevent side walls of latrines collapsing;
- impervious clay soils may exclude any system dependent upon seepage.

Soil conditions can vary over a short distance, and a thorough survey is necessary. Differences in soil conditions between dry and wet seasons must also be noted. Where the water table is high or flooding is likely, excreta must be contained using watertight or raised container systems, since simple dry systems may lead to contamination.

Cost, available materials, expertise, and timing have to be taken into account. The simpler the solution, the quicker and cheaper it is. The choice is usually between community (or shared) and family or household latrines. A household latrine is preferable, since maintenance and cleaning of a shared facility is always a problem. Families tend to look after their own latrines, and usually use them if they understand the benefits. The difficulty in keeping communal latrines clean often leads to a decline in their use.

Latrine systems fall into main two types:

a. Dry systems
- trench latrines
- pit latrines, including ventilated improved pit (VIP) latrines
- borehole latrine
- composting latrine.

b. Wet systems
- water-seal latrines
- aquaprivies
- Oxfam emergency sanitation units.

The advantages and disadvantages of various options are summarised in Table 5.2 in **5.**4.3.6 Sanitation. Detailed technical information can be found in the publications listed in the Resources Section. Information about the Oxfam Sanitation Unit is given in **6** Appendix VII.

6.4.5 Public health and personal hygiene

Personal, domestic, and general environmental hygiene are essential to protect public health. This entails:

- provision of appropriate facilities, soap and utensils for personal hygiene;

- hygienic handling of food;
- elimination of stagnant water, and safe disposal of waste water;
- collection and safe disposal of rubbish;
- dust control;
- health education campaigns to emphasise the importance of sanitation and hygiene;
- vector control.

Personal hygiene: needs for men and women are distinct and it is essential to consult both sexes about what is needed, and what is acceptable to them. Arrangements should be made to ensure that enough water is available for women to be able to wash themselves adequately, and in private. They may also need protected washing areas where they can wash rags or other materials used during menstruation, without fear of being observed or ostracised. Adequate provision needs also to be made at the latrines for the disposal of rags or towels used during menstruation. If latrines are being blocked by rags or other materials, then the provision of bags or other containers at all latrines used by women might be appropriate.

Waste or stagnant water: if waste water is not drained away into soakage pits, it causes a health risk. Waste water not only smells unpleasant but facilitates the spread of infection by providing breeding places for insects, especially mosquitoes.

If stagnant water cannot be removed quickly, it may be necessary to reduce risks to health by chlorinating the water, and spraying to prevent mosquitoes breeding.

Solid refuse and rubbish: The accumulation of refuse or rubbish in a camp can constitute a real health risk. Rodents and insects increase, creating an unpleasant and unhealthy environment. Rubbish should either be removed from the settlement to a safe place, or burned or buried within the camp. A system will need to be established and collection bins distributed. UNHCR recommends one container for every ten families.

Special collection facilities will also be needed when markets are established. It may be advisable to incinerate large amounts of solid waste. Incinerators, for which many designs are available, can be fabricated from corrugated iron sheets and iron bars.

6.5 Vector control

Emergencies often create environments favourable to the proliferation of disease-carrying insects and rodents. In addition to creating a health risk, these pests can also spoil or destroy large quantities of food.

Vector problems develop in densely crowded conditions, and when general environmental sanitation (disposal of excreta, rubbish and waste water) is inadequate. Local expertise should be sought to supplement surveys to establish the incidence of lice, fleas and ticks; and to determine the extent and location of rodent infestations.

Problems should be reviewed with representatives of the affected population to discuss the underlying causes and assess possible eradication measures. Education campaigns should be considered, covering the significant methods of vector control, including the elimination of possible breeding grounds; and ensuring that food is covered against flies. A range of interventions is available to deal with vectors, depending on the severity of infestation. Specific insecticides may be appropriate for mosquitoes, flies, lice, fleas, ticks, and bed bugs. In areas where plague or other arthropod-borne diseases are endemic, action must be taken to control the vectors carried by rats before any large-scale control of rodents is attempted. If this is not done, an epidemic of plague may be precipitated by fleas transferring from dead rats to humans.

Table 6.4 Vectors which may pose significant health risks

Vector	Health risks	Favourable environment
Flies	Eye infections (particularly among infants and children); diarrhoeal diseases	Exposed food; excreta; dead animals.
Mosquitoes	Malaria filariasis encephalitis Yellow fever, dengue	Stagnant water, especially in the periphery of inundated areas;pools and slow-moving water. Stored water in or around dwellings; accumulations of rainwater in old tins and other containers.
Mites	Scabies, Scrub typhus	Overcrowding and poor personal hygiene.
Lice	Epidemic typhus, relapsing fever	
Fleas	Plague (from infected rats), endemic typhus	
Ticks	Relapsing fever, spotted fever	
Rats	Rat bite fever,leptospirosis, salmonellosis	Inadequately protected food; exposed garbage; covered spaces.

(Adapted from UNHCR *Handbook for Emergencies*)

6.6 Key questions

1 What are the key infrastructural needs relating to environmental health in this particular emergency?
2 Is the water supply acceptable in terms of quantity, quality, and accessibility?
3 What domestic water containers for transport and storage are people using? If the water supply is being chlorinated, is there a residual of chlorine in domestic containers?
4 Is any agency taking account of sanitation needs? What efforts have been made to consult with women and men in the affected community, with a view to establishing defaecation zones?
5 Are existing latrines being used? Has consultation taken place to find out about people's perceived problems and preferences? Have steps been taken to design appropriate improved latrines, in consultation with women and men in the affected community?

7 Food security, food aid, and food distribution in emergencies

7.1 Introduction 930
7.2 Security and vulnerability: entitlements and assets 931
    7.2.1 Food production systems 933
    7.2.2 Post-crisis recovery of food production systems 934
7.3 Food aid in emergencies 936
    7.3.1 Types of food aid intervention 937
7.4 Food supplies and distribution 942
    7.4.1 Food supplies 942
    7.4.2 Distribution and monitoring 943
    7.4.3 Monitoring the sale of food aid 945
7.5 Key questions 946

7.1 Introduction

Oxfam believes that every human being has the right to adequate and affordable food; and that hunger and malnutrition are injustices that must be eradicated by every possible means. Oxfam therefore emphasises the need to support local and national efforts to promote food security, and to ensure that basic food is produced and distributed in ways that will meet the needs of poor and marginalised people, producers as well as consumers. Within the context of promoting livelihoods that are equitable and sustainable, Oxfam aims to address the underlying causes of food insecurity, and so reduce people's vulnerability to shortfalls in production, fluctuations in the market, or other food-related crises. However, when severe food shortages threaten people's survival, Oxfam may also become involved in emergency relief programmes that include the distribution of food or agricultural inputs.

Not all national food deficits are associated with widespread hunger; and not all famines are associated with national food shortages. The availability of food within a national economy is not the only key to understanding why systematic or acute deprivation occurs within a society. The reasons why some people go hungry are to be found in the

930

social, political, and economic systems governing the entitlements which people have to food, and their capacity to produce or purchase it. It is important, therefore, that relief programmes to alleviate food-related emergencies address the dysfunctions and injustices which lie behind the specific crisis.

The issues of food security and supplies as they relate to sustainable socio-economic systems and to agricultural production are presented in **1.3 Environment and development**, and **Chapter 5 Production** respectively. The focus of this section is on food security, in the context of relief programmes. It includes a brief consideration of emergency food aid, and practical guidelines for the management of food-distribution programmes.

7.2 Security and vulnerability: entitlements and assets

Famines can and do arise even when sufficient food is available within the national economy as a whole. The work of the Indian economist Amartya Sen demonstrated that the Bangladesh famine of 1974 occurred in a period of peak food availability. However, the normal production pattern had been skewed by crop losses in some areas due to flooding, and increased yield in other, usually drier, areas.

The availability of food supplies within a particular country is not, therefore, the main clue to understanding why some of its citizens go hungry. Far more crucial is the issue of *entitlements*: that is, the capacity of individuals and specific groups to guarantee their rights to a range of commodities, including food, whether through trade, production, labour, or exchange. Different entitlements reflect the differences in power between groups and social sectors, both in the political system and in the economy, and so are connected to factors such as gender relations, socio-economic class, and ethnic or cultural identity. The notion of entitlements thus relates to the ways in which both the State and private sector provide (or fail to provide) individuals with a regular means of income and survival, and with compensatory mechanisms or 'safety nets' for those who are vulnerable to fluctuations in their resource base. At the household level, too, entitlements may be significantly differentiated by age and by gender: in some societies, men and boys are systematically fed better than women and girls, or elderly dependants may fare worse than young adults.

People's vulnerability also depends on their *assets*. In a famine, some people survive and some die, even though they might produce the same amount or are considered equally poor. This is because survival does not just depend on producing enough to eat, although for many poor

6

people this is important. It may also depend on the ability to buy and sell produce and labour, or to exploit family and broader community networks and friendships; or it may depend on receiving food aid or relief assistance. Herders, for example, may resort to selling animals to buy grain. If animal prices go down, they have to sell more to buy the same amount, even if they produce the same number and quality of animals. Such people are vulnerable to market prices as well as to climatic conditions. Landless wage labourers or urban workers are not dependent on their own agricultural production, but on their earnings: they are thus vulnerable to changes in the amount of time they work, and what they are paid.

The assets or resources on which people can call at times of crisis are of three kinds:

- **Investments**
  - ◆ human (such as health and education)
  - ◆ individual (such as animals, houses, wells, farming equipment)
  - ◆ collective or communal (such as irrigation systems, land, grazing areas, trees)
- **Stores**
  - ◆ food or produce (such as granaries or animals)
  - ◆ jewellery, gold, or precious belongings
  - ◆ money, savings, bank accounts.
- **Claims**
  These include lending others something in the hope that this will be reciprocated in times of need; building up contacts or political influence (locally, nationally and internationally); securing alliances by marriage, gifts or tribute; belonging to a union or mutual support association; or paying taxes or *zakat*. They may lead to;
  - ◆ claims on other households for food, labour or animals;
  - ◆ claims on patrons, *caciques*, chiefs, or on other communities;
  - ◆ claims on local or national government;
  - ◆ claims on the international community.

Assets are normally accumulated by investing surpluses in building up physical stores or claims, or are inherited. 'Cashing in' these assets during a crisis helps people to survive. The differences in the types and amounts of such assets held by different households and individuals in part explains differences in their vulnerability.

Investments and stores are usually 'owned' in a legal sense, while claims are established by the social context. For example, if the adult male in a household gets more of its produce — for example, by having first claim on the meat or fish, or receiving greater medical attention in case of illness — this may be accepted as customary practice, although the claim could not be legally enforced. For women, who are widely discriminated against in this manner, such (often invisible) conventions are particularly important in explaining their increased vulnerability compared to men.

The analysis of entitlements and assets can help to identify the *survival strategies* of different groups in the face of adversity, and to reveal these as part of a dynamic process rather than a fixed set of responses. For instance, seen over time, such strategies might include the following:

Table 6.5 Hierarchy of survival strategies over time, with declining food availability

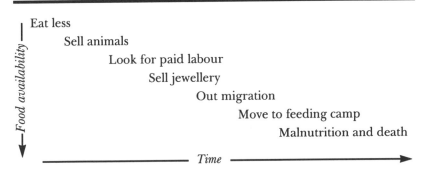

Understanding the hierarchy of responses to crisis can assist in differentiating between different levels of exposure to risk or vulnerability within social groups and households. It is therefore useful as a means of determining a more sensitive range of direct and indirect interventions, whether these are aimed at reducing risk, preventing an intensification in people's existing vulnerabilities, increasing long-term security, or addressing specific emergencies.

7.2.1 Food production systems

Agricultural producers usually develop some capacity to cope with occasional adverse climatic conditions. However, subsistence farmers and small producers may live in conditions of recurrent deficit, and a season that is only slightly worse than usual may result in a crisis. In the absence of savings or alternative sources of income (assets), farming households are pushed further into debt and dependence. If farmers' capacity to meet their own subsistence needs is affected, and they lack the means to purchase food on the open market, their households will suffer hardship unless there are compensatory mechanisms on which they can rely.

933

Provided that stocks of food are available within the overall economy, these compensatory mechanisms are unlikely to involve major food-distribution programmes in the first instance. Other forms of indirect intervention might include tax relief; price control and rationing; support of livestock prices; subsidised sales; insurance of crops; and cash (or cash plus food) wages for public works. The enhancement of food security for the most vulnerable is generally less concerned with immediate food distribution than with indirect economic interventions. The apparent need for emergency food aid often arises from the breakdown, or non-existence, of adequate public or social mechanisms to supply food, or to compensate for major disruptions in normal distribution systems. However, food-aid programmes themselves also have an impact on household, local, and national economies, which may or may not be intended.

As illustrated in Table 6.5, in times of extreme food shortage, people may have a range of responses enabling them to meet a significant proportion of their needs and maintain the long-term sustainability of their livelihoods. Often, however, these responses intensify the vulnerability of poor people — as for example, when women resort to prostitution in order to maintain their families, or when people are forced to sell the few assets they possess in order to survive in the immediate term.

Aid agencies need to understand the background to a food deficit, and the hierarchy of responses to it, in order both to reduce the immediate vulnerability of poor men and women, and enable them to maintain their livelihoods in the longer term. Above all, relief programmes should avoid undermining people and their social structures by drawing them from their normal environment, or restricting their freedom of action. In particular, every effort should be made to avoid the need to establish closed feeding camps.

7.2.2 Post-crisis recovery of food production systems
(See **6**.2.6.1 Capacities and Vulnerabilities Analysis.)

In times of social unrest, new opportunities can arise as the very crisis forces people to work together or to take on new responsibilities within the household or wider community. In Uganda and Somalia this has enabled NGOs to work through community leaders and elders who had hitherto been seen as controlling power and influence to the detriment of others. Gender relations are often radically changed during a crisis, sometimes for the better. A holistic approach to recovery is to use this period to bring about change, or consolidate gains made during the crisis. The aim should not be to return to the 'normality' or *status quo* which led to the crisis in the first place.

However, when crises subside, these openings and gains can also disappear unless they are deliberately protected. For example, it has frequently been observed that as countries emerge from situations of conflict, women who played leading and independent roles during liberation struggles are expected to return to their pre-crisis status. Rights to land are often contested, particularly in situations where refugees are returning to reclaim homes and plots that have since been occupied by others. This is a problem that arose in Guatemala, where war widows had been cultivating land that was subsequently reclaimed by men who were returning to the area after many years.

In situations of crisis or post-crisis, Oxfam has learnt that it is usually better to expand or subsidise existing activities than to introduce totally new initiatives, for which there may not be sufficient time to undertake the necessary background research and consultation. Some of the most successful rehabilitation initiatives have built on existing coping strategies. Rehabilitation activities should not be introduced too soon after a crisis, so that people have a chance to adopt their own traditional systems of recovery. In this context, the question of whether inputs such as seeds and tools should be given, subsidised, sold at cost, or given on credit, needs careful consideration. While loans may keep costs down, they may delay recovery by increasing recipients' economic vulnerability in the short term. Extremely poor people may need additional support in order to avoid their having to sell the relief inputs to raise cash for other essential purchases.

In the specific case of re-stocking to help farmers build up their depleted herds, there are conflicting arguments. Some analysts suggest that loans may have a negative impact on recovery, while others maintain that to draw on existing forms of loan arrangements may best reinforce re-stocking systems that are easily understood. Similarly, there is disagreement about whether re-stocking should be collectively or individually managed, and over what constitutes the minimum viable herd to avoid animals being sold to meet other needs. While it is important to be aware of these dilemmas, the best approach will vary from one situation to another, and will depend on local circumstances.

The distribution of agricultural inputs or other forms of support thus requires administrative and logistic resources as well as local knowledge that may be lacking. It may therefore be necessary to improve absorption capacity at the local level so that resources which are provided from outside can be better coordinated, and more responsive to needs. Adequate monitoring and evaluation should ideally be based on local criteria and participation, though Oxfam also has to ensure that the structures through which its assistance is channelled are equipped to represent the interests of poor and vulnerable people.

6

7.3 Food aid in emergencies

Not every emergency gives rise to a significant disruption in the normal production and availability of food. While there may be some immediate problems concerning food distribution, in many cases these are short-lived and can be tolerated or overcome without resorting to food aid programmes. Often, difficulties are experienced not in the immediate aftermath of the disaster but later, when food and seed stocks are depleted; or as essential reconstruction work takes people away from their normal food-production activities.

However, when emergency food aid is needed, it is often needed rapidly and on a large scale. The most clear-cut examples arise when a large influx of people require food which they cannot purchase, as in the case of refugees or displaced persons. Such people may be dependent on food and services for a considerable time, depending on whether they can find paid employment, or obtain land and agricultural inputs. Where food aid is needed, it must arrive at the right time and in appropriate quantities: the late delivery of emergency food, inappropriate foodstuffs, or inadequate distribution channels, can cause serious problems.

While food aid in general meets only a small proportion of needs in emergencies, one of its most important functions is to enable people to adopt their own survival strategies. For example, public works programmes using cash or food (or a combination of both) can be an efficient means of countering the collapse in entitlements resulting from drought. For poor people, the search for wage labour — either local or through temporary out-migration — is one of the most significant responses to crisis. By guaranteeing work, Food for Work (FFW) can serve to strengthen this strategy, although there may be other problems associated with the FFW approach. (See **6.7.3.1** Types of food aid intervention.)

The design and implementation of food aid programmes is a complex matter. The problems created by delays, inappropriate food consignments or inadequate distribution have in some cases been greater than those they were intended to address. Poorly designed or unnecessarily prolonged food aid interventions may create dependence where it did not exist, by undermining recovery efforts; or undercutting local producers by distributing free food.

While food aid is vital in certain emergencies (or potential emergencies), it is important to be aware of the dangers, and minimise these as far as possible. It is generally agreed that it is counter-productive to prolong the distribution of free food beyond the minimum necessary period. If long-term projects are designed around the availability of food aid, its provision may become institutionalised in a way which fosters dependence rather than self-reliance..

936

NGOs tend to leave major food aid inputs to the specialised government and inter-governmental agencies, mainly because of the scale of resources required. Oxfam is generally drawn into the direct procurement of food aid only:

- where international donors are unable to overcome political obstacles (such as in areas of Ethiopia not under government control up to 1991);
- where local government distribution mechanisms are considered inadequate;
- to demonstrate the need for more international action in delivering relief food.

Oxfam believes that whenever possible, food aid should be procured from nearby sources. (See **6.7.4** Food supplies and distribution.) Whenever Oxfam is involved in handling food aid, it seeks to work through local structures and organisations for distribution purposes.

7.3.1 Types of food aid intervention

The three main systems for food aid intervention are: economic support, payment-in-kind through FFW, and nutritional support.

a. Economic support
This kind of intervention is essentially pre-emptive, in order to enable people to remain in their homes, reduce their vulnerability to fluctuations in the market, or increase their capacity to sustain themselves in the future. Where programmes are aimed at supporting people through a particular food deficit, food aid is not usually intended to cover the entire food needs of the affected population. As such, food aid for economic support is a form of disaster prevention, and so should not be confused with rations intended to meet the entire nutritional need. For example, in Uganda, Oxfam and the WFP jointly distributed a ration amounting to only 25 per cent of total food needs to groups of people who might otherwise have become destitute. This was enough to allow them to continue their usual economic activities.

In situations where the aim is to prevent a collapse of the economic base of society, it may be appropriate to use food aid as animal fodder, enabling farmers to preserve their breeding stock, or in exchange for surplus animals (de-stocking), where herds have to be reduced. Oxfam has supported operations of this type in Mali (1984–85) and Burkina Faso (1990–91). In Mali during the 1983/5 drought, as livestock prices plummeted and cereal prices soared, herders underlined the need to de-stock as rapidly as possible, but at a price that would allow some purchasing power on the cereal market. A 'dried meat' programme

937

involved livestock being purchased by the herders' co-operatives, and slaughtered after examination by their veterinary agents. The meat was then dried using traditional techniques, and purchased by relief agencies for distribution in feeding camps. The main limitations of such an operation are that, since it is a last resort, rural producers will only sell their animals when there is absolutely no alternative. Moreover, since the purchase price of animals in good years bears no relation to their selling price in bad years, the money raised is insufficient to reconstitute lost capital; in this case, livestock. In terms of replicability, it should also be recognised that this particular operation was dependent on a temporary and exogenous market. Nevertheless, it served to strengthen local institutions, and to provide them with a possible solution in the next drought.

In Burkina Faso, the de-stocking operation was combined with reinforcing cereal banks, in recognition of the link between animal and cereal production and prices. Two operations involved the purchase of sheep for fattening in one region, and the purchase of cattle for sale in markets inside and outside the Sahel region. In both cases, the village groups and unions which Oxfam was supporting were involved in the design, execution, and evaluation of the activity. Unfortunately, it was difficult to secure prices that covered the cost of purchase because of intense market competition. In addition, while the programme improved the purchasing power of herders *vis-à-vis* other groups, it tended to favour owners of larger herds. However, the initiative was a means of injecting cash into the local economy, which in turn permitted the purchase of cereals, which stimulated their supply. More importantly, it showed how the institutional support that Oxfam and other NGOs had provided enabled an emergency programme to be developed and run in a much more timely, participatory, and effective way than would otherwise have been the case.

Creative interventions of this kind may also be used to help people to recover from famine. For example, Oxfam was involved in the distribution of food to agro-pastoralists in the Red Sea Province of Sudan, to enable them to build up their herds, without having to sell animals in order to eat. Similarly, Oxfam's approach to food aid in Turkana District of north-west Kenya was based on the view that to support the pastoral economy, it is important to look beyond nutritional indicators alone. Food aid was made available to all but identified wage-earners within the affected population, through elected relief committees of elders (women and men), at each of the distribution points. The insistence on involving women in the relief programme reinforced the existing system of social organisation, whereby it is women who are responsible for livestock management and food security for all household dependants.

Purchasing cereals from surplus-producing areas and redistributing them (at cost or on a subsidised basis) in areas vulnerable to food shortages may be an alternative to international food aid. However, it is likely to become a genuinely long-term answer only if the economic climate and government policies are conducive to this type of operation. In Mali, where Oxfam has some experience of this type of assistance, at least three types of constraint have appeared. Firstly, the transport costs tend to be under-estimated, and may be beyond the means of the communities concerned. Secondly, the operational approaches are not always based on a careful analysis of the organisational capacity and representative status of those structures running the programme, so giving rise to the need for additional support and monitoring. Finally, these problems mean that it may not always be the most vulnerable or destitute people who receive food.

Relief efforts to assist 'the community' will not assist women and men equally, or address the needs of its weaker or less vocal members, unless they are specifically designed to do so. The appropriateness and effectiveness of this kind of intervention depend crucially on how much is known and understood about existing social structures. Gender relations are a crucial dimension of all socio-economic systems, and the distinct roles and needs of women and of men, as well as of other specific groups of people, should routinely be analysed. Crucial questions need to be answered, such as: who cultivates which crops, and when; who markets the crops, and who controls the resources; who cares for which livestock; who decides on changes in cropping or livestock management patterns, and on what basis? (See 1.4.2 Formal methods of information-gathering and appraisal.)

b. Food for Work

Food for Work (FFW) is sometimes seen as an option which avoids some of the pitfalls of free food handouts. It has been used in situations of high unemployment or landless agricultural labour, particularly in Asia and parts of Africa. However, FFW requires an exceptionally high level of local organisation and a detailed understanding by aid agencies of the social and economic mechanisms — such as migration, seasonal labour, informal sector work, gender-based division of paid and unremunerated labour — which might be unintentionally disrupted. (See 1.3.5 Livelihoods analysis.)

FFW has been most successfully used where the activities and level of participation had been agreed beforehand; and where the FFW element was time-bound, and did not extend to the next year's harvest, and so interfere with local production. FFW may also be an effective way to keep speculation, primarily by traders and richer farmers, to tolerable levels. If food prices are kept down through the availability of food aid to poorer social sectors, this tends to improve the entitlements of those who are on the demand-side of the market.

Significantly, both the ILO and the WFP recommend that workers should receive at least half their wages in cash at the prevailing local rate, and only half in the form of food rations. This allows recipients still to participate in the cash economy, without having to resort to selling part of their rations and hence contributing to further distortions in the market. (This recommendation is often ignored by aid agencies that rely heavily on FFW schemes.)

There are a number of well-documented problems in the use of FFW. Some of these relate to the potential distortion in the local market, as demand is suppressed, either because people are buying less or because some of the food aid is sold at lower prices. If this situation continues into the next agricultural cycle, it can serve as a disincentive to local production. Similarly, if FFW programmes using foreign foodstuffs become institutionalised — as they have done in many countries — dietary changes may also result in a reduced demand for local crops.

Other difficulties concern the nature of the activities for which people are remunerated in food. If FFW schemes are designed principally as means to distribute food aid, then people may work simply in order to receive the food, rather than from any sense of commitment to the work itself. This can serve to undermine traditional survival strategies, either by providing an alternative to these, or by discouraging people from moving, or by involving them in work which reduces the time available for other activities. Another complex issue concerning FFW is that of asset-distribution. Often, public works schemes which have used labour paid in food, have been to the long-term disadvantage of the very people given temporary employment through the projects. Improvements to land and infrastructure made by labourers on FFW schemes often consolidate the economic power and control of those who own the resources. For example, FFW projects have been set up in areas such as Bangladesh or north-east Brazil to enable share-croppers to make improvements on rented land — such as terracing or irrigation — only for their landlords to increase the rent as a result. While participants are self-selecting, so that FFW are successful in terms of distributing the food aid to those who need it (except those who are too weak or too heavily burdened to participate), it is rare for FFW schemes to serve as means of redistributing assets to, or strengthening the position of, poorer people.

In assessing whether to support a FFW scheme, it is essential to consider these medium- and longer-term factors in detail, to ensure that the final outcome does not undermine the material, organisational or motivational capacities of poor people, and their households.

940

Finally, while all food aid programmes have an economic impact — which may not always be well defined or targeted — some donors make rigid distinctions between food aid for free distribution (for example through Mother-Child Health (MCH) or therapeutic feeding programmes) and for FFW schemes. Before using donated food for FFW, written agreement must be given by the donor.

c. Nutritional support
(See **6**.5 Health and nutrition in emergencies.)

The extremes of food shortages, mass migration, widespread death, or extensive loss of assets can transform a poor but functioning society of subsistence farmers to destitute migrants. Where food shortages are life-threatening, it may be necessary to distribute a food ration as nutritional support, through organised food distribution or full-scale feeding programmes. For those already suffering starvation, full rations are needed in addition to supplementary and therapeutic feeding for identified groups. In the earlier stages, partial rations may be adequate. It is important to note that men and women have different nutritional needs, in particular women who are pregnant or breast-feeding. Technical detail about feeding programmes is given in section **6**.5.

Traditional or community leaders may have strong views about how such programmes should be organised; and who should benefit from them. The categories of people who are especially vulnerable to malnutrition, and who would normally command the attention of humanitarian relief NGOs (pregnant and breast-feeding women, small children, and elderly, injured or disabled people), may not be regarded as a high priority by these leaders. In situations of conflict, it may be seen as more important to ensure the survival of the stronger members of society, usually younger men, as an effective fighting or military force.

Aid agencies generally have their own criteria with which to determine their priorities for intervention: most obviously, the humanitarian imperative to safeguard human life. Furthermore, beneath the appearance of community cohesion, there are *always* different (sometimes competing) interests at stake. Relief workers should seek to engage in the broadest possible dialogue with the people affected. It may be necessary to negotiate shared criteria about how and to whom to direct food aid interventions, in order to ensure that the more vulnerable members of society are not excluded. (See **6**.4.4 Consulting and involving the affected population.)

6

7.4. Food supplies and distribution

7.4.1 Food supplies

Bulk food can be extremely expensive to purchase, and package and transport may cost at least as much again. (See **6**.8.3 Relief supplies and logistics.) NGOs often choose either to lobby for bilateral food donations, or seek funds from governments or multilateral agencies if they wish to act as a channel for food. The WFP can make modest amounts available through its national offices; but does not itself undertake to organise the distribution of food commodities.

Although donors such as the EU have de-linked the disposal of surpluses from food aid programmes, there is still reluctance to consider local purchase arrangements. The results of such reluctance can be unfortunate. In Mozambique, for example, the national trading organisation, AGRICOM, had substantial stocks remaining unsold while donors concentrated on food shipments from abroad. In Tigray, NGOs funded internal purchases for many years but had extreme difficulty in persuading the British Government and the EU to do likewise, despite detailed economic analyses and elaborate monitoring systems.

Local or regional purchase of food is generally preferable to international food aid. Transport costs are reduced and there are likely to be fewer problems with delays or with the acceptability of the foodstuffs. Above all, such purchases reduce competition with local producers. Where it is necessary to purchase food outside the country or region, the logistics are daunting. The specification of food commodities and packaging are complicated technical areas in which large losses can easily occur.

The experience of relief operations in Africa during 1983-5 indicates that the major factor in the direct delivery of food was adequate logistics, with logistic failure being the main reason for slow or ineffective operations. Despite the provision of a massive amount of food aid (5 million tonnes in 1984), much of it was distributed in an indiscriminate way, with the result that the most vulnerable often did not get enough support. At the same time, while delivery through feeding centres did more to help those at risk, it did little to prevent population movements, and, in certain cases, actually encouraged them. Finally, in many cases, much of the food aid arrived after the next harvest, and so aggravated a glut in local markets.

Oxfam does not normally engage in large-scale purchases direct, but uses the services of Euronaid, the food procurement and logistics agency which acts as the intermediary between NGOs and the EU. Where Oxfam has felt compelled to purchase food, this has usually been in the context of public lobbying for humanitarian aid. For example, a shipment to Ethiopia in 1984 was used to draw attention to the impending famine and the failure of the international community to pledge or deliver adequate quantities of relief food.

7.4.2 Distribution and monitoring

Distribution and monitoring are usually best undertaken by a local agency which has a sensitive understanding of the needs of different groups within the affected population, and which has the organisational capacity to handle a range of different distribution mechanisms. In Oxfam's experience, it is difficult for an international aid agency to guarantee an effective food-distribution programme in the complete absence of such an organisation; yet sometimes these may not exist, or may be unable to assume responsibilities on the scale required. Taking on the distribution of food poses several dilemmas. If it is done through centralised feeding or distribution centres, this may promote a higher level of displacement, along with an increase in the risk of disease, and the likelihood that some very vulnerable people (for example, those who are not readily mobile) will not be reached. If it is distributed in a decentralised manner, it is harder to concentrate resources on the most vulnerable, because of the administrative, logistic, and medical resources required. The choice is often between indiscriminate universal distribution, which means that it may not be possible to provide enough support to the most vulnerable; or using local institutions, which may lack the necessary human, financial, and organisational capacity to give priority to reaching the most vulnerable; or be unwilling to do so.

The use of local groups and leaders to distribute food often leads to uniform rations being given to each household. In the Red Sea Hills, for example, despite having a clear idea of the different needs of various households, such groups did not use this information to determine the allocation of food. There were some cases where newly-arrived displaced people were discriminated against, as local leaders felt less responsible for them. Where an NGO knows a community sufficiently well to be sure that local differences in wealth are not large, and the most vulnerable people can be reached, uniform distribution can be a convenient and relatively simple means of allocating food rations, and avoids creating tension and conflict. Oxfam has found that the active involvement of women, not just in determining priorities but also in controlling the distribution of food, is generally the most reliable means both of ensuring that households are treated equitably, and increasing the chances of equitable intra-household distribution.

Three alternative approaches have also been attempted:

6

- using specific criteria, such as nutritional status
- intervening in the market
- relying on self-selection.

Each of these approaches has some drawbacks.

There have been conflicting claims about the merits of using criteria such as nutritional status, asset ownership, geographic location or ethnic group. Although nutritional status is perhaps the most obvious criterion, it has two important limitations: first, assessment is a highly complicated and skilled task; and, second, once undernourished individuals have been identified, there remains the problem of whether to allocate resources to them or to their families. This has sometimes led to families deliberately keeping the nutritional status of an individual member below the level which qualifies the whole family for support. In situations where families tend in any case to protect the most vulnerable (under-fives), then it is better to avoid introducing criteria that may encourage such behaviour.

Intervening in the market — for example by subsidising food prices or supporting livestock prices — and letting the allocation between individuals depend on their market situation, is also problematic..

While relying solely on the market often discriminates against the poor, at the same time, market responses are crucial in a famine situation, and it is always necessary to take them into account when evaluating alternative forms of intervention. The role of private traders during famines may be both positive and negative. Hoarding, speculation and the large-scale export of food from famine areas have all been commonly observed. But not all traders are portly merchants sitting on sacks of grain; many are poor buyers and sellers, and many are women. State interventions to paralyse private trade during famine have often been disastrous. This also indicates the positive role that private trade can play, for example by moving food from low-price areas to high-price areas, which can in turn bring down prices where there is a positive association between levels of distress and high prices (though the impact may be negative if the reason why demand was low was because people were unable to pay, rather than because their needs were being met); or by moving food at less cost and more flexibly than state marketing boards.

Collusion and manipulation by traders does occur and, along with high transport costs, this can lead to large discrepancies in prices between areas. However, like governments, NGOs should be wary of attempting to replace private trade rather than stimulate and complement it.

The third approach, of relying on self-selection, such as the requirement of work in exchange for relief (as in FFW), in order to discourage less vulnerable groups who might consider this demeaning, or not sufficiently remunerative compared to what they could otherwise do, has advantages and disadvantages. Some of these are mentioned above in the discussion of FFW. Other factors to take into account are that such activities may be most appropriate at an early stage of a crisis when people are already actively looking for alternative employment, but are not yet facing grave hardship or malnutrition; and that family ties can be preserved if such employment does not involve long-range displacement, so that positive intra-household redistribution patterns can be reinforced (for example, if there is positive discrimination in favour of the vulnerable); and that poor people are offered an opportunity to organise around common interests.

However, the negative factors to consider are, firstly, that such work usually increases calorie requirements at a time when it might be argued that they need to be reduced; and, secondly, that women are likely to benefit from such schemes only if deliberate policy decisions are made, for example, to promote female employment.

It is generally better to combine these three approaches, rather than to rely exclusively on one or the other. To think only of direct feeding or only of leaving things to the mercy of the market is clearly too simplistic. Providing subsidies, in the form of employment (using food or wages) or price support to herders (which can stimulate the market as well as protect people from its excesses), combined with unconditional relief for those who need it, is likely to be a more effective response than doing either alone.

The operational costs of distribution and monitoring can be very high, and there may still be substantial losses or diversion of food. The best form of monitoring is through downwards accountability to the intended recipients. It is important that people understand the methods and criteria of the food-distribution programme, so that they can take action if they do not receive their due. Women must be directly involved in this process, given their direct responsibility for the preparation, cooking and distribution of food within the household; and their responsibilities for the welfare of other family members, such as children and disabled, sick, and elderly people. It is also essential that food is distributed in a form in which it can be used; and that appropriate facilities, such as grinding mills, cooking utensils, and fuel, are available.

7.4.3 Monitoring the sale of food aid

A basic food ration does not meet a household's entire needs, and part of it is likely to be exchanged or sold. This should not automatically be interpreted as a sign that food is not needed or that monitoring is lax, though who is doing the selling and buying — women or men, and from which groups or social sectors — should be checked; and also, what is being done with the money. It is vital also to ensure that such sales are not competing in a harmful way with the efforts of local producers to market their goods.

The bags in which food aid is distributed may have a real value. A shortage of bags can be a disincentive to local trade, and the recycling of food aid bags can help to overcome this. Such recycling has occasionally embarrassed donors, as the bags are often photographed in markets, apparently with the contents on sale. It is important to remember that appearances are often deceptive, before concluding that the bags contain food aid for sale.

7.5 Key questions

1 What is already known about food security, food production, and food supplies in the area or country affected, prior to the emergency? Is Oxfam involved in supporting work within the food production sector? What are the different roles and needs of women and men?

2 What are the indicators of crisis in the food sector (increased sale or death of livestock; changes in migration patterns; significant decline in income among food purchasers; increase of market price in food staples or in other essential commodities)? What is the analysis of the underlying cause, and potential impact, of the crisis in terms of food security generally, and the needs of poor and disadvantaged people in particular?

3 What interventions might be made instead of, or in addition to, food-distribution programmes? What are the principal aims of the programme of intervention and on what analysis are these based? How will the food-distribution programme contribute to economic stability in the longer term? How was its design determined and by whom?

4 What are the distribution mechanisms to be adopted and how do these ensure that disadvantaged people will benefit equitably? In particular, how will it be ensured that women and children are covered fairly? If FFW is being used, is it clear that the long-term benefits will accrue to the disadvantaged? What are the guarantees?

5 How has the rationale of a food-distribution programme been explained? Are there differences in the criteria for distribution of the women and men affected, and of the humanitarian NGO? How will such differences be addressed so as to ensure that food is not diverted to other recipients?

6 If food aid is to be used in food-distribution programmes, from where is it to be obtained and how? What are the reasons for the chosen source? How, if at all, will local economies benefit? What is the likely impact on local producers?

7 In supplementary feeding programmes, what guarantees exist that the food will be supplementary to the existing diet rather than substituting for it? How have the rations been determined?

8 What are the criteria for stopping food distribution, and what are the mechanisms for ensuring this will happen?

6

8 Oxfam procedures in emergency relief programmes

8.1 Introduction 948
8.2 Information and assessment 949
    8.2.1 Information needs 951
    8.2.2 Assessment 952
    8.2.3 Sources of funds for emergency programmes 953
    8.2.4 Recommending emergency grants 955
    8.2.5 Internal communications 955
    8.2.6 Reporting 959
    8.2.7 Liaison with other agencies 961
    8.2.8 Evaluation 961
8.3 Relief supplies and logistics 961
    8.3.1 The importance of logistics 961
    8.3.2 Ordering supplies 962
    8.3.3 International transport 963
    8.3.4 Local transport, handling, and storage 966
    8.3.5 Distribution 969
8.4 Administration and staffing 970
    8.4.1 Preparedness and contingency plans 970
    8.4.2 Financial procedures 971
    8.4.3 Staffing and recruitment 972
    8.4.4 Staff health and security 972
    8.4.5 Travel in dangerous circumstances 974
8.7 Key questions 975

8.1 Introduction

The management of emergency programmes depends largely upon good communication within and between each of the various teams of people involved in the relief effort. Where a programme brings together a range of inter-related responses — for example, proactive media work in one country, discreet lobbying of UN agencies, and a major operational relief programme on the ground — the question of internal (often cross-cultural) communication becomes more crucial still.

948

In many cases, an effective emergency response also depends upon co-ordination with a number of other agencies; and these may range from local NGOs or government departments, to multilateral agencies and NGO consortia each with their own needs and dynamics. Good communication lines and efficient decision-making processes are vital to the smooth running of emergency relief programmes.

In practice, however, the rapidly changing and pressing demands of emergency relief programmes often find senior managers spending an inordinate amount of time as 'trouble-shooters' — rushing from one job to another, failing to delegate effectively, duplicating other people's work, and trying to deal with the resulting problems. The management of a crisis easily becomes crisis management. Yet the very nature of emergency relief work makes it imperative that managers dedicate enough efforts to supervising, supporting, and managing their teams in a systematic way. Time spent on motivating staff, facilitating discussions, and generating new initiatives, is time well spent. This in turn means being able to delegate, and to ensure that people are given adequate training to be able to perform their duties responsibly.

This section differs from others in this *Handbook,* in that it is based on Oxfam's recommended procedures for managing in-country emergency relief programmes. While these will not in themselves eliminate management problems, they may be used as a guide to good practice in certain critical areas. It should be read in conjunction with the detailed sections on Planning, Evaluation, Financial management and Financial administration to be found in Chapter 3 Capacity building for development.

The section is not intended to provide a comprehensive guide to the management of operational relief programmes, or to substitute for the detailed policies and guidelines that should be referred to by Oxfam staff in the event of an emergency.

8.2 Information and assessment

a. Sudden-onset disasters
The first priority in a sudden-onset disaster is to have appropriate and reliable information in order to:

• decide whether and how to respond
• inform and respond to the media and general public.

The media profile of sudden-onset disasters is characterised by a pattern of immediate and overwhelming interest, a plateau of intense interest, and a rapid tailing-off. This pattern generally takes place over a ten-day period, and there is rarely any follow-up. Sudden-onset

949

disasters themselves usually fall into three phases, the timing of which rarely follows that of the media focus: search and rescue may cover a week or more, depending on the particular event; relief efforts may commence within days after the event, but may take a week to become fully operational; some rehabilitation and reconstruction activities will commence in the midst of relief work, and will continue for many months afterwards. Media interest is heavily concentrated on the search and rescue phase, at a time when relief efforts have barely started.

In Oxfam's experience, there is a regular pattern of media activity in the wake of such disasters. At first, amid confusion, conflicting reports, and exaggeration (for example, by politicians eager to gain support for their viewpoints), there will be a wide-ranging search for reliable information. When journalists arrive on the scene, the quality of information improves. The coverage often focuses on 'human interest' accounts (escapes, rescues, stories about foreign aid workers), and may concentrate on the international aid operation. Inevitably, as time passes, the 'story' wanes. As the disaster comes under control, journalists begin to leave. Coverage may become dominated by questions about the arrival and efficacy of aid, tales of corruption and incompetence.

This pattern of interest will govern Oxfam's response to the media, but not to the development of the emergency programme itself. Speed is vital in terms of providing information for public use; in the immediate aftermath of a disaster, Oxfam's principal communications purpose is to inform and explain. A system of regular communication between the Head Office and Oxfam's locally-based staff should be established as soon as possible. It is often useful to nominate a spokesperson on the ground for the purpose of interviews or contact with international journalists. This may be supplemented by well-briefed spokespersons for Oxfam, in the UK and Ireland, who can offer informed speculation about what the situation might be like.

Once journalists start arriving on the scene of the disaster, it is ideal to designate a staff member whose work can be reported upon publicly or filmed, as well as staff who may be interviewed. This does not mean that Oxfam staff are expected to act as reporters, simply that they are willing to engage with the media and talk about or show their work. The appropriate way to do this depends largely on the nature of the disaster, and on the character of Oxfam's overall programme.

In the longer term, it may be appropriate for Oxfam to be involved in preparing other materials for the media — for example, documentaries that follow up on the disaster at a later stage; and to provide reliable information to counter false or inaccurate claims about national or international relief efforts.

b. Slow-onset or complex emergencies

In the case of slow-onset or complex emergencies, the role of the media is likely to be more susceptible to proactive work by agencies such as Oxfam, since there is a greater opportunity to prepare in-depth analysis and background documentation as the crisis gains momentum. In situations such as these, while it is not possible to predict how a crisis will actually be played out, it may be possible to engage in creative advocacy and policy-related work to preempt the worst impact of an emergency that is 'waiting to happen'. In a broad sense, disaster preparedness often includes proactive measures (such as fact-finding missions in co-ordination with other agencies, lobbying for institutional reform within the inter-governmental agencies, or drawing up a code of practice within the NGO community) that can themselves be the basis of creative work with sympathetic journalists and reporters from the international media. Many Oxfam publications are related to the need to anticipate emergencies, and to use information in such a way as to preempt or mitigate their impact. *Landmines: Legacy of Conflict* is an example of a publication which brought together practical experience with high level, and high profile, lobbying for active UN intervention in mine-clearing operations. (See **3**.1.3 Communications in development.)

8.2.1 Information needs

In the case of slow-onset emergencies there may be time to monitor the deteriorating situation and to make programme plans. Regular first-hand accounts and analysis will form an invaluable picture against which to plan a relief intervention.

Whatever the nature of the actual or potential emergency, locally-based Oxfam staff should:

- confirm the facts with whatever reliable source they can: the government, UN agencies, the press, local or international NGOs in the area (see **6**.4.2 Assessment of emergencies);
- fax, telex or telephone Oxfam Head Office (or the Regional or Country Office), with the information they have received, and plans for visiting the area (NB — a report on the whereabouts and safety of all staff should form a part of the first communication);
- visit the area affected if possible or appropriate, or delegate an appropriately qualified person or team to do so, to assess the situation at first-hand and find out from local people, or organisations who can speak on their behalf, how they are affected.

The international news media are usually better resourced than the national or local services and may be able to add to the picture of events as they appear on the ground. Reports can also be obtained from DHA-

UNDRO, the International Federation of Red Cross and Red Crescent Societies, ICRC, and other international relief agencies. (See **6**.4.3.2 International agencies involved in relief work, and Resources Directory.)

International coverage, particularly of events which may be subject to widely differing interpretations, is often not freely available in the country actually experiencing the emergency. It is essential also to keep the Country or Regional Office abreast of the media coverage in the UK and Ireland and internationally.

To avoid duplicating or omitting information, it is important to establish lines and regularity of communication between Oxfam Head Office and the Regional or Country office (and, where appropriate, with sub-offices).

8.2.2 Assessment

The principles of assessment in emergencies are described in **6**.4 Assessment, co-ordination, and consultation in emergencies. The type of information needed is given below, in the form of steps to be followed:

- Contact the government or other competent authorities for their assessment of damage and of priority needs, an outline of their relief programme and suggestions as to where help is required.
- Contact other international relief agencies to find out their plans, to share data and impressions, and to liaise about collection and analysis of first-hand information.
- Contact counterpart NGOs, local organisations, and community groups, for their assessment of the situation, to find out what they are doing, their plans, and needs.
- Make an independent assessment of the overall situation, noting the existing capacities of the affected population; establish priorities, and consider what actions to meet them might be possible. Staff should try to travel around, especially in the poorer or less accessible areas which may not be visited by other aid workers. It is vital to seek information from women as well as men, and to assess the distinct ways in which the impact of the emergency is experienced by different social groups. Attention should be given to:
  - food stocks held and food supplies expected, with observations of warehouse stocks, markets, prices and normal household stocks;
  - health and nutritional status, especially of: under-fives, pregnant and breast-feeding women, elderly people;
  - existence, quality, and quantity of water supplies;
  - local availability of immediate relief supplies, such as shelter, building materials, clothes, cloth, cooking utensils, fuel and fuelwood, transport;

- Share this information without delay with Oxfam Head Office (or Regional Office), with recommendations concerning Oxfam's involvement, indicating whether this involvement is likely and whether further assessment is required.

Essential communications should be as direct as possible in the early days of an emergency. Intermediaries and E-mail should not be used if there is any risk of delay. If the telephone is the most rapid and reliable form of communication, then the person initiating the contact should ensure that substantive points of information and specific decisions are properly logged; and followed up with a written record.

8.2.3 Sources of funds for emergency programmes

a. Special appeals

The financing of large-scale emergency relief work may be partly dependent upon donor response in the NGO's home country. Oxfam sets aside an annual budget for emergency work, which is supplemented by special appeals for particular programmes.

The UK-based Disasters Emergency Committee (which includes the British Red Cross Society, The Catholic Fund for Overseas Development (CAFOD), Christian Aid, Save the Children (SCF), Action Aid, Help the Aged, and Oxfam) makes joint appeals for major emergencies.

Funds which are 'earmarked' by the donors for specific programmes may not be used for purposes other than those for which they were originally designated. Hence, special appeals may be couched in rather general terms, in order to allow sufficient flexibility to be able to respond to changing priorities as events unfold. Here, again, the role of the media is crucial; public support for emergency operations depends to a very large extent on the quality and extent of media coverage.

b. Channelling funds for other NGOs

Funding for emergency programmes may be forthcoming from NGOs which do not have a staff presence in the country affected, but which prefer to channel their assistance through a like-minded organisation or sister agency. Oxfam is often approached to channel funds on behalf of other British agencies without locally-based staff.

Agreement to channel funds in this way depends firstly upon Oxfam's own decision to approve a grant for the emergency programme; and, secondly, upon having made the appropriate financial arrangements.

6

Reporting and monitoring arrangements must be established from the outset, and agreed by all parties. It should be made clear whether responsibility for organising visits for personnel from sister agencies has been assumed as one of the conditions for acting as a channel. (See **6**.4.2.4 Co-ordinating assessment with other agencies.)

c. Co-funding from official sources

The Overseas Development Administration (ODA) of the British government funds NGO emergency programmes, provided that these fall within its established criteria for assistance. These mainly concern ODA's technical definitions of what constitutes emergency relief, as opposed to 'rehabilitation' inputs, which would normally be dealt with by a separate department.

Where Oxfam is funding local agencies or organisations, these must have given their consent to act as channels for British government funds before their projects are submitted to the ODA for co-funding. It is Oxfam's responsibility to ensure that these organisations understand what co-funding entails.

While there may be good bilateral contacts between Oxfam staff and the British diplomatic representatives within the country affected, detailed arrangements for co-funding are handled by, and should be referred to, Oxfam's Emergencies Department. In most cases, emergency relief interventions are initially funded either from the existing programme budget or from the catastrophe budget set aside for such purposes, and administered centrally. Submissions are made to the ODA, after a commitment has already been made to fund. Oxfam's normal monitoring and reporting requirements are adequate for ODA purposes.

Emergency funds from the European Union (EU) are handled in a different way, in part because very large sums of money are often involved. As with other official sources of assistance, there are criteria laid down concerning relief as opposed to rehabilitation interventions. These may not always be identical to, or compatible with, those of Oxfam or of the implementing agency. Since they are subject to change from time to time, they are not outlined in detail here.

To qualify for emergency funds, submissions must be made to the EU *before* the commencement of relief programmes, since approval cannot be given retroactively. Even if this means delays, programmes which will depend on securing EU funding should not be initiated with the confidence of reimbursement, until a formal contract has been signed. However, once approval has been given, the programme must be implemented without delay, and certainly within the time limit specified in the contract (normally three months). This means that planning and logistical arrangements need to be in place prior to the submission for funds, to ensure that the programme can start immediately approval is granted.

The contract will also indicate the EU accounting, reporting and evaluation requirements to be met. These can represent a considerable extra administrative demand, and, in Oxfam's experience, it is usually necessary to appoint a staff member whose exclusive responsibility it will be to ensure that the additional procedures are properly followed.

The United Nations High Commissioner for Refugees (UNHCR) funds refugee programmes implemented by NGOs on the basis of a signed contract stipulating the terms of the agreement, including budgets and reporting requirements. As with the EU, these must be stringently observed. It is crucial that Oxfam fully informs the implementing agencies of the implications for them, before such funding is sought.

8.2.4 Recommending emergency grants

Senior staff in Regional or Country Offices may authorise emergency grants from their existing programme budgets. They may also recommend larger emergency grants, with detailed proposals and budgets for an application either to the centrally-held catastrophe budget, or to official aid sources. They may prefer to request a fund from which to make smaller disbursements, within agreed criteria, rather than applying separately for each grant. All grants and proposals should be consistent with an agreed (or proposed) strategy for Oxfam's response to the emergency. It is important to establish a means of receiving funds, drawing cash, and paying grants. This will usually be through a local bank — ideally a branch of a bank with good international links — to facilitate international transfers.

Before making a site visit, staff should consult Oxfam Head Office about the availability of funds, and check procedures for official co-funding. Further assessment by technical specialists may be recommended, before firm proposals are made.

8.2.5 Internal communications

(see also **3.2**.6 Computer management and information technology.)

a. Establishing a communication link

Where a disaster occurs in an area outside the immediate reach of an Oxfam Office, or where there is no programme already in the country or area, a first priority is to establish a base and set up reliable communications. Initially, this may be a hotel, equipped with a fax, phone or telex machine. It may be sensible to use the same hotel as other international NGO representatives, to facilitate formal and informal co-ordination with them. Oxfam staff should ensure that they are equipped with a portable typewriter or laptop computer (battery operated) and extra diskettes, if they expect to be sending in written reports directly from this base.

A telex and/or fax machine may be available at the hotel, or alternatively at the post office, public booth or travel agency. If staff are to be in the area for more than a few days, they should establish a telephone number, and advise the best hours to call. A stay of more than a few weeks may justify establishing a postal address. If this is a PO Box number, staff should advise the exact location of the office or base in case people are to be directed there. International courier services cannot normally deliver to a PO Box, and require a street address.

Well-functioning telex, fax, and telephone facilities are usually adequate. The operation of radios is sensitive, and licences are unlikely to be granted easily. However, ICRC, some UN agencies, national civil defence organisations, and local NGOs, often have established radio networks. Embassies and Consulates may also have facilities. It may be possible to make arrangements with these organisations to use their circuits, if appropriate. In addition, amateur radio operators are often glad to make their services available for humanitarian relief.

If telecommunications have broken down or are inadequate, or in insecure areas, it may be essential to establish independent radio and telecommunications. Within towns, this may be by using portable VHF radios; between towns or operational bases, using HF radios; and between the Regional or Country Office and Oxfam Head Office, using satellite communications equipment. Oxfam is currently developing a package of standard equipment, which is compatible with that used by other agencies, in particular UNHCR, IFRC and ICRC.

b. Communication breakdown

The lines of normal communication may be suspended or severely disrupted because of the emergency. A lack of contact between Regional or Country Office and Oxfam Head Office can give rise to anxiety and frustration, as outside reports come in about a major crisis, which Oxfam can neither confirm or deny; while locally-based staff are desperate to communicate urgent information to Oxfam Head Office. It should not be assumed that 'no news is good news'; and every effort must be made to find a communication link, however unconventional or limited.

A complete communication breakdown in the wake of a major emergency should not be allowed to continue beyond a couple of days. In extreme cases, it may be necessary for a team member or delegated person to fly to a neighbouring country to make telephone contact with

Oxfam Head Office, once all local possibilities have been discounted. The disadvantage is that the amount of information the person will have in the immediate aftermath of a disaster is limited, and not likely to do more than confirm staff safety and well-being. If no news is forthcoming from the Regional or Country Office, Oxfam will consider flying someone to the affected country, possibly from a neighbouring office; or approaching a friendly NGO or Embassy in the area to make a visit on its behalf.

c. Telex and fax procedures

All messages should be dated and numbered sequentially, beginning with the reference of the originator: for example, 'OXMEX 43 — DAY/MONTH/YEAR' indicates that this is the forty third communication from Oxfam Head Office to Mexico concerning the emergency programme. This provides a reference for the message and a check that no message has been missed. A complete record should be kept of all outgoing and incoming messages, and a comprehensive file maintained in sequence.

Where there are three or more administrative centres involved — for example, Oxfam Head Office, the Regional Office and a sub-office in the affected country — a standard procedure must be established determining which correspondence between any two offices is to be copied to the third. Failure to establish such a system can result in confusion and misunderstanding, as number sequences are broken and false assumptions are made about who has what information.

Each separate paragraph of the message should be fully referenced and include project and grant numbers, as well as the title or name of the project where relevant, as follows:

AA NIC 153 A3 — Fee for water engineer. Payment received 26/11/92.
BB NIC 153 H3 — Purchase of water pumps. Please process payment asap.

When supplies are ordered by telex, a purchase request reference number should be included in the message. (See **6**.8.3 Relief supplies and logistics.)

It is important for the sender also to stipulate the staff or departments to whom each item of information is addressed, and to whom the report is to be copied. Communications are internal to Oxfam, but if material is confidential or not to be quoted, this should be clearly indicated.

Frequency of telexes or faxes should be determined by the urgency of the message. Sending *ad hoc* faxes or telexes can be counter-productive and should be avoided, unless the additional communication is absolutely justified. It is also important to establish a communications routine. It is usually possible, once a programme is under way, to limit

6

these to a daily or twice-weekly pattern. The discipline of preparing the communication on a regular basis can be helpful in bringing the respective emergency teams together to assess what has taken place, and ensure that all outstanding queries are attended to promptly.

d. Telephone procedures

Telephone conversations are used to convey information as well as to negotiate, agree, and communicate urgent decisions. It may be useful to keep a brief record of all significant telephone calls, for the benefit of other team members or to confirm agreements with the other party. Copies of such notes should be filed together. An office log-book may also be a useful means to record a brief summary of all relevant calls. This is especially important where various members of staff are dealing with the emergency, and where comprehensive or frequent briefings are not possible.

For conveying straightforward information which is not urgent, written communication is preferable to telephone calls, which may be disruptive or misinterpreted unless they are scheduled in advance and the lines are very clear. On the other hand, a well-organised conference call between three or more people can cover an immense amount of ground and clarify or preempt potential misunderstandings between the respective teams.

e. Communication costs

Faxes are generally the most economical form of telecommunication and can also enable copies of essential documents or newspaper cuttings to be transmitted. To transmit the same message by telex is usually more expensive. International telephone calls are the most expensive means of conveying information, and should be used only in urgent cases or where direct person-to-person discussion is necessary. When lengthy reports, documents and newspaper cuttings, computer diskettes or confidential material are to be sent, it may be more appropriate to send them by courier delivery service.

Communication costs in emergency programmes can be significant, and may be too great to be absorbed by administrative budgets. If necessary, a grant should be raised to cover additional expenditure.

f. Confidentiality

It should not be assumed that telexes, faxes or telephone calls are private, in particular if public or commercial facilities are being used. There are often matters relating to the emergency, or to staff health and welfare, which require confidentiality. If there are matters which should be treated discreetly, alternative means of communication should be found.

8.2.6 Reporting

Reporting is vital to keep each team up-to-date with changes in the situation and progress in the relief programme; to co-ordinate the formulation of policies and recommended courses of action; and to seek additional funds, where necessary. Broadcasters, journalists, other agencies, and the general public will also expect to obtain reliable and current information from Oxfam.

To ensure that information is accurate and consistent requires good, two-way communication from the earliest possible moment. When a relief operation is becoming established, telex or fax reports are often the best and most reliable means of communication. However, much of the background information, personal reflections, observations, opinions, or confidential material cannot be sent by public means. Fortnightly or monthly written 'situation reports' or 'sitreps', ranging over all aspects of the operation, are essential for background and general information as well as for decision-making purposes. A consistent framework for sitreps assists both in compiling and using them for comparative and monitoring purposes. Table 6.6 shows the topics which should be covered.

Table 6.6 Framework for a situation report

AA Main developments in emergency
Summary of main developments and events of the week since the last report, with comments on their significance. Relevant operations of other agencies and relief supplies pledged, delivered and being distributed.

BB General situation
Latest significant information, indicating how different categories of people are differently affected (women, men and children; racial or ethnic groups) with any figures disaggregated by age and by sex wherever possible; official estimates of damage; government requests to agencies and policies towards local and international NGOs.

CC Progress of Oxfam response
Progress and problems of each intervention (whether implemented or funded by Oxfam) since last report. These should explore the social dimensions of their impact, with particular emphasis on gender and on cultural considerations. Reports on individual projects should be attached separately. Progress in implementing previous plans or difficulties in implementation as well as how these will be handled. Plans for immediate and medium-term future, and assumptions on which these are based. List pending requests or likely proposals.

6

DD Review of objectives
Summary of the main uncertainties in situation or in relief efforts overall, and possible outcomes. Whether the overall objectives of Oxfam's intervention have altered since they were last formulated. State where (sitrep, PASF, memorandum) and why.

EE Staffing
Deployment and morale of staff; whether additional personnel required. Workplans (where appropriate), including planned visits.

FF Profile
Report on lobbying activity, formal and informal; what issues should be taken forward, by whom, in the UK and Ireland; visits made to Oxfam by other NGOs, or journalists; joint initiatives with other NGOs in the region or country. Press line: should indicate which information is confidential, what might usefully be used and how, human interest stories and observations.

GG Finances
Summary of actual expenditure against budgets; or accounts submitted up to specific date.

HH Reports produced
List reports written (visits, meetings, projects) since last written sitrep.

Sitreps have to fulfil various functions, from addressing media concerns to recording administrative details. They are the main summary of decisions taken, and description of the practical implications of these decisions. Since they are the basis on which briefings are prepared for Area offices in the UK and Ireland, for public information, and for media and fund-raising work, they should include the more complex social information, and challenge inaccurate stereotypes about 'disaster victims' or about the role of women, and not be simply restricted to matters of logistics. It may be more convenient to assign responsibility for preparing different sections of the sitrep to appropriate members of the team, leaving one person to authorise the final compilation.

Events can move very fast in emergency work, both in the field of operations and in the UK and Ireland (fund-raising campaigns, debates in Parliament, appeals, media pressure). While communications may be difficult and time-consuming, the failure to co-ordinate effectively introduces the risk of developing a double momentum, in which mutual perceptions become increasingly outdated or contradictory. For example, while Oxfam Head Office may be following the direction taken by the media and the fund-raising campaign, the relief programme may be already being reoriented in response to changing local circumstances. The risks are significantly reduced if staff at Oxfam Head Office ensure that they also provide an equivalent sitrep, indicating initiatives taken and the kind of press and other publicity which the emergency programme is attracting.

8.2.7 Liaison with other agencies

On this subject generally, see **6**.4.3.2 International agencies involved in relief work and **6**.4.2.4 Co-ordinating assessment with other agencies. In the context of information-sharing, close liaison with other agencies may be crucial, especially in areas with restricted access. Regular co-ordination meetings with other agencies provide an opportunity to share and to gather information, on the emergency itself and progress of relief work, and on the general context.

8.2.8 Evaluation
(To be read in conjunction with **3**.2.3 Evaluation.)

Evaluation can provide lessons which should inform future practice, and it is necessary for accountability. Staff involved in emergency programmes should identify their operating assumptions and objectives, and how they will monitor progress.

It is Oxfam's policy to conduct a formal evaluation of all emergency operational programmes spending more than £100,000; and all non-operational grants of more than £500,000. In the case of operational programmes, the evaluation team must be headed by a person external to Oxfam. Evaluation entails consultation with the organisations through which funds have been channelled, as well as with representatives of the affected population. It will always examine the different impact of a relief programme on women and on men, and on relations between them. It will cover both the impact of interventions and the internal management of the programme — that is to say, both the work funded by Oxfam and Oxfam's own performance.

8.3 Relief supplies and logistics

8.3.1 The importance of logistics

Since an essential aim of any relief programme is to deliver the right relief items to the right people in the right quantity at the right time, an effective relief programme depends on a good supplies and logistics system. While speed is vital, it is more important that the relief system works, and is sustainable throughout the operation. Good administrative and financial procedures must be established and adhered to from the outset.

In large-scale relief work, the government or other civil authority usually takes a central role: as a rule, international NGOs should refer to these authorities, and endeavour to support their efforts. If other agencies are also involved, it is important to set up an appropriate co-ordination mechanism at an early stage. This should include joint meetings to agree the division of labour and to standardise the relief items to be delivered.

These paragraphs deal with the procurement, moving, and storage of relief items. A distinction is drawn throughout between international transactions and movements (between Oxfam Head Office and the Regional or Country Office) and those confined to the region or country of operation. Before any supplies are purchased, *financial provision must have been made* for such purchase. Oxfam staff should refer to detailed guidelines on emergency grant-making procedures.

8.3.2 Ordering supplies

a. International purchase
Orders made through Oxfam Head Office should use the standard Quotation or Supplies Request forms. Telephoned orders are to be avoided. Orders should include the following information:

- quantity and precise specification;
- project and grant number or budget head;
- exact consignee name, address and telex/fax number (the consignee named may be the only person/organisation entitled to clear the goods: make sure this will be possible);
- transport required (sea/air, with routing if applicable);
- supplies request number: each office should have a system of numbering for easy identification of orders;
- an indication of the urgency of the order: date required and, if appropriate, 'time-marking', or a date after which goods whose procurement had been delayed would no longer be required.

Serious and expensive mistakes can be made if inadequate technical information is given on the supplies request form. Before purchase, particularly of equipment, it may be advisable to send a suitably qualified person to the supplier and to reconfirm that the purchase is exactly what is required.

UNIPAC (the UNICEF Packing and Assembly Centre, in Copenhagen) stocks a wide range of materials, including relief supplies.

NGOs can order supplies through UNIPAC on a reimbursement basis, though order fulfilment can take a long time.

b. Local purchase
If goods are available locally, it is preferable to buy them in or near the country of operation. This is usually quicker, and cuts down on freight costs. The cheapest suppliers are not necessarily the best choice, as they may not be able to deliver the right quantity or quality of goods on time.

Financial arrangements between the UK and a local bank must be made as quickly as possible once the decision has been made to purchase locally. The local bank should preferably be the counterpart of the UK bank.

If there is no experienced buyer in the operational team, it may be better to engage the services of a local purchasing agent. The agent should undertake to procure and deliver the goods to a specified location within a specified time. The agreement with the agent or supplier should be clear and in writing. It should state:

- exact specifications and type of goods required, including samples;
- price agreed, method and timing of payment; not more than 50 per cent should be paid in advance, though suppliers may press for more;
- exact details of what the price agreed covers (to include packing to buyer specifications, delivery, and insurance);
- date of delivery (consider a penalty clause for late delivery).

8.3.3 International transport

The manuals prepared by the ICRC and UNHCR, listed in the Resources Section, provide considerably more detail on matters relating to international transport and should be used for reference. There are different ways of transporting relief goods.

a. Transporting goods by sea
This is much cheaper than by air, and advisable when freighting heavy goods (unless extremely urgent). A shipping agent should be used, because clearance procedures can be technically complicated and time-consuming. If an agent is not available, clearance procedures should be checked before goods are sent. Considerable time will have to be dedicated to the procedures involved in clearance.

Where there is sufficient freight, and container handling facilities are available, it is advisable to hire or buy containers for shipping consignments. They provide weatherproof, secure stores both in transit and on a more permanent basis in-country. Prior to ordering

6

containers, it is important to check that there are adequate handling facilities, and suitable trucks for transport.

b. Transporting goods by air

Air freight is more expensive than sea freight; but it is quick and reliable. Scheduled cargo flights are timetabled, and the airline will have established handling procedures at either end of the route.

The Oxfam Regional/Country Office will receive a pre-alert telex/fax giving details of the flight their consignment is booked on and its Estimated Time of Arrival (ETA). This information should be handed to Oxfam's clearing agent. If Oxfam is clearing the goods itself, contact should already have been made with the airline's handling agent, the customs authorities, and relevant government ministries, for advice on the procedure to be followed.

Booking a consignment does not mean that it will fly on the date given. It may be off-loaded or part-shipped, at the airline's discretion. There is no recourse to the airline in this case, and it can lead to difficulties in clearing since the paperwork will refer to the whole shipment, not the part which has arrived.

Charter flights offer choice of destination and good value if Oxfam has sufficient goods to fill a plane, but flight dates and times are subject to last-minute changes. Charter flights generally require more involvement of receiving staff in handling and clearing the cargo than do scheduled flights. This is because charter operators usually do not have handling agents at the port of destination. Instead, the aircraft captain hands the paperwork over to the airport authorities, who in turn may feel no particular responsibility for it.

The reception of air charters can be frantic and difficult. A plane takes only a few hours to unload a cargo, and the captain is likely to be less concerned with the cargo than with speedy discharge and prompt departure. Where routine airport clearance procedures have broken down, it is particularly important to agree some method of operation with all the responsible authorities (government ministries, customs, security, airport authorities) as to how these goods are to be unloaded and cleared. If charters are planned, the Oxfam office should draw up reception and clearance procedures, which should usually include a member of staff meeting the flight.

c. Transporting goods by land

International shipment by land is subject to the same procedures as any other international shipment. If a specialist agent or contractor is not available, a member of staff should be assigned to accompany the consignments, to sort out problems as they arise, and to report difficulties and delays.

964

d. Documents required

It is important to understand which documents are needed when, and who issues them. This section deals with the routine documents: there may be further paperwork required to clear goods free of duty, or to comply with local regulations governing the importation of certain commodities. Regulations should be checked in each country before importing goods.

An **export invoice** will be raised when goods are dispatched,, detailing the goods sent and their value; and a gift certificate, which states the value of the goods, and certifies that they are a 'free gift and no foreign currency is involved'. These documents are sent by courier with the shipping documents to the consignee if the goods are sent by sea; or sent with the goods if they are air-freighted. They can be sent in advance, by courier or fax, if this is necessary for clearance purposes.

A **bill of lading** is issued by a shipper in three originals and several copies for goods that are dispatched by sea. It is a *receipt* for goods, and a *contract* for their carriage. It is also *evidence of title* to goods, and as such is as valuable as the goods themselves. The bill of lading will normally have a named consignee (if it does not, anybody producing the bill of lading has title to the goods). The named consignee must produce the bill of lading, together with proof of identity, in order to claim the goods. It is possible for the consignee to assign the bill of lading to a third party by evidence in writing from the consignee (for example, by an endorsement on the bill). It is thus a 'negotiable' document.

Bills of lading tend to be issued after the vessel has sailed and then couriered by the shipping agent to their destination, to arrive in advance of the arrival of the vessel.

Air waybills serve the same purpose as bills of lading, guiding handling agents as to the dispatching and ownership of goods. However, unlike a bill of lading, possession of the air waybill is *not* evidence of title to goods, and it cannot be endorsed to pass title to a third party. Air waybills accompany the consignment and are not sent out in advance of the goods. They are handed over by the crew of the aircraft to the handling agents at the airport of destination. The airline may carry several consignments for several consignees under one master air waybill; in this case each consignment should be covered under an agent's own house air waybill. The numbers of both documents may be necessary to identify a shipment.

The shipping of food and seeds may need further documents to prove that they are uncontaminated and of suitable quality. Various internationally recognised certificates exist. The receiving office must find out which one will be needed from the local authorities before shipment is arranged.

In the case of perishable items, such as vaccines that cannot be left in the airport while the formalities are gone through, it is usual to arrange

6

'pre-clearance'. The air waybill numbers and other documents are sent before the goods, and the formalities completed before shipment. In this case, it falls to the Regional/Country Office to advise when the formalities are complete so that the goods can be sent.

e. Insurance

This is always arranged for goods purchased by Oxfam Head Office, to cover them in transit at least as far as their port of entry. Insurance to cover onward transport to a named point, and the storage of the goods, can be arranged by Oxfam Head Office if this is requested at the time of ordering goods. Oxfam insures its property wherever possible.

It may be possible to arrange insurance through the local company that deals with Oxfam's business. However, it is worth asking Oxfam Head Office to quote for insurance, as better rates may be possible.

Insurance certificates are issued for each shipment. In the case of goods shipped by air, these may arrive after the goods. In the event of damaged or missing goods, it is vital that the proper procedure is followed if a claim is not to be prejudiced. The procedure is detailed on the certificate of insurance.

Goods are normally insured for 60 days after their arrival *while in the port*. Once out of the port or airport, unless this has been specifically asked for and agreed in advance, they will *not* be insured, and local cover should be arranged.

8.3.4 Local transport, handling, and storage

a. Commodity control

This is the process by which goods are ordered, stored, and stacked, through to final distribution, in a manner that ensures their security and allows for feedback on their receipt, so as to adjust supply to demand. A system must be put in place, with the staff required to operate it, before goods start arriving. A good commodity-control system not only reduces pilferage and loss, but will also provide vital management information.

Oxfam has a model commodity control system for use in relief operations (see Oxfam Procedures Manual for details). In general, each consignment should be accompanied by a consignment note detailing what it is, who sent it, where it should go, and to whom. The issuer of the goods should get confirmation of their safe receipt before paying the transporter or supplier. Once in the warehouse, details of goods should be entered into a ledger (consignments in date order) and on stock cards (running total of holding of particular item).

Each emergency programme is unique, and the system devised will have to fit in with both government procedures and local practice and custom. This should be checked before a system is established.

b. Warehousing and storage

The choice of warehouses may not be large, but inadequate storage facilities may mean the loss or damage of large quantities of expensive relief items. It is worth spending time and trouble locating and, if necessary, refurbishing storage facilities. Sharing warehouse facilities is not recommended: security is much easier with exclusive access to the site.

A warehouse should:

- be secure from theft
- be weather proof
- have a concrete floor (or floor covered with plastic sheeting)
- have good ventilation
- have reliable all weather truck access (both dry and rainy season)
- be secure against pests (especially rats and birds)
- have a reasonable permissible floor loading (1000 Kg/m2).

The following advice should be followed in storing goods:

- Keep stacks to 2.5m high at most, and do not mix commodities in the same stack. Keep foodstuffs separate from non-food items, especially fuel. Edible oil is notorious for leaking; keep it well away from other commodities and observe the stacking restrictions (printed on the box). Stack commodities on pallets. If these are not available, and cannot be made, a network of wooden poles or plastic sheeting is better than nothing. If pallets are in short supply, bagged products have priority. Keep commodities at least 1.2m clear of walls, and other stacks. Ventilate the warehouse as required so as to keep the stack as cool and dry as possible.
- Make sure that the warehouse is cleaned daily and that sweepings are removed. The outside is as important as the inside. Rank vegetation around a warehouse is a haven for rats. Make provision for fire fighting. Smoking should not be permitted in the warehouse.
- Security of goods is enhanced if clear procedures are in place and staff understand their responsibilities. Try to ensure that the site is fenced. Control access to the site and to the warehouse keys.
- The storekeeper should prepare regular reports on the state of the store and the stock. Make sure stock is utilised in accordance with the rule of 'first in, first out'. Accounting procedures for the stock should be kept up to date. The storekeeper should have somewhere to work and to keep papers.
- Should food stocks become infested with pests, (between 2 and 10 insects per 3kg sample is a heavy infestation), its treatment is a matter for experts. If food is unfit for human consumption, make sure local procedures concerning the condemnation of food are followed.

6

c. Local transport

(To be read in conjunction with 3.2.7 Vehicles.)

Road transport is the main delivery method in most programmes because of its availability and flexibility. It is not practical to buy and operate a fleet of trucks unless the programme will continue for a number of years. The setting up of a truck fleet requires specialist advice and a lead time of about six months. In most cases, Oxfam should use local transport contractors rather than setting up a new fleet. Their knowledge of local conditions can prove invaluable.

Trucking operations tend to be much smaller in developing countries than in industrialised countries. Often a truck will be operated by its owner, who will ply for hire individually. It can be time-consuming to assemble a fleet, as each truck may have to be negotiated for separately. It may be possible to pass on the job of finding sufficient trucks to an agent, who will sub-contract to individual owner-drivers. If a large contractor is available, it is advisable to check their record for reliability and performance before engaging them. The number of trucks that will have to be used and for how long depends on the goods to be moved, and the distance and quality of roads to be travelled. Routes, particularly the strength of bridges and the steepness of river fords, should be checked before commencing the operation.

In drawing up a contract with the trucking firm, Oxfam should ensure that it conforms to any legislation or to local practice concerning freight rates. Contracts agreeing to pay for deliveries (either per ton or per trip) provide an incentive for the contractor to complete the job more quickly.

Responsibility for losses during transit, and for insurance, must be clarified before signing the contract. If substantial trucking is needed, a transport manager who knows the local context might be employed.

The lack of spare parts and the age of the trucks may mean that their reliability is poor. The search for spare parts may keep trucks off the road for extended periods. It is usually easier for an international agency, with its access to hard currency, to import spares. It may be feasible to pay contractors with spare parts. Provision of fuel to contractors can save them time searching for and securing sufficient (and sometimes expensive) fuel. Agreement on how much fuel per trip will be supplied should be made in advance.

Rail transport is good for moving large amounts of material quickly, but railways rarely reach the required destination, so there will need to be some trucking capacity to take cargo to or from the railhead. Cost savings can be achieved where the rail section of the journey is long, (over 500km) but the off-take time from the railhead must be sufficient to avoid overloading the storage facilities. The reliability of the trains must be checked.

Air transport: the use of aircraft for in-country transport may be necessary either because of impossible terrain or security considerations. Aircraft are fast and reliable, but expensive, and normally beyond the means of NGOs. Air operations are complex to set up and manage, because aircraft require special fuels and are subject to rigorous maintenance schedules. Oxfam staff must seek expert advice before embarking on airlift operations. Aircraft are most useful for transporting high-value, low-bulk items such as drugs; and to transport personnel.

8.3.5 Distribution

The administration of relief distribution is a major and complex exercise. Social structures or channels that represent women as well as men should be drawn on to the maximum. It cannot be assumed that the most vocal members of the affected population are necessarily its most accurate representatives. It is vital to look critically at how genuinely representative these people are; and not take claims to be representative at face value. For example, while community 'leaders' or spokespersons are usually men, it is women who hold the major responsibility for producing, processing, and cooking the household's food.

Food-distribution systems must be designed to reflect and build on the actual responsibility for all aspects of food management held by women and men. Steps must be taken to ensure that distribution between and within households does not act to the disadvantage of women and children, as is commonly the case. Similarly, in a seeds, fertilisers, and tools distribution programme, it is important to ensure that those responsible for cultivating food for household consumption are given appropriate supplies. The specific needs of women-maintained households, who may not have access to land, or the opportunity to farm it, should be addressed.

It is crucial to ascertain the extent to which social and household structures have themselves been disrupted by the emergency, and so are not reliable channels. For example, there may be a marked increase in the number of women-maintained households, in which roles previously associated with men are taken on by women, in addition to their existing responsibilities. To set up distribution mechanisms through men might mean that households with no males present were excluded, or disadvantaged.

If distribution is handled by local structures, such as village councils, it is important to check both how representative these councils are and how many people they actually represent. Individual registration may be necessary if reliable records do not exist, perhaps because the named family member is no longer present. This is a labour-intensive operation: 200 helpers are required to hold a registration for 10,000 people. (See *Registration in Emergencies*: Oxfam Practical Guide 6.)

8.4 Administration and staffing

8.4.1 Preparedness and contingency plans

Every Oxfam office is expected to prepare a plan to cover the actions and arrangements required in the event of an emergency. This enables staff to respond quickly and effectively if a disaster occurs. The plans should be regularly reviewed, and should include:

- a review of likely or possible emergencies, including an awareness of past emergencies and disasters and the lessons learnt from responses to them (successes as well as failures);
- information about contingency plans for major emergencies drawn up by central and local government, UN agencies and other NGOs; links with relevant bodies to develop an understanding of the likely role that Oxfam could play;
- details of monitoring and early-warning systems for both slow-onset or sudden-onset emergencies, and for emergencies of a political nature (armed conflict, large-scale migration within natural boundaries, influx of refugees);
- co-ordinating mechanisms to review emergency preparedness of different organisations and to share information on early-warning or monitoring systems;
- assistance being given to local NGOs and groups in vulnerable areas to improve their preparedness and, where appropriate, integrate them into locally-co-ordinated preparedness plans;
- identification of relief items and services likely to be needed in an emergency (food, water supply equipment, shelter materials, medical supplies); and identification of ready sources of supply (including perhaps a stockpile of emergency equipment and supplies), both locally and regionally;
- details of local, national and international bodies with emergency relief capacity, together with up-to-date phone, fax, telex and E-mail numbers for essential contacts (including home numbers, where appropriate);
- register of local professional consultants or technical advisers to assist with assessment: this should include women as well as men, all of whom should be skilled in dealing with the gender dimensions of emergency work;

- likely needs for additional personnel, whether specialist or not (distinguishing between essential and desirable skills or characteristics); and sources for recruiting short-term staff;
- current reference copies of relevant emergency and procedures manuals, in the appropriate languages;
- contingency plans for urgent access to money (loan or overdraft facilities, hard-currency arrangements, credit-card facilities, additional signatories to bank accounts);
- consideration of the additional tasks the office might have to undertake, and how they would be managed and financed (extra communications needs, vehicles, interpreters for visitors, office space, accounting.)

At programme level, more detailed contingency plans are drawn up, and cover:

- programme priorities and allocation of responsibilities and tasks in the event of emergencies;
- lines and forms of communication with other offices (Head Office, other regional offices, NGO co-ordination networks);
- a review of needs of local and expatriate staff and their families;
- security guidelines, in particular to enable women workers to assist in emergencies and not merely be protected from them;
- contact arrangements, assembly points, 'standing orders' for particular situations;
- government and relevant Embassy or Consulate plans for communication, or evacuation;
- contingency stocks of fuel, food, batteries, spares, cash;
- security of office assets, especially vehicles;
- security of confidential documents (files, computer back-up disks);
- security of money, cash books, cheque books;
- up-to-date details of all personnel, including next-of-kin, passport numbers, essential medication; extra copies of standard visa forms or other travel documents; supplies of passport-sized photographs for staff who travel;
- names and home telephone numbers of relevant staff.

8.4.2 Financial procedures
(To be read in conjunction with **3.2.5** Financial administration.)

Financial procedures must be established at the beginning of any relief programme, because in a confused situation it is easy to lose financial control. A basic accountancy system should be set up and, depending on the size of the operation, a qualified person employed to control finances. There are often complications when a large operational programme is being mounted, both because of the many payments and transactions associated with relief distribution programmes, and the number of additional staff on the payroll. Where co-funding from the EU is involved, there are accounting demands on relief programmes which are in excess of Oxfam's standard requirements, and which must be met.

Oxfam staff should refer to current guidelines on financial procedures for use in emergencies. These will provide the basis on which specific procedures for the programme in question will be based.

8.4.3 Staffing and recruitment

Major emergency programmes create the need for extra staff, at least in the short term. Personnel needs will vary according to the type of programme and its scope, as well as on the qualifications and experience already available within the existing staff. It may be necessary to take on additional staff for specific areas of work, such as administration, accounting, technical assessments, liaison or information work. It may be important to complement the range of skills already present in the programme team, by taking on a person who is already familiar with the affected population, with the area, or with the language of a particular ethnic group. The relief team should include enough women to ensure that consultation can readily take place with women from the affected population, especially in areas concerning reproductive health, sanitation needs, personal hygiene, and protection issues. Emergency staff should have the relevant experience and background, but may require detailed induction in Oxfam procedures.

Oxfam's gender policy states that all programme staff should be aware that the impact of relief and development work is different on women and on men, and that they must aim to ensure that interventions actively benefit women, and do not worsen their situation relative to men. (See **2.1** Gender.)

Oxfam's Head Office is ultimately responsible for ensuring that all staff are employed in accordance with the terms and conditions of Oxfam's personnel policies and Staff Charters, and advice may be sought from specialist departments in drawing up contracts. Assistance should be given to help employees to review any private insurance policies, as these may be invalidated by particular work locations, particularly in areas of armed conflict.

8.4.4 Staff health and security
(To be read in conjunction with **6.3.4.2.b** Psycho-social aspects of armed conflict; and **5.4.9** Mental and emotional well-being.)

Within the emergency relief programme, the Representative carries overall responsibility for the health, morale, and general well-being of all Oxfam employees in the Regional/Country Office. These matters are important for the individuals concerned, and their families. They also affect the efficient running of the programme.

Working in the midst of an emergency, particularly for those who have no prior experience in such situations, is highly stressful. The pressure and volume of work may be exceptionally high. The suffering experienced by the victims of large-scale emergencies may be distressing for relief workers. In some situations, staff, and their families, may fear for their own lives or safety. The safety of aid workers in areas of armed conflict is a paramount and growing concern.

Exposure to prolonged stress, fear, and pressure of work affects people in a variety of ways. Emotional tension may be extreme for those who have family and friends in some way caught up in the emergency. Foreign relief workers may be very isolated or without adequate accommodation; and have no support networks outside their immediate colleagues. A culture readily builds up in which aid workers can feel guilty if they are not constantly immersed in their work. People may not themselves recognise the ways in which their responses and behaviour are stress-related. A common reaction is to take refuge in work — by working long hours without proper breaks, and failing to relax or take leave. The individual's health and ability to function may seriously suffer. Fatigue and exhaustion also lead to poor judgements or reckless decisions.

The Representative is responsible for establishing a work culture which enables staff to articulate their concerns and know that they will be listened to sympathetically. Ensuring that every member of the team has workloads which are manageable enough for her or him to be able to take adequate leave is an essential part of such a culture.

When staff are working in areas of political violence or armed conflict, they may be exposed to exceptional physical risks. These may include travelling in areas that have been mined, being caught in cross-fire, being detained for interrogation, or being kidnapped. These risks are in themselves the cause of considerable stress for the individuals, and their families and friends. Even when no physical risks are involved, there are enormous emotional pressures on aid workers who are witnessing, or working with the victims of, human rights violations, torture, air raids, or massacres. These may express themselves in ways not unlike those associated with Post-Traumatic Stress Disorder (PTSD), whose symptoms include sleep disturbance, poor concentration, disruptive 'flashbacks' or depression.

It is Oxfam's policy to ensure that staff are fully debriefed after all assignments. Professional counselling may be made available to staff, if this is required. Oxfam's Privation, Risk and Hardship policy outlines other forms of help which might be offered to staff in certain circumstances — for instance, additional paid leave or travel outside the country. Oxfam's relief programme managers should review how it might apply to their particular location.

Oxfam has a duty to ensure that staff are equipped to make informed choices about the risks they may be running in their work. They should be made aware of any personal dangers involved, and of what support they could expect from Oxfam as an employer (such as personal accident or life assurance cover) in the event of a mishap.

It is not acceptable to allow or encourage staff to run undue, or avoidable, risks in the course of their work for Oxfam. Parameters need to be agreed within the relief team as to what constitutes an unreasonable risk in any specific context. If individual staff members feel that the risks become too great, or outweigh their usefulness in staying, a joint decision should be reached about whether to withdraw. In very extreme cases, staff may be withdrawn if, in the judgement of Oxfam's senior staff and/or Trustees, the situation has become too dangerous to justify their presence.

8.4.5 Travel in dangerous circumstances

Whatever the pressure to undertake site visits to unsafe areas for assessment, monitoring or reporting requirements, the highest priority must be given to assessing the risks involved in doing this, and to planning to avoid unnecessary exposure to danger. This may involve liaison with the relevant government or military authorities, or other reliable sources of information. Precise guidelines for each situation should cover such issues as:

- use of various routes;
- marking of vehicles;
- use of convoys and escorts;
- carrying of first-aid equipment (and basic training in its use);
- tool kit and essential spare parts for vehicle (and basic training in their use);
- reporting and logging procedures;
- respect of curfews;
- travelling alone, on public transport or in agency vehicles with other NGO personnel;
- travelling with armed guards, or under armed protection;
- offering lifts to, or accepting lifts from, armed or uniformed personnel (Oxfam staff are not permitted to carry arms and should in normal circumstances avoid travelling with, or giving lifts to, armed personnel);

974

- contingency plans in the case of being ambushed, caught in cross-fire, questioned, detained or kidnapped;
- communications procedures;
- procedures on obtaining permits to travel to affected areas;
- guidelines on documentation (personal and Oxfam-related) to be carried.

NB Specific recommendations for travelling in land-mined areas are given in Oxfam's manual on this subject (see Resources Section).

8.5 Key questions

1 What reliable background information on the area and people affected is already available, and is it accurately differentiated by gender? What sources exist for supplementary information?
2 What background information is already available on the specific emergency, including analysis of its underlying causes and likely impact? Is this information already differentiated by gender? If not, how will this deficiency be addressed prior to planning an emergency programme?
3 What arrangements for communication already exist between the Regional/Country Office and Oxfam Head Office? How might these need to be modified in the short, medium and longer term of an emergency programme? What staffing arrangements might be required to address increased communications needs?
4 What are the existing lines of responsibility, authority, consultation and decision-making in the Regional/Country Office, in Oxfam Head Office, and between the two? Do these require modification in the context of an emergency programme?
5 How might existing arrangements for personnel management need to be modified in the short, medium and longer term phases of the emergency? If new staff have been recruited, are their job descriptions and contractual arrangements clear and have their induction and training needs been met? Are staff who have been redeployed aware of their duties and responsibilities?
6 How will the current composition of programme staff permit a thorough and sensitive analysis of gender-related concerns to be incorporated into the assessment and/or design of any emergency programme? Will it be necessary to recruit more women, whether as programme staff or as technical advisers, to ensure that effective discussion can take place with women among the population affected by the emergency?

6

7 What personnel requirements has the emergency generated or can be predicted in the short to medium term? How have matters of staff security and health been addressed? What provision been made for briefing and debriefing of staff?

8 What are the financial procedures to be adopted? What is the procedure for supplies request and procurement? What are the transport options? What provision has been made for local transport, handling and storage? What is the commodity control system?

9 What is the division of labour with other agencies?

Appendix I

Relief items for which local suppliers should be identified

1 Food supplies (as appropriate locally): beans, oil, rice, sugar, wheat, maize.
2 Subsistence equipment: blankets, buckets, clothing, housing and construction materials, insecticides and sprayers, kitchen utensils.
3 Water supplies: bleaching powder, drilling rigs, pipes, pumps, tanks.
4 Medical supplies: blood banks, dressings, drugs, equipment.
5 Agricultural supplies: fertiliser, hand tools, pesticides and sprayers, machinery, veterinary supplies.
6 Logistics: transport, fuel, warehousing.
7 Support equipment: generators, office supplies.

6

Appendix II

Oxfam's emergencies store

Oxfam's UK emergencies store holds stocks of:

- blankets;
- plastic sheeting: for use as waterproof shelter (see *Plastic Sheeting :Its use for emergency housing and other purposes,* an Oxfam Technical Guide.) The usual stock is (8mt x 28mt), 375 microns (1,500 gauge) black; (8mt x 28mt), 250 microns (1,000 gauge) black;
- feeding kits: for use in nutritional assessment, supplementary and therapeutic feeding. The original Supplementary Feeding Kit (with equipment for feeding 500 children packed in 2 Triwall boxes) and the Therapeutic Feeding Kit (with equipment for 100 children incorporating a nutritional assessment kit packed in one Triwall box) are being remodelled as 3 separate kits: Nutritional Assessment and Surveillance Kit; Supplementary Feeding Kit (for 250 children); Therapeutic Feeding Kit (for 100 children);
- sanitation units: for use with high density population to provide rapid sanitation;
- water kits: distribution, pumping, storage.

Appendix III

Other relief items

Tents: the British Red Cross Society maintains a stock of family-size ridge tents (floor area 4.25 mt x 2.75 mt, height at walls 1.20 mt, at ridge 2.15mt).

Family cooking sets: available from UNIPAC (see standard specifications appended below).

Soap: Available at short notice from normal commercial suppliers.

Drugs and Medical Equipment: ECHO (The Joint Mission Hospital Equipment Board) exists to supply bona fide charities and missions, etc. with drugs and equipment at low cost. Oxfam purchases through them or through similar organisations in Europe. (See also **5**.4.8 The provision of essential drugs.)

6

Appendix IV

Standard specifications for commonly required relief items

(Reproduced from UNHCR Handbook for Emergencies; UNIPAC numbers in brackets.)

These specifications have been developed with UNICEF to assist staff in drawing up tender requests where local purchase is possible, and to give a clear indication of what could otherwise be supplied at short notice through funding agency headquarters. The UNIPAC catalogue reference is given in brackets where applicable; the actual source of supply through funding agency headquarters would depend on the circumstances and in particular on regional availability.

1 Blankets, heavy (similar E500 35 05)
   Woven, 30-40% wool, the rest other fibres (cotton, polyester) blanket with stitched ends, size 150 x 200 cm, weight 1.3 kg., packed in pressed bales of 50 items. Each bale would be about 0.35 m3 volume and weight 65-70 kg. Large quantities are generally available.

2 Blankets, light
   Cotton size 140 x 190 cm, weight approx 850 gm, usually packed in pressed bales of 100 items. Each bale would be about 0.4m3 volume and weight 85-90 kg. Fairly large quantities generally available ex-stock in Asian region; more limited availability elsewhere.

3 Buckets, plastic (217 00 00)
   Bucket/pail 10 litre capacity, polyethylene with plated steel-wire bail handle, conical seamless design, suitable for nesting, reinforced or turned lip. Plastic or galvanized buckets are likely to be available locally and are very useful. Plastic are generally to be preferred.

4 Family cooking sets, emergency (203 65 10)
   12 items aluminium utensils as follows:
   • Cooking pot, 6 litre, with bail handle and cover
   • Cooking pot, 4 litre, with bail handle
   • Dinner plate, aluminium (4 each)
   • Plastic mug (4 each)
   • Coffee pot, aluminium, 2 litre
   The set is packed in a cardboard carton 25 x 25 x 20 cm, weight 2 kg.

980

The set does not contain cutlery: five stainless steel soup spoons and one stainless steel cook's knife, blade 15-17 cm, can be supplied separately if not available locally. While the set is quite robust, utensils of a heavier gauge aluminium are normally supplied by UNHCR when some delay can be accepted. The advantages of the emergency set are lower weight, packed volume and price. It is therefore particularly suitable when supply by air is necessary.

Also recommended by Oxfam:
5 Plastic sheeting
   Black seamless polyethylene sheeting, 250 microns (1000 gauge), width 5-8m, supplied double-folded in lengths usually of 100-800m, approx. weight 1kg/4m2. For multipurpose use: roofing, walls, ground sheets, linings, etc. Widely available.

6

Appendix V

Oxfam Policy in Emergencies

1 Most activities related to household subsistence (food preparation, fuel-gathering, and childcare), health care, and water management are the responsibility of women. Aid workers responsible for assessing and/or planning these areas of work must be conversant with the implications of gender relations, and specifically the distinct roles of women and men, for public health and community organisation; and able to work effectively with women in the affected population. It may not be possible or appropriate for a male aid worker to do this in some cultures.

2 Many aspects of public health are the official responsibility of government departments. Oxfam should ensure that programme plans are acceptable both to the appropriate authorities, and to representatives of the affected population.

3 In order for public health interventions to be comprehensive and complementary, Oxfam should ensure appropriate consultation and review mechanisms between the various agencies involved.

4 Women and girls constitute the vast majority of registered refugees, and a similar proportion of internally displaced populations. A disproportionate number of women refugees die from preventable causes, such as malnutrition and its related illnesses. Health programmes must address the specific requirements of women as well as men.

Appendix VI

Oxfam water supply scheme for emergencies: the water packs

Oxfam developed the Water Packs, containing a range of equipment for provision of water supplies in emergencies, in the early 1980s. They have been used extensively in most refugee and displaced person crises for over a decade, by Oxfam and by several other multilateral and non-governmental relief agencies. The Packs are subject to constant improvement. They are designed around the main elements of water supply: pumping, storage, treatment and distribution. Each contains a number of kits, to give the flexibility to respond to a wide range of needs.

The packs are designed to be fully self-contained, with the following characteristics:

1 Each Pack is designed to provide a population of 5,000 with 20 litres of water per person. Packs can be easily used in multiples to provide for much larger numbers of people.
2 The Packs are complete with assembly instructions and all tools necessary for installation and maintenance.
3 The Packs are ready for immediate installation, in most cases within hours of arrival on site, by a team of semi-skilled workers under the supervision of an experienced engineer. The services of an experienced water engineer are needed to make best use of the Packs in order to provide an adequate water supply.
4 The equipment used is of reasonable cost and its components are light in weight for transport by air and road, and for handling on site.
5 The Packs will provide drinking water of a suitable quality for general purposes.
6 The Packs are designed for exploitation of a range of surface and groundwater sources and for distribution of water by gravity or by pumping.
7 The equipment requires only simple operation and maintenance and uses minimal external energy.
8 The Packs are easy to dismantle and re-assemble in new locations.

6

They are designed to have a working life of several years.

Each Pack comprises a number of kits as follows:

Pumping: Contains diesel-engine powered, surface-mounted pumps, complete with suction and delivery hoses, tools, and oil. Two sizes of pump are available.

Storage: Four sizes of circular tanks are available, (10.5, 45, 70 and 95cubic meters). They comprise prefabricated, galvanised-steel sheets with a rubber liner, and come complete with interconnecting pipework, fittings, and valves.

Treatment: An easily assembled slow-sand-filter system can be built using all necessary fittings, flowmeters, and sand-washing kit. Chlorine tablets are also supplied for disinfection of filtered or unfiltered water.

Distribution: Contains a 3" diameter PVC supply main, 1" distribution pipework, all necessary fittings and water distribution frames complete with self-closing taps.

The Oxfam/Delagua water testing kit is also invaluable for use with the Packs. It is a complete portable kit, including a battery-operated incubator, for testing the primary indicators of water quality: faecal coliforms, chlorine content, pH, turbidity, electrical conductivity and temperature.

Full details of the Packs are available from Oxfam.

Appendix VII

Oxfam emergency sanitation unit

The Oxfam Sanitation Unit is a complete, packaged system able to be delivered to an emergency site. It comprises a communal collection and treatment system of 20 squatting plates, 2 flexible tanks made of nylon-reinforced butyl rubber for sewage treatment, and all the necessary pipes and fittings.
- It is a proven system which can be assembled quickly and is not affected by soil conditions.
- One unit can service up to 1,000 persons per day.
- It requires about 3,000 litres of water per day at full design capacity.
- A new soakaway is required.
- It is suitable only for those communities who use water for anal cleansing.

The Unit can be used as a self-contained package system for sanitation and sewage treatment, or it can be seen as a kit of parts which can be used in several ways, for different kinds of sanitation. The principle features of the equipment are as follows:
- The Unit can be used with one tank only as a short-term facility.
- When used with two tanks and a percolating filter, the Unit provides continuous treatment of sewage and discharges a 'safe' effluent, providing a long-term public health facility.
- The squatting plates can be used separately within existing drainage systems to improve the latrines.
- The tanks can be connected to existing drains to provide sewage treatment where none was previously provided.
- The squatting plates can be used with borehole or trench latrines.
- The flexible tanks if new can be used to store water if required.

The Sanitation Unit works well in wet conditions where an adequate water supply is available. It is not appropriate in hot, dry conditions.

(**NOTE**: This Unit was developed by Oxfam for use in Bangladesh in the 1970s. A small number are still held at Oxfam's UK-based Emergency Stores. The design information is available from Oxfam.)

6

9 Resources

Many useful articles on emergencies and relief work appear in various journals, notably the quarterly *Disasters* (International Disasters Institute), and *Development in Practice* (Oxfam). Items marked * are available in French, and those # in Spanish.

General

Allen, T and Morsink, H (eds) (1994) *When Refugees Go Home: African Experiences*, UNRISD and James Currey.

Anderson, M B and Woodrow, P J (1989) R*ising from the Ashes: Development Strategies in Times of Disaster*, Paris: Westview Press, UNESCO.

Bennet, J (1994) *Meeting Needs: NGO Coordination in Practice*, Earthscan.

Benthall, J (1993) *Disasters, Relief, and the Media*, I B Tauris.

Blakie, P, Cannon, T, Davis, I and Wisner, B (1994) *At Risk: Natural Hazards, People's Vulnerability and Disasters*, Routledge.

Blomquist, U and Mahlasela, J (1988) *Community Work: Social Work Training in Refugee Camps*, Stockholm: Radda Barnen.

Bonnerjea, L (1985) *Shaming the World: The Needs of Women Refugees*, London: Change.

Brazeau, A (July, 1990), 'Gender Sensitive Development Planning in the Refugee Context': UNHCR.

CAPART (1990) *Disaster Preparedness Handbook: A Handbook for Trainers*, India.

Carter, W N (1992) *Disaster Management*, Asian Development Bank.

Cuny, F (1983) *Disasters and Development*, Oxford: Oxford University Press.

D'Souza, F and Crisp, J (1985) *The Refugee Dilemma*, Minority Rights Group report 43, London.

Duffield, M (1990) *War and Famine in Africa*, Oxfam research paper.

Dye, G, Hughes, L and Penrose, A.(1991) *Children: A Right to Refuge*, Save the Children.

FAO (1988) T*he Global Information and Early Warning System on Food and Agriculture*.

Forbes , M S (1991) *Refugee Women*, Zed/UN/NGO Liaison Service.

IIED (1988) *Famine and Rapid Onset Disaster and Warning Systems*.

Institute of Child Health, *The Refugee Child and the Child-to-Child*

986

Programme, London, Institute of Child Health.

Kelly, N (1989) *Working with Refugee Women: A Practical Guide.*

League of Red Cross and Red Crescent Societies (1991) *Working with Refugees and Asylum Seekers.*

Larkin, M A, Cuny, F C, and Stein, B N (eds) (1991) *Repatriation under Conflict in Central America*, Washington DC: CIPRA and Intertect.

Maskrey, A (1989) *Disaster Mitigation: A Community Based Approach*, Oxford: Oxfam.

McCallin, M (1992) T*he Psychological Well-Being of Refugee Children: Research, Practice and Policy Issues*, Geneva: International Catholic Child Bureau.

McGrath, R (1994), *Landmines: Legacy of Conflict: A Manual for Development Workers*, Oxford: Oxfam.

Minear, L, Weiss, T G (1995) *Mercy Under Fire: War and the Global Humanitarian Community*, Boulder:Westview

Ressler, E M, Boothby, N and Steinbock, D (1988), *Unaccompained Children: Care and Protection in Wars, Natural Disasters and Refugee Movements*, Oxford: Oxford University Press.

Richman, N (1993) *Communicating with Children: Helping Children in Distress*, London: Save the Children.

Summerfield, D (1991), 'The Psychological Effects of Conflict in the Third World', *Development in Practice* 1:3, Oxford, Oxfam.

UNDRO (1991) *Mitigating Natural Disasters.*

UNDRO (1982) *Disasters and the Disabled.*

UNHCR (1982) *Handbook for Emergencies*, Geneva.*#

UNHCR (1984) *Handbook for Social Services*, Geneva.

UNHCR *Regional Emergency Preparedness Profiles.*

UNICEF (1986) *Assisting in Emergencies.**

Wijkman, A and Timberlake, L (1984) *Natural Disasters: Acts of God or Acts of Man?*, Earthscan.

Williams, S *et al* (1994) *Oxfam Gender Training Manual*, Oxfam.

Zolberg, A *et al, Escape from Violence: Conflict and the Refugee Crisis in the Modern World*

Health and nutrition in emergencies

Kuntz, D (1990) *Ensuring the Health of Refugees: Taking a Broader Vision*, Washington DC: RPG.

Mears, C and Chowdhury, S (1994) *Health Care for Refugees and Displaced People*, Oxford: Oxfam.

PAHO (1981, *Emergency Health Management After Natural Disaster.*

PAHO (1990) *International Health Relief Assistance, A Guide for Effective Aid.*

Sandler, R . and Jones, T C (eds.) *Medical Care of Refugees*, New York and Oxford: Oxford University Press.

Simmonds, S, Vaugham, P, William-Gunn (eds.) (1983) *Refugee Community Health Care*, Oxford: Oxford University Press.

UNHCR (1989) *Essential Drugs Policy:* Geneva.

WHO (1990) *The New Emergency Health Kit.*

Environmental health and physical infrastructure
Cairncross, S (1988) *Small Scale Sanitation*, London: Ross Institute.

Davis, I (1978) *Shelter after Disaster*, Oxford Polytechnic Press: New York.

Oxfam (1981) *Plastic Sheeting: Its Use for Emergency Housing and Shelter*, Oxford: Oxfam.

UNICEF, *Handbook*, Chapters 9-12 and Annexes.*

Food security, food aid and food distribution
Keen, D (1993) *Famine, Needs-assessment and Survival Strategies in Africa*, Oxfam Research Paper 8, Oxford: Oxfam

Lusty, T and Diskett P (1984) *Selective Feeding Programmes*, Practical Health Guide 1, Oxford: Oxfam.

Sen, A (1988) *Hunger and Entitlements, Wider Research for Action*, World Institute for Development Economics Research of the United Nations University.

Sen, A (1981) *Poverty and Famines: An Essay on Entitlement and Deprivation*, Oxford: Oxford University Press.

WFP (1989) *Food Aid in Emergencies.*

WFP (1983) *Food Storage Manual.*

Young H (1992) *Food Scarcity and Famine*, Practical Health Guide 7, Oxford: Oxfam.

Management procedures in emergencies
ICRC (1987) *Red Cross Cargo.*

LICROSS (1982) *When Disaster Strikes: Emergency Logistics Handbook*, Volags Steering Committee for Disasters, Geneva.

UNHCR (1989) *Supplies and Food Aid Handbook.*

Index

abortion 653, 654, 744
abuse
  alcohol or drug abuse 647-8
  children 275-6, 281-2
  women 181, 845, 884-5
access and control profile 135, 137, 210 11
accompaniment 127-8
accounts *see* financial administration,
  accounting statements
acidity of soil 82
acquaculture *see* fish farming
Acquired Immune Deficiency Syndrome
  see HIV/AIDS
Action Aid 953
Action on Aid and Disability 314
Action Research 99
activity profile 136, 210
acute respiratory infections 640,
  731-2, 909
adoptions 288
advocacy 377, 378, 388, 392-3
  Charity Commission guidelines
    390-2
  disabled persons 314
  ethnic and race relations 260-1
  human rights action 56-7, 221
  social organisation and 384-7
  visits 389
  women and 221
  see also campaigning
Afghanistan 361, 667, 815
African Charter on Human and People's
  Rights 29, 30
African Commission on Human and
  People's Rights 46
African Development Bank 778
ageing *see* elderly people
Agency for Cooperation and Research in
  Development (ACORD) 342
Agricultural and Forestry Workers'
  Association (Pakistan) 591
agriculture 515-60
  access to resources 520

analysis of rural livelihoods 103-11
biodiversity 89-90
capital-intensive 517
cereal banks 527-8
co-operatives 557-9
control of resources 520
credit 558
crop varieties
  choice 527
  high yield (HYV) 89, 517, 524
  locally-bred or traditional 523-4
  new varieties 524
  types 525-6
cropping systems
  LEISA 83, 532-5
  small-scale farmers 530, 531, 532
fertility maintenance 532-3
fish farming *see* fish farming
fishing *see* fishing
gender inequalities 204, 522-3, 542-4
gleaning 522
'green revolution' 89, 517, 524
high yield varieties (HYV) 89, 517, 524
inappropriate technology 106
land *see* land rights; *main heading* land
livestock production 537-55
  bees and beekeeping 554-5, 593
  breed improvement 545-6
  by-products 542-3
  camels 551
  cattle 549
  chickens 553
  choice of species and breeds 545-6
  cultural considerations 541-2
  diseases 547
  division of labour 542-3
  donkeys 551
  ducks 553
  environmental degradation 539
  extensive systems 538-9
  feeding 546
  geese 553-4
  goats 550

6

guinea fowl 554
guinea pigs 552-3
health 546-7
housing 547
increasing 544-7
land rights 543
llamoids 551
nutrition 546
ownership 542-3
pastoralists 538-9
pigs 551-2
poultry 553-4
rabbits 552
sheep 550
small-scale 541
social considerations 541-2
vaccination 539
water buffaloes 550
water provision 539
wildlife 554
low-external-input sustainable agricul
   ture (LEISA) 83, 533
   fertility maintenance 532-3
   pest control 534-5
   weed control 535
marketing organisations 558
NGO Sustainable Agriculture Treaty 519
non-traditional farming 105
organisations 555-60
   credit 558
   marketing 558-9
   pastoralist 556-7
   small-scale farmers 557-9
   training 559
participatory appraisal 523
pastoralists 538-9
   agropastoralists 538
   assessment of pastoralism 107-8
   associations 556-7
   emergencies and 890-1, 892
   general guidelines for develop-
      ment 547-8
   nomadic pastoralists 538
   reducing vulnerability 548
   supporting basic rights 548
   sustainability 107-8
   threats to livelihood 107
   transhumant pastoralists 538
   see also livestock production
pest control 534-5
preservation 529-30
processing 527, 529-30
production groups 557-9

rehabilitation programmes 838
rights
   crop by-products 522
   crops and income 521
   labour and assistance 522
   land see land rights
risk 516
sharecropping 521
shocks 106
small-scale farmers 517-18
   access to and control of resources 520-2
   cropping systems 530, 531, 532
   increasing production 523-7
   preservation 529-30
   processing 527
   production groups or cooperatives
      557-9
   storage 527-8
   see also livestock production
storage 527-8
sustainable systems 106-7, 518-19
   fertility maintenance 532-3
   low-external-input (LEISA) 83, 532-5
   pest control 534-5
   weed control 535
threats to livelihoods 106
traditional farming 104-5
training 559
trees on farms 587-9
   alley farming 588-9
   fodder 588
   see also trees and forests
vegetable production
   for landless people 535-7
   hydroponics 536-7
   kitchen gardens 536
   nutrient film technique 536-7
weed control 535
women in 204, 522-3, 542-4
   see also land
agro-chemicals 82, 84
AIDS see HIV/AIDS
AIDS Support Organisation (Uganda) 754
air transport
   international 964
   local 969
alcohol abuse 647-8
Alliance of Forest Peoples (Brazil) 593-9
ambulances 639
American Convention on Human Rights
   30, 46
American Council of Churches 873
American Declaration of the Rights and

Duties of Man 46
Amnesty International 45, 47
Angola 76
animals
  social and cultural considerations 541-2
  see also agriculture, livestock production
Annapurna Mandal 505
antenatal care 655, 669
Anti-Slavery International 48, 260
apartheid 76-7, 232
Aquinas, Thomas 28
Arid Lands Information Network (ALIN)
  80, 106-7, 380, 509
armed conflict 812
  asylum seekers 843
  children in 278-80, 841
    displaced children 279, 286
    refugees 279
    soldiers 279-80
  civilians
    dependency-syndrome 857
    learned helplessness 857
    legislation protecting 846-7
    NGO support 853-8
    psycho-social aspects 760-2, 855-8
    'rebel sympathisers' 853, 870
    see also non-combatants
  deforestation during 587
  denial of human rights 841
  disablement cause 307
  displaced persons 25, 75-6, 843-4
    rights 844-6
    see also main heading
  education during 359, 887-8, 889-90
  emergencies 840-59
  environment and 73-8
    destruction of infrastructure 75
    destruction of natural resources 75-6
    landmines 75
    migrations 75-6
    over environmental resources 76-8
  ethnic groups and 76
  Geneva Conventions 842, 846
  health care
    dependency-syndrome 857
    ex-combatants 761-2
    post-traumatic stress disorder 760, 856
    psycho-social aspects 855-8
    trauma 855
  human right to freedom from 27
  humanitarian assistance 842, 849-53
    assessment and monitoring 852-3
    channels for relief 851-2
    dilemmas facing agencies 850-1
    impartiality principle 849-53, 870
    international legislation 842-8
    landmines 75, 307-8, 893
    mental health 760-2, 855-8
    migrations 75-6
    NGOs and 848-59
      lobbying 858-9
      non-operational work 858-9
      practical approaches 849-59
      staff safety 848-9
    non-combatants 38, 74
      see also civilians
    non-international 847-8
    psycho-social aspects 760-2, 855-8
    refugees 25, 75-6, 286, 843
      rights 844-6
      see also main heading
    victim protection 846-7
    women 189-90, 841, 845, 855
    see also emergencies
assessment *see* evaluation; information
  assessment; monitoring
Association for Progressive Communica-
  tions (APC) 459
Association of Prostitutes of Rio de
  Janeiro 752
Association of South-East Asian Nations
  (ASEAN) 37
Association of Women Entrepreneurs
  (Senegal) 381
asylum seekers 843
audits 451-2
  terms of reference 452

Baby Milk Action Coalition (BMAC) 772
Bamako Initiative 778
Bangladesh 343, 505, 877
  Grameen Bank 505, 611
bank accounts 445
  see also financial administration
Bantu Education 357
bees and beekeeping 554-5, 593
Bentham, Jeremy 29
Biafran war 815
bilharzia 734
biodiversity 88-90
  biotechnology 90
  forests 90-1
  in agriculture 89-90
biogas 92-3
biotechnology 90
birth planning 654, 657, 736-44

definitions 737
HIV/AIDS and 739, 742-3
methods
  abortion 744
  barrier methods 742-3
  Billings method 742
  condoms 742-3
  contraceptives 741-2, 743
  hormonal methods 741-2, 743
  injectable contraceptives 741-2, 743
  intra-uterine devices 741, 743
  sterilisation 741, 744
  traditional methods 742
Oxfam interventions 739-40
support for 738-9
population control 737-8
services 740
blankets 970
blindness
  disabled persons 676
  elderly persons 674
bonded labour 235
boreholes 697-8
BRAC 343
Brazil
  agriculture 517
  Alliance of Forest Peoples 593
  Association of Prostitutes of Rio de
    Janeiro 752
  conflict over environmental resources 76
  fishworkers 111, 116-17
    organisations 578-9
  forests 586, 593
  GAPA (Grupo de Apoyo contra AIDS)754
  IBASE 343
  liberation theology 10
  literacy and numeracy training 366
  National Union of Indians 593
  prostitution 199
  rubber tappers 586, 593
  street children 285
  urban livelihoods 116
breast-feeding 668, 669, 681-2
  Baby Milk Action Coalition (BMAC) 772
  International Baby Foods Action Net-
    work (IBFAN) 771-2
Bridge Development Fund 608, 609
British Red Cross Society 953
Brundtland Report *Our Common Future*
  60, 61, 62
buckets, specification 970
budgets *see* financial administration,
  bugeting

buffaloes 550
Burkina Faso 937, 938

Cambodia 74, 381, 870, 893
camels 551
Cameroon 584
campaigning 377, 378, 384-7
  armed conflict and 858-9
  Charity Commission guidelines 378,
    390-2
  choice of issues 385-6
  direct lobbying 387-8
  disabled persons 313-14
  facilitation and training 388-90
  health education 771-2
  lobbying 377, 378, 386-7
  women 222
Canadian International Development
  Agency 129
capacities-vulnerabilities analysis 133-5,
  186, 832-4
capacity building *see* institutional develop
  ment: social organisation
carers
  elderly persons and AIDS orphans 674,
    754
  women as 660-1
Caritas Belgique 873
Caritas International 873
cash-flow forecast 444
caste 233-5, 603
  bonded labour 235
  closed system 234
  human rights 227-8
  quota or reservation policies 234-5
  small-scale industries and 603
  untouchables 228, 234
Catholic Fund for Overseas Development
  (CAFOD) 873, 953
Catholic Relief Services 873
cattle 546
CEDAW (Committee on the Elimination
  of All Forms of DIscrimination Against
  Women) 39, 45-6
cereal banks 527-8
Chad 544
Chagas disease 734
CHANGE (NGO) 39, 221
Charity Commission campaigning guide
  lines 378, 390-2
chickens 553
children 11, 269-91
  abuse 275-6, 281-2

adoption 288
AIDS orphans 674, 754
armed conflict, in 278-80, 286, 841
caring for 274-5, 282-3
  creches and kindergartens 282-3
child-focused approaches 286-8
congresses 289
Convention on the Rights of the Child
  270-1
cultural identity 888
Declaration of the Rights of the Child
  270
definitions of childhood 273-4
demographic trends 272
displaced 279, 286
education
  formal 283-4
  in refugee camps 284
  non-formal 284
  primary 283
emergencies 280, 886-8
  education 887-8
  health 887
employment 271-2
  domestic workers 277, 286
  industrial workers 277
  rural workers 276-7
  sex workers 198-9, 277
feeding programmes 288
fostering 288
health
  antenatal care 669
  breast-feeding 668, 669, 681-2,
    686-7, 771-2
  CHILD to child programme 670-1
  emergency care 887
  foeticide 668
  gender inequality 668
  immunisation see main heading
  infectious diseases 667
  mass screening 671
  maternal death and 654
  mortality
    child 667
    infant 272, 667
  Oxfam support 667
  perinatal care 669-70
  pre-conception care 668-9
  reproductive health 281-2
  schools 671
  sex education 671
  sexual welfare 281-2
  siblings, responsibility for 670-1

under-fives 670
  see also caring for
human rights 54-5, 270-1
legal work for 289-90
orphanages 287
parenting 275
refugees 279, 286, 886-8
residential institutions 287-8
sex work 198-9, 277
social organisation 289-90
soldiers 279-80
sponsoring 288
street children 278, 285, 671
UNICEF 271
World Summit for Children 271
youth clubs 289
Chile 110, 343, 564
China 93
Christian Aid 873, 953
Christian Medical Commission of World
  Council of Churches 758
circumcision 194, 258, 662, 663-5
citizenship 246
civil wars see armed conflict
colonialism 239
Columbia 558
Commission on Human Rights (UN) 41-2
Commission on Inter-Church Aid
  Refugee and World Service 873
Committee Against Torture 45
Committee on the Elimination of All
  Forms of Discrimination Against
  Women (CEDAW) 39, 45-6
commoditisation 69
communicable diseases
  acute respiratory infections 640,
    731-2, 909
  bilharzia 734
  case finding and treatment 728
  Chagas disease 734
  control measures 728-9
  dehydration 730-1, 908-9
  diarrhoeal diseases 729-31, 908-9
    drug treatment 731
    NGO involvement 731
    nutrition and 729-30
    oral rehydration therapy (ORT)
      730-1
    prevention 730
    rehydration 730-1, 908-9
  elephantiasis 734
  emergencies 765
  epidemics 735

6

immunisation *see main heading*
kala azar 734
leprosy 734, 756
malaria 640, 732-3, 756
measles 723, 908
river blindness 734
sleeping sickness 734
sudden-onset emergencies 901
tuberculosis 723, 733-4, 749
vector control 727-8, 927-8
see also immunisation
communications
advocacy *see* advocacy
APC 459
campaigning *see* campaigning
E-mail 381, 458-9
electronic 381
emergencies
breakdown 956-7
confidentiality 958
costs 958
establishing link 955-6
fax 956, 957-8
radio networks 956
satellite communication equip
ment 956
situation reports 959-61
telephone procedure 958
telex 956, 957-8
facsimile transmission 956, 957-8
GEONET 459
information technology and 458-9
lobbying *see* campaigning
networks *see main heading*
Packet Switching Network 459
SATIS 459
social organisation 377-93
telex communication 956, 957-8
UNIENET 459
visits 389-90
Community Aid Abroad Trading
(Australia) 608
Community Development Forestry
Project (Nepal) 582
Community Health Workers 316
Community Water Supply and Sanitation
(CWSS) programme (Nepal) 703-4
comparative advantage 506
computer systems
advice and training 461
backing up 462
equipment 460
health and safety problems 462

in development and relief work 458
maintenance 461
power supply 460
printers 460
replacing equipment 461
software 460
viruses 461
Conference on Environment and
Development (Rio) 61, 518-19
consultation 16
emergencies 861, 879, 880-2
ethnic and race relations 255-6
information gathering 124-5
social differences 255-6
women 217-18, 879, 880-2
context of development
accompaniment 127-8
assessments *see* information assess
ment
consistency 120
cooperation 127-8
mutual understanding 120
openness 120-1
'partnerships' 127
ways of working 119-28
contingency plans 865, 970-1
Control of Diarrhoeal Diseases prgramme
640
Convention on the Prevention and
Punishment of the Crime of Genocide
246
Convention on the Rights of the Child
270-1
cooperation 127-8
Cooperative Committee for Cambodia
381
cooperatives 337
'coping strategies' 830-2
cost-benefit analysis 129, 148, 150
cost-effectiveness analysis 147-50
strengths and weaknesses 149
costing evaluation procedures 420
Council for Non-Governmental
Organisations in Malawi (CONGOMA)
380
credit and savings support
agricultural organisations 558
assessing needs 504-5
banking systems 503
credit groups 502
credit unions 503
fishing credit 577-9
forms of credit and savings 502-3

obstacles to obtaining 503-4
participation 505
revolving credit funds 558
revolving drug funds 778, 779-80
revolving loan funds 502
saveway clubs 503
small-scale industries 610-11
women-only systems 503-4
crop varieties *see* agriculture
culture
emergencies 888, 890-2
gender and 176-7, 215
human rights criticisms 29-3
livestock production 541-2
malnutrition factor 681-2
mental health 760
sanitation 705-6
sensitivity to
clashes of values 257-9
consultation 255-6
information assessment 255
information gathering 253-4, 256-7
oppressed groups 252-3
participation 255-6
social differences 235-6
women's health 193-4, 257-8, 662-6

dams 88
Narmada project 73, 86, 241
DAWN *see* Development Alternatives with
Women for a New Era (DAWN)
Day-care centres
elderly people 299-300
debt
environment and 71-2
Third World debt 485-6
see also structural adjustment policies
Declaration of the Rights of the Child 270
Declaration on Right to Development 245
Declaration on the Elimination of all
forms of Intolerance and of Discrimination based on Religion or Belief 246
deforestation *see* trees and forests
dehydration treatment 730-1, 908-9
demographics
ageing populations 293-5
children 272
depreciation 446-7
Deutsche Caritas 873
development
accompaniment 127-8
anti-poverty approach 206
consistency 120

cooperation 127-8
efficiency approach 206
empowerment approach 206-7
environment and 59-117
see also environment
equity approach 206
gender and 177-8, 205-7
practical needs 209
strategic needs 209-10
human rights in 24-58
see also human rights
limitations of projects 21-3
mutual understanding 120
of institutions *see* institutional devel
opment: social organisation
openness 120-1
participation 14-17
partnerships 127
people-centred 10-12
priorities 17-18
programmes, emergencies and 828-30
right to 9-10
sustainability *see* sustainable development
target groups 17-19
ways of working 119-28
welfare approach 205
wisdom approach 207
women and 205-7
see also empowerment; participation
Development Alternatives with Women
for a New Era (DAWN) 58, 207, 216,
221, 381
DIACONIA 380
diarrhoeal diseases 729-31, 908-9
drug treatment 731
health worker training 731
NGO involvement 731
nutrition and 729-30
prevention 730
rehydration 730-1, 908-9
diphtheria 723
Disability Rights Movement 315
disabled persons 303-18
Action on Aid and Disability 314
advocacy 314
campaigning 313-14
causes of disability 675-6
landmines 307-8
poverty-related 307
war-related 307-9
work-related 309
community-based rehabilitation
315-16

6

definitions 305-6
Disability Rights Movement 315
education and training 312-13
emergencies 892-3
Friends of the Handicapped 314
gender and
  carer 310
  disabled person 309-10
handicap definition 305-6
health 674-6
  artificial limbs 676
  cause *see* causes
  community-based rehabilitation
    315-16
  medical intervention 316
  residential care 316-17
impact of 304
impairment meaning 305
Independent Living Movement 315
interventions 310-17
medical intervention 316
networking 314-15
residential care 316-17
social organisations 313
Disabled Persons International 314
disaster mitigation 834-6
disaster preparedness 865, 970-1
  training programmes 912
  see also emergencies
Disasters Emergency Committee 953
displaced persons
  armed conflict 75-6, 843-4
    rights 844-6
  children 279, 286
  elderly people 296
  ethnic cleansing 238, 267, 845, 890
  health 765, 903
  human rights 25, 55-6
  women 186-9
division of labour (gender) 69, 207-9, 496,
  603, 605
domestic violence 192-3
domestic workers 200-1, 277, 286
donkeys 551
drought 86
drug abuse 647-8, 671
drugs (medicinal) 756-9
  abuses in connection with supply
    758
  donations 758, 778
  financing 779
  revolving drug funds 758, 778, 779-80
  supply and availability 757

WHO 'essential drugs' concept 756, 757
ducks 553

E-mail 381, 458-9
'Earth Summit' 61
ecofeminism 68-9
Ecuador 586
education and training 363-76
  agricultural organisations 559
  Bantu Education 357
  children 283-4
  crisis in 354-5
  development and relief work skills train
    ing 373
  differentiated access and opportunities
    357-8
  disabled persons 312-13
  distance learning 368
  during emergencies 887-8, 889-90
  'education for liberation' 345, 359-
    60
  emergency health care training 912
  ethnic and race relations 261,
    263-5, 266
  'extension work' 372
  family planning *see* birth planning
  for health educators 768-9
  formal education 264, 283-4, 355
    constraints on impact 357-9
  gender
    gender awareness 212-13
    gender skills training 373-4
    inequalities 358, 611-12
    women exclusion 181, 367-8, 603, 605
  health education *see* health
    education
  HIV/AIDS 750-2
  human right 27, 52-3
  in refugee camps 284
  institutional staff training 405-6
  legal rights training 374
  'liberation education' 354
  literacy 363-8, 375
    agents of 365-6
    cascade method 367
    distance learning 368
    oral traditions 364-5
    participation in 367-8
    training of facilitators 366-7
  non-formal education 264-5, 284, 355-6,
    359-61
  numeracy 364, 366
  nutrition 687

organisational and management training 372
Oxfam role 356-7
participatory training 360-1, 363
peace education 267
personal development skills 373
popular education 359-60, 363
  agents of 362
  assessment of achievement 363
  equality 362-3
  goals 361-2
poverty and access to 358-9
primary education 283
production and 508-9
refugees 284, 887-8, 889-90
right to 27, 52-3
skills training 372-3
small-scale industries 611-12
social education *see* popular education
social organisation 342
trade unions 351-2
traditional birth attendants 657-8
training 360-1, 376
  accessibility 370
  aims 369
  analysing need 368-9, 370
  areas of 371-4
  content 370-1
  learning group 369
  methods 371
  monitoring and evaluation 371
  planning 369
  trainers 370
  training the trainers 374-5
  vocational 372-2
war and civil conflict 359
water supply management 704
women exclusion 181, 367-8, 603, 605
'education for liberation' 345, 359-60
Egypt 648
El Salvador 815, 841, 879
elderly people 292-302
  ageing populations 293-5
  caring for 296-7, 299
    day-care centres 299-300
    home care 299
    residential care 300
  displaced 296
  emergencies 300-1, 888-90
  empowerment 299
  health care 672-4

    eyesight 674
    HIV deaths and burden on 674, 754
    mobility 673-4
    nutrition 673
  HIV deaths and burden on 674, 754
  listening to 297-9
  pensions 295-6
  refugees 296
  roles 295-6
electronic communications 381
electronic conferences 381
elephantiasis 734
ELISA test 747-8, 753
emergencies 799-988
  armed conflict *see main heading*
  assessment 861, 862-5, 952-3
    detailed (technical) assessment 864
    for programme management 952
    initial (general) assessment 863
    inter-agency co-ordination 864-5
    preparedness 865
    priority identification 863
    systematic monitoring 862
    see also information
  capacities-vulnerabilities analysis 133-5, 186, 832-4
  changing nature of 812-13
  channels for relief 351-2
  chaos and complexity 821-3
  children in 280, 886-8
    education 887-8
    health 887
    see also armed conflict
  code of conduct for NGOs in disaster relief 802-5
    definitions 801-2
    purpose 801
    recommendations
      to donor governments 806-7
      to governments of disaster-affected countries 805-6
      to intergovernmental organisations 807-8
    working environment 805
  communicable diseases 765
  communications
    breakdown 956-7
    confidentiality 958
    costs 958
    establishing link 955-6

6

fax 956, 957-8
radio networks 956
satellite communication equip
  ment 956
situation reports 959-61
telephone procedure 958
telex 956, 957-8
community liaison work 879
complex emergencies
causes 813-14
see also inter-agency co-ordination
consultation 861, 878-82
  local organisations 878, 879
  women 879, 880-2
contingency plans 865, 970-1
co-ordination see inter-agency coordina
  tion
coping strategies 830-2
crisis defined 810-11
cultural considerations 888, 890-2
deforestation during conflict 587
development
  as response to crisis 829-30
  programmes adapted 828-9
disabled persons and 892-3
disasters 811
  mitigation 834-6
  preparedness 865, 970-1
    training programmes 912
dispersed populations 877-8
displaced persons see main heading
elderly persons 300-1, 888-90
environmental health 764, 896,
  914-29
see also sanitation; water supply
ethnic cleansing 238, 267, 845, 890
ethnicity 250-2, 812-13, 890-2
evaluation 961
feedback 821-2
financial procedures 971-2
food 930-47
  assets or resources 932-3
  deficit 933-4
  distribution 943-5, 969-70
  entitlements 931, 933
  Food for Work 936, 939-41, 944-5
  grinding facilities 917-18
  nutritional support 941
  planning 901-2
  production systems 933-4
    gender relations and 934-5
    post-crisis recovery 934-5
  purchase of bulk supplies 942-3

storage facilities 917
supplies 942-3
survival strategies 933, 934, 940
vulnerability 931-3
see also nutrition
food aid 936-41
  economic support 937-9
  Food for Work 936, 939-41, 944-5
fund sources
  co-funding from official sources
    954-5
  emergency grants 955
  funds from other NGOs 953-4
  special appeals 953
health 894-912
  acute respiratory infections 909
  assessment 764-5
    demographic information 898
    general 896-7
    health information 898
    nutrition 898-900
    slow-onset emergencies 897-900
    sudden-onset emergencies 897
  community health workers 908
  dehydration 908-9
  diarrhoea 908-9
  environmental health 764, 896,
    914-29
  food see food; nutrition
  health information system 909
  measles immunisation 908
  mental health 907
  morbidity data 910
  mortality data 910
  personal hygiene 926-7
  PHC interventions 896
  population data 910
  primary health interventions 908-9
  public health 763-7, 896
  reproductive health 907
  sanitation see sanitation
  services provision 907-8
  slow-onset emergencies
    assessment 897-900
    information 951
    non-displaced people 902-3
    refugees and displaced persons 903
  sudden-onset emergencies
    assessment 897
    casualty management 900-1
    communicable disease control 901
    food planning 901-2
    information 949-50

search and rescue 900
shelter 901
surveillance 909-19
  general living conditions 911-12
  health sector activities 911
  morbidity data 910
  mortality data 910
  nutrition data 910-11
  population data 910
training 912
vector control 927-8
vitamin A supplements 909
see also nutrition; sanitation; water
  supply
housing 916
  reconstruction 918-19
  see also shelter
human rights and 814
humanitarian response 810, 811-12,
  815-17
  agencies 816-17
  military personnel and 815-16
Humanitarianism and War research
  project 810, 866
immunisation 726, 908
impartiality principle 849-53, 870
information
  and public policy 818-19
  and vulnerability 817-18
  interpretation 952
  media 818-19, 949-50
  needs 951-2
  slow-onset emergencies 951
  sudden-onset emergencies 949-50
  see also assessment
infrastructure 763
  food grinding facilities 917-18
  food storage facilities 917
  housing 916
    reconstruction 918-19
  settlements 915-16
  see also shelter
inter-agency co-ordination 866-74
  assessment 864-5
  dispersed populations 877-8
  donor governments 867
  'lead agency' 865
  local authorities 874-5
  local structures 875-7
  NGOs 869
  programme management and 961
  responsibilities, limitations, impacts and
    opportunities (RLIO) grid 867-9

UN peace-support operations 868
see also international agencies
international agencies 870-4
  Caritas International 873
  International Council of Voluntary
    Agencies 874
  Lutheran World Federation 873-4
  Red Cross and Red Crescent societies
    872-3
  Steering Committee for Humanitarian
    Response 873
  UN agencies 871-2
  World Council of Churches 873
  see also inter-agency co-ordination
local authorities 874-5, 878, 879
local structures 875-7, 878, 879
management of programmes see man
  agement of emergency programmes
media and 818-19, 949-50
minority groups 890-2
mitigation 834-6
nutrition 764, 766-7, 894-912
  assessment 898-900
  food planning 901-2
  general rations 903-4
  supplementary foods 904
  surveillance 909, 910-11
  therapeutic feeding 904-5
  vitamin A supplements 909
  see also health
Oxfam and 799-801
Oxfam emergency store 978
planning
  contingency plans 865, 970-1
  for diversity and divergence 820-1
  see also management of emergency
programmes
  potential flash points 823-4
  programmes see management of emer-
    gency programmes
  public health 763-7, 896
  reconstruction 837
  refugees see main heading
  rehabilitation 836-7, 838
  relief programme management see man-
    agement of programmes
  responsibilities, limitations, impacts and
    opportunities (RLIO) grid 867-9
  risk mapping 835
sanitation
  destruction of system 75
  excreta disposal 906, 923
  faecal contamination dangers 923-4

6

immediate interventions 924-5
latrines 925-6
open-surface defaecation 924-5
Oxfam sanitation unit 878, 985
personal hygiene 926-7
social issues 924
trench defaecation 925
self-reliance 830-2
settlements 915-16
shelter 901, 911, 916-17
commercial emergency housing
917
plastic sheeting 917, 981
tents 917, 979
short and long-term interventions
824-8
site visits 974-5
situation reports 959-61
supply distribution 969-70
supply purchase
international 962-3
local 963
support, changing emphasis of 827-8
transport *see main heading*
wars *see* armed conflict
water supply 763, 906
assessment of needs 919-20
disinfection 921-3
mobile drinking-water units 923
Oxfam water packs 978, 983-4
priorities 920-1
quality 919
testing 920, 921-3
women and 920
women 184-90
access to resources and benefits
188-9
armed conflict 189-90, 841, 845,
855
consultation with 879, 880-2
displaced persons 186-9
flight 182
protection 187-8
refugees 186-9, 872, 884
situation of 883-5
water supply 920
water supply responsibility 920
employment
bonded labour 235
children 271-2
domestic workers 277, 286
industrial workers 277
rural workers 276-7

sex workers 198-9, 277
domestic workers
children 277, 286
women 200-1
sexual division of labour 69, 207-9, 496,
603, 605
urban livelihood strategies 113
wage labour 492
women 181
domestic workers 200-1
farmers 204
prostitution 198-200
work-related disablement 309
see also livelihoods; production; small-
scale industries
empowerment 9, 206-7, 345
collective public action 12
demands on the State 13
elderly people 299
meaning 12-14
participation 14-17
personal 12
women 13, 70, 206-7, 216-17
World Bank 11-12
energy
conservation 93-4
fuel economy 94
sources
biogas and producer gas 92-3
biomass 91-2
fossil fuels 92
fuelwood 582-3
human power 91
micro-hydro 93
solar energy 93
wind power 93
environment
armed conflict 73-8
between ethnic groups 76
destruction of infrastructure 75
destruction of natural resources
74-5
landmines 75, 307-8, 893
migrations 75-6
over environmental resources 76-8
assessment
environmental assessment analysis
129, 140-3
environmental impact assessment
(EIA) 95-6, 98
livelihoods analysis 102-17
see also livelihoods
participatory appraisal 99-102, 131-3

participatory mapping 99
participatory rural appraisal 131-3
participatory rural assessment 98-102
profiles 97-8
rapid rural appraisal 147-50
scientific and local knowledge 98-9
screening 141, 142-3
soil maps 99
biodiversity 88-90
  agriculture 89-90
  biotechnology 90
  forests 90-1
country environmental studies 97
debt 71-2
deforestation
  civil conflict and 587
  'crisis' 583-4
  floods caused by 87
degradation 64, 65-6, 81-3, 539, 811
development 59-117
discounting concept 95
economics 94-5
energy *see main heading*
environmental assessment analysis 129,
  140-3
Environmental Impact Assessment (EIA)
  95-6, 98
gender and *see* women
health *see* environmental health
land *see main heading*
macro-policies and 96-7
meaning 59-60
Oxfam approach 68-70
population issue 63-5
poverty and degradation 64, 65-6
profiles 97-8
resource valuation at project level
  95-6
structural adjustment policies 70,
  72-3
sustainability *see main heading*
sustainable livelihoods *see main heading*
sustainable natural resources 81-94
  see also biodiversity: energy: land:
    water sources
trade 70-3
  free trade 71
  Trade-Related Environmental
    Measures (TREMS) 72
  World Trade Organisation 71-2
valuing resources
  economic 94-5
  Environmental Impact Assessment

(EIA) 95-6, 98
  macro-policies 96-7
war and 73-8
water 84-8
  see also water sources; water supply
women 67-70
  ecofeminism 68-9
  gender analysis 69-7
environmental health 688-9
  aims of programmes 689, 691
  atmospheric pollution 693
  comprehensive approach to 693-4
  drainage 693
  emergencies 764, 896, 914-29
  monitoring and evaluation 717-20
  planning 714-17
  urban 691-3
  women 714-17
  see also public health; sanitation; water
    supply
Environmental Impact Assessment (EIA)
  95-6, 98
Enzyme Linked Immuno-absorbent Assay
  (ELISA) test 747-8, 753
epidemics 735
  see also communicable diseases; immuni
    sation
Equipment for Charity Hospitals Overseas
  (ECHO) 757
equity principle 345
erosion *see* environment
Ethiopia 876, 891
Ethiopian Water Works Construction
  Authority 876
ethnic and race relations 225-68
  cohesion and solidarity 251-2
  conflict 250-1
    between ethnic groups 76
    see also ethnic cleansing
  consultation 255-6
  cultural sensitivity 252-3
  emergencies 250-2, 812-13, 890-2
  ethnic cleansing 238, 267, 845, 890
  ethnic minorities 238-9
  ethnicity 231-3
    dress 232
    manipulation of 232
  human rights 227-8, 244-9
    abuses 260
    advocacy 260-1
    awareness raising 259
    campaigning 260-1
    citizenship 246

6

Declaration on Right to Development
    245
education 261, 263-5, 266
health 261-3, 266
interventions 259-60
land tenure 260
legal aid 259
peace education 267
rights to land and resources 247-8
rights to movement 248-9
self-determination 249
Sub-commission on Prevention of
    Discrimination and Protection of
    Minorities 244, 245
indigenous populations 239-43
    Brazil 247-8
    dispossession 240-1
    Guatemala 890
    Indigenous and Tribal Peoples
        Convention 244
    integration and assimilation 242-3
    Miskito indians 74, 891, 892
    Nicaragua 238
    protection 242
    Voluntary Fund 44
    working groups 244, 245, 260
    World Council 260
individual and collective rights 237
information assessment 255
information gathering 253-4, 256-7
institution building 266
land tenure 260
learned behaviour 226
migrants and refugees 243-4
participation 255-6
plural societies 237-8
race 233
tree and forest use 592
see also social differences
ethnic cleansing 238, 267, 845, 890
Euronaid 942
European Fair Trade Organisations 608
European Union
    emergency funds from 954-5
Eurostep network 380
evaluation
    agreeing criteria 418-19
    aim 417
    briefings 426
    costing 420
    documentation 426
    emergency programmes 961
    environmental health 717-20

evaluators
    briefings 426
    expatriate 430
    external 430-1
    internal 429
    local 431
ex-ante 423
ex-post 424
final 424
formal 423-4
health care programmes 784-5
informal 420-3
institutional development 415-34
learning from 433-4
mid-term 423-4
participation in 16, 421-2
principles and purpose confirmation
    425
priority definition 417-18
process evaluation 425-34
projects 22
report 432-3
resource provision 426
sanitation systems 717-20
self(auto)-evaluation 421
supervision 426
team 425-6, 428-31
    see also evaluators
terms of reference
    basic framework 427
    drawing up 425
use 432
user evaluation 422-3
water supply 717-20
exchange rates 454-5
exchange visits 381-3
Exclusive Economic Zones 562
Expanded Programme for Immunisation
    (EPI) 640, 722
exports 607-8

facsimile transmission (fax) 956, 957-8
Fair Trade Federations 608
families
    gender sensitive information 203-4
    women-maintained 182-4
family cooking sets 979, 980
family planning see birth planning
farmers see agriculture
FASIC 343
Federation of Red Cross and Red
    Crescent Societies 817-18
feedback 821-2

feeding programmes 288
  general rations 903-4
  supplementary foods 904
  therapeutic feeding 904-5, 941
  see also food; nutrition
fertility control 196-7
  see also birth planning
financial administration
  accounting statements
    balance sheet 450-1
    income and expenditure 448-9
    profit and loss account 448-9
    receipts and payments 447-8
  audits 451-2
  bank accounts
    current account 445
    deposit account 445
    savings account 445
    third country accounts 445
  books
    bank books 444
    cash books 444
    double entry book keeping 444
    invoices 444
    ledgers 444
    petty cash 444
    vouchers 444
  budgeting
    cash budget 444
    complementary budget 442
    guaranteed budget 442
    optimal budget 443
    survival budget 442
  cash-flow forecast 444
  depreciation 446-7
  emergency procedures 971-2
  exchange rates 454-5
  institutional development 442-57
  inter-agency liaison 456-7
  international transfer of funds
    bank draft 453
    emergency grants 955
    mail payment 453
    telegraphic transfer 453-4
  loans 455
  project assessment 456-7
  staff 456
financial planning
  budgets *see* financial administration,
  budgeting
  core budgets 436-7
  cost-benefit analysis 129, 148, 150
  diversity of income sources 439-40

donor consortium 439
external funding 435-6
generation of income 441
institutional development 434-41
remuneration for community-based
  workers 438-9
salaries 437-9
self-financing activities 440-1
see also funding
financing *see* funding
fish farming 562, 563-4, 566
  disease and depredation 575-6
  feeding 575
  small-scale 566, 572-6
  species choice 574-5
  technical support 572-6
fishing 109-11
  assessment of livelihood 109-11
  'blue revolution' 562
  boats 570-1
  capture fishing 563, 566
    organisations 578
    small-scale 566, 569-71
    technical support 569-71
  communities 562, 566-7
  credit 577-9
  developing countries 561-4
  Exclusive Economic Zones 562
  fish farming *see main heading*
  fish for flour barter systems 579
  fishworker vulnerability 562, 563
  International Collective in Support of
    Fishworkers (ICSF) 579
  Lomé Convention 563
  marketing 577-9
  National Confederation of Fishworkers
    (Chile) 564
  NGO support 564-79
  nurture fishing 571-2
  organisations 564, 577, 578-9
  processing of fish 576-7
  small-scale 561
    capture fishing 566, 569-71
    fish farming 566, 572-6
    technical support 569-76
  sustainability 110-11
  technical support
    fish farming 572-6
    nurture fishing 571-2
    small-scale fishing 569-76
  threats to 110
  traditional 110
  women 567-9

6

flies
  vector control 713, 928
floods 86-7
  deforestation and 87
foeticide 668
food
  distribution 905-6, 943
    cost 945
    emergencies 943-5, 969-70
    interventions in market 944
    monitoring 945
    private traders 944
    reuse of bags 946
    women and 905-6, 943
  emergencies and 930-47
    assets or resources 932-3
    deficit 933-4
    distribution 943-5, 969-70
    entitlements 931, 933
    food aid *see main heading*
    grinding facilities 917-18
    nutritional support 941
    production systems 933-4
      post-crisis recovery 934-5
    purchase 942-3
    storage facilities 917
    supplies 942-3
    survival strategies 933, 934, 940
    vulnerability 931-3
  general rations 903-4
  monitoring
    distribution 945
    sale of aid 945-6
  production systems 933-4
    gender relations and 934-5
    post-crisis recovery 934-5
  supplementary foods 904
  supplies 942-3
  therapeutic feeding 904-5, 941
  see also nutrition
food aid
  dietary changes 940
  economic support 936, 939-41
  emergencies and 936-41
  'Food for Work' 936, 939-41, 944-5
  local market distortion 940
Food and Agriculture Office (FAO) 871
  Global Information and Early Warning
    System 871
'Food for Work' 936, 939-41, 944-5
Forest Stewardship Council (FSC) 586
forests *see* trees and forests
fostering 288

France
  Declaration of the Rights of Man and
    Citizens 29
freedom from armed conflict 27
Freedom from Debt Coalition 342, 379,
  388
freedom of association 333
Freire, Paulo 354, 359-60
Friends of the Earth 584
fuel *see* energy
funding
  diversity of sources 439-40
  donor consortium 439
  emergency fund sources
    co-funding from official sources 954-5
    emergency grant recommendation
      955
    other NGO funds 953-4
    procedures 971-2
    special appeals 953
  external funds 435-6
  generation of income 441
  health care 773-87
    Bamako Initiative 778
    cost sharing 777
    direct transfers and grants 777
    government level 777-8
    NGO level 776-7
    Oxfam approach 780-1
    pre-payment (insurance) 776-7
    preventive or curative services 778-9
    primary health care 775
    rational use of drugs 779
    revolving drug funds 778, 779-80
    user fees 776
  institutional development 435-41
  international transfers
    bank draft 453
    emergency grants 955
    mail payment 453
    telegraphic transfer 453-4
  networking 380
  participation as condition 14
  relief NGOs 400
  'responsible funder' concept 127
  self-financing activities 440-1
  social organisation 339-40
  see also credit and savings support;
    financial planning

Gandhian movement 10
GAPA (Grupo de Apoyo contra AIDS)
  (Brazil) 754

geese 553-4
gender 169-224
  agriculture 522-3
  armed conflict and 189-90, 841, 845, 855
  assessment and planning 186
  awareness 180
  concept of 174-5
  culture and 176-7, 215, 257-8
  development and 177-8
    policy approaches 205-7
    practical needs 209
    strategic needs 209-10
  disablement and
    carer 310
    disabled person 309-10
  discrimination in health care 651-2, 668
  division of labour 69, 207-9, 496, 603,
    605
  education and training 181, 358, 367-8,
    611-12
  emergencies and 184-90, 824
    access to resources and benefits 188-9
    armed conflict 189-90, 841, 845, 855
    consultation with women 879, 880-2
    displaced persons 186-9
    flight 182
    food production 934-5
    refugees 186-9, 872, 884
    situation of women 883-5
    water supply distribution 920
  environment and 67-70
  fishworkers 567-9
  foeticide 668
  food distribution 905-6, 943
  food production systems 934-5
  gender awareness training 212-13
  gender skills training 373-4
  health care inequalities 651-2, 668
    see also health care, women
  human rights 29, 38-40, 54-5, 177-8
  income inequality 496, 497
  information
    access to 220-2
    gathering 211-12
    gender-sensitive analysis 201-4, 210-11
    monitoring and evaluation 211-12
  livelihood system inequality 495-6
  livestock production 542-4
  malnutrition 905-6
  nature and 176-7
  networking 220-1
  organisations and groups 213-22
  Oxfam policy 68-70, 171-3

participation 15, 216-17
patriarchy 172, 173, 176
policy approaches to 205-7
poverty 65-7, 180-2
production and
  division of labour 69, 207-9, 496, 603,
    605
  income 496, 497
  participatory organisations 512
  technology gap 499
  unpaid work 497
sexual division of labour 69, 207-9, 496,
  603, 605
small-scale industries 602-4, 605
social transformation 178-8
tradition and 175-6
trees and forests and 591
violence against women see women, vio
  lence against
women's interests 179-80
see also women
gender framework analysis 129, 135-40,
  210-11
  access and control profile 135, 137,
    210-11
  activity profile 136, 210
  people-oriented planning in refugee
    situations 129
  project cycle analysis 135, 137-40
gender-sensitive analysis 210-11
General Agreement on Tariffs and Trade
  (GATT)
  environment 71
  production and 487-8
  Trade-Related Environmental Measures
    (TREMS) 72
  World Trade Organisation 71-2, 487-8
Geneva Conventions
  non-combatant protection 74
genital mutilation 194, 258, 662, 663-5
Gepa, Dritte-Welt-Laden 608
Ghana 586
gleaning 522
Global Forum 62
Global Information and Early Warning
  System 871
Global Union of Technologies for
  Environment and Sustainable
  Development (SATIS) 459
goats 550
Grameen Bank 505, 611
grassroots support organisations 397-8
'green revolution' 89, 517, 524

6

high yield varieties (HYV) 89, 517, 524
ground water 695-6
Group of 77 37
growth monitoring 685-6
Guatemala 357, 368, 890
guinea fowl 554
guinea pigs 552-3
guinea worm transmission 694

handicap
  definition 305-6
  see also disabled persons
Hansen's disease 734
Harvard Gender Framework Analysis 604
Harvard Institute for International
  Development 129, 210
Health Action International (HAI) 380,
  387, 772
health care
  alcohol abuse 647-8
  Alma Ata conference 631-2, 633, 641
  birth planning 654, 657, 736-44
    definitions 737
    HIV/AIDS and 739, 742-3
    methods
      abortion 744
      barrier methods 742-3
      Billings method 742
      condoms 742-3
      contraceptives 741-2, 743
      hormonal methods 741-2, 743
      injectable contraceptives 741-2, 743
      intra-uterine devices 741, 743
      sterilisation 741, 744
      traditional methods 742
    Oxfam
      interventions 739-40
      support for 738-9
    population control 737-8
    services 740
  buildings 638
  child health
    antenatal care 669
    breast-feeding 668, 669, 681-2, 686-7,
      771-2
    CHILD-to child programme 670-1
    Control of Diarrhoeal Diseases 640
    emergencies 887
    foeticide 668
    gender inequality 668
    infectious diseases 667
    mass screening 671
    maternal death and 654

mortality
  child 667
  infant 272, 667
  Oxfam support 667
  perinatal care 669-70
  pre-conception care 668-9
  reproductive health 281-2
  schools 671
  sex education 671
  sexual welfare 281-2
  siblings, responsibility for 670-1
  under-fives 670
  see also immunisation
collaboration 642-3
communicable diseases
  acute respiratory infections 640, 731-2,
    909
  bilharzia 734
  case finding and treatment 728
  Chagas disease 734
  control measures 728-9
  dehydration 730-1, 908-9
  diarrhoeal diseases 729-31, 908-9
    drug treatment 731
    NGO involvement 731
    nutrition and 729-30
    oral rehydration therapy (ORT) 730-1
    prevention 730
    rehydration 730-1, 908-9
  elephantiasis 734
  emergencies 765
  epidemics 735
  immunisation see main heading
  kala azar 734
  leprosy 734, 756
  malaria 640, 732-3, 756
  measles 723, 908
  river blindness 734
  sleeping sickness 734
  sudden-onset emergencies 901
  tuberculosis 723, 733-4, 749
  vector control 727-8, 927-8
  see also immunisation
community health workers 632, 633,
  638
  in emergencies 908
computer systems 462
consumables 638
dehydration 730-1, 908-9
development and 626-7
diarrhoea see communicable diseases
disabled persons 674-6
  artificial limbs 676

causes of disability 307-9, 675-6
community-based rehabilitation 315-16
medical intervention 316
residential care 316-17
displaced persons 765, 903
district health teams 637
drug abuse 671
urban 647-8
drug provision 756-9
abuses in connection with supply 758
donations 758, 778
financing 779
revolving drug funds 758, 778, 779-80
supply and availability 757
WHO 'essential drugs' concept 756,
757
elderly persons 672-4
caring for
day-care centres 299-300
home care 299
residential care 300
emergency situations 889
eyesight 674
HIV deaths and burden on 674, 754
mobility 673-4
nutrition 673
emergency situations *see* emergencies,
health
environmental health 688-9
aims of programmes 689, 691
atmospheric pollution 693
comprehensive approach to 693-4
drainage 693
emergencies 764, 896, 914-29
monitoring and evaluation 717-20
planning and evaluation 714-17
urban 691-3
women 714-17
see also public health; sanitation; water
supply
epidemics 735
see also communicable diseases; immu
nisation
equipment 639-40
ethnic and race relations 261-3, 266
financing 773-87
Bamako Initiative 778
cost sharing 777
direct transfers and grants 777
government level 777-8
NGO level 776-7
Oxfam approach 780-1
pre-payment (insurance) 776-7

preventive or curative services 778-9
primary health care 775
rational use of drugs 779
revolving drug funds 778, 779-80
user fees 776
genital mutilation 194, 258, 662, 663-5
HIV/AIDS *see main heading*
human right to care 27
immunisation 626, 640, 667, 671, 727
background 722
cold chain
equipment 725
health workers 724-5
emergency situations 726, 908
Expanded Programme for
Immunisation 640, 722
immunisable diseases 722-3
programmes 640, 671, 722
schedule 724
strategies
campaigns 726
emergencies 726, 908
integrated programmes 726
impaired vision
disabled persons 676
elderly persons 674
infrastructure failure 634
laboratories 639
levels
primary level 635-6
secondary level 636
tertiary level 636
life expectancy 626
livestock health 546-7
malaria 732-3
drugs 756
eradication programme 640
malnutrition *see* nutrition
mental health 759-63
armed conflict 760-2, 855-8
cultural concepts 760
emergency situations 760-2, 855-8, 907
ex-combatants 761-2
NGO role 761-2
post-traumatic stress disorder 760, 856
primary health workers and 761
minimum activities package (MAP) 637-8
mobility, elderly persons 673
Mother and Child Health (MCH) pro
grammes 652-3, 654-9
motor vehicle use 467
NGO role 627-9
primary health care 633-5

6

secondary health care 637-8
traditional health care 642-4
urban health care 648-9
nutrition *see main heading*
oral rehydration therapy (ORT) 730-1
physical mutilation 907
post-traumatic stress disorder 760, 856
primary health care 631-4
  Alma Ata conference 631-2, 633, 641
  community health workers 632, 633
  emergency interventions 896
  financing 775
  NGO role 633-5
  principles and components 633
programme planning and evaluation
  781-2
  baseline information 782-3
  evaluation 784-5
  impact evaluation 784
  outcome evaluation 785
  process evaluation 784-5
  see also management of emergency
    programmes
psycho-social aspects 760, 855-8
public health 688-9
  aims of programmes 689, 691
  disease transmission 690
  emergency relief 763-7, 896, 927-8
  vector control 727-8
    emergency situations 927-8
    flies 713, 928
    mosquitoes 711-13, 928
  see also communicable diseases; envi
    ronmental health; sanitation; water
    supply
quality and testing 87-8
refugees 765, 903
reproductive health 627
  abortions 653, 654, 744
  antenatal care 655, 669
  breast-feeding 668, 669, 681-2, 771-2
  delivery 656
  education 281-2, 658, 661
  emergency situations 907
  family planning *see* birth planning
  fertility control 196-7
  maternal mortality 196, 653-4
  Mother and Child Health (MCH) pro
    gramme 652-3, 654-9
  postnatal care 656-7
  reproductive tract infections 196
  rights of women 196-7
  'Safe Motherhood Initiative' 655

traditional birth attendants 638, 657-8,
  669, 765-6
ultrasound scans 639
right to 625-6
sanitation
  anal cleansing methods 710
  communal or household facilities 708-9
  cost and affordability 708
  cultural issues 705-6
  emergency situations 906, 923-6
    Oxfam sanitation union 878, 985
    system destruction 75
  faecal contamination dangers 923-4
  financial management and cost
    recovery 720-1
  ground conditions 709
  latrines 694-5, 906, 925-6
  maintenance 711
  monitoring and evaluation 717-20
  open-surface defaecation 924-5
  Oxfam sanitation unit 878, 985
  personal hygiene 926-7
  population density 709-10
  social issues 705-6, 924
  timing of interventions 710-11
  trench defaecation 925
  upgrading 710
  urban sewerage systems 692
  waste disposal options 706-11
  waste reuse 710
  women's requirements 715, 906
  see also water supply
secondary health care 636, 637-8
sexually transmitted diseases 661-2
staff health and safety 972-4
sterilising equipment 638
surgical equipment 638
traditional 628, 640, 641
  assessment of practices 643-4
  birth attendants 638, 657-8, 669, 765-6
  forms 642
  NGO role 642-4
  support 644
training 912
transport 639
ultrasound scans 639
urban health care 645-9
  accidents 648
  alcohol abuse 647-8
  crowding 646-7
  drug abuse 647-8
  facilities 646
  homelessness 647

malnutrition 645, 647
NGO role 648-9
poverty 645-6
problems 646-8
street life 647
working conditions 647
vector control
communicable diseases 727-8
emergency situations 927-8
flies 713
mosquitoes 711-13
vertical programmes 640
water sources
boreholes 697-8
contamination when collected 88,
699-700
ground water 87, 88, 695-6
hand-dug wells 696-7
rain water 698
springs 88, 696
surface water 698
tubewells 697
village-level operation and mainte
nance handpumps (VLOM) 697
water supply 695-704
contamination when collected 699-700
daily requirement 695
emergency situations 763, 906, 921-3
assessment of needs 919-20
destruction of systems 75
quality 919
testing 920, 921-3
financial management and cost
recovery 720-1
guinea worm transmission 694
industrial pollution and 692-3
industry 692
monitoring and evaluation 717-20
operation and maintenance 703-4
Oxfam water packs 978, 983-4
Oxfam/DelAgua Water testing Kit 920,
921, 984
piped water 699-700
quality and testing 87-8
chemical quality 701-2
emergency situations 919, 920-3
microbiological quality 700-1
physical quality 702
storage 88
contamination during 700
treatment by 702
training in management 704
transportation and distribution 699-700

treatment
aeration 702
disinfection 703, 921-3
filtration 702, 922
sedimentation 921-2
storage 702
used as latrine 694-5
Water User's Committees 703
women and 714-17, 920
see also sanitation; water sources
women 181, 651-66
as carers 660-1
culture and 193-4, 257-8, 662-6
customs 662-3
early marriage and childbearing 663
education
evaluation criteria 419
sex education 661
family planning see birth planning
gender-based discrimination 651-2,
668
genital mutilation 194, 258, 662, 663-5
HIV/AIDS 660, 661, 662
needs 652-3
sanitation requirements 715, 906
sexually transmitted diseases 661-2
taboos 662-3
violence against women 665-6
water supply and 714-17, 920
work-related problems 659-60
see also reproductive health
X-rays 639
health education 767-72
campaigning 771-2
children 671
evaluation criteria 419
HIV/AIDS 750-2, 771
impact 771
KAP (knowledge, attitude and practice)
surveys 771
methods 769-71
mass media 770-1
materials 769
teaching aids 770
working directly with people 769-70
Mother and Child Health programme
658
public education 771-2
sex education 661, 671
traditional care and 642-3
training for 768-9
Help the Aged 953
High Commissioner for Refugees 271,

6

845, 871-2, 955
appraisal methodology 129
funds from 955
Guidelines on the Protection of Refugee Women 872
Handbook for Emergencies 872
Policy on Refugee Women 872
see also refugees
High Commissioner on Human Rights 26
high yield varieties (HYV) 89, 517, 524
Hindu caste system *see* caste
HIV/AIDS 745-55
    appearance of disease 746
    birth planning and 739, 742
    care of people with HIV 753-4
    condoms 641, 742-3
    counselling 754
    deaths and burden on grandparents 674, 754
    discrimination against sufferers 754-5
    health care 641
    health education 419, 750-2, 771
    human rights and 754-5
    magnitude of problem 746-7
    orphans 674, 754
    prevention and control 750
    safe blood promotion 748, 753
    sex workers 660, 752
    signs and symptoms 749
    support organisations 754
    testing for HIV 747-8, 753
    transmission
        infected blood, needles, instruments etc. 748-9
        mother to child 749, 753
        sexual transmission 748, 752-3
    treatment 749
    women and 660, 661, 662
homeworkers 597
Honduras 76
households
    gender sensitive information 203-4
    woman-maintained 182-4
housing
    emergencies 916
        reconstruction 918-19
    for livestock production 547
    see also shelter
Human Development Index (HDI) 37
Human Immune Deficiency Virus *see* HIV/AIDS
human resource development 405-6
human rights

advocacy 56-7, 221
    disabled persons 314
    ethnic and race relations 260-1
African Charter 29, 30
African Commission 46
American Convention 30, 46
American Declaration of the Rights and Duties of Man 46
Amnesty International 45, 47
Anti-Slavery International 48, 260
assessment of situation 50-1
children 54-5, 270-1
civil and political rights 30, 35-6
collective rights 30, 237
Committee Against Torture 45
Committee on the Elimination of All Forms of Discrimination Against Women 39, 45-6
contemporary politics 36-7
cultural criticisms 29-30
denials 26
displaced persons 55-6
economic and social rights 30, 35-6, 227-8
education 27, 52-3
    ethnic and race relations 261, 263-5, 266
emergencies and 814
ethnic and race relations 227-8, 244-9
    abuses 260
    advocacy 260-1
    awareness raising 259
    campaigning 260-1
    citizenship 246
    Declaration on Right to Development 245
    education 261, 263-5, 266
    health 261-3, 266
    interventions 259-60
    land tenure 260
    legal aid 259
    peace education 267
    rights to land and resources 247-8
    rights to movement 248-9
    self-determination 249
freedom from armed conflict 27
freedom of association 333
gender 29, 38-40, 54-5, 177-8
health 625-6
    ethnic and race relations 261-3, 266
health care 27
High Commissioner 26
historical developments 27-30

HIV/AIDS and 754-5
Human Rights Committee 44-5
Human Rights Watch 38, 48
in development and relief work 24-58
individual 237
information gathering 56-7
information provision 53-4
Inter-American Commission on Human Rights 46
Inter-American Court of Human Rights 46
intergovernmental organisations 40-6
Interights 45
International Commission of Jurists 47
International Covenant on Civil and Political Rights 31, 33-4, 44-5
International Covenant on Economic, Social and Cultural Rights 31, 34-5
International Labour Organisation 44
international pressure 57
involuntary displacement 25
legal rights training 374
legal support 53-4, 56-7
Marxist view 29
moral constraints on governments 28-9
nationalism 37-8
natural rights theory 28, 29
networking 57-8
NGOs 46-9
Oxfam and 49-58
refugees 25, 55-6, 844-6
regional bodies 46
religious fundamentalism 37-8
'social contract' theory of government 28
social differences 227-8
sovereignty 36-7
Sub-commission on Prevention of Discrimination and Protection of Minorities 244, 245
Survival International 48-9, 260
sustainable livelihood 27
threats to 37-40
training 27, 52-3
United Nations
  1503 procedure 42
  CEDAW 39, 45-6
  Commission on Human Rights 41-2
  Commission on the Status of Women 42
  indigenous populations 43-4, 244, 245
  Secretary General's 'good offices' 43
  Special Rapporteurs
    on Religious Intolerance 43
    on Violence Against Women 40, 43, 178
  Sub-commission on Prevention of Discrimination and Protection of Minorities 42
  theme mechanisms 43
  Universal Declaration 29, 31-3, 244
    text 151-7
  women 54-5, 177-8
Human Rights Committee 44-5
Human Rights Watch 38, 48
Humanitarianism and War projects 810, 866

IBASE 343
immunisation 626, 640, 667, 671, 727
  background 722
  cold chain
    equipment 725
    health workers 724-5
  emergency situations 726, 908
  Expanded Programme for Immunisation 640, 722
  immunisable diseases 722-3
  programmes 640, 671, 722
  schedule 724
  strategies
    campaigns 726
    emergencies 726
    integrated programmes 726
income
  gender inequality 496, 497
  income-generation projects 219, 598-9, 603-4
  wage labour 492
  see also employment; small-scale industries
Independent Living Movement 315
India
  Annapurna Mandal 505
  fishworker organisations 577, 578
  forest legislation 584
  Gandhian movement 10
  Gharwal Himalayas 89
  Joint Forest Management 592
  Narmada dam 73, 86, 241
  panchayats 336
  Rural Action Committee (BRAC) 505
  South Indian Federation of Fishermen Societies (SIFFS) 578
  women
    in trade unions 349-50
    Self-Employed Women's Association (SEWA) 505

6

Working Women's Forum 505
Indigenous and Tribal Peoples
  Convention 246
indigenous populations 239-43
  Brazil 247-8
  dispossession 240-1
  Guatemala 890
  Indigenous and Tribal Peoples
    Convention 246
  integration and assimilation 242-3
  Miskito indians 74, 891, 892
  Nicaragua 238
  protection 242
  Voluntary Fund 44
  working groups on 43-4, 244, 245, 260
  World Council 260
Indonesia 89, 588
industry
  industrial pollution 692-3
  small-scale see small-scale industries
  water supply for 692
infant mortality 272, 667
information
  assessment see information assessment
  emergencies
    feedback 821-2
    interpretation 952
    media 818-19, 949-50
    needs 951-2
    public policy 818-19
    slow-onset emergencies 951
    sudden-onset emergencies 949-50
    vulnerability 817-18
    see also information assessment
  exchange 509
  feedback 124, 821-2
  gathering see information gathering
  gender sensitive
    analysis see information assessment
    base-line data 201-2
    community 203
    farmers 204
    household or family 203-4
  human right to provision 53-4
  quality of background information 122-3
  women's access to 220-2
information assessment
  capacities-vulnerabilities analysis 133-5,
    186, 832-4
  cost-benefit analysis 129, 148, 150
  cost-effectiveness analysis 147-50
  cultural sensitivity 255
  emergencies 861, 862-3, 952-3

detailed (technical) assessment 864
  for programme management 952
  health care see emergencies, health
    care
  initial (general) assessment 863
  preparedness 865
  priority identification 863
  systematic monitoring 862
environment 95-102
  environmental assessment analysis
    129, 140-3
  Environmental Impact Assessment
    (EIA) 95-6, 98
  livelihoods analysis 102-17
  participatory appraisal 99-102, 131-3,
    523
  participatory mapping 99
  participatory rural appraisal 131-3,
    523
  participatory rural assessment 98-102
  profiles 97-8
  rapid rural appraisal 129, 130-3, 523
  scientific and local knowledge 98-9
  soil maps 99
  ethnic and race relations 255
  gender awareness 186, 211-12
  gender framework analysis 129, 135-40,
    210-11
  gender-sensitive analysis 202-4, 210-11
  informal 121-2
  livelihoods analysis 102-17
    see also livelihoods
  logical framework analysis 129, 143-7
  methods 128-50
  nutritional state 898-900, 909, 910-11
  official agency choice of 129
  preliminary 121-2
  ZOPP 144, 146-7
  see also evaluation
information gathering 122
  consultation 124-5
    with women 217-18, 879, 880-2
  cultural sensitivity 253-4, 256-7
  emergencies 880-2
  gender awareness 211-12
  meetings 123-4
  process 123-6
  socio-cultural mapping 253-4
  technical advice 126
  visits 123-4, 389-90
  women 217-18, 879, 880-2
  workshops 125-6, 383-4
information technology

documentation centres 459
see also communications; computer
  systems
infrastructure
  destruction in armed conflict 75
  health care and failure of 634
  see also sanitation; water supply
institutional development 331
  agricultural organisations 555-60
  communications
    APC 459
    GEONET 459
    information technology and 458-9
    Packet Switching Network 459
    SATIS 459
    UNIENET 459
  computer systems
    advice and training 461
    backing up 462
    equipment 460
    equipment maintenance 461
    health and safety 462
    power supply 460
    replacing machines 461
    software 460
    use 458
    viruses 461
  defining the organisation 397-405
  emergency responses
    local authorities 874-5
    local structures 875-7
  evaluation 415-34
    agreeing criteria 418-19
    aim 417
    briefings 426
    costing 420
    documentation 426
    evaluators
      briefing 426
      expatriate 430
      external 430-1
      internal 429
      local 431
    ex-ante 423
    ex-post 424
    final 424
    formal 423-4
    informal 420-3
    learning from 433-4
    mid-term 423-4
    participatory 421-2
    principles and purpose confirmation
      425

priority definition 417-18
process organisation 425-34
report 432-3
resource provision 426
self(auto)-evaluation 421
supervision 426
team 425-6, 428-31
terms of reference
  basic framework 427
  drawing up 425
use 432
user evaluation 422-3
financial administration
  accounting statements 447-51
    balance sheets 450-1
    income and expenditure 448-9
    profit and loss account 448-9
    receipts and payments 447-8
  audits 451-2
  bank accounts
    current 445
    deposit 445
    savings 445
    third country accounts 445
  books
    bank books 444
    cash books 444
    double entry book keeping 444
    invoices 444
    ledgers 444
    petty cash 444
    vouchers 444
  budgeting
    cash budget 444
    complementary budget 442
    core budgets 436-7
    guaranteed budget 442
    optimal budget 443
    survival budget 442
  cash-flow forecast 444
  depreciation 446-7
  exchange rates 454-5
  inter-agency liaison 456-7
  international transfer of funds 453-4
    bank draft 453
    emergency grants 955
    mail payment 453
    telegraphic transfer 453-4
  loans 455
  project assessment 456-7
  record keeping 444
  staff 456
financial planning 434-41

6

budgets *see* financial administration,
  budgeting
diversity of income sources 439-40
donor consortium 439
external funding 435-6
generation of income 441
remuneration for community-based
  workers 438-9
salaries 437-9
self-financing activities 440-1
fishworker organisations 564, 577, 578-9
growth 403-5
human resource development 405-6
information technology 457-63
  communications and 458-9
  documentation centres 459
  printers 460
  see also computer systems
membership organisations 397-400
mission statements 409
monitoring 413-34
  see also evaluation
planning 406-15
  financial *see* financial planning
  monitoring 413-15
  programme strategy 411-12
  project planning 412-13
  strategic planning 407-11
production organisations 509-12
  gender inequalities 512
  producer groups 510-11, 604-5
  structure and activities 511
relief NGOs 400-3
staff training 405-6
strengthening institutions 395-406
sustainability 395
vehicles
  choice of vehicle 464-5
  costs 464
  donation conditions 465-7
  health care transport 639
  maintenance and running 464
  managing use 465
  safety 467
  transport needs definition 463
  where to buy 465
institutions *see* institutional development:
  social organisation
Inter-American Commission on Human
  Rights 46
Inter-American Court of Human Rights
  46
Inter/Action 812

Interights 45
International Baby Foods Action Network
  (IBFAN) 771-2
International Collective in Support of
  Fishworkers (ICSF) 579
International Commission of Jurists 47
International Committee of the Red Cross
  872
International Consultation on Refugee
  Women 1988 187
International Convention on the
  Elimination of All Forms of
  Discrimination Against Women 39, 45-6
International Convention on the
  Elimination of All Forms of Racial
  Discrimination 246
International Council for Research on
  Agro-forestry (ICRAF) 588
International Council of Voluntary
  Agencies 874
International Covenant on Civil and
  Political Rights 31, 33-4, 44-5
International Covenant on Economic,
  Social and Cultural Rights 31, 34-5
International Dispensary Association
  (IDA) 757
International Drinking Water Supply and
  Sanitation Decade 695
International Federation for Alternative
  Trade 608
International Federation of Red Cross
  and Red Crescent Societies 185, 872
International Institute for Tropical
  Agriculture (IITA) 588
International Labour Organisation 44,
  239-40, 271-2
International Monetary Fund 70, 72-3
  see also structural adjustment policies
International Network for Rational Use of
  Drugs (INRUD) 779
International Red Cross and Red
  Crescent Movement 185, 872
international transfer of funds
  bank draft 453
  emergency grants 955
  mail payment 453
  telegraphic transfer 453-4
International Working Group on
  Indigenous Affairs 260
interviews 217
iodine deficiency 684-5
ISIS 58

kala azar 734
Kenya 590, 754, 891
Kurdistan 815
kwashiorkor 682-3

labour exchange 492
land
  acidity 82
  agro-chemicals 82, 84
  conservation of water and soil 83
  decrease in fertility 81-2
  degradation 81-3
  deterioration of soil structure 81
  dispossession of indigenous populations
    240-1
  erosion 82, 83-4
  improvement measures 83-4
  low external input sustainable agricul
    ture (LEISA) 83
  overgrazing 83
  rights see land rights
  salinisation 82, 84
  soil maps 99
  tenure 260, 521
  terracing 84
  toxic pollution and mining 83
  valuations 96
  see also agriculture; environment
Land Mines Protocol 307
land rights
  ethnic and race relations 247-8
  livestock prodcution 543
  ownership 520-1
  tenancy and sharecropping 521
landmines 75, 307-8, 893
Latin America 53, 76-8, 336, 366, 857
  see also individual countries
latrines 925-6
  emergency situations 906
  water supply used as 694-5
Lebanon 314
legal rights training 374
legal support
  children and 289-90
  right to 53-4, 56-7
leprosy 734, 756
liberation movements 12
liberation theology 10
Licross-Volags Steering Committee for
  Disasters 873
life expectancy 626
literacy 363-8, 375
  agents of 365-6

cascade method 367
distance learning 368
oral traditions 364-5
participation in 367-8
training of facilitators 366-7
livelihoods
  agricultural see agriculture
  analysis 103-11
  changes in systems 494
  fishing see fish farming and fishing (main
    heading)
  forests see trees and forests
  gender inequality 69, 207-9, 496, 603,
    605
  interdependence of systems 495
  labour exchange 492
  ownership 491
  pastoralism see pastoralists
  rural livelihoods
    analysis 103-11
    see also agriculture
  self-employment 492
  sexual division of labour 69, 207-9, 496,
    603, 605
  sustainability see sustainable livelihoods
  urban livelihoods 111-17
    domestic workers 200-1, 277, 286
    employment 113
    neighbourhood associations 116
    population increase 112
    poverty 114
    squatter committees 116
    strategies 113-14
    sustainability 116-17
    threats to 115
    women 198-201
    see also small-scale industries
  use rights 491-2
  wage labour 492
  see also employment; production
livestock production see agriculture
llamoids 551
loans 455
  see also credit and savings support
lobbying see also campaigning
Locke, John 28
logical framework analysis 129, 143-7
  strengths and weaknesses 45-6
  ZOPP 144, 146-7
Lomé Convention 36, 563
Longwe, Sarah Hlupekile 172, 173, 215
low-external-input sustainable agriculture
  (LEISA) 83, 532-5

6

Lutheran World Federation 873-4

Machiguenga indians 260
Madres de la Plaza de Mayo (Mothers of the
    May Square) 218
malaria 732-3
    drugs 756
    eradication programme 640
Malawi 380
Mali 937-8, 939
malnutrition *see* nutrition
management of emergency programmes
    948-76
    communications *see* communications
    contingency plans 865, 970-1
    evaluation 961
    financial procedures 971-2
    information and assessment
        assessment 952-3
        information needs 951-2
        interpretation of events 952
        media liaison 949-50
        slow-onset emergencies 951
        sudden-onset disasters 949-50
    internal communications 955-8
    liaison with other agencies 961
    logistics 961-70
    preparedness 865, 912, 970-1
    recommendation of emergency grants
        955
    situation reports 959-61
    slow-onset emergencies
        information and assessment 951
        information needs 951-2
    sources of funds
        co-funding from official sources 954-5
        emergency grants 955
        funds from other NGOs 953-4
        special appeals 953
    staff
        debriefing 973-4
        health and safety 972-4
        recruitment 972
        staffing 972
        travel in dangerous areas 974-5
    supplies
        distribution 969-70
        purchase
            international 962-3
            local 963
        suppliers 977
    transport, international
        air 964

documents required 965-6
        insurance 966
        land 964
        sea 963
    transport, local
        air 969
        commodity control 966
        rail 968
        road 968
        warehousing and storage 967
        warehousing and storage 967
Manpower Services Commission 360
mapping, participatory 99
marasmus 682
marketing
    agricultural organisations 558
    alternative trading organisations 608-9
    assessing market 505-6
    assistance 506-7
    comparative advantage 506
    fishing industry 577-9
    small producers 507
    small-scale industries 606-9
        advantages and disadvantages of
            markets 606-8
        alternative trading organisations 608-9
        export 607-8
        identification of market 606
        local mass market 607
        local or urban elite market 607
Martineau, Harriet 28
Marx, Karl 29
measles 723, 908
media 818-19, 949-50
meetings 123-4
membership organisations 397-400
mental health 759-63
    armed conflict 760-2, 855-8
    cultural concepts 760
    emergency situations 855-8, 907
    ex-combatants 761-2
    NGO role 761-2
    post-traumatic stress disorder 760, 856
    primary health workers and 761
Mexico 357, 874
migrations
    armed conflict 75-6
    emergency flight of women 182
    ethnic and race relations 243-4
    see also displaced persons; ethnic cleans
        ing; refugees
minimum activities package (MAP) 637-8
mining pollution 83

minorities
  Sub-commission on Prevention of
    Discrimination and Protection of 42
  see also ethnic and race relations; indige-
    nous populations
Miskito indians 74, 891, 892
mission statements 409
mobility 673
monitoring
  environmental health systems 717-20
  food aid sale 945-6
  food distribution 945
  institutional development 413-15
  see also evaluation; information assess-
    ment
mortality
  child 667
  infant 272, 667
  maternal 196, 653-4
mosquitoes, vector control 711-13, 928
Mother and Child Health (MCH) programmes 652-3, 654-9
Mothers' Committees (Latin America) 53
motor vehicles *see* vehicles
Mozambique 74, 75-6

Namibia 221, 357
Narmada dam scheme 73, 86, 241
National Collective of Prostitution (Brazil)
  199
National Council of Rubber Tappers
  (Brazil) 593
National Movement of Street Boys and
  Girls (Brazil) 285
National Union of Indians (Brazil) 593
nationalism 37-8
natural rights theory 28, 29
neighbourhood associations 116
Nepal 93, 582, 703-4, 734
networking 379-84, 392
  Arid Lands Information Network
    (ALIN) 80, 106-7, 380, 509
  combating isolation 57-8
  conferences 383-4
  disabled persons 314-15
  exchange visits 381-3
  funding 380
  human rights and 57-8
  organisational form of network 380
  purpose of network 380
  sustainable livelihoods and 80
  women 220-1
  workshops 383-4

NGO Management Network (Geneva)
  405
NGOs
  assistentialist 401
  change-oriented 401-2
  cooperatives 337
  disaster relief code of conduct 802-5
    definitions 801-2
    purpose 801
    recommendations 806-8
    working environment 805
  funding 339-40
  issue-based groups 337-8
  local structures and mass movements
    340-2
  long-term groups 337
  long-term support from 343-4
  membership organisations and 397-400
  organisational development 347-8
  organisational structures 346-7
  participation promotion 344-6
  practical support for organisations 342-9
  problems and potentials 338-42
  relief NGOs 400-3
  short-term groups 337
  staff safety *see* staff
  see also institutional development; social
    organisation
Nicaragua 74, 233, 238, 249, 365, 891,
  892
nomadic pastoralists 538
non-governmental organisations *see*
  NGOs
non-timber forest products 586
NORDIDA 172
numeracy 364, 366
nutrition 678-88
  assessment 898-900, 909, 910-11
    mid-upper arm circumference
      (MUAC) 899, 900
    MUAC 910-11
    weight for height/length 899, 900
  breast-feeding 668, 669, 681-2, 686-7,
    771-2
  causes of malnutrition 679-82
    cultural factors 681-2
    distribution 680
    environmental factors 681
    food availability 680
    health services and care 681
    national and regional policies 680
    poverty 679
    social factors 681-2

6

consequences of malnutrition 679
diarrhoeal diseases and 729-30
education 687
elderly persons 673
emergencies 764, 766-7, 894-912, 941
feeding programmes 288
general rations 903-4
growth monitoring 685-6
interventions 686-8
  breast-feeding encouragement 686-7
  indirect 686
nutritional rehabilitation units 687-8
poverty and 679
status assessment 685-6
supplementary foods 904
therapeutic feeding 904-5, 941
types of malnutrition 682-6
  iodine deficiency 684-5, 694-5
  iron deficiency anaemia 683-4
  kwashiorkor 682-3
  marasmus 682
  protein-energy malnutrition 682-3
  vitamin A deficiency 683, 909
urban malnutrition 645, 647
vitamin A supplements 683, 909
women 905-6

oral rehydration therapy (ORT) 730-1
Organisation of American States 37
organisations *see* institutional development; NGOs; production, organisations;
  social organisation
overgrazing 83
overpopulation 737-8
Overseas Development Administration
  appraisal methodology 98, 129, 143
  EIA requirements 98, 129, 143
  forest management in Ghana 586
  participation of beneficiaries 14
Oxfam
  birth planning
    interventions 739-40
    support for 738-9
  child health support 667
  education role 356-7
  emergency policy 799-801, 982
  emergency store content 978
  gender approach 68-70, 171-3
  health care financing 780-1
  human rights 49-58
  Humanitarianism and War research
    project 810, 866
  sanitation unit 878, 985

trade union support 350-3
water packs 978, 983-4
ways of working 119-20
see also individual aspects eg participation
Oxfam Trading 608-9
Oxfam/Delagua water testing kit 920, 921,
  984

Packet Switching Network 459
Pakistan 219, 357, 591
Palestine Agricultural Relief Committees
  in the Occupied Territories 343
panchayats 336
participation 489-90
  conflicting interests 15, 16
  consultation 16
  credit and savings support 505
  ethnic and race relations 255-6
  evaluation 16, 421-2
  funding condition 14
  gender and 15
  'head count' approach 16
  levels 14-15
  Popular Participation Learning Group
    14-15
  promotion of 344-6
  social differences 255-6
  women 216-17
Participatory Learning Methods (PALM)
  14-15, 523
participatory mapping 99
participatory rural appraisal 131-3, 523
participatory rural assessment 98-102
partnerships 127
Pastoral Women's Workshops 559
pastoralists 538-9
  agropastoralists 538
  assessment of pastoralism 107-8
  associations 556-7
  emergencies and 890-1, 892
  general guidelines for development
    547-8
  nomadic pastoralists 538
  reducing vulnerability 548
  supporting base rights 548
  sustainability 107-8
  threats to livelihood 107
  transhumant pastoralists 538
patriarchy 172, 173, 176
patronatos 336
peace education 267
people 167-323
  ageing *see* elderly people

disabilities *see* disabled persons
ethnic peoples *see* ethnic and race
    relations: indigenous populations:
    social differences
gender *see* gender: women
old people *see* elderly people
race relations *see* ethnic and race
    relations
social differences *see* caste: ethnic and
    race relations: social differences
personal development skills 373
Peru 110, 260, 564, 593
pest control
    health *see* vector control
    LEISA 534-5
Philippines 73, 89, 605
    fishing and fishworkers 111, 564, 578
    Freedom from Debt Coalition 342, 379,
        388
pigs 551-2
planning 406-15
    birth planning *see main heading*
    contingency plans 865, 970-1
    emergency situations 820-1
    environmental health 714-21
    family planning *see* birth planning
    financial *see* financial planning
    health care programmes 784-5
    mission statements 409
    monitoring 413-15
    programme strategy 411-12
    project planning 412-13
    strategic planning 407-11
plural societies 237-8
polio 723
political parties 336-7
pollution
    atmospheric 693
    fishing and 564
    industrial 692-3
    mining 83
popular movements 336-7
population 63-5, 737-8
    see also birth planning
post-traumatic stress disorder 760, 856
poultry 553-4
poverty
    and environmental degradation 64, 65-6
    disablement cause 307
    education and training 358-9
    feminisation 65-6, 67
    health and, urban 645-6
    malnutrition and 679

NGOs and 482-3
    production and 480-2
    women 65-6, 67, 180-2
    World Bank definition 481
power *see* energy
primary health care 631-4
    Alma Ata conference 631-2, 633, 641
    community health workers 632, 633
    emergency interventions 896
    financing 775
    NGO role 633-5
    principles and components 633
producer gas 92-3
production
    agriculture *see* agriculture
    credit and savings support
        assessing needs 504-5
        forms of credit and savings 502-3
        obstacles to obtaining 503-4
        participation 505
        women-only systems 503-4
    economic interventions 480-2, 488-90
    fishing *see* fishing
    forestry *see* trees and forests
    GATT 487-8
    gender inequalities
        division of labour 496
        income 496, 497
        livelihood systems 495-6
        participatory organisations 512
        technology gap 499
    gender sensitive strategies 496-8
    globalisation 484
    growth 483-5
    information exchange 509
    labour exchange 492
    livelihood system assessment 491-4
        see also livelihoods; sustainable
            livelihoods
    marketing assistance
        alternative trading organisations 608-9
        assessing market 505-6
        comparative advantage 506
        forms of 506-7
        small producers 507
    modernisation 483-5
    NGO interventions 488-90
    organisations 509-12
        gender inequalities 512
        production groups 510-11
        small-scale industries 604-5
        structure and activities 511
    participatory organisations 509-12

6

formal organisations 510-11
gender considerations 512
production groups 510-11
structure and activities 511
poverty and 480-2
self-employment 492
small-scale industries *see main heading*
structural adjustment policies 484, 486-7
technology development 498-501
existing technologies 500
gender technology gap 499
high-input capital intensive technologies 501
intermediate labour-intensive technologies 500-1
small-scale industries 605
Third World debt 485-6
training 508-9
trees *see* trees and forests
wage labour 492
see also employment; livelihoods; sustainable livelihoods
project cycle analysis 135, 137-40
projects
evaluation 22
limitations 21-3
time-bound 22
see also management of emergency programmes and *individual schemes*
prostitution 198-200
children 198-9, 277
public health 688-9
aims of programme 689, 691
disease transmission 690
emergency relief 763-7, 896, 927-8
infrastructure 763
water resources 763
vector control
emergency situations 927-8
flies 713, 928
mosquitoes 711-13, 928
see also communicable diseases; sanitation; water supply

rabbits 552
race relations *see* ethnic and race relations: social differences
radio schools 368
Radio Vox de Nahuala 368
rail transport 968
rapid rural appraisal 129, 130-3
agriculture 523
participatory rural appraisal 131-3

The Realisation of the Right to Development (UN) 9
recycling
food aid bags 946
Red Crescent societies 185, 817-18, 870, 872-3
Red Cross societies 185, 817-18, 870, 872-3, 953
Refugee Policy Group 810
refugees 813
armed conflict 25, 75-6, 286, 843, 844-5
children 279, 286, 886-8
Convention relating to the status of refugees 872
cultural identity 888, 890-2
disaster mitigation 834
dispersed populations 877-8
education of 284, 887-8, 889
elderly people 296
ethnic and race relations 243-4
health care 765, 903
human rights 25, 55-6, 844-6
returning home 837-9
UNHCR 271, 845, 871-2, 955
Handbook for Emergencies 872
women 186-9, 884
Guidelines on the Protection of Refugee Women 872
Policy on Refugee Women 872
rehydration 730-1, 908-9
relief work *see* context of development and *individual aspects*
religion
fundamentalism 37-8
social differences 235-6
Special Rapporteur on Religious Intolerance 43
Renamo 75
reproductive health 627
abortions 653, 654, 744
antenatal care 655, 669
breast-feeding 668, 669, 681-2, 771-2
delivery 656
education 281-2, 658, 661
emergency situations 907
family planning *see* birth planning
fertility control 196-7
see also birth planning
mortality 196, 653-4
Mother and Child Health (MCH) programmes 652-3, 654-9
post-natal care 656-7
reproductive tract infections 196

rights of women 196-7
'Safe Motherhood Initiative' 655
traditional birth attendants 638, 657-8,
    669, 765-6
ultrasound scans 639
reproductive tract infections 196
residential care
    disabled persons 316-17
    elderly persons 300
responsibilities, limitations, impacts and
    opportunities (RLIO) grid 867-9
'responsible funder' concept 127
revolving credit funds, agriculture 558
revolving drug funds 758, 778, 779-80
risk mapping 835
road transport
    international 964
    local 968
    see also vehicles
Rubb-Hall type storage 917
rubber tappers (Brazil)
    National Council of Rubber Tappers 593
    Rubber Tappers' Union 586
Rural Action Committee (BRAC) 505
rural livelihoods
    see also agriculture
Russia, ethnic groups 233

'Safe Motherhood Initiative' 655
safety
    computer system use 462
    motor vehicle use 467
    NGO staff in emergencies 848-9, 972-4
salaries 437-9
    community-based workers 438-9
salinisation 82, 84
Salvador 190
sanitation
    anal cleansing methods 710
    communal or household facilities 708-9
    cost and affordability 708
    cultural issues 705-6
    emergency situations 906, 923-6
        Oxfam sanitation unit 878, 985
        systems destruction 75
    excreta disposal 906, 923
    faecal contamination dangers 923-4
    financial management and cost recovery
        720-1
    ground conditions 709
    latrines 694-5, 906, 925-6
    maintenance 711
    monitoring and evaluation 717-20

open-surface defaecation 924-5
Oxfam sanitation unit 878, 985
personal hygiene 926-7
population density 709-10
social issues 705-6, 924
timing of interventions 710-11
trench defaecation 925
upgrading 710
urban sewerage systems 692
waste disposal options 706-11
waste reuse 710
women's requirements 715, 906
SATIS (Global Union of Technologies for
    Environment and Sustainable
    Development) 459
Save the Children Fund 953
savings see credit and savings support
sea transport 963
Secours Catholique 873
self-determination 249
Self-Employed Women's Association
    (SEWA) 219, 350, 505
self-employment 492
Senegal 381
SERVV Self-Help Handicrafts 608
settlements
    in emergencies 915-16
    site selection 916
    see also housing; shelter
sex education 661, 671
sex workers 198-200
    children 198-9, 277
    HIV/AIDS 660, 752
sexual harassment 188
sharecropping 521
shari'a 30
sheep 550
shelter
    commercial emergency housing 917
    emergencies 901, 911, 916-17
    plastic sheeting 917, 981
    sudden-onset emergencies 901
    tents 917, 979
'silent listening' 217
sitreps see situation reports
situation reports 959-61
    framework for 959-60
    functions 960
skills training 372-3
sleeping sickness 734
small-scale farmers see agriculture
small-scale industries 595-613, 616-17
    credit and savings support 610-11

6

The Oxfam handbook of development and relief

economic content 596-8
entertainment 602
food-processing 601
forms of assistance 600-2
gender and 602-4
handicrafts 601
homeworkers 597
marketing assistance 606-9
  advantages and disadvantages of
    markets 606-8
  alternative trading organisations 608-9
  export 607-8
  identification of market 606
  local mass market 607
  local or urban elite market 607
NGO interventions 598-600
petty trade 602
producer group support 604-5
recycling 602
social considerations 602-4
sub-contracting 597
technology development 605
training 603, 605, 611-12
trans-national corporations 596
types 601-2
women 598-9, 603-4
SMART: Specific, Measurable, Achievable,
  Realistic and Time-bound 413
'social contract' theory of government 28
social differences
  awareness of 228-9
  caste 233-5, 603
  conflicts 250-1
  consultation 255-6
  cultural sensitivity 252-3
  culture and religion 235-6
  emergencies and 250-2
  human rights and 227-8
  information assessment 255
  information gathering 253-4
  livestock production 541-2
  participation 255-6
  sanitation 705-6
  small-scale industries 602-4
  solidarity and cohesion 251-2
  values 257-9
  within NGOs 229-30
  see also ethnic and race relations
social organisation 331, 333-93
  advocacy 377, 378
  agricultural organisations 555-60
  campaigning see campaigning
  communications see communications

development see institutional development
disabled persons 313
education and training see education
  and training
emergencies
  channels for relief 851-2
  local authorities 874-5
  local structures 875-7
fishworkers 564, 577, 578-9
freedom of association 333
funding 339-40
grassroots support organisations 397-8
intermediate agencies 397
issue-based organisations 398
local structures and mass movements
  340-2
membership organisations 397-400
NGOs 337-42
  assistentialist 401
  change-oriented 401-2
  funding 339-40
  issue-based groups 337-8
  local structure and mass movements
    340-2
  long-term support 337-8, 343-4
  membership organisations and
    397-400
  organisational development 347-8
  organisational structures 346-7
  participation promotion 344-6
  practical support from 342-9
  problems and potentials 338-42
  relief NGOs 400-3
  short-term groups 337
  staff see main heading
non-profit making organisations 401
officially promoted institutions 336
Oxfam interpretation of 334
people's organisations 333-53
political parties 336-7
popular movements 336-7
producer groups 604-5
production organisations 509-12
  gender inequalities 512
  production groups 510-11
  structure and activities 511
reasons for forming associations 333-4
trade unions 349-53
traditional institutions 335-6
types 334-8
voluntary agencies 397
Society for Participatory Research in Asia

(PRIA) 360
soil maps 99
solar power 93
SOS Wereldhandel 608
South Africa 76-7, 232, 357
South Indian Federation of Fishermen
   Societies (SIFFS) 578
'South-South' linking projects 80, 107,
   110-11, 352
sovereignty 36-7
special appeals 953
Special Rapporteurs
   on Religious Intolerance 43
   on Violence Against Women 40, 43, 178
sponsoring of children 288
springs 88, 696
squatter committees 116
Sri Lanka 362, 588
staff
   emergencies
      debriefing 973-4
      health and safety 848-9, 972-4
      recruitment 972
      travel in dangerous areas 974-5
   financing 456
'stakeholders' 409, 417
Steering Committee for Humanitarian
   Response 873
sterilising equipment 638
storage
   emergency supplies 967
   food 917
   Rubb-Hall type storage 917
street children 278, 285, 647
   health education 671
street dwellers
   health problems 647
structural adjustment policies 72-3, 401
   environment 70, 72-3
   International Monetary Fund 70, 72-3
   production and 484, 486-7
   trees and forests 584
   women and 181
   World Bank 70, 72-3
Sudan 77-8, 876-7, 938
SUNDEP 172
surgical equipment 638
Survival International 48-9, 260
sustainability 19-21, 490
   development 60-3
   fishing 110-11
   forest livelihoods 109
   institutions 395

pastoralism 107-8
urban livelihoods 116-17
   see also sustainable agriculture; sustainable livelihoods
sustainable agriculture 106-7, 518-19
   fertility maintenance 532-3
   low-external-input sustainable agriculture (LEISA) 83, 532-5
   pest control 534-5
   weed control 535
sustainable livelihoods 20, 490-5
   assessing system 491-4
   capacity to cope 79
   environment and 78-80
   equity and social justice 79, 80
   human right of 27
   networking 80
   Oxfam and 63
   social organisation 80
   sustainability 79-80
   see also livelihoods; production
suti 193, 258

Tanzania 754
target groups 17-19, 67, 68, 230
technology development
   existing technologies 500
   fishing see main heading
   gender technology gap 499
   high-input capital intensive technologies
      501
   intermediate labour-intensive technolo-
      gies 500-1
   production and 498-501
   small-scale industries 605
telex communication 956, 957-8
terracing 84
tetanus 723
Third World debt 485-6
Thomas J Watson Jr Institute for
   International Studies 810
torture
   Committee Against Torture 45
toxic pollution 83
trade
   alternative trading organisations 608-9
   environment and 70-2
   Fair Trade organisations 608
   free trade 71
   GATT 71, 487-8
   Trade-Related Environmental Measures
      (TREMS) 72
   World Trade Organisation 71-2, 487-8

6

trade unions 349-53
  education and training 351-2
  Oxfam support policy 350-3
  women in 349-50
Trade-Related Environmental Measures
  (TREMS) 72
traditional birth attendants 638, 669
  training 657-8
  upgrading 765-6
traditional institutions 335-6
traditional medicine 628, 640, 641
  assessment of practices 643-4
  birth attendants 638, 657-8, 669, 765-6
  forms 642
  NGO role 642-4
  support 644
Traditional Medicine Programme (WHO)
  641
Traidcraft 608
training *see* education and training
trans-national corporations 596
transhumant pastoralists 538
Transnational Information Exchange 384
transport
  international
    air 964
    documents required 965-6
    insurance 966
    land 964
    sea 963
  local
    air 969
    commodity control 966
    rail 968
    road 968
    warehousing and storage 967
  'needs' definition 463
  see also vehicles
trees and forests
  bees and beekeeping in forests 593
  biodiversity 90-1
  common property resources (CPR) 587
  Community Development Forestry
    Project (Nepal) 582
  control rights 591-2
  deforestation
    civil conflict 587
    'crisis' 583-4
    floods caused by 87
  dry forests 91
  economic status and 591-2
  ethnic identity and 592
  farms with trees 587-9

Forest Stewardship Council (FSC) 586
forest user support 592-3
fuelwood 582-3
gender and 591
historical context 581-3
International Council for Research on
  Agro-forestry (ICRAF) 588
International Institute for Tropical
  Agriculture (IITA) 588
Joint Forest management (India) 592
Kenya Agro-forestry Development
  Programme 590
livelihoods in
  sustainability 109
  threats to 108-9
natural forests 585-6
NGO interventions 585-93
non-timber forest products 586
ownership 591-2
people-oriented policies 582
plantations 587
planting
  multi-purpose trees 589-90
  seeds and seedlings 590-1
pressure groups 584
rubber tappers 586, 593
structural adjustment programmes 584
sustainability 109, 584, 586
'sustainable harvested' timber definition
  586
threats to 108-9
trees on farms
  alley farming 588-9
  fodder 588
tropical forests 90-1
tropical rainforest 584
use rights 591-2
water table and 587
World Forestry Congress 582
Tro'caire 873
tuberculosis 723, 733-4, 749

Uganda 72-3, 314, 754, 857
UN Development Programme (UNDP)
  871
UNCED (Conference on Environment
  and Development) 61, 518-19
UNHCR *see* High Commissioner for
  Refugees
UNICEF 271
UNIENET (United Nations International
  Emergencies Network) 459
United Nations

agencies in relief work 871-2
CEDAW 39, 45-6
Commission on Human Rights 41-2
Commission on the Status of Women 42
Conference on Environment and
    Development (UNCED) 61, 518-19
Department of Humanitarian Affairs
    (DHA) 812, 871
Disaster Relief Office 871
Food and Agriculture Office 871
human rights organisations 41-4
International Emergencies Network 459
Law of the Sea Convention 1982 563
peace-keeping forces 815
Special Rapporteur on Religious
    Intolerance 43
Special Rapporteur on Violence Against
    Women 40, 43, 178
Sub-commission on Prevention of
    Discrimination and Protection of
    Minorities 42
theme mechanisms 43
Voluntary Fund for Indigenous
    Populations 44
Working Group on Indigenous
    Populations 43-4, 244, 245
World Food Programme 871
United Nations Children's Fund
    (UNICEF) 871
United Nations International
    Emergencies Network (UNIENET) 459
United States
    Declaration of Independence 29
    Human Rights Watch Committees 38
Universal Declaration of Human Rights
    29, 31-3, 244
    text 151-7
untouchables 228, 234-5
urban health care
    accidents 648
    alcohol abuse 947-8
    crowding 646-7
    drug abuse 647-8
    facilities 646
    homelessness 647
    malnutrition 645, 647
    NGO role 648-9
    poverty 645-6
    problems 646-8
    street life 647
    working conditions 647
urban livelihoods
    employment 113

environmental assessment 111-17
neighbourhood associations 116
population increase 112
poverty 114
squatter committees 116
strategies 113-14
sustainability 116-17
threats to 115
women 198-201
see also small-scale industries

vector control 727-8
    emergency situations 927-8
    flies 713, 928
    mosquitoes 711-13, 928
vegetable production 535-7
    hydroponics 536-7
    kitchen gardens 536
    nutrient film technique 536-7
vehicles
    ambulances 639
    choice 464-5
    costs 464
    donation conditions 465-7
    health care transport 639
    institutional development 463-7
    maintenance and running 464
    managing use 465
    safety 467
    transport needs definition 463
    where to buy 465
    see also transport
village-level operation and maintenance
    handpumps (VLOM) 697
violence against women 190-5
    circumcision 194, 258, 662, 663-5
    domestic violence 192-3
    health care 665-6
    socio-cultural violence 193-4
    Violence Against Women in the Family (UN
    report) 39
visits
    advocacy work 389
    information gathering 123-4, 389-90
vocational training 372-3
Voluntary Fund for Indigenous
    Populations 44
wage labour 492
    see also employment; production
warehousing 967
wars see armed conflict
water
    acid rain 87

control of 85-6
dams 88
  Narmada project 73, 86, 241
  see also individual dams eg Narmada
    dam project
drought 86
floods 86-7
harvesting 88, 699-700
quality 87-8
storage 88, 700, 702
table 587
water sources
  boreholes 697-8
  contamination when collected 699-700
  groundwater 87, 88, 695-6
  hand-dug wells 696-7
  rain water 698
  springs 88, 696
  surface water 698
  tubewells 697
  village-level operation and maintenance
  handpumps (VLOM) 697
water supply 695-704
  contamination when collected 699-700
  daily requirement 695
  emergencies and 763, 906, 921-3
    assessment of needs 919-20
    destruction of systems 75
    quality 919
    testing 920, 921-3
  financial management and cost recovery
    720-1
  for industry 692
  guinea worm transmission 694
  industrial pollution and 692-3
  mobile drinking-water units 923
  monitoring and evaluation 717-20
  operation and maintenance 703-4
  Oxfam water packs 978, 983-4
  Oxfam/Delagua water testing kit 920,
    921, 984
  piped water 699-700
  quality and testing 87-8
    chemical quality 701-2
    emergency situations 919, 920-3
    microbiological quality 700-1
    physical quality 702
  storage
    contamination during 700
    treatment by 702
  training in management 704
  transportation and distribution 699-700
  treatment

aeration 702
disinfection 703, 921-3
filtration 702, 922
sedimentation 921-2
storage 702
used as latrine 694-5
Water User's Committees 703-4
women's responsibilities 714-17, 920
see also water sources
Water User's Committees 703-4
weed control
  LEISA 535
wells
  boreholes 697-8
  hand-dug 696-7
  tubewells 697
  village-level operation and maintenance
    handpumps (VLOM) 697
WHO *see* World Health Organisation
whooping cough 723
wildlife (as protein source) 554
wind power 93
Wollstonecraft, Mary 28
women 11
  abuse 181-2
  agriculture 204, 522-3, 542-4
  armed conflict 189-90, 841, 845, 855
    see also emergencies
  campaigning 222
  circumcision 194, 258, 662, 663-5
  Commission on the Status of Women 42
  Committee on the Elimination of All
    Forms of DIscrimination Against
    Women 39, 45-6
  community 203
  consultation 217-18, 879, 880-2
  control over resources 496-7
  credit and savings support 611
  culture 176-7, 215, 257-8
  DAWN 58, 207, 216, 221, 381
  debt-bond system 199
  decision-making 217-18
  denial or violation of human rights 38-40
  discrimination in health care 651-2, 668
  division of labour 69, 207-9, 496, 603,
    605
  domestic workers 200-1
  education 181, 358, 367-8, 611-12
  emergencies 184-90, 824
    access to resources and benefits 188-9
    armed conflicts 189-90, 841, 845, 855
    consultation 879, 880-2
    displaced persons 186-9

flight 182
protection 187-8
refugees 186-9, 872, 884
situation of 883-5
employment 181
domestic workers 200-1
farmers 204
fishworkers 567-9
food production 934-5
prostitution 198-200
sexual division of labour 69, 207-9,
496, 603, 605
empowerment 13, 70, 206-7, 216-17
environment and 67-70
ecofeminism 68-9
gender analysis 69-7
targeting resources 67
ethnic minority 231-2
exclusions from decision-making 186-7
exploitation 29
farmers 204
fishworkers 567-9
food distribution responsibilities 905-6,
943
food production 934-5
health 181, 651-66
as carers 660-1
culture and 193-4, 257-8, 662-6
customs 662-3
early marriage and childbearing 663
education
evaluation criteria 419
sex education 661
family planning see birth planning
gender-based discrimination 651-2,
668
genital mutilation 194, 258, 662, 663-5
needs 652-3
sanitation requirements 715, 906
sexually transmitted diseases 661-2
taboos 662-3
water supply and 714-17, 920
work-related problems 659-60
see also reproductive health main heading; violence against
HIV/AIDS 660, 661, 662
household and family 182-4, 203-4
human rights 54-5, 177-8
impoverishment 65-7, 180-2
income 496, 497
income-generation projects 219, 598-9,
603-4
information

access 220-2
gathering 211-12, 217-18
gender-sensitive analysis 201-4, 210-11
monitoring and evaluation 211-12
literacy training 367-8
livestock production 542-4
malnutrition 905-6
marginalisation of interests 179-80
networking 220-1
nutrition 905-6
organisations 218-20
participation 216-17
patriarchy 172, 173, 176
policy approaches to 205-7
poverty 65-6, 67, 180-2
production and
inequalities 495-8
participatory organisations 512
see also employment
prostitution 198-200
refugees 186-9, 884
Guidelines on the Protection of Refugee
Women 872
Policy on Refugee Women 872
see also emergencies
reproduction
rights of women 196-7
see also reproductive health main heading
sanitation requirements 715, 906
sex work 198-200
sexual harassment 188
Special Rapporteur on violence against
women 40, 43, 178
structural adjustment programmes and
181
technology gap 499
trade unions 349-50
training exclusion 603, 605, 611-12
trees and forests and 591
unpaid work 497
violence against 39, 40, 190-5, 665-6
domestic violence 192-3
political and structural 194-5
socio-cultural violence 193-4
Special Rapporteur 40, 43, 178
water supply and 714-17, 920
woman-maintained households 182-4
work see employment; production
see also gender; gender framework
analysis
Women in Development (WID) approach
205, 401-2

Women's Desks 67
Women's Development Units 67
Women's Linking Project (Namibia) 221
Women's Ministries 67
Working Group on Indigenous
  Populations 43-4, 244, 245
Working Women's Forum 505
workshops 125-6, 383-4
World Bank
  appraisal methodology 129
  EIA requirements 98
  empowerment 11-12
  Popular Participation Learning Group
    14-15
  poverty definition 481
  structural adjustment policies 70, 72-3
World Commission on Environment and
  Development (WCED) 19-20, 60, 61
World Conference on Human Rights
  (Vienna 1993) 25, 26, 178
World Council for Indigenous People 260
World Council of Churches 177, 873
  American Council of Churches 873
  Christian Aid 873
  Christian Medical Commission 758
  Church World Service 873
  Department of World Service 873

World Food Programme 871
World Forestry Congress (Jakarta) 582
World Health Organisation 271, 871
  Acute Respiratory Infections programme
    640
  Bamako Initiative 778
  community-based rehabilitation 315-16
  Control of Diarrhoeal Diseases pro-
    gramme 640
  Emergency Health Kit 758
  'essential drugs' concept 756, 757
  Expanded Programme for
    Immunisation (EPI) 640, 722
  malaria eradication programme 640
  Traditional Medicine Programme 641
World Summit for Children 271
World Trade Organisation 71-2, 487-8
Worldwide Fund for Nature 584

Yanomami land-rights 260-1
youth clubs 289

Zambia 211-12, 592-3
Zimbabwe 89, 361
ZOPP (objectives-oriented project plan-
  ning system) 144, 146-7